Merrills' International Dispute Settlement

The fully revised seventh edition of this successful textbook explains the legal and diplomatic methods and organisations used to solve international disputes, how they work and when they are used. It looks at diplomatic (negotiation, mediation, inquiry and conciliation) and legal methods (arbitration, judicial settlement). It uses many, up-to-date examples of each method in practice to place the theory of how the law works in real-life situations, demonstrating the strengths and weaknesses of different methods when they are used. Fully updated throughout, the seventh edition includes a new introduction explaining the common principles of international dispute settlement and a chapter on investor–state arbitration, as well as recommended further readings at the end of each chapter. It is an essential resource for advanced undergraduate and postgraduate courses on international dispute settlement.

J. G. MERRILLS was Emeritus Professor of International Law at the University of Sheffield, and held visiting posts at the Universities of Auckland and Toronto. For eight years, he was Alternate Member of the United Nations Sub-Commission on Prevention of Discrimination and Protection of Minorities. He authored seven books and over seventy journal articles, and was on the editorial board of the *Global Community Yearbook of International Law and Jurisprudence*.

ERIC DE BRABANDERE is Professor of International Dispute Settlement Law and Director of the Grotius Centre for International Legal Studies at Leiden University. He is also Attorney-at-Law at the Brussels Bar, practising in international law and investment arbitration, and Editor-in-Chief of the *Leiden Journal of International Law*. Eric De Brabandere is a general international lawyer, with special expertise in international investment law and arbitration, and international dispute settlement. He teaches on international dispute settlement and international investment law and arbitration.

Merrills' International Dispute Settlement

Seventh edition

JOHN MERRILLS
ERIC DE BRABANDERE
Leiden University

CAMBRIDGE
UNIVERSITY PRESS

University Printing House, Cambridge CB2 8BS, United Kingdom

One Liberty Plaza, 20th Floor, New York, NY 10006, USA

477 Williamstown Road, Port Melbourne, VIC 3207, Australia

314–321, 3rd Floor, Plot 3, Splendor Forum, Jasola District Centre, New Delhi – 110025, India

103 Penang Road, #05–06/07, Visioncrest Commercial, Singapore 238467

Cambridge University Press is part of the University of Cambridge.

It furthers the University's mission by disseminating knowledge in the pursuit of education, learning, and research at the highest international levels of excellence.

www.cambridge.org
Information on this title: www.cambridge.org/highereducation/isbn/9781108836814
DOI: 10.1017/9781108872560

Second, third, fourth, fifth and sixth editions © J. G. Merrills 1991, 1998, 2011, 2017
Seventh edition © Cambridge University Press 2022

This publication is in copyright. Subject to statutory exception and to the provisions of relevant collective licensing agreements, no reproduction of any part may take place without the written permission of Cambridge University Press.

First published by Sweet and Maxwell Ltd 1984
Second edition published by Grotius Publications 1991
Reprinted by Cambridge University Press 1993, 1995, 1996
Third edition published by Cambridge University Press 1998
Reprinted 2000
Fourth edition published by Cambridge University Press 2005
Fifth edition published by Cambridge University Press 2011
Sixth edition published by Cambridge University Press 2017
Seventh edition by Cambridge University Press 2022

Printed in the United Kingdom by TJ Books Limited, Padstow Cornwall

A catalogue record for this publication is available from the British Library.

Library of Congress Cataloging-in-Publication Data
Names: Merrills, J. G., author. | DE Brabandere, Eric author.
Title: Merrills' international dispute settlement / John Merrills [and] Eric De Brabandere
Other titles: International dispute settlement
Description: Seventh edition. | Cambridge, United Kingdom ; New York, NY : Cambridge University Press, [2022] | Includes bibliographical references and index.
Identifiers: LCCN 2021038902 | ISBN 9781108836814 (hardback) | ISBN 9781108819220 (paperback)
Subjects: LCSH: Pacific settlement of international disputes. | LCGFT: Textbooks.
Classification: LCC KZ6010 .M47 2022 | DDC 341.5/2–dc23
LC record available at https://lccn.loc.gov/2021038902

ISBN 978-1-108-83681-4 Hardback
ISBN 978-1-108-81922-0 Paperback

Cambridge University Press has no responsibility for the persistence or accuracy of URLs for external or third-party internet websites referred to in this publication and does not guarantee that any content on such websites is, or will remain, accurate or appropriate.

Contents

Preface	*page* ix
Table of Cases	xi
Table of Treaties and Agreements	xx

1 International Dispute Settlement: Principles and Concepts — 1
1.1 The Peaceful Settlement of Disputes — 2
1.2 State Consent and the Free Choice of Means of Settlement — 5
1.3 The Notion of 'Dispute' — 8
1.4 Justiciability and Mootness — 14
1.5 The Notion and Functions of 'Settlement' — 18
1.6 The Means of International Dispute Settlement — 24
1.7 Jurisdiction — 25
1.8 Admissibility — 32
1.9 Further Reading — 36

2 Negotiation — 38
2.1 Consultation — 39
2.2 Forms of Negotiation — 45
2.3 Substantive Aspects of Negotiation — 49
2.4 Negotiation and Adjudication — 54
2.5 Limitations of Negotiation — 61
2.6 Further Reading — 65

3 Mediation — 66
3.1 Mediators — 67
3.2 Consent to Mediation — 69
3.3 Functions of Mediation — 74
3.4 Limits of Mediation — 79
3.5 Further Reading — 83

4 Inquiry — 84
4.1 1899 Hague Convention — 84
4.2 The *Dogger Bank* Inquiry — 85
4.3 Inquiries under the 1907 Hague Convention — 87
4.4 Treaty Practice 1911–40 — 91
4.5 Post-Second World War Practice — 92

4.6 The Value of Inquiry 97
4.7 Further Reading 103

5 Conciliation 104
5.1 Emergence of Conciliation 104
5.2 Work of Commissions of Conciliation 106
5.3 Practice of Conciliation 112
5.4 Place of Conciliation in Modern Treaty Law 116
5.5 Further Developments 122
5.6 Significance of Conciliation 127
5.7 Further Reading 131

6 Arbitration 132
6.1 Forms of Arbitration 132
6.2 Selection and Appointment of Arbitrators 136
6.3 Terms of Reference 144
6.4 Basis of the Decision 152
6.5 Effect of the Award 158
6.6 Utility of Arbitration 165
6.7 Further Reading 170

7 Investment Arbitration 172
7.1 Investment Treaties and Consent to Arbitration 173
7.2 The Jurisdiction of Investment Tribunals 175
7.3 Procedural Law 180
7.4 The Law Applicable to the Merits 185
7.5 The Validity of the Award and its Implementation 188
7.6 Further Reading 192

8 The International Court I: Organisation and Procedure 194
8.1 Contentious Jurisdiction 194
8.2 Incidental Jurisdiction 204
8.3 Advisory Jurisdiction 218
8.4 Membership of the Court 221
8.5 Chambers 224
8.6 Further Reading 229

9 The International Court II: The Work of the Court 231
9.1 Establishing the Facts 231
9.2 Identifying the Law 236
9.3 Extension of the Court's Function 239
9.4 Legal and Political Disputes 244
9.5 Effect of Judgments 248

9.6 Significance of the Court ... 254
9.7 Further Reading ... 259

10 The Law of the Sea Convention ... 261
10.1 The Convention and its Dispute Settlement System ... 262
10.2 Principle of Compulsory Settlement ... 269
10.3 Conciliation ... 281
10.4 Arbitration under Annex VII ... 284
10.5 Special Arbitration under Annex VII ... 288
10.6 The International Tribunal for the Law of the Sea (ITLOS) ... 290
10.7 Seabed Disputes Chamber ... 297
10.8 Significance of the Convention and its Dispute Settlement Provisions ... 301
10.9 Further Reading ... 307

11 International Trade Disputes ... 310
11.1 From GATT (1947) to the World Trade Organization ... 310
11.2 The WTO Dispute Settlement Understanding ... 311
11.3 Consultations ... 316
11.4 Good Offices, Conciliation and Mediation ... 318
11.5 Panel Proceedings ... 320
11.6 Appellate Review ... 326
11.7 Implementation of Rulings and Recommendations ... 333
11.8 Arbitration under Article 25 DSU ... 337
11.9 Regional Trade Systems ... 339
11.10 The WTO System in Context ... 342
11.11 Further Reading ... 345

12 The United Nations ... 347
12.1 Machinery of the Organisation ... 348
12.2 Security Council and General Assembly in Action ... 350
12.3 Role of the Secretary-General ... 360
12.4 Political Organs and the International Court ... 367
12.5 Effectiveness of the United Nations ... 376
12.6 Further Reading ... 382

13 Regional Organisations ... 383
13.1 Range of Regional Organisations ... 383
13.2 Role of Regional Organisations in Disputes ... 390
13.3 Limitations of Regional Organisations ... 398
13.4 Regional Organisations and Adjudication ... 402
13.5 Regional Organisations and the United Nations ... 407
13.6 Further Reading ... 411

14 Trends and Prospects — 413
- 14.1 International Dispute Settlement Today — 413
- 14.2 A Political Perspective — 415
- 14.3 A Legal Perspective — 420
- 14.4 Improving the Capacity of Political Methods and International Organizations — 425
- 14.5 Improving the Capacity of Legal Methods — 429
- 14.6 Conclusion — 437
- 14.7 Further Reading — 438

Appendices — 439
- A. Agreement between Argentina and the United Kingdom establishing an Interim Reciprocal Information and Consultation System, 1990 — 439
- B. Report of the Commission of Inquiry into the Red Crusader Incident, 1962 (extract) — 441
- C. Conciliation Commission on the Continental Shelf Area between Iceland and Jan Mayen, May 1981 — 443
- D. Arbitration Agreement between the United Kingdom and France, July 1975 — 444
- E. Special Agreement for Submission to the International Court of Justice of the Differences between the Republic of Hungary and the Slovak Republic Concerning the Gabcikovo–Nagymaros Project (1993) — 448
- F. Optional Clause Declarations — 451
- G. Ruling Pertaining to the Differences between France and New Zealand Arising from the Rainbow Warrior Affair (extract) — 454

Index — 459

Preface

Professor John G. Merrills sadly passed away in 2018. I had the opportunity to meet Professor Merrills on several occasions, and remember him as an inspiring scholar and lecturer, and considerate colleague. He was Emeritus Professor at the University of Sheffield, and author of, amongst others, this seminal book. This text has been my own international dispute settlement bible for many years, in my teaching of international dispute settlement at Leiden University and elsewhere. Professor Merrills last updated this important textbook in 2016, and I am truly honoured to have been asked to take charge of this new edition.

The writing of a new edition of an existing textbook is a challenge, but one that I have gladly accepted and taken on. This seventh edition is rightly entitled 'Merrills' International Dispute Settlement'. In revising the text, I have not only sought to provide an update on the evolutions which had taken place since the last edition, but I have also, and perhaps most importantly, tried to maintain and be faithful to the approach adopted by Professor Merrills. It has not been my ambition, for that reason, to completely overhaul the structure and approach adopted in this book, with the risk of otherwise transforming it into a completely new text which would have been too remote from the original intention of Professor Merrills. I have approached the new edition above all as an update and revision of Professor Merrills' work, not my own book on international dispute settlement.

I have therefore decided not to move away from the 'institutional' approach adopted by Professor Merrills, and thus left the configuration of the book largely unaltered. I have also retained his approach to not include sections on international courts and tribunals which are technically not concerned with dispute settlement. The overall objective of this book is to look at international dispute settlement; it is not a textbook on international courts and tribunals generally.

That being said, I have taken into account the feedback organised by Cambridge University Press from colleagues around the world who use this book as the main textbook for their courses, and have also been inspired by my own use of the book over the past decade. I have therefore decided to make some additions and modifications to the text. Readers will notice that a general introductory chapter has been added, containing a discussion of the principles of dispute settlement and an introduction to the various categories of dispute settlement methods. Another new chapter covers disputes between states and non-state entities in the field of investor-state arbitration. While the focus of the book has generally been on inter-state dispute settlement, I have found it difficult not to engage with the increased use of investor-state arbitration, especially in light of the fact that most courses on international dispute settlement now cover this topic. However, while several additions have been made to this new edition, I have decided as a matter of principle to limit the removal of Professor Merrills' original work. I have found that most of the existing paragraphs remain highly relevant, though certain parts, notably the role of international organisations in international dispute settlement and the final chapter on 'Trends and Prospects', required updating and some limited deletions.

Structurally, I have made only a few changes in light of my general approach mentioned above. Subheadings were added to make it easier for readers to directly locate one specific aspect, all headings were numbered to clarify the overall structure of the book, and a 'Further Reading' section was added to the end of each chapter.

Revising this textbook, which was one of the first texts on international dispute settlement, has been an immense honour and pleasure, despite the practical limitations I have run into in light of the first year of the Covid-19 pandemic, during which this new edition has been drafted and finalised. But I have not written in intellectual isolation, and hence wish to thank several people who have contributed, in various capacities, to the revision of this book.

First of all, I wish to thank Niamh McCormack and Samantha Tirthdas for research and editorial assistance. My thanks also go to several colleagues at the Grotius Centre for International Legal Studies and elsewhere for having shared their thoughts on the new edition of this book, and for having carefully reviewed some chapters and offered their comments and suggestions: Laurence Boisson de Chazournes, Mamadou Hébié, Larissa van den Herik, Sebastian Lopez Escarcena, Anna Marhold, Brian McGarry and Cecily Rose.

Last but not least, in revising the textbook, I have benefitted much from having co-taught for almost a decade the course of International Dispute Settlement at Leiden University with the late Professor Hugh Thirlway, who passed away in 2019. Notably the newly drafted first chapter's structure has been based on how Professor Thirlway and I used to introduce International Dispute Settlement to our LL.M. students. I will always remain much indebted to Professor Thirlway for his mentoring, counsel and friendship.

Eric De Brabandere
Ghent (Belgium), 19 March 2021

Table of Cases

Abaclat v. Argentine Republic (2011), 35
Abyei Arbitration (2009), 164
Aegean Sea Continental Shelf Case
  Interim Protection (1976), 207, 351, 404
  Judgment (1978), 53, 59, 60, 245, 253
Aerial Herbicide Spraying Case (2013), 46, 254
Aerial Incident Case (1996), 254
Aerial Incident Case (2000), 201–2
African Commission on Human and Peoples' Rights v. Libya (2011), 398
Air Transport Arbitrations (1963, 1965, 1978), 167
Alabama Claims Case (1871/2), 2, 135, 147, 153
Åland Islands Inquiry (1921), 98
Alleged Violation of Sovereign Rights in the Caribbean Case (2013)
  Counter-claims Order (2017), 218
  ICJ Press Release (2013), 252
Ambatielos Case (1953), 248
Application of the Interim Accord Case (2011), 59
Application of the International Convention on the Elimination of All
    Forms of Racial Discrimination (Georgia v. Russian Federation)
  Provisional Measures Order (2008), 223
  Preliminary Objections (2011), 11–12, 16, 30, 49, 55–6, 207–8
Application of the Convention on the Prevention and Punishment of the
    Crime of Genocide (Bosnia and Herzegovina v. Serbia and
    Montenegro)
  Application for Revision (2003), 217
  Judgment (2007), 19, 20–1, 233
  Preliminary Objections (1996), 200
  Provisional Measures (1993), 371
Application of the Convention on the Prevention and Punishment of the
    Crime of Genocide (Croatia v. Serbia), Judgment 2015, 233
"ARA Libertad" (Argentina v. Ghana), Provisional Measures, Order of
    15 December (2012), 264
Arbitral Award Case (1960), 162, 165, 250, 403–4
Arbitral Award of 31 July 1989 (Guinea-Bissau v. Senegal) (1991), 22–3,
    208

Arbitral Award of 3 October 1899 (Guyana v. Venezuela)
  Application Instituting Proceedings (2018), 169
  Preliminary Objections (2020), 25, 54, 59
Arctic Sunrise Arbitration (2013)
  Award on Jurisdiction (2014), 208, 288
  Merits (2015), 264, 272–3, 305
  Provisional Measures (2013), 432
Armed Activities on the Territory of the Congo (New Application: 2002) (Democratic Republic of the Congo v. Rwanda) (2006), 11, 26, 34, 55
Armed Activities on the Territory of the Congo (DRC v. Uganda) (2005)
  Merits (2005), 232, 244, 251
  Order on Experts (2020), 235
Arrest Warrant Case (2002), 196, 237, 257
Article XXVIII Rights Case (1990), 337
Asylum Case (1950), 256
Avena Case
  Interpretation (2009), 252
  Merits (2004), 195
Bank for International Settlements Case (2002/3), 167
Barbados/Trinidad and Tobago Case (2006), 57, 263, 266, 287
Bay of Bengal Maritime Boundary Arbitration (2014), 286
Beagle Channel Award (1977), 68, 71–2, 75, 82, 134, 147, 152, 164
Ben Bella Case (1958), 115, 128
Bering Sea Arbitration (1893), 156
BG Group v. Argentina (2014), 190
Bolivar Railway Company Claim (1903), 133
Border and Transborder Armed Actions Case (Nicaragua/ Honduras) (1988), 14, 55, 117, 199, 394, 405–6
BP v. Libya (1973), 154, 161, 163
Brcko Arbitration (1999), 156, 165
Buraimi Arbitration (1955), 163
Canada – Renewable Energy Case (2013), 330
Carthage Case (1913), 87
Case No. A/18 (1984), 151
Case concerning the Northern Cameroons (Cameroon v. United Kingdom), Preliminary Objections, Judgment of 2 December 1963, 16, 35, 48, 256
Case concerning the Right of Passage over Indian Territory (1960)
  Merits (1960), 31
  Preliminary Objections (1957), 199
Certain Activities carried out by Nicaragua in the Border Area Case (2013), 218, 233
Certain Criminal Proceedings in France Case (2002/3), 198

Table of Cases

Chaco Inquiry (1929), 107–8, 393
Chagos Marine Protected Area Arbitration (Mauritius *v.* United Kingdom) (2015)
  Award (2015), 264, 276
  Reasoned Decision on Challenge (2011), 142–4, 149, 150, 274
Chaisiri Reefer 2 Case (2001), 302
Channel Arbitration (1977/8), 136, 148, 152, 158–9, 161, 165, 251
China – Intellectual Property (2009), 325, 327
China – Raw Materials (2012), 330
Chorzów Factory Case (1927/8), 96
Clipperton Island Case (1931), 134
Compañía de Aguas del Aconquija *v.* Argentina (2010), 190, 198
Construction of a Wall (Advisory Opinion) (2004), 219, 220, 223, 247, 355, 372, 382
Copper Case (1987), 319
Corfu Channel Case
  Merits (1949), 235
Daimler Financial Services AG *v.* Argentina (2012), 35
Delimitation of the Maritime Boundary in the Bay of Bengal Case (2012), 301
Denmark *v.* Turkey (2000), 118
Denmark, France, the Netherlands, Norway and Sweden *v.* Turkey (1985), 118
Dispute Concerning Coastal State Rights in the Black Sea, Sea of Azov and Kerch Strait (Ukraine *v.* the Russian Federation) (2020), 138, 150, 268, 273–4, 279, 280, 288
Dispute concerning delimitation of the maritime boundary between Mauritius and Maldives in the Indian Ocean (Mauritius/Maldives) (2021), 273, 275, 287
Dispute Concerning Delimitation of the Maritime Boundary between Ghana and Côte d'Ivoire in the Atlantic Ocean (Ghana/Côte d'Ivoire) (2015), 294
Dogger Bank Inquiry (1905), 85–9, 97
Dubai/Sharjah Boundary Arbitration (1981), 140, 145
East African Community Case (1981), 110, 111–16, 130–1
East Timor Case (1995), 203
EC – Bananas Case (1997), 330
EC – Biotech Case (2006), 325
EC – Hormones Case (1998), 327, 331, 336–7
EC – Seal Products Case (2014), 328
ELSI (Elettronica Sicula SpA) Case (1989), 227–8
Emilio Agustín Maffezini *v.* The Kingdom of Spain (2000), 30–1
'Enrica Lexie' Incident (Italy *v.* India) (2020), 150–1

Eritrea–Ethiopia Boundary Commission Case (2002), 159
Eritrea–Ethiopia Claims Commission Cases (2003–9), 392
Eritrea/Yemen Arbitration (1998/9), 135, 147, 149, 152, 157, 163, 165
EU Fact-Finding Mission on Georgia (2008), 393
Eurotunnel Case (2007), 167
Expenses Case (1962), 375
Fisheries Jurisdiction Case (1998), 201
Fisheries Jurisdiction Cases (1973/4), 62–3, 199, 237, 253
Franco-Siamese Frontier Case (1947), 108, 113
Franco-Swiss Internment Case (1955), 109
Free Zones Arbitration (1933), 156, 158
Frontier Dispute Case (Benin/Niger) (2005), 226
Frontier Dispute Case (Burkina Faso/Mali)
   Judgment (1986), 226, 240
   Nomination of Experts (1987), 250
   Provisional Measures (1986), 250
Frontier Dispute Case (Burkina Faso/Niger) (2013), 17, 19, 250
Gabcikovo-Nagymaros Project (Hungary/Slovakia) Case (1997), 63, 198, 231–2, 237, 251
Glamis Gold v. United States (2010), 187–8
Gorm and Svava Cases (1952), 108
Grimm v. Iran (1983), 151
Gulf of Maine Case
   Constitution of Chamber (1982), 225
   Merits (1984), 60, 225–8, 241, 243, 245, 250, 292
Guyana/Suriname Case (2007), 287
Hadijatou v. Niger (2008), 398
Haji-Bagherpour v. United States (1983), 151
Haya de la Torre Case (1951), 15, 256
Heathrow Airport Arbitration (1992/3), 136, 145, 155, 166
Impregilo SpA v. Argentine Republic (2017), 5
Impregilo SpA v. Islamic Republic of Pakistan (2005), 11
Indus Waters Arbitration (2013), 136–7, 166
Interhandel Case (1959), 128
Interpretation of Peace Treaties (Advisory Opinion) (1950), 11–12, 138, 219
Ioan Micula v. Romania (2009), 179
Ireland v. UK (App no 5310/71) (1978), 18
Iron Rhine Railway Arbitration
   Award (2005), 135
   Interpretation (2005), 160
Island of Palmas Case (1928), 135
Italian Property Tax Case (1956), 110
Jan Mayen Conciliation (1981), 111–13, 116, 129, 131, 306

Japan – Import Quotas on Dried Laver and Seasoned Laver (2006), 325
Japanese Loan Cases (1955, 1960), 114, 129
Jeronovičs v. Latvia (2016), 18
Jurisdictional Immunities of the State Case
  Application to Intervene (2011), 214
  Counter-Claims Order (2010), 218
Kasikili/Sedudu Island Case (1999), 198, 239, 240
KE 007 Inquiry (1983), 100–2
Kosovo Case (2010), 355
LaGrand Case (2001), 211, 237
Lake Lanoux Arbitration (1957), 40, 44–6, 49, 50, 138, 166
Land, Island and Maritime Frontier Case
  Application for Revision (2003), 217
  Application to Intervene (1990), 213, 214, 424
  Composition of Chamber (1989), 226, 228
  Merits (1992), 227
Land and Maritime Boundary between Cameroon and Nigeria
  Preliminary Objections (1998), 216, 406
  Provisional Measures (1996), 205, 363
  Request for Interpretation (1999), 216
Land Reclamation Case
  Award (2005), 287
  Provisional Measures (2003), 41
Legality of Use of Force (Serbia v. Belgium)
  Merits (2004), 16
  Provisional Measures (2003), 41
Legal Consequences of the Separation of the Chagos Archipelago from
    Mauritius in 1965 (2019), 219, 220–1, 238, 274–5, 355
Letelier and Moffitt Case (1992), 91, 95, 97, 103
Libya–Malta Continental Shelf Case
  Application to Intervene (1984), 213
  Merits (1985), 228, 249
Ligitan and Sipadan Case
  Application to Intervene (2001), 215
Lockerbie Cases
  Discontinuation (2003), 254
  Preliminary Objections (1998), 55
  Provisional Measures (1992), 373
Manouba Case (1913), 87
Maritime Delimitation and Territorial Questions Case (Qatar and Bahrain)
  Judgment (2001), 431
  Jurisdiction and Admissibility (1994), 53, 199
  Jurisdiction and Admissibility (1995), 53, 199
Maritime Delimitation Case (Guinea and Guinea-Bissau) (1985), 136, 160

Maritime Delimitation Case (Guinea-Bissau and Senegal) (1989), 22–3, 136, 208
Maritime Delimitation in the Black Sea Case (Romania v. Ukraine) (2009), 223
Maritime Delimitation in the Indian Ocean (Somalia v. Kenya) (2017), 267
Maritime Dispute (Peru v. Chile) 2014, 243
Mavrommatis Palestine Concessions (Greece v. United Kingdom) (1924), 10–12
Mexico – Taxes on Softdrinks and Other Beverages (2006), 331
MH17 Inquiry (2015), 101
Mike Campbell (Pty) Limited & Others v. The Republic of Zimbabwe (2008), 399
Military and Paramilitary Activities in and against Nicaragua Case, see Nicaragua Case
Minquiers and Ecrehos Case (1953), 249
Monetary Gold Arbitration (1953), 135
Monetary Gold Case (1954), 203, 425
Mosul Inquiry (1925), 98
MOX Plant Case
   Provisional Measures (2001/3), 57, 264, 268
   Suspension of Proceedings (2003), 168, 272, 287, 435
   Termination of Proceedings (2008), 287
M/T 'San Padre Pio' Case (Switzerland v. Nigeria) (2019), 264
MV Saiga No. 2 Case (1999), 301
MV Virginia G Case (2014), 301
Namibia Case (1971), 223–4, 355, 374
Nicaragua Case
   Jurisdiction and Admissibility (1984), 201, 368, 404, 424
   Merits (1986), 199, 232
   Provisional Measures (1984), 207, 404
North Atlantic Coast Fisheries Arbitration (1910), 156
North Sea Continental Shelf Cases (1969), 63, 243, 248–9
Norwegian Loans Case (1957), 200
Nuclear Tests (Australia v. France) (1974), 16–17, 257
Nuclear Tests (New Zealand v. France) (1974), 9, 16, 257
Nuclear Tests II Case (1995), 257
Nuclear Weapons Advisory Opinion (1996), 220, 355
Obligation to Negotiate Access to the Pacific Ocean (Bolivia v. Chile) (2018), 7, 8, 64–5
Obligations concerning Negotiations relating to Cessation of the Nuclear Arms Race and to Nuclear Disarmament (Marshall Islands v. India) (2016), 9, 11–12

Obligations concerning Negotiations relating to Cessation of the Nuclear
   Arms Race and to Nuclear Disarmament (Marshall Islands *v.* United
   Kingdom) (2016), 9, 15, 54, 58
Oil Platforms Case (Islamic Republic of Iran *v.* United States of
   America)
  Counter-Claims Order (1998), 218
  Merits (2003), 34
  Preliminary Objection (1996), 200
OSPAR (Article 9) Arbitration (2003), 136, 153, 162, 166, 287
Palena Case (1966), 134, 165
Palmer Report (2011), 99
Passage through the Great Belt Case (1991), 212, 254
Peace Treaties Case (1950), 138, 162, 255
Philip Morris Asia Limited *v.* The Commonwealth of Australia (2015), 30
Philip Morris *v.* Uruguay (2013), 177
Phosphate Lands in Nauru Case (1992), 203, 254
Pulp Mills on the River Uruguay Case, 42, 234
  Judgment (2010), 42, 234
  Provisional Measures (2006, 2007), 208–9
Questions relating to the Obligation to Prosecute or Extradite Case
   (2012)
  Merits (2012), 11, 57, 204
  Provisional Measures (2009), 209
Questions relating to the Seizure and Detention of Certain Documents and
   Data Case (2014/15), 205–6, 433
Rainbow Warrior Case (1986), 25, 135, 146, 157–9, 169, 364–5
Rainbow Warrior II Case (1990), 160
Rann of Kutch Arbitration (1968), 78, 80, 183, 152, 154, 165
Red Crusader Inquiry (1962), 92–7, 290
Reparation for Injuries Case (1949), 354
Republic of Italy *v.* Republic of Cuba (2005/8), 178
Request for Advisory Opinion submitted by the Sub-Regional Fisheries
   Commission (2015), 297
Responsibilities and Obligations of States with respect to Activities in the
   Area (2011), 300
Rhine Chlorides Case (2004), 166
Rompetrol *v.* Romania (2013), 188
Roula Case (1956), 129
Saghi *v.* Iran (1993), 151
Saint Pierre and Miquelon Case (1992), 151, 165
Sarayaku Case (2012), 42
Sempra Energy International *v.* Argentina (2010), 191

SGS (Société Générale de Surveillance) S.A. v. Republic of the Philippines (2004), 20, 36
South China Sea Arbitration (2015)
  Award (2016), 279, 305
  Jurisdiction and Admissibility (2015), 139, 264, 267–8, 271, 278–9, 288, 304–5, 432
South West Africa Cases (1962), 11–12, 47–8, 55
Southern Bluefin Tuna Case
  Jurisdiction and Admissibility (2000), 18, 167, 265, 268, 276, 277, 288, 304, 435
  Provisional Measures (1999), 11, 57
Sovereignty over Pedra Branca Case (Malaysia/Singapore) (2008), 198
Spiridon Roussalis v. Romania (2011), 18
Swordfish Case (2000), 287, 302, 435
Taba Arbitration (1988), 30, 117, 135, 147, 152, 159, 165
Tavignano Inquiry (1912), 87–9, 92, 97
Temple of Preah Vihear Case (Cambodia v. Thailand) (1961)
  Interpretation (2013), 216
  Jurisdiction (1961), 202
  Merits (1962), 253
Territorial and Maritime Dispute Case (Nicaragua v. Colombia) (2011), 214
Territorial Dispute (Libyan Arab Jamahiriya/Chad) (1994), 431
Tiger Inquiry (1918), 88–9, 90, 97
Timor Sea Conciliation (2018)
  Decision on Australia's objection to competence (2016), 283
  Report and Recommendations (2018), 104
Tinoco Arbitration (1923), 135
Trail Smelter Arbitration (1938/41), 153–4, 161
Tubantia Inquiry (1922), 90–1, 93
Tulip Real Estate Investment and Development Netherlands B.V. v. Republic of Turkey (2015), 21
Tunisia–Libya Continental Shelf Case
  Application to Intervene (1981), 213
  Judgment (1982), 228, 241, 243, 249, 251
  Revision and Interpretation (1985), 215
Tza Yap Shum v. Republic of Peru (2011), 188
United Nations Headquarters Agreement Case (1988), 11, 248
United States v. Iran (2000), 168
United States – Continued Suspension Case (2008), 331
United States – Gambling Case (2005), 336
United States – Shrimp Case (1998), 331
United States – Tuna (2012), 330

United States – Upland Cotton (Article 21.5) Case (2008), 331
US Diplomatic and Consular Staff in Tehran (United States *v.* Iran) (1980), 13
Vannessa Ventures *v.* Venezuela (2013), 187
Venezuela–British Guiana Boundary Case (1899), 164, 169
Vitianu Case (1949), 130
Waste Management Inc *v.* Mexico No 2 (2002), 19
Western Sahara Case (1975), 219, 220, 224, 236, 256, 355
Wet Salted Cod Case (1988), 319
Whaling in the Antarctic Case
  Intervention Order (2013), 215
  Judgment (2014), 204, 234
WHO Regional Headquarters Case (1980), 220
Youmans Claim (1926), 133
Young Loan Arbitration (1980), 166

Table of Treaties and Agreements

1794	Jay Treaty, 133
1814	Treaty of Ghent, 133
1866	Treaties of Bayonne, 45
1872	Arbitration Agreement concerning Claims to Delagoa Bay, 156
1894	Gamez-Bonilla Treaty, 161, 162
1899	Hague Convention for the Pacific Settlement of International Disputes, 2, 15
1902	General Treaty of Arbitration (Argentina–Chile), 134
1904	Declaration of St Petersburg, 86
1907	Arbitration Agreement (Colombia–Ecuador), 156
1907	Hague Convention for the Pacific Settlement of International Disputes, 87
1907	Convention on the Limitation of Employment of Force for Recovery of Contract Debts (Hague, II), 3
1911	Taft (Knox) Treaties of Arbitration, 91
1913–40	Bryan Treaties, 91, 95, 106, 112
1914	Bryan–Suárez Mujica Treaty (Chile–United States), 95
1915	ABC Treaty, 91
1919	Covenant of the League of Nations, 15, 407, 425
1919	Mandate for South West Africa, 48
	Treaty of Conciliation (Brazil–Great Britain), 91
	Treaty of Conciliation (Chile–Great Britain), 91
1920	Treaty of Conciliation (Chile–Sweden), 104
1921	Treaty of Arbitration and Conciliation (Germany–Switzerland), 105
1923	Gondra Treaty, 91, 106–7
	Treaty of Washington, 106
1924	Treaty of Conciliation and Judicial Settlement (Italy–Switzerland), 110
1925	Locarno Treaties, 105
	Treaty of Conciliation (France–Switzerland), 105–7, 117
1927	Treaty of Conciliation, Judicial Settlement and Arbitration (Belgium–Denmark), 109
1928	General Act for the Pacific Settlement of International Disputes, 106

1929	Inter-American General Convention of Conciliation, 106
	Protocol establishing the Chaco Commission, 107, 393
	Treaty of Conciliation (Czechoslovakia, Romania, Kingdom of the Serbs, Croatians and Slovenes), 106
1933	Saavedra Lamas Agreement, 106
	Treaty of Conciliation (Brazil–Poland), 128
1935	Arbitration Agreement concerning the Trail Smelter Dispute, 153
1938	Munich Agreement, 77
1944	Chicago Convention on Civil Aviation, 100
1945	Charter of the United Nations
	Art. 1, 347
	Art. 2(3), 1, 263
	Art. 2(7), 350
	Arts. 10–14, 350
	Art. 10, 350
	Art. 11(2), 350
	Art. 11(3), 349
	Art. 12, 370
	Art. 12(1), 350
	Art. 14, 350
	Art. 24, 368
	Art. 25, 371
	Chapter VI, 348
	Art. 33, 8, 59, 407–8
	Art. 33(1), 39, 348, 350
	Art. 33(2), 350
	Art. 34, 255, 351
	Art. 35(1), 349
	Art. 35(2), 350
	Art. 36(1), 350
	Art. 36(3), 354
	Art. 37(1), 349
	Art. 37(2), 351
	Art. 38, 348
	Chapter VII, 348
	Art. 39, 360
	Art. 41, 360
	Art. 42, 360
	Art. 43, 360
	Art. 51, 386
	Chapter VIII, 407
	Arts. 52–4, 407
	Art. 52(2), 348

Art. 53(1), 408
Art. 94, 252
Art. 96(1), 372
Art. 98, 360, 367
Art. 99, 349, 360
Art. 103, 373
Statute of the International Court of Justice
Art. 1, 368
Art. 2, 222
Art. 9, 222
Art. 17, 233, 291
Art. 24, 233
Arts. 26–9, 224
Art. 36(2), 405, 452
Art. 36(5), 201
Art. 36(6), 27, 198
Art. 37(5), 202
Art. 38(1), 236
Art. 38(2), 240
Art. 41, 371
Art. 50, 235
Art. 53, 252, 286
Art. 60, 216, 252
Art. 61, 215
Art. 62, 212, 323
Art. 63, 212, 323
Art 65(1), 372
Art. 80, 217

1946　Trusteeship Agreement for the Cameroons, 16, 48
Whaling Convention, 215
1947　General Agreement on Tariffs and Trade, 310
Inter-American Treaty of Reciprocal Assistance (Rio Treaty), 386
Treaty of Peace with Italy, 110
Treaties of Peace with Bulgaria, Hungary and Romania, 138
United Nations Headquarters Agreement, 248
1948　American Treaty on Pacific Settlement (Pact of Bogotá), 386
Charter of Bogotá, 386
Genocide Convention, 10, 200, 206, 374
1949　Revised General Act for the Pacific Settlement of International Disputes, 106
1950　European Convention on Human Rights, 117, 271, 290, 384
1953　Agreement on German External Debts, 166

1957	European Convention for the Peaceful Settlement of Disputes, 117, 140, 195, 218
	Washington Agreement (Honduras–Nicaragua), 391
1958	Geneva Convention on Fishing and Conservation of the Living Resources of the High Seas, 269
	Geneva Conventions on the Law of the Sea, 269
	New York Convention on the Recognition and Enforcement of Foreign Arbitral Awards, 189, 190
1959	Antarctic Treaty, 43, 51
	Treaty between the Federal Republic of Germany and Pakistan for the Promotion and Protection of Investments, 173
1960	Indus Waters Treaty, 137, 166
1961	Exchange of Notes concerning Fishing (United Kingdom–Iceland), 50–1, 62
	Exchange of Notes concerning the *Red Crusader* Incident (United Kingdom–Denmark), 92
1961	Regulations on the Procedure of International Conciliation adopted by the Institute of International Law in 1961, 104
1963	Charter of the Organization of African Unity, 117, 387
	Vienna Convention on Consular Relations, 6, 195, 207, 237
1964	Protocol of the Commission of Mediation, Conciliation and Arbitration of the OAU, 117–18
1965	Convention on the Settlement of Investment Disputes between States and Nationals of Other States, 120, 173, 188–9
	Convention on Transit Trade of Land-Locked Countries, 56
	International Convention on the Elimination of All Forms of Racial Discrimination, 49
	Treaty of Conciliation, Judicial Settlement and Arbitration (United Kingdom–Switzerland), 115
1966	Concession Agreement between BP and Libya, 154
	International Covenant on Civil and Political Rights, 118
	UN Covenants on Human Rights, 125
1968	Indonesia–Netherlands BIT, 174
1969	American Convention on Human Rights, 118
	Vienna Convention on the Law of Treaties, 119, 130, 180, 282
1971	Agreement for Arbitration of the Beagle Channel Dispute, 75
	Montreal Convention for the Suppression of Unlawful Acts against the Safety of Civil Aviation, 55, 373
1972	Charter of the Islamic Conference, 389
1975	Algiers Accord (Iran–Iraq), 81
	Arbitration Agreement concerning Delimitation of the Continental Shelf (United Kingdom–France), 444
	Brussels Communiqué (Greece–Turkey), 53

Convention on the Representation of States in their Relations with International Organizations of a Universal Character, 282

Helsinki Agreement, 123, 125

Statute of the River Uruguay, 42, 209

1976 Special Agreement concerning Delimitation of the Continental Shelf (Libya–Malta), 249

1977 Air Services Agreement, 'Bermuda II' (United Kingdom–United States), 146

Special Agreement concerning Delimitation of the Continental Shelf (Tunisia–Libya), 148, 240, 251

Treaty between Czechoslovakia and Hungary concerning the Construction and Operation of the Gabcikovo-Nagymaros System of Locks, 448

1978 Camp David Agreements, 379

Torres Strait Treaty, 50

Vienna Convention on Succession of States in respect of Treaties, 64, 119

Agreement between the Government of Sweden and the Government of the Socialist Federal Republic of Yugoslavia on the Mutual Protection of Investments, 176

1979 Special Agreement concerning Delimitation of the Maritime Boundary in the Gulf of Maine Area, 60

1981 African Charter on Human and Peoples' Rights, 118

Agreement on the Continental Shelf between Iceland and Jan Mayen, 111

Declaration of Algeria concerning the Settlement of Claims by the United States and Iran, 137

Treaty Establishing the Organization of Eastern Caribbean States, 117

1982 Antitrust Cooperation Agreement (United States–Australia), 39

Law of the Sea Convention

Art. 187, 28, 299

Art. 188, 299

Art. 189, 299

Art. 190, 299

Art. 191, 300

Art. 279, 263

Art. 280, 263

Art. 281, 168, 265

Art. 282, 265

Art. 283, 265

Art. 284, 281

Art. 287, 270

                    Art. 288, 270
                    Art. 289, 270
                    Art. 290, 270, 294
                    Art. 290(1), 287, 294
                    Art. 290(5), 294–5
                    Art. 292, 270
                    Art. 293, 272–3, 299
                    Art. 294, 271
                    Art. 295, 271
                    Art. 297, 276–7, 280
                    Art. 298, 276–8, 280–1, 284, 304
                    Art. 298(3), 278
                    Art. 299, 281
                    Art. 308, 261
                    Annex V, 129, 281, 283
                    Annex VI, 263, 290, 298–9, 300
                    Annex VII, 284–8
                    Annex VIII, 288–9, 290
                    Part XI, 298
1983   Special Agreement concerning Frontier Delimitation (Upper Volta/Burkina Faso–Mali), 205
            Special Agreement concerning Maritime Boundary Delimitation (Guinea–Guinea-Bissau), 160
1984   Agreement concerning the Assets of the East African Community, 110
            Treaty of Peace and Friendship (Argentina–Chile), 76
            UN Convention Against Torture, 204
1985   Protocol of Cartagena de Indias, 387
            Vienna Convention for the Protection of the Ozone Layer, 120
1986   Agreement to Arbitrate the Boundary Dispute concerning the Taba Beachfront, 116
            Single European Act, 384
1987   Esquipulas II Accord, 395, 406
            Montreal Protocol to the Vienna Convention for the Protection of the Ozone Layer, 120, 126
1988   Switzerland–Uruguay BIT, 179
1989   ILO Convention No. 169, 43
1990   Agreement establishing an Interim Reciprocal Information and Consultation System (Argentina–United Kingdom), 41, 439
            Argentina – United Kingdom BIT, 32
            Agreement to Settle Dispute concerning Compensation for the Deaths of Letelier and Moffitt (Chile–United States), 95
            Italy – Morocco BIT, 174

1991	Argentina–United States BIT, 32, 191
	Mercosur Treaty, 342
	Treaty Establishing the African Economic Community, 389
1992	Convention for the Protection of the Marine Environment of the North-East Atlantic (OSPAR Convention), 136, 147, 153, 162, 166, 268, 287, 435
	Convention on Biological Diversity, 121, 267–8
	Framework Convention on Climate Change, 121
	North American Free Trade Agreement (NAFTA), 340
	Protocol of Washington, 386
	Stockholm Convention on Conciliation and Arbitration within the CSCE, 125, 394
	Treaty of Maastricht, 384
1993	Commonwealth of Independent States Charter, 385
	Commonwealth of Independent States Treaty on Creation of Economic Union, 385
	Italy–Cuba BIT, 178
	Protocol to the 1976 Convention on the Protection of the Rhine against Pollution by Chlorides, 166
	Revised Treaty of the Economic Community of West African States, 340
	Special Agreement concerning the Gabcikovo–Nagymaros Project (Hungary–Slovak Republic), 448
1994	Agreement establishing the World Trade Organization, 311, 314, 342
	Agreement on Technical Barriers to Trade, 329
	Agreement relating to the Implementation of Part XI of the Law of the Sea Convention, 261
	Convention to Combat Desertification, 121
	Peru–China BIT, 188
	SPS Agreement, 324
	TRIPS Agreement, 314, 326
1995	Dayton Peace Agreement, 70, 156
	Joint Declaration on Cooperation over Offshore Activities in the South West Atlantic (Argentina–United Kingdom), 51, 439
	Straddling Stocks Agreement, 306
1996	Special Agreement concerning the Kasikili/Sedudu Island Dispute (Botswana–Namibia), 239
1997	Convention on the Law of the Non-Navigational Uses of International Watercourses, 121
	Kyoto Protocol, 127
	Treaty of Amsterdam, 384
1998	Aarhus Convention, 127

1999	International Convention for the Suppression of the Financing of International Terrorism, 166
2000	Cartagena Protocol on Biosafety, 127
2001	Constitutive Act of the African Union, 117, 383, 388, 400
2002	Special Agreement concerning a Boundary Dispute (Benin–Niger), 251
	Agreement on encouragement and reciprocal protection of investments between the Kingdom of the Netherlands and the Federal Republic of Yugoslavia, 177
2006	Southern Indian Ocean Fisheries Agreement, 307
	Agreement between the Government of the United Kingdom of Great Britain and Northern Ireland and the Government of the United Mexican States for the Promotion and Reciprocal Protection of Investments, 177
2008	Protocol on the Statute of the African Court of Justice and Human Rights, 389
	Treaty between the Government of the United States of America and The Government of the Republic of Rwanda concerning the Encouragement and Reciprocal Protection of Investment, 176
2009	Lisbon Treaty, 384
	Arbitration Agreement between the Government of the Republic of Croatia and the Government of the Republic of Slovenia, 145
2010	Belgium–Luxembourg Economic Union – Montenegro BIT, 32
2012	PCA Arbitration Rules, 140
2013	Aerial Herbicide Spraying Agreement, 46
2014	Convention on Transparency in Treaty-based Investor-State Arbitration from 10 December 2014, 183
2018	UN Convention on International Settlement Agreements Resulting from Mediation ('Singapore Convention on Mediation'), 81
2020	Multi-Party Interim Appeal Arbitration Arrangement Pursuant to Article 25 of the DSU, 332

1

International Dispute Settlement: Principles and Concepts

Disputes are an inevitable part of international relations, just as disputes between individuals are inevitable in domestic relations. Like individuals, states often want the same thing in a situation where there is not enough of it to go round. Moreover, just as people can disagree about the way to use a river, a piece of land or a sum of money, states frequently want to do different things, but their claims are incompatible. Admittedly, one side may change its position, extra resources may be found, or, on looking further into the issue, it may turn out that everyone can be satisfied after all. But no one imagines that these possibilities can eliminate all domestic disputes and they certainly cannot be relied on internationally. Disputes, whether between states, neighbours, or brothers and sisters, must therefore be accepted as a regular part of human relations and the problem is what to do about them.

A dispute may be defined as a specific disagreement concerning a matter of fact, law or policy in which a claim or assertion of one party is met with refusal, counter-claim or denial by another. In the broadest sense, an international dispute can be said to exist whenever such a disagreement involves governments, institutions, juristic persons (corporations) or private individuals in different parts of the world. However, the disputes with which the present work is primarily concerned are those in which the parties are two or more of the nearly 200 or so sovereign states into which the world is currently divided.

A basic requirement is a commitment from those who are likely to become involved, that is to say, from everyone, that disputes will only be pursued by peaceful means. Within states, this principle was established at an early stage and laws and institutions were set up to prohibit self-help and to enable disputes to be settled without disruption of the social order. On the international plane, where initially the matter was regarded as less important, equivalent arrangements have been slower to develop. The emergence of international law, which in its modern form can be dated from the seventeenth century, was accompanied by neither the creation of a world government nor a renunciation of the use of force by states. In 1945, however, with the consequences of the unbridled pursuit of national objectives still fresh in the memory, the founder members of the United Nations agreed in Article 2(3) of the UN Charter to 'settle their international disputes by peaceful means in such a manner that international peace and security, and justice, are not endangered'. What these peaceful means are and how they are used by states are the subject of this book.

This first introductory chapter aims to identify the basic framework for the settlement of international disputes by discussing the main principles of international dispute settlement and the concepts used in the settlement of disputes. This chapter looks at the general principles of practice across dispute settlement methods and institutions, rather than engaging in a discussion on every court and tribunal individually.

1.1 The Peaceful Settlement of Disputes

International dispute settlement has long been viewed through the lens of the question of whether international law and international relations require a compulsory method to settle disputes, a question which is inextricably linked to the idea that dispute settlement is necessary to avoid recourse to war or armed force.[1] From the 1870s onwards, proposals for the establishment of some system to arbitrate international disputes were becoming common.[2] The trust in international arbitration found confirmation in the increased practice of international arbitration, and the relative successes of arbitration to settle disputes, such as the arbitration of the *Alabama claims* between the United Kingdom and the United States in 1872, and the *Fur Seal Arbitration* between the same parties, concluded in 1892.

These successes resulted in a formalisation of international arbitration as a method of dispute settlement through the creation of the Permanent Court of Arbitration (PCA) during the first Hague Peace Conference of 1899.[3] International arbitration was already then seen in its connection to avoid recourse to war in addition to being considered as a means to ensure implementation of international law. This goal had been vigorously defended during the 1899 Hague Peace Conference and finds reflection in Article 1 of the 1899 Convention for the Pacific Settlement of International Disputes which established the PCA:

> With a view to obviating, as far as possible, recourse to force in the relations between States, the Signatory Powers agree to use their best efforts to insure the pacific settlement of international differences.

---

[1] See M. E. O'Connell, 'Arbitration and Avoidance of War: The Nineteenth-Century American Vision', in C. P. R. Romano (ed.), *The Sword and the Scales: The United States and International Courts and Tribunals*, Cambridge, 2009, pp. 30–45.

[2] W. G. Grewe, *The Epochs of International Law*, Berlin, 2000, p. 517; M. E. O'Connell, 'Arbitration and Avoidance of War: The Nineteenth-Century American Vision', in C. P. R. Romano (ed.), *The Sword and the Scales* (n. 1) pp. 30–45.

[3] Hague Convention on Pacific Settlement of International Disputes (Hague, I) (adopted 29 July 1899, entered into force 4 September 1900).

There was, however, no compulsory submission of disputes to the PCA.

The Second Hague Peace Conference which was convened in 1907 renewed enthusiasm for the idea of a permanent tribunal with compulsory jurisdiction, but no substantial adaptations were made to the PCA. The Second Hague Peace Conference, however, did result in the signature of the Hague Convention on the Limitation of Employment of Force for Recovery of Contract Debts (Hague II, also known as the 'Drago Porter Convention').[4] The Convention was important for the agreement of the states parties to prohibit the use of armed force for the 'recovery of contract debts claimed from the Government of one country by the Government of another country as being due to its nationals'.[5] The Convention links the prohibition of the use of force to recover contract debts to dispute settlement, since it also provides that the undertaking not to use force is 'not applicable when the debtor State refuses or neglects to reply to an offer of arbitration, or, after accepting the offer, prevents any compromise from being agreed on, or, after the arbitration, fails to submit to the award'.[6]

The creation of the Permanent Court of International Justice (PCIJ) in 1920 was another important step in the rise of international dispute settlement and its link to the prohibition of the use of force. The PCIJ had no compulsory jurisdiction, despite proposals to that effect from the Advisory Committee of Jurists headed by the Belgian Baron Descamps,[7] but its permanent and especially its standing character was considered a major achievement. Importantly, the PCIJ was seen as part of the 'system of war prevention',[8] but the PCIJ was also established in the context of a strong belief not only in the settlement of disputes to avoid war, but also in an institutionalisation to bring about peace and development.[9]

After the Second World War, the United Nations (UN) and its principal judicial organ, the International Court of Justice (ICJ) were established. The UN and the ICJ were seen as important institutions in the avoidance of the use of force in international relations. This is reflected by the obligation for UN member states to settle their disputes by peaceful means set out in Article 2(3) of the UN Charter, the first time that the peaceful settlement of disputes was established as a freestanding obligation. It is not a coincidence that the obligation to settle disputes in a peaceful way is

---

[4] Convention on the Limitation of Employment of Force for Recovery of Contract Debts (Hague, II) (adopted 18 October 1907, entered into force 26 January 1910).

[5] Article 1(1) Convention on the Limitation of Employment of Force for Recovery of Contract Debts ('Drago Porter Convention').

[6] Ibid. Article 1(2).   [7] C. Rousseau, *Droit International Public*, Paris, 1979, p. 327.

[8] W. G. Grewe, *The Epochs of International Law*, Berlin, 2000, p. 616.

[9] See L. Tosi, 'The League of Nations: An international relations perspective' (2017) 22 *Uniform Law Review*, 148–57 and M. Erpelding, B. Hess, and H. Ruiz Fabri, *Peace through Law : The Versailles Peace Treaty and Dispute Settlement After World War I*, Baden-Baden, 2019.

provided in Article 2(3) of the UN Charter, before the prohibition on the use of force, provided for in Article 2(4) of the UN Charter. The sequence is notable but also indicates that the principle that states should settle their disputes by resort to peaceful means is the counterpart of the prohibition of the use of force in international relations. Since then, the peaceful settlement of disputes has been repeated and confirmed in various instruments. For example, UNGA Resolution 2626 (XXV) containing the 'Declaration on Principles of International Law concerning Friendly Relations and Co-operation among States in accordance with the Charter of the United Nations' ('Friendly Relations Declaration') contains multiple references to the prohibition of the use of force in international relations, and the obligation for states to settle international disputes by peaceful means.

The obligation on states to settle disputes by peaceful means resulting from Article 2(3) of the UN Charter should primarily be read as an obligation directed to and binding upon all UN member states. Yet it is safe to conclude that the obligation for states to settle disputes by peaceful means also applies beyond the UN member states to all states in their conduct.

At its core, the obligation to settle disputes by peaceful means implies simply that states should use any peaceful means to settle their disputes, with the exclusion of resort to force. While the obligation to settle disputes by peaceful means can therefore be mostly understood and given legal significance in its negative construction by reference to the countervailing prohibition on the use of force, it has a very strong principled and symbolic function.[10]

The obligation does not impose any obligation as such to settle disputes. However, in respect of the latter, reference should be made to Article 33 of the UN Charter which contains an obligation for UN member states to settle 'any dispute, the continuance of which is likely to endanger the maintenance of international peace and security'. This article contains a positive obligation on UN member states to settle their disputes if these are likely to endanger the maintenance of international peace and security. The aforementioned 'Friendly Relations Declaration' both confirms these principles and adds that in the event of failure to reach a solution by any means of settlement chosen, states are under an obligation to continue to seek a settlement of the dispute by other peaceful means to be agreed upon by parties. Moreover, the Declaration adds that all states, including states not parties to the dispute, are under an obligation to 'refrain from any action which may aggravate the situation so as to endanger the maintenance of international peace and security'. The 1982 'Manila Declaration on the Peaceful Settlement of International Disputes' reaffirms these principles.[11]

---

[10] O. Corten, F. Dubuisson, V. Koutroulis and A. Largewall, *Une Introduction Critique au Droit International*, Brussels, 2017, p. 543.

[11] United Nations General Assembly Resolution 37/10 ('Manila Declaration on the Peaceful Settlement of International Disputes').

The obligation to settle disputes by resort to peaceful means also does not impose any specific choice of dispute settlement method. States involved in a dispute need to consent to the settlement of the dispute and retain the choice to freely determine the method of settlement.

1.2 State Consent and the Free Choice of Means of Settlement

The sovereign equality of states, a firmly established principle of public international law which implies that irrespective of size or power states have equal rights and capacities,[12] implies two important principles of international dispute settlement: the need for states to consent to the settlement of a dispute and the free choice of means of settlement.

1.2.1 State Consent to Dispute Settlement

The principled sovereign equality of states in international law entails the need for the states involved in a dispute to consent to the settlement of a dispute and to the means of settlement. Indeed, despite the general obligation to settle international disputes peacefully, general international law does not impose on states a particular means of dispute settlement. No state is, without consenting, under an obligation to agree on a particular means of settlement of disputes – consent is a necessary prerequisite for the settlement of disputes between states. This prerequisite of consent is valid for all methods of settlement, but has also a practical function in the context of diplomatic methods such as negotiation, good offices and mediation where, by necessary implication, the state needs to participate actively in settling the dispute. In such cases, the consent is of both a principled and a practical relevance.

This fundamental principle of international law has long been recognised by international courts and tribunals. In its Advisory Opinion on the 'Status of Eastern Carelia', the PCIJ noted:

> it is well established in international law that no State can, without its consent, be compelled to submit its disputes with other States either to mediation or to arbitration, or to any other kind of pacific settlement.[13]

The principle of state consent is sometimes expressed through the notion of 'jurisdiction *ratione voluntatis*' in international adjudication and arbitration.[14] However, since state consent forms the basis of any dispute

---

[12] M. N. Shaw, *International Law*, 8th ed., Cambridge, 2017, p. 168.
[13] Permanent Court of International Justice, Status of Eastern Carelia, Advisory Opinion, 1923 PCIJ (ser. B) No. 5 (23 July 1923), p. 27.
[14] See e.g. *Impregilo S.p.A. v. Argentine Republic*, ICSID Case No. ARB/07/17, Brigitte Stern dissenting opinion.

settlement method, it has a more fundamental character than the jurisdictional requirements contained in the *expression* of such consent. In other words, jurisdiction is created by consent.[15]

Consent can be expressed in various ways, which are either implicit in the method of settlement chosen or regulated by the statutes or rules governing formalised dispute settlement methods such as international adjudication or arbitration. If states opt for diplomatic dispute settlement methods, the consent to settle a dispute by negotiation or mediation can easily be derived from the participation by states in these procedures. The more formal the dispute settlement method, however, the more the expression of consent is formalised and subject to specific requirements included in the relevant statutes of international courts and tribunals, or the rules of procedure chosen in case of arbitration.

Generally, consent to jurisdiction is expressed by an international instrument such as a treaty, where states parties formally consent to the jurisdiction outlined therein. As a matter of principle, consent to jurisdiction cannot be derived from custom.[16] Where states expressly agree in an international instrument to settle a given dispute by immediate resort to international adjudication or arbitration, such treaty is referred to as a 'special agreement' or 'compromis'.[17]

States may also stipulate an agreement in a bilateral or multilateral treaty covering certain substantial issues to submit disputes relating to the treaty to international adjudication or arbitration or any other method (or combination thereof) of settlement. Such agreement is provided for in a clause referred to as a 'compromissory clause'. An example is Article 1 of the Optional Protocol to the Vienna Convention on Consular Relations Concerning the Compulsory Settlement of Disputes[18] which provides:

> Disputes arising out of the interpretation or application of the Convention shall lie within the compulsory jurisdiction of the International Court of Justice and may accordingly be brought before the Court by an application made by any party to the dispute being a Party to the present Protocol.

States, however, are often free to make reservations to compromissory clauses in treaties, in which case, and depending on the precise formulation of the treaty, states will be bound by the substantive obligations contained therein but not the dispute settlement clause.

The advantage of a 'compromis' compared to 'compromissory clauses' resides in the fact that it guarantees the 'direct and immediate consent of

---

[15] H. Thirlway, *The International Court of Justice*, Oxford, 2016, p. 36.   [16] *Ibid.*, 36.
[17] H. Thirlway, 'Compromis', in *Max Planck Encyclopedia of Public International Law*, Oxford, 2006, para. 1.
[18] Optional Protocol to the Vienna Convention on Consular Relations Concerning the Compulsory Settlement of Disputes (adopted 24 April 1963, entered into force 19 March 1967) UNTS 596.

both parties',[19] and to that extent is different from 'compromissory clauses' which contain a generalised advance consent of states.

Another form of consent may be found in a 'compromissory treaty', a particular form of treaty containing the consent of a group of states, where a certain set of defined disputes may, if they occur, be submitted to international adjudication or arbitration. The difference between this type of treaty and the two other forms of consent lies in the fact that in the case of a 'compromissory treaty' the subject matter of the treaty is the organisation of the settlement of disputes. An example is the so-called 'Pact of Bogotá' signed in 1948[20] which has often been invoked as a basis for the jurisdiction of the International Court of Justice.[21]

In the case of compromissory treaties or compromissory clauses, states consent in advance to having a range of disputes settled in a particular manner. In such instances, there may be a certain lapse of time between consent expressed by states and the actual submission of a dispute to a defined method of settlement. Similarly, treaties may contain a compromissory clause without the possibility for states to make reservations or opt out of the compromissory clause. In such cases, despite the remoteness between the consent and the actual submission of a dispute, and the impossibility for states to sign and ratify a treaty without accepting the compromissory clauses, the fundamental principle that states have consented to submit a dispute to adjudication or arbitration remains intact.

It is important to note at this point that specific methods of settlement or courts and tribunals may also provide for specific modes for consent, such as the so-called 'optional clause' provided in Article 36(2) of the Statute of the ICJ. These specific modes for consent will be discussed throughout this book in the various chapters dedicated to the particular dispute settlement methods.

1.2.2 Free Choice of Means of Settlement

The principle of sovereign equality of states and the need for states to consent to have their disputes settled imply that states are free to choose the means of dispute settlement. As explained by the ICJ in the *Obligation to Negotiate Access to the Pacific Ocean* case,[22] in the context of the discussion on whether there exists an obligation to negotiate based on the general principle of the peaceful settlement of disputes:

---

[19] H. Thirlway, 'Compromis' (n. 17), para. 26.
[20] American Treaty on Pacific Settlement (signed 30 April 1948, entered into force 6 May 1949) 30 UNTS 55.
[21] See E. Valencia-Ospina, 'Bogotá Pact (1948)', in *Max Planck Encyclopedia of Public International Law*, Oxford, 2006.
[22] *Obligation to Negotiate Access to the Pacific Ocean (Bolivia v. Chile)*, Judgment of 1 October 2018, [2018] ICJ Rep. 507.

The Court recalls that, according to Article 2, paragraph 3, of the Charter of the United Nations, '[a]ll Members shall settle their international disputes by peaceful means in such a manner that international peace and security, and justice, are not endangered'. This paragraph sets forth a general duty to settle disputes in a manner that preserves international peace and security, and justice, but there is no indication in this provision that the parties to a dispute are required to resort to a specific method of settlement, such as negotiation. Negotiation is mentioned in Article 33 of the Charter, alongside 'enquiry, mediation, conciliation, arbitration, judicial settlement, resort to regional agencies or arrangements' and 'other peaceful means' of the parties' choice. However, this latter provision also leaves the choice of peaceful means of settlement to the parties concerned and does not single out any specific method, including negotiation. Thus, the parties to a dispute will often resort to negotiation, but have no obligation to do so.[23]

The free choice of means is a fundamental principle of international dispute settlement and is sometimes explicitly included in dispute settlement provisions of international treaties.[24] It is explicitly included in the 'Friendly Relations Declaration', which links the free choice of means to the sovereign equality of states,[25] as does the 1982 Manila Declaration.[26] To a large extent, the freedom of choice is implicit in the need for states to consent to have their disputes settled, since the expression of consent to have a dispute settled necessarily implies choosing a *particular* type of procedure or method of settlement in the expression of consent. The free choice of means is only subjected to the limitation that all parties to the dispute need to consent to the *same* method of settlement.

1.3 The Notion of 'Dispute'

What constitutes a dispute is central to any discussion of international dispute settlement. The question of whether a 'dispute' exists between parties is of fundamental importance, with the existence of a dispute often forming one of the bases upon which a court or tribunal's jurisdiction is

---

[23] *Ibid.*, para. 165.

[24] See e.g. Article 280 of UNCLOS: 'Nothing in this Part impairs the right of any States Parties to agree at any time to settle a dispute between them concerning the interpretation or application of this Convention by any peaceful means of their own choice.'

[25] See e.g. the following statement of the 'Friendly Relations Declaration': 'International disputes shall be settled on the basis of the sovereign equality of States and in accordance with the principle of free choice of means. Recourse to, or acceptance of, settlement procedure freely agreed to by States with regard to existing or future disputes to which they are parties shall not be regarded as incompatible with sovereign equality'. See also, for a discussion of the Declaration on this precise point: *Obligation to Negotiate Access to the Pacific Ocean (Bolivia v. Chile)*, Judgment of 1 October 2018, [2018] ICJ Rep. 507, para. 166.

[26] General Assembly Resolution 37/10 ('Manila Declaration on the Peaceful Settlement of International Disputes').

grounded,[27] and directly relates the exercise by a court or tribunal of its arbitral or judicial function.[28] More fundamentally, the question whether a 'dispute' exists between parties is essential to establish and delimit the issues upon which a court or tribunal is empowered to pronounce itself resulting in a final and binding decision.[29] However, certain dispute settlement methods, such as that provided by the GATT and the World Trade Organization Dispute Settlement Understanding does not limit settlement to 'disputes', but extends also to 'situations' and 'non-violation complaints' in case a benefit under a WTO Agreement is being nullified or impaired.[30]

The existence of a dispute, as put by the ICJ, is 'a condition of the Court's jurisdiction'.[31] It is a question that precedes those relating to the existence of jurisdiction of a court or tribunal:

> Even before turning to the questions of jurisdiction and admissibility, the Court has first to consider the essentially preliminary question as to whether a dispute exists and to analyse the claim submitted to it.[32]

In the *Obligations concerning Negotiations relating to Cessation of the Nuclear Arms Race and to Nuclear Disarmament (Marshall Islands v. United Kingdom)* case, the Court noted that

> The Court's jurisprudence treats the question of the existence of a dispute as a jurisdictional one that turns on whether there is, in substance, a dispute, not on what form that dispute takes or whether the respondent has been notified (see paragraph 38 above).[33]

---

[27] See generally: J. McIntyre, 'Put on notice: the role of the dispute requirement in assessing jurisdiction and admissibility before the International Court' (2018) 19 *Melbourne Journal of International Law*, 546 and B. I. Bonafé, 'Establishing the existence of a dispute before the International Court of Justice: Drawbacks and implications' (2017) 45 *Questions of International Law*, 3–32.

[28] As emphasized by Judge Crawford: 'the rationale behind requiring a legal dispute is to ensure that the Court has something to determine: it protects the Court's judicial function which, in a contentious case, is to determine such disputes' (*Obligations concerning Negotiations relating to Cessation of the Nuclear Arms Race and to Nuclear Disarmament (Marshall Islands v. United Kingdom), Preliminary Objections*, Judgment of 5 October 2016, Dissenting Opinion of Judge Crawford, [2016] ICJ Rep. 833, para. 3.

[29] M. N. Shaw, *Rosenne's Law and Practice of the International Court (1920–2015)*, 5th ed., Leiden, 2016, Volume II (Jurisdiction), p. 527.

[30] See Art. 3(3) WTO DSU and Article XXIII (1)(b)-(c) GATT.

[31] *Obligations concerning Negotiations relating to Cessation of the Nuclear Arms Race and to Nuclear Disarmament (Marshall Islands v. India), Jurisdiction and Admissibility*, Judgment [2016] ICJ Rep. 255, para. 33.

[32] *Nuclear Tests (New Zealand v. France)* (Merits), Judgment, 20 December 1974 [1974] ICJ Rep. 457, paras 22–4.

[33] *Obligations concerning Negotiations relating to Cessation of the Nuclear Arms Race and to Nuclear Disarmament (Marshall Islands v. United Kingdom), Preliminary Objections*, Judgment of 5 October 2016, [2016] ICJ Rep. 833, para. 45.

The need for the existence of a dispute most often results from the fact that statutes of courts and tribunals, international treaties containing compromissory clauses and arbitration rules require the existence of 'a (legal) dispute' for the establishment of jurisdiction.

Article 36(2) of the Statute of the ICJ thus provides that

> The states parties to the present Statute may at any time declare that they recognize as compulsory *ipso facto* and without special agreement, in relation to any other state accepting the same obligation, the jurisdiction of the Court in all *legal disputes* concerning [...].[34]

Article 21 of the Statute of the ITLOS provides that

> The jurisdiction of the Tribunal comprises all *disputes* and all applications submitted to it in accordance with this Convention and all matters specifically provided for in any other agreement which confers jurisdiction on the Tribunal.[35]

Article IX of the Genocide Convention contains a compromissory clause which states

> *Disputes* between the Contracting Parties relating to the interpretation, application or fulfilment of the present Convention, including those relating to the responsibility of a State for genocide or for any of the other acts enumerated in article III, shall be submitted to the International Court of Justice at the request of any of the parties to the dispute.[36]

The UNCITRAL Arbitration Rules, which are widely used in international commercial arbitration and investor-state arbitration, and have also been used in inter-state arbitrations, also refer to the existence of disputes between parties:

> Where parties have agreed that *disputes* between them in respect of a defined legal relationship, whether contractual or not, shall be referred to arbitration under the UNCITRAL Arbitration Rules, then such *disputes* shall be settled in accordance with these Rules subject to such modification as the parties may agree.[37]

While these examples recognise the requirement of the existence of a dispute, they do not provide a definition of what constitutes a 'dispute'. The PCIJ famously posited in its decision in the *Mavrommatis Palestine Concessions* case that a dispute can be defined as 'a disagreement on a point of law or fact or, a conflict of legal views or of interests between

---

[34] Emphasis added. [35] Emphasis added.
[36] Convention on the Prevention and Punishment of the Crime of Genocide (adopted 9 December 1948, entered into force 12 January 1951) 78 UNTS 277 (emphasis added).
[37] Article 1(1) UNCITRAL Arbitration Rules (emphasis added).

two persons'.[38] The definition of the PCIJ, drafted in general terms and not necessarily being limited to international disputes only, has since been widely referred to as the basic description of what can be considered to constitute a 'dispute' in international law. Reference to the definition of the PCIJ can be found not only in the jurisprudence of the ICJ[39] but also in decisions of the International Tribunal for the Law of the Sea (ITLOS),[40] arbitral tribunals in inter-state disputes[41] and in investor-state arbitrations.[42]

The definition nonetheless is very broad, and a 'conflict of interests' does not always amount to an international legal dispute. The ICJ has on several occasions stated that a mere conflict of interest is insufficient for such to qualify as a 'dispute'. Rather, '[i]t must be shown that the claim of one party is positively opposed by the other'.[43] What 'positively opposed claims' means, was further explained by the Court in the *Headquarters Agreement* case:

> In the view of the Court, where one party to a treaty protests against the behaviour or a decision of the other party, and claims that such behaviour or decision constitutes a breach of the treaty, the mere fact that the party accused does not advance any argument to justify its conduct under international law does not prevent the opposing attitudes of the parties from giving rise to a dispute concerning the interpretation or application of the treaty...[44],[45]

---

[38] *Mavrommatis Palestine Concessions* (Greece v. United Kingdom), Judgment of 30 August 1924 (Objection to the Jurisdiction of the Court) 1924 PCIJ (ser. A) No. 2, p. 11.

[39] See e.g. *Interpretation of Peace Treaties*, Advisory Opinion, 30 March 1950 [1950] ICJ Rep. 65, 74; South West Africa cases (1962, at 328).

[40] E.g. *Southern Bluefin Tuna* (New Zealand v. Japan; Australia v. Japan) Provisional Measures, Order of 27 August 1999, ITLOS Reports 1999, p. 293, para. 44 and *M/V "Norstar"* (Panama v. Italy), Preliminary Objections, Judgment of 4 November 2016, ITLOS Reports 2016, p. 44, para. 85.

[41] E.g. Permanent Court of Arbitration, *Ecuador v. United States*, PCA Case No. 2012-05, Award, 29 September 2012, para. 212.

[42] E.g. *Maffezini v. Spain*, Decision on Jurisdiction of 25 January 2000, 40 ILM 1129, at paras 93–94 and *Impregilo SpA v. Islamic Republic of Pakistan*, Decision on Jurisdiction, 22 April 2005 (ICSID Case No. ARB/03/3) 12 ICSID Rep. 245, at paras. 302–3.

[43] *South West Africa Cases* (Ethiopia v. South Africa; Liberia v. South Africa), Preliminary Objections, Judgment of 21 December 1962 [1962] ICJ Rep. 319, 328. See also *Armed Activities on the Territory of the Congo (New Application: 2002)* (Democratic Republic of the Congo v. Rwanda), Jurisdiction and Admissibility, Judgment [2006] ICJ Rep. 40, para. 90; *Application of the International Convention on the Elimination of All Forms of Racial Discrimination* (Georgia v. Russian Federation), Preliminary Objections, Judgment [2011] ICJ Rep. 70, para. 30; *Questions relating to the Obligation to Prosecute or Extradite* (Belgium v. Senegal), Judgment [2012] ICJ Rep. 422, para. 46.

[44] *Application of the Obligation to Arbitrate under Section 21 of the United Nations Headquarters Agreement*, Advisory Opinion of 26 April 1988, [1988] ICJ Rep. 28, para. 38.

[45] *Obligations concerning Negotiations relating to Cessation of the Nuclear Arms Race and to Nuclear Disarmament* (Marshall Islands v. India), Jurisdiction and Admissibility, Judgment, 5 October 2016 [2016] ICJ Rep. 255.

The definition of the PCIJ in the *Mavrommatis Palestine Concessions* case does not in itself enable courts and tribunals to *identify* the existence of a dispute in a particular case. Since the decision, however, notably the ICJ has on several occasions clarified the means for identification of the existence of a dispute.

The ICJ has acknowledged that a dispute can be determined based on objective criteria, and the existence of a dispute thus does not depend on the qualifications given by the parties to the dispute. As posited by the ICJ in its opinion in the *Interpretation of Peace Treaties with Bulgaria, Hungary and Romania* case:

> Whether there exists an international dispute is a matter for objective determination. The mere denial of the existence of a dispute does not prove its non-existence.[46]

In its decision in the *South West Africa* cases, the ICJ also held that a 'mere assertion is not sufficient to prove the existence of a dispute any more than a mere denial of the existence of the dispute proves its non-existence'.[47] In *Application of the International Convention on the Elimination of All Forms of Racial Discrimination*, the ICJ further held that 'the existence of a dispute may be inferred from the failure of a State to respond to a claim in circumstances where a response is called for'.[48] In the same case, the ICJ also explained that '[t]he Court's determination must turn on an examination of the facts. The matter is one of substance, not of form'.[49]

More recently, the ICJ appears to have moved away from the pure objectivity by which a dispute can be identified in its decisions in *Obligations concerning Negotiations relating to Cessation of the Nuclear Arms Race and to Nuclear Disarmament*. The Court first restated the principle, derived from its previous decisions that the existence of a dispute 'is a matter for objective determination', and that this can be derived from statements or documents exchanged between the parties, exchanges made in multilateral settings and the conduct of the parties.[50] The Court nonetheless went on to decide that a dispute can only exist when it is 'demonstrated, on the basis of the evidence, that the respondent was aware, or could not have been unaware, that its views were "positively opposed" by

---

[46] *Interpretation of Peace Treaties*, Advisory Opinion of 30 March 1950 (first phase) [1950] ICJ Rep. 65, 74.
[47] *South West Africa Cases (Ethiopia v. South Africa; Liberia v. South Africa)*, Preliminary Objections, Judgment of 21 December 1962 [1962] ICJ Rep. 319, 328.
[48] *Application of the International Convention on the Elimination of All Forms of Racial Discrimination (Georgia v. Russian Federation), Preliminary Objections*, Judgment of 1 April 2011 [2011] ICJ Rep. 70, at 84, para. 30.
[49] *Ibid.*
[50] *Obligations concerning Negotiations relating to Cessation of the Nuclear Arms Race and to Nuclear Disarmament (Marshall Islands v. India)*, Jurisdiction and Admissibility, Judgment of 5 October 2016, [2016] ICJ Rep. 255, paras. 32–7.

the applicant'.[51] In doing so, the Court added a subjective element, requiring the awareness of both parties of the existence of a legal dispute.

Disputes of a legal nature must be distinguished from 'conflicts'[52] or 'situations'.[53] A 'situation' can be a general state of disagreement, opposition or antagonism. It is broader than the concept of 'dispute' and refers to the overall factual environment[54] or context in which one or more disputes exist. A 'conflict' can be described as 'a general state of hostility between the parties'.[55] Most often, one or more disputes in a legal and technical sense can be identified within a broader situation or within a conflict: 'legal disputes between sovereign States by their very nature are likely to occur in political contexts, and often form only one element in a wider and long-standing political dispute between the States concerned'.[56] This implies that solving a dispute does not always result in a resolution of the broader situation or state of hostility between parties.

Conversely, the mere fact that a legal dispute is part of a broader situation or conflict does not in itself imply that a court or tribunal should decline jurisdiction. As put by the ICJ in its order on provisional measures in *United States Diplomatic and Consular Staff in Tehran*:

> no provision of the Statute or Rules contemplates that the Court should decline to take cognizance of one aspect of a dispute merely because that dispute has other aspects, however important.[57]

The ICJ has subsequently reaffirmed that the broader political aspects of a dispute are no impediment to the Court exercising its jurisdiction. In *Nicaragua* v. *Honduras*, the Court recognized that 'the issues of which

---

[51] *Ibid.*, para. 38.
[52] J. Collier and V. Lowe, *The Settlement of Disputes in International Law: Institutions and Procedures*, Oxford, 1999, p. 1.
[53] See e.g. Article 12(1) UN Charter, which distinguished between disputes and situations: 'While the Security Council is exercising in respect of any dispute or situation the functions assigned to it in the present Charter, the General Assembly shall not make any recommendation with regard to that dispute or situation unless the Security Council so requests.' See also *Interpretation of the Peace Treaties with Bulgaria, Hungary and Romania*, Advisory Opinion of 30 March 1950 (first phase), [1950] ICJ Rep. 65, at 74: 'There has thus arisen a situation in which the two sides hold clearly opposite views concerning the question of the performance or non-performance of certain treaty obligations.'
[54] See C. Schreuer, 'What Is a Legal Dispute', in I. Buffard, J. Crawford, A. Pellet, and S. Wittich (eds), *International Law between Universalism and Fragmentation. Festschrift in Honour of Gerhard Hafner*, Leiden/Boston, 2008, 959–80, at p. 966.
[55] J. Collier and V. Lowe, *The Settlement of Disputes in International Law: Institutions and Procedures*, Oxford, 1999, p. 1.
[56] *US Diplomatic and Consular Staff in Tehran (United States* v. *Iran)*, Judgment of 24 May 1980, [1980] ICJ Rep. 3, para. 37.
[57] *US Diplomatic and Consular Staff in Tehran (United States* v. *Iran)* Request for the indication of Provisional Measures, Order of 15 December 1979 [1979] ICJ Rep. 7, para. 24. See also International Court of Justice, *US Diplomatic and Consular Staff in Tehran (United States* v. *Iran)*, Judgment of 24 May 1980, [1980] ICJ Rep. 3, para. 37.

the Court has been seized may be regarded as part of a wider regional problem.'[58] Citing its decision in *United States Diplomatic and Consular Staff in Tehran*, the Court then explained that

> The Court, as a judicial organ, is however only concerned to establish, first, that the dispute before it is a legal dispute, in the sense of a dispute capable of being settled by the application of principles and rules of international law [...] The purpose of recourse to the Court is the peaceful settlement of such disputes; the Court's judgment is a legal pronouncement, and it cannot concern itself with the political motivation which may lead a State at a particular time, or in particular circumstances to choose judicial settlement.

The question of whether a 'dispute' exists also takes special importance in relation to the jurisdiction *ratione temporis* of courts and tribunals. This will be discussed in the section 'jurisdiction *ratione temporis*'.[59]

Finally, it should be pointed out that not all international courts and tribunals settle disputes. International criminal courts and tribunals, such as the International Criminal Court (ICC), are tasked with establishing the international criminal responsibility of individuals and hence their decisions cannot as such be seen as settling international disputes.[60] International criminal courts and tribunals will therefore not be dealt with in this book.

1.4 Justiciability and Mootness

Not all disputes are capable of settlement by courts and tribunals. While the definition and requirement of 'legal disputes' set out in the previous section essentially corresponds with the issue of *what* constitutes a legal dispute and which criteria are regularly used to establish the existence of a dispute, the question of whether that dispute is capable of settlement by the application of (international) law is a different yet related question. To a large extent, the requirement for disputes to be justiciable is inherent in the idea that the jurisdiction of courts and tribunals is dependent upon the existence of a *legal* dispute.

The general objective underpinning the requirement for disputes to be justiciable is to distinguish disputes that are suitable for settlement by courts and tribunals by application of law, from those that are not.[61] The roots of the concept of 'justiciability' date back to a time when disputes between states were divided between legal disputes and political disputes,

---

[58] *Border and Transborder Armed Actions (Nicaragua/Honduras)*, Jurisdiction and Admissibility, Judgment, 20 December 1988 [1988] ICJ Rep. 69, para. 54.
[59] See *infra* Section 1.7.3.
[60] A. Pellet, 'Judicial Settlement of International Disputes' in R. Wolfrum, *Max Planck Encyclopedia of Public International Law*, Oxford, 2006, para. 3.
[61] J. Collier and V. Lowe, *The Settlement of Disputes in International Law* (n. 55) p. 191.

which was then translated into the legal-technical term of 'justiciable' versus 'non-justiciable' disputes – those which are capable of settlement by international adjudication or arbitration and those which are not.[62] One can find, for example, an implicit reference to the distinction in Article 13 of the League of Nations Covenant which enumerates in its second paragraph the types of disputes which are 'declared to be among those which are generally suitable for submission to arbitration'. The First Hague Convention of 1899 on the Pacific Settlement of International Disputes, which created the PCA, also explicitly refers to the use of arbitration for 'questions of a legal nature, and especially in the interpretation or application of International Conventions'.[63] The same convention further recommends settlement by international commissions of enquiry for 'differences of an international nature involving neither honour nor vital interests, and arising from a difference of opinion on points of fact', thus excluding and considering as non-justiciable disputes involving 'honour' or 'vital interests' or states.[64]

The debate on the distinction between political and legal disputes has lost much of its relevance today. Vice-President Yusuf, in his dissenting opinion in the case *Obligations concerning Negotiations relating to Cessation of the Nuclear Arms Race and to Nuclear Disarmament (Marshall Islands* v. *United Kingdom)*, described the 'justiciability' of disputes as an 'old and controversial concept'.[65] With the expansion of international law into new areas in the past decades, and considering the notion expressed above that the political aspects of a dispute do not as such disqualify the dispute as a 'legal dispute', a finding of non-justiciability is not common.

In the past, however, the ICJ has on occasion refused to pronounce itself on (certain aspects of) a dispute because it was not capable of settlement by application of law. The *Haya de la Torre* case revolved around the political asylum given to Mr Victor Ratil Haya de la Torre by Colombia in its embassy in Peru. After a first judgment rendered by the Court, the parties submitted a new case requiring from the Court, amongst others, to 'make a choice amongst the various courses by which the asylum may be terminated'.[66] The Court held that it was 'unable to give any practical advice as to the various courses which might be followed with a view to

---

[62] For a discussion, see H. Lauterpacht, *The Function of Law in the International Community*, Oxford, 2011, p. 147 ff.
[63] Article 16 First Hague Convention of 1899 on the Pacific Settlement of International Disputes.
[64] Ibid., Article 9.
[65] *Obligations concerning Negotiations relating to Cessation of the Nuclear Arms Race and to Nuclear Disarmament (Marshall Islands v. United Kingdom), Preliminary Objections*, Judgment of 5 October 2016, [2016] ICJ Rep. 833, Dissenting Opinion of Vice-President Yusuf, para. 10.
[66] *Haya de la Torre Case (Colombia/Peru)* (Merits), Judgment of 13 June 1951, [1951] ICJ Rep. 71, p. 79.

terminating the asylum, since, by doing so, it would depart from its judicial function'.[67]

The idea that a court or tribunal cannot depart from its judicial or arbitral function, which underlies the concept of justiciability, has relevance in the context of cases which have become 'moot'. Mootness implies that a court or tribunal cannot exercise its jurisdiction because the case no longer has a substantial object.[68] The concept of 'mootness' is linked to the fact that courts and tribunals settle disputes, and in doing so exercise a judicial or arbitral function, which is to pronounce on a dispute by applying international law. When the 'object of the dispute' no longer exists, a court or tribunal cannot exercise its function. While a dispute must exist when the parties to the dispute submit their application to the court,[69] a case can become moot if the dispute ceases to exist while it is pending before the court. While the concept of mootness pertains to a fundamental aspect of jurisdiction, cases in which courts and tribunals decline to exercise jurisdiction based on mootness are rare.

An example of an international court discussing mootness[70] is the decision of the ICJ in the *Northern Cameroons* case, which related to a claim for breach of a Trusteeship Agreement which had in fact been validly terminated. Considering this, the Court found that a decision on the claims in relation to the operation and administration of the Trusteeship for the Northern Cameroons by the United Kingdom 'can have only an academic interest'.[71] More generally, the Court explained that

> The function of the Court is to state the law, but it may pronounce judgment only in connection with concrete cases where there exists at the time of the adjudication an actual controversy involving a conflict of legal interests between the parties. The Court's judgment must have some practical consequence in the sense that it can affect existing legal rights or obligations of the parties, thus removing uncertainty from their legal relations. No judgment on the merits in this case could satisfy these essentials of the judicial function.[72]

A second example is the *Nuclear Tests* case, which had been brought by Australia and New Zealand against France and related to the legality of atmospheric nuclear tests conducted by France in the South Pacific

---

[67] Ibid., 78. See also PCIJ, *Free Zones of Upper Savoy and District of Gex (France v. Switzerland)*, 1932 PCIJ (ser. A/B) No. 46 (7 June 1932), pp. 153 ff.
[68] Hugh Thirlway, *The International Court of Justice*, Oxford, 2016, p. 57.
[69] *Application of the International Convention on the Elimination of All Forms of Racial Discrimination (Georgia v. Russian Federation)* (Preliminary Objections) [2011] ICJ Rep. 70, para. 30.
[70] Other examples where the Court discussed mootness are amongst others: *Legality of the Use of Force (Serbia v. Belgium)* [2004] ICJ Rep. 295–6, para. 38.
[71] *Case concerning the Northern Cameroons (Cameroon v. United Kingdom)*, Preliminary Objections, Judgment of 2 December 1963 [1963] ICJ Rep. 15, p 35.
[72] Ibid., 34.

region.[73] After the initiation of the case, the French authorities had repeatedly stated that they would no longer conduct atmospheric nuclear tests and given assurances that the tests would cease.[74] The ICJ held that it 'must not fail to take cognizance of a situation in which the dispute has disappeared because the object of the claim has been achieved by other means'.[75] As a consequence, the Court decided it could not exercise its functions: 'the object of the claim having clearly disappeared, there is nothing on which to give judgment'.[76] It is important to note that the ICJ linked this finding to the need for the Court to act 'in accordance with the proper interpretation of its judicial function'.[77]

A third example is the decision of the Court in *Frontier Dispute (Burkina Faso/Niger)*.[78] The significance of this decision lies in the fact that the Court was confronted with the submission of a dispute based on a special agreement. While the Court recognised that parties can therefore freely determine the limits of the Court's jurisdiction, the parties cannot by doing so 'alter the limits of the Court's judicial function', since these 'are not at the disposal of the parties, even by agreement between them, and are mandatory for the parties just as for the Court itself'.[79] The Court expanded on this, explaining that 'the requests that parties submit to the Court, must not only be linked to a valid basis of jurisdiction, but must also always relate to the function of deciding disputes'.[80] Based on these general considerations, the Court found that an aspect of the dispute between the parties, which related to the delimitation of two sectors on which the parties had reached an agreement during negotiations and before the institutions of proceedings, no longer existed and that it could not 'endorse' in the operative part of the judgment the agreement reached.[81] Technically, however, the decision of the court here may also be interpreted not necessarily as a question of 'mootness', but also the absence of any dispute between the parties on that precise point when the proceedings were instituted.[82] This interpretation highlights the fundamental aspect of mootness: in order for a dispute to *become* moot, it must have existed at the point of the institution of proceedings.

---

[73] *Nuclear Tests (Australia v. France)* (Merits) Judgment, 20 December 1974, [1974] ICJ Rep. 253, para. 16.
[74] *Ibid.*, paras 32, 51 and 55–6. [75] *Ibid.*, para. 55 [76] *Ibid.*, para. 59. [77] *Ibid.*, para. 57.
[78] *Frontier Dispute (Burkina Faso/Niger)*, Judgment of 16 April 2013, [2013] ICJ Rep. 44.
[79] *Ibid.*, para. 46. [80] *Ibid.*, para. 46. [81] *Ibid.*, para. 53.
[82] The refusal by the Court to incorporate the agreement of the parties in the operative paragraph may seem surprising, but the fact that the agreement had been reached by the parties *before* the institution of proceedings may explain the position of the Court. In any event, arbitral tribunals have shown much more flexibility in incorporating agreements of the parties reached during the proceedings especially if they have jurisdiction to hear the claim. This is notably the case in commercial arbitration and in the context of investor-state arbitrations. See Y. Kryvoi and D. Davydenko, 'Consent awards in international arbitration: from settlement to enforcement' (2015) 40 *Brooklyn Journal of International Law*, 827–68.

The question of mootness transcends the law and practice of the ICJ, and has been discussed in the context of inter-state arbitration under the Law of the Sea Convention[83] and in investor-state arbitration.[84] It must still be noted that not all international courts follow the approach of the International Court of Justice. The European Court of Human Rights stated in its 1978 judgment in the *Ireland* v. *United Kingdom* case that its judgments 'serve not only to decide cases brought before the Court but, more generally, to elucidate, safeguard and develop the rules instituted by the Convention'.[85] At that time, the Rules of the Court explicitly stated that the Court could 'decide that, notwithstanding the notice of discontinuance, friendly settlement, arrangement or other fact referred to in the two preceding paragraphs, it should proceed with the consideration of the case'.[86] In the meantime, changes were made to the Rules of the Court, but it is still enshrined in Article 37 of the Convention that the Court 'shall continue the examination of the application if respect for human rights as defined in the Convention and the Protocols thereto so requires'.[87] Even after an application has been struck out, the Court 'may restore it to its list if it considers that exceptional circumstances so justify'.[88] In its 2016 decision in *Jeronovičs* v. *Latvia*, the European Court of Human Rights noted that

> the Court's rulings serve not only to decide those cases brought before it but, more generally, to elucidate, safeguard and develop the rules instituted by the Convention, thereby contributing to the observance by the States of the engagements undertaken by them as Contracting Parties.[89]

1.5 The Notion and Functions of 'Settlement'

International dispute settlement implies that at a certain point in time, a dispute is considered to be settled. Here, the difference between the means of settlement plays an important role. Diplomatic means of settlement do

---

[83] See e.g. *Southern Bluefin Tuna (Australia* v. *Japan; New Zealand* v. *Japan)*, Award on Jurisdiction and Admissibility, Decision of 4 August 2000, 119 ILR 508; RIAA Vol. XXIII pp. 1–57, paras 46 ff.

[84] E.g. *Spiridon Roussalis* v. *Romania*, ICSID Case No. ARB/06/1, Award, 7 December 2011, paras 255 and 312.

[85] *Ireland* v. *UK* (App no 5310/71) (1978) ECtHR, Series A no 25, para. 154. See also, more recently, *Jeronovičs* v. *Latvia* [GC], no. 44898/10, ECHR 2016, para. 109.

[86] Amendments to the Rules of Procedure of the European Court of Human Rights, Yearbook 1974, vol. 17, p. 30, rule 47(3).

[87] Council of Europe, European Convention for the Protection of Human Rights and Fundamental Freedoms *as amended by Protocols Nos. 11 and 14*, 4 November 1950, ETS 5, article 37(1).

[88] Rules of the Court, ECtHR, rule 43(5).

[89] *Jeronovičs* v. *Latvia* [GC], no. 44898/10, 5 July 2016, para. 109.

not in principle result in a binding decision or outcome. This implies that any agreement reached by the parties after successful resort to a diplomatic means of settlement requires incorporation in a binding instrument in order to bind the states parties to the dispute to the outcome. Most often, parties will sign a treaty subsequent to the successful outcome to incorporate the agreement reached. The treaty embodying the agreement of the parties then implies settlement of the dispute, provided of course that the agreement reached comprises all aspects of the dispute.[90]

Legal means of dispute settlement on the other hand imply that the parties in advance accept that the outcome of the chosen procedure will be binding. In other words, the agreement as to the binding outcome of the procedure precedes the outcome, the reversed situation in case of resort to diplomatic means. The use of legal means of dispute settlement therefore results in a settlement of the dispute upon the final decision of the court or tribunal.

The binding nature of a decision of a court or arbitral tribunal is often referred to by the term *res judicata* and has also been expressed through the notion of "finality'. This implies not only an obligation for the states which were party to the dispute to respect the judgment or award in good faith, but also that the dispute is considered as settled and cannot be reopened or relitigated. As put by the ICJ:

> the principle of *res judicata* [...] signifies that once the Court has made a determination, whether on a matter of the merits of a dispute brought before it, or on a question of its own jurisdiction, that determination is definitive both for the parties to the case, in respect of the case (Article 59 of the Statute), and for the Court itself in the context of that case.[91]

The principle of *res judicata* as barring any relitigation of the case applies only to subsequent cases where the parties, the object of the dispute and the cause of action are identical.[92] It also covers in principle the operative

---

[90] See e.g. *Frontier Dispute (Burkina Faso/Niger)*, Judgment of 16 April 2013, [2013] ICJ Rep. 44, in which the parties only agreed on the delimitation of certain zones only during negotiations prior to the submission of the dispute to the ICJ. The special agreement signed between the parties to submit the dispute to the ICJ had recorded the agreement reached, but asked the Court nonetheless to include the agreement reached in the *dispositif* of the decision, which the ICJ refused. The Court however proceeded to the delimitation of the contested boundaries between the two states to the extent that those were not included in the agreement reached by the parties.

[91] *Application of the Convention on the Prevention and Punishment of the Crime of Genocide (Bosnia and Herzegovina v. Serbia and Montenegro)*, Judgment of 26 February 2007 (merits), [2007] ICJ Rep. 43, para. 138.

[92] Doubts have been expressed as to the question whether the identity of the 'cause of action' is tenable. See A. Pellet, 'Judicial Settlement of International Disputes' in R. Wolfrum, *Max Planck Encyclopedia of Public International Law*, Oxford, 2006, para. 38. For a general discussion, see N. Ridi, 'Precarious finality? Reflections on res judicata and the question of the Delimitation of the Continental Shelf Case' (2018) 31 *Leiden Journal of International Law*, 383–401. For an application of the principle, see *Waste Management Inc v. Mexico No 2*, ICSID Case No ARB (AF)/00/3 [NAFTA], Decision of 26 June 2002.

part of the decision and the *ratio decidendi*, but the ICJ has in past affirmed that it also applies to issues 'which are necessarily entailed in the decision of those issues'.[93]

The main rationales behind the finality of decisions and of the principle of *res judicata* are twofold and relate closely to the function of international dispute settlement more generally. The first rationale can be termed the 'public' function of finality or international dispute settlement,[94] which is based on the idea that international litigation and arbitration, and disputes more generally, cannot continue for an indefinite period. Settling disputes serves a public goal of stability in international relations in that the settlement of disputes puts an end to legal controversies which may endanger international peace and security. The principle of certainty is also advanced by dispute settlement, since the final and binding decision of courts and tribunals clarifies the law and the respective rights and obligations for parties. While decisions of courts and tribunals are not binding beyond parties to the dispute, the clarification of the law made by courts and tribunals also serves the broader purpose of predictability and providing guidance to states for future behaviour. Ultimately, settlement contributes to the broader goal of providing enforcement of international law and hence a form of 'international justice' and respect of the rule of law.[95]

The second is the private dimension of finality or international dispute settlement. The rationale here is to end the dispute *between the parties* by 'doing justice' between the parties to the dispute.[96] In practical terms, this translates to mean that the dispute cannot be relitigated. The binding nature of the decision of courts and tribunals, and the application of the principle of *res judicata* to the decision, is often found in the statutes of international courts and tribunals and in the procedural rules of arbitral tribunals. Article 59 of the Statute of the ICJ provides that 'the decision of the Court has no binding force except between the parties and in respect of that particular case'. The same principle is included in Article 53 (1) of the ICSID Convention, which provides that the award rendered by the arbitral tribunal is binding upon the parties.[97]

---

[93] *Application of the Convention on the Prevention and Punishment of the Crime of Genocide (Bosnia and Herzegovina v. Serbia and Montenegro)*, Judgment of 26 February 2007 (merits), [2007] ICJ Rep. 43, para. 126.

[94] On the idea that international courts and tribunals exercise 'public authority', see A. von Bogdandy and I. Venzke, 'In whose name? An investigation of international courts' public authority and its democratic justification' (2012) 23 *European Journal of International Law*, 7–41.

[95] C. Brown, 'The Inherent Powers of International Courts and Tribunals', (2006) 76 *British Yearbook of International Law*, 195, 230.

[96] Ibid.

[97] See also *SGS (Société Générale de Surveillance) S.A. v. Republic of the Philippines*, ICSID Case No. ARB/02/6, Decision on Jurisdiction, 29 January 2004, para. 97 (footnotes omitted).

The finality of decisions however does not imply that a final and binding decision can in no circumstances be re-opened. The principle of *res judicata* leaves intact the possibility for the parties to the dispute to seek rectification, interpretation and revision of decisions in accordance with the specific requirements and procedures made available to the parties in the statutes and rules of courts and tribunals. This was also confirmed by the ICJ:

> That principle [of *res judicata*] signifies that the decisions of the Court are not only binding on the parties, but are final, in the sense that they cannot be reopened by the parties as regards the issues that have been determined, *save by procedures, of an exceptional nature, specially laid down for that purpose.*[98]

These specific procedures will be discussed in the next chapters when we look at the specific legal means of dispute settlement and courts and tribunals.

Furthermore, parties can always agree that a certain decision may be subjected to appeal. Decisions of international courts and tribunals are in principle final and without appeal,[99] as are decisions of arbitral tribunals.[100] That decisions of international courts and tribunals are final and without appeal flows from the absence of a hierarchical relationship between international courts and tribunals, and arbitral tribunals, in international law.[101] This implies that as a matter of principle, no international court or tribunal would have automatic competence to rule over the correctness of the interpretation and application of international law by another court or tribunal. The ad hoc committee in the investor-state arbitration *Tulip* v. *Turkey*, tasked with the assessment of a claim in annulment of the awards of the arbitral tribunal in the same case, posited that 'the principle of finality typically takes precedence over the principle of correctness'.[102] Although advanced in relation to arbitral proceedings, the principle is valid for international adjudication more generally.

However, the principle of consent and the ensuing choice given to the parties to the dispute to decide the method of dispute settlement opens the possibility for the parties to the dispute to also agree to an appeals procedure or mechanism. This possibility is, moreover, sometimes explicitly included in international treaties, such as Annex VII of the UNCLOS,

---

[98] *Application of the Convention on the Prevention and Punishment of the Crime of Genocide (Bosnia and Herzegovina v. Serbia and Montenegro)*, Judgment of 26 February 2007 (merits), [2007] ICJ Rep. 43, para. 115 (emphasis added).
[99] E.g. Article 60 ICJ Statute.
[100] E.g. Article 34(2) UNCITRAL Arbitration Rules which provides that 'awards shall be made in writing and shall be final and binding on the parties.'
[101] See generally, K. Oellers-Frahm, 'International Courts and Tribunals, Appeals', in R. Wolfrum, *Max Planck Encyclopedia of Public International Law*, Oxford, 2006.
[102] *Tulip Real Estate Investment and Development Netherlands B.V. v. Republic of Turkey*, ICSID Case No. ARB/11/28, Decision on Annulment, 30 December 2015, para. 4.

which contains the procedure for international arbitration under that Convention.[103] Appeals mechanisms or the provision of an appeal are however very exceptional.

The most important example of an institutional appeal is the World Trade Organization Dispute Settlement Understanding (WTO DSU). The dispute settlement system established in the WTO DSU is *sui generis* and cannot be easily categorised within the usual classification scheme of methods of dispute settlement.[104] However, the dispute settlement system envisaged in the WTO allows the parties to a dispute to appeal the report of a panel (which decides disputes in first instance) before a standing Appellate Body.[105]

Finally, in the case of the arbitration of international disputes, international law recognizes the possibility for the parties to the dispute to request the annulment of an arbitral award. Annulment is to be distinguished from appeal in that the former is only concerned with assessing the procedure before the tribunal and the validity of the decisions reached which are evaluated against a limited set of grounds of annulment. In other words, claims in annulment of a decision do not in principle concern the correctness of the interpretation or application of international law by the tribunal, and, as a consequence, a court or tribunal which has competence to hear such claims will not in principle re-hear the case in full. As put by the ICJ:

> The Court is not called upon to pronounce on whether the arbitrator's decision was right or wrong. These and cognate considerations have no relevance to the function that the Court is called upon to discharge in these proceedings, which is to decide whether the Award is proved to be a nullity having no effect.[106]

The outcome of a decision of annulment is, contrary to appeal, either the confirmation of the decision subject of the claim in annulment or the partial or total nullification of the decision. In the latter case, the original decision is considered 'null and void' or as having no effect. A claim of annulment is best categorised as a new dispute between the parties, the object of which is the validity of the decision and the procedure leading to that decision.[107]

---

[103] Article 11, Annex VII of UNCLOS: 'The award shall be final and without appeal, unless the parties to the dispute have agreed in advance to an appellate procedure'.
[104] See *infra* Chapter 11.   [105] Art. 16 (4) and 17 DSU.
[106] *Case concerning the Arbitral Award made by the King of Spain on 23 December 1906*, Judgment of 18 November 1960 [1960] ICJ Rep. 192, at 214. On the distinction between appeal and annulment, see F. Baetens, 'Judicial review of international adjudicatory decisions: a cross-regime comparison of annulment and appellate mechanisms' (2016) 8 *Journal of International Dispute Settlement*, 1–28.
[107] Cf. *Arbitral Award of 31 July 1989 (Guinea-Bissau v. Senegal)*, Judgment of 12 November 1991 [1991] ICJ Rep. 53, para. 24.

There is general agreement on the grounds on which decisions may be annulled. These grounds are included in Article 52 of the ICSID Convention, which lays out the grounds for annulment of arbitral awards under the ICSID Convention, and have also been discussed by the ICJ in its decisions on claims in annulment. The grounds are in general terms as follows:

- improper constitution of the tribunal (the tribunal was constituted in violation of the agreement of the parties);
- *Excès de pouvoirs* or 'excess of authority' (deciding in excess of or failing the exercise jurisdiction);
- failure to render a reasoned award;
- transgression of a fundamental rule of procedure, such as the equality of the parties;
- fraud, deceit and corruption.

The principle that the parties can claim the nullity of decisions of arbitral awards[108] does not necessarily imply that a specific court or tribunal has automatic competence to hear such claims. Parties must consent to the exercise by a court or tribunal of its competence to hear a claim in annulment. Such claims can therefore only be brought to the extent that a court or tribunal is endowed with the competence to hear the claim by the parties. However, in the absence of specific consent expressed prior to the arbitral award (which is the subject of the challenge) or of general consent to the jurisdiction of a court or tribunal, it would be difficult to imagine that one of the parties would consent ad hoc to the competence of a court or tribunal to hear a claim in annulment once the decision has been rendered.

On several occasions, the ICJ has had the opportunity to hear claims in annulment of arbitral awards rendered in inter-state disputes.[109] The jurisdiction of the Court was in both cases based on the consent expressed by both states to the Court's jurisdiction for legal disputes under Article 36 (2) of the Statute of the ICJ.

The possibility for parties to file a claim in annulment can also be institutionalised. This is notably the case for investor-state arbitration under the ICSID Convention, which will be discussed in Chapter 7.

---

[108] While in principle decisions of international courts and tribunals could also be subjected to claims in annulment, the practice so far has mainly been relevant for arbitral awards, since it would be very difficult to find a court or tribunal which would have competence to hear such a claim. See K. Oellers-Frahm, 'Judicial and arbitral decisions, validity and nullity', in R. Wolfrum, *Max Planck Encyclopedia of Public International Law*, Oxford, 2006, para. 6.

[109] *Case concerning the Arbitral Award made by the King of Spain on 23 December 1906*, Judgment of 18 November 1960 [1960] ICJ Rep. 192 and *Arbitral Award of 31 July 1989 (Guinea-Bissau v. Senegal)*, Judgment of 12 November 1991 [1991] ICJ Rep. 53.

1.6 The Means of International Dispute Settlement

As mentioned earlier in this chapter, the principle of sovereign equality of states and the requirement of states to consent to have their disputes settled implies that states are free to choose the means of dispute settlement. The free choice of means also implies that any method of settlement of international disputes can be agreed upon subjected only to the condition that it is a peaceful dispute settlement method.

The various methods of settlement available to the parties are usually categorised into diplomatic means and legal means. Diplomatic means of settlement do not in principle result in a binding decision or outcome. They are based not only on the consent of the parties, but most importantly on the cooperation of both parties during the procedure of settlement. Agreements on the settlement of a dispute by virtue of diplomatic means of dispute settlement should be incorporated in a binding instrument in order to be binding for the parties to the dispute. Legal means of settlement, on the contrary, are based on the idea that the parties agree in advance that the outcome will be binding upon the parties.

There are several other differences between both categories of methods, such as the role of law in the settlement of the dispute and the extent to which the third party involved in the settlement of the dispute in fact decides autonomously, but the essential difference between both is a question of 'language'. Diplomatic methods greatly and in most parts rely on the willingness and possibility for the parties to 'talk to each other' and reach an agreement, either by themselves (in case of negotiations) or with the (minimal) intervention of a third party, which may arise in case of good offices or mediation. The agreement does not necessarily need to rely exclusively on international law, meaning the parties can agree to modify in their relations the applicable rules of international law (safe for *jus cogens* norms). On the contrary, legal means rely exclusively on a third party to objectively interpret and apply international law, except if the parties agree on a decision *ex aequo et bono* (equity). Parties are therefore by necessary implication opposing litigants in a formal procedure which usually leaves little room for diplomacy and mutually agreed solutions.

The means of settlement are usually listed as negotiation, good offices, mediation, inquiry/fact-finding, conciliation (diplomatic means of settlement), and arbitration and judicial settlement (legal means of settlement), mirroring closely Article 33 of the UN Charter. This book proceeds on the basis of these categories, to which settlement through regional or universal international organisation is added. The latter is technically not a means of settlement, but rather a setting in which disputes can be settled.

The order in which Article 33 of the UN Charter lists the methods of settlement is not random. As one moves along the list, the formality and the implication of a third party's participation increases. Also, the potential role of and reliance on international law increases, although it is never entirely absent in diplomatic means of settlement. It should however be noted that the methods listed do not constitute an exhaustive or exclusive enumeration of the various possibilities for states to settle their disputes. Parties to a dispute can either use one of the methods listed, use several methods successively, or combine various methods. In the *Rainbow Warrior* case, for example, following unsuccessful negotiations, the parties had agreed to task the Secretary-General of the United Nations to issue a binding 'equitable and principled' ruling[110] on the dispute opposing of parties. It is difficult to categorise the ruling, especially since it is based on *equity* rather than law, contains aspects of conciliation[111] and was in advance agreed to be binding upon the parties.[112]

Finally, as mentioned before, the free choice of means implies that there is no hierarchical relationship between the various means of settlement. States are free to consent to any means of settlement as they see fit, and there is no obligation, save for the application of *lex specialis*, to exhaust a diplomatic method before turning to another legal method of settlement.

Moreover, as was recently confirmed by the ICJ, the submission of a dispute to judicial settlement does not imply that the parties can no longer attempt to settle the dispute via other diplomatic means such as negotiations or good offices. In such case, the Court noted that 'parallel attempts at settlement of a dispute by diplomatic means do not prevent it from being dealt with by the Court'.[113]

1.7 Jurisdiction

Jurisdiction is 'the power to decide according to law (*jus dicere*) a dispute of a particular nature between specific parties'.[114] Jurisdiction determines whether a court or tribunal is empowered by the parties to the dispute to render a decision on that dispute, which is binding.[115] Jurisdiction is often

---

[110] *Case concerning the differences between New Zealand and France arising from the Rainbow Warrior affair*, Ruling of 6 July 1986 by the Secretary-General of the United Nations, *UNRIAA* Volume XIX pp. 199–221, at pp. 200 (para. 5) and 212.

[111] See e.g. *ibid.*, at p. 213: 'On this point, if I am to fulfil my mandate adequately, I must find a solution in respect of the two officers which both respects and *reconciles* these conflicting positions' (emphasis added).

[112] *Case concerning the differences between New Zealand and France arising from the Rainbow Warrior affair*, Ruling of 6 July 1986 by the Secretary-General of the United Nations, *UNRIAA* Volume XIX pp. 199–221, at pp. 200 (para. 5) and 212.

[113] *Arbitral Award of 3 October 1899 (Guyana v. Venezuela)*, Preliminary Objections, Judgment of 18 December 2020, para. 109.

[114] Thirlway, *The International Court of Justice* (n. 68) p. 36.

[115] S. Rosenne, 'International courts and tribunals, jurisdiction and admissibility of inter-state applications', in R. Wolfrum, *Max Planck Encyclopedia of Public International Law*, Oxford, 2012, para. 2.

used interchangeably with 'competence', which derives from the French word for jurisdiction: *compétence*.

The jurisdiction of courts and tribunals should be clearly distinguished from the creation itself of a court or tribunal by agreement of the states: 'to exist is one thing; to have competence in respect of particular states in regard to particular claims is another'.[116] It should also be clearly distinguished from the requirement of consent of states. First, meeting the jurisdictional requirements set by the founding instruments, statutes and rules of the specific courts and tribunals does not absolve the parties to the dispute from consenting to submitting a given dispute to that court or tribunal.[117] Second, states can in expressing consent in advance of a dispute, either in a compromissory clause or compromissory treaty, define the conditions under which such consent is given and hence further delineate the jurisdictional conditions under which disputes may be settled. To establish jurisdiction, one therefore needs to combine both the founding instruments, statutes and rules of the specific courts and tribunals which contain the jurisdictional requirements of each, and the specific instrument containing the consent of the parties to the dispute. As put by the ICJ:

> the Court has jurisdiction in respect of States only to the extent that they have consented thereto. When a compromissory clause in a treaty provides for the Court's jurisdiction, that jurisdiction exists only in respect of the parties to the treaty who are bound by that clause and within the limits set out therein.[118]

There are four dimensions to jurisdiction: (i) personal jurisdiction (jurisdiction *ratione personae* or jurisdiction *in personam*), (ii) subject matter jurisdiction (jurisdiction *ratione materiae* or jurisdiction *in rem*), (iii) temporal jurisdiction (jurisdiction *ratione temporis*), and (iv) territorial jurisdiction (jurisdiction *ratione loci*).[119] In principle, a court or tribunal may only exercise its powers to the extent that the requirements set by the four dimensions of jurisdictions are met. The precise contours within which states can consent to the jurisdiction of a court or tribunal are often set by the founding instruments, statutes and rules of the specific courts and tribunals. These will be discussed in general terms in this section, and

---

[116] R. Higgins, *Problems and Process – International Law and How We Use It*, Oxford, 1995, p. 186.

[117] See e.g. the following paragraph of the Preamble to the ICSID Convention: 'Declaring that no Contracting State shall by the mere fact of its ratification, acceptance or approval of this Convention and without its consent be deemed to be under any obligation to submit any particular dispute to conciliation or arbitration.'

[118] *Armed Activities on the Territory of the Congo (New Application: 2002) (Democratic Republic of the Congo v. Rwanda)*, Jurisdiction of the Court and Admissibility of the Application, Judgment of 3 February 2006, [2006] ICJ Rep. 6, para. 65 (references omitted).

[119] See Y. Shany, 'Jurisdiction and Admissibility', in C. P. R. Romano, K. J. Alter, and C. Avgerou (eds), *The Oxford Handbook of International Adjudication*, Oxford, 2014, pp. 779–805.

for each court and tribunal in this book in the relevant chapters. Territorial jurisdiction (jurisdiction *ratione loci*) mostly is relevant for courts and tribunals having a geographically limited competence and for the question whether the competence of a court of tribunal extends to (overseas) territories of a state; it will not be discussed in detail in this introductory chapter.

Before turning to the various dimensions of jurisdiction, however, two important points need to be made.

First, courts and tribunals are competent to decide on the existence of their own jurisdiction to settle a dispute. This is referred to as the principle of *compétence de la compétence* or *kompetenz-kompetenz*, which is a general principle widely recognized in international dispute settlement.[120] The principle thus implies that it is up to the courts and tribunals to decide and establish the existence and contours of their own jurisdiction based on the instrument(s) containing the consent of the parties and the applicable statutes and rules of the court or tribunal in question. The principle is often included in the statutes of courts and tribunals and in arbitration rules.[121]

Second, the question of jurisdiction is different from that of the 'applicable law'.[122] The 'applicable law' defines the law to be applied by the court or tribunal to the merits of the case. There is, however, a close interaction between jurisdiction and the applicable law. The limited jurisdiction of courts and tribunals implies that the law to be applied by a court or tribunal also is in principle limited to the instrument containing the consent of the states, although there are several possibilities in which the applicable law may also extend to general international law.[123]

1.7.1 Jurisdiction *Ratione Personae*

Personal jurisdiction defines who can be a party to a dispute before a court or tribunal. Irrespective of the subject matter of the dispute, courts and tribunals often have limits on who is entitled to consent to the jurisdiction of, and hence appear as a party before, that court or tribunal. Jurisdiction *ratione personae* is intertwined with the jurisdiction *ratione materiae* of

---

[120] Thirlway, *The International Court of Justice* (n. 68) p. 38. See L. Boisson de Chazournes, 'The Principle of Compétence de la Compétence in International Adjudication and its Role in an Era of Multiplication of Courts and Tribunals', in M. Arsanjani, J. Cogan and S. Weissner (eds), *Looking to the Future: Essays in Honor of W. Michael Reisman*, Leiden, 2010, pp. 1027–64.

[121] See e.g. Article 36(6) ICJ Statute; Article 288(4) UNCLOS; Article 23 UNCITRAL Arbitration Rules.

[122] On the distinction and its consequences, see M. Wood, 'The International Tribunal for the Law of the Sea and General International Law', (2007) 22 *International Journal of Marine and Coastal Law*, 351.

[123] Wood, 'The International Tribunal for the Law of the Sea and General International Law' (n. 122) 351, 358 ff.

courts and tribunals, since the subject matter of the disputes capable of being settled before a given court or tribunal will affect the entities who can be party to a case before that court or tribunal, and vice versa.

For instance, the ICJ can only adjudicate disputes between states.[124] Furthermore, only states which are party to the ICJ Statute can appear before the Court,[125] which thus limits the states that can consent to the jurisdiction of the Court to the UN[126] and those states who are not a UN Member but have been nonetheless authorized to be party to the ICJ Statute.[127] Which particular member states can submit a dispute before the Court is then further defined by the instrument containing the consent of states – in the case of a compromissory clause in a treaty, only the states parties to that treaty will for example be able to submit a case to the Court provided that they also are party to the ICJ Statute.

The ITLOS dispute resolution mechanism is open to states parties to UNCLOS, but also to 'other entities' than states parties for disputes involving non-state entities under Part XI of UNCLOS and in case of 'any other agreement conferring jurisdiction on the Tribunal which is accepted by all the parties to that case'.[128] Part XI of UNCLOS relates to the deep seabed, and provides amongst others that the Seabed Disputes Chamber of ITLOS has jurisdiction for disputes between states, but also disputes involving states, an international organisation ('the International Seabed Authority') and private parties.[129]

A final example is the ICSID Convention, established to settle investment disputes through recourse to arbitration. The jurisdiction of ICSID is limited to disputes between a Contracting State party to the ICSID Convention, and a national of another Contracting State.[130] As a consequence, disputes between two member states, or between two private parties, cannot be brought under the ICSID Convention. The jurisdiction *ratione personae* moreover is often further defined in international investment agreements which, if these contain consent to arbitration under the ICSID Convention, include definitions as to who can be considered 'a national' of one of the states parties to the international investment agreements.[131]

1.7.2 Jurisdiction *Ratione Materiae*

Jurisdiction *ratione materiae*, or subject matter jurisdiction, defines which categories of disputes can be brought before a court or tribunal. Only the legal and factual questions of disputes as defined by the applicable

---

[124] Article 34(1) ICJ Statute.   [125] Article 35(1) ICJ Statute.   [126] Article 93(1) UN Charter.
[127] Article 93(2) UN Charter and Article 35(2) ICJ Statute.   [128] Article 20 ITLOS Statute.
[129] See Article 187 UNCLOS.   [130] Article 25 ICSID Convention.
[131] See *infra* Chapters 6 and 7.

founding instruments, statutes and rules can be the subject of a decision by that court or tribunal.

The ICJ is the only permanent court which has unlimited subject matter jurisdiction: 'all cases which the parties refer to it and all matters specially provided for in the Charter of the United Nations or in treaties and conventions in force'.[132] There is in principle no limit to the subject matter of disputes which can be submitted to the Court, provided that these are legal disputes and raise issues of international law.[133]

All other courts and tribunals have a more limited subject matter jurisdiction. The jurisdiction of ITLOS, for instance, is limited to disputes arising under the UNCLOS.[134] Although the Tribunal's competence can be extended by agreement of the parties to a dispute so as to encompass jurisdiction over disputes concerning the interpretation or application of an international agreement related to the UNCLOS,[135] the Tribunal in principle has no jurisdiction over disputes arising under general international law.[136]

In the context of arbitration between states, there are in principle no limitations as to the types of disputes which can be settled by arbitral tribunals. States can agree to submit any international legal dispute to an arbitral tribunal. Of course, here also, the principled absence of a limitation in the arbitration rules of the *types* of disputes for which the arbitration rules can be used[137] needs to be combined with the consent to arbitrate expressed in an international instrument which will often be confined to a certain category of disputes or a specific dispute. For example, the use of international arbitration to settle disputes by relying on the procedure established in Annex VII of the UNCLOS is limited to disputes arising under the UNCLOS or disputes concerning the interpretation or application of an international agreement related to the UNCLOS, as is the case for the ITLOS.[138]

An exception to the principled neutrality of arbitration rules towards the types of disputes which can be submitted to arbitration is the mentioned ICSID Convention, which not only comprises rules of arbitration but has also established an arbitration institution (the International Centre for Settlement of Investment Disputes – ICSID) which has a limited jurisdiction. Article 25(1) of the ICSID Convention limits the jurisdiction of the ICSID to 'any legal dispute arising directly out of an investment'. Furthermore, the jurisdiction of an arbitral tribunal established under the

---

[132] Article 36(1) ICJ Statute.   [133] Cf Article 36(2) ICJ Statute.
[134] Article 21 ITLOS Statute; Article 288(1) UNCLOS.
[135] Articles 21(2) and 22 ITLOS Statute; Article 288(2) UNCLOS.
[136] Wood, 'The International Tribunal for the Law of the Sea and general international law' (n. 122), 351, 357.
[137] The UNCITRAL Arbitration Rules for example are neutral towards the type of disputes.
[138] Article 288 UNCLOS.

ICSID Convention may be further defined in an international investment agreement containing the consent to arbitration; such agreements typically contain a definition of what constitutes an 'investment', which thus further defines the jurisdiction *ratione materiae* of arbitral tribunals established under such treaties.

1.7.3 Jurisdiction *Ratione Temporis*

Jurisdiction *ratione temporis* defines which disputes can be submitted to an international court or tribunal from a temporal perspective. Jurisdiction *ratione temporis* will often limit the jurisdiction of a court or tribunal for legal disputes arising before or after a certain date, or for disputes based on facts or situations having occurred before or after a certain date.

As mentioned in the section discussing the notion of 'dispute', the question whether a 'dispute' exists takes special importance in relation to the jurisdiction *ratione temporis* of courts and tribunals. The link between the existence of a dispute and the jurisdiction *ratione temporis* of courts implies first of all that the 'dispute must in principle exist at the time the Application is submitted to the Court'.[139]

Second, foundational instruments and statutes of international courts and tribunals often do not contain any temporal limits on the competence of that court or tribunal to adjudicate cases. However, temporal limits can be included in the relevant instrument which contains the parties' consent to jurisdiction.[140] In principle, and absent any contrary indication in the treaty, consent to jurisdiction is valid for disputes arising after the entry into force of a treaty containing the consent to adjudication or arbitration.[141] The question when a dispute in a legal sense has arisen is therefore primordial. This was discussed by the arbitral tribunal in *Mafezzini v. Spain*, an investor-state arbitration based on a bilateral investment treaty (BIT) between Argentina and Spain.[142] The BIT provided in its investor-state arbitration clause that the agreement 'shall not apply to disputes or claims originating before its entry into force'.[143]

---

[139] *Application of the International Convention on the Elimination of All Forms of Racial Discrimination (Georgia v. Russian Federation), Preliminary Objections*, Judgment, [2011] ICJ Rep. 70, at p. 84, para. 30.

[140] Y. Shany, 'Jurisdiction and Admissibility', in C. P. R. Romano, K. J. Alter, and C. Avgerou (eds), *The Oxford Handbook of International Adjudication*, Oxford, 2014, p. 792.

[141] In the context of investor-state arbitration, see *Philip Morris Asia Limited v. The Commonwealth of Australia* (PCA Case No. 2012-12). Award on Jurisdiction and Admissibility, 17 December 2015, para. 525.

[142] *Emilio Agustín Maffezini v. The Kingdom of Spain*, ICSID Case No. ARB/97/7, Decision of the Tribunal on Objections to Jurisdiction (25 January 2000).

[143] Article II (2) the Argentine-Spain BIT (1991) (signed 3 October 1991, entered into force 28 September 1992).

The precise point in time when a dispute in a legal sense thus exists in the case was essential, since several facts on which the claim was in part based had occurred before the BIT's entry into force. The Tribunal considered that:

> there tends to be a natural sequence of events that leads to a dispute. It begins with the expression of a disagreement and the statement of a difference of views. In time these events acquire a precise legal meaning through the formulation of legal claims, their discussion and eventual rejection or lack of response by the other party. The conflict of legal views and interests will only be present in the latter stage, even though the underlying facts predate them[144] ... in this case the dispute in its technical and legal sense began to take shape in 1994 ... At that point, the conflict of legal views and interests came to be clearly established, leading not long thereafter to the presentation of various claims that eventually came to this Tribunal.[145]

The specific provisions contained in the instrument containing consent are therefore fundamental, especially in case of compromissory clauses. Beyond the regularly found provision that the jurisdiction of the court or tribunal does not extend to disputes or claims arising before the entry into force of the treaty, one can also find a limitation to jurisdiction for disputes based on 'situations and facts' arising before the date of the instrument containing consent.[146]

1.7.4 Jurisdictional Conditions

In addition to the general jurisdictional requirements set by the founding instruments, statutes and rules of courts and tribunals, and in the instruments containing the consent of states to adjudication or arbitration, one regularly finds in the latter instruments additional *conditions* under which states consent to the settlement of their disputes.[147] Jurisdictional conditions or further limitations to jurisdiction are primarily found in the constitutive instruments or statutes of courts and tribunals. An important example is the WTO DSU, which limits the rights of the parties to a dispute to request the Dispute Settlement Body to establish a panel to

---

[144] *Emilio Agustín Maffezini v. The Kingdom of Spain*, ICSID Case No. ARB/97/7, Decision of the Tribunal on Objections to Jurisdiction (25 January 2000), para. 96.

[145] *Ibid.*, para. 98.

[146] See e.g. the declaration of Belgium recognizing the jurisdiction of the ICJ as compulsory under Article 36(2) of the ICJ Statute, which limits the jurisdiction of the Court to 'legal disputes arising after 13 July 1948 concerning situations or facts subsequent to that date'. For a discussion, see *Case concerning the Right of Passage over Indian Territory*, Judgment of 12 April 1960, [1960] ICJ Rep. 6.

[147] Y. Shany, 'Jurisdiction and Admissibility' in C. P. R. Romano, K. J. Alter, and C. Avgerou (eds), *The Oxford Handbook of International Adjudication*, Oxford, 2014, p. 793 ff.

settle the dispute to a prior exhaustion of a mandatory consultation for 60 days.[148]

More often, jurisdictional conditions will be contained in the instrument containing the consent of states. Article 283 of the UNCLOS, for instance, contains an obligation on the states parties to a dispute under the Convention to 'proceed expeditiously to an exchange of views regarding its settlement by negotiation or other peaceful means'. Other examples are Article 29(1) of the Convention on Discrimination against Women, which provides:

> Any dispute between two or more States Parties concerning the interpretation or application of the present Convention which is not settled by negotiation shall, at the request of one of them, be submitted to arbitration. If within six months from the date of the request for arbitration the parties are unable to agree on the organization of the arbitration, any one of those parties may refer the dispute to the International Court of Justice by request in conformity with the Statute of the Court.

The Convention on Discrimination against Women thus requires not only an attempt to settle the dispute by negotiation but also to agree on the organisation of arbitration of the dispute for a period of six months.

International investment treaties also often include jurisdiction conditions in the clauses providing for investor-state arbitration. Such conditions frequently relate to the requirement of a formal notification of the existence of a dispute and an attempt to settle the dispute by negotiations within a set time frame following the notification.[149] Certain treaties also included a (time-limited) exhaustion of domestic remedies, that is a requirement to first submit a dispute to the domestic courts of the host state.[150]

1.8 Admissibility

Admissibility relates to the question of whether a court or tribunal, upon having established that it has jurisdiction to hear a case, can in fact exercise its jurisdiction.[151] Admissibility may therefore imply that even where the jurisdictional requirements are fulfilled, a court or tribunal may nonetheless decide to not hear the claim. In essence, admissibility determines

---

[148] Article 7(4) WTO DSU.
[149] E.g. Article 12 BLEU (Belgium-Luxembourg Economic Union) – Montenegro BIT (2010) (signed 16 February 2010), available at https://investmentpolicy.unctad.org/international-investment-agreements/treaty-files/389/download.
[150] E.g. Article 8 Argentina – United Kingdom BIT (1990) (signed 11 December 1990; entry into force 19 February 1993), available at https://investmentpolicy.unctad.org/international-investment-agreements/treaty-files/126/download.
[151] Admissibility is sometimes referred to as receivability, based on the French word for admissibility '*recevabilité*', but the preferred term is admissibility.

'whether, in the light of all the relevant circumstances, that court or tribunal *should* entertain the case'.[152] As stated by the ICJ:

> Objections to admissibility normally take the form of an assertion that, even if the Court has jurisdiction and the facts stated by the applicant State are assumed to be correct, nonetheless there are reasons why the Court should not proceed to an examination of the merits.[153]

The precise nature of admissibility becomes clear when contrasted to the notion of jurisdiction. As put by Fitzmaurice:

> [T]here is a clear jurisprudential distinction between an objection to the jurisdiction of the tribunal, and an objection to the substantive admissibility of the claim. The latter is a plea that the tribunal should rule the claim to be inadmissible on same ground other than its ultimate merits: the former is a plea that the tribunal itself is incompetent to give any ruling at all whether as to the merits or as to the admissibility of the claim.[154]

Jurisdiction precedes the admissibility of the claim, and, as a consequence, a court or tribunal must first establish the existence of jurisdiction in a particular case before assessing any claims as to the (in)admissibility of a claim.[155]

Admissibility entails an element of discretion, but this discretion must be exercised 'strictly in accordance with legal criteria having regard to the place of judicial settlement of international disputes in the conduct of international affairs, the manner in which an international court or tribunal works, and how it obtains its authority to decide a case'.[156] The dismissal of a claim based on its inadmissibility therefore is not left to the full discretion of the court or tribunal, but rather is based on *legal* grounds, separate to grounds related to the merits of the case.[157]

The question of what grounds lead to a finding of inadmissibility precisely is still open to debate. It is in any event difficult to categorise

---

[152] S. Rosenne, 'International Courts and Tribunals, Jurisdiction and Admissibility of Inter-State Applications' in R. Wolfrum, *Max Planck Encyclopedia of Public International Law*, Oxford, 2012, para. 2.

[153] *Oil Platforms (Islamic Republic of Iran v. United States of America)* (Merits) [2003] ICJ Rep. 161, para. 29.

[154] G. Fitzmaurice, *The Law and Procedure of the International Court of Justice*, Cambridge, 1986, pp. 438–9.

[155] H. Thirlway, *The Law and Procedure of the International Court of Justice: Fifty Years of Jurisprudence*, Oxford, 2013, Volume I, p. 807.

[156] S. Rosenne, 'International Courts and Tribunals, Jurisdiction and Admissibility of Inter-State Applications' in R. Wolfrum, *Max Planck Encyclopedia of Public International Law*, Oxford, 2012, para. 2.

[157] G. Fitzmaurice, 'The law and procedure of the International Court of Justice, 1951–4: questions of jurisdiction, competence and procedure', (1958) 34 *British Yearbook of International Law*, 1, 12. See also S. Rosenne, 'International Courts and Tribunals, Jurisdiction and Admissibility of Inter-State Applications' in R. Wolfrum, *Max Planck Encyclopedia of Public International Law*, Oxford, 2012, para. 2.

objections to admissibility and hence these are best described as contentions 'that are neither matters of jurisdiction, nor questions of the merits'.[158] Nonetheless, there is common ground that the requirement of exhaustion of local remedies in the context of claims in the exercise of a state's exercise of diplomatic protection of one of its nationals is a requirement to the admissibility of the claim.[159] Other examples are the mootness of the claim, discussed in Section 1.4 ('('Justiciability and Mootness'), and the objection that the parties to the dispute have agreed to settle the dispute via other means which would take priority of the exercise of jurisdiction by another court or tribunal which otherwise is competent to hear the claim.[160]

The distinction between jurisdiction and admissibility is complex, as witnessed by the discussion on whether jurisdiction conditions are properly categorised as questions of *jurisdiction* of the court or tribunal, or as questions of *admissibility* of the claim. This question still is the subject of discussion and diverging opinions. The debate essentially revolves around two different perspectives on the precise nature of the conditions: either one views these as conditions under which the parties *consent* to jurisdiction, in which case objections based on such requirements are jurisdictional in nature, or one can view these as conditions *to the exercise of jurisdiction* or the *fulfilment of the consent*, in which case they are more properly categorised as relating to the admissibility of the claim.

The ICJ has unambiguously categorised jurisdictional conditions as a question of jurisdiction:

> When that consent is expressed in a compromissory clause in an international agreement, any conditions to which such consent is subject must be regarded as constituting the limits thereon. The Court accordingly considers that the examination of such conditions relates to its jurisdiction and not to the admissibility of the application.[161]

Similarly, in *Georgia* v. *Russia*, the Court unambiguously posited that the prior obligation to negotiate is a question of jurisdiction.[162]

Judge Fitzmaurice, in a separate opinion in the *Northern Cameroons* case offered further explanation on the test to be applied in distinguishing both, following the position of the ICJ to treat jurisdictional conditions as a question of jurisdiction:

---

[158] H. Thirlway, 'The International Court of Justice', in M. D. Evans (4th ed.), *International Law*, Oxford, 2014, p. 600.
[159] Thirlway, *The International Court of Justice* (n. 68) p. 171.   [160] *Ibid.*
[161] *Armed Activities on the Territory of the Congo (New Application: 2002) (Democratic Republic of the Congo v. Rwanda)*, Jurisdiction and Admissibility, Judgment, [2006] ICJ Rep. 40, para. 88.
[162] *Convention on the Elimination of All Forms of Racial Discrimination (Georgia v. Russia)*, Preliminary Objections, 1 April 2011, paras. 173–177.

the real distinction and test would seem to be whether or not the objection is based on, or arises from, the jurisdictional clause or clauses under which the jurisdiction of the tribunal is said to exist. If so, the objection is basically one of jurisdiction. If it is founded on considerations lying outside the ambit of any jurisdictional clause, and not involving the interpretation or application of such a provision, then it will normally be an objection to the receivability of the claim.[163]

The situation is more nuanced in investor-state arbitration. One can find both arbitral awards which treat jurisdictional conditions as going to the admissibility of the claim[164] and arbitral awards which treat these as a question of jurisdiction.[165]

The discussion on whether certain conditions expressed in dispute settlement clauses relate to the jurisdiction of a court or tribunal or the admissibility of the claim has been summarised by Kolb, who discusses both perspectives in relation to the requirement of the existence of a 'dispute':

> It is thus possible to say that in the absence of a dispute the Court will have no subject-matter jurisdiction, its duty (in contentious cases) being to decide between opposing positions on the basis of law. Thus, if there is no dispute, there is nothing for a court of justice to do in terms of its particular task of deciding disputes. The fault lies not simply in the claim, but in the material scope of the Court's jurisdiction. Equally, however, it is possible to say that the absence of a dispute indicates a defect in the claim as a formulated application as, in those circumstances, it is not based on a genuine 'claim'. This perspective leads quite naturally to a decision that the claim is inadmissible.[166]

The distinction between jurisdiction and admissibility might seem theoretical, but it has been argued that it has important consequences. These consequences are subject to divergent opinions and practice and hence it is, as with the distinction itself, difficult to enounce firm principles in this

---

[163] *Case concerning the Northern Cameroons (Cameroon v. United Kingdom)* (Preliminary Objections) Judgment of 2 December 1963, Separate Opinion of Judge Sir Gerald Fitzmaurice, [1963] ICJ Rep. 97, p 35.

[164] E.g. *Abaclat and others (Case formerly known as Giovanna a Beccara and Others)* v. *Argentine Republic* (ICSID Case No. ARB/07/5), Decision on Jurisdiction and Admissibility, 4 August 2011, para. 496: 'The Tribunal is of the opinion that the negotiation and 18 months litigation requirements relate to the conditions for implementation of Argentina's consent to ICSID jurisdiction and arbitration, and not the fundamental question of whether Argentina consented to ICSID jurisdiction and arbitration. Thus, any non-compliance with such requirements may not lead to a lack of ICSID jurisdiction, and only – if at all – to a lack of admissibility of the claim, and will thus be addressed when dealing with issues of admissibility.'

[165] E.g. *Daimler Financial Services AG* v. *Argentina*, ICSID Case No. ARB/05/1, Award, 22 August 2012, para. 194: 'since the 18-month domestic courts provision constitutes a treaty-based precondition to the Host State's consent to arbitrate, it cannot be bypassed or otherwise waived by the Tribunal as a mere "procedural" or "admissibility-related" matter'.

[166] R. Kolb, *The Elgar Companion to the International Court of Justice*, Cheltenham, 2014, pp. 169–70.

respect. An important distinction relates to the question of resubmission of a claim or dispute after either the lack of admissibility or failure to meet the jurisdictional requirements and conditions that are remedied. If a claim is declared inadmissible, it has been argued that there is no legal obstacle in a resubmission of the claim once the admissibility requirements are met,[167] provided of course that the inadmissibility of the claim can be cured.[168] Conversely, if a court or tribunal establishes that it lacks jurisdiction to hear the case, certain authors have claimed that there is no possibility for the parties to resubmit the claim to the tribunal: a defect in jurisdiction, accordingly, could not be cured in relation to that particular dispute and taking into account the facts as they are at the time of the submission of the claim.[169] A second important distinction between jurisdiction and jurisdictional conditions, and admissibility, which one finds in scholarship is the fact that only *admissibility* requirements could be the subject of a waiver by the parties, while jurisdiction conditions could not.[170] The consequences of the categorical distinction between jurisdiction and jurisdictional conditions, and admissibility, are not unequivocal. Ultimately, these categories are important to distinguish but nevertheless difficult to delimit.

1.9 Further Reading

1.9.1 General References on the Principles of International Dispute Settlement

Amerasinghe, C. F., *Jurisdiction of International Tribunals*, The Hague, 2003.
von Bogdandy, A., and I. Venzke, *In Whose Name? A Public Law Theory of International Adjudication*, Oxford, 2014.
Brown, C., *A Common Law of International Adjudication*, Oxford, 2007.
Boisson de Chazournes, L., M. G. Kohen and J. E. Viñuales (eds), *Diplomatic and Judicial Means of Dispute Settlement*, Leiden, 2013.
Collier, J., and V. Lowe, *The Settlement of Disputes in International Law: Institutions and Procedures*, Oxford, 1999.
De Brabandere, E. (ed.), *International Procedure in Interstate Litigation and Arbitration: A Comparative Perspective*, Cambridge, 2021.
French, D., M. Saul and N. D. White (eds), *International Law and Dispute Settlement: New Problems and Techniques*, Oxford, 2010.

---

[167] As noted by the Tribunal in *SGS* v. *the Philippines*: 'Normally a claim which is within jurisdiction but inadmissible (e.g., on grounds of failure to exhaust local remedies) will be dismissed, although this will usually be without prejudice to the right of the claimant to start new proceedings if the obstacle to admissibility has been removed (e.g., through exhaustion of local remedies)' (*SGS Société Générale de Surveillance* v. *Republic of the Philippines*, ICSID Case No. ARB/02/6, Decision of the Tribunal on Objections to Jurisdiction, 29 January 2004, para 171).

[168] C. F. Amerasinghe, *Jurisdiction of International Tribunals*, The Hague, 2003, p. 243.

[169] Ibid. [170] Ibid., pp. 286 ff.

Giorgetti, C.,*The Rules, Practice, and Jurisprudence of International Courts and Tribunals*, Leiden, 2012.

Mackenzie, R., C. P. R. Romano, Y. Shany and P. Sands, *The Manual on International Courts and Tribunals* (2nd ed.), Oxford, 2010.

Orrego Vicuña, F., *International Dispute Settlement in an Evolving Global Society*, Cambridge, 2004.

Romano, C. P. R., K. J. Alter and C. Avgerou (eds), *The Oxford Handbook of International Adjudication*, Oxford, 2014.

Schabas, W. A., and S. Murphy (eds), *Research Handbook on International Courts and Tribunals*, Cheltenham, 2017.

Shany, Y., *Questions of Jurisdiction and Admissibility before International Courts*, Cambridge, 2016.

Tanaka, Y., *The Peaceful Settlement of International Disputes*, Cambridge, 2018.

1.9.2 Treaties, Official Documents and Collections of Documents

Hague Convention on Pacific Settlement of International Disputes (Hague, I) (adopted 29 July 1899, entered into force 4 September 1900).

Convention on the Limitation of Employment of Force for Recovery of Contract Debts (Hague, II) (adopted 18 October 1907, entered into force 26 January 1910) ('Drago Porter Convention').

American Treaty on Pacific Settlement (signed 30 April 1948, entered into force 6 May 1949) 30 UNTS 5 ('Pact of Bogota').

United Nations General Assembly Resolution 37/10 (1982) ('Manila Declaration on the Peaceful Settlement of International Disputes').

Tams, C., and A. Tzanakopoulos, *Basic Documents on the Settlement of International Disputes*, Oxford, 2012.

2

Negotiation

Article 33(1) of the UN Charter lists the various methods of peaceful settlement. The methods listed are not set out in any order of priority, but the first mentioned, negotiation, is the principal means of handling all international disputes.[1] In fact in practice, negotiation is employed more frequently than all the other methods put together. Often, indeed, negotiation is the only means employed, not just because it is always the first to be tried and is often successful, but also because states may believe its advantages to be so great as to rule out the use of other methods, even in situations where the chances of a negotiated settlement are slight. The importance of negotiation as a method of dispute settlement was recognized in Article 10 of the 1982 'Manila Declaration on the Peaceful Settlement of International Disputes',[2] which states that

> States should, without prejudice to the right of free choice of means, bear in mind that direct negotiations are a flexible and effective means of peaceful settlement of their disputes. When they choose to resort to direct negotiations, States should negotiate meaningfully, in order to arrive at an early settlement acceptable to the parties. States should be equally prepared to seek the settlement of their disputes by the other means mentioned in the present Declaration.

On the occasions when another method is used, negotiation is not displaced, but directed towards instrumental issues, for example the terms of reference for an inquiry or conciliation commission or the arrangements for implementing an arbitral decision.

Thus, in one form or another, negotiation has a vital part in international disputes. But negotiation is more than a possible means of settling differences, it is also a technique for preventing them from arising. Since

---

[1] For discussion of the meaning and significance of negotiation, see H. Darwin, 'Negotiation', in C. M. H. Waldock (ed.), *International Disputes: The Legal Aspects*, London, 1972, ch. 2A; F. S. Northedge and M. D. Donelan, *International Disputes: The Political Aspects*, London, 1971, ch. 12; P. J. I. M. De Waart, *The Element of Negotiation in the Pacific Settlement of Disputes between States*, The Hague, 1973; United Nations, *Handbook on the Peaceful Settlement of Disputes between States*, New York, 1992, ch. 2A; B. Starkey, M. A. Boyer and J. Wilkenfeld, *Negotiating a Complex World*, Lanham, MD, 1999; I. W. Zartman and J. Z. Rubin (eds), *Power and Negotiation*, Ann Arbor, MI, 2000; and V. A. Kremenyuk (ed.), *International Negotiation*, 2nd ed., San Francisco, 2002.

[2] General Assembly Resolution 37/10 ('Manila Declaration on the Peaceful Settlement of International Disputes').

prevention is always better than cure, this form of negotiation, known as 'consultation', is a convenient place to begin.

2.1 Consultation

When a government anticipates that a decision or a proposed course of action may harm another state, discussions with the affected party can provide a way of heading off a dispute by creating an opportunity for adjustment and accommodation. Quite minor modifications to its plans, of no importance to the state taking the decision, may be all that are required to avoid trouble, yet may only be recognised if the other side is given a chance to point them out. The particular value of consultation is that it supplies this useful information at the most appropriate time – before anything has been done. For it is far easier to make the necessary modifications at the decision-making stage, rather than later, when exactly the same action may seem like capitulation to foreign pressure, or be seized on by critics as a sacrifice of domestic interests.

2.1.1 Consultation and Dispute Prevention

A good example of the value of consultation is provided by the practice of the United States and Canada in antitrust proceedings. Writing of the procedure employed in such cases, a commentator has noted that:

> While it is true that antitrust officials of one state might flatly refuse to alter a course of action in any way, it has often been the case that officials have been persuaded to modify their plans somewhat. After consultation, it may be agreed to shape an indictment in a less offensive manner, to change the ground rules of an investigation so as to require only 'voluntary' testimony from witnesses, or that officials of the government initiating an investigation or action will keep their antitrust counterparts informed of progress in the case and allow them to voice their concerns.[3]

This policy of cooperation, developed through a series of bilateral understandings, has been incorporated in an agreement providing for coordination with regard to both the competition laws and the deceptive marketing practices laws of the two states.

Consultation should be distinguished from two related ways of taking foreign susceptibilities into account: notification and the obtaining of prior consent. Suppose state A decides to notify state B of imminent action likely to affect B's interests, or, as will sometimes be the case, is obliged to do so

---

[3] See B. R. Campbell, 'The Canada–United States antitrust notification and consultation procedure' (1978) 56 *Canadian Bar Review*, 459 at 468. On arrangements with Australia, see S. D. Ramsey, 'The United States–Australian Antitrust Cooperation Agreement: a step in the right direction' (1983–4) 24 *Virginia Journal of International Law*, 127.

as a legal duty. Such advanced warning gives B time to consider its response, which may be to make representations to A, and in any case avoids the abrasive impact of what might otherwise be regarded as an attempt to present B with a *fait accompli*. In these ways notification can make a modest contribution to dispute avoidance, though naturally B is likely to regard notification alone as a poor substitute for the chance to negotiate and influence the decision that consultation can provide.

Obtaining the consent of the other state, which again may sometimes be a legal obligation, lies at the opposite pole. Here, the affected state enjoys a veto over the proposed action. This is clearly an extremely important power and its exceptional nature was properly emphasised by the tribunal in the *Lake Lanoux* case:

> To admit that jurisdiction in a certain field can no longer be exercised except on the condition of, or by way of, an agreement between two States, is to place an essential restriction on the sovereignty of a State, and such restriction could only be admitted if there were clear and convincing evidence. Without doubt, international practice does reveal some special cases in which this hypothesis has become reality; thus, sometimes two States exercise conjointly jurisdiction over certain territories (joint ownership, *co-imperium*, or *condominium*); likewise, in certain international arrangements, the representatives of States exercise conjointly a certain jurisdiction in the name of those States or in the name of organizations. But these cases are exceptional, and international judicial decisions are slow to recognize their existence, especially when they impair the territorial sovereignty of a State, as would be the case in the present matter.[4]

In that case, Spain argued that, under both customary international law and treaties between the two states, France was under an obligation to obtain Spain's consent to the execution of works for the utilisation of certain waters in the Pyrenees for a hydroelectric scheme. The argument was rejected, but the tribunal went on to hold that France was under a duty to consult with Spain over projects that were likely to affect Spanish interests. Speaking of the nature of such obligatory consultations, the tribunal observed that:

> one speaks, although often inaccurately, of the 'obligation of negotiating an agreement'. In reality, the engagements thus undertaken by States take very diverse forms and have a scope which varies according to the manner in which they are defined and according to the procedures intended for their execution; but the reality of the obligations thus undertaken is incontestable and sanctions can be applied in the event, for example, of an unjustified breaking off of the

---

[4] *Lake Lanoux Arbitration (France v. Spain)* (1957) 24 ILR 101 at 127. For discussion of the significance of the case, see J. G. Laylin and R. L. Bianchi, 'The role of adjudication in international river disputes: the *Lake Lanoux* case' (1959) 53 *American Journal of International Law*, 30.

discussions, abnormal delays, disregard of the agreed procedures, systematic refusals to take into consideration adverse proposals or interests, and, more generally, in cases of violation of the rules of good faith.[5]

2.1.2 The Role of Consultation in Dispute Settlement

The role of consultation at different stages of a dispute may be seen in the *Land Reclamation* case.[6] Here, Malaysia brought proceedings against Singapore in response to reclamation activities being undertaken by the latter in the Straits of Johor, claiming that, as the activities were damaging and had been carried out without notification or consultation, Singapore had breached its obligations under the 1982 Law of the Sea Convention. Malaysia first sought provisional measures of protection from the International Tribunal for the Law of the Sea, and, in its order in 2003, the Tribunal put on record various undertakings from the parties with regard to the sharing of information and cooperation and required them to set up a group of independent experts to investigate the dispute and make recommendations. The group submitted its recommendations as requested, which provided the basis for an agreement settling the dispute which shortly afterwards was incorporated in an arbitration award on agreed terms. Under the settlement, the two states set up a joint mechanism designed to promote cooperation between them in the future. Thus, here consultation played a triple role, providing the basis for Malaysia's initial claim, then forming part of a transitional framework in the provisional measures order, and finally supplying a major component of the final settlement.

Another example of how the various ways of coordinating activities may be constructively combined is provided by the 'Interim Reciprocal Information and Consultation System', established in 1990 to regulate the movement of British and Argentine forces in the south-western Atlantic.[7] The system involved the creation of a direct communication link with the aim of reducing the possibility of incidents and limiting their

---

[5] 24 ILR 101 at 128. See further C. B. Bourne, 'Procedure in the development of international drainage basins: the duty to consult and negotiate' (1972) 10 *Canadian Yearbook of International Law*, 212; and F. L. Kirgis, *Prior Consultation in International Law*, Charlottesville, VA, 1983, ch. 2.

[6] *Case Concerning Land Reclamation by Singapore in and around the Straits of Johor (Malaysia v. Singapore)*, Provisional Measures Order of 8 October 2003, 126 ILR 487; and see J. G. Merrills, 'New horizons for international adjudication' (2006) 6 *Global Community YBILJ* 47 at 48–57.

[7] Text in (1990) 29 ILM 1296; and see document A in Appendix A. For discussion, see M. Evans, 'The restoration of diplomatic relations between Argentina and the United Kingdom' (1991) 40 *International & Comparative Law Quarterly*, 473 at 478–80. For later developments, see R. R. Churchill, 'Falkland Islands: maritime jurisdiction and co-operative arrangements with Argentina' (1997) 46 *International & Comparative Law Quarterly*, 463.

consequences if they occur. These facilities for consultation are supported by a provision under which at least 25 days' written notice is required for air and naval movements, and exercises of more than a certain size. This is a straightforward arrangement for notification, but two-component features of the system are worth noticing. First, the notification provision is very specific as to the areas in which the obligation exists and the units to which it applies, and thereby minimises the possibilities for misunderstanding. Second, in relation to the most sensitive areas, those immediately off the parties' respective coasts, the notifying state must be informed immediately of any movement which 'might cause political or military difficulty' and 'mutual agreement will be necessary to proceed'. Here, therefore there is not only a right and a corresponding duty in respect of notification, but in some circumstances at least a need to obtain consent.

When arrangements for consultation are agreed upon in advance, questions may naturally arise as to whether they have been complied with if one party adopts measures to which the other takes exception. In the *Pulp Mills on the River Uruguay* case,[8] for example, Argentina took Uruguay to the International Court of Justice claiming, inter alia, that the latter had failed to notify and consult with Argentina before authorising the construction of two large pulp mills on the river which forms the international boundary. The obligations in question were contained in a bilateral treaty, the 1975 Statute of the River Uruguay, and, after examining the parties' conduct, the Court ruled that Uruguay had indeed breached its procedural obligations under the Statute. Argentina further claimed that Uruguay had violated its substantive obligations under the treaty, on account of the ecological impact of the pulp mills, but the Court found that this claim was not made out. Cooperative arrangements for utilising shared resources such as boundary rivers are increasingly common nowadays, and this case is a good illustration of their significance.

In the *Sarayaku* case,[9] the Inter-American Court of Human Rights was required to examine the scope of a state's obligation to consult an indigenous community when undertaking development projects that may affect their lands. The case arose because in 1996 Ecuador had granted oil concessions in the ancestral lands of the Sarayaku community without any consultation. Although it was recognised that the community had suffered harm from the concessions because it was unable to practice its traditional means of subsistence and had lost freedom of movement, Ecuador argued that a duty to consult only arose

---

[8] *Pulp Mills on the River Uruguay (Argentina v. Uruguay)*, Judgment [2010] ICJ Rep. 14 and see C. R. Payne, Note (2011) 105 *AJIL*, 94.

[9] *Kichwa Indigenous Community of Sarayaku v. Ecuador*, Inter-American Court of Human Rights (ser. C) No. 245 (2012). See also L. Brunner and K. Quintana, 'The duty to consult in the Inter-American system: legal standards after Sarayaku' (2012) 16 *ASIL Insights*, 35.

when Ecuador subsequently ratified the International Labour Organization's 1989 Convention No. 169. The Court, however, disagreed and, holding that the obligation to consult is a general principle of international law, found Ecuador liable. Although necessarily to be seen in the context of its rather specialised subject matter, this decision clearly has important implications for the responsibilities of states towards their indigenous peoples.

2.1.3 The Difficulty of Institutionalising Consultation

The advantages of consultation in bilateral relations are equally evident in matters which are of concern to a larger number of states. In a multilateral setting, consultation usually calls for an institutional structure of some kind. These can vary widely and do not have to be elaborate in order to be useful. The Antarctic Treaty system, for example, now operates on the basis of annual meetings but until recently had no permanent organs. It nevertheless exemplified the value of what has been called 'anticipatory cooperation' in addressing environmental and other issues in a special regional context. When closer regulation is needed, more complex institutional arrangements may be appropriate. Thus, the International Monetary Fund at one time required a member which had decided to change the par value of its currency to obtain the concurrence of the IMF before doing so. It is interesting to note that the term 'concurrence' was chosen 'to convey the idea of a presumption that was to be observed in favour of the member's proposal'.[10] Even so, the arrangement meant that extremely sensitive decisions were subject to international scrutiny. As a result, until the par value system was abandoned in 1978, the provision gave rise to considerable difficulties in practice.

Consultation between states is usually an ad hoc process and, except where reciprocity provides an incentive, as in the cases considered, has proved difficult to institutionalise. Obligatory consultation is bound to make decision-making slower and, depending on how the obligation is defined, may well constrain a government's options. In the *Lake Lanoux* case, the tribunal noted that it was a 'delicate matter' to decide whether such an obligation had been complied with, and held that, on the facts, France had done all that was required. If consultation is to be compulsory, however, the circumstances in which the obligation arises, as well as its content, need careful definition, or an allegation of a failure to carry out the agreed procedure may itself become a disputed issue.

Whether voluntary or compulsory, consultation is often easier to implement for executive than for legislative decision-making, since the former is usually less rigidly structured and more centralised. But legislative action

---

[10] See J. Gold, 'Prior consultation in international law' (1983–4) 24 *Va JIL*, 729 at 737.

can also cause international disputes; therefore procedures designed to achieve the same effect as consultation can have an equally useful part to play. Where states enjoy close relations, it may be possible to establish machinery for negotiating the coordination of legislative and administrative measures on matters of common interest. There are clear advantages in having uniform provisions on such matters as environmental protection, where states share a common frontier, or commerce, if trade is extensive. The difficulties of achieving such harmonisation are considerable, as the experience of the European Union has demonstrated, though, if uniformity cannot be achieved, compatibility of domestic provisions is a less ambitious alternative. In either case, the rewards in terms of dispute avoidance make the effort well worthwhile.

Consultation, then, is a valuable way of avoiding international disputes. It is therefore not surprising to find that, in an increasingly interdependent world, the practice is growing. The record, however, is still very uneven. Although, as we shall see in Chapters 5 and 7, consultation is increasingly important in international trade and to a lesser extent also in investor-state arbitration, on other issues with the potential to cause disputes, such as access to resources and the protection of the environment, progress in developing procedures for consultation has been slower than is desirable. Similarly, while there is already consultation on a number of matters between Canada and the United States and in Europe, in other parts of the world the practice is scarcely known. Finally, when such procedures have been developed, there is, as we have noted, an important distinction between consultation as a matter of obligation and voluntary consultation, which states prefer.

The author of a comprehensive review of consultation was compelled by the evidence of state practice to conclude that:

> Despite the growth of prior consultation norms, it is unlikely that there will be any all-encompassing prior consultation duty in the foreseeable future. Thus, to the extent that formal procedural structures for prior consultation may be desirable, they should be tailored to recurring, relatively well defined, troublesome situations.[11]

The difficulty of persuading states to accept consultation procedures and the ways in which they operate when established are reminders of the fact that states are not entities, like individuals, but complex groupings of institutions and interests. If this is constantly borne in mind, the salient features of negotiation and the means of settlement discussed in later chapters will be much easier to understand.

---

[11] Kirgis, *Prior Consultation* (n. 5) p. 375. See also I. W. Zartman (ed.), *Preventive Negotiation*, Lanham, MD, 2001.

2.2 Forms of Negotiation

Negotiations between states are usually conducted through 'normal diplomatic channels', that is, by the respective foreign offices, or by diplomatic representatives, who in the case of complex negotiations may lead delegations including representatives of several interested departments of the governments concerned. As an alternative, if the subject matter is appropriate, negotiations may be carried out by what are termed the 'competent authorities' of each party, that is, by representatives of the particular ministry or department responsible for the matter in question; for example, between trade departments in the case of a commercial agreement, or between defence ministries in negotiations concerning weapons procurement. Where the competent authorities are subordinate bodies, they may be authorised to take negotiations as far as possible and to refer disagreements to a higher governmental level. One of the treaty provisions discussed in the *Lake Lanoux* dispute, for example, provided that:

> The highest administrative authorities of the bordering Departments and Provinces will act in concert in the exercise of their right to make regulations for the general interest and to interpret or modify their regulations whenever the respective interests are at stake, and in case they cannot reach agreement, the dispute shall be submitted to the two Governments.[12]

In the case of a recurrent problem or a situation requiring continuous supervision, states may decide to institutionalise negotiations by creating what is termed a mixed or joint commission.

2.2.1 'Mixed Commissions'

Neighbouring states commonly employ mixed commissions to deal with boundary delimitation, or other matters of common concern. Mixed commissions usually consist of an equal number of representatives of both parties, and may be given either a broad brief of indefinite duration, or the task of dealing with a specific problem. An outstanding example of a commission of the first type is provided by the Canada–United States International Joint Commission, which, since its creation in 1909, has dealt with a large number of issues, including industrial development, air pollution and a variety of questions concerning boundary waters.[13]

---

[12] See The Additional Act to the three Treaties of Bayonne (1866), Art. 16, (1957) 24 ILR 104.
[13] For an excellent survey of the work of the International Joint Commission, see M. Cohen, 'The regime of boundary waters: the Canadian–United States experience' (1975) 146 *Hague Recueil des Cours*, 219 (with bibliography). For a review of another commission, see L. C. Wilson, 'The settlement of boundary disputes: Mexico, the United States and the International Boundary Commission' (1980) 29 *ICLQ*, 38.

A commission of the second type was created in the Agreement of 2013 which settled the *Aerial Herbicide Spraying* case.[14] Ecuador had brought a case in the International Court against Colombia over the alleged spraying of toxic chemicals near, at and across their common border. However, the two states then concluded an agreement which established an exclusion zone in which Colombia would not conduct aerial spraying and which also set up a joint commission to ensure that spraying outside the zone did not cause herbicides to drift into Ecuador. The agreement also provided for the possibility of reducing the width of the exclusion zone, as well as operational parameters for Colombia's spraying programme, arrangements to exchange information and a mechanism for dispute settlement. Ecuador regarded the agreement as fully satisfying its claims. Accordingly, it arranged for the court proceedings to be discontinued.

An illustration of the different functions that may be assigned to ad hoc commissions is to be found in the *Lake Lanoux* dispute. After being considered by the International Commission for the Pyrenees, a mixed commission established as long ago as 1875, the matter was referred to a France–Spain Commission of Engineers, set up in 1949 to examine the technical aspects of the dispute. When the Commission of Engineers was unable to agree, France and Spain created a special mixed commission with the task of formulating proposals for the utilisation of Lake Lanoux and submitting them to the two governments for consideration. It was only when this commission was also unable to agree that the parties decided to refer the case to arbitration, though not before France had put forward (unsuccessfully) the idea of a fourth mixed commission which would have had the function of supervising execution of the water-diversion scheme and monitoring its day-to-day operation.

2.2.2 'Summit Discussions'

If negotiation through established machinery proves unproductive, 'summit discussions' between heads of state or foreign ministers may be used in an attempt to break the deadlock. Though the value of such conspicuous means of negotiation should not be exaggerated, summit diplomacy may facilitate agreement by enabling official bureaucracies to be bypassed to some extent, while providing an incentive to agree in the form of enhanced prestige for the leaders concerned. It should be noted, however, that summit diplomacy is usually the culmination of a great deal of conventional negotiation, and in some cases at least reflects nothing

---

[14] See *Aerial Herbicide Spraying (Ecuador v. Colombia)*, Order of 13 September 2013 [2013] ICJ Rep. 278.

more than a desire to make political capital out of an agreement that is already assured.

A disadvantage of summit meetings is that, unlike conventional negotiations, they take place amid a glare of publicity and so generate expectations which may be hard to fulfil. The idea that a meeting between world leaders has failed unless it produces a new agreement of some kind is scarcely realistic yet is epitomised by the mixture of hope and dread with which meetings between the leaders of the United States and the Soviet Union used to be surrounded. In an attempt to change this unhealthy atmosphere, in November 1989 President George H. Bush described his forthcoming meeting with Mr Gorbachev as an 'interim informal meeting' and emphasised that there would be no specific agenda.[15] It is doubtful if such attempts to damp down expectations can ever be wholly successful and even less likely that politicians would wish the media to treat their exploits on the international stage with indifference. However, as the solution of international problems is primarily a matter of working patiently with regular contact at all levels, there is much to be said for attempting to remove the unique aura of summit meetings and encouraging them to be seen instead as a regular channel of communication.

The public aspect of negotiations which is exemplified in summit diplomacy is also prominent in the activity of international organisations. In the United Nations General Assembly and similar bodies, states can, if they choose, conduct diplomatic exchanges in the full glare of international attention. This is undoubtedly a useful way of letting off steam and, more constructively, of engaging the attention of outside states which may have something to contribute to the solution of a dispute. It has the disadvantage, however, that so visible a performance may encourage the striking of attitudes which are at once both unrealistic and difficult to abandon. It is therefore probable that, for states with a serious interest in negotiating a settlement, the many opportunities for informal contact which international organisations provide are more useful than the dramatic confrontations of public debate.

2.2.3 Negotiations in a Multilateral Setting

Whether discussion of a dispute in an international organisation can be regarded as equivalent to traditional diplomatic negotiation is an issue which may also have legal implications. In the *South West Africa* cases (1962),[16] one of South Africa's preliminary objections was that any dispute between itself and the applicants, Ethiopia and Liberia, fell outside the terms of the International Court's jurisdiction (which rested on Article 7 of

---

[15] See L. Freedman, 'Just two men in a boat', *Independent*, 3 November 1989, p. 19.
[16] *South West Africa*, Preliminary Objections, Judgment [1962] ICJ Rep. 319.

the Mandate), because it had not been shown that the dispute was one which could not be settled by negotiation. The Court rejected the objection on the ground that extensive discussions in the United Nations on the question of South West Africa, in which South Africa and the applicants had been involved, constituted negotiations in respect of the dispute and the fact that those discussions had ended in deadlock indicated that the dispute could not be settled by negotiation.

In their joint dissenting opinion, Judges Spender and Fitzmaurice disagreed. In their view, what had occurred in the United Nations did not amount to negotiation within Article 7. Those discussions, they argued, failed to satisfy the requirements of Article 7 because such discussions had not been directed to the alleged dispute between the applicants and South Africa, merely to points of disagreement between the General Assembly and South Africa. Even if this had not been so, proceedings within an international organisation could never be regarded as a substitute for direct negotiations between the parties because:

> a 'negotiation' confined to the floor of an international Assembly, consisting of allegations of Members, resolutions of the Assembly and actions taken by the Assembly pursuant thereto, denial of allegations, refusal to comply with resolutions or to respond to action taken there under, cannot be enough to justify the Court in holding that the dispute 'cannot' be settled by negotiation, when no direct diplomatic interchanges have ever taken place between the parties, and therefore no attempt at settlement has been made at the statal and diplomatic level.[17]

The *Northern Cameroons* case[18] raised a very similar issue. Article 19 of the Trusteeship Agreement for the Cameroons, like Article 7 of the Mandate, covered only disputes incapable of settlement by negotiation. The International Court, which decided the case on other grounds, did not discuss this aspect of Article 19. Fitzmaurice, however, examining the requirement in light of his opinion in the *South West Africa* cases, observed that 'negotiation' did not mean 'a couple of states arguing with each other across the floor of an international assembly, or circulating statements of their complaints or contentions to its member states. That is disputation, not negotiation',[19] and repeated his view that direct negotiations were essential. Finding that the only 'negotiations' in the present case had taken the form of proceedings in the General Assembly, Fitzmaurice upheld a British objection that the requirements of Article 19 had not been satisfied. The issue here is clearly one that is unavoidable. International organisations, as already noted, provide an attractive forum for the airing of certain types of international disputes. How far it is appropriate to regard such exchanges as an alternative to conventional negotiation is a question which

---

[17] *Ibid.*, 562. [18] *Northern Cameroons*, Judgment [1963] ICJ Rep. 15. [19] *Ibid.*, 123.

judicial institutions must expect to resolve as part of the larger process of determining their relationship with their political counterparts.

More recently, the ICJ had to address a similar question in the *Application of the International Convention on the Elimination of All Forms of Racial Discrimination (Georgia v. Russian Federation)* case.[20] The case concerned the International Convention on the Elimination of All Forms of Racial Discrimination (CERD) which was relied on by Georgia to establish the jurisdiction of the Court. Article 22 of CERD reads:

> Any dispute between two or more States Parties with respect to the interpretation or application of this Convention, which is not settled by negotiation or by the procedures expressly provided for in this Convention, shall, at the request of any of the parties to the dispute, be referred to the International Court of Justice for decision, unless the disputants agree to another mode of settlement.

2.3 Substantive Aspects of Negotiation

The Court had to establish, *inter alia*, whether statements made during a Security Council meeting could (in conjunction with other statements) qualify as 'negotiations' for the purpose of Article 22 of CERD. The Court first considered that the subject matter of the negotiations should be the treaty containing the respective compromissory clause.[21] It then, in relation to the question whether statements made during a Security Council meeting could qualify as 'negotiations' for the purposes of the compromissory clause, considered that the statements made during a press briefing by the Georgian President and at the Security Council were not 'genuine attempts by Georgia to negotiate matters falling under CERD', and that while the statements 'attest to the existence of a dispute' between Georgia and Russia, they 'fail to demonstrate an attempt at negotiating these matters'.[22]

For a negotiated settlement to be possible, the parties must believe that the benefits of an agreement outweigh the losses. If their interests are diametrically opposed, an arrangement which would require one side to yield all or most of its position is therefore unlikely to be acceptable. This appears to have been the situation in the *Lake Lanoux* dispute, where the various attempts at a negotiated settlement encountered an insuperable obstacle in the irreconcilability of Spain's demand for a veto over works

---

[20] *Application of the International Convention on the Elimination of All Forms of Racial Discrimination (Georgia v. Russian Federation)*, Preliminary Objections, Judgment [2011] ICJ Rep. 70.

[21] *Ibid.*, paras 161 and 180.   [22] *Ibid.*, para. 181.

affecting border waters with France's insistence on its complete freedom of action.

There are a number of ways in which such an impasse may be avoided. If negotiations on the substantive aspects of a dispute are deadlocked, it may be possible for the parties to agree on a procedural solution. This is not an exception to the principle that gains must outweigh losses but an illustration of it, as the *Lake Lanoux* case demonstrates. For there, the parties' eventual agreement to refer the dispute to arbitration provided both states with the benefits of a definitive settlement to a question which had been under discussion for almost 40 years and the removal of a serious irritant in Franco-Spanish affairs.

Another approach is to consider whether the issue at the heart of a dispute can be split in such a way as to enable each side to obtain satisfaction. A solution of this kind was devised in 1978 to the problem of maritime delimitation between Australia and Papua New Guinea in the Torres Strait.[23] Having identified the different strands of the dispute, the parties succeeded in negotiating an agreement which dealt separately with the interests of the inhabitants of islands in the Strait, the status of the islands, seabed jurisdiction, fisheries jurisdiction, conservation and navigation rights. The virtue of this highly functional approach to the problem is underlined by the fact that earlier attempts to negotiate a single maritime boundary for the area had all ended in failure.

If splitting the dispute is not possible, a procedural agreement may be used to compensate one side for yielding on the substantive issue. In 1961, the United Kingdom and Iceland ended a dispute over the latter's fishing limits with an agreement which provided for the recognition of Iceland's claims in return for phasing out arrangements to protect British interests and an undertaking that future disputes could be referred to the International Court. The agreement provided that Iceland:

> will continue to work for the implementation of the Althing Resolution of May 5, 1959, regarding the extension of fisheries jurisdiction around Iceland, but shall give the United Kingdom Government six months' notice of such extension and, in the case of a dispute in relation to such extension, the matter shall, at the request of either party, be referred to the International Court of Justice.[24]

Two points are worth noting about this provision. First, while it is phrased in terms which permit recourse to the Court by either party, it is clear from the *travaux préparatoires* that it was included at Britain's request. Second, the reference to the Althing Resolution shows how a compromise can be

---

[23] See H. Burmester, 'The Torres Strait Treaty: ocean boundary delimitation by agreement' (1982) 76 *AJIL*, 321; also D. Renton, 'The Torres Strait Treaty after 15 years: some observations from a Papua New Guinea perspective', in J. Crawford and D. R. Rothwell (eds), *The Law of the Sea in the Asian Pacific Region*, Dordrecht, 1995, p. 171.

[24] [1973] ICJ Rep. 8.

agreed without prejudicing what one side regards as an important point of policy or principle.

Agreements like the one just quoted in which the parties are able to bring their negotiations to a successful conclusion, while agreeing to differ on what may appear to be a major obstacle to agreement, are not uncommon. Like other diplomatic techniques, such 'without prejudice' clauses are as useful in multilateral as in bilateral negotiations, where the need to avoid sensitive issues may be even greater. A particularly good example may be seen in the Antarctic Treaty of 1959,[25] which succeeded in creating the basis for international administration of the area, while providing in Article 4 for existing rights and claims to be preserved, but not improved. A comparable bilateral example is the informal agreement between the United Kingdom and Argentina in 1989 to the effect that discussions between them would take place relating to various aspects of the Falkland Islands issue, but that the question of sovereignty would not be raised.[26] As in the case of Antarctica, the effect of this was that each side reserved its position on the sovereignty question, in order that negotiations could proceed on other matters.

It is easy to appreciate why such arrangements are popular with negotiators and to recognise their value in not so much bridging, as creating a detour around, incompatible positions. It seems improbable that in 1959 the question of Antarctica could have been dealt with in an acceptable way without the ingenious formula of Article 4. Similarly, it is only necessary to recall that in 1984 a previous attempt to discuss the Falkland Islands broke down when Argentina insisted on raising the issue of sovereignty, to appreciate the importance of a 'without prejudice' arrangement in that context. Such arrangements are not a panacea, however. The issues on which states agree to differ are unlikely to disappear and, to the extent that they are really important, far from being forgotten, will remain as a source of future problems. Within ten years of the 1961 agreement, Iceland was extending its fishing limits again, and it is scarcely necessary to point out that at present neither the status of Antarctica nor the future of the Falkland Islands can be regarded as completely settled. 'Without prejudice' arrangements should therefore be thought of less as a means of settling disputes by negotiation than as a way of managing them. By allowing attention to be focused on

---

[25] Antarctic Treaty, 1959. Text in (1960) 54 *AJIL* 477. For discussion of this and other aspects of the treaty, see J. Hanessian, 'The Antarctic Treaty 1959' (1960) 9 *ICLQ*, 436. Also J. Crawford, 'The Antarctic Treaty after 50 years', in D. French, M. Saul and N. D. White (eds), *International Law and Dispute Settlement: New Problems and Techniques*, Oxford, 2010, p. 271.

[26] The parties agreed to place the sovereignty issue under a so-called 'umbrella', while other differences were discussed. See Evans, 'The restoration of diplomatic relations' (n. 7) 476–7. For the text of the informal agreement, see (1990) 29 ILM 1291. The same formula was subsequently employed in the two states' Joint Declaration on Co-operation over Offshore Activities in the South West Atlantic, 1995; text in (1996) 35 ILM 301.

those matters which can be negotiated, they allow progress to be made until such time as other more intractable issues can be addressed.

It often happens that the nature of a dispute and the parties' interests are such that in an agreement, one side is bound to gain at the other's expense. A possible way of providing compensation in such a situation is to give the less-favoured party control of details such as the time and place of the negotiations. The latter in particular can assume considerable symbolic importance and thus constitutes an element which may be used to good effect. A more radical solution is to link two disputes together so that a negotiated settlement can balance gains and losses overall and be capable of acceptance by both sides. Such 'package deals' are particularly common in multilateral negotiations such as the Third United Nations Conference on the Law of the Sea, where the large number of states involved and the broad agenda made the trading of issues a conspicuous feature of the proceedings.[27]

The fact that today the public dimension of diplomacy has much greater importance than in the past is another factor with a bearing on the substance of international negotiations. For, if negotiation is a matter of exchanging proposals and counter-proposals in an attempt to arrive at an agreement from which both sides can derive a measure of satisfaction, the parties' awareness of an audience consisting of the general public in one or both of the states concerned, and the international community as a whole, can seriously affect the outcome. The element of give and take which is usually an essential part of a successful negotiation is likely to be inhibited if every step is being monitored by interested pressure groups at home, while the suspicion that the other side may simply be interested in eliciting a favourable audience reaction may lead serious proposals to be dismissed as mere propaganda. The difficulty of negotiating arrangements for arms limitation and disarmament in the era of the Cold War illustrates both points.

It follows that, in sensitive negotiations, precautions may be necessary to ensure that the demands of the media do nothing to jeopardise agreement. In 1982, when the British military commander was negotiating the surrender of the Argentine forces in Port Stanley at the end of the conflict over the Falkland Islands, he insisted that the official photographer wait in an adjoining room until agreement had been secured. He explained afterwards that he had taken this step to avoid anything that might interfere with the final stages of the negotiations. While these were in progress, the British government imposed a news blackout on Port Stanley for the same reason.[28]

Besides inhibiting possible agreement, the real or supposed need to keep the public informed as to the state of negotiations can itself be a cause of

---

[27] See H. Caminos and M. R. Molitor, 'Progressive development of international law and the package deal' (1985) 79 *AJIL*, 871.
[28] For an account of the negotiations, see L. Freedman and V. Gamba-Stonehouse, *Signals of War: The Falklands Conflict of 1982*, London, 1990, ch. 23.

avoidable controversy. In the *Aegean Sea Continental Shelf* case, the International Court was called upon to examine the legal significance of a joint communiqué issued to the press by the Prime Ministers of Greece and Turkey, following a meeting between them in May 1975. The key passage in the communiqué was the paragraph which stated that:

> In the course of their meeting the two Prime Ministers had an opportunity to give consideration to the problems which led to the existing situation as regards relations between their countries. They decided that those problems should be resolved peacefully by means of negotiations and as regards the continental shelf of the Aegean Sea by the International Court at the Hague.[29]

Greece argued that this constituted an agreement to refer the dispute over the continental shelf to the Court and that it permitted unilateral recourse in the event of a refusal by either side to conclude any subsequent agreement that might be needed to implement the obligation. Turkey denied that the communiqué had any legal force and argued that in any event it could not be said to contemplate recourse to the Court prior to the negotiation of a special agreement.

In its decision in 1978, the Court held that both the terms of the disputed instrument and the circumstances of its conclusion were relevant to its interpretation. The background to the communiqué was, the Court found, a situation in which in previous diplomatic exchanges and at an earlier meeting of foreign ministers in Rome, the parties had discussed the possibility of a joint submission to adjudication. The Court found no evidence in the terms of the communiqué to suggest that at the meeting of Prime Ministers this situation had changed and that the possibility of a unilateral reference had been in the parties' contemplation. Indeed, a reference in the communiqué to a subsequent meeting of the parties' experts confirmed that only a joint reference of the matter had been envisaged. Further support for this construction was found in the parties' subsequent practice. From the first, Turkey had insisted that a special agreement must be negotiated, and even Greece had not sought to argue that the communiqué alone provided a basis for the Court's jurisdiction until the initiation of the present proceedings. Thus, the Court's conclusion was that the communiqué provided no basis for its jurisdiction.

In the *Maritime Delimitation and Territorial Questions* case[30] between Qatar and Bahrain, which raised a rather similar issue, the Court reached the opposite conclusion. The first question in that case was whether the

---

[29] [1978] ICJ Rep. 39, 40. For a comprehensive review of this decision, see D. H. N. Johnson, 'The International Court of Justice declines jurisdiction again' (1976–77) 7 *Aust. Year Book Int. L*, 309.

[30] *Maritime Delimitation and Territorial Questions between Qatar and Bahrain*, Jurisdiction and Admissibility, Judgments of 1 July 1994 and 15 February 1995 [1994] ICJ Rep. 112 and [1995] ICJ Rep. 6. For comment, see M. D. Evans, Note (1995) 44 *ICLQ*, 691.

minutes of a meeting of the Cooperation Council of Arab States, held in 1990, constituted an agreement between the two states capable of providing the International Court with a basis of jurisdiction. The Court decided that the minutes were an agreement, rather than a 'simple record of negotiations' as Bahrain maintained, and, having established this point, then had to determine the content of the agreement. This called for decisions as to both the subject matter of the dispute and how it should be submitted, which presented considerable difficulties. When states discuss submission of a dispute to the Court, they therefore need to be clear about the nature and scope of their commitments if subsequent argument on these matters is to be avoided.

2.4 Negotiation and Adjudication

Although negotiation is usually involved at some stage in every international dispute and in that sense is related to all of the other methods of settling disputes we shall be considering, its relation to one of them, adjudication, is particularly significant. Much of the discussion in this section however is *mutatis mutandis* applicable in relation to international arbitration.

Negotiation is a process which allows the parties to retain the maximum amount of control over their dispute; adjudication, in contrast, takes the dispute entirely out of their hands, at least as regards the court's decision. It is therefore not surprising that defining the point of transition from one to the other, and establishing the relation between them, when a court first becomes involved, then while it is functioning, have been matters to which states and international courts alike have had to give a good deal of attention.

2.4.1 Negotiation as a Pre-Condition to Adjudication

One situation in which the connection is important is when states choose to make the exhaustion of attempts to settle a dispute by negotiation a condition of an adjudicator's jurisdiction. It is important to note that, generally, prior negotiations are not required unless the parties have agreed otherwise.[31] When negotiations are a condition of an adjudicator's jurisdiction, questions which may arise here are, first, what is to be regarded as negotiation for jurisdictional purposes? And, then, how is it to be

---

[31] *Obligations concerning Negotiations relating to Cessation of the Nuclear Arms Race and to Nuclear Disarmament (Marshall Islands v. United Kingdom)*, Preliminary Objections, Judgment of 5 October 2016, [2016] ICJ Rep 833, paras 38–45; *Arbitral Award of 3 October 1899 (Guyana v. Venezuela)*, Preliminary Objections, Judgment of 18 December 2020, para. 98: 'The Court also recalls that the Charter of the United Nations does not require the exhaustion of diplomatic negotiations as a precondition for the decision to resort to judicial settlement.'

established that the possibilities of a negotiated settlement have been exhausted? We have already seen that the *South West Africa* cases and the *Application of the International Convention on the Elimination of All Forms of Racial Discrimination (Georgia v. Russian Federation)* case, posed the first question with reference to diplomatic exchanges in the United Nations and the issue can also arise in other contexts. In the *Border and Transborder Armed Actions* case,[32] for example, where the question was whether negotiations in a dispute between Honduras and Nicaragua were still in progress, the International Court decided that the multilateral diplomacy of the Contadora process constituted mediation rather than negotiation, and accordingly rejected an argument from Honduras to the effect that the Court's jurisdiction had not yet been established.

Whether the prerequisites for negotiation had been satisfied was also an issue in the *Armed Activities* case[33] between the Democratic Republic of the Congo (DRC) and Rwanda. Here, the DRC sought to base the International Court's jurisdiction on a number of treaties, including the 1971 Montreal Convention, which provides in Article 14 that any dispute between the parties 'which cannot be settled by negotiation' shall at the request of one of them be referred to arbitration and may then be referred to the Court if the parties cannot agree on the organisation of the arbitration. In its decision on admissibility and jurisdiction, the Court decided that this provision did not provide a basis for its jurisdiction because the DRC had failed to show that it had ever tried to begin negotiations and also did not appear to have suggested arbitration. In the earlier *Lockerbie* cases,[34] on the other hand, Libya was able to rely on Article 14 because its request for arbitration had been rejected by the United States and the United Kingdom and the Court agreed that the dispute could not be settled by negotiation.

In the *Application of the International Convention on the Elimination of All Forms of Racial Discrimination (Georgia v. Russian Federation)* case,[35] Article 22 of CERD required negotiations before submission of the dispute to the Court. The ICJ explained that the requirement of negotiations 'requires — at the very least — a genuine attempt by one of the disputing

---

[32] *Border and Transborder Armed Actions*, Jurisdiction and Admissibility, Judgment [1988] ICJ Rep. 69. The Court's decision on this point and the significance of the Contadora Process are further discussed in Chapter 13.

[33] *Armed Activities on the Territory of the Congo (New Application: 2002) (Democratic Republic of the Congo v. Rwanda)*, Jurisdiction and Admissibility, Judgment [2006] ICJ Rep. 6; and see A. Orakhelashvili, Note (2006) 55 *ICLQ*, 753.

[34] *Questions of Interpretation and Application of the 1971 Montreal Convention Arising from the Aerial Incident at Lockerbie*, Preliminary Objections, Judgment [1998] ICJ Rep. 9 and 115; and see F. Beveridge, Note (1999) 48 *ICLQ*, 658.

[35] *Application of the International Convention on the Elimination of All Forms of Racial Discrimination (Georgia v. Russian Federation)*, Preliminary Objections, Judgment [2011] ICJ Rep. 70.

parties to engage in discussions with the other disputing party, with a view to resolving the dispute.'[36] The Court further argued that such negotiations should also 'relate to the subject-matter of the treaty containing the compromissory clause. In other words, the subject-matter of the negotiations must relate to the subject-matter of the dispute which, in turn, must concern the substantive obligations contained in the treaty in question'.[37] Showing that the possibilities of a negotiation have been exhausted might seem to require a demonstration that negotiations of some kind have taken place. Usually this will be so, but if one party to a dispute makes it clear that it is unwilling to negotiate, the absence of negotiations will not be regarded as an obstacle to an international court's exercising jurisdiction.[38] Consequently, when the parties to a dispute specify that negotiations are to have priority as a means of settlement, it will not be open to either of them to delay legal proceedings by the simple expedient of refusing to negotiate. While it is easy to appreciate that any other view would deprive the parties' reference to adjudication of its intended force, a more difficult situation arises when negotiations take place but fail to yield a solution. Here, the party which wishes to avoid litigation is likely to argue that further efforts at negotiation should be made, while its opponent will seek to persuade the court or tribunal that nothing more is needed to enable it to exercise jurisdiction. To spare the adjudicator the delicate task of deciding whether there is still a chance to reach a negotiated settlement, treaties such as the 1965 Convention on Transit Trade of Land-Locked Countries[39] lay down a time limit for use of the preferred procedure. Time limits are also very often included in the investor-state arbitration clauses of international investment treaties.[40]

Absent time limits, the appreciation of the exhaustion of prior negotiations will be difficult. The ICJ reiterated in the *Application of the International Convention on the Elimination of All Forms of Racial Discrimination* case its position that, once negotiations have commenced, there should be evidence that 'there has been a failure of negotiations', or that they 'have become futile or deadlocked'.[41] In *Questions relating to the*

---

[36] *Ibid.*, para. 157.   [37] *Ibid.*, para. 161.
[38] See, e.g. *United States Diplomatic and Consular Staff in Tehran*, Judgment [1980] ICJ Rep. 3.
[39] 597 UNTS 3. Article 16(1) of the Convention provides: 'Any dispute which may arise with respect to the interpretation or application of the provisions of this Convention which is not settled by negotiation or by other peaceful means of settlement within a period of nine months shall, at the request of either party, be settled by arbitration.'
[40] See Chapter 7. See generally: A. Ganesh, 'Cooling off Period', in H. Ruiz-Fabri (ed.), *Max Planck Encyclopedia of International Procedural Law [MPEiPro]*, Oxford University Press, online edition.
[41] *Application of the International Convention on the Elimination of All Forms of Racial Discrimination (Georgia v. Russian Federation)*, Preliminary Objections, Judgment [2011] ICJ Rep. 70, para. 159.

Obligation to Prosecute or Extradite case,[42] the Court further explained that the requirement that a dispute cannot be settled through negotiation cannot be understood 'as referring to a theoretical impossibility of reaching a settlement' and that meeting the requirement implies that 'no reasonable probability exists that further negotiations would lead to a settlement'.[43]

Under Article 283(1) of the UN Convention on the Law of the Sea, the parties to a dispute concerning the interpretation or application of the Convention 'shall proceed expeditiously to an exchange of views regarding its settlement by negotiation or some other peaceful means'. Accordingly, when a dispute is referred to a court or tribunal under Part XV of the Convention, an 'exchange of views' is a jurisdictional prerequisite, making the interpretation of this requirement potentially very important. Moreover, under Article 283(2), there is a similar obligation where a procedure 'has been terminated without a settlement or where a settlement has been reached and the circumstances require consultation regarding the manner of implementing the settlement'. Thus, an exchange of views is more than an initial requirement when a dispute first arises, but, depending on how it progresses, may be a continuing obligation.

Since an exchange of views is a condition of the resort to compulsory procedures entailing binding decisions under the Law of the Sea Convention, it is not surprising that the fulfilment of the requirement has often been the subject of argument. At the provisional measures stage of the *Southern Bluefin Tuna* cases,[44] Japan denied that sufficient efforts to resolve the dispute by negotiation had been made, and similar arguments were put forward by the United Kingdom in the *MOX Plant* case[45] and by Singapore in the *Land Reclamation* case. In all three cases, however, the International Tribunal for the Law of the Sea (ITLOS) reviewed the communications between the parties and concluded that they satisfied the requirements of Article 283. In the last case, for example, finding that Malaysia had informed Singapore of its concerns, the Tribunal ruled that 'in the circumstances of the present case Malaysia was not obliged to continue with an exchange of views when it concluded that this exchange could not yield a positive result'.[46]

---

[42] *Questions relating to the Obligation to Prosecute or Extradite (Belgium v. Senegal)*, Judgment of 20 July 2012, [2012] ICJ Rep. 422.

[43] *Ibid.*, para 57.

[44] *Southern Bluefin Tuna* cases, Request for Provisional Measures, Order of 27 August 1999, (1999) 38 ILM 1624.

[45] The *MOX Plant* case, Request for Provisional Measures, Order of 3 December 2001, (2002) 41 ILM 405.

[46] (2005) 126 ILR 487, para. 48. See also on Art. 283 the *Barbados/Trinidad and Tobago* case, Award of 11 April 2006, (2006) 45 ILM 798.

Even if the parties are not required to explore the possibility of a negotiated settlement as a condition of international jurisdiction, diplomatic exchanges will usually be necessary to focus a disagreement to the point where it can be treated as an international dispute. In relation to adjudication this is particularly important because, as we shall see later, adjudication is a rather specialised way of resolving conflicts, and cannot be regarded as appropriate for every sort of disagreement. One reflection of their specialised function is that courts, unlike international political institutions, cannot be asked to deal with situations in which there is pervasive tension, but no specific questions to be resolved. It follows that one of the functions of negotiation is to bring such situations into focus so that any issues which might be put to a legal tribunal can be identified. Thus, quite apart from its jurisdictional significance, negotiation will often be needed to make the points of disagreement sufficiently concrete for reference to a court or tribunal to be possible.

Although this screening or concretising function is another significant facet of the relation between negotiation and adjudication, it would be wrong to see a linkage between the two processes as vital, or to believe that negotiation is indispensable. To prove that a dispute exists, it is necessary to show that the claim of one party is positively opposed by the other. Usually this will be done by using the parties' diplomatic exchanges to demonstrate that official representations have defined the points in issue and that efforts to resolve the matter by negotiation have failed. However, there is no rule of law to the effect that a dispute exists only if it is reflected in a formal exchange of representations. As was discussed in Chapter 1, if the subject of a disagreement is perfectly clear, then the International Court has indicated that it will be prepared to hold that a dispute exists, even if there has been no official contact. This was the situation in the *Diplomatic Staff in Tehran* case, where the actions of Iran had caused a break in relations but the Court had no hesitation in finding that there was a dispute with the United States, arising out of the interpretation or application of the relevant international conventions. Here, it should be reminded that in the *Marshall Islands* case[47] the Court refused to consider that statements made by the Marshall Islands in multilateral fora were sufficient to establish the existence of a dispute, since on the basis of these statements the other party to the dispute could not be aware, or could not have been unaware, of an allegation of a breach of an international obligation.[48]

---

[47] *Obligations concerning Negotiations relating to Cessation of the Nuclear Arms Race and to Nuclear Disarmament (Marshall Islands* v. *United Kingdom),* Preliminary Objections, Judgment of 5 October 2016, [2016] ICJ Rep. 833.

[48] *Ibid.*, paras 48–52.

2.4.2 The Substantive Relation between Negotiation and Adjudication

Referring a case to a court or tribunal is merely one way of attempting to settle international differences and, as several of the cases we have been considering demonstrate, even when judicial settlement has been agreed on by the parties in advance, there is no guarantee that it will appeal to them equally when a dispute arises. A further question to be considered, therefore, is whether, as a matter of principle, the competence of an international court is affected if negotiation is also under way. To avoid misunderstanding it should be emphasised that the issue here is not whether it is open to the parties to agree to give negotiation formal priority. For, as we have seen, this can easily be arranged by including an appropriate provision in the instrument establishing jurisdiction. Rather, the question is whether the relation between negotiation and adjudication is such that it is inappropriate or impermissible for the two methods of settlement to be pursued simultaneously; whether in short the judge must be ready to defer to the negotiator.

This issue was one of the preliminary matters considered in the *Aegean Sea Continental Shelf* case. Certain observations by the Turkish government were interpreted by the International Court as perhaps suggesting that it ought not to proceed while Greece and Turkey continued to negotiate, and that the existence of active negotiations was a legal impediment to the exercise of its jurisdiction. All this the Court emphatically rejected. It drew attention to the fact that negotiation and judicial settlement are enumerated together in Article 33 of the Charter and pointed out that on several occasions both methods have been pursued simultaneously. Moreover, in some cases judicial proceedings have been discontinued when negotiations resulted in a settlement. In light of this, said the Court, 'the fact that negotiations are being actively pursued during the present proceedings, is not, legally, any obstacle to the exercise by the Court of its judicial function'.[49] Recently, the ICJ also confirmed in its judgment in *Arbitral Award of 3 October 1899 (Guyana* v. *Venezuela)* that the submission of a dispute to judicial settlement does not imply that the parties can no longer attempt to settle the dispute via other diplomatic means such as negotiations or good offices. The Court noted that 'parallel attempts at settlement of a dispute by diplomatic means do not prevent it from being dealt with by the Court'.[50]

Thus, while negotiation is a basic means of attempting to settle disputes, any priority or privileged status which it is to enjoy depends on the parties,

---

[49] *Aegean Sea Continental Shelf,* Judgment [1978] ICJ Rep. 3 at 12. See also *Application of the Interim Accord of 13 September 1995 (Former Yugoslav Republic of Macedonia* v. *Greece),* Judgment of 5 December 2011, [2011] ICJ Rep. 644.

[50] *Arbitral Award of 3 October 1899 (Guyana* v. *Venezuela),* Preliminary Objections, Judgment of 18 December 2020, para. 109.

and not on considerations of principle bearing on justiciability. This is a sensible approach because it avoids placing unnecessary constraints on the actions of states and recognises that, as international disputes are complex, the chances of a peaceful settlement are enhanced by allowing different procedures to be employed simultaneously. Though relevant to the relation between negotiation and adjudication, this point is no less pertinent in other contexts. For, as we shall see in later chapters, the approach adopted in the *Aegean Sea Continental Shelf* case has been followed in cases where the relation between adjudication and other political procedures was in issue.

The final aspect of negotiation which needs to be mentioned concerns what may be termed the substantive relation between negotiation and adjudication. When the parties to an international dispute attempt to deal with it by diplomacy, they may say and do things in the course of negotiation which could prejudice their case if the dispute is subsequently referred to adjudication. Although the dangers here should not be exaggerated and a state's actions can sometimes have the effect of improving its case, if such a prejudicial link exists (or is thought to exist) it may make a state reluctant to refer a dispute to adjudication. The answer to this type of problem is to insulate the judicial proceedings from the previous negotiations concerning the substance of the dispute. An example of how this can be done is provided by the Special Agreement under which the United States and Canada agreed to refer the *Gulf of Maine* case[51] to a chamber of the International Court. Article 5(1) of the Agreement stated:

> Neither party shall introduce into evidence or argument, or publicly disclose in any manner, the nature or content of proposals directed to a maritime boundaries settlement, or responses thereto, in the course of negotiations or discussions between the parties undertaken since 1969.[52]

This type of provision is rather rare, which perhaps suggests that excluding the evidence of diplomatic exchanges is only likely to be important when negotiations have been prolonged, or when criteria of reasonableness or acceptability are expected to play a significant part at the judicial stage. In the first situation, however, the value of being able to move from profitless negotiation to a definitive settlement is particularly marked; moreover, the tendency to use equitable criteria for certain kinds of decisions means, as we shall see, that, in some areas of international law, the line between adjudication, based on rules, and conciliation, emphasising accommodation, has

---

[51] *Delimitation of the Maritime Boundary in the Gulf of Maine Area*, Judgment [1984] ICJ Rep. 246. This case is discussed in Chapters 8 and 9.
[52] Text in (1981) 20 ILM 1378. A further reference to negotiations is to be found in Art. 7(1) which provided that: 'Following the decision of the Chamber, either party may request negotiations directed toward reaching agreement on extension of the maritime boundary as far seaward as the Parties may consider desirable.'

become somewhat blurred. If, therefore, negotiation is not to be a barrier to adjudication, prohibitions on referring to diplomatic material at the stage when a dispute is being litigated may be increasingly necessary.

2.5 Limitations of Negotiation

Negotiation is plainly impossible if the parties to a dispute refuse to have any dealings with each other. Serious disputes sometimes lead the states concerned to sever diplomatic relations, a step that is especially common when force has been used. Prominent examples include the severance of relations between the United States and Iran, following the seizure of the embassy in Tehran in 1979, and the breaking of diplomatic relations between Britain and Argentina after the invasion of the Falkland Islands in 1982. Of course, the termination of official relations need not entail the elimination of all contact between the states concerned. It does, however, preclude the use of the various standard arrangements for diplomatic contact, described earlier, and thus places a substantial obstacle in the path of negotiation.

Similar consequences flow from the use of non-recognition to deny standing to the other party to a dispute, or as a general mark of disapproval. Here, the problem is that official channels are never established. The consequences of this are demonstrated by the Arab–Israeli situation, where for many years the refusal of the Arab states to recognise Israel and Israel's refusal to acknowledge the Palestine Liberation Organization (PLO) prevented direct negotiations. It is again possible for the absence of official communication to be mitigated by alternative means, as the extensive discussions between US and Chinese representatives in the years before American recognition of the Beijing government demonstrate. But, where non-recognition is essentially a reflection of the substantive issues in dispute, as in the case of the Arab states and Israel, there may be little reason for such links to be established. Negotiation will be ineffective if the parties' positions are far apart and there are no common interests to bridge the gap. The variety of ways in which an agreement can be constructed so as to satisfy both sides has already been pointed out. But it must frankly be recognised that in many situations no arrangement, however ingenious, is capable of fulfilling this function. In a territorial dispute, the party in possession may see no reason to negotiate at all. In any dispute, if one party insists on its legal rights, while the other, recognising the weakness of its legal case, seeks a settlement on some other basis, there is little room for agreement on matters of substance, and even a procedural agreement, to refer the dispute to arbitration, for example, may be difficult to negotiate without seeming to prejudice one side or the other.

Disagreement on the agenda for discussion, which may mean that negotiations never get beyond the stage of 'talks about talks', is usually a reflection of a wide gulf between the parties on some such substantive matter. For example, the reluctance of the United Kingdom to place the issue of sovereignty on the agenda of its discussions with Spain on the subject of Gibraltar is a clear indication of unwillingness to yield on the crucial issue of legal title. While it is true that relations between states are not static and that concessions which are unthinkable today may be regarded with equanimity tomorrow, in many disputes, including some of the most serious, until the time is ripe, negotiation can have little to offer.

Even when it is obvious that negotiation has only a small chance of success, it is commonly assumed that the parties to a dispute are duty-bound to try. Whether this assumption is correct depends on whether negotiation is ever to be regarded as an inappropriate means of settlement. The answer must be yes. If a different arrangement has already been agreed between the parties, a state which demands negotiation and refuses to use the agreed procedure is in breach of its obligations and has no reason to complain if its demands are refused. This was the position in the 1972 'Cod War', when Iceland repudiated the provisions for judicial settlement in the treaty quoted earlier and the United Kingdom referred the dispute to the International Court.[53]

A more general objection is that the idea that states should always be prepared to negotiate ignores the fact that the terms of any agreement will generally reflect not the merits of each party's case, but their relative power.[54] Admittedly, 'a less powerful party in an international negotiation is not necessarily at the mercy of a more powerful party',[55] and the concept of power itself is a complex one. The fact remains, however, that a state with a completely unjustified claim may well be able to secure a favourable negotiated settlement by bringing superior power to bear. A party which possesses this kind of advantage will naturally tend to demand negotiations and to portray any resistance as unreasonable. But, since it is clear that to negotiate in such a situation is to guarantee that the solution will be unjust, the weaker party has excellent grounds for refusing the invitation.

Another drawback appears if we consider the possibility that the attempt to resolve a dispute by negotiation may be unsuccessful. For negotiations which are unsuccessful do not, as might be thought, simply leave a dispute where it was to begin with. On the contrary, although they can sometimes improve matters by demonstrating that the parties are slowly moving closer together, they can also have the opposite effect. Indeed, because

---

[53] See *Fisheries Jurisdiction (United Kingdom v. Iceland)*, Jurisdiction of the Court, Judgment [1973] ICJ Rep. 3.
[54] See Northedge and Donelan, *Political Aspects* (n. 1) p. 282.
[55] J. W. Salacuse, 'Lessons for practice', in I. W. Zartman and J. Z. Rubin (eds), *Power and Negotiation*, Ann Arbor, MI, 2000, p. 255 at p. 257.

negotiations involve exploring the possibilities for resolving a dispute peacefully, lack of progress may encourage the use of force by seeming to eliminate every alternative. As a commentator on the Falklands dispute put it:

> While negotiations can control a conflict for a certain time while alternatives are being considered, every time an alternative is considered and discarded by mutual agreement, the dispute ... has less and less room to evolve toward settlement. The successful control of a conflict – not necessarily its resolution – seems to lie in the ability to avoid running short of viable alternatives.[56]

Events in the 20-year period preceding the war of 1982 appear to bear out this analysis. Initially, the United Kingdom denied that there was any dispute with Argentina, then, when this was no longer feasible, delayed formalising negotiations for as long as possible. The wisdom of this strategy became apparent when negotiations eventually began, because, as one alternative after another was discussed and rejected, the prospects of securing a settlement which both sides could accept soon receded to a vanishing point. This does not mean that Argentina was justified either legally or morally in attempting to seize the islands by force, nor that the failure of the parties' negotiations should be thought of as making the war inevitable. It does, however, suggest that the ending of negotiations can sometimes be the signal for a dispute to enter a new and more dangerous phase and, as a corollary, that an awareness of these implications can make governments reluctant to become involved with them.

A state can of course bind itself to negotiate by treaty, or find itself in a situation where an obligation to negotiate arises under the general law. In 1997, for example, the International Court decided that Hungary and Slovakia were under a legal obligation to negotiate in good faith to determine how the objectives of a treaty concerning a project on the Danube could best be carried out.[57] In an earlier case, it decided that, according to customary international law, the delimitation of continental shelf boundaries between neighbouring states 'must be effected by agreement in accordance with equitable principles'.[58] Similarly, in 1974 it found that the United Kingdom and Iceland were 'under mutual obligations to undertake negotiations in good faith for the equitable solution of their differences'[59] concerning their respective fishery rights in the waters of Iceland. In all three cases, what the Court was saying was that, since the rights of more than one state were in issue, the matter in question was not

---

[56] R. de Hoyos, 'Islas Malvinas or Falkland Islands: the negotiation of a conflict, 1945–1982', in M. A. Morris and V. Millán (eds), *Controlling Latin American Conflicts*, Boulder, CO, 1983, p. 185 at pp. 192–3.
[57] *Gabcikovo-Nagymaros Project (Hungary/Slovakia)*, Judgment [1997] ICJ Rep. 7.
[58] *North Sea Continental Shelf*, Judgment [1969] ICJ Rep. 3.
[59] *Fisheries Jurisdiction (United Kingdom v. Iceland)*, Merits, Judgment [1974] ICJ Rep. 3.

open to unilateral regulation, but had to be negotiated. In the above situations, like the cases of consultation considered earlier, the duty to negotiate exists even before there is a dispute.

Recently, the Court posited in the *Obligation to Negotiate Access to the Pacific Ocean* case,[60] that there is, in general terms, no autonomous obligation on states to negotiate. The case had been submitted by Bolivia against Chile, and revolved around the question of whether Chile was under an obligation to negotiate Bolivia's access to the Pacific Ocean. The Court, before turning the several specific arguments invoked by Bolivia to establish such an obligation, explained:

> In international law, the existence of an obligation to negotiate has to be ascertained in the same way as that of any other legal obligation. Negotiation is part of the usual practice of States in their bilateral and multilateral relations. However, the fact that a given issue is negotiated at a given time is not sufficient to give rise to an obligation to negotiate. In particular, for there to be an obligation to negotiate on the basis of an agreement, the terms used by the parties, the subject-matter and the conditions of the negotiations must demonstrate an intention of the parties to be legally bound. This intention, in the absence of express terms indicating the existence of a legal commitment, may be established on the basis of an objective examination of all the evidence.[61]

Often, however, negotiation is laid down as a requirement when a dispute arises and forms either the exclusive procedure, or, more commonly, a necessary preliminary to the use of other methods. An illustration of this type of obligatory negotiation may be seen in Article 41 of the 1978 Vienna Convention on Succession of States in respect of Treaties,[62] which provides:

> If a dispute regarding the application or interpretation of the present Convention arises between two or more Parties to the Convention, they shall, upon the request of any of them, seek to resolve it by a process of consultation and negotiation.

It is clear, then, that in some situations, there is a duty to negotiate. Moreover, in others, as we have seen, the parties to a dispute may have a lesser obligation such as to 'proceed expeditiously to an exchange of views' regarding the means of settlement to be adopted. However, it is worth emphasising that, just as there is no general duty to consult other states before taking action which may affect them, so there is no general duty to

---

[60] *Obligation to Negotiate Access to the Pacific Ocean (Bolivia v. Chile)*, Judgment of 1 October 2018, [2018] ICJ Rep. 507.
[61] *Ibid.*, para. 91.
[62] See R. Lavalle, 'Dispute settlement under the Vienna Convention on Succession of States in respect of Treaties' (1979) 73 *AJIL*, 407.

attempt to settle disputes by negotiation.[63] The various means of settlement in Article 33 of the UN Charter are listed as alternatives, and so, in the absence of a specific obligation to negotiate, a state is entitled to suggest that another procedure should be used. In a dispute concerning sovereignty over territory, for example, a state which is confident of its legal title may well advocate judicial settlement, as the United Kingdom did in the case of Gibraltar. Naturally, the offer is unlikely to be accepted if the other party's claim is political rather than legal. But that is hardly the point. Negotiation is simply one means of settlement and, in the absence of a legal duty to negotiate, states are entitled to use it or not as they see fit.

None of the above is intended to imply that negotiation is not an extremely important means of dealing with international disputes. In almost all cases, diplomatic exchanges will be necessary before a disagreement becomes sufficiently specific to be called a dispute, and, once a dispute has arisen, negotiation will often provide the best prospect of a solution. We have seen, however, that, although negotiation must be regarded as basic, it may also be impossible, ineffective or inappropriate. As a consequence, use of the methods described in the following chapters may be essential if any progress is to be made.

2.6 Further Reading

Brunner, L., and K. Quintana, 'The duty to consult in the Inter-American system: legal standards after *Sarayaku*' (2012) 16 *ASIL Insights*, 35.

Darwin, H., 'Negotiation', in C. M. H. Waldock (ed.), *International Disputes: The Legal Aspects*, London, 1972.

De Waart, P. J. I. M., *The Element of Negotiation in the Pacific Settlement of Disputes between States*, The Hague, 1973.

Ganesh, A., 'Cooling off Period', in H. Ruiz-Fabri (ed.), *Max Planck Encyclopedia of International Procedural Law [MPEiPro]*, Oxford University Press, online edition available at https://opil.ouplaw.com/view/10.1093/law-mpeipro/e3168.013.3168/law-mpeipro-e3168?rskey=Y49ISv&result=1&prd=OPIL.

Gold, J., 'Prior consultation in international law' (1983–4) 24 *Va JIL*, 729.

Kirgis, F. L., *Prior Consultation in International Law*, Charlottesville, 1983, ch. 2.

Kremenyuk, V. A. (ed.), *International Negotiation*, San Francisco, 2002.

Starkey, B., M. A. Boyer and J. Wilkenfeld, *Negotiating a Complex World*, Lanham, MD, 1999.

Zartman, I. W. (ed.), *Preventative Negotiation*, Lanham, MD, 2001.

Zartman, I. W., and J. Z. Rubin (eds), *Power and Negotiation*, Ann Arbor, 2000.

---

[63] See *Obligation to Negotiate Access to the Pacific Ocean (Bolivia v. Chile)*, Judgment of 1 October 2018, [2018] ICJ Rep. 507, para. 165.

3

Mediation

When the parties to an international dispute are unable to resolve it by negotiation, the intervention of a third party is a possible means of breaking the impasse and producing an acceptable solution. Such intervention can take a number of different forms. The third party may simply encourage the disputing states to resume negotiations, or do nothing more than provide them with an additional channel of communication. In these situations, the intermediary is said to be contributing 'good offices'. On the other hand, the assignment may be to investigate the dispute and to present the parties with a set of formal proposals for its solution. As we shall see in Chapter 5, this form of intervention is called 'conciliation'. Between good offices and conciliation lies the form of third-party activity known as 'mediation'.[1]

Like good offices, mediation is essentially an adjunct to negotiation, but with the mediator as an active participant, authorised, and indeed expected, to advance fresh proposals and to interpret, as well as to transmit, each party's proposals to the other. What distinguishes this kind of assistance from conciliation is that a mediator generally offers proposals informally and on the basis of information supplied by the parties, rather than independent investigations, although in practice such distinctions tend to be blurred. In a given case, it may therefore be difficult to draw the line between mediation and conciliation, or to say exactly when good offices ended and mediation began.

Mediation may be sought by the parties or offered spontaneously by outsiders. Once under way, it provides the governments in dispute with the possibility of a solution, but without any prior commitment to accept the mediator's suggestions. Consequently, it has the advantage of allowing

---

[1] Useful discussions of mediation are to be found in F. S. Northedge and M. D. Donelan (eds), *International Disputes: The Political Aspects*, London, 1971, ch. 13; C. M. H. Waldock (ed.), *International Disputes: The Legal Aspects*, London, 1972, ch. 2B; K. V. Raman (ed.), *Dispute Settlement through the United Nations*, New York, 1977, ch. 3; S. Touval and I. W. Zartman (eds), *International Mediation in Theory and Practice*, Boulder, CO, 1985; United Nations, *Handbook on the Peaceful Settlement of Disputes between States*, New York, 1992, ch. 2C; D. J. Bercovitch and J. Z. Rubin (eds), *Mediation in International Relations*, London, 1992; J. Bercovitch (ed.), *Resolving International Conflicts: The Theory and Practice of Mediation*, London, 1996; M. Kleiboer, *The Multiple Realities of International Mediation*, Boulder, CO, 1998; and M. C. Greenberg, J. H. Barton and M. E. McGuinness (eds), *Words over War*, Lanham, MD, 2000.

them to retain control of the dispute, probably an essential requirement if negotiations are deadlocked on a matter of vital interest. On the other hand, if a face-saving compromise is what is needed, it may be politically easier to make the necessary concessions in the course of mediation than in direct negotiation. If a dispute concerns sensitive issues, the fact that the proceedings can be completely confidential is an advantage in any case. As with other means of dispute settlement, however, not every international dispute is suitable for mediation. The first requirement is a willing mediator.

3.1 Mediators

Mediation may be performed by international organisations, by states or by individuals acting independently. For the United Nations and a number of regional organisations, the settlement of disputes is a basic institutional objective, and, as a result, the Secretary-General and their regional counterparts are often engaged in providing good offices and mediation. In certain situations, non-governmental organisations can act as mediators. The International Committee of the Red Cross (ICRC), for example, avoids involvement in political disputes, but regularly intervenes where armed conflict or the treatment of detainees raise humanitarian issues.[2] Since it offers the opportunity to become involved in a dispute and to influence its outcome, the role of mediator also has attractions for states concerned to see a dispute resolved peacefully, or with an interest in a particular solution. Thus, it is not unusual to find the course of an international dispute punctuated by offers of mediation from one or more outside parties.

In the dispute between Britain and Argentina over the invasion of the Falkland Islands in 1982, first the United States, in the person of Secretary of State Alexander Haig, offered to mediate, then the United Nations Secretary-General, Javier Pérez de Cuéllar, tendered his good offices.[3] From the American perspective, a war between a North Atlantic Treaty Organization (NATO) ally and a leading member of the Organization of American States (OAS) would force a choice between allies which it strongly wished to avoid. The Secretary-General, on the other hand, was involved in the dispute because Argentina's invasion had already been condemned by the Security Council and almost all members of the

---

[2] See D. P. Forsythe, 'Humanitarian mediation by the International Committee of the Red Cross', in S. Touval and I. W. Zartman (eds), *International Mediation in Theory and Practice*, Boulder, CO, 1985, p. 233.

[3] For an excellent account of these initiatives and the attempt by President Belaunde of Peru to develop the results of the Haig mediation, see L. Freedman and V. Gamba-Stonehouse, *Signals of War: The Falklands Conflict of 1982*, London, 1990, chs. 12–18; and Kleiboer, *Multiple Realities* (n. 1) ch. 5.

United Nations were anxious for a fresh initiative to avert the threat of further bloodshed.

In 1978, when war between Chile and Argentina seemed to be imminent over the implementation of the *Beagle Channel* award,[4] the Pope offered the services of Cardinal Antonio Samoré as mediator, a proposal which both governments accepted. As in the Falklands crisis, the motives for intervention are not hard to identify, for the concern naturally aroused by the prospect of war between two Catholic states was here reinforced by both the promptings of the United States and a tradition of Papal involvement in South American affairs stretching back over five centuries.

In an earlier territorial dispute, the conflict between India and Pakistan over Kashmir in 1965, the mediation of the Soviet Union was instrumental in securing a cease-fire when war had already broken out. The historical and religious connections which inspired the offer of mediation in the previous example were here replaced by a political interest in restoring stability to an area close to the southern borders of the Soviet Union and avoiding the risk of Chinese intervention, while at the same time advancing Soviet influence in the region.[5]

The desire to extend influence is by no means confined to major powers. Indeed, mediation can provide small or middle-rank states with an opportunity to improve relations with larger states, while also safeguarding other interests. In 1980, for example, Algeria pursued a combined good offices and mediation role in the diplomatic hostages dispute between the United States and Iran. The dispute, after some very complex negotiations over Iranian assets in the United States, was eventually settled. The settlement not only enhanced Algeria's reputation in the eyes of Americans, but, more importantly, resolved a crisis which could have led to war between a superpower and a Muslim state.[6] In a similar way, Algeria's constructive intervention in the dangerous tension between Iran and Iraq in 1975 again served to increase the mediator's prestige and influence in the Muslim world, while also preserving the unity of the Organization of the Petroleum

---

[4] *Beagle Channel Award* (1977) 52 ILR 91. Text also in (1978) 17 ILM 634. For discussion of this case, see Chapter 5.

[5] See T. P. Thornton, 'The Indo-Pakistan conflict: Soviet mediation at Tashkent, 1966', in S. Touval and I. W. Zartman (eds), *International Mediation in Theory and Practice*, Boulder, CO, 1985, p. 141. Similar motives probably lay behind an unsuccessful Soviet attempt to mediate in the Gulf crisis of 1990: see L. Freedman and E. Karsh, *The Gulf Conflict 1990–1991*, London, 1993, pp. 175–9.

[6] See G. Sick, 'The partial negotiator: Algeria and the US hostages in Iran', in S. Touval and I. W. Zartman (eds), *International Mediation in Theory and Practice*, Boulder, CO, 1985, p. 21; and R. M. Slim, 'Small state mediation in international relations: the Algerian mediation in the hostage crisis', in D. J. Bercovitch and J. Z. Rubin, *Mediation in International Relations* (n. 1). For Algeria's unsuccessful attempt to mediate when Iraq invaded Kuwait, see Freedman and Karsh, *The Gulf Conflict* (n. 5) p. 248.

Exporting Countries (OPEC), an organisation in which Algeria, as an oil exporter, had a major interest.[7]

In the crisis which accompanied the break-up of Yugoslavia between 1991 and 1995, mediation was attempted by a number of intermediaries, including at various times the European Community (EC), the United Nations working in conjunction with the EC, and the United States. Incentives for EC involvement were the historical and geographical links of many of the member states with Yugoslavia[8] and, for the UN, a combination of humanitarian considerations and the issue of peace and security which led the Security Council to adopt measures under Chapter VII of the Charter. The United States, which became involved in mediation at a relatively late stage, had throughout been closely concerned with the crisis in its capacities as a member of the Security Council and of NATO and had witnessed the failure of earlier efforts to deal with a critical threat to regional stability.

The cases just considered indicate the kinds of concerns that may induce an offer of mediation. It should be noted, however, that in a significant number of disputes mediation will be out of the question because no mediator is able or willing to act. Third states are unlikely to regard themselves as qualified to act as mediators between superpowers, which are moreover rarely willing to entertain the idea of outside intervention in their disputes. In most situations, too, mediation is an exhausting and often thankless task, which therefore requires a correspondingly strong incentive. Shuttling between Buenos Aires and London in an effort to reconcile the governments of General Galtieri and Mrs Thatcher called for more than patience and an iron constitution. As the Haig mission demonstrates, a state which puts itself forward in the role of mediator may antagonise an erstwhile ally, while sacrificing its own freedom of action. Yet, there can never be any guarantee that these and other diplomatic costs will be repaid by a successful outcome to the mission. In such circumstances, the calculations that must temper an inclination to mediate and the result – that in some disputes a willing mediator may be hard to find – are not difficult to understand.

3.2 Consent to Mediation

Mediation cannot be forced on the parties to an international dispute, but only takes place if they consent. So, unless they have taken the initiative

---

[7] See D. Lieb, 'Iran and Iraq at Algiers, 1975', in S. Touval and I. W. Zartman (eds), *International Mediation in Theory and Practice*, Boulder, CO, 1985, p. 67.

[8] See K. Webb, V. Koutrakou and M. Walters, 'The Yugoslavian conflict, European mediation, and the contingency model: a critical perspective' in Bercovitch (ed.), *Resolving International Conflicts* (n. 1); and M. C. Greenberg and M. E. McGuinness, 'From Liston to Dayton: international mediation and the Bosnia crisis', in M. C. Greenberg, J. H. Barton and M. E. McGuinness (eds), *Words over War* (n. 1), p. 35.

and appointed a mediator already, their unwillingness to consider this form of assistance may prove a major stumbling block. This is because, although a mediator's proposals are not binding, the very act of mediation has implications which may be unacceptable to either or both of the governments concerned.

3.2.1 The Politics of Accepting Mediation

By accepting mediation, a government acknowledges that its dispute is a legitimate matter of international concern. If, therefore, a question of international accountability lies at the heart of the controversy, as in the furore over South Africa in the apartheid era, mediation will be out of the question. Moreover, a mediated settlement is always likely to be a compromise of some kind. So, if a government believes either that it can win the dispute, or that the time to make concessions has not yet arrived, there is again unlikely to be room for mediation. The clearest example of the former situation is when a state's position is effectively unchallengeable, as when the Soviet Union refused to accept the mediation of the United Nations Secretary-General following its intervention in Hungary in 1956. An example of the 'no compromise' situation is provided by Nigeria's refusal to accept mediation over the secessionist war in Biafra, which it also claimed was a matter of domestic jurisdiction.

The elements that may induce a government to accept mediation may be illustrated from the disputes already considered. In the Falklands crisis, both Britain and Argentina were anxious to secure and maintain the sympathy of regional allies and to avoid alienating outside states, whose political or economic support might be useful in the event of armed conflict. Here, then, acceptance of mediation was motivated by a desire to project an image of political reasonableness as much as by any expectation of success. In the Yugoslavia crisis, on the other hand, Serbia was under severe pressure from economic sanctions imposed by the UN, the beleaguered Bosnian government desperately needed outside support and neither Croatia, nor the Serbian minority in Bosnia, were in a position to challenge international involvement. These factors made mediation possible from an early stage, although the complexity of the situation and its constantly changing character meant that only the final effort, led by the United States and culminating in the Dayton Peace Agreement of 1995, was successful.

In many disputes, outside opinion is not as important, but other inducements may be present. Unlike the Falklands dispute, where the forcefulness of the British response appears to have taken the Argentine government by surprise, the *Beagle Channel* controversy concerned a situation in which the use of force by Argentina was certain to lead to war. Since Argentina was ruled by a military junta, war could have radical domestic repercussions. In light of this, and the fact that, by setting up the ill-starred arbitration, Chile and Argentina had sought an external resolution of this dispute once already, it is perhaps not too surprising that, following the Pope's timely intervention, they were willing to accede to mediation and try again.[9]

In the Kashmir dispute, on the other hand, war, the product of two decades of hostility between India and Pakistan, had already broken out. What seems to have been the main incentive to accept mediation here was that, having used force to make the point that their respective claims would be defended, neither side had the power to go further and impose its own solution unilaterally. Thus, if hostilities cannot always be avoided, a military stalemate may provide a convenient opportunity for second thoughts.

Mediation is likely to be particularly relevant when a dispute has progressed to a stage which compels the parties to rethink their policies. A stalemate is clearly one such situation; another is when the parties come to recognise that the risks of continuing a dispute outweigh the costs of trying to end it. In the dispute between Iran and Iraq, for example, Iraq's determination to crush the Kurds presented Iran with a choice between increasing its support, leading, almost certainly, to war with Iraq, and offering to withdraw its support for the Kurds in return for Iraq's recognition of Iran's boundary claims. Since Iraq had concluded that the Kurds were currently a more pressing issue than the disputed boundary, the way was clear for the two states to accept a fact-finding mission from the United Nations, a diplomatic initiative by Egypt and finally Algeria's mediation.

In the diplomatic hostages dispute between Iran and the United States, where Algeria was also involved, there had been a deadlock for almost a year when Iran eventually made approaches to the United States. A significant factor here was that the domestic turmoil which had accompanied the Islamic Revolution, and which was to complicate the dispute throughout, was beginning to subside. If this made a new policy towards the hostages easier to formulate and put into effect, such a move was also becoming increasingly necessary. Politically, the hostages had probably served their purpose, a presidential election in the United States was imminent and Iran was suffering from financial and diplomatic isolation. When Iraq seized the opportunity to attack Iran in September 1980, the pressure to seek a deal which would release Iranian assets in the United States was

---

[9] See M. Laudy, 'The Vatican mediation of the Beagle Channel dispute: crisis intervention and forum building', in M. C. Greenberg, J. H. Barton and M. E. McGuinness (eds), *Words over War*, Lanham, MD, 2000, p. 293; T. Princen, 'International mediation: the view from the Vatican' (1987) 3 *Negotiation Journal*, 347; T. Princen, 'Mediation by a transnational organisation: the case of the Vatican', in D. J. Bercovitch and J. Z. Rubin (eds), *Mediation in International Relations*, London, 1992, p. 149; and G. R. Moncayo, 'La mediation pontificale dans l'affaire du Canal Beagle' (1993) 242 *Hague Recueil des Cours*, 197.

further increased. Much hard bargaining would be needed before a settlement was secured, but the United States and Iran were now both in a frame of mind to accept an offer of mediation.

3.2.2 Agreeing on the Mediator

For mediation to get under way, the parties in dispute must do more than accept that it is a good idea. They must also agree upon the mediator. If the governments concerned believe that a would-be mediator has little understanding of their position, is unsympathetic, wholly committed to the other party, or less concerned with their interests than with a selfish agenda, the candidate is unlikely to be acceptable, though if there is no objection to mediation in principle, an offer from a different quarter may be more successful.

An individual's ability to pose as a prospective mediator depends on relevant personal qualities and reputation; a state's on the circumstances, including the time and place of the dispute. In the *Beagle Channel* controversy, for example, not only was the Pope a singularly appropriate mediating authority, but his envoy revealed himself as an immaculate exponent of the art of personal diplomacy. Described as 'tireless, bubbling over with humour and goodwill, a beaming Pickwickian prelate who was also the soul of discretion',[10] Cardinal Samoré was clearly a shrewd choice for this exacting role.

It is sometimes suggested that mediation will only be acceptable if the mediator is perceived to be strictly neutral. Neutrality is certainly important for some mediators and in some situations. The ICRC, for example, is always careful to avoid taking sides in political disputes and recognises that its standing to act on humanitarian issues depends on preserving its neutrality. The same is true of the wider type of intervention practised by the Secretary-General of the United Nations. As we shall see in Chapter 12, the Secretariat has a power of initiative in dispute situations, as well as a role in carrying out functions assigned by the political organs; in both cases, it must act impartially. Elsewhere, however, acceptability is likely to depend more on what a mediator can offer and on being in a position to talk to both sides. Thus, Algeria, an uncommitted Muslim state, was in an ideal position to mediate between Iran and Iraq in 1975, and, as the state which had been entrusted with the representation of Iran's interests in Washington since diplomatic relations were broken off, was also well placed to mediate in the hostages crisis.

In the Kashmir dispute, neither the United States nor the United Kingdom was in a position to act as mediator. The first was too closely

---

[10] *The Economist*, 13 January 1979, p. 54.

aligned with Pakistan, and though the United Kingdom had successfully mediated in the same parties' dispute over the Rann of Kutch only a few months earlier, it had now cut off military aid and was attempting to have India condemned in the United Nations. In contrast, the acceptability of the Soviet Union rested on its interests and influence as a regional power, and the fact that, though more attention had been paid to developing relations with India than with Pakistan, this policy had recently been modified. When war broke out, the Soviet Union refused to condemn Pakistan and so, despite maintaining its military assistance to India, was able to satisfy Pakistan as to its suitability as a mediator.[11]

When states offer to mediate, it is usually because they see either a settlement in itself, or a settlement on particular terms, as furthering some interest of their own. This is well recognised and is therefore not a disqualification, provided the mediator can offer the parties something which they want, or cannot afford to refuse. Thus, the fact that a state has interests of its own and may have close relations with one party to a dispute will not normally be an objection so long as it is on speaking terms with the other party. Indeed, a special relationship with one side may actually be an advantage, for, as a leading commentary notes, when a state which is close to one party offers to act as mediator, 'the closeness that implies a possibility to "deliver" its friend may stimulate the other party's co-operativeness'.[12]

The inducements to accept particular mediators are well illustrated by the Falklands crisis. There, neither side could challenge the authority of the Secretary-General, who could explore the possibilities of a settlement on behalf of the United Nations, while the situation of the United States bore some resemblance to the Soviet position in the Kashmir dispute. Allied with Britain through NATO, and a potential source of logistical support for the British task force, the United States had also recently sought to develop closer relations with Argentina. Any doubts the latter may have had as to the objectivity of the United States were outweighed by the influence it was in a position to exercise over its ally[13] and by another consideration that may have been present in the previous case: the political cost of rejecting mediation, especially when offered by a powerful neighbour.

---

[11] See N. Schwiesow, 'Mediation', in E. Luard (ed.), *The International Regulation of Frontier Disputes*, London, 1970, pp. 161–2.

[12] Touval and Zartman, *International Mediation* (n. 1) p. 257. See also P. J. Carnevale and S. Arad, 'Bias and impartiality in international mediation', in J. Bercovitch (ed.), *Resolving International Conflicts: The Theory and Practice of Mediation*, London, 1996, p. 39.

[13] Indeed, according to a leading study, 'The Argentines were generally pleased with the idea of American mediation: securing it had been one of the original objectives behind the occupation of the Islands'. Freedman and Gamba-Stonehouse, *Signals of War* (n. 3) p. 168.

3.3 Functions of Mediation

If mediation becomes possible when the parties suspect that a settlement on their own terms may no longer be achievable at an acceptable cost, then the mediator's task is to devise or promote a solution from which both can devise a measure of satisfaction. This may, of course, be impossible, in which case mediation will fail. But a resourceful mediator has a variety of means at their disposal to avoid this result.

3.3.1 Facilitating Communication and Channelling Information

Much can be achieved by simply providing good offices and facilitating communication between the parties. If a dispute is serious enough to call for the services of a mediator, it is possible that events have already had the effect of restricting the parties' contact, or have made it difficult for them to deal with each other openly. In the diplomatic hostages crisis, for example, formal relations between the United States and Iran were broken off following the seizure of the American embassy in Tehran in November 1979 and a subsequent unsuccessful rescue mission. Moreover, since the revolutionary authorities had presented the United States as the enemy of Iran, and corrupter of its spiritual values, it was impossible for Iran to deal directly with the United States, even when Iran had decided that it was in its interests to end the crisis. The elimination of official contact therefore meant that the task of re-establishing communication was performed by a highly diverse group of intermediaries and ultimately by the Algerians, whom the parties were prepared to entrust with good offices and mediation.[14]

Once the parties are in contact, a mediator can be useful in loosening the tension, which may have developed in the course of the dispute, and creating an atmosphere conducive to negotiation.[15] Such an intermediary can also be an effective channel of information. Thus, in the hostages crisis, Algeria was able to suggest how certain proposals from Washington could be modified to improve their chances of acceptance and in a subtle way convey the message from Tehran that, though Iranian assets in the United States were of great symbolic importance, the financial implications of the arrangements for dealing with them were a secondary consideration.[16] It is

---

[14] For a vivid account of the unconventional arrangements preceding Algeria's involvement, see P. Salinger, *America Held Hostage*, London, 1982.

[15] See H. G. Darwin, 'Mediation and good offices', in C. M. H. Waldock (ed.), *International Disputes: The Legal Aspects*, London, 1972, p. 83 at p. 85.

[16] Sick, 'The partial negotiator' (n. 6) p. 35. For an excellent account of the value of mediation in situations of this type, see R. Cohen, 'Cultural aspects of international mediation', in J. Bercovitch (ed.), *Resolving International Conflicts: The Theory and Practice of Mediation*, London, 1996, p. 107. See also G. O. Faure, 'International negotiation: the cultural dimension', in V. A. Kremenyuk (ed.), *International Negotiation*, 2nd ed., San Francisco, 2002, p. 392.

naive to believe that all international disputes can be solved by the removal of misunderstandings, but, since the attitude of a party is determined by its appreciation of its own position in relation to its adversary's capabilities and intentions, a mediator's reports may be important in encouraging a realistic assessment of the situation and inducing a conciliatory frame of mind. In the Falklands crisis, for example, there is good reason to believe that one of Mr Haig's first tasks was to convince the Argentine government that Britain's threat to use force to recover the islands was not a bluff, and that the price of intransigence on the terms of a possible settlement would be correspondingly high.[17]

The value of mediation as a source of information should not be overstated. Mediators are not infallible and, as we have seen, often have interests of their own which may influence what they say and how their messages are received. It is therefore as well to remember that:

> Governments generally do not lend absolute credibility to mediators (or to any other sources or channels). Instead, information received is interpreted in light of the assumed motives and interests of the source or the channel, and in terms of its usefulness in furthering the recipient's own goals.[18]

There is therefore no guarantee that the information brought by a mediator will always be believed; nevertheless, its presence will certainly tend to discourage wishful thinking, while sometimes providing critics of official policy (whose pressure may be important in encouraging a settlement) with a source of valuable intelligence.

3.3.2 Achieving a Mediated Settlement of the Dispute

What of the mediator's substantive contribution? The aim, as already noted, must be to satisfy both parties. In some situations it will be possible to do this by giving each state all or most of what it wants. This is because the aims of the parties in an international dispute are rarely identical and often quite different. Of course, the fact that there is a dispute indicates that the parties' aims are not entirely compatible, but unsuccessful negotiations may cause these differences to become the exclusive focus of attention. A mediator who can remind the parties of their essential objectives (or cause them to be redefined) may therefore be in a position to suggest a mutually satisfactory arrangement.

In the *Beagle Channel* controversy, for example, Argentina's main interest evidently lay in the effect of the controversial award on its maritime sovereignty, while Chile's centred on respect for the decision and the territorial consequences. The settlement promoted by Cardinal Samoré's

---

[17] See Freedman and Gamba-Stonehouse, *Signals of War* (n. 3) p. 176.
[18] Touval and Zartman, *International Mediation* (n. 1) pp. 15, 16.

mediation therefore confirmed Chile's sovereignty over the disputed islands, in return for relinquishing its rights in South Atlantic waters.[19] Similarly, in the Iran–Iraq dispute of 1975, Iran's support for the Kurds was evidently regarded by the Shah as a means to an end, rather than an essential interest. Consequently, when Iraq decided that its main concern was to secure an end to Iranian intervention, Algeria was able to arrange a settlement containing concessions by Iraq on the border issue.

A state in a strong position will naturally expect a settlement to reflect its aims, though acceptance of mediation usually denotes a readiness to make at least some concessions. If both parties regard themselves as relatively strong and their aims are truly incompatible, then mediation, if it is possible at all, will generally fail. To reduce this risk, the mediator may be able to put extra inducements into the scale of the parties' calculations. In both the Falklands crisis and the Kashmir dispute, the fact that the mediating state was a substantial source of military support for one party was clearly capable of manipulation as an incentive to both sides to make concessions. Moreover, in the Kashmir dispute, India relied on Soviet influence to protect it from condemnation in the Security Council. The possibility of Soviet protection being withdrawn, whether or not the threat was actually made, accordingly increased the leverage which Mr Kosygin could exercise as mediator.[20]

One of the reasons why powerful states are so often called upon to act as mediators is this ability to influence the parties' behaviour by exploiting the strength of their own position. In the negotiations over the future of Namibia, for example, a prominent role was played by a Contact Group consisting of representatives of five Western members of the Security Council.[21] By acting together, the members of the Group were in a position to threaten South Africa with the prospect of economic sanctions, a form of leverage which requires concerted action if it is to be credible. An illustration of the opposite technique, the rewarding of cooperation, is the settlement of the Indus Waters dispute through the mediation of the International Bank for Reconstruction and Development in 1960. By providing Pakistan with the resources needed to control its own water supply, the Bank in effect bought one party its objective, while relieving the other, India, of the burden of the dispute: a settlement in

---

[19] For the Papal Proposal of 1980 and the 1984 Treaty of Peace and Friendship, which settled the dispute, see (1985) 24 ILM 7 and 10.

[20] Thornton, 'The Indo-Pakistan conflict' (n. 5) pp. 158–9. The possibility of the Soviet veto being used against Pakistan meant that Mr Kosygin was also in a good position to put pressure on Pakistan. On the value of this type of influence see further Carnevale and Arad, 'Bias and impartiality' (n. 12) *passim*.

[21] See M. A. Spiegel, 'The Namibia negotiations and the problem of neutrality' in S. Touval and W. Zartman (eds), *International Mediation in Theory and Practice*, Boulder, CO, 1985, p. 111.

which, with the aid of outside intervention, both parties were able to realise their aims.[22]

Although a mediated settlement must be a compromise of some kind, it does not follow that the parties must be treated equally. Each must be given something, but need only receive whatever it is ready to settle for as the price of ending the dispute. A state in a relatively weak position may be prepared to sacrifice its original objective and accept some substitute satisfaction as a way of cutting losses and saving face.[23] Thus, a party may be content with some symbolic or token recognition of its claims. Here, mediation can be useful in improvising such expedients, especially when there are obstacles to direct negotiation. In the Falklands mediation, for example, there was talk of dual flags and a symbolic Argentine presence on the islands, either of which in other circumstances might have been a suitable inducement for withdrawal.

Because the costs of a dispute end with its settlement, the fact that a dispute has been settled peacefully can itself be treated as an achievement, regardless of the terms obtained. This is often a key factor in promoting the peaceful settlement of disputes, and a skilful mediator is likely to emphasise the credit which a settlement will reflect on the parties, while reminding them of the serious consequences of any failure. The Iran–Iraq Agreement was announced to general acclaim at the closing session of the first OPEC summit in 1975, and shows how a successful outcome can be orchestrated. On the other hand, as the 1938 Munich Agreement demonstrates, a desire for peace at any price may enable what is really nothing more than the appeasement of an aggressor to be presented as a diplomatic masterstroke.

Closely related to peaceful settlement as prominent values are observance of international law and the United Nations Charter, and compliance with judicial decisions and the resolutions of international organisations. These work best when backed by other pressures and even then may not be enough to produce a settlement. Their force, however, should not be underestimated. The humanitarian mediation practised by the ICRC relies very heavily on the desire of governments to secure the Red Cross 'good house-keeping seal of approval'[24] and the odium which attaches to those who seem to have something to hide. These factors are also relevant to the mediation of political disputes. In the Falklands crisis, for example, if Argentina had wanted to avoid hostilities, Security Council

---

[22] For an account of the background to the dispute and the details of the Indus Waters Treaty (1960) by which it was resolved, see A. H. Garretson, C. J. Olmstead and R. D. Hayton (eds), *The Law of International Drainage Basins*, New York, 1967, ch. 9. See also S. C. McCaffrey, *The Law of International Watercourses*, Oxford, 2001, pp. 248–50.

[23] See F. Edmead, 'Analysis and prediction in international mediation', in K. V. Raman (ed.), *Dispute Settlement through the United Nations*, New York, 1977, p. 221 at pp. 260–7.

[24] Forsythe, 'Humanitarian mediation' (n. 2) p. 242.

Resolution 502, which called for Argentine forces to leave the islands, would have provided a respectable reason for withdrawal.

In a dispute which neither side can win, both may be looking for such a way out. In the Kashmir dispute, the military stalemate meant that both parties were more concerned with cutting their losses than with achieving their initial objectives. There, mediation provided an honourable escape route in the form of a cease-fire and arrangements for continuing discussions between India and Pakistan on issues of outstanding concern. Agreements like this on future procedure are among the most important kinds of substitute satisfaction. They provide the parties with respite and a sense of progress, while postponing the day of reckoning. Such an arrangement may lead eventually to the resolution of a dispute, as when the mediation of the United Kingdom inspired a successful arbitration in the Rann of Kutch dispute.[25] The difficulty, however, is that, by failing to grapple with the substance of the dispute, a procedural agreement points the parties in the direction of a solution, while leaving scope for second thoughts.

Although mediation is not a panacea, it clearly has an important role to play in many international disputes. It is therefore not surprising that its significance has been recognised by the UN General Assembly which in 2011 passed a Resolution entitled 'Strengthening the role of mediation in the peaceful settlement of disputes, conflict prevention and resolution'.[26] As well as urging states to recognise the value of mediation, and expressing support for the noteworthy actions of the United Nations, the Resolution requested the Secretary-General to develop guidance for more effective mediation, taking into account recent and current experience. In response to this invitation, the Secretary-General produced a detailed report[27] outlining the progress made in implementing the General Assembly Resolution. Annexes to the report set out the Guidance for Effective Mediation and the views of member states. As a reference document, the Guidance aims to produce a better understanding of approaches to mediation, as well as advice on how to organise and manage mediation effectively.

In a related sphere of dispute settlement and in the same year as the Secretary-General's report, the International Bar Association (IBA) produced a set of Rules for Investor–State Mediation.[28] As we shall see in Chapter 7, since the end of the last century the number of disputes between states and foreign investors has increased markedly, with the result that today several hundred such cases are pending. Although arbitration is now

---

[25] *Rann of Kutch* Arbitration, 50 ILR 2. For further discussion, see Chapter 6.
[26] UN Doc. A/65/L. 79 (2011).   [27] UN Doc. A/66/811 (2012).
[28] International Bar Association Mediation Committee State Mediation Sub-committee, *IBA Rules for Investor–State Mediation* (2012).

the standard method for dealing with these disputes, certain deficiencies in the process have prompted states, investors and international organisations to explore the possibilities of mediation, not as a substitute for, but as a supplement to arbitration. Although bilateral investment treaties (BITs) and multilateral investment treaties (MITs), encourage the use of mediation, they do not specify how this may be done. It is this omission that the IBA Rules are intended to rectify. The Rules are quite short, but cover all the essential elements, including, for example, the arrangements for appointing mediators and a clear definition of their role. Among several novel elements is provision for a 'Mediation Management Conference' (Article 9) to ensure mediation actually begins. Rules, cannot, of course, ensure that mediation will always be successful, but can at least facilitate its use. If the new IBA Rules have this effect, they will have achieved their purpose.

Enough has been said to indicate that, as a means of dispute settlement, mediation is subject to important limitations. The readiness to mediate and the need for a mediator have already been considered. Once mediation has begun, its prospects of success rest on the parties' willingness to make the necessary concessions. Although this can be encouraged by a skilful mediator in the ways described, the chances of a successful mediation often hinge on its timing.

3.4 Limits of Mediation

3.4.1 The Timing of Mediation

In the Falklands crisis, the aims of the parties were diametrically opposed. Argentina's objective was to rule the islands. Although Britain was not committed to retaining the Falklands indefinitely, it was prepared to relinquish sovereignty only on the condition that the wishes of the inhabitants were respected, which in the circumstances made Argentine rule extremely unlikely. A mediated settlement therefore depended on whether either party was prepared to abandon its original aim and cut its losses. But mediation took place before the battles between the Argentine Air Force and the Royal Navy had established who had the military advantage. Thus, mediation had to be tried at a time when both sides could still think in terms of a military solution and in that situation had little chance of success.[29]

In the diplomatic hostages dispute, on the other hand, Algeria was called upon to act when Iran had decided that it was time to end the crisis. Since this was what the United States had been trying to do from the beginning,

---

[29] It has also been suggested that, for the Argentine leadership, 'the prospect of defeat in battle was preferable to dishonor. Anglo-Saxon material commonsense, in this instance, did not coincide with the imperative requirements of Argentinean *machismo* and *dignidad*.' See Cohen, 'Cultural aspects' (n. 16) p. 120.

the mediator's role was to bring the parties into contact and help them to work out the details of a settlement. The timing of Algeria's intervention in the Iran–Iraq dispute was equally felicitous. There, too, the parties were ready for a settlement; moreover, the ground had already been prepared by a diplomatic initiative taken by Egypt and the constructive assistance of a UN fact-finding and mediation mission.

A well-timed offer of mediation will often be able to exploit the efforts of others who may have been involved at earlier stages, or who may still be present in the background. In the Kashmir negotiations, for example, both sides were aware that, if they failed to agree, the dispute would go to the Security Council. In that event, the Soviet attitude would be crucial, which, as we have seen, gave Mr Kosygin considerable leverage as mediator.

Exhaustion or the risks of escalation are other factors which can help the mediator. Thus, in the Kashmir and Rann of Kutch disputes, military action had been tried and the offer of mediation could be timed to take advantage of the parties' search for some alternative. These disputes were therefore ripe for mediation. It is worth recalling, however, that, despite this critical similarity, the effect of mediation in the two disputes was quite different. In the Rann of Kutch dispute, as already noted, mediation led eventually to a binding arbitration. In the Kashmir dispute, however, following the agreement on a cease-fire, no progress was made in resolving the basic issue. When important interests are at stake, as in Kashmir, it will generally be much easier to negotiate a provisional solution than to achieve a permanent settlement. A cease-fire is better than nothing, of course, but, like a temporary filling in a bad tooth, it may mean even more trouble in the future if steps are not taken to get to the root of the problem.

3.4.2 Implementing Mediated Settlement

A related point is that, if an agreement concerns future procedures, it may be ineffective unless there is someone to ensure its implementation. The mediator should therefore recognise that, 'left to their own devices, the parties may fall out of an agreement just as it is being made or implemented'[30] and to forestall this possibility may seek to extend the mediator's role. In the Iran–Iraq dispute, Algeria not only supervised the negotiation of the 1975 peace treaty, but also arranged for its representative to be present when the mixed commissions which the parties had agreed upon were created and subsequently during the commissions' deliberations.[31] At all three stages, the presence of a third party helped to maintain the parties' commitment to the agreement and avoided the stalemate and recriminations which had characterised their earlier negotiations.

---

[30] Touval and Zartman, *International Mediation* (n. 1) p. 268.
[31] Lieb, 'Iran and Iraq at Algiers' (n. 8) pp. 83–4.

Despite the negotiation of the Algiers Accord and the careful arrangements for its implementation, in September 1980 Iraq attacked Iran and attempted to recover the territory conceded in the earlier agreement. The war, which lasted for eight years, ended only when both sides were exhausted and again ready to accept outside mediation, on this occasion by the UN Secretary-General. The fact that the war took place is not, of course, a ground for criticising the 1975 settlement, which achieved all that was possible at that time. It is, however, a reminder that there are two types of temporary settlement: those like the Kashmir Agreement, which never purport to be anything more than interim arrangements, and those like the Algiers Accord which, though addressed to the basic issues in dispute and intended to be permanent, are unable to withstand the pressure of changing circumstances.

The problem of ensuring the implementation of agreements reached after a successful mediation also occurs in the context of international commercial disputes. To facilitate the enforcement of international settlement agreements resulting from mediation, a Convention was negotiated within the United Nations Commission on International Trade Law (UNCITRAL). The UN Convention on International Settlement Agreements Resulting from Mediation ('Singapore Convention on Mediation')[32] was adopted by the UN General Assembly in 2018 and entered into force in September 2020.

The Singapore Convention applies to international settlement agreements resulting from mediation to resolve an international commercial dispute (Article 1(1)). The international nature of the dispute can result from the fact that the parties 'have their places of business in different states', or the fact that both parties have their places of business in the same state but a substantial part of the obligations under the settlement is performed in another state or the State with which the subject matter of the settlement agreement is most closely connected with is different. The Convention does not apply to settlement agreements which relate to consumer, family, inheritance and employment matters, nor to settlement agreements that have been approved by a court or concluded in the course of court proceedings and that are enforceable as a judgment, or to settlement agreements that have been recorded and are enforceable as an arbitral award (Article 1(2–3)). The main idea behind the Convention is that a signed settlement agreement which was the result of international mediation must be enforced in accordance with the provisions of the Convention, *the rules of procedure* of the state in which enforcement is sought and provisions of the Convention (Articles 3 and 4). The Convention also lists the grounds under which enforcement under the Singapore Convention can be refused (Article 5).

---

[32] UN Convention on International Settlement Agreements Resulting from Mediation ('Singapore Convention on Mediation'), General Assembly Resolution 73/198 (20 December 2018).

Sometimes, then, mediation may only be able to achieve a partial solution. Even that degree of progress will be impossible if the parties cling tenaciously to fundamentally incompatible positions; if, for example, they are not prepared to acknowledge that a political solution is what is needed, rather than an endorsement of existing rights. In the *Beagle Channel* dispute, Cardinal Samoré's proposals would have been stillborn if Chile had insisted on the implementation of the original award with all its jurisdictional implications, just as a mediation in the Falklands crisis would have been pointless had Britain refused to discuss the future status of the islands.

In the same way, mediation is likely to be ineffective in situations where any solution would require one side to abandon its main objective and receive little in return. This was the position during the crisis which led to the Gulf War of 1991.[33] Following Iraq's invasion of Kuwait in August 1990 and the imposition of sanctions by the UN Security Council, the Secretary-General, France, the Soviet Union and a number of others made several attempts to bring about a peaceful solution. All were unsuccessful, essentially because a key demand was that Iraq should withdraw from Kuwait and not be rewarded for its aggression. This clearly restricted what Iraq could be offered as an inducement and meant that the main incentive for withdrawal was that it would remove the threat of military conflict. It is therefore perhaps not surprising that, from the very beginning, this was a crisis in which few considered that mediation would produce a solution.

Mediation may also founder if a dispute has become an issue in the domestic politics of one or both of the parties. A government may have adopted a position from which it cannot retreat without attracting accusations of betrayal, or the subject matter of a dispute may be so emotive that the very act of negotiating will be contentious. The situation is even more difficult if either of the parties has a government which is unstable or divided. In the former case, a government is likely to be particularly sensitive to criticism, and in the latter may find it impossible to follow a consistent policy. The fact that an international dispute is a major issue in domestic politics need not preclude effective mediation, as the settlement of the hostages crisis demonstrates. However, it is clear that, where there are domestic repercussions, strict confidentiality is essential during the negotiations. Moreover, since mediation is in this respect subject to the same limitations as other means of dispute settlement, in some cases of this type the gulf between the parties' respective positions will simply be too wide to be bridged.

Thus, mediation can only be as effective as the parties wish it to be, and this is governed largely by their immediate situation. Although this is a

---

[33] See Freedman and Karsh, *The Gulf Conflict* (n. 5) pp. 430–2.

major limitation on the usefulness of mediation, it is important to retain a sense of perspective. It would be quite wrong to think that a mediator is merely someone who lends authority to an agreement that is already virtually made. On the contrary, by facilitating the parties' dialogue, providing them with information and suggestions, identifying and exploring their aims and canvassing a range of possible solutions, mediation can play a vital role in moving them towards agreement. Although success will often be incomplete and failure sometimes inevitable, the mediator's job is to spare no effort for the parties, and trust that they will reciprocate.

3.5 Further Reading

3.5.1 General References on Mediation

Beardsley, K., *The Mediation Dilemma*, Ithaca, 2011.
Ben Hamida, W., and S. Bostanji, *La médiation dans tous ses états*, Paris, 2018.
Bercovitch, D. J. (ed.), *Resolving International Conflicts: The Theory and Practice of Mediation*, London, 1996.
Bercovitch, D. J., and J. Z. Rubin (eds), *Mediation in International Relations*, London, 1992.
Kleiboer, M., *The Multiple Realities of International Mediation*, Boulder, CO, 1998.
Northedge, F. S., and M. D. Donelan (eds), *International Disputes: The Political Aspects*, London, 1971, ch. 13.
Titi, C., and K. Fach Gomez, *Mediation in International Commercial and Investment Disputes*, Oxford, 2019.
Touval, S., and I. W. Zartman (eds), *International Mediation in Theory and Practice*, Boulder, CO, 1985.
Waldock, C. M. H. (ed.), *International Disputes: The Legal Aspects*, London, 1972, ch. 2B.

3.5.2 Treaties and Official Documents

UN Convention on International Settlement Agreements Resulting from Mediation, General Assembly Resolution 73/198 (20 December 2018) ('Singapore Convention on Mediation').

4

Inquiry

When a disagreement between states on some issue of fact, law or policy is serious enough to give rise to an international dispute, their views on the matter in question may be difficult or impossible to reconcile. In such a case, either or both of the parties may refuse to discuss the matter on the ground that their position is 'not negotiable'. Alternatively, negotiations may drag on for years until one side abandons its claim or loses patience and attempts to impose a solution by force. It follows that negotiation, even if assisted by good offices or mediation, cannot be regarded as an adequate means of resolving all international disputes.

With states, as with individuals, experience demonstrates that the risks of stalemate are greatly reduced when a disinterested third party is brought into a dispute to provide the parties with an objective assessment. Internationally, a number of methods of achieving this have been developed. The method with which this chapter is concerned is called 'inquiry'.

'Inquiry' as a term of art is used in two distinct, but related, senses. In the broader sense, it refers to the process that is performed whenever a court or other body endeavours to resolve a disputed issue of fact. Since most international disputes raise such issues, even if legal or political questions are also present, it is clear that inquiry in this operational sense will often be a major component of arbitration, conciliation, action by international organisations and other methods of third-party settlement. The place of inquiry in the work of the United Nations, the International Court and other bodies will be examined in later chapters. Our present concern is with inquiry in another sense, not as a process which any tribunal may be required to perform as part of its work, but as a specific institutional arrangement which states may select in preference to arbitration or other techniques, because they desire to have some disputed issue independently investigated. In its institutional sense, then, inquiry refers to a particular type of international tribunal, known as the commission of inquiry and introduced by the 1899 Hague Convention.

4.1 1899 Hague Convention

On 15 February 1898, the United States battleship *Maine*, at anchor in Havana harbour, was destroyed by an explosion which killed 259 of her officers and crew.[1] Relations between the United States and Spain were already strained, and American opinion needed little encouragement to see the *Maine* disaster as the work of the European power. Although Spain denied liability and held a commission of inquiry which found the explosion to have had an internal cause, American suspicions were confirmed when a rival commission, composed of US naval personnel, decided that the *Maine* had been destroyed by a submarine mine.

While it would be wrong to suppose that the *Maine* incident was the fundamental cause of the Spanish–American war which followed, the precipitating effect of what was really no more than a disagreement about the interpretation of evidence sufficiently impressed the delegates to the Hague Peace Conference of 1899 for them to give serious attention to the issue of fact finding in international disputes. The focus of debate at the conference was a proposal from the Russian delegation for the replacement of national commissions of inquiry of the kind that had proved so unsatisfactory in the *Maine* episode with international commissions for the impartial investigation of the facts and circumstances of international disputes.

After discussion had revealed, among other sources of doubt, a fear on the part of some of the smaller states that inquiry commissions might be used as a cloak for foreign intervention, the conference eventually agreed that such commissions were acceptable, provided a number of important conditions were fulfilled. These were that inquiry commissions should only be used for disputes 'involving neither honour nor essential interests', that they should handle only questions of fact and not questions of law, and finally that neither the creation of a commission nor the implementation of its findings should be regarded as obligatory. With these qualifications, arrangements for the creation and operation of inquiry commissions were outlined in six articles of the 1899 Hague Convention.[2] Their value was soon to be demonstrated.

4.2 The *Dogger Bank* Inquiry

In the early hours of 9 October 1904, a squadron of Russian warships, on their way from the Baltic to the Far East to take part in the Russo-Japanese war, unwittingly steamed into the Hull fishing fleet near the Dogger Bank. In the ensuing confusion, the Russian admiral formed the erroneous impression that he was being attacked by Japanese torpedo boats, which were rumoured to be in the area, and opened fire. The firing, which lasted about ten minutes, caused considerable damage. One of the trawlers was

---

[1] For details of the *Maine* incident, see *Annual Register*, 1898, pp. 362–3.
[2] Hague Convention for the Pacific Settlement of Disputes, 1899, Arts 9–14. See also A. Eyffinger, *The 1899 Hague Peace Conference*, The Hague, 1999, ch. 10.

sunk and five others were damaged, and two crew members were killed and six wounded.[3]

When news of the incident reached England, feelings ran high and preparations were made to intercept the Russian fleet which, in ignorance of its error, was by now approaching Gibraltar. Before matters could deteriorate any further, intense diplomatic activity by France, which strongly desired to avoid a rupture of Anglo-Russian relations, persuaded the two states to establish a commission of inquiry in accordance with the Hague Convention.

The Commission, which was set up in November 1904, was composed of an admiral from each of the parties, together with one each from France, Austro-Hungary and the United States. Its terms of reference were to:

> inquire into and report on all the circumstances relative to the North Sea Incident, and particularly on the question as to where the responsibility lies and the degree of blame attaching to the subjects of the two High Contracting Parties, or to the subjects of other countries, in the event of their responsibility being established by the inquiry.[4]

The Commission spent two months hearing witnesses and preparing its report, which was delivered in February 1905. In it, the Commission found that there had been no torpedo boats either among the trawlers or anywhere nearby and concluded that the Russian admiral had therefore had no justification for opening fire. It added, however, that these findings were not, in the Commissioners' opinion, 'of a nature to cast any discredit upon the military qualities or the humanity of Admiral Rojdestvensky, or the personnel of his squadron'.[5] Following acceptance of the report by both parties, Russia made a payment to Britain by way of damages of some £65,000 and the incident was closed.

The *Dogger Bank* episode furnishes a striking example of the value of the international inquiry commission as an instrument of dispute settlement. Had the issue been investigated by two national inquiries, it is almost certain that, as in the *Maine* case, they would have exacerbated matters by coming to opposite conclusions. Although it may be doubted whether such an outcome would necessarily have resulted in war, since neither Britain nor Russia had previously contemplated such a step, their decision to establish a commission of inquiry effectively removed the risk that a dispute involving issues of considerable sensitivity might get out of hand.

---

[3] For an account of the incident and the subsequent fate of Admiral Rojdestvensky, see R. Hough, *The Fleet that Had to Die*, London, 1975.

[4] Declaration between Great Britain and Russia, relating to the constitution of an international commission of inquiry on the subject of the North Sea incident, signed at St Petersburg, 12/25 November 1904, Art. 2. See J. B. Scott, *The Hague Court Reports*, New York, 1916, p. 411. The original French text is at *ibid.*, 614.

[5] *Ibid.*, 410.

In this respect, the inquiry also demonstrated that, provided no actual clash of policy was involved, even disputes involving 'honour' and 'essential interests' might be amenable to the inquiry process. Indeed, it is evident that it was the very sensitivity of the issue that prompted the setting up of the inquiry as a way of relaxing the tension.

In another way, too, the inquiry departed from the pattern envisaged by the Hague Convention. The duty to apportion 'blame' appeared to assign the Commission an arbitral as well as a fact-finding function. The admirals who made up the Commission, no doubt wisely, sought to underplay this aspect of their work and, in a decision of somewhat ambiguous legal import,[6] demonstrated what later experience was to confirm, that in the interests of dispute settlement, legal and factual issues need not always be sharply distinguished.

4.3 Inquiries under the 1907 Hague Convention

There was one further respect in which the *Dogger Bank* episode was significant. Before it could begin its investigation, the Commission had to spend precious time deciding upon its rules of procedure. With a view to expediting the work of future commissions, the Hague Convention of 1907 expanded the somewhat skeletal provisions of the 1899 Convention with a series of articles devoted to organisation and procedure.[7] As a result, it was these new arrangements that were followed when the next international inquiry commission was convened.

4.3.1 The *Tavignano* Inquiry

The first case under the new Convention concerned a series of incidents off the Tunisian coast during the Turco-Italian war of 1911–12. Although France was neutral in that war, the Italian government strongly suspected that French vessels were involved in the shipment of Turkish contraband. The interception of French ships by the Italian navy had already led to two disputes which had been referred to arbitration[8] and when, on 25 January 1912, the French mail steamer *Tavignano* was arrested and two other vessels were fired on, according to Italy on the high seas, but according to France in Tunisian territorial waters, it was agreed to refer the matter to a commission of inquiry in accordance with the 1907 Convention.

---

[6] For an excellent summary and analysis of scholarly responses to the case, see N. Bar-Yaacov, *The Handling of International Disputes by Means of Inquiry*, Oxford, 1974, pp. 72–81. See also R. N. Lebow, 'Accidents and crises: the Dogger Bank affair' (1978) 31 *Naval War College Review*, 66.

[7] Hague Convention for the Pacific Settlement of International Disputes, 1907, Arts 9–35. For commentary, see Bar-Yaacov, *Inquiry* (n. 6) ch. 4.

[8] The Franco-Italian disputes referred to arbitration were the *Carthage* and *Manouba* cases. For the Awards of 6 May 1913, see Scott, *Hague Court Reports* (n. 4) p. 330 and p. 342.

The main question for the Commission, which consisted of a French, an Italian and a British naval officer, was to determine exactly where the controversial incidents had occurred. In an attempt to resolve the serious conflict of evidence on this point, the Commission did not confine itself to an examination of witnesses and documents, but also visited the scene of the incident. In its unanimous report, however, it concluded that it could do no more than indicate the general areas in which the incidents had taken place.[9] From the Commission's findings, it was clear that, though the arrest of the *Tavignano* may or may not have been in Tunisian waters, the firing incidents certainly were.

The decision to establish the commission of inquiry had been accompanied by an agreement which envisaged that the next step might be a reference of the legal aspects of the dispute to arbitration. Following receipt of the Commission's report, a decision to this effect was taken; but, before the case could be heard, the issue was settled out of court when the Italian government agreed to pay 5,000 francs in satisfaction of the claim. If the *Dogger Bank* case had demonstrated the value of inquiry in defusing an explosive situation, the *Tavignano* case showed how in other circumstances it could be used to provide the basis for subsequent arbitration.

By assigning the disputed issues of fact to a commission of inquiry, the parties ensured that the evidence was reviewed at the earliest opportunity by a tribunal with the requisite expertise. The Tavignano Commission, like its predecessor, was ideally constituted for the work in hand and, relieved by the provisions of the 1907 Convention of the need to settle procedural issues, it was able to complete its investigation in less than a month. Although, as we have seen, the Commission was compelled to leave a crucial issue unresolved, the French and Italian governments were sufficiently satisfied with its work to include in their arbitral agreement a provision requiring the use of its report.

Paradoxically, the fact that the dispute was not in the end resolved by arbitration is also significant. For it indicates that, though fact finding may be envisaged as a preliminary to arbitration, and can certainly function in that way, in practice, as the sponsors of the Hague Convention foresaw, an elucidation of the facts, or even only some of them, may be all that is needed to induce a negotiated settlement.

4.3.2 The *Tiger* Inquiry

The next inquiry to be held under the 1907 Convention concerned a situation not unlike the previous case. On 7 May 1917, during the First World War, a German submarine pursued and sank a Norwegian ship, the

---

[9] See Scott, *Hague Court Reports* (n. 4) p. 413.

Tiger, off the northern coast of Spain. As in the *Tavignano* incident, the justification advanced was that the vessel was a neutral carrying contraband and the crucial question was the vessel's location. Spain, also a neutral, alleged that the arrest had taken place in her territorial waters; Germany maintained that it had taken place on the high seas.

Following lengthy diplomatic exchanges, Spain and Germany agreed to set up a commission of inquiry under the 1907 Convention, charged with the task of determining where the crucial events had occurred. The Tiger Commission, like its predecessor, was made up of naval officers from the parties in dispute, with a neutral (here, Danish) chairman. Once again, the evidence concerning the vessel's navigation sharply conflicted and the Commission experienced great difficulty in coming to a decision as to exactly what had occurred. In the end, however, it concluded that the pursuit and arrest had occurred in Spanish waters.[10]

Although similar in many respects to the previous case, the *Tiger* inquiry contains several points of interest. This was the first case in which the parties to an international inquiry agreed in advance to accept the report of the Commission as binding. This departure from the Hague Conventions underlined the determination of the states concerned to use the fact-finding process to achieve a settlement of the dispute, and, like the inclusion of a legal question in the terms of reference of the Dogger Bank Commission, showed how in appropriate circumstances the inquiry procedure was flexible enough to act as a substitute for arbitration.

But, if the binding nature of the decision brought the *Tiger* proceedings close to arbitration in one respect, the Commission's treatment of the evidence served to emphasise the distinctive character of the inquiry procedure. The evidence concerning the location of the submarine and its victim at the material time proved exceptionally difficult to interpret. In part, this was because, as the *Tavignano* case had already shown, the location of a ship at sea is often difficult to determine with great precision and after the event; in part, it was because, unlike the earlier case, the lapse of time between the incident and the inquiry had resulted in the destruction of much important evidence, including the submarine with its crew and vital logbook, all of which had been lost on a subsequent operation. An arbitration in this situation might have been expected to generate a major argument over the burden of proof. The fact that the commission of inquiry was not a court of arbitration enabled it to assess the evidence and ultimately settle the dispute without addressing this notoriously thorny legal issue.[11]

---

[10] See Bar-Yaacov, *Inquiry* (n. 6) pp. 156–71. The Commission's report was not published; the documents are in the Library of the Permanent Court of Arbitration at The Hague.

[11] The importance which the burden of proof argument might have assumed is clear from the separate opinion of the German Commissioner who examined the issue in some detail. On the

4.3.3 The *Tubantia* Inquiry

The last case also involved a German submarine. On 16 March 1916, the Dutch steamer *Tubantia* was sunk by a torpedo on the high seas. The Dutch government claimed that the sinking was the work of a U-boat and that, since Holland was neutral, Germany must pay compensation. Germany, on the other hand, though unable to deny that the sinking had been caused by a German torpedo, since identifiable fragments of the torpedo had been recovered, maintained that the torpedo in question had actually been fired at a British destroyer, which it had missed, and must have remained afloat to claim the *Tubantia* some ten days later.

When the war was over, the two governments established a commission of inquiry with the aim of establishing the cause of the sinking. The Commission, consisting of naval officers from Denmark, Sweden, the Netherlands and Germany, together with a Swiss jurist as chairman, heard a variety of witnesses and experts and delivered its report in February 1922.[12] In it, the Commission decided that the *Tubantia* had indeed been the victim of a submarine attack. This was a clear finding of German responsibility, though the Commission was careful to add that it was not in a position to determine whether the torpedoing had taken place knowingly or as a result of error. The German government accepted the conclusions of the report and paid an indemnity of 6.5 million florins to the Dutch government in satisfaction of the claim.

This was the first case in which a commission of inquiry had included a lawyer among its members. Although the Commission's interpretation of its mandate was broad enough to include questions of knowledge and motive among the 'facts' to be investigated, it is clear that there were no specifically legal issues to be decided in this case. The inclusion of a jurist has been seen therefore as a reflection of the seriousness of the matter under investigation – virtually a criminal charge – and an indication that, in view of the exceptional quantity of very diverse technical evidence, the parties regarded a legally qualified chairman as essential.[13]

The *Tubantia* inquiry is also notable for the extent to which the proceedings resembled arbitration. For, although, as we have seen, no legal issue was in dispute and, in contrast to the *Tiger* inquiry, the parties had not undertaken to accept the Commission's report in advance, the exchange of memorials and the handling of the oral evidence were both more reminiscent of a judicial proceeding than of the inquiry provisions of the Hague Conventions.

---

general significance of such evidential factors in the work of inquiry commissions, see the comments of H. Darwin in C. M. H. Waldock (ed.), *International Disputes: The Legal Aspects*, London, 1972, p. 169.

[12] See J. B. Scott, *The Hague Court Reports* (Second series), New York, 1932, p. 135.

[13] Bar-Yaacov, *Inquiry* (n. 6) p. 178.

4.4 Treaty Practice 1911–40

The desire of states to depart from the pattern of the Hague Conventions, which was so evident in the *Tubantia* case, had already inspired a number of important developments on the other side of the Atlantic. In 1911, the United States negotiated treaties with France and the United Kingdom which provided that all differences or controversies between the parties must be submitted either to arbitration or to a Joint High Commission of Inquiry. These treaties, known as the Taft (or Knox) treaties of arbitration, laid down that the organisation and procedure of the commissions were, in general, to be governed by the relevant provisions of the 1907 Hague Convention. However, in a series of significant departures from the latter, the new treaties contained no limitations as to the kinds of dispute which could be investigated, authorised the commissions to make recommendations as well as findings of fact and went so far as to lay down that decisions by a commission as to whether a dispute was subject to arbitration were binding on the parties.

Between 1913 and 1940, the United States concluded a further series of treaties, known as the Bryan treaties, again based on the Hague Convention. Though unrestricted as to subject matter, these treaties conferred no power to make recommendations, but contained another innovation in that the commissions provided for by the treaties were to be permanent rather than ad hoc bodies. Inspired by the early Bryan treaties, Argentina, Brazil and Chile concluded the so-called ABC Treaty in 1915, the United Kingdom made rather similar agreements with Brazil and Chile in 1919, and in 1923 sixteen American states concluded the Gondra Treaty with arrangements for inquiry along the same lines.[14]

Though quite extensive, the treaty practice just described did not produce a series of inquiries like those generated by the Hague Conventions.[15] But, if its significance in that sense is negligible, it represents an important step in the development of dispute settlement. For these treaties were an early recognition of the three principles essential to further progress: that permanent or standing commissions offer significant advantages over ad hoc bodies like the Dogger Bank Commission; that the types of disputes which can be investigated should be unrestricted; and that the ability of commissions to contribute to the settlement of disputes could be increased by authorising them to make recommendations. As we shall see in the next chapter, when these elements were finally brought together, the product was the institutional technique known as conciliation.

---

[14] See D. V. B. Galeano, 'The Gondra Treaty' (1929) 15 *Grotius Soc. Trans.I*, 1.

[15] The Taft treaties never came into force, and the procedures laid down by the Bryan treaties have so far been used only once, in the *Letelier and Moffitt* case (1992), discussed below. For further discussion of these treaties and their significance, see Bar-Yaacov, *Inquiry* (n. 6) pp. 113–17; and J.-P. Cot, *International Conciliation*, London, 1972, pp. 66–74.

4.5 Post-Second World War Practice

After the *Tavignano* inquiry in 1922, almost 40 years passed before the next international commission was appointed. This was the inquiry set up by the United Kingdom and Denmark to investigate the *Red Crusader* incident in 1961.

4.5.1 The *Red Crusader* Inquiry

As in the other cases we have considered, the incident arose out of events at sea. On 29 May 1961, the Danish fisheries protection vessel *Niels Ebbesen* encountered the British trawler *Red Crusader* close to the Faroe Islands and with its fishing gear in the water. Accusing the trawler of illegal fishing, the Danish commander forced it to stop and effected an arrest by putting two members of his crew on board. While en route to a port in the Faroes, the crew of the *Red Crusader* succeeded in incapacitating their guards and reversed course. Pursued by the Danish vessel, the trawler was fired at with solid shot and suffered damage to its prow, masts, wireless aerials and radar installation. A British frigate came on the scene and, after the abducted Danes had been returned to their ship, all three vessels headed for Aberdeen.

In the diplomatic exchanges which followed, it was clear that the Danish government took a serious view of the incident, not least because the Danish boarding party had been unarmed in accordance with a previous request from the British government that this step would reduce tension when British trawlers had to be arrested. With a view to settling the dispute, the United Kingdom and Denmark, after some negotiation, eventually agreed to establish a commission of inquiry to investigate the incident.

The three-member commission was composed of distinguished international lawyers from Belgium, France and the Netherlands Inspector-General of Shipping. Its terms of reference were to investigate and report to the two governments:

(i) the facts leading up to the arrest of the British trawler *Red Crusader* on the night of 29 May 1961, including the question of whether the *Red Crusader* was fishing, or with her fishing gear not stowed, inside the blue line on the map annexed to the Agreement between the two Governments concerning the regulation of fishing around the Faroe Islands constituted by the Exchange of Notes of 27 April 1959;
(ii) the circumstances of the arrest; and
(iii) the facts and incidents that occurred thereafter before the *Red Crusader* reached Aberdeen.[16]

---

[16] Exchange of Notes of 15 November 1961, para. (b), UKTS No. 118 (1961, Cmnd No. 1575), also in Bar-Yaacov, *Inquiry* (n. 6) p. 185.

The Commission received written submissions from Britain and Denmark and held oral hearings at The Hague. Its sizeable report was delivered to the parties in March 1962. In it, the Commission set out a detailed description of the events which comprised the incident and drew the following main conclusions:[17]

1. There was no proof that the *Red Crusader* had been fishing within the forbidden area, although the vessel was within the area with her gear not stowed.
2. The *Red Crusader* was arrested, but the skipper, having changed his mind, 'attempted to escape and to evade the jurisdiction of an authority which he had at first, rightly, accepted'.
3. In opening fire after the escape, the Danish commander 'exceeded legitimate use of armed force' because the circumstances did not 'justify such violent action'.
4. The British naval officers 'made every effort to avoid any recourse to violence' between the Danish vessel and the *Red Crusader*, and exhibited an attitude and conduct that were 'impeccable'.

As in the cases already considered, the report of the commission of inquiry facilitated the settlement of the dispute, though on this occasion only after some delay since it was nearly a year from the delivery of the Commission's report to the announcement that Britain and Denmark had agreed to settle the issue by a mutual waiver of their claims.

If inquiries under the Hague Conventions had shown how the desire of states for highly specific types of third-party settlement could be accommodated by investing the procedure of pure inquiry with overtones of arbitration, the *Red Crusader* inquiry displays the process of assimilation taken a good deal further. For, in respect of its composition, its procedure and its findings, the Red Crusader Commission was a fundamentally judicial operation.[18] A majority of the Commission were jurists, and had the tribunal been a court of arbitration, its blend of legal and non-legal expertise would have been in no way unusual. Moreover, like many arbitral tribunals, but unlike any of the previous commissions of inquiry, no member of the tribunal was a national of either of the parties to the dispute.

As in the *Tubantia* inquiry, the *Red Crusader* proceedings were divided into a written and an oral stage. But an important innovation in the latter was that, as in an arbitration, the principal examination of the witnesses was conducted by the representatives of the parties instead of by the members of the Commission. Scarcely less significant was the parties' decision that the report of the Commission should not be published

---

[17] See 35 ILR 485 and document B in Appendix B.   [18] Bar-Yaacov, *Inquiry* (n. 6) p. 192.

automatically, as had been the case with the reports of previous commissions of inquiry, but, like an arbitral award, should be published only with the consent of the two governments.

The findings of the Commission, though mainly devoted to the facts of the incident, clearly included important legal rulings. The Commission's findings that Danish authority had been 'rightly' accepted by the skipper of the *Red Crusader* and that the subsequent firing 'exceeded legitimate use of armed force' are, as has been pointed out,[19] legal judgments which, like other features of the case, suggest arbitration rather than inquiry.

What, then, was the difference between the *Red Crusader* inquiry and an arbitration? Two important distinctions can be identified and may well explain the parties' preference for this mode of settlement.

First, by creating a tribunal whose primary concern was to establish the facts, the parties were able to avoid debating the full legal implications of the case. Of course, legal issues of immediate significance, such as the lawfulness of the shooting, had to be considered. Had the matter been dealt with by arbitration, however, it is likely that the legality of the Faroese fishery limits would also have been the subject of argument, because this issue was currently the subject of a clear difference of opinion between Britain and Denmark.[20] Thus, by handling the matter by means of a commission of inquiry rather than by arbitration, the two states were able to obtain a solution to the immediate problem without the delay and precedential implications of a more broadly based adjudication.

Second, because the proceedings were in the form of an inquiry, the outcome was a report rather than an award. Despite the Commission's findings of fault on both sides, the question of the effect to be given to the report remained in the hands of the parties. The fact that it then took them almost a year to agree upon a settlement suggests that in this respect a binding arbitration award, specifying damages or some other remedy, might have provided a more expeditious solution. The delay is, however, also a reminder of the importance which governments attach to freedom of action even in relatively minor disputes, and, as a corollary, the usefulness of the inquiry procedure as a means of accommodating this demand.

---

[19] E. Lauterpacht, *The Contemporary Practice of the UK in the Field of International Law 1962 (I)*, London, 1962, p. 53.

[20] The 'blue line' mentioned in the terms of reference of the Commission was the six-mile fishery line which Britain had recognised in the 1959 agreement in return for Denmark's recognition of the British right to fish beyond the limit. By 1961, however, Denmark was seeking revision of this arrangement and, following the termination of the earlier agreement in 1962, unilaterally imposed a twelve-mile limit in March 1964. For a review of this episode and contemporaneous developments, see D. H. N. Johnson, 'European fishery limits', in *Developments in the Law of the Sea 1958–1964*, British Institute of International and Comparative Law Special Publication No. 6, London, 1965, pp. 48–92.

4.5.2 The *Letelier and Moffitt* Case

The *Red Crusader* inquiry was followed almost 30 years later by the decision in the *Letelier and Moffitt* case, the first, and so far the only, investigation by a commission established under one of the Bryan treaties. The circumstances which gave rise to the case were unusual and account for a number of features which distinguish the work of this Commission from that of its predecessors. The dispute had its origin in the murder in 1976 of Mr Orlando Letelier, a former foreign minister of Chile, who was killed in Washington, DC when a bomb which had been placed in his car exploded. The explosion also killed an American lady, Mrs Moffitt, and seriously injured her husband, both of whom were also travelling in the car. Mr Moffitt, Mr Letelier's estate and relatives of the deceased then brought proceedings against Chile in the United States, alleging that the state was responsible for the explosion. Following the rejection of a plea of sovereign immunity, the claim was successful and the plaintiffs were awarded approximately US$5 million in damages.[21] However, the judgment was not satisfied and the US courts then rejected an attempt to obtain execution against the assets of the Chilean national airline.[22]

In 1988, the United States made an international claim against Chile in respect of the deaths and injuries, subsequently invoking the provisions of the Bryan–Suárez Mujica Treaty of 1914 between the two states.[23] Although Chile denied responsibility for the incident, it indicated that it was prepared to make an *ex gratia* payment to the United States, on behalf of the families of the victims. In view of this concession, the United States and Chile were able to conclude an agreement in 1990 under which Chile agreed to make an *ex gratia* payment corresponding to the sum payable if liability had been established.[24] The agreement went on to provide that the amount of this payment was to be determined by a commission established under the 1914 Treaty and that this was to be the sole question to be determined.

The five-member Commission, appointed in a *compromis* appended to the agreement, was composed of Judge Aguilar Mawdsley of the International Court of Justice, from Venezuela, as president, and four other jurists, including a national from each of the parties. The Commission received written submissions from the United States and Chile and at the parties' request had the benefit of facilities provided by the Inter-American Commission on Human Rights. In its decision, which was delivered in January 1992, the Commission reviewed the numerous

---

[21] See 63 ILR 378; see also the note in 88 ILR 747.   [22] See 79 ILR 561.
[23] Treaty for the Settlement of Disputes that May Occur between the United States and Chile, 1914, US Treaty Series No. 621.
[24] Chile–United States: Agreement to Settle Dispute Concerning Compensation for the Deaths of Letelier and Moffitt, 1990, (1991) 30 ILM 422.

legal and factual issues pertaining to the question of compensation, and, after considering the various individual claims, unanimously awarded sums amounting in total to just over US$2.5 million.[25]

In accordance with the parties' original intentions, the decision effectively settled the dispute. It will be recalled that the parties had already undertaken to treat the Commission's decision as binding and within a month of the ruling Chile agreed to pay the total sum awarded, to be divided among the relatives of those killed.

As in the *Red Crusader*, the task given to the Commission in this case was essentially judicial, and this was reflected in all stages of its work. Its membership included prominent international lawyers, and, though the nature of the issues made the examination of witnesses unnecessary, the parties filed what in effect were written pleadings and could comment in writing on the other's observations. No arrangements for publication of the decision were made, although in the event it was not treated as confidential.

The Commission's decision, like the report in the *Red Crusader*, included several important legal rulings, as well as numerous findings of fact. Indeed, the former was much more important here than in the earlier case, because where compensation is in issue the principles governing assessment supply the framework for identifying the relevant facts. In this respect, it is notable that the *compromis* specifically required the Commission to give its decision 'in accordance with applicable principles of international law', which led it to refer, inter alia, to the decision of the Permanent Court of International Justice in the *Chorzów Factory* case,[26] and to the practice of judicial and arbitral tribunals with regard to non-pecuniary loss, as well as to questions such as remoteness and compensation for special expenses. The significance of the decision as a contribution to international law was further explored in Professor Orrego Vicuña's concurring opinion.

The Commission did not, of course, decide that Chile was responsible for the act of terrorism, but the fact that the sum involved was paid *ex gratia* affects neither the legal basis of the decision, nor the genuine nature of the argumentation. As Professor Orrego Vicuña observed, the parties argued their cases with professional skill and 'every relevant point of law and fact [was] controverted by the parties with precision during the proceedings'.[27] Thus, although the United States originally invoked the 1914 Treaty 'to investigate and report upon the facts' surrounding the victims' deaths, the Commission which was eventually set up functioned less as a commission of inquiry of the traditional type and more like a court of arbitration, producing a binding decision and deciding issues of law as

---

[25] See 88 ILR 727; also in (1992) 31 ILM 1.   [26] *Chorzów Factory* case, PCIJ Series A, No. 17.
[27] *Orrego Vicuña*, concurring opinion, section 5, 88 ILR 741.

well as fact. The *Letelier and Moffitt* case thus confirms a general point made earlier that commissions of inquiry can sometimes be used in unexpected ways, and a specific point, as we shall encounter again in Chapter 6, that when a face-saving solution is wanted, procedures such as inquiry and arbitration can help by enabling certain issues to be resolved authoritatively, while leaving others, such as responsibility, undecided.

4.6 The Value of Inquiry

It is clear from the cases we have considered that, from its inception in the *Dogger Bank* case to its latest use in the *Letelier and Moffitt* case, the international commission of inquiry has compiled a worthwhile yet curiously ambivalent record. Envisaged by the Hague Conventions as an institution for the management of a relatively narrow range of disputes, inquiry has been employed in cases in which 'honour' and 'essential interests' were unquestionably involved, for the determination of legal as well as factual issues, and by tribunals whose composition and proceedings more closely resembled courts than commissions of inquiry as originally conceived. On the other hand, this lateral extension of the role of the commission of inquiry has not, as might have been expected, generated a corresponding increase in business. On the contrary, the four inquiries between 1905 and 1922 were followed by a 40-year gap until the *Red Crusader* in 1962, and, despite the elaborate provisions of various treaties and a General Assembly Resolution[28] urging the use of fact-finding procedures, there has been only one case since. These apparently contradictory tendencies tell us a good deal about the settlement of international disputes in the modern world.

The utilisation of inquiry for disputes as varied as the *Dogger Bank* and *Tavignano* cases is a reminder that, where sovereign states are concerned, form is subordinate to function. Since international disputes are infinitely various in their circumstances and subject matter, it is not surprising that in their search for acceptable procedures states have adapted the inquiry technique to provide a range of institutional solutions, from the 'pure' fact-finding of the *Tiger* inquiry, to the near arbitration of the *Red Crusader* and *Letelier and Moffitt* inquiries.

Why, then, if the inquiry procedure is so flexible, is it not more widely used? Here, the answer is more complex.

First – and the point is so obvious it may easily be overlooked – it is sometimes unnecessary to set up an inquiry because a situation in which the facts are open to different interpretations proves amenable to

---

[28] Resolution 2329 (XXII), 18 December 1967. Text in Waldock, *Legal Aspects* (n. 11) p. 175. See also United Nations, *Handbook on the Peaceful Settlement of Disputes between States*, New York, 1992, ch. 2B.

negotiation. In May 1999, for example, during the 11-week NATO air campaign against the Federal Republic of Yugoslavia, a US aircraft bombed the Chinese embassy in Belgrade, killing three Chinese nationals and wounding 20 others. The attack was evidently a mistake, as those who planned the raid were under the impression that the building was a Yugoslav arms agency, having relied on incorrect intelligence information from the US authorities. As the attack was highly controversial and the circumstances initially unclear, the matter could in principle have been investigated through an international inquiry. In the event, however, it was resolved through discussions involving an explanation and apology and the payment of compensation by the United States.[29]

A second point is that, when an inquiry is needed, there are a number of ways in which it can be carried out without recourse to the machinery of the Hague Conventions. The League of Nations set up its own commissions of inquiry in seven cases, including the *Åland Islands* dispute between Finland and Sweden in 1921 and the *Mosul* dispute between Britain and Turkey in 1925.[30] These commissions, which did not include representatives of the parties, examined the circumstances of each dispute in considerable detail and in some cases also attempted conciliation. The United Nations has used inquiry in a similar way. In 1982, for example, the Security Council established a fact-finding commission to investigate an attempted coup led by foreign mercenaries in the Seychelles, and when chemical weapons were used in the Iran–Iraq war in 1984, Secretary-General Pérez de Cuéllar sent a commission of Swiss, Swedish, Spanish and Australian experts to study the situation at the front and report back.[31] More recently, the UN Human Rights Council (UNHRC) set up an investigation into the armed conflict in Gaza. Published in 2009, the *Gaza Report*[32] concluded that both Israeli and Palestinian armed groups violated their duties under international humanitarian law, thereby committing war crimes. The Report was adopted by both the UNHRC and the UN General Assembly, which called upon both sides to investigate the allegations made against them. Israel subsequently admitted a number of breaches of humanitarian law, but denied allegations of systematic and deliberate violations of international law, while the Palestinian authorities, for their

---

[29] See (2000) 94 *AJIL*, 127, and for another episode involving these states (2001) 95 *AJIL*, 630. See also the acceptance by the United States in March 1989 of an offer of compensation by Iraq for the attack on the USS *Stark* while on station in the Persian Gulf in 1987. See (1989) 83 *AJIL* 561.

[30] See Cot, *International Conciliation* (n. 15) p. 250.

[31] See R. R. Probst, '"Good offices" in international relations in light of Swiss practice and experience' (1987) 201 *Hague Recueil des Cours*, 211 at 372.

[32] *Human Rights in Palestine and Other Occupied Palestinian Territories: Report of the United Nations Fact-Finding Mission on the Gaza Conflict*, UN Doc. A/HRC/12/48 (2009), also known as the Goldstone Report. And see Z. Yihdego, 'The Gaza Mission: Implications for international humanitarian law' (2012) 13 *Melbourne JIL*, 158.

part, claimed to have undertaken investigations, but failed to address key allegations directed at the armed group Hamas. The *Gaza Report* demonstrates the value of outside investigation of disputed factual and legal issues, but also the difficulties where the parties' cooperation is lacking and they are unwilling to accept the investigators' findings.

A more specific aspect of the Gaza situation was the subject of investigation of the *Mavi Marmara* incident in 2010. Here, a flotilla of six vessels was boarded and taken over by Israeli military forces while trying to break the Israeli blockade of Gaza. In the course of the operation, nine activists on board the Turkish ship *Mavi Marmara* were killed and many more were injured. The raid was widely condemned and caused tension between Israel and Turkey, both of which set up inquiries that reached different conclusions. Following an investigation by the UNHRC, the UN Secretary-General set up a four-member inquiry, consisting of one representative each from Israel and Turkey, and with Geoffrey Palmer, the former Prime Minister of New Zealand, as Chair and Alvaro Uribe, the outgoing president of Colombia, as Vice-Chair. In its report,[33] which was published in 2011, the Commission concluded that the blockade of Gaza was legal, but criticised both the decision to board the vessels and the conduct of the flotilla. Both the national members disagreed with the report's conclusions, with the result that it was adopted by the Chair and Vice-Chair, as previously agreed. Despite this rather unsatisfactory outcome, the report seems to have contributed to an improvement in Israeli–Turkish relations.

In 2011, the UNHRC established an international commission of inquiry 'to investigate all alleged violations of international human rights law in Libya, to establish the facts and circumstances of such violations and of the crimes perpetrated and, where possible, to identify those responsible, to make recommendations, in particular, on accountability measures, all with a view to ensuring that those individuals responsible are held accountable'.[34] In the following year, the Commission issued its report. It found that the Libyan government had committed crimes against humanity and war crimes, including murder, enforced disappearances and torture, in attacks against the civilian population. It also found that anti-governmental forces had committed serious violations, but that when NATO had intervened in the conflict it had sought to avoid civilian casualties, though not always successfully. This inquiry, like a number of others conducted by the UNHRC, investigated both factual and legal

---

[33] *Report of the Secretary-General's Panel of Inquiry on the 31 May 2010 Flotilla Incident* (2011) also known as the Palmer Report. And see R. Buchan, 'The Palmer Report and the legality of Israel's naval blockade of Gaza' (2012) 61 *ICLQ*, 264.
[34] *Situation of Human Rights in the Libyan Arab Jamahiriya*, HRC Res, S-15/2, UN Doc. A/HRC/RES/S-15/1 (2011).

issues, and also supplied authoritative evidence as a basis for further action.[35]

An unusual procedure similar in some respects to inquiry is the process established by the Security Council to deal with claims arising from the invasion of Kuwait by Iraq in 1990. Using a body called the UN Compensation Commission,[36] the process enables governments, companies and international organisations to have claims for compensation assessed by expert panels and to receive payment from a special fund financed from a levy on Iraqi oil sales. A very large number of such claims have now been reviewed, resulting in the payment of several billion dollars of compensation. Contrary to what might be thought, the process involved here is not arbitration or adjudication, but administrative in nature as the broad issue of Iraq's liability was settled by Security Council Resolution 687 in 1991, and the proceedings before the Commission are not adversarial and are usually conducted through written submissions. Thus, in the words of the Secretary-General, the Commission 'performs an essentially fact-finding function of examining claims, verifying their validity, evaluating losses, assessing payments and resolving disputed claims'.[37]

The UN's specialised agencies can also conduct inquiries in certain situations. Thus, the International Labour Organization (ILO) has on several occasions created commissions of inquiry to deal with complaints relating to labour conventions, and in September 1983 the International Civil Aviation Organization (ICAO) instructed its Secretary-General to investigate the *KE 007* incident, which involved the shooting down of a South Korean jumbo jet in Soviet airspace. The inquiry report,[38] which was ready by the end of the year, complained of the lack of Soviet cooperation and was unable to shed light on all aspects of the incident. It did, however, serve to establish many of the facts and provided the basis for a resolution in which the ICAO Council condemned the Soviet attack. The resolution in turn facilitated the adoption in May 1984 of an amendment to the Chicago Convention on Civil Aviation,

---

[35] On the role of commissions of inquiry in the context of international criminal law, armed conflicts and atrocities, see L. J. van den Herik, 'An Inquiry into the Role of Commissions of Inquiry in International Law: Navigating the Tensions between Fact-Finding and International Law Application' (2014) 13 *Chinese Journal of International Law*, 507 and C. Harwood, *The Roles and Functions of Atrocity-Related United Nations Commissions of Inquiry in the International Legal Order: Navigating between Principle and Pragmatism*, Leiden/Boston, 2019.

[36] For a description of the Commission, see J. R. Crook, 'The United Nations Compensation Commission: a new structure to enforce state responsibility' (1993) 87 *AJIL*, 144; and, for an account of some of its recent work, see M. Kazazi, 'Environmental damage in the work of the UN Compensation Commission', in M. Bowman and A. E. Boyle (eds), *Environmental Damage in International and Comparative Law*, Oxford, 2002, p. 111.

[37] UN Doc. S/2259 (2 May 1991), para. 20, quoted in J. Collier and V. Lowe, *The Settlement of Disputes in International Law*, Oxford, 1999, p. 42.

[38] *Destruction of Korean Air Lines Boeing 747 over Sea of Japan 31 August 1983, Report of ICAO Fact-Finding Investigation*, ICAO Doc. C-WP/7764 (1983), Attachment, p. 1, reproduced in part in (1984) 23 ILM 864.

designed to reduce the risk of such incidents in the future. Here, then, an inquiry by an organisation was possible without the consent of one of the states involved, and, though the report cannot be said to have settled the dispute, it had an important bearing on its consequences.

A somewhat similar investigation was required in the *MH17* incident[39] in 2014. Here, an airliner on a scheduled passenger flight was shot down over the Ukraine, killing all on board. Since the cause of the crash was unclear, the Dutch Safety Board was commissioned to conduct an inquiry. The reason for Dutch involvement was that under the ICAO Convention the state in which an aviation incident occurs is allowed to delegate an investigation of it to another state, which Ukraine did in this case. In its report, which was published in 2015, the investigation team concluded that the plane was brought down by a ground-to-air missile of a type used by the Russian military. The report also identified an area from which the missile could have been fired and criticised all parties' risk assessment in light of the fact that the route of the flight was known to pass over a conflict area. As in the *KE 007* incident, the inquiry did not settle the dispute, but by pointing to the strong likelihood of the involvement of Russian-backed separatists, it answered some key questions.

In 1993, the World Bank created a kind of standing inquiry procedure when it established an Inspection Panel[40] to receive and review requests from communities, organisations or groups who believe they may be adversely affected by a project funded by the Bank and claim the project may contravene the Bank's operational policies and practices. The Panel's task is first to recommend to the Executive Directors whether the matter should be investigated and then, if asked to do so, to carry out an inspection. The findings of the Panel are not binding, but, based as they are on impartial investigation, utilising visits and consultations, carry considerable weight. As evaluation has a quasi-judicial aspect, Panel reports go beyond inquiry in the strict sense, but clearly incorporate a significant fact-finding element. The World Bank's Panel has begun to develop a useful practice[41] and both the Inter-American Development Bank and the Asian Development Bank now have similar mechanisms.

---

[39] See R. Abeyratne, 'Flight MH17 and state responsibility for ensuring safety and security of air transport' (2014) *J Transp. Secur.*, 347.

[40] For comment on the Panel and its significance, see C. Chinkin, 'Alternative dispute resolution under international law', in M. D. Evans, *Remedies in International Law: The Institutional Dilemma*, Oxford, 1998, p. 123 at pp. 134–7; and P. Sands, *Principles of International Environmental Law*, 2nd ed., Cambridge, 2003, pp. 210–11.

[41] See R. E. Bissell, 'Recent practice of the Inspection Panel of the World Bank' (1997) 91 *AJIL*, 741; and A. N. Gowlland Gualtieri, 'The environmental accountability of the World Bank to non-state actors: insights from the Inspection Panel' (2001) 72 *BYBILI*, 213. Also D. French and R. Kirkham, 'Complaint and grievance mechanisms in international dispute settlement', in D. French, M. Saul and N. D. White (eds), *International Law and Dispute Settlement: New Problems and Techniques*, Oxford, 2010, p. 57 at pp. 68–72.

Regional organisations also set up inquiry commissions from time to time and, as we shall see in Chapter 10, the 1982 Law of the Sea Convention has provision for inquiry in its articles on 'special arbitration'. It was noted earlier that inquiry in the operational sense is a frequent component of judicial settlement. Presumably, therefore, with the creation of standing judicial tribunals in the form of the Permanent Court of International Justice and its successor, the present International Court of Justice, litigation has been employed in a number of disputes which might otherwise have provided subjects for inquiry. Likewise, we shall see in the next chapter that the early inquiry commissions were followed in the interwar period and afterwards by commissions of conciliation, which suggests that the blending of inquiry with conciliation in the League of Nations era also had a diversionary effect.

The fact that there are now many alternatives to the traditional inquiry commission is therefore another reason for the relatively small number of cases. There is, however, a third and more fundamental explanation. All forms of third-party settlement have proved less popular than was once anticipated. States have no compelling reason to regard inquiry as more attractive than, say, judicial settlement, and, as will be seen later, they are prepared to refer disputes to international courts and tribunals only in somewhat exceptional circumstances. The fact of the matter is that states are often less interested in settling a dispute than in having their view prevail. The *KE 007* incident illustrates the point perfectly. This incident, in some ways reminiscent of the *Dogger Bank* affair, might be thought well suited to an inquiry commission of the traditional type. It is true that a dispute involving security interests, accusations of spying and perhaps questions about the Soviet chain of command, is not the kind of dispute which those who drew up the Hague Conventions had in mind. Yet, as we have seen, the commission of inquiry can be, and has been, adapted to deal with just this type of case. From the technical point of view, there would therefore have been no difficulty in establishing an international commission of inquiry to investigate the incident. What prevented this from being done was not any lack of flexibility in the procedures available for dispute settlement, but an unwillingness on the part of the Soviet Union to have its account of the incident or its actions challenged in an international forum. Although this could not prevent the matter from being investigated by the ICAO, it clearly ruled out any possibility of a consensual inquiry commission of the type we have been considering.

It is therefore only in situations in which certain special conditions are satisfied that there is scope for setting up a traditional inquiry commission. As already indicated, these are that the disputed issue is largely one of fact, rather than law or policy; that no other procedure is being employed; and, most important of all, that the parties are willing to accept that their version of events may be shown to be wrong. Such a combination of circumstances evidently does not occur very often. When it does, the highly satisfactory outcome of the *Red Crusader* and *Letelier and Moffitt* cases demonstrates that as a means of dispute settlement, the international commission of inquiry can still produce useful results.

4.7 Further Reading

4.7.1 General References on Inquiry

Bar-Yaacov, N., *The Handling of International Disputes by Means of Inquiry*, Oxford, 1974.

Buchan, R., 'The Palmer Report and the legality of Israel's naval blockade of Gaza' (2012) 61 *ICLQ*, 264.

Chinkin, C., 'Alternative dispute resolution under international law' in M. D. Evans (ed.), *Remedies in International Law: The Institutional Dilemma*, Oxford, 1998.

Harwood, C., *The Roles and Functions of Atrocity-Related United Nations Commissions of Inquiry in the International Legal Order: Navigating between Principle and Pragmatism*, Leiden/Boston, 2019.

van den Herik, L. J., 'An inquiry into the role of commissions of inquiry in international law: navigating the tensions between fact-finding and international law application' (2014) 13 *Chinese Journal of International Law*, 507.

Hyde, C. C., 'The place of commissions of inquiry and conciliation treaties in the peaceful settlement of disputes' (1929) 10 *BYBIL*, 96.

4.7.2 Treaties and Official Documents

Hague Convention on Pacific Settlement of International Disputes (Hague, I) (adopted 29 July 1899, entered into force 4 September 1900), Arts 9–14.

5

Conciliation

Conciliation has been defined as:

> A method for the settlement of international disputes of any nature according to which a Commission set up by the Parties, either on a permanent basis or an *ad hoc* basis to deal with a dispute, proceeds to the impartial examination of the dispute and attempts to define the terms of a settlement susceptible of being accepted by them or of affording the Parties, with a view to its settlement, such aid as they may have requested.[1]

The eclectic character of the method is at once apparent. The Conciliation Commission in the 'Timor Sea Conciliation' explained that conciliation 'seeks to combine the function of a mediator with the more active and objective role of a commission of inquiry'.[2] If mediation is essentially an extension of negotiation, conciliation puts third-party intervention on a formal legal footing and institutionalises it in a way comparable, but not identical, to inquiry or arbitration. For the fact-finding exercise that is the essence of inquiry may or may not be an important element in conciliation, while the search for terms 'susceptible of being accepted' by the parties, but not binding on them, provides a sharp contrast with arbitration and a reminder of the link between conciliation and mediation.

5.1 Emergence of Conciliation

The first treaty to provide for conciliation was concluded between Sweden and Chile in 1920.[3] Its emphasis, however, was on inquiry and the only

---

[1] The quotation is from Art. 1 of the Regulations on the Procedure of International Conciliation adopted by the Institute of International Law in 1961. See (1961) 49(ii) *Annuaire* 385–91. For comment on these provisions, see H. Fox, 'Conciliation', in C. M. H. Waldock (ed.), *International Disputes: The Legal Aspects*, London, 1972, p. 93. N. Bar-Yaacov, *The Handling of International Disputes by Means of Inquiry*, Oxford, 1974, chs 5 and 7, gives a good account of conciliation from the inquiry aspect. For general surveys, see J.-P. Cot, *International Conciliation*, London, 1972; and United Nations, *Handbook on the Peaceful Settlement of Disputes between States*, New York, 1992, ch. 2E. Also S. M. G. Koopmans, *Diplomatic Dispute Settlement*, The Hague, 2008.

[2] 'Timor Sea Conciliation', Report and Recommendations of the Compulsory Conciliation Commission between Timor-Leste and Australia on The Timor Sea, PCA Case No. 2016-10 (9 May 2018), para. 52.

[3] For discussion of the treaty between the United States and Canada relating to boundary waters (1909) and the activities of the International Joint Commission, see Chapter 1. For detailed accounts of the development of conciliation, see J. Efremoff, 'La conciliation internationale'

reference to conciliation is in an article putting it forward as an optional procedure. A number of treaties at about this time dealt with conciliation in a similar way, though in others it was given a more prominent place. In 1921, for example, conciliation and arbitration were laid down as alternative means of settlement in a treaty between Germany and Switzerland. If conciliation were chosen, a Permanent Board of Conciliation would be charged with the twofold task of investigating the facts and the law and formulating proposals for a solution. In 1922, the Assembly of the League of Nations, after some debate, adopted a resolution in which it recommended member states to conclude agreements providing for the submission of disputes to conciliation commissions, and with this encouragement more than twenty treaties providing for some form of conciliation were signed in the first five years of the decade.

The year 1925 was marked by two important developments. First, a treaty between France and Switzerland defined the functions of Permanent Conciliation Commissions in terms which were to become the model for later treaties:

> The duty of the Permanent Conciliation Commission shall be to elucidate the questions in dispute, to collect with that object all useful information by inquiry or otherwise, and to endeavour to bring the Parties to an agreement. It may, after examining the case, intimate to the Parties the terms of settlement which seem to it suitable, and lay down a time-limit within which they are to reach their decision.
>
> At the close of its proceedings the Commission shall draw up a report stating, as the case may be, either that the Parties have come to an agreement and, if need be, the terms of the agreement, or that it has proved impossible to effect a settlement.
>
> The Commission's proceedings must, unless the Parties otherwise agree, be concluded within six months of the day on which the dispute was laid before the Commission.[4]

Then, shortly afterwards, in the four bilateral Locarno treaties,[5] Germany agreed with Belgium, France, Czechoslovakia and Poland that, except where the parties agreed to refer a legal dispute to judicial settlement or arbitration, all disputes between them should be subject to conciliation. The powers of the Permanent Commissions provided for in the Locarno treaties were virtually identical to those provided for in the France–

(1927) 18 *Hague Recueil des Cours*, 5, and 'L'organisation de la conciliation comme moyen deprévenir les guerres' (1937) 59 *Hague Recueil des Cours*, 103. See also C. C. Hyde, 'The place of commissions of inquiry and conciliation treaties in the peaceful settlement of disputes' (1929) 10 BYBIL, 96.

[4] M. Habicht, *Post War Treaties for the Pacific Settlement of International Disputes*, Cambridge, MA, 1931, p. 226.

[5] There were seven Locarno treaties in total: the four mentioned in the text and three treaties of guarantee.

Switzerland Treaty, and this formula was again employed when the Locarno approach was endorsed by the Assembly of the League of Nations and embodied in the multilateral General Act for the Pacific Settlement of International Disputes in 1928.

Under the General Act, the parties agreed to set up permanent bilateral commissions, or an ad hoc commission if no permanent commission was in existence at the time of the dispute. Conciliation was to be compulsory unless the states concerned had accepted the jurisdiction of the Permanent Court of International Justice (PCIJ) and if conciliation was unsuccessful the dispute had to be taken to arbitration. The General Act was revised in 1949, but no change was made in these arrangements, which had also been incorporated in a treaty between Czechoslovakia, Romania and the Kingdom of the Serbs, Croatians and Slovenes in 1929.

Although much influenced in its early period by the example of the Bryan treaties, conciliation acquired its prominence as a means of dispute settlement from treaty practice in Europe. It was not long, however, before the new process crossed the Atlantic. As early as 1923, the United States and five Central American states signed the Treaty of Washington, which provided for the creation of commissions with powers of conciliation as well as inquiry. As already noted, the Gondra Treaty of the same year reverted to the Bryan arrangements for enlarged inquiry, but, in response to the General Act and the vogue for conciliation in Europe, the Inter-American General Convention of Conciliation (1929) revised the Gondra Treaty to enable commissions of inquiry, established under Article IV, to exercise wide powers of conciliation. These developments were taken a stage further in 1933, when a protocol to the 1929 Treaty provided for the creation of permanent bilateral commissions, and at the same time the multilateral Saavedra Lamas Agreement[6] incorporated conciliation provisions modelled on those of the General Act.

The period between 1925 and the Second World War saw the climax of the worldwide movement in favour of conciliation, and by 1940 nearly 200 treaties had been concluded. The majority were patterned on the 1925 France–Switzerland Treaty, though there were significant differences of approach to such important matters as the function of commissions of conciliation and their procedure which, as we shall see, were subsequently reflected in their work.

5.2 Work of Commissions of Conciliation

In 1931, a Germany–Lithuania Commission met to consider a dispute occasioned by the expulsion of five Germans from Memel. Three years

---

[6] See P. C. Jessup, 'The Argentine Anti-War Pact' (1934) 28 *AJIL*, 538.

later, a Belgium–Luxembourg Commission examined a dispute over contraband traffic, and in 1938 a dispute between Denmark and Lithuania over the construction of a railway was referred to conciliation. It is known that all three disputes were eventually settled on the basis of the Commissions' recommendations, but information concerning the activities of these and other commissions in the inter-war period is scant, owing to the confidential nature of the procedure and the fact that their reports were never published.[7] The work of later commissions is better documented, and, by studying some of the more prominent cases, it is possible to grasp the purposes for which the machinery described in the previous section has been employed.

5.2.1 The Chaco Commission

The Chaco Commission[8] was set up after an outbreak of fighting at Fort Vanguardia on the border between Bolivia and Paraguay. Established as a result of the good offices of the Conference of American States, meeting to revise the Gondra Treaty, the Commission consisted of two delegates from each party to the dispute and one each from the United States and four other American States. Under the terms of the protocol creating the Commission, its functions were to carry out an inquiry and to submit proposals for a settlement. If its proposals were not accepted, it was to draw up a report and, if it was not able to effect conciliation, it was 'to establish both the truth of the matter investigated and the responsibilities which, in accordance with international law, may appear as a result of its investigation'.[9]

The Commission met for six months and studied a large quantity of evidence from each of the parties, as well as the testimony of both sides' prisoners. In September 1929, it unanimously adopted a resolution of conciliation, in which it was able to announce that the parties had agreed to a mutual waiver of their claims, to a restoration of the territorial status quo and to a resumption of diplomatic relations.

The success of the Commission meant that it had no need to draw up a report. It is clear, nonetheless, that a large part of the Commission's time was taken up with the investigation of how the fighting had broken out and other disputed questions of fact. In this respect, the Chaco Commission bears an obvious resemblance to the cases considered in the previous

---

[7] An outline of the work of pre-war commissions of conciliation can be found in Cot, *International Conciliation* (n. 1) pp. 91–2; and Koopmans, *Diplomatic Dispute Settlement* (n. 1) pp. 87–9.
[8] See *Proceedings of the Commission of Inquiry and Conciliation, Bolivia and Paraguay, March 13, 1929–September 13, 1929* (1929). For commentary, see L. Woolsey, 'Commission of inquiry and conciliation, Bolivia and Paraguay' (1929) 23 *AJIL*, 110 and (1930) 24 *AJIL*, 122 and 573.
[9] See (1929) 23 *AJIL*, 98.

chapter, with the important difference that here inquiry was not the sole, nor even the primary, function of the Commission, but simply a way of preparing the ground for the parties' reconciliation.

5.2.2 The France–Siam Conciliation Commission

A very different kind of frontier dispute came before the France–Siam Conciliation Commission in 1947.[10] Siam claimed that its frontier with French Indo-China should be altered for a combination of ethnic, geographical and economic reasons; France disagreed. An agreement between the two states established a conciliation commission, composed of one representative of each party and three neutral Commissioners, to consider the question. Both the composition and the powers of the Commission were established in accordance with the 1928 General Act.

After hearing the parties' evidence and their replies to certain questions, the Commission tried to move the parties towards agreement. When this proved unsuccessful, the Commission drew up a report in which it summarised the parties' arguments and its own conclusions and made a number of specific recommendations. Although it suggested minor adjustments of the frontier, together with certain modifications to the frontier regime, the Commission's report was effectively a rejection of the Siamese claim. The Siamese request for the transfer of the whole of Laos was rejected as beyond the Commission's competence, while its examination of the ethnic, geographical and economic evidence led the Commission to conclude that there would be no advantage in moving the frontier in any of the other disputed areas.

In the Franco-Siamese dispute, the Commission's investigation of the facts was not concerned with specific events, as in the *Chaco* case, but rather with the whole ethnic, geographical and economic situation in the frontier region. Moreover, the Commission's concern was not merely to identify the relevant material on these matters, but also to determine its significance with respect to the issue of frontier rectification and conciliation, a matter of interpretation of the evidence with no counterpart in the earlier case.

The *Franco-Siamese* dispute was unusual in the sense that it was a straightforward conflict of political interests. In most disputes submitted to conciliation, law, as well as politics, has been involved. In 1952, the Belgium–Denmark Commission[11] was asked to examine the circumstances in which two Danish merchant ships, the *Gorm* and the *Svava*, had been

---

[10] See S. Bastid, 'La Commission de conciliation franco-siamoise', in *Etudes en l'honneur de Georges Scelle*, vol. I, Paris, 1950, p. 1.

[11] See H. Rolin, 'Une conciliation belgo-danoise' (1953) 57 *RGDIP*, 353.

evacuated from Antwerp when Belgium was overrun by the Germans in 1940. Both vessels had subsequently been lost and the Commission, which was established in accordance with a Belgium–Denmark Treaty of 1927, was required to advise on whether Belgium should pay compensation. To answer this question, the Commission sought first to determine the legal character of the actions taken by the Belgian authorities. The Commission was agreed that the vessels had not been seized as prize, but was divided as to whether they could be said to have been requisitioned. If the Commission had been a court of arbitration, a ruling on this point would have been essential. However, since its task was conciliation, it was able to leave the issue unresolved, and to propose an agreement, which the parties accepted, under which Belgium paid a reduced amount of compensation to reflect the element of uncertainty in the Danish claim.

5.2.3 The 1955 France–Switzerland Commission

In 1955, the France–Switzerland Commission,[12] acting under the influential 1925 Treaty mentioned earlier, handled another dispute with a significant legal dimension. Like the *Belgian–Danish* case, it arose from the traumatic events of 1940. When France surrendered to the Germans, a Polish division which had fought as part of the French army crossed into Switzerland and was interned. The internment lasted until 1945 and the dispute was over who should pay the cost. Switzerland maintained that, as the unit had been fighting for France, the responsibility was French; France stated that, as the soldiers were Poles, the responsibility was Poland's. Since the facts were not really in dispute, the Commission's investigation was largely concerned with legal issues. After hearing the parties' arguments, the Commission proposed that France should pay the costs of the internment up to February 1941, the date when French internees had been freed, and that for reasons of equity France should pay Switzerland a substantial sum as compensation for the remaining years. If the dispute had been referred to arbitration, this result, which was accepted by the parties, might have been different. As in the previous case, however, it is clear that the Commission's appreciation of the parties' legal rights formed the framework of its proposals for conciliation.[13]

---

[12] See F. M. Van Asbeck, 'La tâche et l'action d'une Commission de conciliation' (1956) 3 *NTIR*, 1, and 'La procédure suivie par la Commission permanente de conciliation franco-suisse' (1956) 3 *NTIR*, 209. Also S. Bastid, 'La commission de conciliation franco-suisse' (1956) 2 *AFDI*, 436; and A. Gros, 'Remarques sur la conciliation internationale', in *L'Evolution du Droit Public: Etudes Offertes à Achille Mestre*, Paris, 1956, p. 279.

[13] The Commission also succeeded in resolving another dispute at the same time. This concerned the alleged violation of Swiss territorial sovereignty by French customs officials and appears mainly to have turned on the facts. See Bar-Yaacov, *Inquiry* (n. 1) pp. 220–4.

5.2.4 The 1956 Italy–Switzerland Commission

Legal issues were even more prominent in the next case to be considered, a dispute which was brought to the Italy–Switzerland Commission[14] in 1956 over whether Swiss nationals could claim exemption from a special Italian property tax. The nationals of allied states already enjoyed exemption under the Treaty of Peace with Italy (1947) and an earlier treaty between Switzerland and Italy contained a most favoured nation clause. The question therefore was whether that clause applied to the preferential arrangements contained in the Peace Treaty.

The Commission, set up in accordance with the Italy–Switzerland Treaty of Conciliation and Judicial Settlement of 1924, took the view that its duty was 'to consider in the first place the legal aspects of the dispute'[15] and found that Swiss nationals were not entitled to exemption from the tax. However, it also decided that the treaty provision in question did entitle Swiss nationals to equality of treatment under Italian law, and that the disputed legislation violated this standard of equality by discriminating against foreign corporations. Taking this and the various facts which had emerged in the course of the proceedings into account, the Commission proposed as an 'equitable settlement' of the dispute that Swiss nationals should pay the tax, but that its impact should be lightened in various ways.[16] This proposal was accepted by the parties.

5.2.5 The *East African Community* case

In the cases considered so far, conciliation was carried out by commissions containing several members, and this is the usual arrangement under bilateral or multilateral treaties. It is, however, open to states to refer a dispute to a single conciliator, and this was the procedure adopted in 1977 when Kenya, Uganda and Tanzania asked the experienced Swiss diplomat, Dr Victor Umbricht, to make proposals for the distribution of the assets of the former East African Community (EAC).[17] The dispute had arisen because the partner states, having integrated their economic activities both before and after independence, had now decided to go their separate ways. Before this could be done, it was necessary for an agreement

---

[14] See M. Breton-Jokl, 'La Commission permanente de conciliation italo-suisse' (1957) 3 *AFDI*, 210.
[15] (1958) 25 ILR 316.   [16] See the annex to the report of the Commission, *ibid.*, p. 322.
[17] For a comprehensive account of this case, see V. Umbricht, 'Principles of international mediation: the case of the East African Community' (1984) 187 *Hague Recueil des Cours*, 307. Although termed by the parties a 'mediator', Dr Umbricht was clearly engaged in conciliation. For a less successful contribution by an individual mediator/conciliator, see K. R. Simmonds, 'The Belize mediation' (1968) 17 *ICLQ*, 996; and J. G. Merrills, 'The Belize–Guatemala territorial dispute and the legal opinion of January 2002' (2002) *Global Community YBILJ*, 77 at 80–1 and 91–2.

to be reached on the extent of the EAC's assets and liabilities and, more contentiously, on their allocation. As the three states were unable to resolve these matters by negotiation, they were encouraged by the World Bank to give Dr Umbricht a wide-ranging brief to investigate the whole issue and bring forward proposals for its resolution.

From the first it was apparent that the conciliator's task was one of outstanding difficulty. The assets of the EAC included land, ships, aircraft, railways and rolling stock, as well as plant, machinery and spares and various non-physical assets. These were spread across East Africa and, along with the Community's liabilities, had to be located and valued. Less than a year had been allowed for compiling an inventory, but, not surprisingly, the process actually took four years and eventually revealed assets with a net value exceeding US$1 billion.

The conciliator then had to find appropriate criteria for distribution. Various possibilities were rejected as unsuitable, but at last a formula was found which gave Kenya 42.7 per cent of the assets, Tanzania 34.3 per cent and Uganda 23 per cent. When this was put to the parties, they did not immediately accept it, but, as they were entitled to do, used the conciliator's proposals as a basis for negotiation. With further assistance from Dr Umbricht, an agreement winding up the affairs of the EAC was finally concluded in May 1984. Although the division of assets under the agreement differed slightly from that originally proposed, it is clear that the reports and findings of the conciliator made a vital contribution to the settlement.

5.2.6 The *Jan Mayen* case

A later dispute referred to conciliation involved a commission of the conventional type and, though it raised some difficult issues of law and fact, was more straightforward than the *East African Community* case. In 1980, Iceland and Norway set up a commission to make recommendations with regard to the dividing line for the area of continental shelf between Iceland and Jan Mayen Island. The Commission was directed to take into account Iceland's 'strong economic interests' in the sea areas in question, together with 'the existing geographical and geological factors and other special circumstances'. Following a detailed investigation of the evidence pertaining to these matters, the Commission proposed a joint development agreement covering substantially all of the area offering any significant prospect of hydrocarbon production. This recommendation (see Appendix D) was subsequently accepted by the parties, and in 1981 was incorporated into a treaty which ended the dispute.[18]

---

[18] For the Commission's report, see (1981) 20 ILM 797 and 62 ILR 108. For the treaty, which substantially incorporated the Commission's recommendations, see (1982) 21 ILM 1222. For

5.3 Practice of Conciliation

All conciliation commissions have the same functions: to investigate the dispute and to suggest the terms of a possible settlement. However, as our review of some of the cases has already indicated, within this broad mandate, arbitration panels have performed a variety of different tasks. What a commission does and how it goes about its work depend, in the first place, on the instrument setting it up. But much also depends on how the parties choose to present the particular case, and how the members of the commission see their role. Consequently, though the practice of conciliation commissions exhibits many common features, significant differences of approach to the most basic matters are also to be found.

5.3.1 The Nature of Conciliation

What sort of process is conciliation? One view is that it is to be regarded as a kind of institutionalised negotiation. The task of the commission is to encourage and structure the parties' dialogue, while providing them with whatever assistance may be necessary to bring it to a successful conclusion. This approach, which proceeds from the premise that the resolution of disputes depends on securing the parties' agreement, finds an affinity between conciliation and mediation and can best be seen in the work of the Chaco Commission, the France–Siam Commission and the Commission in the *Jan Mayen* dispute.[19] Another view is that conciliation is closer to inquiry or arbitration,[20] that the commission's function is to provide information and advice as to the merits of the parties' positions and to suggest a settlement that corresponds to what they deserve, not what they claim. This approach, which can be seen in the work of the Belgium–Denmark Commission and the *East African Community* conciliation, reflects the historical link between conciliation and the procedure for enlarged inquiry contained in the Bryan treaties.

Clearly, a commission's views as to the nature of conciliation are likely to exercise an important influence on its work. A commission which sees conciliation as a form of quasi-arbitration, or which is required to perform this function by the parties, will naturally tend to operate more formally than one which sees itself primarily as a forum for negotiation. Thus, in the

---

reflections on the case by the chairman of the Commission, see E. L. Richardson, 'Jan Mayen in perspective' (1988) 82 *AJIL*, 443. And see also R. R. Churchill, 'Maritime delimitation in the Jan Mayen area' (1985) *Marine Policy*, 16.

[19] See also the 'Facilitation Process' initiated by Belize and Guatemala assisted by the OAS in 2000, discussed in Merrills, 'The Belize–Guatemala territorial dispute' (n. 17) 81 and 93–4, and in Koopmans, *Diplomatic Dispute Settlement* (n. 1) pp. 102–4.

[20] See the views expressed in Professor Rolin's report to the Institute of International Law in (1959) 48(i) *Annuaire*, 30–42.

Belgian–Danish case, both written and oral proceedings were reminiscent of an arbitration. In the *Jan Mayen* case, on the other hand, the Commission decided that, since its purpose was to submit unanimous recommendations and its two national members had participated in all previous diplomatic negotiations, pleadings of any kind were unnecessary. An intermediate position was taken in the *Franco-Siamese* case where written and oral proceedings were intermingled, and in the *Franco-Swiss* and *Italo-Swiss* cases where the oral proceedings were quite informal and the parties' agents sat alongside the members of the commission and participated fully in its work.

5.3.2 The Role and Powers of Conciliation Commissions

A conciliation commission has a duty to examine the nature and background of a dispute and so is usually equipped with wide powers of investigation. Unlike an inquiry, however, whose whole *raison d'être* is to illuminate the dispute, a conciliation commission has as its objective the parties' conciliation. Its investigative powers are thus simply a means to an end. As a result, if it becomes apparent that the exposure of some matter might make conciliation more difficult, that line of investigation is unlikely to be pursued. In 1958, a France–Morocco Conciliation Commission was set up to investigate the French authorities' diversion of an aircraft carrying Ben Bella and four other leaders of the Algerian revolt from Morocco to Tunis.[21] The Commission was asked by Morocco to permit the questioning of all the passengers on the diverted plane, but refused to do so on the ground that 'to have taken this evidence would, in the opinion of the Commission, have been likely to embitter Franco–Moroccan relations and thus defeat the purpose of the mission with which the Commission had been entrusted by the two governments'.[22]

A commission can obtain information in different ways. The commission in the *Jan Mayen* case obtained its evidence on technical matters by convening a meeting at Columbia University at which geologists and geophysicists who had conducted research in the area described their findings. The Chaco Commission declined to carry out a survey to establish the location of Fort Vanguardia, but arranged for each side's prisoners to be questioned by neutral committees in Argentina and Brazil. The France–Siam Commission neither visited the disputed area, nor took testimony from witnesses, but relied for its information on a questionnaire, devised in consultation with the parties.

---

[21] See Note, 'L'Affaire du F-OABV' (1958) 4 *AFDI* 282; and C. Rousseau, 'Echec de la procédure d'enquête et de conciliation dans l'affaire du déeroutement de l'avion transportant de Rabat à Tunis les chefs nationalistes algériens le 22 octobre 1956' (1958) 62 *RGDIP*, 691.

[22] Cot, *International Conciliation* (n. 1) p. 193.

In the *East African Community* case, the nature of the conciliator's remit was such as to make the gathering of information a vital part of his work. Identifying and listing the assets of the Community, and then putting a value on them, was, however, an enormous and complex task. Recognising that, if he was to carry this out, Dr Umbricht would need assistance, the partner states authorised him to appoint consultants and full advantage was taken of this facility.[23] One of the conciliator's first actions was to set up an auditing board composed of experts in accounting, finance and engineering to advise him on the formulation of guidelines and their application. In addition to this body, which met at regular intervals, Dr Umbricht also engaged more than forty technical and financial experts for limited periods to assemble and check information. These were organised into working groups and between them prepared draft reports on all the EAC institutions. The draft reports were passed to the governments for comment and eventually provided the basis both for the preparation of the conciliator's proposals relating to the distribution of assets and for the parties' subsequent negotiations.

As already noted, many of the disputes handled by conciliation commissions have raised questions of law, and this is reflected in their membership, which has usually been made up of lawyers, though diplomats, like Dr Umbricht, and individuals with technical expertise have also been employed. In a case involving the complex financial consequences of a pre-war Japanese loan, the parties appointed the President of the International Monetary Fund as sole conciliator,[24] and, in a later case[25] with similar subject matter, the President of the International Bank for Reconstruction and Development served in the same capacity.

How active should the commission be in seeking to bring the parties together? In the earliest conciliation treaties, the duties of the commission were to hold its investigation and make its proposals, leaving the parties to perform the act of conciliation. Though this approach was followed by the conciliators in the two *Japanese loan* cases, other commissions have tried to play a more active role. Both the France–Siam Commission and the Italy–Switzerland Commission attempted to bring the parties together after the completion of the investigation and prior to the presentation of the report, and in the second case the Commission was successful. The Chaco Commission adopted a more radical approach and began its work of conciliation before it had begun its investigation, an unusual procedure, redolent of mediation rather than conciliation.

---

[23] See Umbricht, 'Principles of international mediation' (n. 17) 328–41.
[24] See *In re Imperial Japanese Government 4% Loan of 1910 Issued in France – Methods of Resumption of Service*, 29 ILR 4. In the event, another expert, M. von Steyern, deputised for the IMF President.
[25] *In re City of Tokyo 5% Loan of 1912 – Plan for Resumption of Payment and Interest on the French Tranche of the Loan*, 29 ILR 11.

Whether a commission is engaged upon investigation, or the formulation of proposals and the work of conciliation, the confidentiality of its proceedings is essential to its prospects of success. Disputes invariably raise delicate issues; it is much easier for governments to offer concessions privately, and so secrecy has been the general rule. In the *Ben Bella* affair, a request by Morocco for public hearings was rejected, presumably on the ground that, in a case which had already aroused the bitterest feelings, the cause of conciliation would not be furthered by the spotlight of publicity.[26] Even the Chaco Commission, which did conduct some of its proceedings in public, held its most sensitive sessions behind closed doors.

As previously noted, one of the distinctive features of conciliation is that a commission's report takes the form of a set of proposals, not a decision. Thus, even in cases where law has been a major consideration, the report is quite different from an arbitral award and not binding on the parties. This feature of conciliation has presented commissions with something of a dilemma. On the one hand, they wish to make their proposals as persuasive as possible by supporting them with reasons; on the other hand, they are unwilling to provide the parties with legal arguments or findings of fact that may be cited in subsequent litigation. The Belgium–Denmark Commission adopted the curious expedient of accompanying a written statement of its conclusions with an oral explanation of its reasons. The France–Switzerland and Italy–Switzerland Commissions adopted the more satisfactory practice of providing a written account of both conclusions and reasons, subject to a restriction that 'the opinion of the Commission on points of law may not be invoked by the parties before any tribunal, judicial or arbitral'.[27] A later treaty of conciliation[28] contains a provision to the same effect, indicating that the need for such precautions is well recognised.

Because the proposals of a conciliation commission can be either accepted or rejected, the usual practice is for the commission to give the parties a specified period of a few months in which to indicate their response. If its proposals are accepted, the commission draws up a *procès verbal* (agreement) recording the fact of conciliation and setting out the terms of the settlement. If the proposed terms are rejected, then conciliation has failed and the parties are under no further obligation. Thus, in the normal case, the functions of a conciliator come to an end with the presentation of a report, and everything thereafter is in the hands of the parties. It is, however, open to states to agree on a different arrangement and to ask the conciliator to perform a more extensive role. In this respect the *East African Community* case is again instructive.

---

[26] On the damaging consequences of the sensationalism of the French journal *L'Express* in this case, see Cot, *International Conciliation* (n. 1) pp. 166–7.
[27] (1958) 25 ILR 321. See also Koopmans, *Diplomatic Dispute Settlement* (n. 1) pp. 153–5.
[28] Treaty for Conciliation, Judicial Settlement and Arbitration between the United Kingdom and the Swiss Confederation (1965) Cmnd 2741.

After identifying the relevant assets and liabilities and valuing them, both processes in which the partner states were closely involved, Dr Umbricht heard their legal, economic and financial arguments, and, in October 1981, produced a report containing his proposals on distribution. A series of ministerial meetings was then held with a view to negotiating an agreement. At these meetings, it became apparent that the parties were divided as to the choice of criteria for distribution and the weight to be given to each. With a view to bridging the financial gap between what the parties wanted and what was available, Dr Umbricht approached a number of foreign governments to explore possible sources of financial assistance. These efforts, which had the consent of the partner states, were unsuccessful, and so, in February 1983, the conciliator, at the request of the parties, presented a further report to the Presidents of the partner states. Between the presentation of this report and the meeting of the Presidents in November, Dr Umbricht engaged in shuttle diplomacy in an attempt to bring the positions closer together. As noted earlier, this was successful, and the final agreement was signed in May 1984, seven years after the breakdown of the Community.[29] Thus, in this case, the conciliator's involvement was both varied and unusually protracted, first supervising a far-reaching inquiry and bringing forward proposals for a settlement, then acting as mediator in the final phases of the dispute.

5.4 Place of Conciliation in Modern Treaty Law

In the period since 1945, conciliation has retained a place in bilateral treaty practice, though on a much diminished scale. A handful of treaties were concluded in the years after the war, and more recently Switzerland, the leading exponent of conciliation, has concluded treaties with the United Kingdom and a number of other states. Apart from treaties of this kind, which establish general obligations, it is, of course, open to states to make an agreement setting up a commission for an individual dispute. Ad hoc arrangements of this type were the basis of the conciliators' jurisdiction in the *Jan Mayen* dispute and the *East African Community* case, and, in 1986, formed part of an agreement between Egypt and Israel relating to the settlement of a boundary dispute in the Taba area.[30] This latter treaty was

---

[29] For an account of events after the presentation of the conciliator's report, see Umbricht, 'Principles of international mediation' (n. 17) 356–8. A rather similar function was performed by Sir Arthur Watts who was appointed Special Negotiator for Succession Issues by the High Representative for Yugoslavia in 1996. In that capacity he provided drafts of a framework for negotiation by the parties which eventually led to a settlement in 2001. See Koopmans, *Diplomatic Dispute Settlement* (n. 1) p. 49.

[30] See Agreement to Arbitrate the Boundary Dispute concerning the Taba Beachfront, Egypt–Israel (1986), text in (1987) 26 ILM 1. Also, Koopmans, *Diplomatic Dispute Settlement* (n. 1) pp. 63–6.

unusual because, although it was primarily an arbitration agreement, it included detailed arrangements for conciliation while the arbitration was in progress. However, conciliation, when attempted, was unsuccessful and so in the end this dispute had to be settled by arbitration.[31]

5.4.1 Conciliation in Multilateral Treaties

If conciliation has rather fallen out of favour in bilateral treaty practice, multilateral treaties show a quite different pattern. The Pact of Bogotá (1948) provides for conciliation, along with a variety of other procedures and, as we shall see in Chapter 13, the relation between the provisions in the Pact dealing with conciliation and those providing for judicial settlement was one of the issues considered by the ICJ in a case in 1988.[32] The European Convention for the Peaceful Settlement of Disputes (1957) similarly provides for conciliation in a provision modelled on the France–Switzerland Treaty of 1925. Other regional agreements containing references to conciliation include the Charter of the Organization of African Unity (1963) and the Treaty Establishing the Organization of Eastern Caribbean States (1981).[33] In the former, conciliation was one of the functions of the Commission of Mediation, Conciliation and Arbitration envisaged in a protocol of 1964;[34] in the latter agreement, on the other hand, conciliation is provided for in an annex to the treaty which establishes a panel of conciliators from which commissions can be drawn when required.

Conciliation is also available under the settlement provisions of a number of treaties on particular topics. It is not the purpose of this book to describe the arrangements for settling disputes in particular fields in any detail, but it is appropriate to mention that conciliation is a favoured procedure in agreements concerned with international trade[35] and is also prominent in treaties for the protection of human rights. Thus, under Article 38 of the European Convention on Human Rights, one of the functions of the European Court of Human Rights is to 'place itself at the disposal of the parties concerned with a view to securing a friendly settlement of the matter on the basis of respect for human rights as defined

---

[31] See *Boundary Dispute concerning the Taba Area*, Arbitration Award, 1988, text in (1988) 27 ILM 1421, summarised in (1989) 83 *AJIL*, 590. For further discussion, see Chapter 6.
[32] See *Border and Transborder Armed Actions*, Jurisdiction and Admissibility, Judgment [1988] ICJ Rep. 69.
[33] Text in (1981) 20 ILM 1166.
[34] See Chapter 13. In the event, the Commission never became operational and was dropped when the OAU was replaced in 2001 by the new African Union: see C. A. A. Packer and D. Rukare, 'The new African Union and its Constitutive Act' (2002) 96 *AJIL*, 365 at 376.
[35] See Chapter 11.

in the Convention and the protocols thereto', and equivalent provisions are to be found in other instruments.[36]

Under the Convention in its original form, the promotion of friendly settlements was one of the responsibilities of the European Commission of Human Rights, a group of human rights experts which dealt with all cases taken to Strasbourg. Since the restructuring of the system and the abolition of the Commission in 1999, this function has passed to the Court which in practice means that it is now carried out by the Registrar.[37] Although the vast majority of cases, and consequently friendly settlements, involve claims brought by individuals, in the rarer inter-state cases the same possibilities are available. Thus, in 2000, the case of *Denmark* v. *Turkey*[38] was settled in this way. The claim, which involved alleged maltreatment of a Danish citizen, was resolved following an agreement in which Turkey acknowledged various incidents of wrongdoing, undertook to pay a substantial sum by way of compensation and committed itself to certain human rights projects. This was fundamentally a bilateral settlement to which the Registry, acting under Article 38, contributed advice on drafting.

In the present context, two general points are particularly worth noting about Article 38. One is that, as part of a functioning system of rights protection, this is a type of conciliation provision which is regularly used. The other is that, by referring to a friendly settlement 'on the basis of respect for human rights', the Convention makes it clear that the purpose of this provision is not simply to achieve a settlement without further recourse to Strasbourg, but to enable cases to be disposed of informally, while at the same time observing the Convention's basic values. The fact that here, and in other human rights treaties, conciliation is more than a means of securing a settlement which the parties can accept, but has an additional – and crucial – substantive component, is clearly something which distinguishes friendly settlement under these arrangements from conciliation as generally understood.

Conciliation in the conventional sense is provided for in numerous treaties on other topics. Indeed, the inclusion of arrangements for conciliation either in combination with, or as an alternative to, other procedures,

---

[36] See International Covenant on Civil and Political Rights (1966), Arts. 41 and 42; International Convention on the Elimination of All Forms of Racial Discrimination (1965), Art. 12; American Convention on Human Rights (1969), Arts. 48 and 49; and African Charter on Human and Peoples' Rights (1981), Art. 52. For discussion of conciliation in these and other human rights treaties, see A. H. Robertson and J. G. Merrills, *Human Rights in the World*, 4th ed., Manchester, 1996.

[37] On the evolution of the friendly settlement procedure, see Koopmans, *Diplomatic Dispute Settlement* (n. 1) pp. 184–99.

[38] *Denmark* v. *Turkey*, Case No. 34382/97, ECtHR (Friendly Settlement), 5 April 2000. On an earlier inter-state case brought by Denmark, France, the Netherlands, Norway and Sweden against Turkey and also resolved by a friendly settlement, see Koopmans, *Diplomatic Dispute Settlement* (n. 1) p. 190.

has become almost a routine feature of modern multilateral treaties. The 1969 Vienna Convention on the Law of Treaties,[39] for example, provides for disputes concerning the interpretation or application of the articles on *ius cogens* to be referred to the International Court and for other disputes relating to the validity or termination of treaty obligations to be dealt with by compulsory conciliation. The arrangements for setting up a commission are set out in some detail in an annex to the Convention. The annex provides for the Secretary-General to maintain a list of qualified jurists as available conciliators. Commissions are created by each party nominating two members, not necessarily from the list; the four members so appointed then appoint a fifth, who acts as chairman. A feature of the procedure is that any appointment not made within the specified period can be made by the Secretary-General, so preventing frustration of the process. The commission 'hears the parties, examines the claims and objections and makes proposals to the parties with a view to reaching an amicable settlement of the dispute'[40] and must submit its report within twelve months of its constitution. In light of a point raised earlier, it is interesting to note that the annex envisages a commission's report including 'conclusions regarding the facts or questions of law', but, as well as stating that it is not binding on the parties, lays down that it 'has no other character than that of recommendations submitted for the consideration of the parties in order to facilitate an amicable settlement of the dispute'.[41]

The 1975 Convention on the Representation of States in their Relations with International Organizations of a Universal Character[42] and the 1978 Vienna Convention on Succession of States in respect of Treaties[43] contain arrangements for conciliation along lines which are generally similar. In both Conventions, consultation is a prerequisite for activating the conciliation machinery and, as in the 1969 Convention, the setting up of a commission cannot be prevented by default. The 1975 Convention is unusual in that it provides for commissions of three, rather than five, members and also mentions the possibility of a commission recommending that the international organisation concerned seek an advisory opinion from the International Court. The 1978 Convention, on the other hand, is unique in providing for the expenses of its conciliation commissions to be borne by the United Nations. Both conventions provide in the usual way that the recommendations of a commission shall not be regarded as binding. However, the earlier convention adds the words 'unless all the parties to the dispute have accepted them' (Article 85(7)) and also provides for a party to declare that it will abide by such recommendations unilaterally.

---

[39] Text in (1969) 63 *AJIL*, 875. [40] Annex, para. 5. [41] *Ibid.*, para. 6.
[42] Text in (1975) 69 *AJIL*, 730. [43] Text in (1978) 72 *AJIL*, 971.

The 1965 ICSID Convention[44] contains elaborate arrangements for the settlement of disputes between foreign investors and the host state, including a substantial section on conciliation. Although, as will be seen in Chapter 7, the emphasis in the Convention is on arbitration, the provisions on conciliation are sufficiently detailed to enable the parties to an investment dispute to employ it, if they wish. The Convention thus provides for a conciliation commission to be set up, on the request of either party, consisting of 'persons of high moral character and recognised competence in the fields of law, commerce, industry or finance, who may be relied upon to exercise independent judgment' (Article 14(1)). The commission's task is to hear the parties' representations and then recommend terms for a settlement. Finally, whether the parties have accepted the settlement or not, the Commission is to draw up a report (Article 34). In practice, however, the conciliation procedure has been little used. The ICSID reports that as of 30 June 2020, it has administered only 12 investor-state conciliation cases, which starkly contrasts with the 756 investor-state arbitrations it has administered in the same period under both the ICSID Arbitration Rules (689) and the ICSID Additional Facility Rules (67). Moreover, the same statistics show that in 86 per cent of the conciliation cases parties fail to reach an agreement, leaving thus a meagre 14 per cent of successful conciliation cases.[45] It is the disuse of the conciliation procedure that prompted the International Bar Association to produce its Rules for Investor–State Mediation, described in Chapter 3.

5.4.2 Conciliation in Combination with other Methods of Settlement

Striking examples of the use of conciliation in combination with other methods of settlement can also be seen in a number of treaties concerned with the environment. For example, the 1985 Vienna Convention for the Protection of the Ozone Layer[46] provides that, in the event of a dispute relating to the interpretation or application of the Convention, the parties must first attempt to settle the dispute by negotiation. If negotiation is unsuccessful, they may jointly seek the good offices or mediation of a third party. To deal with disputes which are still outstanding, states may further declare that they accept either arbitration or the jurisdiction of the International Court. Finally, if the parties have each accepted a different

---

[44] See A. Broches, 'The Convention on the Settlement of Investment Disputes between States and Nationals of Other States' (1972) 136 *Hague Recueil des Cours*, 331.
[45] International Centre for Settlement of Investment Disputes, 'The ICSID Caseload — Statistics' (Issue 2020-2), pp. 9 and 15.
[46] Text in (1987) 26 ILM 1516. It should be noted, however, that Art. 8 of the 1987 Montreal Protocol to the Vienna Convention provides for the creation of a noncompliance procedure which has made the dispute settlement provisions described above much less important. See the text accompanying note 59 below.

procedure, or if they have accepted no procedure, they are obliged to submit the dispute to conciliation, unless they can agree on some other means of settlement. The Convention deals rather briefly with the arrangements for constituting a commission, but the essential points are covered.

Similar arrangements are to be found in the 1992 Convention on Biological Diversity,[47] the 1992 Framework Convention on Climate Change[48] and the 1994 Convention to Combat Desertification.[49] The Biodiversity Convention sets out its conciliation procedure in an annex, whereas in the other conventions this is left for later adoption at a Conference of the Parties. On the other hand, the latter Conventions provide for conciliation to begin twelve months after the notification that a dispute exists, whereas the Biodiversity Convention, like the 1985 Vienna Convention, simply requires conciliation to be used without specifying a time limit. Conciliation, then, has a role to play in all these conventions and in the event of a dispute relating to their interpretation or application, which cannot be resolved by other means, a compulsory, though non-binding, procedure is available.

Related to the above are the arrangements for dispute settlement to be found in the 1997 United Nations Convention on the Law of the Non-Navigational Uses of International Watercourses.[50] After providing in Article 32 for non-discriminatory access to domestic remedies by private parties, the Convention establishes a staged procedure in Article 33 for dealing with disputes at the inter-state level. This involves first negotiations, then various other options, followed, if necessary, by a compulsory fact-finding process which can be invoked by any party. The process, which is carried out by a three-member commission, one of whom is from a third country and acts as chair, results in a non-binding report and is primarily conceived as a form of inquiry. Its relevance in the present context is that the commission's report, in addition to its findings (with reasons), is also to include 'such recommendations as it deems appropriate for an equitable solution of the dispute, which the Parties concerned shall consider in good faith'. Commissions under Article 33 thus also have a significant conciliatory function since their reports, as an authority on water resources has pointed out, 'could point to solutions not foreseen by the parties, or that they, for domestic political or other reasons, would otherwise have difficulty in adopting on their own initiative'.[51]

Finally, it should be pointed out that an elaborate and potentially very important treatment of conciliation is to be found in the 1982 Law of the Sea Convention. However, these arrangements can most conveniently be studied alongside the extensive provisions of the Convention concerned

---

[47] Text in (1992) 31 ILM 818.   [48] Text in (1992) 31 ILM 849.
[49] Text in (1994) 33 ILM 1332.   [50] Text in (1997) 36 ILM 700.
[51] S. C. McCaffrey, *The Law of International Watercourses*, Oxford, 2001, p. 444.

with other means of settlement. Discussion of this aspect of conciliation will therefore be postponed until Chapter 10.

5.5 Further Developments

Interest in conciliation as a possible means of handling disputes is evident in a number of further developments. The first of these is the effort within the United Nations to produce a code of rules on the subject. In 1990, the Sixth Committee submitted a report to the General Assembly containing a set of Draft Rules for the Conciliation of Disputes between States. The General Assembly asked the Secretary-General to circulate the Draft Rules for comment, and decided that they should be examined as part of the programme of the UN Decade of International Law and in the Special Committee on the Charter of the United Nations and on the Strengthening of the Role of the Organization. The Special Committee completed its work in 1995 and submitted its report, containing a revised version of the Model Rules, which was approved by the General Assembly.[52]

5.5.1 Model Rules on Conciliation

In their revised form, the Model Rules contain twenty-nine articles covering all aspects of conciliation from the initiation of proceedings to the submission of the report. As Model Rules they have no binding force, but are intended as a set of norms which states between whom a dispute has arisen can agree to adopt, either by simply referring to them in a bilateral agreement, or, if they wish to amend them, by making the desired changes. The Model Rules may be particularly useful where states are already parties to a convention which lays down conciliation as a mandatory procedure, but which does not prescribe the necessary arrangements. Naturally, if the convention does contain its own arrangements, the Model Rules are less useful, although it is worth noting that, even here, the parties can, if they wish, use the Model Rules instead by following the appropriate formalities. There is likewise no difficulty if the parties to a dispute are already under an obligation to submit a dispute to the International Court or to arbitration, since it is normally open to states to agree that they will first try conciliation, and to postpone recourse to binding procedures until alternative methods have been explored.

---

[52] See GA Res. A/50/50 (1996); and V. Morris and M. C. Bourloyannis-Vrailas, 'The work of the Sixth Committee at the Fiftieth Session of the UN General Assembly' (1996) 90 *AJIL*, 491 at 497. The Permanent Court of Arbitration adopted a set of Model Rules in the same period. For discussion and comparison of the two approaches, see Koopmans, *Diplomatic Dispute Settlement* (n. 1) pp. 106–20.

Unless states decide to employ conciliation more frequently than hitherto, the Model Rules seem unlikely to have a major impact on the way international disputes are handled. However, as a modest step forward, they are useful in supplying a framework for conciliation and in drawing attention to its potential.

5.5.2 Conciliation and the OSCE

Developments of a more far-reaching nature are to be found in various initiatives utilising conciliation taken by the Organization for Security and Co-operation in Europe (OSCE), formerly the Conference on Security and Co-operation in Europe (CSCE). We shall see in Chapter 13 that this is a quasi-regional political organisation with its origins in the Helsinki Agreement of 1975. Although that Agreement itself committed the participating states to settle their disputes by peaceful means, it was not until the Vienna Follow-Up Meeting, which concluded in 1989, that measures were adopted to implement this principle. That this was possible was a consequence of the ending of the confrontation between East and West which had held up progress across the whole range of issues. Now, however, significant steps have been taken to address the issue of dispute settlement and, although their effect should not be exaggerated, the central place assigned to conciliation is certainly of interest.

The first step was the creation of a CSCE Dispute Settlement Mechanism involving a combination of mediation and conciliation.[53] The Concluding Document of the Vienna Follow-Up Meeting accepted the concept of 'mandatory involvement of a third party in certain categories of disputes' and the details were agreed at a meeting of experts at Valletta in 1991, then endorsed at the Berlin Meeting of the CSCE in the same year and in the Helsinki Document of 1992. The Valletta Procedure, as it is known, provides for disputes to be dealt with in two stages. At the first stage, the parties to a dispute which they have failed to resolve establish a 'Mechanism' by selecting one or more individuals from a central register to provide 'comment or advice' on the procedure to be adopted to deal with the dispute.[54] At the second stage, the individual or panel is authorised to comment or advise on the substance of the dispute. At either stage, the parties can, by agreement, modify or adapt the procedure to perform fact-finding or other functions.

---

[53] See K. Oellers-Frahm, 'The mandatory component in the CSCE dispute settlement system', in M. W. Janis (ed.), *International Courts for the Twenty-First Century*, Dordrecht, 1992, p. 195. The text of the CSCE Procedure for Peaceful Settlement of Disputes can be found in *ibid.*, 206, and in (1991) 30 ILM 390.

[54] The procedure for appointing a Mechanism was simplified at the third meeting of the CSCE Council at Stockholm in 1992. See Annex 1 to the Council's Decision on Peaceful Settlement of Disputes, text in (1993) 32 ILM 551 at 556.

It is important to note that the process can be initiated by any party to the dispute and does not depend on agreement. In that sense, submission to the procedure is mandatory and there is a provision to ensure that a Mechanism can be established even if a party refuses cooperation. However, although comments or advice emanating from the Mechanism must be considered 'in good faith and in a spirit of co-operation', they are not binding. Thus, the process is essentially one of conciliation, with elements of mediation, particularly at the first stage, and also inquiry if the parties so desire. A further limitation to the Mechanism is that, if another party 'considers that because the dispute raises issues concerning its territorial integrity, or national defence, title to sovereignty over land territory, or competing claims with regard to jurisdiction over other areas, the Mechanism should not be established or continued' (Section XII). This is clearly a major exclusion.

At the Stockholm Meeting of the Council of the CSCE in 1992, the participating states decided to complement the Valletta Procedure by creating a formal conciliation procedure.[55] The arrangements agreed enable the parties to a dispute to refer it to a conciliation commission either by agreement, or unilaterally where both have accepted its jurisdiction in advance by making declarations analogous to those under Article 36(2) of the Statute of the International Court of Justice.[56] A commission consists of one conciliator selected by each party from the Valletta register, who then select a third person from the register as chairman. The powers and procedure of the commission are set out in provisions rather like those of the UN Model Rules, but there are some significant differences. Thus, while the parties are normally free to reject the commission's proposals, a party may declare either generally, or in relation to a specific dispute, that it will accept them as binding on a condition of reciprocity. Likewise, to reflect the institutional setting of its work, a commission must forward a report to the Senior Council of the OSCE.[57]

Another decision taken at Stockholm was intended to take the use of conciliation even further. Whereas the procedure just described is essentially voluntary, the Stockholm Meeting the Council of Ministers decided that it, or the Senior Council, can direct any two participating states to seek conciliation if they have been unable to settle a dispute within a reasonable time.[58] Such 'directed conciliation' is therefore mandatory and to ensure that the new power can be used, the parties to the dispute are not allowed to participate in the initial decision. Directed conciliation uses the same

---

[55] See Annex 3 to the Council's Decision on Peaceful Settlement of Disputes, *ibid.*, 568.
[56] The procedure established by Art. 36(2), known as the 'optional clause', is described in Chapter 8.
[57] Formerly known as the Committee of Senior Officials of the CSCE.
[58] See Annex 4 to the CSCE Council's Decision on Peaceful Settlement of Disputes, text in (1993) 32 ILM 570.

procedure as if the parties had made a joint request, subject to minor variations, and, although the process itself is not optional, the parties remain free to reject the conciliation commission's recommendations. Furthermore, not all disputes are subject to directed conciliation. In addition to those which are already covered by other processes, conciliation may not be ordered with regard to disputes falling within the categories excluded from the Valletta Process. As before, this is a crucial limitation.

A general point about all the arrangements mentioned so far is that, in so far as they can be thought of as creating obligations for OSCE states, these obligations are of a political and not a legal character. This stems from the fact that, from the 1975 Helsinki Agreement onwards, CSCE undertakings took the form not of treaties, but of political commitments. This does not make such developments meaningless, or mean that they can safely be ignored,[59] but when surveying current arrangements for dispute settlement it is at least something to be borne in mind. The remaining OSCE development to be considered is different, however, because it is in the form of a treaty and thus comparable to the various conventions already discussed. This is the Stockholm Convention on Conciliation and Arbitration within the CSCE,[60] another achievement of the 1992 Meeting.

As the name indicates, this Convention is concerned with two distinct methods for dealing with disputes: arbitration, which is further discussed in Chapter 6, and conciliation. The Convention provides for the creation of a panel of conciliators and arbitrators, nominated by the states parties, and collectively known as the Court of Conciliation and Arbitration. The Court, which is based in Geneva, establishes its own rules of procedure, and is competent to provide conciliation for cases which are referred either by agreement or unilaterally by the states parties. A commission is appointed for each case, and includes one member chosen by each party from the panel, together with an uneven number (normally three), selected by the Court's Bureau. The commission's function is 'to assist the parties to the dispute in finding a settlement in accordance with international law and their CSCE commitments' (Article 24). If the dispute is not settled in the course of the proceedings, the Commission draws up a report containing its proposals which the parties are free to accept or reject. However, if the Commission's proposals are not accepted, its report is forwarded to the OSCE Council.

The Convention came into force in 1994 when it had been accepted by twelve, mainly Western European, states. Although it creates obligations

---

[59] As regards the issue of human rights, for example, the signature of the Soviet Union and the communist governments of Eastern Europe to the 1975 Helsinki Agreement had far greater consequences than their ratifications of the 1966 UN Covenants on Human Rights. See further Robertson and Merrills, *Human Rights in the World* (n. 36) pp. 179–90.

[60] Text in (1993) 32 ILM 557. The Convention forms Annex 2 to the CSCE Council's 1992 Decision on Peaceful Settlement of Disputes.

only for the parties, it is significant, at least potentially, because a state which has accepted the Convention can be obliged to submit to conciliation unless another procedure for settling the dispute has been agreed. In this respect, it is particularly important that there is no category of excluded disputes, in sharp contrast to the Valletta Process, and that the Convention contains no provision enabling states to make reservations which would exempt specific types of dispute from conciliation. Becoming a party to the Convention thus entails a general and unqualified commitment to conciliation by the OSCE state concerned. However, none of these elaborate arrangements for OSCE conciliation has so far been used, suggesting perhaps that here, as elsewhere, the need is not so much for new mechanisms and procedures, as for a readiness on the part of governments with unresolved disputes to use established arrangements wisely.

5.5.3 Conciliation and Compliance Procedures

The last development which should be noted concerns the emergence of novel 'compliance procedures' constituting a special form of conciliation in recent environmental agreements. The first agreement of this kind was the 1987 Montreal Protocol on Substances that Deplete the Ozone Layer,[61] under which an Implementation Committee consisting of ten parties to the Protocol has been established to hear submissions relating to a party's noncompliance which may be put forward by the Secretariat or any other party. The Committee may then make recommendations 'with a view to securing an amicable resolution of the matter on the basis of respect for the provisions of the Protocol'. Implementation of the ozone regime is reviewed through a number of institutions, of which the compliance procedure is only one. But, by dealing with disputes both 'in house' and informally, the new procedure is particularly suitable for an evolving regulatory regime, as it can reflect the expectations and understandings of the parties, but at the same time avoid crystallising the law in a fast-changing area. Not surprisingly, therefore, following this example, non-compliance procedures have been introduced or provided for under a number of other environmental treaties.

---

[61] Text in (1987) 26 ILM 154. See D. G. Victor, 'The operation and effectiveness of the Montreal Protocol's non-compliance procedure', in D. G. Victor, K. Raustiala and E. B. Skolnikoff, *The Implementation and Effectiveness of International Environmental Commitments*, Laxenburg, 1998, p. 137; C. Chinkin, 'Alternative dispute resolution under international law', in M. D. Evans (ed.), *Remedies in International Law: The Institutional Dilemma*, Oxford, 1998, p. 123 at pp. 128–34; and P. Sands, *Principles of International Environmental Law*, 2nd ed., Cambridge, 2003, pp. 205–10. Also J. Klabbers, 'Compliance procedures', in D. Bodansky, J. Brunneé and E. Hey (eds), *The Oxford Handbook of International Environmental Law*, Oxford, 2007, p. 995; and K. N. Scott, 'Non-compliance procedures and dispute resolution mechanisms under international environmental agreements', in D. French, M. Saul and N. D. White (eds), *International Law and Dispute Settlement: New Problems and Techniques*, Oxford, 2010, p. 225.

A good example of the noncompliance procedure in operation may be seen in the case of Russia, the issue of whose record under the Montreal Protocol was raised before the Implementation Committee in 1995. By 2002, following public scrutiny and the provision of funds and assistance, Russia had achieved compliance. While not all cases have been so successful, there are clear advantages in supervisory arrangements which engage all parties to a treaty and are aimed at providing incentives for compliance, rather than grounds for recrimination. The traditional law of state responsibility, though necessarily the basis of treaty obligations, is at the same time a crude and unsatisfactory instrument for encouraging performance. With environmental treaties in particular, it has been suggested that traditional methods 'simply do not work: they are hardly ever applied, are antagonistic and ... offer little scope for win-win solutions'.[62] The emergence of noncompliance procedures to rectify these deficiencies may thus be seen as a logical progression.

In addition to the Montreal Protocol, more than twenty other treaties now provide for noncompliance procedures, including the 1997 Kyoto Protocol,[63] for which a compliance regime was established in 2001, the 1998 Aarhus Convention,[64] the parties to which set up a Compliance Committee in 2002, and the 2000 Cartagena Protocol on Biosafety,[65] where a non-compliance procedure was adopted in 2004. Equivalent arrangements for other treaties are currently under negotiation. As a relatively new means of monitoring states' international commitments and resolving disagreements, noncompliance procedures represent an important development, but raise a number of issues which have yet to be resolved, not least their relation to more traditional ways of handling disputes. Nevertheless, noncompliance procedures are a type of multilateral conciliation with unique advantages, and as such are likely to be increasingly prominent.

5.6 Significance of Conciliation

In the ninety or so years in which conciliation has been available, around twenty cases have been heard. Although this is rather more than the number of cases handled by commissions of inquiry over a slightly longer period, it is hardly an impressive record. When one bears in mind the more than 200 bilateral treaties and the various multilateral instruments with

---

[62] Koopmans, *Diplomatic Dispute Settlement* (n. 1) p. 227. See also M. Asada, 'The OPCW's arrangements for missed destruction deadlines under the Chemical Weapons Convention: an informal non-compliance procedure' (2014) 108 *AJIL*, 448.
[63] Text in (1998) 37 ILM 22.　[64] Text in (1999) 38 ILM 517.
[65] Text in (2000) 39 ILM 1027.

similar provisions, it is clear that conciliation has failed to become the routine procedure that its promoters expected. Why?

The treaties themselves suggest one set of explanations. Some bilateral treaties are restricted to particular categories of disputes; some multilateral treaties, the General Act, for example, are subject to wide-ranging reservations, which have the same effect of restricting the parties' obligations. Moreover, the significance of some treaties was always likely to lie more in the example they set than in their application, since disputes between, say, Sweden and Chile, or Brazil and Poland,[66] have never been very common.

As in the case of inquiry, the influence of other means of dispute settlement must also be taken into account. We shall see in later chapters that a government which is interested in settling a dispute can be helped to do so through informal conciliation within an international organisation. Likewise, a government which merely wishes to ventilate a grievance has in the United Nations a forum which a conciliation commission cannot hope (and should not try) to match. The more bilateral conciliation acquires the overtones of arbitration, the more the tendency to take disputes of a political character to international organisations will be encouraged. But, since to convene and operate a conciliation commission is neither easy nor cheap, even states with legal disputes will often have reason to prefer the tried and tested procedures of arbitration to the uncertainties of conciliation.

In the *Interhandel* case,[67] the United States rejected a proposal for conciliation on the ground that the facts were clear. This suggests that sometimes the possibilities of conciliation may not be fully appreciated, a problem which is exacerbated by the limited amount of practice and the paucity of published material. The fact that conciliation is a relatively elaborate procedure probably discourages its use for minor disputes; but a conciliation commission, unlike a mediator, usually has no political authority to back up its proposals and so, quite apart from other considerations, conciliation is not a particularly attractive option for major disputes either.

In 1938, Czechoslovakia's request for conciliation in the Sudeten crisis was ignored by Nazi Germany. Goodwill and a readiness to compromise are clearly prerequisites of conciliation and in virtually all the cases in which it has been attempted the parties have been neighbours, or near neighbours, with an interest in maintaining friendly relations. Conciliation, like inquiry, can provide the parties with a better understanding of their opponent's case and an objective appraisal of their own, and, like mediation, with the assistance of a third party in negotiation and an opportunity to make concessions without loss of face.

---

[66] Brazil and Poland signed a treaty of conciliation in 1933.
[67] See *Interhandel*, Judgment [1959] ICJ Rep. 6.

Conciliation has so far proved most useful for disputes where the main issues are legal, but the parties desire an equitable compromise. The *Belgian-Danish*, *Franco-Swiss* and *Swiss-Italian* cases were all of this type, as were the two Japanese loan cases, the *Roula* case[68] (1956) between Italy and Greece, and the more recent *Jan Mayen* case. In cases of this type, conciliation would appear to offer two advantages over arbitration *ex aequo et bono*, the obvious alternative.

First, because of the way conciliation is conducted – through a dialogue with and between the parties – there is no danger of it producing a result that takes the parties completely by surprise, as sometimes happens in legal proceedings. Second, a commission's proposals, as already noted, are not binding and, if unacceptable, can be rejected. The importance which states attach to retaining control of a dispute has been mentioned earlier, and would appear to be equally relevant here.

It is perhaps also for these reasons that the recent conciliation between Australia and the Democratic Republic of Timor-Leste ('Timor-Leste') in the establishment of their maritime boundaries in the Timor Sea proved successful. The case will be discussed in detail in Chapter 10, but its success is nonetheless worth noting here already. The dispute between Australia and Timor-Leste in relation to the maritime boundary between the two states was submitted to the compulsory conciliation procedure under Section 2 of Annex V of the UNCLOS in 2016, making it the first instance of conciliation under the Convention. Previous negotiations on the dispute had not resolved it, but conciliation successfully resulted in the settlement of the dispute. The proceedings notably resulted in the signature of the 'Treaty Between Australia and the Democratic Republic of Timor-Leste Establishing Their Maritime Boundaries in the Timor Sea' (the Maritime Boundary Treaty) on 6 March 2018. The successful conciliation of this dispute is an important example of the significance of the role played by conciliation in international dispute settlement in recent years.[69]

In all the cases just mentioned, conciliation was successful. Significantly, all involved issues that were both legal and of secondary importance. The difficulties that have been experienced in utilising conciliation for other types of disputes indicate its limitations. The Chaco Commission was instructed to confine its attention to the incident at Fort Vanguardia, and, though it subsequently obtained authority to investigate the whole of the long-standing border dispute in the area, its proposals for a solution were not taken up. The France–Siam Commission prudently sought to limit its brief by excluding the issue of Laos; even so, its report was rejected by Siam. In the *Ben Bella* affair, the Moroccan delegate resigned when the

---

[68] See J. P. A. François, 'Le Palais de la Paix en 1956' (1957) 4 *NTIR*, 69 at 71.
[69] See for a discussion D. Tamada, 'The Timor Sea conciliation: the unique mechanism of dispute settlement' (2020) 31 *European Journal of International Law*, 321.

commission refused to allow the passengers on the diverted aircraft to be called as witnesses. And, in the *Vitianu* case (1949), an attempt to achieve a conciliated settlement in a dispute involving a Romanian diplomat collapsed when the Swiss authorities refused to discontinue proceedings for espionage.[70] In all these cases, a substantial interest of a political nature was in issue, and strong feelings made it difficult for the parties to accept a compromise.

It is worth noting, however, that the *East African Community* case was resolved by conciliation, though substantial sums were at stake, and that, even when it is less successful, conciliation can still have significant results. Although the Chaco Commission failed to resolve the underlying issue, it succeeded in patching up the immediate quarrel. Likewise, despite the rejection of the France–Siam Commission's report, when a new government came to power in Siam, it indicated that it regarded the border dispute as over. While it is tempting to believe that there ought to be ways of resolving disputes once and for all, partial or step-by-step solutions may often be the best that can be managed.

When assessing the significance of conciliation, it is also worth bearing in mind that, while the conciliation provisions in many treaties have still to be utilised, this does not, as might be thought, make such arrangements meaningless. A former legal adviser, who was closely involved with the negotiation of the Vienna Convention on the Law of Treaties, has observed that:

> the chief value of the automatic procedures for settlement of disputes now written into the Convention lies not in their precise content but in their mere existence. Paradoxically, the less they are utilised the more effective they will be. No state is anxious to indulge in lengthy and expensive international conciliation or litigation. This imposes a very heavy burden upon Foreign Offices and upon their legal advisers, with the outcome far from certain. What is important – what is indeed crucial – is that there should always be in the background, as a necessary check upon the making of unjustified claims, or upon the denial of justified claims, automatically available procedures for the settlement of disputes.[71]

The comment is, of course, equally applicable to other multilateral conventions, whether general or particular, and indeed to arrangements for conciliation in bilateral treaties, whether or not they are employed in practice.

Currently, then, conciliation is regularly included in provisions dealing with dispute settlement and retains a modest place among the procedures actually used by states when disputes arise. While the number of cases

---

[70] See Cot, *International Conciliation* (n. 1) p. 93.
[71] I. Sinclair, *The Vienna Convention on the Law of Treaties*, 2nd ed., Manchester, 1984, p. 235.

handled by conciliation is small and there can be no guarantee that if attempted the procedure will be successful, the *Jan Mayen* case and the *East African Community* case have provided timely reminders of its value. As these cases demonstrate, the ad hoc use of conciliation is no less handy in practice than the standing arrangements laid down in treaties, and, as noted above, informal conciliation through organisations is a further possibility. Like inquiry, the process from which it developed, conciliation offers a procedure adaptable to a variety of needs, and demonstrates the advantage to be derived from the structured involvement of outsiders in the settlement of international disputes.

5.7 Further Reading

5.7.1 General References on Conciliation

Efremoff, J., 'La conciliation internationale' (1927) 18 *Hague Recueil des Cours*, 5.

Efremoff, J., 'L'organisation de la conciliation comme moyen deprévenir les guerres' (1937) 59 *Hague Recueil des Cours*, 103.

Fox, H., 'Conciliation', in C. M. H. Waldock (ed), *International Disputes: The Legal Aspects*, London, 1972, p. 93.

Gros, A., 'Remarques sur la conciliation internationale', in *L'Evolution du Droit Public: Etudes Offertes à Achille Mestre*, Paris, 1956, p. 279.

Hyde, C. C., 'The place of commissions of inquiry and conciliation treaties in the peaceful settlement of disputes' (1929) 10 *BYBIL*, 96.

Koopmans, S. M. G., *Diplomatic Dispute Settlement*, The Hague, 2008.

Tamada, D., 'The Timor Sea conciliation: the unique mechanism of dispute settlement', (2020) 31 *European Journal of International Law*, 321.

Van Asbeck, F. M., 'La tâche et l'action d'une Commission de conciliation' (1956) 3 *Netherlands International Law Review*, 1.

5.7.2 Treaties and Official Documents

Hague Convention on Pacific Settlement of International Disputes (Hague, I) (adopted 29 July 1899, entered into force 4 September 1900).

Regulations on the Procedure of International Conciliation adopted by the Institute of International Law in 1961, (1961) 49(ii) *Annuaire* 385–91.

6

Arbitration

The means available for the settlement of international disputes are commonly divided into two groups. Those considered so far, namely, negotiation, mediation, inquiry and conciliation, are termed diplomatic means because the parties retain control of the dispute and may accept or reject a proposed settlement as they see fit. Arbitration and judicial settlement, on the other hand, are employed when what is wanted is a binding decision, usually on the basis of international law, and hence these are known as legal means of settlement.

Judicial settlement involves the reference of a dispute to the International Court or some other standing tribunal, such as the International Tribunal for the Law of the Sea or the European Court of Human Rights. Arbitration, in contrast, requires the parties themselves to set up the machinery to handle a dispute, or series of disputes, between them. Historically, arbitration was the first to develop and provided the inspiration for the creation of permanent judicial institutions. The focus of this chapter will therefore be on the earlier institution.[1]

6.1 Forms of Arbitration

Arbitration may be prescribed in a treaty providing for its use in the event of a dispute relating to the interpretation or application of the agreement, or arranged by the parties when a dispute arises. In the former situation, as we shall see in Chapter 10 in relation to dispute settlement under the UNCLOS, the treaty usually establishes the procedural framework for the arbitration. In the latter, on the other hand, this is a matter for the parties.

---

[1] For general reference, see J. G. Wetter, *The International Arbitral Process: Public and Private*, 5 vols., New York, 1979, an outstanding collection of cases and materials; J. L. Simpson and H. Fox, *International Arbitration: Law and Practice*, London, 1959; C. M. H. Waldock (ed.), *International Disputes: The Legal Aspects*, London, 1972, ch. 2; United Nations, *Handbook on the Peaceful Settlement of Disputes between States*, New York, 1992, ch. 2F; C. Gray and B. Kingsbury, 'Developments in dispute settlement: inter-state arbitration since 1945' (1992) 63 BYBIL, 97; and S. Muller and W. Mijs (eds), *The Flame Rekindled: New Hopes for International Arbitration*, Dordrecht, 1994. See also J. Collier and V. Lowe, *The Settlement of Disputes in International Law*, Oxford, 1999, chs 3, 4 and 8; and R. Y. Jennings, 'The differences between conducting a case in the ICJ and in an ad hoc tribunal: an inside view', in N. Ando, E. McWhinney and R. Wolfrum (eds), *Liber Amicorum Judge Shigeru Oda*, The Hague, 2002, p. 893.

But whether states are drafting a general undertaking to refer future disputes to arbitration, or negotiating a *compromis* (special agreement) for the submission of a dispute that has already arisen, the first step is to decide the kind of tribunal to be appointed.

One possibility is to set up a commission consisting of equal numbers of national arbitrators, appointed by the parties, and a neutral member (or umpire) to whom cases are referred if the national members cannot agree. The origins of this form of tribunal, frequently used to deal with claims arising out of injury to aliens, can be traced back almost 200 years. In the Treaty of Ghent (1814), the United States and the United Kingdom agreed that certain disputes between them should be arbitrated by national commissioners with reference to a disinterested third party in the event of disagreement. Under the earlier and more famous Jay Treaty (1794), on the other hand, national commissioners alone were employed. These early Anglo-American commissions were not judicial tribunals in the modern sense, but were supposed to blend juridical with diplomatic considerations to produce (in effect) a negotiated settlement. In the modern form of mixed commission, however, the juridical element predominates, with the result that cases like the *Bolivar Railway Company* claim[2] (1903), decided by the Britain–Venezuela Commission, and the *Youmans* claim[3] (1926), decided by the United States–Mexico General Claims Commission, are regarded as authoritative applications of international law.

Another form of arbitration derives from the long-established practice of referring a dispute to a foreign head of state or government for decision (sometimes referred to as 'sovereign arbitration'). Examples can be found in classical times and also in the medieval period when the Pope was often called upon to act in this capacity. Because the effect is to involve an influential outside party in the dispute, arbitration in this form has some of the same advantages as mediation. A powerful arbitrator, like a powerful mediator, can be useful when pressure or inducements are needed to encourage a party to accept an unfavourable decision, or expertise and resources are needed to implement a settlement by carrying out tasks such as mapping or surveying. One disadvantage of this form of arbitration was that it used to be common for sovereign arbitrators to answer the parties' question without giving reasons. It was therefore impossible to know what part, if any, juridical considerations had played in the decision. Towards the end of the nineteenth century, however, as arbitration came to be recognised as an essentially judicial process, reasoned decisions, based on

---

[2] *Bolivar Railway Company Claim (Great Britain v. Venezuela)* (1903) 9 RIAA 445.
[3] *Youmans Claim (United States v. Mexico)* (1926) 4 RIAA 110. For discussion of the significance of cases of this type, see B. J. Bederman, 'The glorious past and uncertain future of international claims tribunals', in M. W. Janis (ed.), *International Courts for the Twenty-First Century*, Dordrecht, 1992, p. 161.

advice tendered by jurists, became the norm. As a result, by 1931, arbitral decisions like that of the King of Italy in the *Clipperton Island* case,[4] were regularly settling disputes on the basis of international law.

Although sovereign arbitration is now a rarity, its flexibility and adaptability to modern circumstances were demonstrated in two modern arbitrations. Under a treaty of 1902, the Queen, as successor to her great-grandfather King Edward VII, was empowered to act as arbitrator in territorial disputes between Chile and Argentina. In the *Palena* case[5] between these two countries in 1966, these powers were delegated to a tribunal consisting of a jurist, Lord McNair, and two geographical experts. In the *Beagle Channel* case[6] (1977), in contrast, Argentina would have preferred a reference of the matter to the International Court and so the tribunal appointed was composed entirely of jurists, all of them members of the permanent body.

If neither a mixed commission nor a sovereign arbitrator is considered appropriate, another possibility is to refer the dispute to a specially qualified individual for a decision. The 1899 Hague Convention established a list of arbitrators, styled, inappropriately, 'the Permanent Court of Arbitration' (PCA), and created a bureau with premises, library and staff, which still exists and plays a major role in facilitating arbitration and other forms of peaceful settlement. In 2019, the PCA administered 199 cases, of which forty-nine were initiated in that year.[7] Of the total number of PCA-administered cases in 2019, four cases were inter-state arbitrations, 125 were treaty-based investor-state arbitrations, and 60 were arbitrations in contract disputes involving states, state entities or international organisations. And this varied and extensive level of activity seems likely to continue.[8]

Provided a suitable individual can be found, using a single arbitrator can be quicker and less expensive than convening a larger body, though the demands on the person chosen are correspondingly increased. For this reason, it cannot be regarded as appropriate for all types of cases, though

---

[4] *Clipperton Island Case (France v. Mexico)* (1931), (1932) 26 *AJIL*, 300.

[5] *Argentine–Chile Frontier Case* (1966) 38 ILR 10; 16 RIAA 109. For discussion, see H. Fox, 'Arbitration', in E. Luard (ed.), *The International Regulation of Frontier Disputes*, London, 1970, pp. 172–91.

[6] *Beagle Channel Arbitration (Argentina v. Chile)* (1977) 52 ILR 93. For discussion, see M. Shaw, 'The Beagle Channel Arbitration Award' (1978) 6 *Int. Rel.*, 415.

[7] Permanent Court of Arbitration (PCA), Annual Report 2019, at 10, available at https://docs.pca-cpa.org/2020/03/7726c41e-online-pca-annual-report-2019-final.pdf.

[8] After a period of neglect the role of the PCA has recently been given renewed attention; see J. L. Bleich, 'A new direction for the PCA: the work of the expert group', in S. Muller and W. Mijs (eds), *The Flame Rekindled: New Hopes for International Arbitration*, Dordrecht, 1994, p. 17; and W. E. Butler, 'The Hague Permanent Court of Arbitration' in M. W. Janis (ed.), *International Courts for the Twenty-First Century*, Dordrecht, 1992, p. 43. See also P. Hamilton, H. C. Requena, L. van Scheltinga and Bette E. Shifman (eds), *The Permanent Court of Arbitration: International Arbitration and Dispute Resolution*, The Hague, 1999.

the decisions of Chief Justice Taft in the *Tinoco* arbitration[9] and Max Huber in the *Island of Palmas* case[10] show what can be achieved. A variant of this method was employed in the *Monetary Gold* arbitration,[11] where the single arbitrator, George Sauser-Hall, was a member of the Permanent Court of Arbitration and appointed in response to a request from the parties by the President of the International Court. Normally, where a single arbitrator is appointed, he or she will be a jurist. Exceptionally, however, an arbitrator with other qualifications may be chosen. Thus, in 1986, France and New Zealand asked the Secretary-General of the United Nations to act as arbitrator in the *Rainbow Warrior* case,[12] and his ruling, which was unreasoned but covered the outstanding issues, settled the dispute.

The form of tribunal most commonly found in modern treaty practice is the collegiate body consisting of an uneven number of persons, generally three or five, with the power to decide the case by majority vote. This type of tribunal was first used in the famous *Alabama Claims* case[13] (1871–2), which concerned the United Kingdom's responsibilities as a neutral during the American Civil War. There, the British and American governments established a five-member tribunal, containing only two national members, and it is this feature, together with the fact that the tribunal followed a strictly juridical procedure and issued a reasoned award, which makes the case a decisive step in the development of arbitration. Cases in which a five-member court has been employed include the *Taba* dispute[14] between Egypt and Israel; the earlier *Channel* arbitration[15] between the United Kingdom and France; the two-stage *Eritrea/Yemen* arbitration;[16] and the *Iron Rhine Railway* arbitration[17] between Belgium and the Netherlands.

---

[9] *Tinoco Arbitration (Great Britain v. Costa Rica)* (1923) 1 RIAA 369.

[10] *Island of Palmas Case (The Netherlands v. United States)* (1928) 2 RIAA 829.

[11] *Gold Looted by Germany from Rome in 1943 (United States, France, United Kingdom, Italy)* (1953) 20 ILR 441.

[12] *Ruling Pertaining to the Differences between France and New Zealand Arising from the Rainbow Warrior Affair* (1986) 74 ILR 241. Text also in (1981) 81 *AJIL*, 325, (1987) 26 ILM 1346 and document J in Appendix G below. For discussion, see M. Pugh, 'Legal Aspects of the Rainbow Warrior Affair' (1987) 36 *ICLQ*, 655.

[13] B. Moore, *History and Digest of the International Arbitrations to Which the United States Has Been a Party*, London, 1898, vol. I, p. 653; also in A. G. La Pradelle and N. Politis, *Recueil des Arbitrages Internationaux*, Paris, 1957, vol. II, p. 713. The award and a valuable collection of background material can be found in Wetter, *The International Arbitral Process* (n. 1) vol. I, pp. 27–173. See also T. Bingham, 'The Alabama Claims Arbitration' (2005) 54 *ICLQ*, 1.

[14] *Arbitral Award in the Dispute concerning Certain Boundary Pillars between the Arab Republic of Egypt and the State of Israel* (1988) 80 ILR 224, summarised in (1989) 83 *AJIL*, 590.

[15] *Delimitation of the Continental Shelf (United Kingdom of Great Britain and Northern Ireland and the French Republic)* (1977) 54 ILR 6. For analysis and commentary, see J. G. Merrills, 'The United Kingdom–France Continental Shelf Arbitration' (1980) 10 *Calif. Western Int. LJ*, 314.

[16] *Eritrea–Yemen Arbitration*, Phase I (1998), Phase II (1999), (2001) 40 ILM 900 and 983. For discussion, see N. S. M. Antunes in (1999) 48 *ICLQ*, 362 and (2001) 50 *ICLQ*, 299.

[17] *Iron Rhine Railway Arbitration (Belgium/Netherlands)* (2005), available at www.pca-cpa.org.

A five-member tribunal also is the default for inter-state arbitration under Annex VII of the UNCLOS.[18] On the other hand, in the *Maritime Delimitation* cases[19] between Guinea and Guinea-Bissau and Guinea-Bissau and Senegal, the *Heathrow Airport* case[20] between the United States and the United Kingdom, and the *OSPAR (Article 9)* arbitration[21] between Ireland and the United Kingdom, a smaller three-member tribunal was used. In the *Indus Waters Kishenganga* arbitration *(Pakistan v. India)* arbitration[22] a seven-member tribunal was agreed upon.

6.2 Selection and Appointment of Arbitrators

The membership of a collegiate tribunal, like the appointment of a single arbitrator, is a matter for negotiation between the parties, with each side generally appointing one or more 'national' arbitrators and the remaining 'neutral' members being agreed between them. If the parties can settle the composition of the tribunal at an early stage, it will be possible to name the members in the arbitration agreement. In the *Channel* arbitration, for example, the *compromis* listed the five jurists who the parties had agreed should constitute the tribunal (see Appendix D). Frequently, however, the identity of the members is left to be settled later. In that case, the agreement will simply define the membership of the tribunal and lay down the procedure to be followed in setting it up. A provision of this type may be seen in the agreement setting up the Arbitral Tribunal for the *Maritime Delimitation* case between Guinea and Guinea-Bissau.[23]

When setting up the Iran–United States Claims Tribunal in 1981, following the diplomatic hostages crisis, it was necessary to create a plenary body from which smaller chambers could be created for determining particular cases. For this reason, the arrangements for the nomination of arbitrators had to be more elaborate than for a conventional arbitration. The instrument establishing the Tribunal therefore provides:

> The Tribunal shall consist of nine members or such larger multiple of three as Iran and the United States may agree are necessary to conduct its business

---

[18] Article 3(a), Annex VII of the UNCLOS: 'For the purpose of proceedings under this Annex, the arbitral tribunal shall, unless the parties otherwise agree, be constituted as follows: (a) Subject to subparagraph (g), the arbitral tribunal shall consist of five members.'

[19] *Guinea–Guinea-Bissau Maritime Delimitation* Case (1985) 77 ILR 636; *Guinea-Bissau–Senegal Maritime Delimitation Case* (1989) 83 ILR 1.

[20] *United States–United Kingdom Arbitration concerning Heathrow Airport User Charges* (1992–3) 102 ILR 216. For analysis, see S. M. Witten, 'The US–UK arbitration concerning Heathrow Airport user charges' (1995) 89 *AJIL*, 174.

[21] *Access to Information under Article 9 of the OSPAR Convention* (Ireland v. United Kingdom) (2003), (2003) 42 ILM 1118, summarised in (2004) 98 *AJIL*, 330.

[22] *Indus Waters Kishenganga Arbitration (Pakistan v. India)*, PCA Case No. 2011-01, available at www.pca-cpa.org.

[23] For the text of this agreement, see 77 ILR 642.

expeditiously. Within ninety days after the entry into force of this agreement, each government shall appoint one-third of the members. Within thirty days after their appointment, the members so appointed shall by mutual agreement select the remaining third of the members and appoint one of the remaining third President of the Tribunal. Claims may be decided by the full Tribunal or by a panel of three members of the Tribunal as the President shall determine. Each such panel shall be composed by the President and shall consist of one member appointed by each of the three methods set forth above.[24]

While the parties usually appoint (international) jurists to an arbitral tribunal which is to decide disputes relating to international law, it occasionally happens that the states also appoint scientific experts to sit in arbitral tribunals. The Indus Waters Treaty,[25] for instance, which formed the basis for the *Indus Waters Kishenganga* Arbitration *(Pakistan v. India)*, mentions that the arbitrators may be either lawyers or 'highly qualified engineers'.

6.2.1 Appointment of Arbitrators

For obvious reasons, the result of a collegiate arbitration often turns on the decision of the other member or members of the tribunal; that is, those that are not the party-appointed arbitrators, sometimes called the 'neutral' member or members. Deciding who they shall be is therefore extremely important to the governments concerned, which may sometimes find it difficult to agree on suitable candidates. To take account of this, arbitration treaties often provide that, in the event of disagreement, the neutral members may be appointed by an 'appointing authority' such as the President of the International Court, the Secretary-General of the Permanent Court of Arbitration[26] or by some other disinterested party. In case of arbitration under Annex VII of the UNCLOS, the President of the ITLOS will make the appointment, unless the parties agree otherwise.[27]

---

[24] Declaration of the Government of the Democratic and Popular Republic of Algeria concerning the Settlement of Claims by the Government of the United States of America and the Government of the Islamic Republic of Iran, 1981, Art. III(1), I Iran–US CTR 10; (1981) 20 ILM 230. For various reasons the composition of the Tribunal gave rise to a number of problems in practice. For discussion of these, see R. Khan, *The Iran–United States Claims Tribunal*, Dordrecht, 1990, chs. 3 and 4; and G. H. Aldrich, *The Jurisprudence of the Iran–United States Claims Tribunal*, Oxford, 1996, pp. 9–44.

[25] The Indus Waters Treaty, signed at Karachi, on 19 September 1960, 126 UNTS 1962 No. 6032.

[26] See Article 6(1) UNCITRAL Arbitration Rules: 'Unless the parties have already agreed on the choice of an appointing authority, a party may at any time propose the name or names of one or more institutions or persons, including the Secretary-General of the Permanent Court of Arbitration at The Hague (hereinafter called the "PCA"), one of whom would serve as appointing authority.'

[27] Article 3(d)-(e), Annex VII of the UNCLOS

Such arrangements have proved useful on a number of occasions. In the *Lake Lanoux* arbitration,[28] for example, the French and Spanish governments referred the selection of the president of the tribunal to the King of Sweden, and in the *Rann of Kutch* case[29] the Secretary-General of the United Nations performed the same service for India and Pakistan. In the *Dispute Concerning Coastal State Rights in the Black Sea, Sea of Azov, and Kerch Strait (Ukraine* v. *the Russian Federation)* arbitration, the three remaining 'neutral' members could not be agreed upon by the parties. They were thus appointed by the Vice-President of the ITLOS, who acted as appointing authority in replacement of the President of ITLOS who in that dispute had been appointed by Russia as arbitrator.[30] Authorising a third party to take the steps necessary to complete the membership of a tribunal is beneficial in a double sense. In the above-mentioned cases, it enabled states which were experiencing genuine difficulties to avoid an impasse. However, it also prevents a state which has conceived an objection to the whole idea of arbitration from frustrating the process by a blank refusal to cooperate in the appointment of neutral members. But, suppose that a state which wishes to be obstructive refuses even to appoint its own members? The effect of this form of non-cooperation had to be considered in the *Peace Treaties* case.[31]

The peace treaties with Bulgaria, Hungary and Romania provided that disputes arising out of their interpretation or execution were to be referred to arbitral commissions. In accordance with the usual practice, these were to consist of a national member appointed by each side and a third member appointed by agreement, or, failing that, by the Secretary-General of the United Nations. Soon after the treaties came into force in 1947, the United Kingdom and the United States complained that the three former enemy states were violating their human rights obligations. However, when an attempt was made to set in motion the arbitral procedure, the respondent states refused to appoint their representatives to the commissions. In 1950, the whole matter came to the International Court, when the General Assembly asked for an advisory opinion as to the legal consequences of this action.

In the first phase of the case, the Court rejected the respondents' argument that there was no dispute to which the settlement provisions of

---

[28] *Lake Lanoux Arbitration (France* v. *Spain)* (1957) 24 ILR 101. See further Chapter 1.
[29] *Indo-Pakistan Western Boundary (Rann of Kutch) (India* v. *Pakistan)* (1968) 50 ILR 2. For commentary, see J. G. Wetter, 'The Rann of Kutch Arbitration' (1971) 65 *AJIL*, 346.
[30] *Dispute Concerning Coastal State Rights in the Black Sea, Sea of Azov, and Kerch Strait (Ukraine* v. *the Russian Federation)* PCA Case No. 2017-06, Award on Preliminary Objections, 21 February 2020, para. 13.
[31] *Interpretation of Peace Treaties with Bulgaria, Hungary and Romania*, Advisory Opinion, First Phase [1950] ICJ Rep. 65; Second Phase [1950] ICJ Rep. 221. For commentary, see K. S. Carlston, Note (1950) 44 *AJIL*, 728.

the peace treaties could apply, and held that Bulgaria, Hungary and Romania were under an obligation to appoint their members of the commissions. When it became clear that, despite the opinion, this duty would not be performed, the Court had to consider whether the provision in the treaties for recourse to the Secretary-General could be invoked to save the arbitration. The Court was urged to decide that the term 'third member' in the treaties meant simply 'neutral member' and was not intended to make the appointment of both national members a prerequisite for the exercise of the Secretary-General's power. This was, however, held to be an unconvincing reading of the text which, the Court held, must be interpreted to cover only situations in which the parties had failed to agree. Consequently, although the respondents' failure to make their appointments incurred international responsibility, it could not in itself justify the creation of a commission by the method proposed.

More recently, several states have also failed to appoint the member(s) of an arbitral tribunal, occasionally because they have altogether objected to the whole idea to arbitrate the dispute. In the *South China Sea* arbitration *(the Philippines v. China)*, China had refused to participate in the arbitration. China had issued a Note Verbale to the Department of Foreign Affairs of the Philippines (who had initiated the arbitral proceedings) thereby 'rejecting the arbitration and returning the Notification and Statement of Claim to the Philippines'.[32] Because of China's refusal to participate in the proceedings, the Philippines had requested the President of the ITLOS to appoint China's party-appointed arbitrator, and subsequently the three remaining members of the Tribunal.[33]

Another example is the *Arbitration Between the Republic of Croatia and the Republic of Slovenia*. The dispute relates to the maritime and land boundary between the two states. At a certain point in time, before the Tribunal rendered its award on the merits, Serbian and Croatian newspapers published transcripts and audio files of several telephone conversations reportedly involving Slovenia's party-appointed arbitrator and one of the agents presenting Slovenia in the dispute.[34] Slovenia's party-appointed arbitrator immediately resigned from the Tribunal, and Slovenia informed the Tribunal that the agent of Slovenia also resigned. Slovenia soon thereafter appointed Ronny Abraham, President of the ICJ, who in turn resigned from the Tribunal a couple of days later. In the meantime, Croatia's party-appointed arbitrator had also resigned from the Tribunal.

---

[32] *The South China Sea* arbitration *(The Republic of Philippines v. The People's Republic of China)*, PCA Case No. 2013-19, Award on Jurisdiction and Admissibility, 29 October 2015, para. 27.

[33] *The South China Sea* arbitration *(The Republic of Philippines v. The People's Republic of China)*, PCA Case No. 2013-19, Award on Jurisdiction and Admissibility, 29 October 2015, paras 29–30.

[34] See for an overview of these facts: *Arbitration Between the Republic of Croatia and the Republic of Slovenia (Croatia v. Slovenia)*, PCA Case No. 2012-04, Partial Award, 30 June 2016, paras 37 ff.

Croatia considered that Slovenia had 'engaged in one or more material breaches of the Arbitration Agreement' and consequently refused to further 'apply the Arbitration Agreement'. Slovenia in turn requested the Tribunal to continue the proceedings, finding that the Arbitration Agreement was still in force between the parties.

Based on the foregoing, both Croatia and Slovenia had refused to appoint an arbitrator in replacement of the two party-appointed arbitrators who had resigned from the Tribunal. Applying the Arbitration Agreement which provided that the President of the Arbitral Tribunal was authorized to appoint the party-appointed arbitrators if the parties failed to do so, the President of the Arbitral Tribunal thus appointed the two party-appointed members of the Tribunal.

These cases are striking illustrations of the obstacles which an unwilling state can place in the way of arbitration and the care which must be taken to cover all contingencies when drafting provisions dealing with the appointment of arbitrators. As in the case of disagreement over the neutral members, the simplest solution is a provision to the effect that, after a suitable period, the necessary appointment may be made by an outside party, the 'appointing authority'. Though not always included even today, such provisions have been a feature of bilateral treaties for more than fifty years and were endorsed by both the International Law Commission and the Permanent Court of Arbitration.[35] Similar arrangements have been incorporated into the major multilateral agreements on peaceful settlement, including the 1928 Geneva General Act (Article 23), the 1948 Pact of Bogotá (Article 45) and the 1957 European Convention for the Peaceful Settlement of Disputes (Article 21). As we shall see in Chapter 10, arrangements of this type are also to be found in the arbitral provisions of the 1982 Law of the Sea Convention.

When an arbitration is held before a standing body, such as the Iran–United States Claims Tribunal, arbitrators will already have been appointed, and so the issue of default should not arise. On the other hand, even in that case, it is still possible for the party-appointed arbitrators to disagree about the appointment of the 'neutral' members, or about selecting the president. To cover these possibilities, the instrument establishing the tribunal provides for any outstanding appointments to be made by an 'appointing authority', chosen by the Secretary-General of the

---

[35] See the ILC Model Rules of Arbitral Procedure (1958), *ILC Year Book*, 1958, vol. II, p. 12; text also in Simpson and Fox, *International Arbitration* (n. 1) p. 295, and Wetter, *The International Arbitral Process* (n. 1) vol. V, p. 232; and Article 6 of the Permanent Court of Arbitration's Arbitration Rules of 2012, available at https://pca-cpa.org/en/resources/pca-conventions-and-rules/. It is interesting to see that, in the *Dubai/Sharjah Boundary* arbitration, 91 ILR 543, the ILC Model Rules were regarded as an authoritative statement of customary international law and used to identify the salient characteristics of a true arbitral award. See D. W. Bowett, 'The Dubai/Sharjah Boundary Arbitration of 1981' (1994) 65 *BYBIL*, 103 at 116.

Permanent Court of Arbitration. The person designated to act in this capacity often also has the task of resolving any challenges which may be made to the neutral members.[36]

6.2.2 Independence and Impartiality of Arbitrators

The independence and impartiality of arbitrators is a fundamental principle of arbitral procedure. Independence and impartiality, although often taken as forming one concept, have different understandings. Independence relates to the absence of any relation between an arbitrator and one of the parties which may influence the arbitrator's decision. Impartiality on the other hand implies the absence of bias or predisposition of an arbitrator towards the parties or the substance of the dispute.

Members of an arbitral tribunal need to be independent and impartial, and this applies both to the party-appointed arbitrators and the 'neutral' members of an arbitral tribunal. Provisions to this effect are usually found in the applicable arbitration rules. The PCA Arbitration Rules (2012) for example require that persons which are approached to be appointed as arbitrator in a dispute need to 'disclose any circumstances likely to give rise to justifiable doubts as to his or her impartiality or independence'.

The PCA Arbitration Rules further require that 'an arbitrator, from the time of his or her appointment and throughout the arbitral proceedings, shall without delay disclose any such circumstances to the parties and the other arbitrators unless they have already been informed by him or her of these circumstances'.[37] This provision is identical to Article 11 of the UNCITRAL Arbitration Rules. Article 12 of the PCA Arbitration Rules, identical to Article 12 of the UNCITRAL Arbitration Rules, further provides that 'any arbitrator may be challenged if circumstances exist that give rise to justifiable doubts as to the arbitrator's impartiality or independence'.

The requirement that members of an arbitral tribunal need to be independent and impartial not only exists at the time of appointment but continues throughout the proceedings, as shown in the *Arbitration Between the Republic of Croatia and the Republic of Slovenia*. The allegations of unauthorized contacts between Slovenia's party-appointed arbitrator and one of the agents presenting Slovenia in the dispute,[38] resulted in Slovenia's party-appointed arbitrator immediately resigning from the

---

[36] For accounts of work of Sir Robert Jennings in this role, see (2000) 94 *AJIL*, 378 and (2001) 95 *AJIL*, 895.
[37] Article 11 PCA Arbitration Rules (2012), available at https://pca-cpa.org/en/resources/pca-conventions-and-rules/.
[38] See for an overview of these facts: *Arbitration Between the Republic of Croatia and the Republic of Slovenia (Croatia v. Slovenia)*, PCA Case No. 2012-04, Partial Award, 30 June 2016, paras 37 ff.

Tribunal. Failing to have done so may have in all likelihood resulted in a challenge of the arbitrator by Croatia.

Arbitration agreements may also contain references to the requirement of independence and impartiality, although this occurs only rarely. More often, arbitration agreements contain specific qualifications or qualities arbitrators need to possess, and these may in turn refer to the requirements of independence and impartiality. Article 2 Annex VII of UNCLOS, as we will also see in Chapter 10, for instance, requires the states parties to the UNCLOS to nominate to the 'list of arbitrators' which is maintained by the UN Secretary-General, arbitrators which need to be persons 'experienced in maritime affairs and enjoying the highest reputation for fairness, competence and integrity'. While the parties to the dispute may appoint other persons than those included on the list, the arbitrators appointed by the President of the ITLOS 'shall be of different nationalities and may not be in the service of, ordinarily resident in the territory of, or nationals of, any of the parties to the dispute'.[39] The Tribunal in the *Chagos Marine Protected Area* arbitration *(Mauritius v. United Kingdom)* considered moreover that the requirements of 'fairness, competence and integrity' are equally applicable to party-appointed arbitrators from outside the list, since these requirements are derived from 'general principles of international law and from the practice of international courts and tribunals'.[40]

As regards arbitration generally, challenges to arbitrators have recently increased,[41] partly because the increasing use of arbitration to resolve disputes has not been accompanied by a corresponding increase in the pool of arbitrators, with the result that real or perceived conflicts of interest have multiplied. Although challenges are not upheld very often, this seems likely to continue to be a problem.

A recent example is the challenge of Christopher Greenwood as a member of the Arbitral Tribunal in the *Chagos Marine Protected Area Arbitration (Mauritius v. United Kingdom)*.[42] Mauritius sought to challenge the appointment by the United Kingdom of Christopher Greenwood, then Judge at the ICJ, on the basis that he had a 'long, close and continuing relationship with the Government of the United Kingdom',[43] evidenced, amongst others, by Christopher Greenwood's participation in the appointment procedure of the new legal advisor to the UK's Foreign and

---

[39] Article 3(e) Annex VII UNCLOS.
[40] *Chagos Marine Protected Area Arbitration (Mauritius v. United Kingdom)*, PCA Case No. 2011-03, Reasoned Decision on Challenge, 30 November 2011, para. 135.
[41] See on the question of challenges: Chiara Giorgetti (ed.), *Challenges and Recusals of Judges and Arbitrators in International Courts and Tribunals*, Leiden, 2015.
[42] *Chagos Marine Protected Area Arbitration (Mauritius v. United Kingdom)*, PCA Case No. 2011-03, Reasoned Decision on Challenge, 30 November 2011.
[43] *Chagos Marine Protected Area Arbitration (Mauritius v. United Kingdom)*, PCA Case No. 2011-03, Reasoned Decision on Challenge, 30 November 2011, para. 39.

Commonwealth Office (FCO) slightly before the initiating of the proceedings.

The decision of the four other members of the Tribunal on the challenge provides, besides the decision on the challenge, interesting insights on the applicable rules and principles. The four members of the Tribunal, who decided on the challenge, confirmed that the applicable rules are the provisions found in Article 2 Annex VII of UNCLOS mentioned in the previous paragraphs. Second, the decision notes that the 'Declaration of Acceptance and a Statement of Impartiality and Independence' which is used for PCA-administered arbitrations and reflects the contents of Article 11 of the PCA Arbitration Rules,[44] implies the requirement of the absence of 'circumstances that might give rise to justifiable doubts as to the arbitrators' impartiality or independence'.[45]

The Tribunal then considered whether any other rules can be found in general principles of international law as evidenced by the practice of international courts and tribunals relating to the qualifications of judges and arbitrators. It first looked at Articles 16 and 17 of the ICJ Statute and Articles 7, 8 and 17 of the Statute of ITLOS which cover the rules on independence and impartiality of judges at the ICJ and the ITLOS respectively. These rules in essence consider the prior involvement in the subject matter of the case as constituting a conflict of interest. The Tribunal also considered Article 10 of the PCA 'Optional Rules for Arbitrating Disputes Between Two States', which provides that 'Any arbitrator may be challenged if circumstances exist that give rise to justifiable doubts as to the arbitrator's impartiality or independence', a provision identical to Article 12 of the more recent PCA Arbitration Rules of 2021 discussed above. While the PCA Rules had not been adopted by the parties to the *Chagos* arbitration, the Tribunal considered that the standard of independence and impartiality adopted in the Rules 'can be considered to form part of the practice of inter-State arbitral tribunals', having been relied on by various other inter-state arbitral tribunals.[46]

The Tribunal did not find the rules and practices of international criminal courts and tribunals, and rules developed by non-governmental bodies such as the IBA Guidelines on Conflicts of Interest in International Arbitration and those developed by international commercial arbitration institutions, to be applicable to inter-state arbitration. Based on the foregoing, the Tribunal thus limited the applicable standard to the existence of 'justifiable grounds for doubting the independence and impartiality of that

---

[44] The Declaration can be found annexed to the PCA Arbitration Rules (2012).
[45] *Chagos Marine Protected Area Arbitration (Mauritius v. United Kingdom)*, PCA Case No. 2011-03, Reasoned Decision on Challenge, 30 November 2011, para. 136.
[46] *Chagos Marine Protected Area Arbitration (Mauritius v. United Kingdom)*, PCA Case No. 2011-03, Reasoned Decision on Challenge, 30 November 2011, para. 151.

arbitrator in a particular case'.[47] The Tribunal added that it did not consider that, in the context of an arbitration based on Annex VII of the UNCLOS, it could have been the intention of the parties to set standards of independence and impartiality that are different from those that apply to judges at the ICJ or ITLOS (which are alternative forums to settle disputes under the UNCLOS as we will see in Chapter 10). The so-called 'Appearance of Bias Standard' which is more regularly used in international commercial arbitration and in investment arbitration,[48] was according to the Tribunal not applicable to the present case.[49] The Tribunal concluded that Greenwood's prior activities did not 'give rise to justifiable doubts as to his independence or impartiality'.[50]

6.3 Terms of Reference

Just as the appointment of arbitrators is in the hands of the parties, so it is for them to determine how the proceedings are to be conducted and what question or questions the arbitrator will be asked to decide. The 1899 and 1907 Hague Conventions laid down rules which have provided the procedural framework for many subsequent arbitrations; more recently, these have been elaborated through the work of the International Law Commission, UNCITRAL, the PCA and other bodies. Ultimately, however, it is for the parties to agree on the procedural arrangements, and so here, as elsewhere, they can exercise a high degree of control over the handling of their dispute.

6.3.1 Procedural Rules

The procedural arrangements determine the way in which the arbitration is to be conducted, where it is to be held and how the proceedings are to be paid for. The parties may agree to conduct the proceedings according to existing sets of rules of arbitration such as the UNCITRAL Arbitration Rules or the PCA Arbitration Rules. The advantage of using existing rules of procedure may be the acquaintance with these rules and the possibility to rely on previous decisions interpreting and applying the rules. The

---

[47] *Chagos Marine Protected Area Arbitration (Mauritius v. United Kingdom)*, PCA Case No. 2011-03, Reasoned Decision on Challenge, 30 November 2011, para. 166.
[48] See, however, for a decision in the context of investment arbitration which applies a less stringent standard than the 'appearance of bias': *ConocoPhillips Company et al. v. Bolivarian Republic of Venezuela*, ICSID Case No. ARB/07/30, Decision on the Proposal to Disqualify L. Yves Fortier, Q.C., Arbitrator, 27 February 2012.
[49] *Chagos Marine Protected Area Arbitration (Mauritius v. United Kingdom)*, PCA Case No. 2011-03, Reasoned Decision on Challenge, 30 November 2011, paras. 168–70.8885
[50] For a discussion of the standard applied, see Chiara Giorgetti, 'Challenges of arbitrators in international disputes: two tribunals reject the "appearance of bias" standard' (2012) *ASIL Insights*, 16.

procedure may also be complemented by the treaty containing the consent to arbitrate disputes. The use of the PCA Arbitration Rules for instance was agreed by the parties in the *Croatia/Slovenia* arbitration,[51] complemented by several specific provisions in relation to the appointment of the arbitrators amongst others. The UNCITRAL Arbitration Rules also are often used, notably for investment arbitration as we will see in Chapter 7. On occasion, the parties may also agree that the tribunal decides on the procedure to be followed, as was the case in the *Arbitration under the Timor Sea Treaty (Timor-Leste v. Australia)*.[52] If procedural issues need to be decided, arbitral tribunals will issue a procedural order to that effect.[53]

It is usual to include quite detailed provisions relating to the constitution of the tribunal including challenges to arbitrators, number and order of the written pleadings, the oral stage of the proceedings and the important issue of time limits. Other matters which are normally covered in the *compromis*, compromissory clause or procedural rules may be how the tribunal is to obtain evidence, whether it may appoint experts or conduct visits, whether it can order provisional measures, what languages will be used, how the decision will be taken, whether separate opinions are allowed and whether the decision will be published, and more generally the powers of the arbitral tribunal. Although each of these matters can be negotiated separately, it is clearly convenient if the parties can agree on the use of standard provisions. In the same way, when dealing with the finer procedural details, time can be saved by following established practice or by referring to existing procedural rules.

In the 1985 *Maritime Delimitation* case, for example, it was agreed at the first session of the tribunal that the arbitration 'would follow the same rules of procedure as the International Court of Justice, and more specifically that Articles 30–31, 49–50, 52, 54, 56–58, 60–68, 71, 72, 94–95 and 98 of the Rules of the Court would be applicable *mutatis mutandis*'.[54]

Similarly, in the *Heathrow Airport* arbitration, the parties agreed that the tribunal should use rules of procedure adapted from those of the International Centre for Settlement of Investment Disputes.[55] The use of rules developed for international investment arbitration is explained by the complex economic issues involved in this dispute and the same factor

---

[51] Article 6 of the Arbitration Agreement between the Government of the Republic of Croatia and the Government of the Republic of Slovenia, 4 November 2009, available at https://pcacases.com/web/sendAttach/2165.

[52] *Arbitration under the Timor Sea Treaty (Timor-Leste v. Australia)*, PCA Case No. 2013-16.

[53] See e.g. *Arbitration under the Timor Sea Treaty (Timor-Leste v. Australia)*, PCA Case No. 2013-16, Procedural Order No 1 (Rules of Procedure), 6 December 2013, available at https://pcacases.com/web/sendAttach/2107.

[54] Award, para. 9, 77 ILR 647. A similar approach was employed in the *Dubai/Sharjah Boundary* arbitration where the vagueness of the *compromis* caused a number of problems; see Bowett, 'The Dubai/Sharjah Boundary Arbitration' (n. 35) 108–9.

[55] See Witten, 'The US–UK arbitration' (n. 20) 182–3.

accounts for a number of other procedural innovations. Thus, the United States and the United Kingdom agreed that staggered, rather than simultaneous, pleadings should be filed,[56] while the tribunal decided that the proceedings should be divided into two phases: an initial phase to decide whether the US claims were well-founded; then, if necessary, a remedial phase to determine compensation. In the event, the second phase was never concluded because the case was settled. However, it is interesting to note that, during the pre-hearing period of the remedial phase, the tribunal was persuaded by the United States to direct the United Kingdom to produce hundreds of pages of financial documentation for inspection. Pre-trial discovery is, of course, common in domestic civil litigation, but rather unusual in intergovernmental arbitration. The fact that it was used so extensively here again highlights the special nature of the issues in this case and, like the innovations already described, shows how the procedural framework of an international arbitration can be adapted to meet the parties' needs.

6.3.2 The Issues to be Decided by the Tribunal

The definition of the issue is important because it establishes the scope of the arbitrator's jurisdiction. By defining the issue broadly, the parties can use arbitration to remove a major obstacle to good relations. Conversely (and more commonly), by defining the issue narrowly, they can prevent an investigation of wider questions which might create more problems than it would resolve, or exclude from arbitration particular issues for which negotiation or some other means of settlement is considered more appropriate. In the *Rainbow Warrior* case, for example, France and New Zealand asked the Secretary-General for a ruling on a number of aspects of the dispute, including the amount of compensation to be paid by France for sinking the vessel in Auckland harbour and the future of the two French intelligence agents who were serving prison sentences in New Zealand for carrying out this action. The Secretary-General was not asked to decide whether compensation was due, because this responsibility was admitted, nor whether New Zealand was justified in detaining the agents, because both states were more concerned with finding an acceptable solution to the dispute than with justifying their past actions. Although, therefore, the Secretary-General had to deal with a range of issues, in the interests of settling the dispute the parties chose to focus on certain matters to the exclusion of others.

---

[56] See *ibid.*, 183, n. 20. This departure from the procedure laid down in the 1977 'Bermuda II' Agreement, which prescribes two rounds of simultaneous pleadings, allowed the parties to respond to each other's submissions.

The framing of the question or questions is normally a matter for negotiation between the parties and, because of its importance, may be difficult to agree. This was the case in the *Beagle Channel* dispute where sovereignty over the islands of Picton, Nueva and Lennox was clearly the central issue, but Chile and Argentina were unable to devise a mutually acceptable formulation for the *compromis*. The solution was to include two versions of the question, and refer both to the tribunal for decision. A different solution was adopted in the *Eritrea/Yemen* arbitration, where territorial sovereignty was in issue, but the parties could not agree on whether certain islands fell within the scope of the arbitration. The two states therefore left the question for the tribunal itself to determine, asking it to decide this as a preliminary issue, taking into account 'the respective positions of the two Parties'. A matter on which they did agree was that, as their maritime boundaries were also disputed, and largely dependent on their territorial titles, the arbitration should take place in two stages. They therefore included in their *compromis* a requirement that the issue of titles, along with the scope of the dispute, should be decided at the first stage of the arbitration, followed by a second on the question of maritime delimitation.

In case of compromissory clauses, the treaty containing the clause will define the issues which may be submitted to an arbitral tribunal established under that treaty. Article 32(1) of the OSPAR Convention for example provides that

> any disputes between Contracting Parties relating to the interpretation or application of the Convention, which cannot be settled otherwise by the Contracting Parties concerned, for instance by means of inquiry or conciliation within the Commission, shall at the request of any of those Contracting Parties, be submitted to arbitration under the conditions laid down in this Article.

The parties may then further define the issue in the request for arbitration, provided that the overall issue to be decided by the Tribunal remains within the overall limits set by the treaty containing the consent to arbitration.

If the parties fail to define the issues on which they want a decision with sufficient particularity, damaging disputes over exactly what has been agreed are likely to arise. In the *Alabama Claims* case, for example, disagreement between Great Britain and the United States over whether the tribunal was authorised to award compensation for indirect damage almost led to a failure of the arbitration. On the other hand, defining the issue too narrowly can sometimes create difficulties of a different kind. In the *Taba* dispute, which concerned the location of certain pillars marking an international boundary, Egypt and Israel set out their respective submissions in an appendix to the *compromis* and asked the tribunal to decide the location of the pillars in dispute. However, in an annex to the agreement, they stated that the tribunal was not authorised to establish a location of a boundary pillar other than a location advanced by Israel or Egypt and recorded in the appendix to the agreement. In other words, the tribunal had to choose between the rival locations put forward by the parties and could not select a different solution. This type of directive was not unprecedented and is, of course, perfectly clear. It does, however, create a problem if neither party can make out a persuasive case. One of the arbitrators considered that, if Israel's argument was rejected, Egypt's was even less convincing and so the tribunal should declare that neither had proved its case.[57] Although the majority rejected this conclusion, there is no doubt that restricting the powers of a tribunal so severely can generate problems.

A rather similar difficulty has arisen in a number of cases concerned with the delimitation of maritime zones. Here, the parties must not only decide whether they wish the tribunal to draw a boundary line on a map, or to indicate merely the principles and rules applicable to the delimitation, or to do something in between.[58] They must also decide whether they wish the tribunal to deal with the continental shelf alone, or with the whole exclusive economic zone, and, if the latter, whether the tribunal must establish a single boundary for all purposes, or whether it is to be allowed to deal separately with jurisdiction over the sea and the seabed. The tendency in recent arbitral agreements has been to require a single boundary line and it is easy to see the advantages of this solution. From the juridical point of view, however, a directive of this kind can make it difficult for a tribunal to discharge its task adequately, because the considerations relevant to the sea and the seabed will often be quite distinct and it might therefore be better to have different boundaries for different purposes.

6.3.3 Limits to the jurisdiction of arbitral tribunals

Arbitrators only have authority to answer the question or questions referred, and if they exceed their jurisdiction the award can be challenged as a nullity. As a result, when jurisdictional questions arise in the work of arbitral tribunals, they are treated with the same scrupulous regard for the principle of consensuality as in proceedings before the International Court. For example, it emerged in the course of the proceedings in the *Channel* arbitration that to delimit a seabed boundary in the area between the

---

[57] See the elaborate dissenting opinion of Professor Lapidoth in 80 ILR 312 at 347–8.
[58] For example, to identify the relevant principles and rules and 'to specify precisely the practical way in which the aforesaid principles and rules apply to this situation so as to enable the experts of the two countries to delimit those areas without difficulty', see the Special Agreement in the *Tunisia–Libya Continental Shelf* case in [1982] ICJ Rep. 21. The problems of interpreting this type of directive are discussed in the penultimate part of Chapter 9.

Channel Islands and the coasts of Normandy and Brittany, it would be necessary to decide a number of disputed issues concerning each party's territorial sea. Since this would be to go beyond the terms of the *compromis* which the United Kingdom and France were evidently unwilling to extend, the Court decided that a delimitation of this area was outside its competence and must be left for the parties themselves to determine. In the *Eritrea/Yemen* case, on the other hand, the tribunal, having identified certain islands as belonging to Yemen, went on to hold that this did not affect the traditional rights of Eritrean fishermen in the surrounding seas. Since the arbitration agreement asked only for a decision 'on sovereignty', the tribunal's approach might be questioned, but on practical grounds can be justified as a sensible interpretation of its remit.[59]

Several jurisdictional questions have arisen in the work of arbitral tribunals established under Annex VII of the UNCLOS on precisely the question of whether certain claims could be considered to fall under the issues referred to by the parties to the dispute. While these will be discussed in Chapter 10, several decisions of arbitral tribunals established under Annex VII of the UNCLOS deserve attention here, since they touch upon the jurisdiction of tribunals in inter-state arbitration generally, and the relation with consent of states.

An issue that has arisen in several recent international arbitrations concerns the question of whether an arbitral tribunal is authorized to settle questions of territorial sovereignty of states parties to the dispute as 'ancillary' questions. The questions which arose in several recent cases of course result from the specific nature of arbitration under Annex VII of the UNCLOS. Questions relating to the application and interpretation of the UNCLOS often imply questions in respect of a dispute over land sovereignty, and hence trigger the question of whether the tribunal has jurisdiction to decide that aspect of the case. The question is more broadly of importance to international arbitration generally.

In the *Chagos* arbitration, the Arbitral Tribunal confirmed that 'where a dispute concerns the interpretation or application of the Convention, the jurisdiction of a court or tribunal pursuant to Article 288(1) [UNCLOS] extends to making such findings of fact or ancillary determinations of law as are necessary to resolve the dispute presented to it'.[60] The Tribunal further explained that 'where the "real issue in the case" and the "object of the claim" do not relate to the interpretation or application of the Convention, however, an incidental connection between the dispute and

---

[59] See N. S. M. Antunes, 'The Eritrea–Yemen Arbitration: first stage – the law of title to territory re-averred' (1999) 48 *ICLQ*, 362 at 383–4. See also, however, the text accompanying note 87 below.

[60] *Chagos Marine Protected Area Arbitration (Mauritius v. United Kingdom)*, PCA Case No. 2011-03, Reasoned Decision on Challenge, 30 November 2011, para. 220.

some matter regulated by the Convention is insufficient to bring the dispute, as a whole, within the ambit of Article 288(1) [UNCLOS]'.[61] The Tribunal did, however, note that in some instances 'a minor issue of territorial sovereignty could indeed be ancillary to a dispute concerning the interpretation or application of the Convention'.[62] Applied to the case, the Tribunal declined jurisdiction of certain parts of Mauritius' claim, including the question of whether the United Kingdom was entitled to declare a 'Marine Protected Area' or other maritime zones in the Chagos Archipelago, since this would have implied for the Tribunal to decide whether the United Kingdom was the 'coastal State' and hence had territorial sovereignty.

The *Dispute Concerning Coastal State Rights in the Black Sea, Sea of Azov, and Kerch Strait (Ukraine* v. *the Russian Federation)* arbitration[63] concerned the question of coastal state rights of both states in the Black Sea, the Sea of Azov and the Kerch Strait. The Tribunal established that a sovereignty dispute existed, and then engaged in the question of whether deciding that part of the dispute fell within its jurisdiction. The tribunal followed the approach taken in the *Chagos* arbitration and concluded that the dispute regarding sovereignty over Crimea 'is not a minor issue ancillary to the dispute concerning the interpretation or application of the Convention'.[64] The Tribunal, as a consequence, concluded that it had no jurisdiction over Ukraine's claims, to the extent that a ruling of the tribunal would necessarily require it to decide, directly or implicitly, on the sovereignty of either party over Crimea.

In *The 'Enrica Lexie' Incident (Italy* v. *India)*[65] arbitration, the question did not concern the jurisdiction of the tribunal over sovereignty questions, but whether the two Italian marines involved in a shooting incident enjoyed immunity from criminal proceedings. The dispute revolved around the question of which party was entitled to exercise jurisdiction over a shooting incident which had involved two Italian Navy Marines on an Italian oil tanker (the *Enrica Lexie*) which had allegedly killed two Indian fishermen aboard an Indian vessel (the *St. Antony*). The Tribunal in this case confirmed jurisdiction over the question of the immunity of the Italian marines:

---

[61] *Chagos Marine Protected Area Arbitration (Mauritius* v. *United Kingdom)*, PCA Case No. 2011-03, Reasoned Decision on Challenge, 30 November 2011, para. 220.
[62] *Chagos Marine Protected Area Arbitration (Mauritius* v. *United Kingdom)*, PCA Case No. 2011-03, Reasoned Decision on Challenge, 30 November 2011, para. 221.
[63] *Dispute Concerning Coastal State Rights in the Black Sea, Sea of Azov, and Kerch Strait (Ukraine* v. *the Russian Federation)* PCA Case No. 2017-06, Award on Preliminary Objections, 21 February 2020.
[64] *Dispute Concerning Coastal State Rights in the Black Sea, Sea of Azov, and Kerch Strait (Ukraine* v. *the Russian Federation)* PCA Case No. 2017-06, Award on Preliminary Objections, 21 February 2020, para. 195.
[65] *The 'Enrica Lexie' Incident (Italy* v. *India)*, PCA Case No. 2015-28, Award, 21 May 2020.

The Arbitral Tribunal considers that, while the Convention may not provide a basis for entertaining an independent immunity claim under general international law, the Arbitral Tribunal's competence extends to the determination of the issue of immunity of the Marines that necessarily arises as an incidental question in the application of the Convention.[66]

In the *St. Pierre and Miquelon* case,[67] the issue of consent arose in relation to a third party. France sought a delimitation of the continental shelf appertaining to islands situated off the Canadian coast and also asked the tribunal to determine their entitlement beyond the 200-mile limit. However, the court held that this would involve determining France's rights *vis-à-vis* the international community which was not a party to the arbitration. It therefore decided that it had no jurisdiction to extend its ruling in the way requested. We shall see later that the International Court operates under a similar limitation. Thus, not only is the consent of the litigants essential to the arbitrator's competence, but so is the consent of any third party whose rights may be in issue.

In the above examples, the courts concerned were able to decide (some of) the main points in dispute, and so the limitations on their authority were not very important. Sometimes, however, the issue of jurisdiction goes to the root of the arbitrators' competence. In its decision in the case of *Haji-Bagherpour* v. *United States*,[68] the Iran–United States Claims Tribunal decided that it had no jurisdiction over a claim by an Iranian national whose oil tanker was destroyed by American forces during the abortive attempt to rescue the diplomatic hostages in April 1980. Similarly, in the case of *Grimm* v. *Iran*,[69] the Iran–United States Claims Tribunal decided that it had no jurisdiction over a claim by a wife based on her husband's assassination on the ground that the claimant's 'property rights' were not in issue. In these cases, then, individual claims failed and were rejected on jurisdictional grounds.

Even more significant are those decisions in which the effect of a ruling is to settle the fate of a whole class of cases. In *Case No. A/18*,[70] for example, the Tribunal decided that, in view of the purpose for which it had been established, it had jurisdiction to entertain the claims of dual Iranian and United States nationals, provided they satisfied the dominant or effective nationality test in accordance with general international law. In an earlier ruling, the Tribunal decided that, under the terms of the Settlement Agreement, it had no general jurisdiction over claims which

---

[66] *The 'Enrica Lexie' Incident (Italy* v. *India)*, PCA Case No. 2015-28, Award, 21 May 2020, para. 808.
[67] *Case Concerning Delimitation of Maritime Areas between Canada and the French Republic (St Pierre and Miquelon)* (1992) 95 ILR 645, summarised in (1993) 87 *AJIL*, 452.
[68] (1983) 2 Iran–US CTR 38; 71 ILR 600.   [69] (1983) 2 Iran–US CTR 78; 71 ILR 650.
[70] (1984) 5 Iran–US CTR 25; 75 ILR 176. The scope of this decision was subsequently considered in *Saghi* v. *Iran* (1993), 14 Iran–US CTR 3; 84 ILR 609.

might be filed by Iran against nationals of the United States.[71] This, too, was a critical decision because it had the effect of limiting the Tribunal's competence to Iranian counter-claims against Americans with cases already before the Tribunal.

6.4 Basis of the Decision

No less important than the definition of the issue is the parties' directive to the tribunal as to the criteria to be applied in making its decision. Frequently, the tribunal's instructions are to decide the matter in accordance with international law. However, municipal law also may form the basis of the decisions. Moreover, if the parties wish to increase a tribunal's freedom, they can authorise it to take into account what is fair and reasonable, as well as the rules of international or municipal law.

6.4.1 The Law Applicable to the Merits

The court was called upon to decide the boundary of the British and French portions of the continental shelf on this basis in the *Channel* arbitration, and the *compromis* in the *Beagle Channel* case, after formulating the rival versions of the point at issue, was in similar terms. When the directive is less explicit, the applicable law must be inferred. In the *Rann of Kutch* case, for example, the parties asked the court to decide the case in light of their respective claims and the evidence produced before it, and in the *Taba* dispute the *compromis* contained no reference at all to the applicable law, but merely asked the tribunal to decide the location of the boundary pillars 'of the recognised international boundary'. Despite these unhelpful instructions, the respective courts followed the usual practice in such cases, assumed that what the parties wanted was a decision based on international law and gave their judgments accordingly.

Sometimes, the parties want international law to provide the basis for the tribunal's decision, but wish particular aspects to be emphasised. For example, when Eritrea and Ethiopia set up a boundary commission to define their disputed frontier in 2000, they required it to perform its task on the basis of 'pertinent colonial treaties' and applicable international law, but explicitly laid down that 'the Commission shall not have the power to make decisions *ex aequo et bono*'.[72] Similarly, in the *Eritrea/Yemen* case,

---

[71] Iran–United States Claims Tribunal, Decision with regard to Jurisdiction over Claims Filed by Iran against US Nationals (1981) 1 Iran–US CTR 101; 62 ILR 595.
[72] On this and other aspects of the Commission's work, see J. G. Merrills, 'Reflections on dispute settlement in light of recent arbitrations involving Eritrea', in A. Constantinides and N. Zaikos (eds), *The Diversity of International Law*, Leiden, 2009, p. 109. Also M. N. Shaw, 'Title, control and closure? The experience of the Eritrea–Ethiopia Boundary Commission' (2007) 56 *ICLQ*, 755.

the tribunal was asked to rule on territorial sovereignty 'in accordance with the principles, rules and practices of international law applicable to the matter, and on the basis, in particular, of historic titles'. Likewise, at the second stage of the arbitration, it was requested to delimit the maritime boundaries between Eritrea and Yemen in light of the decision reached in the first stage and 'taking into account . . . the United Nations Convention on the Law of the Sea and any other pertinent factor'. Given the matters in dispute and the parties' respective positions, no decision based on law could have ignored the elements mentioned even without these directives. By including them specifically, however, the two states indicated clearly what they saw as key features of the case and therefore expected the tribunal to deal with in its decision.

If the parties are agreed that a solution in accordance with international law would not be appropriate, they can instruct the arbitrator to decide the dispute on some other basis. This can sometimes be another way of isolating a dispute from surrounding complications. In the *Alabama Claims* case, for example, the parties instructed the tribunal to apply a particular set of rules concerning neutrality which the United States regarded as international law, but Great Britain did not. Here, then, the parties' willingness to have the rules applied as *lex specialis* meant that the wider disagreement as to their status was no longer an obstacle to settlement of the dispute. If, on the other hand, the arbitrators' remit is not extended, then the scope for such initiatives is restricted. Thus, in the *OSPAR (Article 9)* case, an arbitration founded on Article 32 of the 1992 OSPAR Convention, the tribunal held that the only applicable law was the Convention itself, and no less crucially that, when interpreting the Convention, it could not take account of evolving international law and practice, or developments that were 'almost law', in the absence of express authority to do so.[73]

The parties' ability to specify the law the arbitrator is to apply also enables them to employ municipal law, either alone or in combination with some other system. In the *Trail Smelter* case,[74] the tribunal was instructed to apply 'the law and practice followed in dealing with cognate questions in the United States of America as well as international law and practice'. Since the dispute concerned liability for trans-frontier air pollution, an issue on which international law had only recently begun to develop, authorising the use of municipal law here provided the tribunal with a recognisably legal basis for its decision, as well as an

---

[73] The tribunal reached this decision by a majority of two to one. For criticism of its conclusion, see P. Sands, *Principles of International Environmental Law*, 2nd ed., Cambridge, 2003, pp. 857–8, but compare T. L. McDorman, Note (2004) 98 AJIL, 330 at 337–9.

[74] *Trail Smelter Arbitration (United States v. Canada)* (1938 and 1941) 3 RIAA 1905. For commentary, see J. E. Read, 'The Trail Smelter dispute' (1963) 1 *Can. Yearbook Int. L.*, 213.

invaluable opportunity to advance the development of international environmental law.

Reference to municipal law is, of course, particularly common in commercial arbitration and in investment arbitration as we will see in Chapter 7. The concession agreement involved in the important case of *BP v. Libya*,[75] for example, provided that:

> This concession shall be governed by and interpreted in accordance with the principles of the law of Libya common to the principles of international law and in the absence of such common principles then by and in accordance with the general principles of law, including such of those principles as may have been applied by international tribunals.

This kind of dispute, involving an entity other than a state, is strictly speaking beyond the scope of this study but similar provisions can be found in arbitration agreements between states. The Iran–United States Claims Tribunal, for example, is instructed to 'decide all cases on the basis of respect for law', and to apply 'such choice of law rules and principles of commercial and international law as the Tribunal determines to be applicable, taking into account relevant usages of the trade, contract provisions and changed circumstances' – a directive which clearly reflects the predominantly commercial character of the Tribunal's business, as well as an intention to give it considerable freedom of action.[76]

6.4.2 Municipal Law and *Ex Aequo et Bono*

If the parties wish to increase a tribunal's freedom still further, they can authorise it to take into account what is fair and reasonable, as well as the rules of international or municipal law. There is a hint of this in the reference to 'changed circumstances' in the provision just mentioned, and the direction to the *Trail Smelter* Tribunal to 'give consideration to the desire of the high contracting parties to reach a solution just to all parties concerned' was quite explicit. In the absence of such instructions, arbitral tribunals have frequently achieved the same result by using 'equitable' considerations of various kinds to qualify or expand their application and interpretation of the law. This technique has been particularly prominent in arbitrations concerning territorial and boundary disputes, where the best solution may sometimes be difficult to justify in strictly legal terms. Thus, in the *Rann of Kutch* case, the award of certain territory to Pakistan was held to be justified on the ground that 'it would be inequitable

---

[75] *BP Exploration Company (Libya) Ltd v. Government of the Libyan Arab Republic* (1973) 53 ILR 297. For analysis, see R. C. A. White, 'Expropriation of the Libyan oil concessions: two conflicting international arbitrations' (1981) 30 *ICLQ*, 1.

[76] See J. R. Crook, 'Applicable law in international arbitration: the Iran–US Claims Tribunal experience' (1989) 83 *AJIL*, 278; and Aldrich, *The Jurisprudence* (n. 24) ch. 4.

to recognise these inlets as foreign territory. It would be conducive to friction and conflict. The paramount consideration of promoting peace and stability in the region compels the recognition and confirmation that this territory, which is wholly surrounded by Pakistan territory, also be regarded as such'.[77]

It is worth noting that, in some situations, it is unnecessary to give arbitrators express authority to apply equity because such considerations are already incorporated in the relevant legal rule. In the *Heathrow Airport* arbitration, for example, the question before the tribunal was whether the United Kingdom had fulfilled its obligations under Article 10 of the 1977 Air Services Agreement with the United States, allowing the imposition of charges which were 'just and reasonable' and subject to 'equitable apportionment' among airport users. This very general language clearly gave the arbitrators a good deal of freedom, but at the same time made their task difficult because there was little in the way of international precedent to guide them.[78] Another example of this state of affairs is in the law relating to the delimitation of maritime zones, where, as a result of judicial pronouncements, developing state practice and international conventions, it is now accepted that the law requires delimitation in accordance with equitable principles, taking into account all relevant circumstances, so as to reach an equitable result. This clearly leaves a great deal of scope for argument as to the content of the applicable principles, the relevance of particular circumstances and the appropriate result in a specific case.

It is interesting, however, that in deciding the various cases which have arisen, international courts and tribunals have consistently made the point that their decisions must be based on law, and that without further authorisation they are not 'endowed with discretionary powers or ... authorised to decide *ex aequo et bono*'.[79] It follows that, while certain criteria are accepted as relevant to delimitation, attempts to refashion nature or to compensate for the economic inequalities of states are not. In this way, tribunals dealing with maritime delimitation have sought to utilise the flexibility inherent in the idea of equity, while at the same time retaining their legal character and avoiding approaches which would

---

[77] 50 ILR 530. For a penetrating analysis of the use of equity and related considerations by international tribunals in such cases, see A. L. W. Munkman, 'Adjudication and adjustment: international judicial decision and the settlement of territorial and boundary disputes' (1972–3) 46 *BYBIL*, 1. On equity in other contexts, see C. W. Jenks, *The Prospects of International Adjudication*, London, 1964, ch. 7.
[78] See Witten, 'The US–UK arbitration' (n. 20) 191. As the same writer points out, the general language of the terms which were being applied also had the effect of depriving the decision of most of its value as a precedent.
[79] *Maritime Delimitation* case, 77 ILR 635 at 675–6.

smack of conciliation. Whether this delicate distinction can actually be sustained is an issue to which we shall return in Chapter 9.

When arbitrators are asked by the parties to have regard to equitable considerations, or take it upon themselves to do so, they are no longer simply adjudicators, applying the relevant rules, but begin to assume the role of legislators, creating law for the case in hand. In the cases considered above, equity was employed as part of the law, or as a supplement to it, and the arbitrator thus combined the two functions. Sometimes, however, what is wanted is a wholly legislative solution, a decision, that is, in which the question of current rights is completely subordinated to the search for a fair and reasonable solution. Arbitration is flexible enough to allow for such a solution, which the parties can obtain by asking the tribunal to render its decision *ex aequo et bono*.

Numerous examples of tribunals being given the authority to decide cases on this basis can be found in treaties of arbitration. The convention between Great Britain and Portugal of 1872 regarding claims to Delagoa Bay provided that 'should the Arbiter be unable to decide wholly in favour of either of the respective claims, he shall be requested to give such a decision as will, in his opinion, furnish an equitable solution of the difficulty'. And a treaty on the arbitration of boundary disputes concluded between Colombia and Ecuador in 1907 went even further in providing that 'the arbiters ... may, leaving to one side strict law, adopt an equitable line in accordance with the necessities and convenience of the two countries'.[80]

In several of the cases decided on this basis, an arbitrator has been called upon to lay down the rules of a new regime to regulate aspects of the parties' relations, a matter which would normally be settled by diplomatic negotiation. In both the *Bering Sea* arbitration[81] and the *North Atlantic Coast Fisheries* case,[82] a framework for the future conduct of the United States and the United Kingdom was created in this way, while in the *Brcko* arbitration[83] a tribunal set up under the 1995 Dayton Peace Agreement created a special regime for a disputed area of Bosnia and Herzegovina, and, in the *Free Zones* arbitration,[84] a tribunal undertook the onerous task of laying down new customs regulations to govern the exchange of goods

---

[80] See Munkman, 'Adjudication and adjustment' (n. 77) 24.
[81] *Bering Sea Arbitration (Great Britain v. United States)* (1893) in Moore, *International Arbitrations* (n. 13) vol. I, p. 935; also in (1912) 6 *AJIL*, 233.
[82] *North Atlantic Coast Fisheries Arbitration (Great Britain v. United States)* (1910) 11 RIAA 173.
[83] *Arbitral Tribunal for Dispute over Inter-Entity Boundary in Brcko*, Final Award, (1999) 38 ILM 534; and see M. G. Karnavas, 'Creating the legal framework of the Brcko district of Bosnia and Herzegovina' (2003) 97 *AJIL*, 111. It should be noted, however, that in setting up this regime the tribunal adopted an extremely broad interpretation of its terms of reference.
[84] *The Free Zones of Upper Savoy and the District of Gex*, Arbitral Award (1933), (1933–4) 10 PCIJ Ann. R. (Ser. E) 106; also in Wetter, *The International Arbitral Process* (n. 1) vol. I, p. 596.

between the free zones and Switzerland 'in a manner more appropriate to the economic conditions of the present day'.

In the unusual circumstances of the *Rainbow Warrior* affair, the Secretary-General interpreted his function in a rather similar way. Here, the parties appear to have given no indication at all of the basis on which the case was to be decided, and the Secretary-General, whose decision was in the form of an elaborate set of conclusions, saw no necessity to explore the issue. However, in dealing with the crucial question of the future of the imprisoned French agents, he outlined the parties' opposing submissions, and then said that he saw his task as to 'find a solution in respect of the two officers which both respects and reconciles these conflicting positions'.[85] This certainly suggests that he considered that his function was to find an acceptable result, rather than to determine the parties' legal rights, and this is borne out by the solution which he arrived at. For, as well as settling the question of compensation and various other issues, the Secretary-General decided that the agents should be transferred from New Zealand and spend the next three years under military discipline on a base in a remote island in French Polynesia. This ingenious solution, which was subsequently implemented, would clearly not have been open to an arbitrator concerned only with the parties' legal rights, and in this respect the case resembles those in which arbitral tribunals have created new regimes. On the other hand, the explicit emphasis on reconciling the parties' positions suggests a process closer to conciliation than arbitration *ex aequo et bono*.

In the *Eritrea/Yemen* arbitration, having ruled at the first stage of the case that its decision on territorial title was without prejudice to the parties' traditional fishing rights, the tribunal then had to establish the scope and basis of such rights at the second stage, a matter on which Eritrea and Yemen, perhaps not surprisingly, expressed very different views. The tribunal thus found itself with the task of identifying, or (more accurately) creating, a regime for fishing, a consequence not of the arbitral *compromis* but of its own earlier decision. Although unusual, this self-imposed task, as already mentioned, can be regarded as both necessary and justified in the circumstances. Less easy to defend, however, is the tribunal's decision to account for the new regime in terms of Islamic law, a legal system which it had not been asked to apply. As one critic of the case has observed, tribunals in international arbitrations 'would be well advised to stick to international law, particularly when the parties have expressly indicated that they wish it to be applied and when it contains all the elements necessary for achieving the tribunal's objectives'.[86]

---

[85] *Rainbow Warrior* ruling, 74 ILR 241 at 272.
[86] See W. M. Reisman, Note (2000) 94 *AJIL*, 721 at 729, and, for a more detailed analysis, N. S. M. Antunes, 'The second stage of the Eritrea–Yemen arbitration and the development of international law' (2001) 50 *ICLQ*, 299 at 301–16.

How significant is the distinction between, on the one hand, arbitration *ex aequo et bono* in a case like the *Free Zones*, or the 'binding conciliation' of the *Rainbow Warrior* case, and, on the other hand, arbitration according to law in, say, the *Channel* arbitration? It has often been pointed out that adjudication is never simply a mechanical process of applying rules, but always involves an element of creativity. Conversely, in cases where the arbitrator is deliberately given freedom, he legislates not in a vacuum, but against the background of the parties' legal rights. Arbitration according to law and arbitration *ex aequo et bono* should be seen, then, as points on a continuum rather than as fundamentally different operations, and the question is not so much whether law is relevant in a given arbitration, but how far the arbitrator is authorised to base his decision on other grounds.

But, if the distinction between arbitration according to law and arbitration *ex aequo et bono* should not be exaggerated, it should not be minimised either. Arbitration of the *Free Zones* type calls for the decision-maker to review a broader and more diverse range of evidence than a conventional legal arbitration, and therefore imposes a different and perhaps more onerous task. This clearly has implications for the composition of the tribunal and the organisation of its work. If technical issues of a non-legal nature are to be a prominent feature of the parties' submissions, the tribunal is likely to require the services of an expert, or, as in the *Free Zones* case, may itself be made up of non-lawyers with the appropriate skills. Here, there is an obvious parallel between arbitration and the processes of inquiry and conciliation which, as we have just seen, the *Rainbow Warrior* case has served to underline.

A more fundamental point is that the parties' directive to the tribunal normally defines the limits of its authority and must always be respected. A request for a decision according to law, for a decision *ex aequo et bono*, or for something in between, reflects the parties' wish that the tribunal settle their dispute on a narrower or a broader basis. If it turns out that the framework prescribed by the parties has not in fact guided the tribunal's approach to the case, this may, as we shall see, be grounds for setting aside the decision.

6.5 Effect of the Award

An arbitral award is binding, but not necessarily final. For it may be open to the parties to take further proceedings to interpret, revise, rectify, appeal or nullify the decision, as was discussed in Chapter 1. Whether such steps are permissible, and, if so, whether the new case can be heard by the original tribunal, or must be brought before another body such as the International Court, depends partly on general international law, but mainly on the terms of the arbitration agreement.

6.5.1 Interpretation, Revision and Rectification

The power to interpret an award, or to appeal against it, must normally be the subject of an express grant. Since the object of the parties in going to arbitration is to end the dispute, provision for appeal is relatively rare. Interpretation, on the other hand, which concerns the clarification of the award, not its correctness, is easier to justify and more commonly allowed. Thus, in the *Taba* case, the *compromis* provided that any dispute between the parties 'as to the interpretation of the award or its implementation' could be referred to the tribunal for clarification at the request of either party, within thirty days of the rendering of the award. Similarly, the agreement in the *Channel* arbitration allowed disputes 'as to the meaning and scope of the decision' to be referred back within a period of three months. In the second case, the arrangements for interpretation were to prove important because a serious disagreement arose relating to two parts of the award. This was resolved only after further proceedings in which the scope of the power of the Court of Arbitration to review its award became a crucial issue.

The *Channel* arbitration demonstrates that, when a tribunal is asked to revisit a decision, it must be careful not to exceed its authority. The same point emerges from the rejection by the Eritrea–Ethiopia Boundary Commission of a 'Request for Interpretation, Correction and Consultation' from Ethiopia on the ground that what was sought went beyond the Commission's powers of interpretation or revision, and as such was inadmissible.[87] On the other hand, the tribunal in the *Iron Rhine Railway* case, having made a minor correction at the request of Belgium, went on to issue an interpretation of its award,[88] answering a number of questions from the same state relating to its scope and implications. While it is true that 'judicial and arbitral practice on the exercise of the power of interpretation is somewhat limited',[89] these cases reflect the varying situations that can arise, and show how practice on interpretation is accumulating.

One of the many unusual features of the *Rainbow Warrior* case was that the question of disputes relating to implementation, instead of being dealt with in the initial agreement, was addressed in the award itself. New Zealand was anxious to ensure that the agreements which would be necessary to implement the Secretary-General's ruling would be subject to compulsory arbitration in the event of a dispute arising as to their interpretation or application. Observing that France was not averse to this, the Secretary-General decided that such a procedure should be created.

---

[87] Eritrea–Ethiopia Boundary Commission, Decision on Interpretation of 24 June 2002, available at www.pca-cpa.org.
[88] *Iron Rhine Railway*, Award on Interpretation of 20 September 2005, available at www.pca-cpa.org.
[89] C. Brown, *A Common Law of International Adjudication*, Oxford, 2007, p. 173.

This reinforces the point already made, that the ruling was concerned to create a framework for regulating the parties' relations in the future, as well as the suggestion outlined above to the effect that some of the elements of arbitration were here displaced by factors reminiscent of conciliation. It is also of interest that, in outlining the arrangements for the arbitration of future disputes, the Secretary-General gave himself the power to designate both the neutral member and the national members of the three-member tribunal if the parties failed to do so. Like the other parts of the ruling, these arrangements were subsequently incorporated in an agreement between the parties,[90] and their value was soon to be demonstrated.

The dispute which prompted the *Rainbow Warrior II* arbitration[91] arose because, having sent the two agents to the island of Hao in accordance with the Secretary-General's ruling, the French government returned them both to metropolitan France before the expiry of the stipulated three-year period of isolation. When New Zealand protested and maintained that this unilateral action was a violation of France's obligations, the issue was referred to arbitration in accordance with the parties' earlier agreement. A three-member tribunal was established to decide the case on the basis of the *lex specialis* established in the agreement and 'the applicable rules and principles of international law'. Unlike the original arbitration, the tribunal's award, which was handed down in 1990, was fully reasoned, containing important rulings on the law relating to state responsibility, remedies and various other matters. Although the tribunal upheld most of New Zealand's arguments, it decided for technical reasons not to award damages, making instead a declaration of illegality, and, in an unusual further step, recommended the creation of a joint fund to promote friendly relations between the two states, to which France agreed to make an initial contribution equivalent to US$2 million. If the French government had carried out its original obligations in good faith, the Secretary-General's decision in the first arbitration would have concluded the matter. When regrettably it did not, New Zealand's foresight at least meant that there was a forum which could finally lay the dispute to rest.

Without an express grant, there is no general power to revise an award in order to take account of new facts. There is, however, nothing to prevent the parties from including a provision to this effect, if they think that it could be useful. So, for example, the agreement under which Guinea and Guinea-Bissau referred the *Maritime Delimitation* case to arbitration included both a provision permitting further proceedings in the event of a dispute concerning the implementation and interpretation of the award

---

[90] See 74 ILR 276.
[91] *Rainbow Warrior (New Zealand* v. *France)* (1990) 82 ILR 499. For analysis and commentary, see J. S. Davidson, 'The Rainbow Warrior arbitration concerning the treatment of the French agents Mafart and Prieur' (1991) 40 *ICLQ*, 446.

and a provision allowing for the possibility of revision. The latter laid down that it was open to either party to request revision of the award 'if any new element has been discovered which could have decisively influenced the award, provided that before the delivery of the award this new element was unknown to the Tribunal and to the Party which requests the revision, and there is no fault on the part of this Party'. The wording of this article was modelled on Article 61 of the Statute of the International Court of Justice, and its inclusion is perhaps explained by the difficulty which the lack of such a provision caused for the United Kingdom in the *Channel* arbitration.

In this connection, it should also be noted that a decision which contains an error in expression or calculation can probably be corrected, at least until the award has been executed, and, since this is an inherent power, no express authorisation is required. This point was made in the *Channel* arbitration, and, at the second stage of the proceedings in the case of *BP v. Libya*, the claimant went so far as to argue that a tribunal which is not *functus officio* also has an inherent power to re-open an award, if it has made a fundamental error of law, and if the earlier decision was not intended to be final. The arbitrator in that case found that it was unnecessary to decide the point, but the fact that, in the *Trail Smelter* case and a number of others, a limited power to re-open appears to have been recognised suggests that the argument may be well-founded.

6.5.2 Annulment of Arbitral Awards

States take a case to arbitration with the intention of obtaining a decision which both parties will be bound to carry out and which will put an end to the dispute. But a decision is only binding in international law if the tribunal has been properly constituted, has carried out its instructions and has produced an adequate award. It is therefore possible for a party to deny that an award is effective by invoking the doctrine of nullity.[92]

An arbitrator clearly has no jurisdiction to make an award if the instrument from which he claims to derive his authority is invalid, is not yet in force or has terminated. In the *Arbitral Award* case[93] (1960), this was one of the grounds on which Nicaragua challenged a boundary award made in 1906 by the King of Spain. Nicaragua argued that the Gamez-Bonilla Treaty under which the King had been appointed, and which had been signed with Honduras in 1894, had lapsed before he had agreed to act as arbitrator. The International Court, however, held that, because the

---

[92] For a comprehensive review of the issue of nullity, see W. M. Reisman, *Nullity and Revision*, New Haven, CT, 1971.

[93] *Arbitral Award Made by the King of Spain on December 23, 1906*, Judgment [1960] ICJ Rep. 192. For commentary and analysis, see D. H. N. Johnson, Note (1961) 10 *ICLQ*, 328.

Treaty had not come into force until the exchange of ratifications in 1896, it was in force at the crucial time and so provided the necessary basis for the King's appointment.

Since an arbitrator's authority derives from the parties' agreement, it may be possible to dispute an award on the ground that the arbitrator's appointment was not in accordance with the agreement. This, of course, is why it was necessary to seek an advisory opinion as to the propriety of appointing a neutral arbitrator in the *Peace Treaties* case, and the same issue provided the basis for Nicaragua's other main argument in the *Arbitral Award* case.

The Gamez-Bonilla Treaty provided for the appointment of the King of Spain only after various other possibilities had been exhausted. Nicaragua maintained that this requirement had not been observed, with the result that the appointment of the King was invalid. However, the Court again disagreed and held that Nicaragua had failed to show that the Treaty had not been complied with. With regard to both this and the earlier issue, the Court noted that Nicaragua had clearly approved the appointment of the King as arbitrator at the time and had raised no objection until 1911. In these circumstances, said the Court, whatever the effect of the Treaty, Nicaragua was in no position to challenge the setting up of the arbitration. Cases in which the legality of the arbitrator's appointment is in question are rather rare. More commonly, the issue is whether an arbitrator has exceeded his authority by failing to follow instructions. A clear case of excess of jurisdiction will arise if an arbitrator fails to obey the parties' directive as to the law to be applied, which explains the caution of tribunals like that in the *OSPAR (Article 9)* case. Likewise, an award can be challenged if the arbitrator, asked to choose between two alternatives, devises a third solution, or if the award fails to answer the questions referred, or deals with others which were not presented. In another *Arbitral Award* case[94] in 1991, Guinea-Bissau asked the International Court to declare that the award in the 1989 *Maritime Delimitation* case was a nullity on the ground that the tribunal had failed to answer the second of two questions in the *compromis* and consequently had failed to settle its dispute with Senegal. The Court, however, rejected the argument, finding that the agreement between the two states made an answer to the second question conditional on a negative answer to the first. Accordingly, the tribunal, which had given a positive answer to the first question, had done what it was asked to do.[95]

---

[94] *Arbitral Award of 31 July 1989*, Judgment [1991] ICJ Rep. 53. For analysis, see F. Beveridge, Note (1992) 41 *ICLQ*, 891; and C. A. Hartzenbusch, Note (1992) 86 *AJIL*, 553.

[95] If the tribunal had interpreted its task more broadly, it could, as its president suggested, have answered both questions. However, while the availability of an alternative line of argument

Guinea-Bissau also argued that the award, which had been made by two votes to one, was a nullity because it lacked a true majority. This was because the president of the arbitral tribunal, though voting for the decision, had made a declaration in which he appeared to support the views of the dissenting arbitrator. The Court, however, rejected this argument also, finding that the voting was clear and the president's declaration reflected a preference rather than a contradiction. The conclusion to be drawn is that, while it is perhaps unwise for an arbitrator to display too much enthusiasm for conclusions he has rejected, if the decision itself is clear, indiscipline alone is not a ground for nullification.[96]

An award will be a nullity if in its handling of the case the tribunal has transgressed a basic rule of judicial procedure. The principle that no one may be a judge in his own cause prohibits the members of an arbitral tribunal from identifying with, or taking instructions from, either of the parties. The common practice of appointing 'national' arbitrators is not inconsistent with this principle, since national arbitrators, though nominated by the parties, are still required to act judicially. But, if there are grounds for believing that an arbitrator has rehearsed with a witness the evidence the latter is about to give, as in the *Buraimi* arbitration,[97] the award could be set aside.

The principle that both sides must be given a fair opportunity to present their respective cases is likewise of fundamental importance. A party which refuses to appear cannot, of course, claim that an award is a nullity because its arguments have not been heard. It may be different, however, if a tribunal bases its decision on considerations which were never put to the parties. That is why it was a risk for the tribunal to introduce Islamic law at the second stage of the *Eritrea/Yemen* arbitration and was actually one of the grounds on which the claimant sought to re-open the proceedings in *BP v. Libya*.[98] Though the application in that case was dismissed on other grounds, there seems no reason in principle why such a judicial bolt from the blue should not have the effect of nullifying the award in an appropriate case.

Failure to give reasons for a decision can be another ground for nullifying an award. As already mentioned, unreasoned awards, particularly from sovereign arbitrators, were common in the early part of the last century, but were displaced by reasoned awards as the distinction between legal and

---

would have been relevant to an appeal from the decision, the ICJ held that it had no bearing on the issue of nullity. The case thus provides a clear illustration of the difference between appellate and nullification proceedings, especially the more limited scope of the latter.

[96] See further S. Schwebel, 'The majority vote of an international arbitral tribunal' in S. Schwebel, *Justice in International Law*, Cambridge, 1994, p. 213.

[97] A useful collection of materials relating to the *Buraimi* arbitration will be found in Wetter, *The International Arbitral Process* (n. 1) vol. III, pp. 357–87.

[98] *BP v. Libya: Competence to Re-open First Stage of Proceedings*, Award (1974) 53 ILR 375.

political means of settlement became clearer. As late as 1899, however, the tribunal in the *Venezuela–British Guiana Boundary* case issued an unreasoned decision, the validity of which on this, and other grounds, must be considered doubtful.[99] Reasoned awards are important because, unless the parties are interested only in the result, they are entitled to know the tribunal's response to their argument and, more fundamentally, because a reasoned award is the best way of ensuring that the tribunal resists the temptation to simply 'split the difference' and bases its decision on the merits of the case.

In the *Abyei* arbitration,[100] a tribunal set up by the Government of Sudan and the Sudanese People's Liberation Movement (SPLM) was asked to decide whether a Committee of Experts assigned to establish the boundaries of the Abyei Area had 'exceeded their mandate'. It decided that in certain respects they had, on account of a failure to support some of their decisions with adequate reasons. The focus of argument in this case was on the scope for subsequent review when a decision is challenged, not by way of appeal, but on the more limited ground of an 'excess of mandate'. The award therefore contains a wealth of material on this rather technical issue, including a discussion of the subtle relationship between the mandate in a given case and the general principles of judicial review, in which the tribunal's treatment of the obligation to provide a reasoned decision is particularly interesting.

Other grounds for nullifying an award are fraud, which includes deceit in the presentation of a case to the tribunal or corruption of one of its members, and 'essential error', of which it has been said 'the ramification of the views of writers ... demonstrates the looseness, vagueness and lack of legal exactness of the term'.[101] It has, nonetheless, often been advanced – sometimes it must be said in desperation – as a ground for challenging a decision. Some cases can be more precisely classified under one of the headings already considered. In others, the plea is no more than a transparent attempt to challenge the merits of the decision, grounds for an appeal perhaps, but nothing more. The 'imbalance in the evaluation of the argumentation and evidence submitted by each party' and 'interpretation defects'[102] which Argentina claimed to detect in the *Beagle Channel* award

---

[99] *Venezuela–British Guiana Boundary Arbitration (Venezuela v. Great Britain)* (1899), *British and Foreign State Papers*, vol. 92, 1899–1900, p. 160. Also in Wetter, *The International Arbitral Process* (n. 1) vol. III, p. 81, together with valuable ancillary documentation. For further discussion, see A. O. Cukwurah, *The Settlement of Boundary Disputes in International Law*, Manchester, 1967, pp. 161–2 and 214–16.

[100] *Abyei Arbitration (Sudan/Sudan People's Liberation Movement)* (2009), available at www.pca-cpa.org.

[101] K. S. Carlston, *The Process of International Arbitration*, New York, 1946, pp. 191–2.

[102] The Argentine Government's Declaration of Nullity may be found in (1978) 17 ILM 738; text also in Wetter, *The International Arbitral Process* (n. 1) vol. I, p. 380.

clearly fall into this category. When a similar argument was advanced in the *Arbitral Award* case, the International Court of Justice simply observed:

> The instances of 'essential error' that Nicaragua has brought to the notice of the Court amount to no more than evaluation of documents and of other evidence submitted to the arbitrator. The appraisal of the probative value of documents and evidence appertained to the discretionary power of the arbitrator and is not open to question.[103]

Clearly, then, it is not enough to have lost; if essential error is a ground for nullifying awards at all, the decision must be wrong in some vital and obvious respect.

6.6 Utility of Arbitration

Arbitration as it has developed over the last 200 years provides the parties to a dispute with the opportunity to obtain a decision from a judge or judges of their own choice. This is important because, if governments are to be persuaded to refer disputes to third parties they must have confidence in those who are to give the decision. An arbitral tribunal, as we have seen, also has the subject matter of the dispute and the criteria for its decision laid down by the parties. Thus, another advantage of arbitration is that it can be used to produce a solution to a selected problem and on any agreed basis. Finally, arbitration, unlike inquiry and conciliation, results in a decision which is binding. Consequently, provided that no problems of interpretation, nullity, etc., arise, an arbitral award should dispose of the dispute.

In view of these advantages, it is not surprising that, in the period since 1945, states have continued to regard arbitration as an appropriate way of handling certain types of dispute. Of the various cases referred to ad hoc tribunals,[104] the majority have concerned territorial or quasi-territorial disputes in which the issues were primarily legal and the outcome of secondary importance. The *Palena* case, the *Lake Lanoux* case, the *Rann of Kutch* case, the *Channel* arbitration, the *St Pierre and Miquelon* case, the *Taba* dispute and the *Eritrea/Yemen* case all fall into this category, while in the *Brcko* case arbitration was used in an analogous way to deal with a territorial dispute between the Bosniac/Croat and Serb communities in Bosnia and Herzegovina. Of course, arbitration can also be used to dispose of a whole series of disputes. In 2000, for example, Eritrea and Ethiopia set

---

[103] [1960] ICJ Rep. 215–16.
[104] For a useful summary, see Gray and Kingsbury, 'Developments in dispute settlement' (n. 1) pp. 99–109; and, for an earlier survey, see D. H. N. Johnson, 'International arbitration back in favour?' (1980) 34 *Yearbook of WA*, 305.

up a Claims Commission[105] to deal with a variety of disputes stemming from their recent war, and its decisions, like those in single cases, show the value of arbitration as a means of removing obstacles to friendly relations.

Arbitration has also retained an important place in international treaty practice and, sometimes in combination with conciliation, is to be found in the dispute provisions of multilateral and bilateral conventions on a wide variety of subjects. The 1960 Indus Waters Treaty, for example, contains a provision permitting disputes between India and Pakistan relating to the use of the Indus system of rivers to be referred to arbitration. In 2010, Pakistan instituted proceedings against India in a dispute over the permissibility of a controversial hydroelectric project which India was currently constructing in the area. In a Partial Award in 2013,[106] the tribunal ruled that India was allowed to continue the project subject to ensuring a minimum downstream flow of water to be determined later. India was also prohibited from employing certain methods of sediment control which were found to be contrary to the Treaty. Towards the end of 2013 the tribunal issued a Final Award which resolved the outstanding issues. The case, which was organised by the PCA, is a good illustration of how an arbitral clause can enhance the effectiveness of a treaty, as well as the value of arbitration in enabling tense and complex disputes to be resolved peacefully.

Further examples are the 1999 International Convention for the Suppression of the Financing of Terrorism,[107] which provides for the reference to arbitration of disputes relating to the Convention, and the treaties comprising the provisional post-war settlement with Germany which provided for arbitration through a series of tribunals each with its own jurisdiction. Thus, the Arbitral Tribunal for the Agreement on German External Debts on several occasions decided disputes between governments over the interpretation of the Agreement,[108] and the Arbitral Commission on Property Rights and Interests in Germany dealt with property and property-related claims from both states and private individuals. The *OSPAR (Article 9)* case, as already noted, was referred to arbitration on the basis of Article 32 of the 1992 OSPAR Convention, the *Rhine Chlorides* case[109] was referred under the 1993 Protocol to the 1976 Convention on the Protection of the Rhine against Pollution by Chlorides, and the earlier *Heathrow Airport* case was one of a series in

---

[105] For a description of the Commission's work, see J. R. Weeramantry, Notes (2005) 99 *AJIL*, 465; (2006) 100 *AJIL* 201; and (2007) 101 *AJIL*, 616.

[106] *In re Indus Waters Kishenganga Arbitration, Pakistan v. India*, Partial Award (2013) and see J. R. Crook, Note (2014) 108 *AJIL*, 308.

[107] Text in (2000) 39 ILM 270. However, although Article 24(1) provides for compulsory arbitration, Article 24(2) permits reservations to this provision.

[108] See, for example, *Young Loan Arbitration* (1980) 59 ILR 494.

[109] *Rhine Chlorides Case (Netherlands/France)* (2004), available at www.pca-cpa.org.

which the United States has been involved in the arbitration of disputes arising out of bilateral international air services agreements.[110] More recently, as we shall also see in Chapter 10, there have been several arbitrations under the dispute settlement provisions of the 1982 Law of the Sea Convention which have also been referred to in this chapter.

It is also worth noting that international arbitration is not the exclusive prerogative of states. Investment arbitration involving states and individuals has already been described and such 'mixed' arbitration is also possible in other contexts. In the *Bank for International Settlements* case,[111] for example, a tribunal decided that private shareholders in the Bank had been lawfully dispossessed and also decided the level of compensation due. Here the respondent was an international institution. In the *Eurotunnel* case,[112] on the other hand, the respondents were the British and French governments who were sued by two companies alleging breach of the concession agreement under which they had built and were operating the Channel Tunnel. This too was a complex case raising factual as well as legal issues and exemplifying the use of internationalised contracts for major projects, as well as the value of arbitration in enabling disputes over the meaning of such contracts to be resolved.

Arbitration, then, is an important means of handling international disputes. It must be recognised, however, to have significant limitations. As we shall see in the next chapter, states are reluctant to make a general commitment to judicial settlement, and for much the same reasons resist the idea of arbitration. For an individual dispute, on the other hand, negotiation or another diplomatic means may be preferred. Consequently, as we shall see later, the 1982 Convention on the Law of the Sea, which contains extensive provisions on arbitration, also makes use of conciliation and a variety of other techniques of peaceful settlement.

The availability of other means of dealing with disputes and the high value which states attach to retaining flexibility mean that, even when arbitration is specified in the provisions of a treaty, to see whether it can be used in practice may require the arbitrators to examine the relation between arbitration and other means of settlement. In the *Southern Bluefin Tuna* case,[113] for example, as we shall see in Chapter 10, an attempt by

---

[110] See *Air Transport Services Agreement Arbitration (United States* v. *France)* (1963) 38 ILR 182; *Italy–United States Air Transport Arbitration* (1965) 45 ILR 393; *Case Concerning the Air Services Agreement of 27 March 1946* (1978) 54 ILR 304. For discussion of the last case, see F. Damrosch, 'Retaliation or arbitration – or both? The 1978 United States–France aviation dispute' (1980) 74 *AJIL*, 785.

[111] *Bank for International Settlements Arbitration* (2002/3) and see D. J. Bederman, 'The unique legal status of the Bank for International Settlements comes into focus' (2003) 16 *Leiden JIL*, 78.

[112] *Eurotunnel Arbitration (The Channel Tunnel Group Ltd and France-Manche SA* v. *United Kingdom and France)* (2007) and see M. Audit, Note (2008) 57 *ICLQ*, 724.

[113] *Southern Bluefin Tuna Case (Australia and New Zealand* v. *Japan),* Award on Jurisdiction and Admissibility (2000), text in (2000) 39 ILM 1359.

Australia and New Zealand to have a dispute with Japan dealt with by arbitration under Annex VII to the Law of the Sea Convention failed when the tribunal ruled that its jurisdiction was barred by Article 281. In the *MOX Plant* case,[114] on the other hand, another Annex VII tribunal decided in 2003 that considerations of judicial comity required suspension of the proceedings pending clarification of the position of the European Court of Justice which might also be dealing with this case.[115] Such jurisdictional constraints are plainly not peculiar to arbitration, but something all courts and tribunals must work with as the legal world becomes more complex. They do, however, underline the point that, useful though arbitration can be, it must always be seen in the context of other techniques and procedures.

Another limitation concerns enforcement. Although arbitration produces a binding decision, there is usually no guarantee that the unsuccessful party will carry out its obligation to recognise the award. This does not mean that arbitral decisions are widely disregarded. On the contrary, since states often prefer to end a dispute rather than incur the political costs which would follow from refusing to accept a decision, arbitral awards are usually implemented. This is another parallel with judicial settlement. In the International Court, the major difficulty is usually persuading the states concerned to accept the jurisdiction of the Court. Once that hurdle has been surmounted, the question of enforcement will normally not arise. But, if there are practical reasons for carrying out unfavourable decisions, in some circumstances the factors arguing against performance predominate, and in these situations the lack of a procedure for enforcement is certainly a conspicuous limitation.

There are several ways in which the problem of enforcing arbitral awards may be overcome. The best, but also the rarest, is to devise a procedure which makes it difficult for the unsuccessful party to go back on its obligations. The awards of the Iran–United States Claims Tribunal, for example, are paid out of a fund which was established by the original agreement and which Iran is required to replenish whenever it falls below US$500 million. Of course, even an arrangement like this depends ultimately on the performance of the underpinning obligation and, when the scope of Iran's commitment itself became a matter of dispute in 1992, the issue had to be referred to the Tribunal for a ruling.[116] Clearly, then, no scheme of this kind is entirely without risk, but, as a consequence of its funding arrangements, American claimants who are successful before the

---

[114] See *MOX Plant Case (Ireland v. United Kingdom)*, Order No. 3, text in (2003) 42 ILM 1187.

[115] See R. R. Churchill and J. Scott, 'The MOX Plant litigation: the first half-life' (2004) 53 *ICLQ*, 643 at 652. As noted in Chapter 10, following the decision of the European Court of Justice, the proceedings were discontinued.

[116] See *United States* v. *Iran*, Decision No. 130-A28 FT, 19 December 2000, noted in (2001) 95 *AJIL*, 414.

Tribunal have enjoyed a good deal more security than their less fortunate counterparts elsewhere.[117]

Another approach is to try to make rejection unlikely by framing the tribunal's decision in a way which is acceptable to both parties. This used to be thought of as one of the features which distinguished arbitration from judicial settlement, and we have seen that the Secretary-General approached his task in the *Rainbow Warrior* case very much in this spirit. However, there are clearly limits on how far a tribunal can go in this direction while respecting the boundaries of its jurisdiction. States which request a decision on the basis of international law, for example, and argue a case in these terms, are unlikely to be satisfied by a decision which is merely conciliatory and which says more about the arbitrator's fondness for compromise than about their legal rights. It is therefore doubtful if the *Rainbow Warrior* approach, though appropriate in the unusual circumstances of that case, is of more than limited application.

A final possibility, which would be of real value in improving compliance with awards and increasing the attractiveness of arbitration generally, would be to improve the arrangements for dealing with allegations of nullity. As noted earlier, it is an unfortunate fact that, at the present time, disputes over the validity of international arbitral awards can rarely be settled by judicial means. The *Venezuela–British Guiana Boundary* case, decided in 1899, of doubtful validity, is a typical example. The award has never been the subject of authoritative review, but an application to confirm the validity of the award has been submitted by Guyana to the International Court of Justice in 2018.[118] Cases in which the issue of nullity was laid to rest by the parties' reference of the matter to the International Court, remain, however, exceptional.

This situation, accurately described by the International Law Commission as 'anarchic', means that nullity claims are handled diplomatically. This is a serious practical weakness of inter-state arbitration. On the one hand, if a state is unable to challenge a dubious or unsatisfactory award, submission to arbitration is made more hazardous and less attractive than it ought to be. On the other hand, if it is open to a state to challenge the validity of an award on grounds which are legally worthless, but cannot be tested, the 'binding' effect of an arbitral award is emptied of most of its meaning.

As we will see in Chapter 7, nullity claims in the context of investment arbitration under the ICSID Convention are the subject of a specific

---

[117] It should be noted that successful Iranian claimants are in a different position. See M. Aghahosseini, 'The enforcement mechanism provided for the awards of the Iran–United States Claims Tribunal' (2003) 3 *Global Community YBILJ*, 3.
[118] *Arbitral Award Of 3 October 1899 (Guyana v. Venezuela)*, Application Instituting Proceedings (29 March 2018), available at https://www.icj-cij.org/.

procedure contained in the ICSID Convention, which thus guarantees that disputes over the validity of international arbitral awards are settled.

We have already seen that the advantages of using the institutions and procedures of municipal law to deal with the enforcement and validity of arbitral awards in investment cases have led to the development of new forms of arbitration for these kinds of disputes. This trend, exemplified by the creation of the Iran–United States Claims Tribunal, with its many unique features, is no doubt likely to continue. Aware of the deficiencies of traditional arbitration, as far as the review of awards is concerned, some have suggested that the answer is for the issue of nullity always to be subject to compulsory adjudication. There is no doubt that compulsory adjudication would avoid many problems. However, at present, it appears to have little prospect of being adopted. Of course, states with a genuine desire to see a dispute settled do not repudiate arbitral awards on flimsy pretexts, while those that are prepared to take such action might not be discouraged by having their cynicism exposed in further litigation. The real answer, then, as regards the specific issue of nullity and the more general issue of compliance, lies with the parties. Arbitration, like other means of settling disputes in a world of sovereign states, depends for its effectiveness on responsible behaviour from the governments concerned.

6.7 Further Reading

6.7.1 General References on Arbitration

Amerasinghe, C. F., *International Arbitral Jurisdiction*, Leiden, 2011.

Blackaby, N., C. Partasides, A. Redfern and M. Hunter, *Redfern and Hunter on International Arbitration*, Oxford, 2015.

Caron, D. D., M. Pellonpää and L. M. Caplan, *The UNCITRAL Arbitration Rules: A Commentary*, Oxford, 2006.

Caron, D. D., S. W. Schill, A. C. Smutny and E. E. Triantafilou (eds), *Practising Virtue: Inside International Arbitration*, Oxford, 2015.

Daly, B. W., E. Goriatcheva and H. E. Meighen, *A Guide to the PCA Arbitration Rules*, Oxford, 2014.

De Brabandere, E. (ed.), *International Procedure in Interstate Litigation and Arbitration: A Comparative Perspective*, Cambridge, 2021.

Franke, U., A. Magnusson and J. Dahlquist Cullborg, *Arbitrating for Peace: How Arbitration Made a Difference*, Alphen aan den Rijn, 2016.

Giorgetti, C. (ed.), *Challenges and Recusals of Judges and Arbitrators in International Courts and Tribunals*, Leiden/Boston, 2015.

Hamilton, P., H. C. Requena, L. van Scheltinga and Bette E. Shifman (eds), *The Permanent Court of Arbitration: International Arbitration and Dispute Resolution*, The Hague, 1999.

Lalive, P., 'On the reasoning of international arbitral awards' (2010) 1 *Journal of International Dispute Settlement* 55–65.

Levine, J., and S. Kimani, 'Peace, water and the Permanent Court of Arbitration: supporting dispute settlement from the Rhine to the Corentyne', in *A Bridge over Troubled Waters*, Leiden/Boston, 2020.

Paulsson, J., and G. Petrochilos, *UNCITRAL Arbitration*, Alphen a/d Rijn, 2018.

Petrochilos, G., *Procedural Law in International Arbitration*, Oxford, 2004.

Schultz, T., and F. Ortino, *The Oxford Handbook of International Arbitration*, Oxford, 2020.

Talmon, S., 'The South China Sea arbitration and the finality of "final" awards', (2017) 8 *Journal of International Dispute Settlement* 388–401.

6.7.2 Treaties and Official Documents

Hague Convention on Pacific Settlement of International Disputes (Hague, I) (adopted 29 July 1899, entered into force 4 September 1900).

7

Investment Arbitration

So far we have been concerned largely with arbitration between states and such disputes are, of course, the focus of this book. However, in some circumstances it is possible for private persons, who may be individuals or corporations, to engage in litigation with states. This is the situation in international investment arbitration when the home state of an investor and the host state (where the investment is located), are parties to an investment treaty containing a dispute settlement clause. Such a treaty may be a bilateral investment treaty (BIT), or a multilateral investment treaty (MIT) such as the Energy Charter Treaty (ECT), but in either case arbitration may be employed by the private investor without the involvement of the investor's state. Although this is obviously not inter-state litigation, since this use of arbitration is now increasingly important, it merits discussion in a separate chapter. Since investment arbitration is a specific form of arbitration, much of what has been discussed in Chapter 6 is also applicable to this chapter. For example, the questions relating to the terms of reference, and how the proceedings are to be conducted and the definition of the issues to be decided by the arbitral tribunal are similarly decided by the parties.

The types of disputes settled through investment arbitration under treaties are nevertheless distinguishable from other forms of arbitration. In relation to the subject matter of the disputes, investment arbitration, when based on an investment treaty, is not concerned generally with adjudication of private rights between two parties established under a contract, but rather concerns the international responsibility of the state for breaches of its international obligations towards a foreign investor which are contained in investment treaties. In some instances, however, a treaty-based tribunal may also consider contract claims. Similarly, one should also keep in mind that the broad notion of 'investment arbitration' also captures contractual disputes in relation to foreign investments which are based on an arbitration clause in a contract. This chapter will, however, focus on treaty-based arbitrations chiefly (referred to as investment treaty arbitration).

Most frequently, investment arbitration is conducted by the International Centre for the Settlement of Investment Disputes (ICSID) under the ICSID Convention or the UNCITRAL Arbitration Rules. ICSID is the most used forum for the settlement of investment disputes. The recent statistics of the caseload of ICSID show an important increase in the number of investor-state arbitrations starting in the late 1990s, with thirty-five new registered cases in 2020.[1] As of 1 January 2020, ICSID had registered a total number of 745 cases. The Centre is similar to the PCA, in that it provides arbitral facilities for parties to settle their investment disputes. The ICSID Convention equally contains a complete set of procedural rules to be applied. It is important to note that ICSID has no jurisdiction for inter-state claims, which are thus to be settled through the customary means available to states.

The ICSID Convention was established under the auspices of the World Bank, and was notably based on several successful interventions of the Bank in investment disputes in the early 1960s.[2] The Convention entered into force on 14 October 1966. In the early years, ICSID was not regularly used to settle disputes between investors and states. Only nine arbitrations had been registered in the 1970s and another sixteen during the 1980s. The 1980s saw the registration of the first treaty-based investment arbitration under the ICSID Convention, *AAPL* v. *Sri Lanka*[3] under the United Kingdom–Sri Lanka BIT of 1980. Investment arbitration is now widely employed.

7.1 Investment Treaties and Consent to Arbitration

Most investment disputes involve a BIT or an MIT, although other possibilities exist, for example where a contract between an investor and a host state contains an arbitration clause or through the adoption of national legislation to that effect. The value of these arrangements may be seen from the fact that over 150 states are currently parties to ICSID and around 3,000 BITs are in force.

The first BITs emerged in the late 1950s. It is generally considered that the BIT signed between Germany and Pakistan in 1959[4] was the first genuine BIT, that is a treaty focusing in most parts on foreign investment only. In the 1960s, BITs started to increase, but the proliferation or 'baby-boom'[5] of investment treaties occurred towards the end of the 1980s and

---

[1] ICSID, Caseload Statistics (2020–1), available at https://icsid.worldbank.org/resources/publications/icsid-caseload-statistics.
[2] See T. St John, *The Rise of Investor-State Arbitration: Politics, Law and Unintended Consequences*, Oxford, 2018, p. 127 ff.
[3] *Asian Agricultural Products Limited* v. *Democratic Socialist Republic of Sri Lanka* (ICSID Case No. ARB/87/3) – July 20, 1987.
[4] Treaty between the Federal Republic of Germany and Pakistan for the Promotion and Protection of Investments, 25 November 1959, available at https://investmentpolicy.unctad.org/international-investment-agreements/treaty-files/1387/download.
[5] S. Alexandrov, 'The "baby boom" of treaty-based arbitrations and the jurisdiction of ICSID tribunals', (2005) 6 *The Journal of World Investment & Trade*, 387–411.

1990s. The emergence of BITs in the 1960s was soon followed by the inclusion of international arbitration as the forum to settle disputes between foreign investors and home states. Originally, arbitration was only included for disputes between states. It was only in the late 1980s that investor-state arbitration clauses started to increase. Despite the absence of investor-state arbitration in the first BIT between Germany and Pakistan, the inclusion of a provision in BITs providing for the arbitration of investment dispute directly between the foreign investor and the host state gradually made its way into BITs and is one of the most important innovations of the 1960s.[6] The Indonesia–Netherlands BIT of 1968 was the first investment treaty to refer to ICSID arbitration, requiring however additional consent from both parties to the dispute.[7]

BITs usually contain standards of treatment aimed at promoting and protecting foreign investors, and often also contain the consent of the states parties to the BIT to settle disputes between the foreign investor and the host state arising out of such treaties through arbitration. The consent to arbitration is given by the states parties to the BIT in advance of the dispute. Consent in a treaty is generally considered to constitute an 'offer to arbitrate' by the state, which may then be accepted by the foreign investor[8] through the submission of a request for arbitration provided for in the instrument containing the consent of the host state.[9] States, when expressing consent to direct investment arbitration, may condition their consent and, for example, require foreign investors to exhaust local remedies, either generally or for a limited time period, or insert a 'fork-in-the-road' clause which obliges investors to choose between international arbitration or domestic courts.[10]

An example of an arbitration clause in a BIT is Article 8 of the BIT between Italy and Morocco (1990):[11]

Article 8

1) All disputes or differences, including disputes related to the amount of compensation due in the event of expropriation, nationalisation, or similar measures, between a Contracting Party and an investor of the

---

[6] K.J. Vandevelde, 'A brief history of international investment agreements' (2005) 12 *UC Davis Journal of International Law and Policy*, 157, 174.
[7] Indonesia–Netherlands BIT 1968, Article 11.
[8] See on the need for the consent of the foreign investor, *American Manufacturing and Trading, Inc. v. Zaire*, ICSID Case No. ARB/93/1, Award, 21 February 1997, 23 ff.
[9] See generally C. Schreuer, L. Malintoppi, A. Reinisch, and A. Sinclair, *The ICSID Convention: A Commentary*, Cambridge, 2009, pp. 1279–82.
[10] See R. Dolzer and C. Schreuer, *Principles of International Investment Law*, Oxford, 2012, pp. 264–70.
[11] Most international investment treaties can be found at https://investmentpolicy.unctad.org/international-investment-agreements.

other Contracting Party concerning an investment of the said investor on the territory of the first Contracting Party should, if possible, be resolved amicably.

2) If the disputes cannot be resolved in an amicable manner within six months of the date of the request, presented in writing, the investor in question may submit the dispute either:
   a) to the competent court of the Contracting Party concerned;
   b) to an ad hoc tribunal, in accordance with the [UNCITRAL] Arbitration Rules;
   c) to the International Centre for Settlement of Investment Disputes [...].

As is visible from this example, investment treaties may give a choice to the parties to conduct arbitration before an ad hoc arbitral tribunal applying the UNCITRAL Arbitration Rules, or through the ICSID. BITs may also offer other arbitration options, such as the Arbitration Institute of the Stockholm Chamber of Commerce (SCC) or the International Chamber of Commerce (ICC) in Paris. When arbitration is conducted under the UNCITRAL Arbitration Rules, or through any other venue such as SCC or ICC, the procedure largely follows the practice of international commercial arbitration. Irrespective of the forum chosen to settle investment disputes, the jurisdictional requirements derived from the BIT or MIT which contains the consent apply equally. However, the ICSID Convention contains several specific features.

7.2 The Jurisdiction of Investment Tribunals

When a dispute under an investment treaty arises, the first question is whether the tribunal involved has jurisdiction. Several issues may arise here. The dispute must concern an 'investment' within the meaning of the investment treaty and the ICSID Convention if it is applicable. Another jurisdictional requirement is that the investment must have been made by an investor or national within the meaning of the investment treaty. Treaties may also contain requirements relating to the temporal application of the treaty, and consequently the jurisdiction of arbitral tribunals established under such treaties.

In case arbitration under the ICSID Convention, additional jurisdictional requirements are included in Article 25 of the ICSID Convention:

> The jurisdiction of the Centre shall extend to any legal dispute arising directly out of an investment, between a Contracting State (or any constituent subdivision or agency of a Contracting State designated to the Centre by that State) and a national of another Contracting State, which the parties to the dispute consent in writing to submit to the Centre. When the parties have given their consent, no party may withdraw its consent unilaterally.

7.2.1 Jurisdiction *Ratione Materiae*

To benefit from the protection of an international investment treaty, and as a consequence, for an arbitral tribunal to have jurisdiction over the dispute, investors need to have made an 'investment' as defined in the applicable BIT or MIT. Moreover, in case disputes that are brought to arbitration under the ICSID Convention, such assets need to be captured also by the notion of 'investment' under Article 25 of the ICSID Convention which defines and delimits the jurisdiction of the ICSID.

The vast majority of investment treaties contain wide and broad definitions of what constitutes an 'investment'. The wide definitions usually present in investment treaties often are similarly structured and consequently follow a similar approach. Yet international investment treaties are not identical, which means that most treaties, while containing similar definitions of 'investment', do leave room for nuance in defining what constitutes an 'investment'.

Broad definitions employ a so-called 'asset-based definition'. Any 'asset' can then constitute an investment. An example of a broad 'stand-alone' asset-based definition is the 2006 Mexico–United Kingdom BIT: '"investment" means an asset acquired in accordance with the laws and regulations of the Contracting Party in whose territory the investment is made (...)'.[12] Treaties may also use a broad asset-based definition which adds substantive characteristics to investments, such as the 'commitment of capital or other resources, the expectation of gain or profit, or the assumption of risk'.[13]

The broad definition may be followed by a non-exhaustive list of examples of forms investments can take with or without exclusions.[14] While the level of detail of the list varies, most lists can be brought down to five categories: (1) movable and immovable property, (2) various interests in companies and enterprises such as shares, (3) claims or titles to money, (4) intellectual property rights and (5) concessions or licences.[15]

Even when treaties include a broad asset-based definition, purely commercial transactions may be excluded from the scope of application of investment treaties. The Mexico–UK BIT, for instance, excludes purely commercial transactions, such as 'claims to money' if these are not part of

---

[12] Agreement between the Government of the United Kingdom of Great Britain and Northern Ireland and the Government of the United Mexican States for the Promotion and Reciprocal Protection of Investments (signed 12 May 2006, entered into force 25 July 2007) (Mexico–UK BIT) Article 1.

[13] Treaty between the Government of the United States of America and The Government of the Republic of Rwanda concerning the Encouragement and Reciprocal Protection of Investment (signed 19 February 2008, entered into force 1 January 2012) (US–Rwanda BIT) Article 1.

[14] See, e.g. Agreement between the Government of Sweden and the Government of the Socialist Federal Republic of Yugoslavia on the mutual protection of investments (signed 10 November 1978, entered into force 21 November 1979) (Serbia–Sweden BIT) Article 1.

[15] J. W. Salacuse, *The Law of Investment Treaties* 2nd ed., Oxford, 2015, 177.

or related to a form of investment which falls under the scope of application of the treaty.[16] Other treaties, however, include generic references to 'claims to money, to other assets or to any performance having an economic value'.[17]

In case of arbitration under the ICSID Convention, the 'investment' must not only be captured by the definition contained in the investment treaty, but also fall under the scope of Article 25 of the ICSID Convention. Article 25 ICSID extends the jurisdiction of the Centre to 'any legal dispute arising directly out of an investment' but fails to further define 'investment'. In view of the lack of a clear definition of what constitutes 'investment' for the purposes of Article 25 ICSID, two main approaches on the question can be identified.

The first approach consists of considering that the notion of 'investment' under Article 25 ICSID has an objective meaning that is independent of the parties' understanding of the concept. Thus construed, 'investment' under Article 25 ICSID requires four features: a contribution, a certain duration of performance, participation in the risks of the transaction, and a contribution to the development of the host state.[18] These criteria were set out by the Tribunal in *Salini* v. *Morocco*[19] and have since then been referred to as the 'Salini criteria'. The second approach consists of operating a *renvoi* to the definition of investment agreed by the states in their investment treaty which contains the consent to arbitration, thus emphasizing party autonomy in defining what constitutes an 'investment'.[20] Irrespective of the approach taken, certain tribunals have considered that the term 'investment' under the ICSID Convention does not include 'a single commercial transaction, such as the mere delivery of goods against payment of the price'.[21]

The existence of an 'investment' is an issue in most investment arbitrations. It was one of the issues in *Philip Morris* v. *Uruguay*,[22] where a Swiss tobacco company challenged measures adopted by Uruguay aimed at preventing

---

[16] Agreement between the Government of the United Kingdom of Great Britain and Northern Ireland and the Government of the United Mexican States for the promotion and reciprocal protection of investments (signed 12 May 2006, entered into force 25 July 2007) (Mexico–UK BIT) Article 1 (i)-(J).

[17] Agreement on encouragement and reciprocal protection of investments between the Kingdom of the Netherlands and the Federal Republic of Yugoslavia (signed 29 January 2002, entered into force 1 March 2004) (Netherlands–Serbia BIT) Article 1(a)(iii).

[18] Dolzer and Schreuer, *Principles of International Investment Law* (n. 10), 66.

[19] *Salini Costruttori SpA and Italstrade SpA* v. *Kingdom of Morocco*, ICSID Case No ARB/00/4, Decision on Jurisdiction (23 July 2001) para 52.

[20] See for a discussion: Dolzer and Schreuer, *Principles of International Investment Law* (n. 10) 68–76. See also, e.g., *Pantechniki SA Contractors & Engineers (Greece)* v. *The Republic of Albania*, ICSID Case No ARB/07/21, Award (30 July 2009) para. 42ff.

[21] *Philip Morris Brands Sàrl* v. *Oriental Republic of Uruguay*, ICSID No. ARB/10/7, Decision on Jurisdiction (2 July 2013), para. 203.

[22] *Philip Morris Brands Sàrl* v. *Oriental Republic of Uruguay*, ICSID No. ARB/10/7, Decision on Jurisdiction (2013) and see B. Sabahi and K. Duggal, Note (2014) 108 *AJIL*, 67.

smoking-related illnesses and deaths. Uruguay claimed that the claimant's activities, which according to the claimant included manufacturing facilities, shares in a local company, rights to royalty payments and trademarks, did not amount to an 'investment' within the meaning of Article 25 of the ICSID Convention. The tribunal, however, rejected this interpretation. The tribunal argued that the term 'investment' under Article 25(1) of the ICSID Convention 'is to be given a broad meaning', and that the activities in question were covered by the definition of 'investment' in the BIT.[23]

The case of *Italy* v. *Cuba*[24] posed a similar question. This case, a rare example of an inter-state BIT dispute, raised the question because Italy claimed that a variety of companies had suffered loss as a result of acts attributable to Cuba. In an Interim Award, the tribunal defined what it regarded as 'investments' and invited Italy to confine itself to such cases in a subsequent stage of the proceedings.

7.2.2 Jurisdiction *Ratione Personae*

Another jurisdictional requirement is that the investment must have been made by an investor or national within the meaning of the investment treaty. In order for an investor to fall under the scope of application of an investment treaty and initiate a treaty claim against the host state under that treaty, the investor should prove that it is a 'national' of the other state. Nationality typically is defined differently for natural persons and legal persons in international investment treaties. Natural persons usually are defined as nationals of a state by mere reference to the fact that they have the nationality of a state party to the treaty. The Netherlands–Argentina BIT for instance contains the following definition:

> natural persons having the nationality of that Contracting Party in accordance with its law

As far as legal persons are concerned, investment treaties may use different criteria, such as the place of incorporation, the seat or head office of the corporation, or the persons controlling the company. Art. 1(4) Bahrain–Germany BIT defines the nationality of companies as follows:

> The term 'companies' means
>
> (a) in respect of the Kingdom of Bahrain:
>
>> natural persons, partnerships, corporations and other legal entities created and organised according to the laws of the Kingdom of Bahrain and having its head office in its territory,

---

[23] *Ibid.*, paras 202–3.
[24] *Republic of Italy* v. *Republic of Cuba*, Interim Award, (2005) and see M. Potestà, Note (2012) 106 *AJIL*, 341.

(b) in respect of the Federal Republic of Germany:

> any juridical person as well as any commercial or other company or association with or without legal personality having its seat in the territory of the Federal Republic of Germany, irrespective of whether or not its activities are directed at profit.

The Netherlands–Argentina BIT conversely defines the nationality of legal persons not only by reference to the place of incorporation, but also through the controlling shareholders:

> legal persons, wherever located, controlled, directly or indirectly, by nationals of that Contracting Party

Article 25 of the ICSID Convention contains the requirement that the dispute brought under ICSID is a dispute between a 'national of one contracting State' and 'another contracting State'. 'National of one contracting State' is defined for natural persons, as 'any natural person who had the nationality of a Contracting State other than the State party to the dispute'. Article 25 of the ICSID Convention does exclude natural persons who have dual nationality; that is, natural persons who also have the nationality of the other state party to the dispute.

As far as legal persons are concerned, Article 25 of the ICSID Convention requires legal persons to have the 'nationality of a Contracting State other than the State party to the dispute' without setting any criteria to identify nationality. Article 25 of the ICSID Convention does allow the parties to treat a company incorporated in the host state as a national of another state 'because of foreign control'. In the latter case, a company incorporated in the host state may thus be considered a national of the home state, if the parties have agreed to this, for example in the applicable investment treaty.

As with the notion of 'investment', the question of the nationality of legal persons often is an issue in investment arbitration. This condition can be illustrated by the case *of Ioan Micula* v. *Romania*.[25] The case concerned two individuals who were born in Romania, but then moved to Sweden, and three corporations which they controlled. The respondent argued that the claimants' effective ties were with Romania and also challenged their acquisition of Swedish nationality. Although Romania maintained that the rule of effective nationality should apply under both the ICSID Convention and the Sweden–Romania BIT, the tribunal rejected the argument and, after carefully examining the applicants' circumstances, concluded that they satisfied the requirements of both conventions.

---

[25] *Ioan Micula, Viorel Micula, S.C. European Food S.A., S.C. Starmill S.R.L. and S.C. Multipack S.R.L. v. Romania*, ICSID Case No. ARB/05/20, Decision on Jurisdiction and Admissibility (2008), (2009) 48 ILM 51 and see C. Knahr, Note (2010) 104 *AJIL*, 81.

7.2.3 Jurisdiction *Ratione Temporis*

Investment treaties will usually contain a provision confirming or not that the treaty applies not only to investments made after the entry into force of the treaties but also to investments which have been made before the date of entry into force of the treaty. Such provisions concern only the scope of application of the treaty to either investments made after or to those made after and before the treaty's entry into force. This question needs to be distinguished from the application of the treaty itself and the substantive investment protection provisions it contains to situations occurring before the entry into force of the treaty. In line with the Vienna Convention on the Law of Treaties, the provisions of the treaty in principle apply only from the date of entry into force of the treaty. As a consequence, the treaty, unless otherwise agreed, applies and provides protection to foreign investors as of its entry into force. That protection may also apply to investments which were made before the entry into force of the treaty, but the provisions of the treaty would not apply retroactively to acts and omissions of the host state occurring before the entry into force of the treaty.

This principle of non-retroactivity in relation to substantive provisions in turn needs to be distinguished from the temporal application of jurisdictional provisions. Some BITs do include a provision explicitly excluding disputes which have arisen prior to their entry into force from its application. In most cases the BIT is silent, or not explicit, on the question. This was discussed by the Tribunal in *Ping An* v. *Belgium*.[26] The tribunal first considered that substantive obligations do not apply retroactively, unless there is an explicit provision to the contrary in the treaty.[27] The Tribunal also found that there is almost no support in investor-state arbitration for a 'presumption that the jurisdiction of a Tribunal extends to disputes which arose prior to its establishment'.[28]

7.3 Procedural Law

Most frequently, investment arbitration is conducted under the ICSID Convention or the UNCITRAL Arbitration Rules. In case of arbitration under the ICSID Convention, that Convention and the ICSID Arbitration Rules, will apply to the proceedings, complemented by specific arrangements in the applicable investment treaty where the ICSID Convention and Arbitration Rules allow this. On questions of procedure, much of what has been discussed in Chapter 6, is applicable to investment arbitration as well, such as the questions relating to the terms of reference, how the

---

[26] *Ping An Life Insurance Company of China, Limited and Ping An Insurance (Group) of China, Limited* v. *Kingdom of Belgium*, ICSID Case No ARB/12/29, Award, 30 April 2015, paras 173 and 186.
[27] *Ping An* v. *Belgium*, (n. 26), para. 167.   [28] *Ping An* v. *Belgium*, (n. 26), paras 184–5.

proceedings are to be conducted and the definition of the issues to be decided by the arbitral tribunal. This section will thus focus mostly on specific procedural questions that arise in the context of investment arbitration and in particular arbitration under the ICSID Convention.

7.3.1 Procedural law in general

The method used to settle international investment disputes is clearly modelled on the rules and principles of international commercial arbitration. International commercial arbitration and investment treaty arbitration thus share many common features. Many of these common features are moreover inherent to the very concept of arbitration as was discussed in the previous chapter. Thus, in both mechanisms, parties decide to bring a claim before a party-appointed panel of arbitrators, and in principle define the applicable law and the procedural rules. The latter is, in the case of ICSID arbitration, limited because the procedural rules are established under the ICSID Convention and the adopted rules of arbitration. Likewise, the conduct of the proceedings is influenced by the common principles of arbitral procedures, such as those governing the constitution of the tribunal, the challenge of arbitrators, and the rules in respect of the rendering of the final award. In respect of these questions, we can refer to the previous chapters, and to the specific rules of procedure contained in either the ICSID Convention and Arbitration Rules, or the UNCITRAL Arbitration Rules.

From a procedural perspective, investment treaty arbitration under the ICSID Convention is a supranational or a-national form of arbitration since it is completely detached from the laws of any particular state, including the state in which the arbitration takes place.[29] The home state of the investor is completely eliminated from the arbitral process, as is the domestic legal system of the state in which the arbitration takes place. As noted by the Arbitral Tribunal in *Electrabel* v. *Hungary*, an arbitration conducted under the Energy Charter Treaty (ECT),

> ... this Tribunal is placed in a public international law context and not a national or regional context. Moreover, this ICSID arbitration does not have its seat or legal place of arbitration in Hungary or elsewhere in the European Union. Such an arbitral seat could trigger the application of the lex loci arbitri and give rise to the jurisdiction of the local courts in regard to the arbitral process, including challenges to the award. This ICSID arbitration is a dispute resolution mechanism governed exclusively by international law. As a result of the Tribunal's international status under the ECT and the ICSID Convention, several of the Commission's submissions cannot be taken into account in this

---

[29] See Santiago Montt, *State Liability in Investment Treaty Arbitration: Global Constitutional and Administrative Law in the BIT Generation*, Oxford, 2009, p. 135.

arbitration, because they are based on a hierarchy of legal rules seen only from the perspective of an EU legal order applying within the EU, whereas this Tribunal is required to operate in the international legal framework of the ECT and the ICSID Convention, outside the European Union.[30]

This supranational nature of investment treaty arbitration under the ICSID Convention is notably visible in the provisions relating to the validity of the award, which will be discussed later in this chapter.

Investment treaty arbitration conducted under the UNCITRAL Arbitration Rules, or under other mechanisms such as arbitration through the facilities of the International Chamber of Commerce (ICC), the London Court of International Arbitration (LCIA) or the facilities of the Stockholm Chamber of Commerce (SCC) still maintains a territorial link with the state of the seat of the arbitration. In those instances, national laws, in particular the laws of the seat of the arbitration, and national courts retain a certain degree of relevance.[31]

7.3.2 Transparency

One of the specific features of investment treaty arbitration is the transparency of the proceedings. Investment treaty arbitration, and investment arbitration under the ICSID Convention, have departed from the secrecy of the proceedings, by making available to the public information about the proceedings and the final outcome thereof and allowing hearings to be made open to the public, without impinging on the arbitral character of the proceedings. The rules in this respect, however, are still very much subjected to the consent of the parties.

Article 48(5) of the ICSID Convention provides that 'the Centre shall not publish the award without the consent of the parties'. Rule 48(4) of the ICSID Arbitration Rules reiterates this provision, but adds that 'the Centre shall, however, promptly include in its publications excerpts of the legal reasoning of the Tribunal'. This latter section was modified in 2006, to enhance the transparency of investment arbitration under the ICSID Convention. Previously, Rule 48(4) provided that ICSID *may* publish excerpts of the award, which in turn was a modification of the initial rule which prohibited publication. If parties have agreed to publish the award of the tribunal, the Secretary-General is mandated to take the necessary steps to arrange for the publication of the award.[32] It should be noted here that

---

[30] *Electrabel S.A. v. Republic of Hungary*, ICSID Case No. ARB/07/19, Decision on Jurisdiction, Applicable Law and Liability, 30 November 2012, para. 4.112.
[31] For a discussion of the various ways in which national courts and national laws may 'interfere' in the proceedings, see N. Blackaby, C. Partasides, A. Redfern and M. Hunter, *Redfern & Hunter on International Arbitration*, 5th ed., Oxford, 2009, paras 7.01–7.64.
[32] Regulations 22 and 23, ICSID Administrative and Financial Regulations.

the ICSID Secretary-General is equally under an obligation to register and make publicly available all requests for conciliation or arbitration brought under the ICSID Convention, which includes at least the names of the parties involved in the dispute and the date of registration of the case.[33]

In practice, the vast majority of awards rendered under the ICSID Convention have been made available to the public, by the ICSID Secretariat and the consent of the parties, by (one of) the parties to the dispute, or by subsequent litigation in domestic courts or tribunals.

Outside the formal context of ICSID, awards and decisions of investment tribunals have been less published. The UNCITRAL Arbitration Rules generally provide that hearings are to be held in camera and that awards are to be made public only with the consent of both parties. The 2014 UNCITRAL Rules on Transparency in Treaty-based Investor-State Arbitration[34] however show a clear departure from the principle of confidentiality as far as investment treaty arbitration is concerned, by provisions in relation to publication of information of the dispute and under certain circumstances the award. These rules apply to arbitration based on investment treaties concluded after 1 April 2014, but the parties may nonetheless agree to apply the rules.

An issue of importance in relation to transparency is the practice of *amicus curiae* submissions or non-disputing party submissions, by which non-disputing parties are granted the right to submit a written statement during the proceedings. They do not, however, by doing so become a party to the dispute.[35] The capacity for third parties to participate as *amicus curiae* in international investment arbitration has been explicitly accepted under the ICSID Arbitration Rules since 2006, and more recently in the 2014 UNCITRAL Rules on Transparency in Treaty-based Investor-State Arbitration.

Certain tribunals had already accepted the possibility for third parties to make *amicus curiae* submissions based on Article 44 of the ICSID Convention which grants the arbitral tribunal the power to decide on procedural questions which are not regulated by the rules of the ICSID Convention. The ICSID Arbitration Rules were amended in 2006 to explicitly include, under certain conditions, the capacity for a tribunal to allow a third party which has a significant interest in the case to file a written submission (Article 37(2)). The specific conditions under which non-disputing parties are included in Rule 37(2) of the ICSID Arbitration Rules:

---

[33] *Ibid.*
[34] UNCITRAL, Rules on transparency in treaty-based investor-State arbitration (2014), available at https://uncitral.un.org/sites/uncitral.un.org/files/media-documents/uncitral/en/rules-on-transparency-e.pdf.
[35] See for a discussion of the concept, P. Sands and R. Mackenzie, 'International Courts and Tribunals, Amicus Curiae', in Rüdiger Wolfrum, *Max Planck Encyclopedia of Public International Law*, Oxford, 2012.

(2) After consulting both parties, the Tribunal may allow a person or entity that is not a party to the dispute (in this Rule called the 'non-disputing party') to file a written submission with the Tribunal regarding a matter within the scope of the dispute. In determining whether to allow such a filing, the Tribunal shall consider, among other things, the extent to which:

(a) the non-disputing party submission would assist the Tribunal in the determination of a factual or legal issue related to the proceeding by bringing a perspective, particular knowledge or insight that is different from that of the disputing parties;
(b) the non-disputing party submission would address a matter within the scope of the dispute;
(c) the non-disputing party has a significant interest in the proceeding.

The Tribunal shall ensure that the non-disputing party submission does not disrupt the proceeding or unduly burden or unfairly prejudice either party, and that both parties are given an opportunity to present their observations on the non-disputing party submission.

Article 4 of the UNCITRAL Transparency Rules regulates the conditions of third-party submissions in a similar manner.

7.3.3 Selection and Appointment of Arbitrators

In general, the qualification requirements and selection of arbitrators in investment arbitration do not therefore differ substantially from arbitrators involved in international commercial arbitration, and much of what has been discussed in Chapter 6 in this respect therefore applies equally in investment arbitration.

Article 37 of the ICSID Convention thus provides that a tribunal may consist of a sole arbitrator, or an uneven number of arbitrators appointed in accordance with the agreement of the parties, and that in the absence of agreement, the Tribunal will consist of three arbitrators: one arbitrator appointed by each party, and the third presiding arbitrator, appointed by agreement of the parties.

Article 39 requires that the majority of the arbitrators be nationals of states other than the state party to the dispute and the state whose national is a party to the dispute, except where each individual member of the Tribunal has been appointed by agreement of the parties. Rule 1(3) of the ICSID Arbitration Rules further contains additional procedural rules in this respect, and inter alia provides that the appointment by a party of an arbitrator which has the nationality of the home or host state requires the agreement of the other party. As far as the qualifications of the arbitrators are concerned, Article 14 of the ICSID Convention requires that they need to be 'persons of high moral character and recognized competence in the fields of law, commerce, industry or finance, who may be relied upon to exercise independent judgment. Competence in the field of law shall be of particular importance in the case of persons on the Panel of Arbitrators.'

Article 14 of the ICSID Convention contains the basic rule in respect of the independence and impartiality of arbitrators: 'persons designated to serve on the Panels shall be persons of high moral character and recognized competence in the fields of law, commerce, industry or finance, who may be relied upon to exercise independent judgment'. Arbitrators, either party-appointed or appointed by the chairman, need thus to possess three essential qualities: be of 'high moral character', have the necessary competence and be independent. Although Article 14 does not explicitly contain the requirement of 'impartiality', even though the Spanish official text refers to impartiality rather than independence, it is generally accepted that Article 14 requires arbitrators to be both independent and impartial.[36]

As far as the challenge of arbitrators and members of ad hoc committees is concerned, Article 57 of the ICSID Convention provides that a party to the dispute may propose the commission or tribunal[37] to disqualify a member 'on account of any fact indicating a manifest lack of the qualities required by paragraph (1) of Article 14'. The ICSID Convention may seem to impose a relatively heavy burden on a party which seeks to challenge an arbitrator, because of the use of the word 'manifest'. Recently, however, some decisions have sought to limit the requirement for the lack of independence and impartiality to be 'manifest', bringing it more closely to a standard of 'reasonableness'.[38]

7.4 The Law Applicable to the Merits

In principle, the legal instrument providing for the jurisdiction of an arbitral tribunal to settle the dispute determines the legal rules to be applied for the settlement of the dispute. If the instrument contains no specific provision in relation to the applicable law, the procedural rules chosen by the parties will often contain a clause which will enable the tribunal to determine the law it should apply. Thus, in accordance with Article 42(1) of the ICSID Convention, an investment tribunal is required to 'decide a dispute in accordance with such rules of law as may be agreed by the parties'. At the same time, Article 42(1) of the ICSID Convention

---

[36] See *AWG Group Limited* v. *Argentina*, UNCITRAL, Decision on a Second Proposal for the Disqualification of a Member of the Arbitral Tribunal, 12 May 2008, para. 27.

[37] The ICSID Convention indeed uses a system whereby the challenge by a party of an arbitrator or an *ad hoc* committee member will be decided by the remaining arbitrators or members of the *ad hoc* committee (Article 58 of the ICSID Convention).

[38] See *Blue Bank International & Trust (Barbados) Ltd.* v. *Bolivarian Republic of Venezuela*, ICSID Case No. ARB 12/20, Decision on the Parties' Proposals to Disqualify a Majority of the Tribunal, 12 November 2013. See generally Chiara Giorgetti, *The Selection and Removal of Arbitrators in Investor-State Dispute Settlement*, Leiden, 2019, p. 44.

provides that 'in the absence of such agreement, the Tribunal shall apply the law of the Contracting State party to the dispute (including its rules on the conflict of laws) and such rules of international law as may be applicable'. A similar rule is provided for under the UNCITRAL Arbitration Rules, although tribunals operating under those rules of procedure have a larger discretion in determining the applicable law, failing a specific choice of law made by the parties: 'The arbitral tribunal shall apply the rules of law designated by the parties as applicable to the substance of the dispute. Failing such designation by the parties, the arbitral tribunal shall apply the law which it determines to be appropriate.'[39]

Article 42 of the ICSID Convention thus establishes that the law chosen by the parties constitutes the applicable law, and in the absence thereof that the tribunal should apply the law of the host state and the relevant rules of international law. It should moreover be added that a tribunal established under the ICSID Convention is prohibited from making a finding of *non liquet* on the ground of silence or obscurity of the law,[40] and that a failure to apply the law may under the ICSID system be a ground for annulment because of 'manifest excess of power'.[41] Many BITs today include applicable provisions very similar to the second limb of Article 42(1) of the ICSID Convention. Still, a certain number of BITs do not contain any specific applicable law clause, which implies that the applicable law will be determined in accordance with the second limb of Article 42(1) of the ICSID Convention.[42]

In practice, since the main objective of an international investment tribunal mandated to settle claims arising out of the provisions of an investment treaty is to rule upon the international legal responsibility of the host states, international law applies because the subject matter of the dispute before the international investment tribunal is regulated by international rather than municipal law. In *LG&E* v. *Argentine Republic*, the Tribunal thus held that 'the fact that there is no contract between the Argentine Republic and LG&E favours in the first place the application of international law, inasmuch as we are dealing with a genuine dispute in matters of investment which is especially subject to the provisions of the Bilateral Treaty complemented by the domestic law'.[43]

Of course, municipal laws may play an important role. Municipal law is the applicable legal system in order to assess whether there has been a breach of a contractual obligation. This assessment might be necessary, either because the contract itself has provided that the arbitral tribunal has

---

[39] Article 35(1) UNCITRAL Arbitration Rules.
[40] Article 42(2) ICSID Convention.
[41] Article 52(1) (lit b) of the ICSID Convention.
[42] See for instance the Model BITs of France and Germany.
[43] *LG&E Energy Corp., LG&E Capital Corp. and LG&E International Inc.* v. *Argentine Republic*, ICSID Case No. ARB/02/1, Decision on Liability, 3 October 2006, para. 98.

jurisdiction in this respect, or because the analysis of whether a treaty obligation has been breached requires first an analysis of the existence of a contract breach. Such an enquiry may lead the tribunal to investigate whether or not contractual obligations have been met or not. As noted by the Committee in *Vivendi I*:

> whether there has been a breach of the BIT and whether there has been a breach of contract are different questions. Each of these claims will be determined by reference to its own proper or applicable law—in the case of the BIT, by international law; in the case of the Concession Contract, by the proper law of the contract.[44]

If the requirements of jurisdiction and admissibility are satisfied, the next question is whether the claim is good on the merits. This too may raise a number of different issues. In many cases the question is whether the investor has been accorded 'fair and equitable' treatment which investment treaties usually guarantee. Thus in *Vannessa Ventures v. Venezuela*,[45] a Canadian mining company complained that delays in domestic court proceedings breached the respondent's obligations under the relevant BIT. Due process is certainly one element of fair and equitable treatment, but the tribunal concluded that here the obligation had not been violated. It reached the same conclusion on a further complaint of lack of independence and impartiality of the domestic courts. As with the first complaint, the tribunal recognised that such impropriety may in principle amount to a breach of obligation, but rejected the complaint on the facts.

In *Glamis Gold v. United States*,[46] a case involving interpretation and application of an MIT (NAFTA), the tribunal arrived at a similar conclusion. The complainant, a Canadian mining company, complained that through legislative and other measures the respondent had wrongfully delayed approval of an open-pit gold-mining project in California, causing it loss. An unusual feature of this case was that the tribunal decided it by reference to the minimum standard of customary international law relating to due process, since the standard of fair and equitable treatment in the NAFTA contained a *renvoi* to the minimum standards of treatment under customary international law. Arguments in the case thus turned on the issue of what customary law requires, a matter on which the tribunal sided with the respondent.

Another commonly included guarantee in investment treaties is a promise of compensation in the event of expropriation. This raises a

---

[44] *Compañiá de Aguas del Aconquija S.A. and Vivendi Universal*, Decision on Annulment, 3 July 2002, para. 96. On the applicable law generally, see H.E. Kjos, *Applicable law in investor-state arbitration: the interplay between national and international law*, Oxford, 2013.
[45] *Vannessa Ventures Ltd v. Bolivarian Republic of Venezuela*, ICSID Case No. ARB(AF)/04/6, Award (2013) and see A. Reinisch, Note (2014) *Global Community YBILJ*, 837 at 851–2.
[46] *Glamis Gold Ltd v. United States*, Award (2009) and see S. W. Schill, Note (2010) 104 *AJIL*, 253.

question that has been an issue in several cases, namely what exactly constitutes an expropriation. This was another issue in the *Vannessa Ventures* case where the tribunal decided that a company's assignment of its rights to another company amounted to a breach of contract and entitled the respondent to terminate the contract, with the result that there had been no expropriation. Similarly, in the *Glamis Gold* case the tribunal ruled that despite various actions of the respondent by way of regulation, mining was still possible, with the result that there had been no expropriation. Expropriation need not always be direct, but can sometimes be indirect if the respondent's actions have the effect of rendering an investment valueless. This was the situation in *Tza Yap Shum* v. *Peru*,[47] where the tribunal decided that the arbitrary exercise of taxing power by the respondent amounted to indirect expropriation, and as such violated the 1994 Peru–China BIT.

Other obligations in investment treaties include guarantees of full protection and security and provisions relating to non-discrimination. When breach of an investment treaty is identified, the usual remedy is financial compensation for the loss suffered. In addition to the question of whether such loss can be proved, legal issues may sometimes arise relating to what amounts to compensatable loss. In *Rompetrol* v. *Romania*,[48] for example, an ICSID tribunal had to consider whether 'moral damages', here in the form of reputational loss, could be awarded. In their award the arbitrators explained that this was an issue on which previous tribunals had expressed divergent views. In the present case the tribunal took something of a middle course. While declining to reject moral damage in principle, the tribunal held that the notional and discretionary character of this type of loss called for a cautious approach. Here the tribunal ruled that the investor's request did not qualify as moral damage, but rather as part of the actual economic loss or damage suffered, and as such merited compensation in the usual way.

7.5 The Validity of the Award and its Implementation

An arbitral award rendered in investment arbitration is final and binding between the parties to the dispute, whether the proceedings were conducted under the ICSID Convention or the UNCITRAL Arbitration Rules.

Under the ICSID Convention, a valid arbitral award must be recognised and may be enforced through the courts of any state party. One of the specific features of ICSID arbitration is that the awards can easily be recognized and enforced through the ICSID Convention, especially in

---

[47] *Tza Yap Shum* v. *Republic of Peru*, ICSID Case No. ARB/07/6, Award (2011) and see Shen Wei, Note (2014) 108 *AJIL*, 315.
[48] *Rompetrol Group N.V.* v. *Romania*, ICSID Case No. ARB/06/3, Award (2013) and see A. Reinisch, Note (2014) *Global Community YBILJ*, 837 at 861–2.

comparison to the recognition and enforcement of foreign arbitral awards in domestic courts, and even compared to enforcement of arbitral awards under the New York Convention.[49] This is essentially a consequence of the fact that investment treaty arbitration under the ICSID Convention has been fully 'internationalised' and detached from the control of the national courts and tribunals of states. Article 54(1) of the ICSID Convention indeed imposes an obligation on all states which are parties to the Convention to enforce an ICSID award 'as if it were a final judgment of a court in that State'.[50] There is no possibility of review by the national courts of ICSID member states in which enforcement is sought. Although this is specific to ICSID Arbitration, the international character of ICSID arbitration is a fundamental characteristic of and is specific to investment treaty arbitration under the ICSID Convention.

Recognition and enforcement of awards in investment arbitration under rules other than the ICSID Convention, such as ad hoc arbitrations, is subject to the 1958 New York Convention on the Recognition and Enforcement of Foreign Arbitral Awards. Although it facilitates enforcement, the New York Convention contains several possibilities for review by domestic courts which are broader than the grounds of annulment provided for under the ICSID Convention.[51] National courts and tribunals have held that awards of non-ICSID investment tribunals are reviewable as 'commercial' arbitral awards for the purposes of Article 1(3) of the New York Convention.[52]

The emergence of investment arbitration highlights the way in which supply can be adapted to meet demand in the field of dispute settlement. Prior to this development, a dispute before a foreign investor and a host state would have been handled as a case of diplomatic protection and transformed into an inter-state dispute between the host and the national state of the investor. Today, this is no longer so. Although diplomatic protection is still possible, and is sometimes used, the development of investment arbitration has provided investors and states alike with an alternative procedure and one moreover that utilises national courts to promote the effective enforcement of awards.

Finally, what is the legal position if an arbitration of the kind we are considering takes place, and then one of the parties wishes to challenge the award? The decisions of investment arbitration tribunals are not normally subject to appeal, but, depending on the circumstances, a review of the award may be possible. Where a claimant has chosen ad hoc arbitration,

---

[49] Convention on the Recognition and Enforcement of Foreign Arbitral Awards, 10 June 1958, 330 UNTS 38 (1959) [hereafter 'the New York Convention'].
[50] Article 54(1) ICSID Convention.
[51] See E. Baldwin, M. Kantor and M. Nolan, 'Limits to enforcement of ICSID awards' (2006) 23 *Journal of International Arbitration*, 1, 1, 4–5.
[52] See Campbell McLachlan, Laurence Shore and Matthew Weiniger, *International Investment Arbitration. Substantive Principles*, Oxford, 2008, p. 65.

rules for enforcement and challenge are laid down in the New York Convention, Article V of which lists various grounds which may be invoked. This will normally be done either through the courts of the state where the tribunal had its seat, or in the courts of any state where enforcement of the award is sought. In *BG Group* v. *Argentina*,[53] for example, the United States Supreme Court considered the standard of review applicable by a US court when it is alleged that an arbitral tribunal exceeded its powers. The case, which concerned a British investor in Argentina's gas industry, involved a challenge to the arbitrators' award from the respondent. The Court, however, adopted a deferential approach to the original decision and dismissed the case.

If an arbitration is carried out through ICSID, the role of the national courts is limited to enforcement and they are prohibited from dealing with disputes over validity. Instead, such disputes are dealt with by annulment committees of ICSID, applying the five criteria laid down in Article 52(1) of the ICSID Convention (see Appendix K). The annulment mechanism provided for by the ICSID Convention applies to all arbitrations conducted under the ICSID Convention. The system was incorporated since Article 54 of the ICSID Convention contains an obligation for all states to 'recognize an award rendered pursuant to this Convention as binding and enforce the pecuniary obligations imposed by that award within its territories as if it were a final judgment of a court in that State'. This implies that there is no review of the award before the domestic courts where the tribunal had its seat, or in the courts of any state where enforcement of the award is sought, as for ad hoc arbitration as discussed in the previous paragraph. The rules for enforcement and challenge as laid down in the New York Convention are thus not applicable to ICSID arbitration.

Article 52(1) of the ICSID Convention mentions the criteria to be applied in case of a request in the annulment of an arbitral award rendered under the ICSID Convention:

(a) that the Tribunal was not properly constituted;
(b) that the Tribunal has manifestly exceeded its powers;
(c) that there was corruption on the part of a member of the Tribunal;
(d) that there has been a serious departure from a fundamental rule of procedure; or
(e) that the award has failed to state the reasons on which it is based.

Thus in *Compañia de Aguas* v. *Argentina*,[54] an ICSID annulment committee had to decide amongst others whether an award was vitiated by the fact

---

[53] *BG Group PLC* v. *Republic of Argentina*, 134 S. Ct. 1198 (2014) and see A. Roberts and C. Trahanas, Note (2014) 108 *AJIL*, 750.
[54] *Compañia de Aguas* v. *Argentina*, ICSID Case No. ARB/02/16, Annulment Decision (2010), and see S. L. Karamanian, Note (2011) 105 *AJIL*, 553.

that one of the original arbitrators held a position with a Swiss bank which in turn held shares in one of the claimants. According to Argentina, this meant that the arbitration panel had not been properly constituted and also that the principles of impartiality and due process had been compromised. The Annulment Committee decided that the Convention's requirements had not been violated. The validity of the award was therefore upheld.

In *Sempra Energy International* v. *Argentina*,[55] an annulment committee had to consider a different point. In this case, one of several concerning Argentina's response to its severe economic and financial crisis, the respondent adopted various measures which could be argued to contravene its obligations under the 1991 United States–Argentina BIT. When the claimant complained, Argentina invoked necessity as a defence, but the arbitral tribunal rejected it, relying for this purpose on customary international law. In the subsequent annulment proceedings Argentina argued, among other points, that the tribunal's approach was wrong and that by giving insufficient weight to the wider provisions of the BIT, the tribunal had committed a manifest error of law. The annulment committee agreed, and ruling that by not giving priority to the BIT the original arbitrators had exceeded their powers, nullified the award. In cases such as this, where an award is invalidated, the claim may then be referred to a new tribunal for a hearing.

The *Sempra Energy International* case is not only a valuable contribution to the jurisprudence on the scope of the defence of necessity in investment arbitration, but more generally is a reminder of the interests of states, as well as those of investors in disputes involving foreign investments. It is true, of course, that one of the functions of investment arbitration is to create a secure environment in which arbitrary and unjust interference with investments by host states is discouraged and investors are provided with reliable remedies in the event of wrong doing. However, it must not be forgotten that respect for foreign investments is just one element in a state's responsibilities and may not always be the highest priority. Investment treaties recognise this both in the way they define the host state's obligations and the provision of defences such as the necessity to cover exceptional situations. It is therefore the task of arbitrators when interpreting and applying investment treaties to strike the appropriate balance and ensure that the legitimate interests of both sides are properly taken into account.

---

[55] *Sempra Energy International* v. *Argentine Republic*, ICSID Case No. ARB/02/16, Annulment Decision (2010), (2010) 49 ILM 1445 and see B. M. J. Szewczyk, Note (2011) 105 *AJIL*, 547. Also A. O. Sykes, 'Economic "necessity" in international law' (2015) 109 *AJIL*, 296 and A. Roberts, 'Clash of paradigms: actors and analogies shaping the investment treaty system' (2013) 107 *AJIL*, 45.

7.6 Further Reading

7.6.1 General References on Investment Arbitration

Bungenberg, M., J. Griebel, S. Hobe and A. Reinisch (eds), *International Investment Law: a Handbook*, München/Oxford/Baden-Baden, 2015.

Chaisse, J., L. Choukroune and S. Jusoh (eds), *Handbook of International Investment Law and Policy*, Singapore, 2021.

Collins, D., *An Introduction to International Investment Law*, Cambridge, 2017.

Crawford, J., 'Treaty and contract in investment arbitration' (2008) 24 *Arbitration International* 351.

De Brabandere, E., *Investment Treaty Arbitration as Public International Law: Procedural Aspects and Implications*, Cambridge, 2014.

Dolzer, R., and C. Schreuer, *Principles of International Investment Law*, Oxford, 2012.

Douglas, Z., *The International Law of Investment Treaty Claims*, Cambridge, 2009.

Giorgetti, C. (ed), *Litigating International Investment Disputes*, Leiden, 2014.

McLachlan, C., L. Shore and M. Weiniger, *International Investment Arbitration: Substantive Principles*, Oxford, 2017.

Muchlinski, P., F. Ortino and C. Schreuer, *The Oxford Handbook of International Investment Law*, Oxford, 2008.

de Nanteuil, A., *Droit international de l'investissement* (3rd ed.), Paris, 2020.

Newcombe, A., and L. Paradell, *Law and Practice of Investment Treaties: Standards of Treatment*, The Hague, 2009.

Radi, Y., *Rules and Practices of International Investment Law and Arbitration*, Cambridge, 2020.

Reinisch, A. (ed.), *Standards of Investment Protection*, Oxford, 2008.

Salacuse, J. W., *The Law of Investment Treaties*, Oxford, 2015.

Sornarajah, M., *The International Law on Foreign Investment*, Cambridge, 2017.

Subedi, S., *International Investment Law: Reconciling Policy and Principle*, Oxford, 2020.

UNCTAD, 'International Investment Agreements' ('Pink Series'), covering various issues of investment law and arbitration in separate volumes; all volumes are available at https://investmentpolicy.unctad.org/publications/series/2/international-investment-agreements.

Van Harten, G., *Investment Treaty Arbitration and Public Law*, Oxford, 2007.

7.6.2 Treaties, Official Documents and Collections of Documents

Convention on the Recognition and Enforcement of Foreign Arbitral Awards from 10 June 1958, signed in New York, 330 UNTS 3.

Convention on the Settlement of Investment Disputes between States and Nationals of other States from 14 October 1966, signed in Washington, 575 UNTS 159.

Convention on Transparency in Treaty-based Investor-State Arbitration from 10 December 2014, signed in New York, UNTS I- 54749.

Crawford, J., R. Doak Bishop and W. M. Reisman, *Foreign Investment Disputes. Cases, Materials and Commentary*, The Hague, 2005.

Hober, K., and J. Dahlquist Cullborg, *Investment Treaty Arbitration: Problems and Exercises*, Cheltenham, 2018.

Lim, C. L., J. Ho, and M. Paparinskis, *International Investment Law and Arbitration: Commentary, Awards, and Other Materials*, Cambridge, 2018.

Paparinskis, M., *Basic Documents on International Investment Protection. Seconded. Documents in International Law*, Oxford, 2018.

Tanzi, A., and F. Cristani, *International Investment Law and Arbitration. An Introductory Casebook*, Padova, 2013.

8

The International Court I: Organisation and Procedure

Judicial settlement involves the reference of disputes to permanent tribunals for a legally binding decision. It developed from arbitration, which accounts for the close similarity between the two, and in various forms is now available through a number of courts of general or specialised jurisdiction. Examples of the latter will be considered when we examine the Law of the Sea Convention in a later chapter, but the advantages and limitations of tribunals of specialised jurisdiction will be more readily appreciated if we first consider the International Court.

The term 'International Court' embraces two courts, the Permanent Court of International Justice, set up as part of the 1919 peace settlement, and its successor, the International Court of Justice (ICJ), founded in 1945 as the principal judicial organ of the United Nations. Interest in both Courts has generated a literature of high quality, dealing with all aspects of their activity in considerable detail.[1] The focus of this chapter will be on features of the organisation and procedure of the Court, with a particular bearing on its role in the settlement of disputes.

8.1 Contentious Jurisdiction

The Court's powers to decide disputes are defined in its Statute and are known as its contentious jurisdiction. According to the Statute, only states may be parties to contentious proceedings and the Court's authority in such cases depends on the consent of the states concerned. The principle of

---

[1] For an excellent introduction, see A. Eyffinger, *The International Court of Justice 1946–1996*, The Hague, 1996. Two standard works on the Court are M. N. Shaw, *Rosenne's Law and Practice of the International Court (1920–2015)*, 5th edn, Brill, 2016; and H. Thirlway, *The Law and Procedure of the International Court of Justice: Fifty Years of Jurisprudence (2 Volumes)*, Oxford, 2013. See also A. Zimmermann, C. Tomuschat and K. Oellers-Frahm (eds), *The Statute of the International Court of Justice. A Commentary*, Oxford, 2006. Essays on particular aspects of the Court's work, some of which are referred to below, may be found in L. Gross (ed.), *The Future of the International Court of Justice*, New York, 1976; L. F. Damrosch (ed.), *The International Court of Justice at a Crossroads*, New York, 1987; V. Lowe and M. Fitzmaurice (eds), *Fifty Years of the International Court of Justice*, Cambridge, 1996; A. S. Muller, D. Raic and J. M. Thuranszky (eds), *The International Court of Justice*, The Hague, 1997; and C. Peck and R. S. Lee (eds), *Increasing the Effectiveness of the International Court of Justice*, The Hague, 1997. See also G. I. Hernandez, *The International Court of Justice and the Judicial Function*, Oxford, 2014 and C. J. Tams and J. Sloan (eds) *The Development of International Law by the International Court of Justice*, Oxford, 2013.

consensuality is as fundamental to adjudication by the Court as to arbitration and means that, unless all the states involved in a particular dispute have given their consent, there is no jurisdiction to give a decision.

8.1.1 Basis of the Court's Jurisdiction

As discussed in Chapter 1, a state's consent can be given in a number of different ways. Consent can be given before the dispute arises by means of a compromissory clause in a treaty, or a declaration under Article 36(2) of the Court's Statute. Alternatively, consent can be given after a dispute has arisen by means of a special agreement between the parties, or in response to the unilateral reference of a dispute to the Court. Once a legal act indicating consent has been performed, jurisdiction may be established, even if the state is unwilling to litigate when an actual case arises. There is thus no contradiction between the consensual basis of the Court's jurisdiction and the fact that the Court is regularly called upon to consider – and frequently rejects as ill-founded – objections to its jurisdiction from unwilling respondents.

Treaties providing in advance for the reference of disputes to the Court are of two types. A number of multilateral instruments have been concluded with the general aim of promoting peaceful settlement (sometimes referred to as 'compromissory treaties'). These treaties, which include the General Act (1928), the Pact of Bogotá (1948) and the European Convention for the Peaceful Settlement of Disputes (1957), constitute general acceptances of judicial settlement with far-reaching implications for the states concerned. For this reason, they have usually been either not widely supported, or accepted only with substantial reservations. Multilateral arrangements of this kind have therefore proved rather unsatisfactory. More successful has been the attempt to ensure that treaties on particular subjects include an article providing that disputes as to the interpretation or application of the agreement can be referred to the Court. Treaties of this second type have been concluded in considerable numbers, as reference to any recent volume of the Court's *Yearbook* will show, and have provided a basis for the Court's jurisdiction in several cases. In 2004, for example, the Court was able to decide a dispute over duties with regard to Mexicans on 'death row' in the United States because both Mexico and the United States were parties to the Protocol concerning the Compulsory Settlement of Disputes attached to the Vienna Convention on Consular Relations of 1963.[2]

The other method of submitting to the Court's jurisdiction in advance is by a declaration under Article 36(2) of the Court's Statute, known as the

---

[2] *Avena and Other Mexican Nationals (Mexico v. United States)*, Judgment [2004] ICJ Rep. 12; and see D. L. Shelton, Note (2004) 98 *AJIL*, 559.

'optional clause'. An optional clause declaration denotes a state's acceptance of judicial settlement on certain terms and conditions, and, when both parties have made declarations which cover the dispute, as in the *Arrest Warrant* case,[3] the Court's jurisdiction is established. Declarations are unilateral acts and thus have the advantage that a state can accept the Court's jurisdiction, and demonstrate its support for the principle of judicial settlement, without the need for the agreement of other states. On the other hand, since declarations function in much the same way as agreements, their effectiveness in practice depends on how many states are prepared to participate in the optional clause system and the terms on which they are willing to do so. Here, there is certainly room for improvement. Only about one-third of the members of the United Nations have made declarations under Article 36(2); and of those declarations in force, many are emasculated by reservations.[4]

The Declaration of India of 27 September 2019, one of the most recent ones, is telling in this respect. The 2019 declaration is an update of India's 1974 declaration which in turn had replaced earlier declarations of 1959 and 1956. While accepting the jurisdiction of the Court for all disputes, the declaration provides a list of over eleven types of dispute which are excluded from India's acceptance of the jurisdiction of the Court:

(1) disputes in regard to which the parties to the dispute have agreed or shall agree to have recourse to some other method or methods of settlement;
(2) disputes with the government of any State which is or has been a Member of the Commonwealth of Nations;
(3) disputes in regard to matters which are essentially within the domestic jurisdiction of the Republic of India;
(4) disputes relating to or connected with facts or situations of hostilities, armed conflicts, individual or collective actions taken in self-defence, resistance to aggression, fulfilment of obligations imposed by international bodies, and other similar or related acts, measures or situations in which India is, has been or may in future be involved, including the measures taken for protection of national security and ensuring national defence;
(5) disputes with regard to which any other party to a dispute has accepted the compulsory jurisdiction of the International Court of

---

[3] *Arrest Warrant of 11 April 2000 (Democratic Republic of the Congo v. Belgium)*, Judgment, [2002] ICJ Rep. 3; and see C. Wickremasinghe, Note (2003) 52 *ICLQ*, 775.
[4] For a fuller account of this problem, see J. G. Merrills, 'Does the optional clause still matter?', in K. H. Kaikobad and M. Bohlander (eds), *International Law and Power: Perspectives on Legal Order and Justice*, Leiden, 2009, p. 431; and, earlier, 'The optional clause revisited' (1993) 64 *BYBIL*, 197. For sample declarations, see document F in Appendix F.

Justice exclusively for or in relation to the purposes of such dispute; or where the acceptance of the Court's compulsory jurisdiction on behalf of a party to the dispute was deposited or ratified less than 12 months prior to the filing of the application bringing the dispute before the Court;

(6) disputes where the jurisdiction of the Court is or may be founded on the basis of a treaty concluded under the auspices of the League of Nations, unless the Government of India specially agree to jurisdiction in each case;

(7) disputes concerning the interpretation or application of a multilateral treaty to which India is not a party; and disputes concerning the interpretation or application of a multilateral treaty to which India is a party, unless all the parties to the treaty are also parties to the case before the Court or the Government of India specially agree to jurisdiction;

(8) disputes with the Government of any State with which, on the date of an application to bring a dispute before the Court, the Government of India has no diplomatic relations or which has not been recognized by the Government of India;

(9) disputes with non-sovereign States or territories;

(10) disputes with India concerning or relating to:
   (a) the status of its territory or the modification or delimitation of its frontiers or any other matter concerning boundaries;
   (b) the territorial sea, the continental shelf and the margins, the exclusive fishery zone, the exclusive economic zone, and other zones of national maritime jurisdiction including for the regulation and control of marine pollution and the conduct of scientific research by foreign vessels;
   (c) the condition and status of its islands, bays and gulfs and that of the bays and gulfs that for historical reasons belong to it;
   (d) the airspace superjacent to its land and maritime territory; and
   (e) the determination and delimitation of its maritime boundaries;

(11) disputes prior to the date of this declaration, including any dispute the foundations, reasons, facts, causes, origins, definitions, allegations or bases of which existed prior to this date, even if they are submitted or brought to the knowledge of the Court hereafter.[5]

The optional clause provides a potentially important source of jurisdiction, but its possibilities, as yet, are far from realisation.

The most commonly used method of consenting to the exercise of the Court's jurisdiction after a dispute has arisen is the negotiation of a special agreement. Such an agreement is similar to an arbitral *compromis* in that it provides the parties with an opportunity to define the issues in dispute and,

---

[5] The declaration, as all others, is available at www.icj-cij.org/en/declarations.

subject to the provisions of the Statute, to indicate the basis on which the Court should give its decision. This flexibility makes special agreements attractive to states as a way of utilising the Court, and as a result they are employed quite regularly. In 2008, for example, the Court was able to decide the *Sovereignty over Pedra Branca* case[6] following a special agreement between Singapore and Malaysia, having also recently decided the *Kasikili/Sedudu Island* case[7] between Botswana and Namibia, and the *Gabcikovo-Nagymaros* case[8] between Hungary and Slovakia on a similar basis.

It has been clear since the time of the Permanent Court that, once jurisdiction is established through the optional clause or on some other basis, the parties may widen its scope by an informal indication of consent in the course of the proceedings. Subsequently, the principle was extended to allow jurisdiction to be based on a unilateral application, followed by an acceptance from the respondent state, something which occurred in 2003 when France informed the Court that it consented to proceedings against it initiated by the Republic of the Congo a few months earlier.[9] This doctrine, known as *forum prorogatum*, avoids the need to conclude a special agreement and so provides states with an alternative means of accepting the Court's jurisdiction in a current dispute. In the normal course of events, however, a state which is prepared to litigate will wish to negotiate a special agreement, while one which is not will be careful to avoid actions which might be construed as indications of consent.

8.1.2 Jurisdictional Disputes

Since jurisdiction to decide a dispute is based on consent shown by a legal act, there is sometimes disagreement as to whether the states concerned have given the Court the necessary competence.

In case of disagreement as to whether the states concerned have given the Court the necessary competence, the question of jurisdiction is resolved by the Court, acting under Article 36(6) of the Statute, which confers what is known as the *compétence de la compétence*. It is therefore possible for a state to raise objections to the Court's jurisdiction but, if these are

---

[6] *Sovereignty over Pedra Branca/Pulau Batu Puteh, Middle Rocks and South Ledge (Malaysia/Singapore)*, Judgment [2008] ICJ Rep. 12; and see C. G. Lathrop, Note (2008) 102 *AJIL*, 828.
[7] *Kasikili/Sedudu Island (Botswana/Namibia)*, Judgment [1999] ICJ Rep. 1045; and see M. N. Shaw, Note (2000) 49 *ICLQ*, 964.
[8] *Gabcikovo-Nagymaros Project (Hungary/Slovakia)*, Judgment [1997] ICJ Rep. 7; and see P. N. Okowa, Note (1998) 47 *ICLQ*, 688.
[9] See ICJ Press Releases 2002/37 (9 December 2002) and 2003/14 (14 April 2003) relating to the *Certain Criminal Proceedings in France* case. On the origins of this doctrine, see H. Waldock, 'Forum prorogatum or acceptance of a unilateral summons to appear before the International Court' (1948) 2 *ILQ*, 377.

unsound, to find that its arguments are rejected. In the *Right of Passage* case,[10] for example, India raised no less than six preliminary objections based on the terms of the parties' respective optional clause declarations, but the Court rejected them all and went on to decide the substantive issue. Even when an objection is accepted, its effect may sometimes be merely to restrict the Court's competence, not to remove it altogether. For example, in the *Nicaragua* case,[11] which was brought by Nicaragua against the United States in 1984, the Court accepted the respondent's argument that a reservation covering certain multilateral treaties was applicable, but held that it was still competent to decide the case on the basis of customary international law. In *Immunities and Criminal Proceedings* the Court also accepted France's objection to jurisdiction in relation to Article 35 of the United Nations Convention against Transnational Organized Crime, but accepted competence on the basis of the Optional Protocol to the Vienna Convention on Diplomatic Relations concerning the Compulsory Settlement of Disputes.[12]

Disputes over jurisdiction must be dealt with at the beginning and often form a separate stage of the proceedings, resulting in a judgment on 'preliminary objections'. Thus, in a case between Nicaragua and Honduras in 1988, the Court considered a number of issues of jurisdiction and admissibility before deciding that its competence had been established on the basis of Article 31 of the Pact of Bogotá.[13] Similarly, in the *Fisheries Jurisdiction* case,[14] where jurisdiction was based on an agreement between the United Kingdom and Iceland, the Court established its competence in 1973 by examining and rejecting various arguments concerned with the validity and scope of the treaty, before going on to decide the main dispute the following year.

The range of legal issues which can arise when the Court is examining the question of jurisdiction is very wide. Thus, in the *Maritime Delimitation and Territorial Questions* case,[15] the Court had to decide whether Qatar and Bahrain had made a legally binding agreement and

---

[10] *Right of Passage over Indian Territory*, Preliminary Objections, Judgment [1957] ICJ Rep. 125.
[11] *Military and Paramilitary Activities in and against Nicaragua*, Merits, Judgment [1986] ICJ Rep. 14. This issue was held over from the earlier proceedings concerned with jurisdiction and admissibility.
[12] *Immunities and Criminal Proceedings (Equatorial Guinea v. France)*, Preliminary Objections, Judgment, [2018] ICJ Rep 292.
[13] *Border and Transborder Armed Actions*, Jurisdiction and Admissibility, Judgment [1988] ICJ Rep. 69. For further discussion, see Chapter 9.
[14] *Fisheries Jurisdiction (United Kingdom v. Iceland)*, Jurisdiction of the Court, Judgment [1973] ICJ Rep. 3. Parallel proceedings were instituted by the Federal Republic of Germany.
[15] *Maritime Delimitation and Territorial Questions between Qatar and Bahrain*, Jurisdiction and Admissibility, Judgments of 1 July 1994 and 15 February 1995 [1994] ICJ Rep. 112 and [1995] ICJ Rep. 6. For comment, see M. D. Evans, Note (1995) 44 *ICLQ*, 691.

then determine its precise scope and effect. In the *Oil Platforms* case,[16] on the other hand, which was brought by Iran against the United States, a treaty between the two states had certainly been concluded, but the respondent sought to argue that the dispute over acts involving the use of force lay outside its ambit. In further contrast, much wider issues, including questions of recognition and statehood, were involved in the *Genocide Convention* case[17] between Bosnia and Herzegovina and the Federal Republic of Yugoslavia. Because the case arose out of events following the break-up of Yugoslavia, the Court had to consider whether Bosnia had become a party to the 1948 Genocide Convention and, if so, when; the scope of the Court's jurisdiction *ratione temporis*; and the relevance of a number of other alleged bases of jurisdiction, including *forum prorogatum*. Questions of recognition and statehood will likely also be discussed in the case *Relocation of the United States Embassy to Jerusalem (Palestine v. United States of America)* initiated in 2018.

8.1.3 The Optional Clause

Optional clause declarations have proved a particularly fruitful source of jurisdictional problems. In the *Norwegian Loans* case,[18] for example, the Court decided that it had no jurisdiction to decide a case brought by France against Norway because the former had made a reservation excluding 'differences relating to matters which are essentially within the national jurisdiction as understood by the Government of the French Republic'. Although there was no such reservation in the Norwegian declaration, the Court followed its previous practice and held that Norway, as respondent, was entitled to invoke the reservation in the French declaration and remove the case from the Court's competence. Limitations on a state's acceptance of the Court's jurisdiction are thus a double-edged weapon. While they provide a state with protection in the sense that they stop certain claims from being brought against it, they also have a disabling effect because they may prevent the reserving state from taking disputes to the Court in which it could appear as plaintiff.

If a state wishes to avoid litigation, it will naturally try to take advantage of any reservations in its own or its opponent's declaration. In the *Aerial*

---

[16] *Oil Platforms (Islamic Republic of Iran v. United States of America)*, Preliminary Objection, Judgment [1996] ICJ Rep. 803. For comment, see M. D. Evans, Note (1997) 46 *ICLQ*, 693; and P. H. F. Bekker, Note (1997) 91 *AJIL*, 518.

[17] *Application of the Convention on the Prevention and Punishment of the Crime of Genocide (Bosnia and Herzegovina v. Yugoslavia)*, Preliminary Objections, Judgment [1996] ICJ Rep. 595. For comment, see P. H. F. Bekker and P. C. Szasz, Note (1997) 91 *AJIL*, 121; and C. Gray, Note (1997) 46 *ICLQ*, 688.

[18] *Certain Norwegian Loans*, Judgment [1957] ICJ Rep. 9.

Incident case,[19] Pakistan sought to limit this power by arguing that reservations not expressly authorised by the Statute are 'illicit' and may not be relied upon, but the Court ruled that there is no such restriction and upheld India's right to invoke a reservation in its declaration covering disputes with states which were, or had been, members of the British Commonwealth. Shortly before, in the *Fisheries Jurisdiction* case[20] between Spain and Canada, the Court had rejected another attempt to limit the impact of reservations. Spain had argued that reservations must be interpreted consistently with legality; in other words, that they cannot protect illegal acts. As the Court pointed out, however, the aim of a reservation may well be to prevent acts of dubious legality from being challenged. It could therefore defeat the purpose of a reservation to accept the Spanish argument.

An important point raised by the *Nicaragua* case was how a state can terminate a declaration. The United States declaration provided that it was terminable on six months' notice. The Nicaraguan declaration, on the other hand, contained no provision on termination and arguably could be terminated instantly. Anticipating that Nicaragua was about to bring a case against it, the United States terminated its declaration without giving six months' notice and made a new declaration containing a reservation which covered the Nicaraguan claim. When this manoeuvre was challenged as inconsistent with the requirement of notice in the original declaration, the United States reply was that, since Nicaragua could have terminated its declaration with immediate effect, reciprocity required that the United States should enjoy the same facility. The Court, however, rejected the argument and held that the new reservation was ineffective.[21]

The optional clause system, like other ways of accepting the Court's jurisdiction, was originally part of the Statute of the Permanent Court of International Justice and a significant number of declarations under Article 36(2) were made in the inter-war period. When the present Court was established in 1945, arrangements were made in Article 36(5) of the Statute to permit those declarations which were still in force to operate as acceptances of the new Court. The aim was to ensure that the new Court began with a nucleus of acceptances of its jurisdiction, and to maintain a sense of

---

[19] *Aerial Incident of 10 August, 1999 (Pakistan v. India)*, Jurisdiction, Judgment [2000] ICJ Rep. 12; and see J. G. Merrills, Note (2001) 50 *ICLQ*, 657.

[20] *Fisheries Jurisdiction (Spain v. Canada)*, Jurisdiction of the Court, Judgment [1998] ICJ Rep. 432; and see L. de La Fayette, Note (1999) 48 *ICLQ*, 664.

[21] *Military and Paramilitary Activities in and against Nicaragua*, Jurisdiction and Admissibility, Judgment [1984] ICJ Rep. 392. And see generally E. B. Weiss, 'Reciprocity and the optional clause', in L. F. Damrosch (ed.), *The International Court of Justice at a Crossroads*, New York, 1987, p. 82. The main reason given by the Court was that the duration of an optional clause is governed by its own terms and not by reciprocity. A subsidiary reason was that declarations with no termination clause are not terminable instantly but only on reasonable notice.

continuity with the old Court. All this was achieved, though at a cost, for the application of this provision, and Article 37(5) which contains a similar arrangement for treaty-based jurisdiction, have raised technical questions of surprising complexity.

The Court's transferred jurisdiction under Article 36(5) was another of the preliminary matters which had to be addressed in the *Nicaragua* case. Nicaragua made its declaration in 1929 but for reasons which were obscure never ratified the Protocol of Signature of the Statute of the Permanent Court. Recognising that, in these circumstances, it might be difficult to persuade the Court that its declaration was 'in force' in 1945 and could therefore be maintained by Article 36(5), Nicaragua argued that it had sufficiently manifested its intent to accept the Court's jurisdiction by allowing its declaration to be reproduced in successive volumes of the Court's *Yearbook* without any protest. Although this concept of 'jurisdiction by acquiescence' was not entirely novel,[22] the position was naturally less clear-cut than if Nicaragua had shown its consent unequivocally by either making a new declaration or ratifying the Protocol. A majority of the Court nevertheless accepted the argument and amid considerable controversy held that the combined effect of Nicaragua's resuscitated declaration and a declaration which the United States had failed to extinguish was enough to give it jurisdiction over the dispute.

Transferred jurisdiction under Article 37(5) was in issue in the *Aerial Incident* case where, as an alternative to its optional clause argument, Pakistan claimed that the Court had jurisdiction on the basis of the 1928 General Act. India rejected this conclusion on various grounds, arguing that the General Act was no longer in force and that, even if it was, neither state had succeeded to it when they became independent in 1947. In ruling on the issue of jurisdiction, however, the Court avoided pronouncing on these questions, and instead decided the case on a narrower ground, holding that, even if the General Act was originally binding on both states, India had validly denounced it, and so ceased to be bound by the Act in 1979. It followed therefore that the General Act did not provide a basis of jurisdiction and Pakistan could not employ Article 37(5).

In the majority of cases in which the Court is required to decide whether its jurisdiction has been accepted, the question will arise because some deficiency is alleged in the instrument by which either or both of the states which are before the Court has ostensibly accepted the Court's jurisdiction.

---

[22] An analogous point was considered in *Temple of Preah Vihear*, Preliminary Objections, Judgment [1961] ICJ Rep. 17. In addition to the reason mentioned in the text, the Court supported its conclusion that Nicaragua's declaration was still in force by holding that Art. 36(5) had the effect of reviving valid declarations even if they were not previously in force. This, however, does not seem very convincing.

However, this situation, which is exemplified by the complex issues in the optional clause cases, is not the only way in which the issue of consent can arise.

8.1.4 Jurisdiction and the Scope of Consent

The principle, it will be recalled, is that all the states involved in a given dispute must have indicated their consent, and from this it follows that it is not open to two states to bring a case directly concerning the rights of a third, unless the latter has also consented to the exercise of jurisdiction. A clear demonstration of this principle may be seen in the *Monetary Gold* case,[23] where the four states which had brought the case had all accepted the Court's jurisdiction, but the Court declined to adjudicate because Albania, whose property rights formed the subject matter of the case, had not.

The scope of the principle of consent was further clarified in the *Nicaragua* case. For there, in addition to the matters already considered, the United States argued that the Court should rule the application inadmissible because the dispute concerned the legal interests of Honduras, Costa Rica and El Salvador which were not parties to the case. The Court rejected the argument and held that the principle in the *Monetary Gold* case applied only to situations in which the legal interests of a non-party 'would not only be affected by a decision, but would form the very subject-matter of the decision'.[24] As this was not the situation here, the Court held that it was entitled to proceed. In rejecting the idea of a broad 'indispensable parties' rule in the *Nicaragua* case, the Court adopted an approach which indicates that the consent of third states will usually be unnecessary. Thus, by denying the need for their presence save in exceptional circumstances, the Court's approach removes a potential obstacle to the exercise of its jurisdiction. On the other hand, the political reality is that international disputes are not exclusively bilateral, and judgments which ignore the interests of third states are unlikely to be fully effective. An awareness of this point led to the inclusion in the Court's Statute of provisions permitting intervention. These are part of the Court's incidental jurisdiction, which is examined below.

---

[23] *Monetary Gold Removed from Rome in 1943*, Judgment [1954] ICJ Rep. 19. For commentary, see D. H. N. Johnson, 'The case of the Monetary Gold Removed from Rome in 1943' (1955) 4 *ICLQ*, 93.

[24] [1984] ICJ Rep. 431. See also on this issue *Certain Phosphate Lands in Nauru (Nauru v. Australia)*, Preliminary Objections, Judgment [1992] ICJ Rep. 240. For summary, see A. Anghie, Note (1993) 87 *AJIL*, 282; and *East Timor (Portugal v. Australia)*, Judgment [1995] ICJ Rep. 90. For comment, see C. Chinkin, Note (1996) 45 *ICLQ*, 712; and P. F. Bekker, Note (1996) 90 *AJIL*, 94.

A further point meriting consideration is whether the Court is entitled to deal with a dispute if the applicant has no specific legal interest in the case, but is simply concerned to enforce the law. Strictly speaking this is a question of admissibility rather than jurisdiction, but it is relevant here because the issue, the permissibility of what is known as an *actio popularis*, determines who is and who is not entitled to bring a case in a wide range of situations. Until recently the conventional view of the Court's competence was that an *actio popularis* was not allowed. However, in the *Whaling in the Antarctic* case,[25] Australia was permitted to challenge Japan's whaling programme and New Zealand was able to intervene in the case despite the fact that the disputed activity had not been carried out in either states' waters. Similarly, in the *Questions relating to the Obligation to Prosecute or Extradite* case,[26] Belgium was able to challenge Senegal's compliance with the 1984 UN Convention Against Torture, even though the matter had no connection with Belgium.

8.2 Incidental Jurisdiction

In addition to its contentious jurisdiction, the Statute entitles the Court to exercise two further kinds of jurisdiction: an incidental jurisdiction, which is linked to the Court's contentious jurisdiction, and an advisory jurisdiction. By virtue of its incidental jurisdiction, the Court has the power to indicate interim measures of protection, to allow intervention and to interpret or revise a judgment. Because these powers are conferred by the Statute, their exercise by the Court does not require a further expression of consent on the part of states and in appropriate circumstances these and other incidental powers can make a constructive contribution to the settlement of disputes. In contrast, the advisory jurisdiction, which is chiefly concerned with the rights and duties of international organisations, is not as important in the present context, although, as we shall see shortly, its bearing on inter-state disputes is sometimes closer than might be assumed.

8.2.1 Interim Measures of Protection

Interim measures of protection, or provisional measures, are governed by Article 41 of the Statute and, as the name indicates, are concerned with the preservation of the parties' rights while litigation is in progress.[27] Their

---

[25] *Whaling in the Antarctic (Australia v. Japan: New Zealand intervening)*, Judgment [2014] ICJ Rep. 226 and see S. E. Rolland, Note (2014) 108 *AJIL*, 496.
[26] *Questions relating to the Obligation to Prosecute or Extradite (Belgium v. Senegal)*, Judgment [2012] ICJ Rep. 422.
[27] See on interim measures: C. A. Miles, *Provisional Measures before International Courts and Tribunals*, Cambridge, 2017.

justification stems from the elementary juridical principle that the judgment of a court should be effective and that to ensure this it may, while a case is before the Court, be essential to restrain either party, or both, from disrupting the situation, or attempting to present its adversary with a *fait accompli*. Arrangements to protect the legal rights of litigants are, of course, a familiar feature of municipal legal systems. At the international level, such procedures are particularly necessary because litigation is often protracted, especially if there are jurisdictional issues to determine, and also because, if a dispute has precipitated an international crisis, the parties may be acting in a way which threatens to destroy the possibility of a peaceful settlement.

In the *Frontier Dispute* case,[28] between Burkina Faso and Mali, for example, both states asked the Court to resolve a boundary question which less than ten years before had caused a war between them. However, before the Court could give its decision, the dispute flared up and fighting broke out again. A cease-fire was arranged and, in order that the eventual judgment should not be prejudiced, both sides asked the Court to indicate interim measures. After examining the parties' requests, which were in somewhat different terms, the Court decided that interim measures were required to prevent the possible destruction of evidence and, more generally, to prevent the extension or aggravation of the dispute. It therefore ordered the parties to respect the cease-fire, to withdraw their armed forces from the frontier, and to do nothing to change the administration of the disputed area, to intensify the dispute or to interfere with each other's rights.

In the *Questions relating to the Seizure and Detention of Certain Documents* case an unusual situation occurred. Timor-Leste initiated proceedings against Australia complaining of the seizure and retention by Australia of documents, data and other property relating to a pending arbitration. At the same time, Timor-Leste filed a request for various interim measures which it claimed were necessary to protect its rights. The Court agreed and in 2014 ordered Australia, among other requirements, to ensure that the seized material should not be used to the disadvantage of Timor-Leste until the case was concluded. In the following year Australia indicated that it wished to return the seized material and asked the Court to modify another part of the order requiring it to keep the material under seal. This the Court agreed to and modified the original order accordingly. Finally, a month later, following the return of the material, Timor-Leste informed the Court that, having achieved the

---

[28] *Frontier Dispute*, Provisional Measures, Order of 10 January 1986 [1986] ICJ Rep. 3. For a more recent case involving a rather similar situation, see the *Land and Maritime Boundary between Cameroon and Nigeria*, Provisional Measures, Order of 15 March 1996 [1996] ICJ Rep. 13, summarised in J. G. Merrills, Note (1997) 46 *ICLQ*, 676.

purpose of the litigation, it wished to discontinue the case. The Court therefore made an order removing the case from the Court's list.[29]

The Court will not make an order for interim measures of protection unless there is some instrument which prima facie recognises its jurisdiction to decide the main dispute. This is unlikely to be a problem in a case referred by a special agreement, such as the *Frontier Dispute* case, but may be an obstacle where the basis is declarations under the optional clause or a treaty, the effect of which is contested. In the *Legality of Use of Force* cases,[30] for example, Yugoslavia brought claims against ten NATO states arising out of the bombing campaign over Kosovo in 1999, relying as regards six of the respondents on their declarations under the optional clause, and as regards all ten on the 1948 Genocide Convention. But, when Yugoslavia asked for interim measures of protection, its request was rejected on the ground that the Court lacked prima facie jurisdiction. In relation to the Genocide Convention, this was because the Court's provisional view was that the acts complained of could not be said to qualify as genocide, and in relation to the optional clause on account of reservations and limitations in either the applicant's or the respondents' declarations which seemed to exclude jurisdiction.

If the requirement of prima facie jurisdiction is satisfied, the Court must then decide whether interim measures are needed. The conditions under which provisional measures can be ordered by the Court are, besides the requirement of prima facie jurisdiction, the risk of irreparable prejudice, urgency, a link between the provisional measures requested and the rights which are in issue in the case, and the plausibility of the rights asserted by the party requesting such measures.

The risk of irreparable prejudice is linked to the requirement of 'urgency' and is often discussed jointly. As explained by the Court:

> the power of the Court to indicate provisional measures will be exercised only if there is urgency, in the sense that there is a real and imminent risk that irreparable prejudice will be caused to the rights in dispute before the Court gives its final decision. The condition of urgency is met when the acts susceptible of causing irreparable prejudice can 'occur at any moment' before the Court rules on the merits.[31]

---

[29] *Questions relating to the Seizure and Detention of Certain Documents and Data (Timor-Leste v. Australia)*, Provisional Measures, Order of 3 March 2014 [2014] ICJ Rep. 147 and see R. J. Bettauer, Note (2014) 108 *AJIL*, 762. For subsequent developments see the Orders of 22 April and 11 June 2015 [2015] ICJ Rep. 147.

[30] *Legality of Use of Force*, Provisional Measures, Order of 2 June 1999 [1999] ICJ Rep. 124 (Belgium); and see C. Gray, Note (2000) 49 *ICLQ*, 730.

[31] *Application of the International Convention on the Elimination of All Forms of Racial Discrimination (Qatar v. United Arab Emirates)*, Provisional Measures, Order of 23 July 2018, [2018] ICJ Rep 406, para. 60 (internal references omitted).

The risk of irreparable prejudice and the existence of 'urgency' depends very much on the specific facts of the case. The Court must take account of a range of factors, including any steps which the parties may already have taken to reduce the tension. Thus, in the *Aegean Sea Continental Shelf* case,[32] which concerned a dispute which had brought Greece and Turkey to the brink of war, the Court decided that it was unnecessary to consider an order prohibiting the use of force because the Security Council had already adopted a resolution, which both states had welcomed, calling upon them to resolve their dispute peacefully. In the *Nicaragua* case,[33] on the other hand, the United States failed to persuade the Court that it should refuse interim measures because these might affect the Contadora process. While these rulings reflect different assessments of whether interim measures were 'necessary', they also demonstrate a broader point which has been emphasised throughout this study – that methods of dispute settlement are interconnected.

The Court has considered that a risk of irreparable prejudice can exist 'when the persons concerned are exposed to danger to health and life'.[34] This was an issue in the *Jadhav* case, which related to a dispute concerning the application of the Vienna Convention on Consular Relations in relation to Mr Jadhav, an Indian national who had been sentenced to death by a court martial in Pakistan. Because of the risk of execution of the death sentence, the Court considered that 'the mere fact that Mr. Jadhav is under such a sentence and might therefore be executed is sufficient to demonstrate the existence of such a risk'.[35]

The Court also has on several occasions determined that individuals forced to leave their own place of residence without the possibility of return may be subject to a serious risk of irreparable prejudice.[36] In *Qatar v. United Arab Emirates*, the Court also considered that a risk of irreparable prejudice may occur

> when individuals are subject to temporary or potentially ongoing separation from their families and suffer from psychological distress; when students are

---

[32] *Aegean Sea Continental Shelf*, Interim Protection, Order of 11 September 1976 [1976] ICJ Rep. 3.

[33] *Military and Paramilitary Activities in and against Nicaragua*, Provisional Measures, Order of 10 May 1984 [1984] ICJ Rep. 169.

[34] *Alleged Violations of the 1955 Treaty of Amity, Economic Relations, and Consular Rights (Islamic Republic of Iran v. United States of America)*, Provisional Measures, Order of 3 October 2018, [2018] ICJ Rep. 623, para. 91.

[35] *Jadhav (India v. Pakistan)*, Provisional Measures, Order of 18 May 2017, [2017] ICJ Rep. 243, para. 53.

[36] *Application of the International Convention on the Elimination of All Forms of Racial Discrimination (Georgia v. Russian Federation)*, Provisional Measures, Order of 15 October 2008, [2008] ICJ Rep, para. 142; *Application of the International Convention on the Elimination of All Forms of Racial Discrimination (Qatar v. United Arab Emirates)*, Provisional Measures, Order of 23 July 2018, [2018] ICJ Rep. 406, para. 69.

prevented from taking their exams due to enforced absence or from pursuing their studies due to a refusal by academic institutions to provide educational records; or when the persons concerned are impeded from being able to physically appear in any proceedings or to challenge any measure they find discriminatory.[37]

The third condition is the requirement of a link between the provisional measures requested and the rights which are in issue in the case. This is to a certain extent inherent in the object of provisional measures and the fact that the Court's competence is limited by the title which grants it jurisdiction. As noted by the Court, 'the power of the Court to indicate provisional measures has as its object to permit the Court to preserve the respective rights of the parties to a case "[p]ending the final decision" in the judicial proceedings, provided such measures are necessary to prevent irreparable prejudice to the rights that are in dispute'.[38]

A case which illustrates this requirement is the *Arbitral Award of 31 July 1989 (Guinea-Bissau v. Senegal)* case, which related to a request for annulment of an arbitral award. Guinea-Bissau had requested the Court to order provisional measures requiring both parties to 'abstain in the disputed area from any act or action of any kind whatever, during the whole duration of the proceedings'.[39] The Court however declined to order provisional measures. The main reason was that the case pending before the Court related to the annulment of the 1989 arbitral award, and not the respective rights of the parties in relation to the delimitation of the maritime areas which was the subject of the arbitral award. The Court considered, consequently, that 'the alleged rights sought to be made the subject of provisional measures are not the subject of the proceedings before the Court on the merits of the case'.[40]

The importance of the link between the provisional measures requested and the rights which are in issue in the case may be seen from the *Pulp Mills on the River Uruguay* case,[41] where the situation was rather unusual. Argentina began proceedings against Uruguay alleging violations of the treaty governing the river that forms the boundary between them. Argentina complained that Uruguay authorised the construction of two

---

[37] *Application of the International Convention on the Elimination of All Forms of Racial Discrimination (Qatar v. United Arab Emirates)*, Provisional Measures, Order of 23 July 2018, [2018] ICJ Rep. 406, para. 69.

[38] *Pulp Mills on the River Uruguay (Argentina v. Uruguay)*, Provisional Measures, Order of 13 July 2006 [2006] ICJ Rep. 113, para. 61.

[39] *Arbitral Award of 31 July 1989 (Guinea-Bissau v. Senegal)*, Provisional Measures, Order of 2 March 1990, [1990] ICJ Rep. 64, para. 3.

[40] *Arbitral Award of 31 July 1989 (Guinea-Bissau v. Senegal)*, Provisional Measures, Order of 2 March 1990, [1990] ICJ Rep. 64, para. 26.

[41] *Pulp Mills on the River Uruguay (Argentina v. Uruguay)*, Provisional Measures, Orders of 13 July 2006 and 23 January 2007 [2006] ICJ Rep. 113 and [2007] ICJ Rep. 3.

pulp mills on the river without observing the notification and consultation procedure required by the 1975 Statute of the River Uruguay. In its request for interim protection, Argentina asked the Court to order Uruguay to suspend construction of the pulp mills and also to cooperate with measures to protect the aquatic environment. The Court, however, ruled that the circumstances were not such as to require the exercise of its powers under Article 41. Although Argentina's request was rejected, the Court explained that it was at liberty to submit a future request based on new facts. But it was then Uruguay that returned to the Court by submitting its own request for interim measures. Uruguay's complaint was that 'organised groups of Argentine citizens' were blockading a bridge over the river and Uruguay requested that Argentina should be ordered to put an end to this. Argentina in turn contested that the measures requested by Uruguay were not linked to the subject matter of the proceedings which was confined to the construction of the pulp mills and the application of the treaty governing the River Uruguay. The Court, however, found that the right Uruguay may have to continue the construction and to begin the commissioning of one of the pulp mills in conformity with the provisions of the treaty governing the River Uruguay 'effectively constitutes a claimed right in the present case, which may in principle be protected by the indication of provisional measures'.[42] The Court, however, having considered all the circumstances, again decided that the measures requested were unnecessary.

The next condition, the plausibility of the rights asserted by the party requesting such measures, can be linked to the need for a link between the provisional measures requested and the rights which are in issue in the case. The 'plausibility' requirement was added by the Court only recently and first explicitly appeared in the *Belgium* v. *Senegal* case in 2009.[43] While initially targeting the plausibility of the rights asserted by the parties in the dispute, recent case law suggests that the Court is now assessing the plausibility of the *claims*.[44]

Since the *Belgium* v. *Senegal* case, the requirement has consistently appeared in decisions on provisional measures of the Court. Recently, in *Application of the International Convention on the Elimination of All Forms of Racial Discrimination (Qatar* v. *United Arab Emirates)*, the Court explained the requirement as follows:

---

[42] *Pulp Mills on the River Uruguay (Argentina* v. *Uruguay)*, Provisional Measures, Order 23 January 2007 [2007] ICJ Rep. 3, para. 29.
[43] *Questions relating to the Obligation to Prosecute or Extradite (Belgium* v. *Senegal)*, Order on Provisional Measures of 28 May 2009, [2009] ICJ Rep. 139, at 151, paras. 57–60.
[44] See M. Lando, 'Plausibility in the provisional measures jurisprudence of the International Court of Justice' (2018) 31 *Leiden Journal of International Law*, 641–68.

the Court must be concerned to preserve by such measures the rights which may subsequently be adjudged by it to belong to either party. Therefore, the Court may exercise this power only if it is satisfied that the rights asserted by the party requesting such measures are at least plausible.

At this stage of the proceedings, the Court, however, is not called upon to determine definitively whether the rights which Qatar wishes to see protected exist; it need only decide whether the rights claimed by Qatar on the merits, and for which it is seeking protection, are plausible. Moreover, a link must exist between the rights whose protection is sought and the provisional measures being requested.[45]

In *Qatar* v. *United Arab Emirates*, the Court was seized by Qatar which requested provisional measures along with the institution of proceedings. The dispute concerns allegations of violation of the Convention on the Elimination of All Forms of Racial Discrimination (CERD), such as discriminatory measures taken by the United Arab Emirates against Qataris and their families. The dispute, however, is part of a broader situation of tension between Qatar and several other states, including Saudi Arabia, the United Arab Emirates, Bahrain and Egypt. In 2018, the Court indicated certain provisional measures directed at the United Arab Emirates, and ordered that both parties refrain from any action which might aggravate or extend the dispute before the Court or make it more difficult to resolve.[46] It found that

> at least some of the rights asserted by Qatar under Article 5 of CERD are plausible. This is the case, for example, with respect to the alleged racial discrimination in the enjoyment of rights such as the right to marriage and to choice of spouse, the right to education, as well as freedom of movement, and access to justice.[47]

Some eight months after that order, the United Arab Emirates in turn submitted a request for the indication of provisional measures and requested amongst others that Qatar immediately withdraw its Communication submitted to the Committee on the Elimination of Racial Discrimination, which it had submitted in parallel to the proceedings before the Court. The United Arab Emirates also requested measures relating to the non-aggravation of the dispute. The Court however considered that request relating to the proceedings before the CERD

---

[45] *Application of the International Convention on the Elimination of All Forms of Racial Discrimination (Qatar v. United Arab Emirates)*, Provisional Measures, Order of 23 July 2018, [2018] ICJ Rep. 406, paras 43 and 44.

[46] *Application of the International Convention on the Elimination of All Forms of Racial Discrimination (Qatar v. United Arab Emirates)*, Provisional Measures, Order of 23 July 2018, [2018] ICJ Rep. 406.

[47] *Application of the International Convention on the Elimination of All Forms of Racial Discrimination (Qatar v. United Arab Emirates)*, Provisional Measures, Order of 23 July 2018, [2018] ICJ Rep. 406, para. 54.

Committee was not related to the protection of plausible rights under the CERD. In relation to the other requested measures, the Court made a point of general importance. It considered that provisional measures with a view to preventing the aggravation or extension of a dispute can 'only be indicated as an addition to specific measures to protect rights of the parties', and that it 'cannot indicate measures solely with respect to the non-aggravation of the dispute'.[48] As to the types of measures ordered, it is important to note that the Court has often emphasised that it has discretion to decide which measures need to be indicated. The Court's power in this respect is not limited by the measures requested by the parties. This was explained by the Court in *Qatar v. United Arab Emirates:*

> The Court recalls that it has the power, under its Statute, when a request for provisional measures has been made, to indicate measures that are, in whole or in part, other than those requested. Article 75, paragraph 2, of the Rules of Court specifically refers to this power of the Court.[49]

Interim measures are legally binding,[50] and so, when the Court makes such an order, states are expected to carry it out. In practice, however, interim measures are likely to be most effective in situations, like that in the *Frontier Dispute* case, where both parties are prepared to recognise the value of judicial intervention. They are less useful in situations like that in the *Nicaragua* case, where one side rejects the whole idea of judicial settlement, for, like the judgment on the merits in such cases, they cannot effectively be enforced. As noted above, the Court will not make an order for interim measures of protection unless there is some instrument which prima facie recognises its jurisdiction to decide the main dispute. Thus, it is not open to a state to use the Court's power to indicate interim measures as a way of by-passing the principle of consensuality. On the other hand, as we saw earlier, consent and willingness may not coincide, and it is not unusual for a state which finds a case brought against it to attempt to repudiate its previous acceptance of the Court. It is precisely in these cases, where steps to restrain the unwilling state from disregarding the applicant's rights may well be needed, that interim measures are often least effective.

It should be noted, however, that the significance of Article 41 is not limited to cases in which the Court makes an order for interim protection

---

[48] *Application of the International Convention on the Elimination of All Forms of Racial Discrimination (Qatar v. United Arab Emirates)*, Provisional Measures, Order of 14 June 2019, [2019] ICJ Rep. 361, paras 25–9.

[49] *Application of the International Convention on the Elimination of All Forms of Racial Discrimination (Qatar v. United Arab Emirates)*, Provisional Measures, Order of 23 July 2018, [2018] ICJ Rep. 406, para. 73.

[50] See *LaGrand (Germany v. United States)*, Judgment [2001] ICJ Rep. 466, paras 99–103; and see M. Menneke and C. J. Tams, Note (2002) 51 *ICLQ*, 449. Prior to this decision, the status of interim measures was a matter of uncertainty.

which is then observed. While that is the ideal situation, a state whose request is granted obtains widespread exposure for its claims at an early stage and, notwithstanding the provisional character of the Court's assessment, can be thought of as having won the first round of the contest, and wrong-footed its opponent. Indeed, even a request which is rejected can sometimes prove beneficial. In the *Passage through the Great Belt* case,[51] for example, Finland challenged Denmark's right to build a bridge across one of the exits from the Baltic Sea. Finland made a request for interim protection, and in the course of the proceedings under Article 41, Denmark undertook not to complete the bridge before the hearing on the merits, while the Court for its part decided to accelerate the proceedings. These represented gains for Finland, despite the Court's ruling that interim protection was unnecessary.[52]

8.2.2 Intervention

The powers of the Court to allow a state to intervene in a case are set out in Articles 62 and 63 of the Statute.[53] The latter entitles a state to intervene as of right when a case involves the interpretation of a treaty to which it is a party. Article 62, on the other hand, authorises a state to make a request to intervene if it considers that it has 'an interest of a legal nature which may be affected by the decision in the case'. Neither provision has been much used, but Article 62, which makes intervention a matter for the Court's discretion, has already posed a number of problems.

It is clearly undesirable for the Court, whose jurisdiction is consensual, to deal with the interests of states that are not present; hence the need to provide such states with an opportunity to intervene. But, although the function of Article 62 is plain, difficulties have arisen over two related issues: the question of what constitutes 'an interest of a legal nature' and the question of the circumstances, if any, in which a state seeking to rely on Article 62 must be able to point to a jurisdictional link between itself and the main parties to the case.

---

[51] *Passage through the Great Belt (Finland v. Denmark)*, Provisional Measures, Order of 29 July 1991 [1991] ICJ Rep. 12. For commentary, see C. Gray, Note (1993) 42 *ICLQ*, 705.

[52] Moreover, the Court indicated that a decision on the merits in favour of Finland might not merely require the payment of compensation, but could result in Denmark's having to abandon the bridge project altogether. This may well have strengthened Finland's bargaining position in the subsequent negotiations between the two states. See further J. G. Merrills, 'Interim measures of protection in the recent jurisprudence of the International Court of Justice' (1995) 44 *ICLQ*, 112, 112–13 and 140–1.

[53] For a review of the issues raised by these provisions, see C. M. Chinkin, 'Third party intervention before the International Court of Justice' (1986) 80 *AJIL*, 495; and J. M. Ruda, 'Intervention before the International Court of Justice', in V. Lowe and M. Fitzmaurice (eds), *Fifty Years of the International Court of Justice*, Cambridge, 1996, p. 487.

Both questions were prominent in the *Tunisia–Libya Continental Shelf* case, where the third state was Malta, seeking to intervene when the two North African states asked the Court to indicate the rules and principles of international law applicable to the delimitation of their respective areas of continental shelf in the central Mediterranean. There was no jurisdictional link between Malta and the main parties, but what led the Court to reject the request was that, while Malta sought permission to submit its views with respect to the law concerning a large area, it attached to its request an express reservation that its intervention was not to have the effect of putting in issue its own claims *vis-à-vis* Tunisia and Libya. This qualification the Court found to be unacceptable, concluding that 'the very character of the intervention for which Malta seeks permission shows ... that the interest of a legal nature invoked by Malta cannot be considered to be one "which may be affected by the decision in the case" within the meaning of Article 62 of the Statute'.[54]

The effect of this decision was that, in 1982, the *Tunisia–Libya* case was decided on the merits without Malta's participation. Malta and Libya then referred their delimitation dispute to the Court. This, in turn, prompted an application to intervene from Italy which, like Malta in the earlier case, found its request opposed by the main parties. The basis of Italy's case was that the continental shelf area which Libya and Malta had referred to the Court included areas over which Italy considered that it had rights. Italy therefore maintained that it had 'an interest of a legal nature' within the meaning of Article 62. To meet the objection which had proved fatal to Malta in 1981, Italy also made it clear that, if permitted to intervene, it would submit to whatever decision the Court might make with regard to its own asserted rights.

The Italian case looked strong but had one weakness. There was no jurisdictional link between Italy and Libya. Was this important? In its decision in 1984, the Court held that it was.[55] The way the Court construed the Italian request in the *Libya–Malta* case meant that it did not need to decide whether a jurisdictional link is always required before a state can intervene under Article 62, and it is clear from the individual opinions that this was a point on which the judges were divided. However, in the *Land, Island and Maritime Frontier* case[56] in 1990, a ruling on the issue of

---

[54] *Continental Shelf (Tunisia/Libyan Arab Jamahiriya)*, Application by Malta for Permission to Intervene, Judgment [1981] ICJ Rep. 3 at 19.

[55] *Continental Shelf (Libyan Arab Jamahiriya/Malta)*, Application by Italy for Permission to Intervene, Judgment [1984] ICJ Rep. 3. For discussion, see G. P. McGinley, 'Intervention in the International Court: The Libya/Malta Continental Shelf Case' (1985) 34 *ICLQ*, 671.

[56] *Land, Island and Maritime Frontier Dispute (El Salvador/Honduras)*, Application to Intervene, Judgment [1990] ICJ Rep. 92. This judgment was given by a chamber in accordance with the Court's Order of 28 February 1990. For comment on the Order and subsequent Judgment, see M. D. Evans, Note (1992) 41 *ICLQ*, 896.

jurisdiction could not be avoided when a chamber of the Court decided that Nicaragua had shown the existence of 'an interest of a legal nature' in the regime of the waters of the Gulf of Fonseca, one of the matters in contention between Honduras and El Salvador. The chamber decided that it was unnecessary to demonstrate a jurisdictional link between Nicaragua and the litigating states on the ground that, when a state intervenes as a 'non-party', the Court's competence with regard to intervention derives not from the consent of the parties to the case, but from their consent to the Court's exercise of its powers under the Statute. This approach has been endorsed by the full Court in later cases and is clearly correct. For it not only treats intervention in the same way as interim measures and other aspects of the Court's incidental jurisdiction, which has the merit of consistency, but also makes intervention possible whenever a state can show the requisite interest, thus enabling Article 62 to achieve its purpose.

In another way, too, the decision in the *Land, Island and Maritime Frontier* case seems likely to facilitate intervention. From the two earlier cases, it appeared that, if, to prove that it had an 'interest of a legal nature', a state specified rights which might be infringed, it could be accused of submitting a dispute to the Court. But if, on the other hand, it refrained from doing this, it could find, as Malta did, that it was held to have no 'interest of a legal nature'. In the *Land, Island and Maritime Frontier* case, however, the chamber provided a way out of this dilemma by examining Nicaragua's alleged legal interest in a balanced and constructive manner and upholding part of its claim. It is important to note that a general interest in the relevant rules of international law is not sufficient to ground an intervention under Article 62, and a number of Nicaragua's other claims were rejected on this basis. Nevertheless, by accepting Nicaragua's claim to intervene in relation to the status of the waters of the Gulf of Fonseca, the first case in which a request to intervene under Article 62 was accepted, the chamber set an important and encouraging precedent.

Subsequent cases have further clarified when intervention under Articles 62 or 63 is possible. Thus in the *Territorial and Maritime Dispute*[57] between Nicaragua and Colombia, both Costa Rica and Honduras sought to intervene as non-parties on the basis that their coastlines on the Caribbean gave them an interest in the issues of maritime delimitation raised in the case. However, the Court dismissed both requests on the ground that they had each failed to demonstrate an interest of a legal nature that might be affected by its decision. On the other hand, in the *Jurisdictional Immunities of the State* case[58] between Germany and Italy,

---

[57] *Territorial and Maritime Dispute (Nicaragua v. Colombia)*, Application for Permission to Intervene, Judgments [2011] ICJ Rep. 348 and 420.
[58] *Jurisdictional Immunities of the State (Germany v. Italy: Greece intervening)*, Application for Permission to Intervene, Order of 4 July 2011 [2011] ICJ Rep. 494.

which concerned, among other matters, the enforceability of Greek judgments in Italy, the Court unanimously allowed a request from Greece for permission to intervene and reached a similar conclusion when New Zealand applied to intervene under Article 63 in the *Whaling in the Antarctic* case,[59] which concerned the interpretation and application of the 1946 Whaling Convention.

It would be wrong to leave this topic without pointing out that, for a would-be intervenor, the opportunity to invoke Article 62 may in itself be quite valuable. For example, in the *Ligitan and Sipadan* case,[60] the Philippines attempted to intervene in a dispute between Indonesia and Malaysia in order to protect its claim to North Borneo, but the application was rejected on the ground that it had failed to show the necessary 'interest of a legal nature'. However, the Court assured the Philippines that the parties' submissions had no bearing on its territorial claim and also indicated that, despite the Court's rejection of the application to intervene, it remained 'cognizant of the positions stated before it by Indonesia, Malaysia and the Philippines in the present proceedings'. There is thus a parallel here between Article 62 and Article 41 since, as we saw earlier, even requests for interim protection which are denied may have certain benefits.

8.2.3 Revision and Interpretation

The power to revise a judgment is contained in Article 61 of the Statute and can only be exercised if new facts come to light and these would have had a decisive effect on the decision. Interpretation of a judgment, in contrast, is a broader power and according to Article 60 can be performed at the request of any party. Like the provisions on intervention, these powers have been little used, but in the right situation can be employed to make judicial settlement more effective. Thus, in the final stage of the proceedings in the *Tunisia–Libya* case,[61] the Court refused a request by Tunisia that it should revise its 1982 judgment on the ground that the new facts could have been discovered earlier and because in any event they were not sufficiently important. It did, however, respond positively to a subsidiary request that it should interpret the previous judgment. There was considerable argument in this case over whether Tunisia's request for 'interpretation' was simply another attempt to secure a revision of the

---

[59] *Whaling in the Antarctic (Australia v. Japan: New Zealand intervening)*, Declaration of Intervention of New Zealand, Order of 6 February 2013 [2013] ICJ Rep. 3.
[60] *Sovereignty over Pulau Ligitan and Pulau Sipadan (Indonesia/Malaysia)*, Application to Intervene, Judgment [2001] ICJ Rep. 575; and see J. G. Merrills, Note (2002) 51 *ICLQ*, 718.
[61] *Application for Revision and Interpretation of the Judgment of 24 February 1982 in the Case concerning the Continental Shelf (Tunisia/Libyan Arab Jamahiriya)* [1985] ICJ Rep. 192.

judgment, and the Court, though acceding to the request, was careful to emphasise the distinction between the two.

A rather similar point was made in the *Land and Maritime Boundary* case when, in an unusual move, Nigeria requested an interpretation of the Court's judgment on jurisdiction and admissibility, while the proceedings on the merits were still pending.[62] There had been no previous requests of this kind, but the Court accepted that the language of Article 60 is sufficiently general to allow for interpretation of judgments on preliminary objections, as well as of those on the merits. It pointed out, however, that by laying down that judgments are 'final and without appeal', Article 60 reflects a fundamental principle, that of *res judicata*, which must always be respected. As regards the particular point in issue, the Court explained that in its earlier judgment it had rejected the pertinent objection of Nigeria in terms which could not be reconciled with its current request. The Court would therefore not be able to 'interpret' that judgment without transgressing the principle of *res judicata*, from which it followed that Nigeria's request was inadmissible.

The significance of Article 60 may perhaps best be seen from the latest proceedings in the *Temple* case.[63] In 1962 the Court decided the *Temple* case, a territorial dispute between Cambodia and Thailand, and gave judgment in favour of Cambodia. In 2011, following disagreement over the implementation of the judgment, leading to armed clashes in the area, Cambodia requested an interpretation of the judgment under Article 60 and at the same time asked for interim measures of protection under Article 41. The latter request was granted soon afterwards and, in 2013, finding that there was a dispute between the parties over the meaning and scope of the 1962 judgment, the Court decided the issue of interpretation in favour of Cambodia. The judges who decided the original case would no doubt have been surprised to find the Court revisiting the case half a century later. But Article 60 contains no time limits and successful requests can significantly enhance the effectiveness of a decision. Therefore, although interpretation so long after the initial decision is certainly unprecedented, the *Temple* case is a timely reminder of the value of Article 60.

Requests to revise a judgment, like requests for interpretation, can relate either to a previous judgment on the merits, or to one on admissibility and jurisdiction. Thus, in the *Genocide Convention* case, Yugoslavia requested a revision of the Court's 1996 judgment on admissibility and jurisdiction, claiming that the earlier judgment rested on a mistaken view of

---

[62] See *Request for Interpretation of the Judgment of 11 June 1998 in the Case concerning the Land and Maritime Boundary between Cameroon and Nigeria (Cameroon v. Nigeria)*, Preliminary Objections, *(Nigeria v. Cameroon)*, Judgment [1999] ICJ Rep. 31.
[63] *Request for Interpretation of the Judgment of 15 June 1962 in the Case concerning the Temple of Preah Vihear (Cambodia v. Thailand)*, Judgment [2013] ICJ Rep. 281 and see J. D. Ciociari, Note (2014) 108 *AJIL*, 288.

Yugoslavia's legal status;[64] while in the *Land, Island and Maritime Frontier* case a chamber of the Court had to deal with a request from El Salvador calling for a revision of its earlier judgment on the merits on the basis of new documentary evidence.[65] Significantly, however, both requests were rejected: Yugoslavia's on the ground that its claim was not based on facts in existence at the time of the original judgment; and El Salvador's because its new facts were not of a decisive nature. While both decisions were justified, they confirm the impression from the *Tunisia–Libya* case that so compelling is the presumption of finality that the circumstances must be exceptional for a claim based on Article 61 to succeed.

8.2.4 Counter-claims

In addition to the matters already described, which are all covered in the Statute, the Court has a further incidental power, to consider counter-claims, which are provided for in its Rules. Under Article 80 of the Rules, the conditions under which a counter-claim may be entertained are that it 'comes within the jurisdiction of the Court and is directly connected with the subject matter of the claim of the other party'. It follows that, when a dispute is referred to the Court by application,[66] the Court is not limited to dealing with the claims of the state initiating proceedings, but can also address various related issues, should they be raised by its opponent. A respondent cannot, of course, use a counter-claim as a way of bringing a separate dispute before the Court, nor can it be used as a device to expand the basis of the Court's jurisdiction in the case. Counter-claims may, however, enable a complex dispute to be dealt with more fully than might otherwise be possible, and as such may help to promote international justice.

Although the facility to present counter-claims goes back to the days of the Permanent Court, until recently it had been little used. However, in the *Genocide Convention* case in 1997, the Court had to consider a counter-claim by Yugoslavia concerning alleged acts of genocide committed by Bosnia and Herzegovina, and shortly afterwards was presented with

---

[64] See *Application for Revision of the Judgment of 11 July 1996 in the Case concerning Application of the Convention on the Prevention and Punishment of the Crime of Genocide (Bosnia and Herzegovina v. Yugoslavia)*, Preliminary Objections *(Yugoslavia v. Bosnia and Herzegovina)*, Judgment [2003] ICJ Rep. and see N. Tsagourias, Note (2004) 53 *ICLQ*, 731.

[65] *Application for Revision of the Judgment of 11 September 1992 in the Case concerning the Land, Island and Maritime Frontier Dispute (El Salvador/Honduras: Nicaragua intervening) (El Salvador v. Honduras)*, Judgment [2003] ICJ Rep. 392; and see M. N. Shaw, Note (2005) 54 *ICLQ*, 1013.

[66] When a case is brought by special agreement, the claims of each party will normally be contained in the agreement and so no question of a counter-claim will arise: see H. Thirlway, 'The law and procedure of the International Court of Justice 1960–1989 (part twelve)' (2001) 72 *BYBIL*, 37 at 175.

counter-claims from the United States, relating to the use of force by Iran, in the *Oil Platforms* case. As the admissibility of the counter-claims was contested in both cases, the Court carefully examined the requirements of Article 80 before deciding they were admissible.[67] More recently, the Court rejected an application by Italy to enter a counter-claim in the *Jurisdictional Immunities of the State* case[68] on the ground that it lay outside the 1957 European Convention for the Peaceful Settlement of Disputes on which Italy based the Court's jurisdiction. In the *Certain Activities Carried out by Nicaragua in the Border Area* case,[69] the Court was required to rule on no less than four counter-claims raised by Nicaragua, but on various grounds rejected them all. Similarly, in *Alleged Violations of Sovereign Rights and Maritime Spaces in the Caribbean Sea (Nicaragua v. Colombia)*[70] the Court was confronted with four counter-claims submitted by Colombia. The Court ultimately accepted two counter-claims, but found the other two, which related to Nicaragua's purported violations of its obligation to protect and preserve the marine environment, inadmissible, since these were found to not relate to the same factual complex and to lack a direct legal connection with Nicaragua's principal claims.[71]

In general terms, counter-claims, even when found to be admissible, have not so far proved to be very significant in practice. They do, however, provide the respondent with a useful, if limited, option which may be worth considering as one of the tactics of litigation.

8.3 Advisory Jurisdiction

The purpose of the Court's advisory jurisdiction is to enable it to give legal opinions at the request of international organisations. Although the details and functioning of the advisory jurisdiction are outside the scope of this work, two points are worth mentioning, one relating to the contentious jurisdiction, the other of a more general nature.

As the principal judicial organ of the United Nations, the Court may find itself asked by the General Assembly, or some other body, for an advisory opinion on a legal dispute between states. Bearing in mind that the Court's contentious jurisdiction is consensual, how should it respond

---

[67] See the Court's Orders of 17 December 1997 (*Genocide Convention* case) [1997] ICJ Rep. 243, and 19 March 1998 (*Oil Platforms* case) [1998] ICJ Rep. 190, discussed by P. H. F. Bekker, Note (1998) 92 *AJIL*, 508; and Thirlway, 'The law and procedure' (n. 66) 174.
[68] *Jurisdictional Immunities of the State (Germany v. Italy)*, Counter-Claim, Order of 6 July 2010 [2010] ICJ Rep. 310.
[69] *Certain Activities carried out by Nicaragua in the Border Area (Costa Rica v. Nicaragua)*, Counter-Claims, Order of 18 April 2013 [2013] ICJ Rep. 200.
[70] *Alleged Violations of Sovereign Rights and Maritime Spaces in the Caribbean Sea (Nicaragua v. Colombia)*, Counter-Claims, Order of 15 November 2017, [2017] ICJ Rep. 289.
[71] *Ibid.*, Paras 37–8.

to such a request? Aside from the question of whether the Court has jurisdiction to respond to a request, which is regulated by Article 96 of the UN Charter and Article 65 of the ICJ Statute, Article 65 of the ICJ Statute adds that the Court *may* give an advisory opinion on any legal question at the request of a body authorised under Article 96 of the UN Charter. The inclusion of the word 'may' has consistently been interpreted by the Court to give it a discretionary authority to respond or refuse to respond to a request for an advisory opinion.[72]

This issue, which is linked with the question of ad hoc judges in advisory proceedings to be considered shortly, has been examined by the Court on several occasions. In the *Western Sahara* case,[73] the Court developed its earlier reasoning in the *Peace Treaties* opinion[74] and held that the discretion whether or not to respond to a request for an advisory opinion exists so as to protect the integrity of the Court's judicial function as the principal judicial organ of the United Nations. The question of discretion therefore does not relate to the Court's jurisdiction. The factors to be taken into account include the object and purpose of the request, the origin and nature of the dispute and the adequacy of the available evidence. The practice of the Court indicates that in assessing these factors there is a weighty presumption in favour of taking the case, a reflection perhaps of the United Nations background of many of the Court's members, and of the fact that disputes over human rights, decolonisation and a number of other issues are no longer simply affairs between states, but a proper concern of international organisations. In general, the Court considers that its answer to a request for an advisory opinion 'represents its participation in the activities of the Organization, and, in principle, should not be refused'.[75] Only when the Court finds 'compelling reasons', will it refuse to respond to a request, provided the request falls within its jurisdiction.[76]

The general point is simply that even advisory opinions which do not relate to legal disputes between states in the strict sense are usually concerned directly or indirectly with matters of inter-state controversy.

The advisory opinion in the *WHO Regional Headquarters* case,[77] for example, though ostensibly concerned with the circumstances in which a

---

[72] See recently, *Legal Consequences of the Separation of the Chagos Archipelago from Mauritius in 1965*, Advisory Opinion, [2019] ICJ Rep. 95, paras 54 and 63.

[73] *Western Sahara*, Advisory Opinion [1975] ICJ Rep. 12. For commentary, see P. V. Lalonde, 'The death of the Eastern Carelia doctrine' (1979) 37 *U. Toronto Fac. L. Rev.*, 80.

[74] *Interpretation of Peace Treaties with Bulgaria, Hungary and Romania*, First Phase, Advisory Opinion [1950] ICJ Rep. 65.

[75] *Legal Consequences of the Construction of a Wall in the Occupied Palestinian Territory*, Advisory Opinion [2004] ICJ Rep. 136, para. 44.

[76] Ibid.

[77] *Interpretation of the Agreement of 25 March 1951 between the WHO and Egypt*, Advisory Opinion [1980] ICJ Rep. 73. For commentary, see C. Gray, 'The International Court's advisory opinion on the WHO–Egypt Agreement of 1951' (1983) 32 *ICLQ*, 534.

specialised agency could move its seat, in reality arose out of animosity between Egypt and its Arab neighbours. Similarly, the advisory opinion in the *Nuclear Weapons* case,[78] although concerned with the abstract question of whether the threat or use of nuclear weapons is permitted by international law, addressed an issue on which the members of the United Nations are deeply divided. In holding here, and in previous cases, that political circumstances are no bar to complying with a request for an advisory opinion, the Court has demonstrated that the clashes of states' interests which occur within international institutions can, when presented in legal form, be a proper object of judicial attention.

In other cases, the link between a request for an advisory opinion and inter-state disputes can be more direct, which raises the question of whether this constitutes a 'compelling reason' which would lead the Court to decline the respond to a request. Because the request for an advisory opinion relates directly to an inter-state dispute which the parties have not consented to submit to settlement by the Court via its contentious jurisdiction, the lack of consent may be a 'compelling reason' for the Court to decline to exercise its advisory jurisdiction:

> In certain circumstances ... the lack of consent of an interested State may render the giving of an advisory opinion incompatible with the Court's judicial character. An instance of this would be when the circumstances disclose that to give a reply would have the effect of circumventing the principle that a State is not obliged to allow its disputes to be submitted to judicial settlement without its consent.[79]

The Court however has consistently held that, while this may in principle be the case, the opinion is given to the body requesting it in order to enable that body to exercise its functions; the purpose therefore is not to settle a dispute between states.[80] The relation between advisory opinions and dispute settlement also was discussed in the *Construction of a Wall* case[81] which arose out of a request from the General Assembly for the Court's assessment of the legal consequences of the security wall being built by Israel in the Occupied Palestinian Territory. After confirming that it was competent to deal with the request, the Court considered that there was no reason to decline to exercise its jurisdiction. The Court examined the legal issues in considerable detail, concluding both that the wall was illegal and

---

[78] *Legality of the Threat or Use of Nuclear Weapons*, Advisory Opinion [1996] ICJ Rep. 66. For comment, see N. Grief, Note (1997) 46 *ICLQ*, 681; and M. J. Matheson, 'The opinions of the International Court of Justice on the threat or use of nuclear weapons' (1997) 91 *AJIL*, 417.
[79] *Western Sahara*, Advisory Opinion [1975] ICJ Rep. 12, paras 32–3.
[80] See e.g. *Western Sahara*, Advisory Opinion [1975] ICJ Rep. 12, para. 39 and *Legal Consequences of the Separation of the Chagos Archipelago from Mauritius in 1965*, Advisory Opinion, [2019] ICJ Rep. 95, para. 86.
[81] *Legal Consequences of the Construction of a Wall in the Occupied Palestinian Territory*, Advisory Opinion [2004] ICJ Rep. 136; and see S. C. Breau, Note (2005) 54 *ICLQ*, 1003.

that this had serious consequences for Israel and for other states. Notable features of the opinion are the Court's assertion of its competence, despite the political aspects of the question and its obviously contentious character, and the near unanimity of the judges. Also interesting, though in no way surprising, is that, in the final part of its opinion, and to put the matter in context, the Court emphasised to the General Assembly the need to encourage efforts to achieve a negotiated settlement and the establishment of a Palestinian state with peace and security for all in the region.

The issue also arose in the recent advisory opinion of the Court in *Legal Consequence of the Separation of the Chagos Archipelago from Mauritius in 1965*, issued on 25 February 2019. The proceedings arose from the process of decolonisation of Mauritius, with the UN General Assembly referring several questions to the ICJ. The Court confirmed jurisdiction and refused to decline to give a response to the request. In relation to the argument raised, that the dispute concerned a bilateral dispute between Mauritius and the United Kingdom regarding sovereignty over the Chagos Archipelago, the Court replied that 'the issues raised by the request are located in the broader frame of reference of decolonization, including the General Assembly's role therein, from which those issues are inseparable'.[82] The Court added that 'the fact that the Court may have to pronounce on legal issues on which divergent views have been expressed by Mauritius and the United Kingdom does not mean that, by replying to the request, the Court is dealing with a bilateral dispute'.[83]

The Court decided that the process of decolonisation of Mauritius was not lawfully completed when Mauritius acceded to independence in 1968, following the separation of the Chagos Archipelago. The Court also decided that the UK has an obligation to bring an end to its administration of the Chagos Archipelago as rapidly as possible, and that all member states must cooperate with the UN to complete the decolonisation of Mauritius.

8.4 Membership of the Court

The Court is composed of fifteen judges, elected for a nine-year term by the Security Council and General Assembly of the United Nations. At the end of this term, a judge is eligible to stand for re-election, and elections are staggered in such a way that five judges – one-third of the Court – are elected every three years. According to the Statute (Article 9), the election of judges is to be carried out in such a way that 'in the body as a whole the representation of the main forms of civilization and of the principal legal

---

[82] *Legal Consequences of the Separation of the Chagos Archipelago from Mauritius in 1965*, Advisory Opinion, [2019] ICJ Rep. 95, para. 88.
[83] Ibid., para. 89.

systems of the world should be assured'. The importance of this requirement can hardly be over-emphasised. Unless the distribution of seats on the Court is seen to reflect the balance and diversity of the international community, it is likely that states which consider their culture to be inadequately represented will not regard the Court as an appropriate body to handle their legal disputes. Moreover, in such circumstances, the Court's authority, perhaps even competence, to interpret and apply law for the world must be considered doubtful. Article 9, then, is directly concerned with the political underpinnings of adjudication and international law.

Elections to the International Court have always been the prerogative of political institutions, first the League and then the United Nations. Consequently, the changes which have taken place in the composition of the Court since 1919 reflect the shifting balance of institutional power over the same period.[84] African and Asian representation, for example, has risen from two in the colonial era (1922) to six at the present time, while European representation in the same period has fallen from ten to six, including France, the United Kingdom and the Russian Federation. As Permanent Members of the Security Council, the states just mentioned, together with the United States and China, are regarded as entitled to have a judge of their nationality on the Court. However, that unwritten entitlement has recently been challenged with the non-election of a judge from the United Kingdom in 2017. It now seems also to be agreed that the ten remaining seats on the Court should follow the pattern of 'equitable geographical distribution' agreed for the Security Council after its enlargement in 1965. The agreement currently is as follows: three Judges from Africa, three judges from Latin America and the Caribbean, three judges from Asia, five judges from Western Europe and other states and two judges from Eastern Europe.

To establish and maintain its authority to handle disputes and complex questions of international law, the members of the Court must be demonstrably competent as individuals to decide the cases which come before them. Article 2 of the Statute requires that the judges shall be 'persons of high moral character, who possess the qualifications required in their respective countries for appointment to the highest judicial offices, or are jurisconsults of recognised competence in international law'. With the distribution of seats on the Court a matter of broad agreement, the fulfilment of Article 2 is a matter of nominations, rather than elections. In theory, nominations are the prerogative of national groups of the Members of the Permanent Court of Arbitration, but in practice governments exercise a major influence. Although disquiet has been expressed at

---

[84] For a lucid examination of this and other aspects of the Court's composition, see S. Rosenne, 'The composition of the Court' in L. Gross (ed.), *The Future of the International Court of Justice*, New York, 1976, p. 377.

the relative lack of experience of some members of the Court, and the nominating process could certainly be improved, the judges in general can hardly be described as insufficiently qualified.

Since it is vital that the judges are not only qualified in a general sense, but also capable of dealing impartially with the particular case, two provisions of the Statute, Articles 17 and 24, provide respectively for disqualification if a judge has been previously involved in a case in another capacity, and that he or she should stand down for other special reasons. Although the purpose of these provisions is obvious, a tendency to elect former legal advisers, members of the International Law Commission and career diplomats to the Court has made decisions as to whether individual judges should be disqualified from sitting in a particular case increasingly difficult. In the *Namibia* case, for example, the eligibility of three members of the Court was challenged on the ground of previous involvement in the dispute in another capacity, and, more recently, in the *Construction of a Wall* case, Israel challenged the eligibility of the Egyptian judge, a former diplomat, on similar grounds. All the challenges were rejected by the Court,[85] though in one case only by a majority of ten votes to four, and it seems clear that, in this respect at least, the previous experience of members of the Court may continue to raise problems.

In a contentious case, if neither party has a judge of its nationality currently on the Court, both sides may appoint an ad hoc judge who becomes a member of the Court for that case only. In the *Maritime Delimitation in the Black Sea* case,[86] for example, between Romania and Ukraine, both states appointed a judge ad hoc. Similarly, if one party currently has a national on the Court and the other has not, the unrepresented party may also appoint a judge ad hoc. Thus, in the *CERD* case,[87] where the respondent was Russia, the applicant, Georgia, appointed an ad hoc judge. However, members of the Court sit as individuals, not as representatives of their national states. In view of this, and of the predictable tendency of ad hoc judges to accept the submissions of the state appointing them, the legitimacy of what one commentator has termed this 'concession to diplomatic susceptibilities'[88] has been seriously questioned.

---

[85] See, for the *Namibia* case [1971] ICJ 3, 6 and 9; and for the *Construction of a Wall* case, ICJ Press Release 2004/4 (3 February 2004). See also Thirlway, 'The law and procedure' (n. 66) 42–6.

[86] *Maritime Delimitation in the Black Sea (Romania v. Ukraine)*, Judgment [2009] ICJ Rep. 61. See C. G. Lathrop, Note (2009) 103 *AJIL*, 543.

[87] *Application of the International Convention on the Elimination of All Forms of Racial Discrimination (Georgia v. Russian Federation)*, Provisional Measures Order of 15 October 2008 [2008] ICJ Rep. 353. See S. Ghandhi, Note (2009) 58 *ICLQ*, 713.

[88] Rosenne, 'Composition of the Court' (n. 84) p. 407. For another critical view, see D. D. Nsereko, 'The International Court, impartiality and judges ad hoc' (1973) 13 *Ind. J Int. L*, 207.

In light of municipal judicial practice, the institution of the ad hoc judge certainly appears anomalous. But is the comparison really relevant? Municipal courts are composed of individuals from a single legal culture, draw on that culture to justify their decisions and enjoy compulsory jurisdiction. None of this is true in the international field. Thus, for a government to refer a dispute to the International Court calls for something of an act of faith. The vote of the ad hoc judge, like that of the 'national' member of a court of arbitration, is never likely to change the result of a case, but their presence provides an important link between the parties and the Court. Accordingly, it has been suggested that, while ad hoc judges have a duty to be impartial, they also have a responsibility to ensure that the factual and legal arguments of the state that has appointed them are fully understood and considered by the other judges.[89] In these circumstances, the institution of the ad hoc judge is perhaps still too useful to be dispensed with.

A question which has exercised the Court on several occasions concerns the circumstances in which ad hoc judges may be appointed in advisory proceedings. The question arises because advisory opinions, which can only be requested by international organisations, sometimes relate to disputes between states, which if they were the subject of contentious proceedings would justify the appointment of a judge ad hoc. Recognising that the purpose of appointing such a judge is the same in both cases, the Court has sought to assimilate its advisory and contentious jurisdiction. Although in the *Namibia* case it held (controversially) that South Africa was not entitled to a judge ad hoc and that the Court had no residual discretion to authorise such an appointment,[90] in the later *Western Sahara* case,[91] it held on more convincing grounds that a similar application from Morocco should be allowed.

8.5 Chambers

Cases in the International Court are normally heard by the full Court. However, Articles 26–29 of the Statute provide for the creation of chambers composed of fewer judges for particular categories of cases, for the speedy dispatch of business, or to deal with an individual case. For many years, these procedures were hardly used, but their potential to enhance the Court's activity is now being realised. In 1972, as part of an effort to

---

[89] See the separate opinion of Judge ad hoc Lauterpacht in the *Genocide Convention* case [1993] ICJ Rep. 408–9. See also S. M. Schwebel, 'National judges and judges ad hoc of the International Court of Justice' (1999) 48 *ICLQ*, 889.
[90] See [1971] ICJ Rep. 12. For discussion, see M. Pomerance, 'The admission of judges ad hoc in advisory proceedings: some reflections in the light of the Namibia case' (1973) 67 *AJIL*, 446.
[91] See [1975] ICJ Rep. 6. For discussion, see I. R. Suh, 'National judges in advisory proceedings of the International Court' (1979) 19 *Ind. J Int. L.*, 20.

encourage greater use of its facilities, the Court revised its Rules so as to promote the use of ad hoc chambers and enable prospective litigants to influence the composition as well as the size of the bench. Similarly, in 1993, the Court decided to establish a chamber of seven judges to deal with disputes concerning international environmental law. The environmental chamber was never used and so was discontinued in 2006. However, ad hoc chambers have been employed in several cases to date, from which certain conclusions may be drawn.[92]

The procedure for ad hoc chambers was used for the first time in the *Gulf of Maine* case, brought to the Court by Canada and the United States in 1981. The new Rules provide that the parties must be consulted about the composition of a chamber, although the question is finally determined by the Court after a secret ballot. To avoid the possibility that the ballot might produce the 'wrong' result, Canada and the United States made it clear that, unless their wishes as to the composition of the Court were carried out, they would withdraw the case and refer the dispute to arbitration. In these circumstances, the Court, over the protests of two of its members, elected the chamber requested by the parties.[93]

It is unlikely that, in normal circumstances, the Court will ignore the parties' wishes, for, as this case made plain, they are at liberty to go elsewhere, if dissatisfied. Consequently, though the Court retains the ultimate control over its composition, the secret ballot will usually be something of a formality. However, the situation here is the natural and not unexpected consequence of the effort to encourage the use of chambers. Not surprisingly, therefore, in subsequent cases in which the Court has been asked to create an ad hoc chamber, it has followed its approach in the *Gulf of Maine* case and elected the bench requested by the parties.[94]

There is currently no provision which establishes the minimum size for a chamber, and in theory it would be possible to set up a chamber consisting of a single judge. Likewise, no maximum is laid down, but, since a quorum of the full Court is nine, a chamber of more than seven judges appears unlikely. In the *Gulf of Maine* case and in subsequent cases in which a chamber has been formed, the Court has consisted of five judges, and this number, which is frequently used for courts of arbitration, now

---

[92] For discussion of the chambers procedure, elaborating many of the points made in the text, see S. M. Schwebel, 'Ad hoc chambers of the International Court of Justice' (1987) 81 *AJIL*, 831; R. Ostrihansky, 'Chambers of the International Court of Justice' (1988) 37 *ICLQ*, 30; and E. Valencia-Ospina, 'The use of chambers of the International Court of Justice', in V. Lowe and M. Fitzmaurice (eds), *Fifty Years of the International Court of Justice*, Cambridge, 1996, p. 503. See also Thirlway, 'The law and procedure' (n. 66) 46–57.

[93] *Delimitation of the Maritime Boundary in the Gulf of Maine Area*, Constitution of Chamber, Order of 20 January 1982 [1982] ICJ Rep. 3. For discussion, see R. H. Brauer, 'International conflict resolution: the ICJ chambers and the Gulf of Maine dispute' (1982–3) 23 *Va. JIL*, 463.

[94] This is not expressly stated in the Orders in the various cases but may be inferred from the academic writings of Judges Oda and Schwebel, as well as from circumstantial evidence.

seems to have become standard. The judges selected for a chamber must normally be current members of the Court, but it is important to note that ad hoc judges may also be appointed, just as for conventional cases. Thus, in the *Gulf of Maine* case, Canada appointed a judge to act in this capacity,[95] while, in the *Land, Island and Maritime Frontier* case,[96] both states nominated judges, when the original chamber was set up in 1989 and again in 2002 when El Salvador requested revision of the judgment. As a result, the chambers in these proceedings contained three regular and two ad hoc judges.

The attraction of the chambers procedure is that it provides states with a method of resolving disputes which combines a major advantage of arbitration, namely, control over the size and composition of the court, with an acknowledged advantage of the International Court of Justice, which is that it comes equipped with a panel of available judges, a court building and the facilities needed for international litigation, all of which are paid for by the United Nations. The parties have to pay the costs of preparing and presenting their case in the normal way, but this is significantly cheaper than arranging and financing an arbitration. The Court also has its constitution, in the form of the Statute, and its established rules of procedure. These also relieve the parties of certain responsibilities, though they also, of course, place limitations on what the Court can be asked to do. Consequently, although the chambers procedure offers considerable flexibility, it remains distinct from arbitration.

The cases referred to chambers, though not very numerous, already suggest when the procedure is likely to be used. It might be thought that chambers are particularly suited to the resolution of relatively straightforward disputes where the use of the time and resources of the full Court would not be justified. This may well be so, but it has to be said that, of the cases decided so far, only El Salvador's request for revision really falls into this category. The *Gulf of Maine* case[97] raised extremely complex issues relating to continental shelf delimitation and as a result the chamber's judgment is actually longer than either of the full Court's previous decisions in this field. The *Frontier Dispute* cases[98] between Burkina Faso and Mali (1986) and Benin and Niger (2005) both required their chambers to unravel tangled skeins of historical and geographical evidence typical of territorial

---

[95] Judge Ruda, who had been originally elected to the chamber, stood down in order that this might happen.
[96] *Land, Island and Maritime Frontier Dispute (El Salvador/Honduras)*, Composition of Chamber, Order of 13 December 1989 [1989] ICJ Rep. 162.
[97] *Delimitation of the Maritime Boundary in the Gulf of Maine Area*, Judgment [1984] ICJ Rep. 246.
[98] *Frontier Dispute*, Judgment [1986] ICJ Rep. 554; and *Frontier Dispute (Benin/Niger)*, Judgment [2005] ICJ Rep. 90. And see S. Allen, 'Case concerning the Frontier Dispute (Benin/Niger)' (2006) 55 *ICLQ*, 729.

disputes. In the *ELSI* case,[99] which involved a dispute between the United States and Italy, the evidence related to corporate financing and again was abstruse and voluminous. Similarly, in the original *Land, Island and Maritime Frontier* case,[100] the chamber again delivered a long judgment in which it dealt with a mass of detailed evidence and addressed important questions concerning both the acquisition of land territory and the law of the sea.

The above cases suggest that, whatever its merits as a way of disposing of straightforward cases, states also see the chambers procedure as a way of ensuring that cases which raise highly technical issues are heard by small tribunals selected for their expertise. This, it will be recalled, has traditionally been regarded as an important advantage of arbitration. Thus, recourse to chambers to decide cases of this type is further evidence of how the two procedures are drawing together. It is perhaps worth adding that, on account of its complexity, the *Gulf of Maine* litigation is estimated to have cost the United States and Canada about US$14 million.[101] The cheapness of litigation before a chamber is therefore very much a relative notion. On the other hand, if the dispute had been arbitrated, the parties would also have had to pay for the tribunal, rendering litigation which was never going to be cheap even more expensive. The saving which comes from using the Court may therefore be particularly attractive in complicated disputes where the parties are already committed to substantial expenditure.

Before states began to use the chambers procedure, the fear was sometimes expressed that to allow the parties to influence the composition of the Court would encourage the formation of chambers with a particular ideological orientation, and that this in turn would affect both the quality and the authority of their decisions. Unlike the position with regard to the full Court, there is no requirement that a chamber should represent 'the main forms of civilization' and 'the principal legal systems of the world', and in practice, as we have seen, the composition of a chamber is determined by the parties. The chambers appointed so far, as might be expected, do reflect certain preferences. The judges for the *Gulf of Maine* case were drawn exclusively from North America and Western Europe. The chamber for the 1986 *Frontier Dispute* case, on the other hand, included no judge from these regions, while the judges for the *ELSI* case, which concerned an alleged expropriation, all came from industrialised states. Chambers,

---

[99] Case concerning Elettronica Sicula SpA (ELSI), Judgment [1989] ICJ Rep. 15.
[100] Land, Island and Maritime Frontier Dispute (El Salvador/Honduras: Nicaragua intervening), Judgment [1992] ICJ Rep. 351. For comment, see M. Shaw, Note (1993) 42 *ICLQ*, 929.
[101] See D. R. Robinson, D. A. Colson and B. C. Rashkow, 'Some perspectives on adjudicating before the World Court: the Gulf of Maine case' (1985) 79 *AJIL*, 578 at 588.

however, consistently make use of a range of judicial expertise. The risk of parochialism is therefore one that should not be exaggerated.

As far as the composition of chambers is concerned, then, practice does not suggest an undue narrowness of outlook, and this is confirmed if we consider the other matters of concern, the quality and authority of the decisions. The judgment in the *Gulf of Maine* case, far from reflecting an Anglo-European view of the law, closely followed the full Court's approach in the *Tunisia–Libya* case.[102] Similarly, the judgments in both *Frontier Dispute* cases, though largely taken up with analysis of the particular facts, applied well-established principles relating to the acquisition of territory; while the reasoning in the *ELSI* case again follows conventional lines. In the *Land, Island and Maritime Frontier* case, the chamber concluded that the waters of the Gulf of Fonseca were governed by a special historical regime rather than by the general law. On the other hand, in its treatment of the various territorial issues, it gave careful attention to the scope and application of *uti possidetis juris* and other recognised principles, and the subsequent decision to reject the request to revise the judgment, as noted earlier, was adequately explained. It is idle to speculate on whether the full Court would have made an identical decision in each of these cases, but, if its application of the law might sometimes have varied, it is improbable that its treatment of basic principles would have been very different. As regards their weight as precedents, if, as just suggested, their legal analysis is sound, one would expect to see these cases regularly cited and relied on. The fact that the decision in the *Gulf of Maine* case was extensively referred to when the full Court addressed similar issues in the *Libya–Malta Continental Shelf* case, and that there have been several references to the decisions of chambers in later cases, bears out this view.[103]

When the new rules were first put forward, fears were expressed in some quarters that the chambers procedure might prove so popular that states would no longer wish to use the full Court. As only a handful of cases have been referred to chambers, it now seems that such fears were groundless. But, if states generally prefer to use the full Court, the attempt to encourage the use of chambers can still be regarded as worthwhile. States have recognised that the new rules provide an opportunity to combine the convenience of the Court with several of the advantages of arbitration. The cases which have been referred suggest that chambers are seen as particularly useful for disputes which involve complex evidence, and perhaps also for issues with a strong regional dimension. The decisions themselves, though inevitably lacking some of the weight which attaches

---

[102] See J. Schneider, 'The Gulf of Maine case: the nature of an equitable result' (1985) 79 *AJIL*, 539.
[103] See M. Shahabuddeen, *Precedent in the World Court*, Cambridge, 1996, pp. 171–7. As indicated earlier, the full Court has now endorsed the approach to Art. 62 taken by the chamber in the *Land, Island and Maritime Frontier* case.

to judgments of the full Court, can certainly stand comparison with those judgments and are far from the blinkered pronouncements which might have been feared.

In making an assessment of the value of the chambers procedure, two further points should be borne in mind. The first is that, although use of the chambers procedure has not been extensive, preferences in dispute settlement can change and the alternative procedure is now available if states wish to use it. The other point is that, in each of the cases to date, the chamber's decision settled the dispute, something which unfortunately cannot be said of every decision of the full Court. The background of the members of the Court is now so diverse and the subject matter of certain disputes so specialised, that the preference of states for a smaller and more select bench for certain cases is readily understandable. Like the issue of ad hoc judges, disqualification and the other matters considered earlier, the current revitalisation of the chambers procedure demonstrates that the question 'who decides?' is as relevant to judicial settlement as to arbitration.

8.6 Further Reading

8.6.1 General References on the International Court of Justice

Akande, D., 'Selection of the International Court of Justice as a forum for contentious and advisory proceedings (including jurisdiction)' (2016) 7 *Journal of International Dispute Settlement*, 320–44.

Aljaghoub, M. M., *The Advisory Function of the International Court of Justice 1946–2005*, Berlin, 2006.

Boisson de Chazournes, L., and P. Sands, *International Law, The International Court of Justice and Nuclear Weapons*, Cambridge, 1999.

Couvreur, P., *The International Court of Justice and the Effectiveness of International Law*, Leiden, 2016.

Greenwood, C., 'Judicial Integrity and the Advisory Jurisdiction of the International Court of Justice', in G. Gaja and J. Grote Stoutenburg (eds), *Enhancing the Rule of Law through the International Court of Justice*, Leiden, 2014, pp. 63–73.

Guillaume, G., *La Cour internationale de Justice à l'aube du XXI e siècle. Le regard d'un juge*, Paris, 2003.

Hernandez, G. I., *The International Court of Justice and the Judicial Function*, Oxford, 2014.

Kolb, R., *The International Court of Justice*, Oxford, 2013.

Kulick, A., 'Article 60 ICJ Statute, interpretation proceedings, and the competing concepts of res judicata' (2015) 28 *Leiden Journal of International Law*, 73–89.

Lando, M., 'Plausibility in the provisional measures jurisprudence of the International Court of Justice' (2018) 31 *Leiden Journal of International Law*, 641–68.

Lowe, V., and M. Fitzmaurice (eds), *Fifty Years of the International Court of Justice*, Cambridge, 1996.

Milanović, M., and M. Wood (eds), *The Law and Politics of the Kosovo Advisory Opinion*, Oxford, 2015.

Miles, C. A., 'Provisional measures and the margin of appreciation before the International Court of Justice' (2017) 8 *Journal of International Dispute Settlement*, 1–21.

Miron, A., 'Working methods of the court' (2016) 7 *Journal of International Dispute Settlement*, 371–94.

Palchetti, P., 'Responsibility for breach of provisional measures of the ICJ: between protection of the rights of the parties and respect for the judicial function' (2017) 100 *Rivista di diritto internazionale*, 5–22.

Quintana, J.J., *Litigation at the International Court of Justice: Practice and Procedure*, Leiden, 2015.

Rosenne, S., *Provisional Measures in International Law: The International Court of Justice and the International Tribunal for the Law of the Sea*, Oxford, 2005.

Ruiz Fabri, H., and J.-M. Sorel (eds.), *Indépendance et impartialité des juges internationaux*, Paris, 2010.

Scobbie, I., '"Une hérésie en matière judiciaire"?: the role of the Judge Ad Hoc in the International Court' (2005) 4 *The Law and Practice of International Courts and Tribunals*, 421–64.

Shaw, M. N., *Rosenne's Law and Practice of the International Court (1920–2015)* (5th ed.) Leiden, 2016 (4 volumes).

Thirlway, H., 'The drafting of ICJ decisions: some personal recollections and observations' (2006) 5 *Chinese Journal of International Law*, 15–28.

Thirlway, H., *The Law and Procedure of the International Court of Justice: Fifty Years of Jurisprudence*, Oxford, 2013 (2 Volumes).

United Nations, *Handbook of the International Court of Justice* (7th ed.), 2019, available at https://legal.un.org/avl/pdf/rs/other_resources/manuel_en.pdf.

Xue, H., *Jurisdiction of the International Court of Justice*, Leiden, 2017.

Yee, S., 'Provisional measures in international law: the International Court of Justice and the International Tribunal for the Law of the Sea' (2006) 5 *Chinese Journal of International Law*, 503–5.

Yusuf, A. A., 'Compulsory Jurisdiction of the Court under the Optional Clause', in S. van Hoogstraten (ed.), *New Challenges to International Law: A View from The Hague*, Leiden, 2018, pp. 8–13.

Zimmermann, A., C. Tams, K. Oellers-Frahm, and C. Tomuschat (eds), *The Statute of the International Court of Justice. A Commentary*, Oxford, 2019.

8.6.2 Treaties, Official Documents and Collections of Documents

Patel, B., *The World Court Reference Guide. Judgments, Advisory Opinions and Orders of the Permanent Court of International Justice and the International Court of Justice (1922–2000)*, The Hague, 2002.

Patel, B., *The World Court Reference Guide and Case-Law Digest. Judgments, Advisory Opinions and Orders of the Permanent Court of International Justice and the International Court of Justice (2001–2010) and Case-Law Digest (1992–2010)*, The Hague, 2014.

9

The International Court II: the Work of the Court

The institutional features of the International Court, as we have just seen, exercise a major influence on both the readiness of states to employ international adjudication and the ability of the Court to respond to their requests. However, the judgments which the Court hands down show how it deals with disputes when given the opportunity, and are no less important. This is not the place to describe the Court's jurisprudence in detail, nor to consider its contribution to the development of international law.[1] What is needed therefore is not a survey of the Court's case law, but rather an indication of what its day-to-day work reveals about the relation between the settlement of disputes and adjudication. The decision itself is a good place to start.

9.1 Establishing the Facts

Proving a case at the international level is primarily a matter of finding and presenting suitable documentary evidence. This material, which is relevant to both fact and law, includes treaty texts, official records of international organisations and national parliaments, diplomatic correspondence, archive material, maps, films, photographs and affidavits. Where the Court has to deal with a case involving technical and scientific evidence, the question of how the Court addresses scientific evidence requires special consideration.

9.1.1 Documentary Evidence

The quantity of evidence may be extremely large and as there are virtually no exclusionary rules, states can and do bring forward everything which might assist their case. Although the facility is little used, documentary evidence may be augmented by the oral testimony of witnesses and experts, or even by the Court itself visiting the scene. In the *Gabcikovo-Nagymaros*

---

[1] On these questions, see C. J. Tams and J. Sloan (eds), *The Development of International Law by the International Court of Justice*, Oxford, 2013; H. Thirlway, *The Law and Procedure of the International Court of Justice: Fifty Years of Jurisprudence*, Oxford, 2013 (2 Volumes) and P. Wojcikiewicz Almeida, and J.-M. Sorel (eds), *Latin America and the International Court of Justice: Contributions to International Law*, London, 2017.

case, for example, which concerned the construction of a barrage system on a boundary river between Hungary and Slovakia, the Court decided in 1997 to visit the relevant area at the parties' request.[2] Site visits, however, remain exceptional.

Evaluating the evidence is a task for the Court and, since the factual matrix is always the key to the application of the law, this can be a long and elaborate process. In some cases, much of the parties' material can be dismissed as inconclusive or irrelevant to the issues to be decided. In disputes over maritime delimitation, for example, the Court has tended to ignore elaborate evidence relating to ecology or geomorphology in favour of less contentious material relating to geography. In some disputes, however, narrowing the focus in this way is impossible and there is no alternative to grappling with the facts. Thus, in the *Nicaragua* case,[3] where the legal issues concerned border-crossing and the use of force in Central America, the Court had to evaluate a huge amount of confusing material and its findings of fact alone occupy fifty-five pages of the judgment.

The Court's difficulties in the *Nicaragua* case were compounded by the fact that, after a controversial ruling on the issue of jurisdiction, the United States decided to take no further part in the proceedings. Although this did not prevent the Court from deciding the case, it meant that, without evidence from one side, the Court was deprived of the interplay of argument which is a vital feature of the judicial process. In this case, as in others where a respondent has failed to appear, the Court made extensive use of admissions, inferences, judicial notice of matters of public knowledge and circumstantial evidence to establish the facts, and when drafting the judgment took unusual care to avoid any impression of bias.[4] It is clear, nonetheless, that by refusing to present its side of the case the United States put itself at an irretrievable disadvantage. However conscientious the Court may be, there is no way in which it can ensure that, if a state is absent, important points in its case will not be lost by default.

The problems that fact-finding can present may be seen in several later cases where the Court was faced with exceptionally complex situations. In the *Armed Activities on the Territory of the Congo* case,[5] the Democratic Republic of the Congo (DRC) complained that Uganda had engaged in

---

[2] See the *Gabcikovo-Nagymaros Project*, Order of 5 February 1997 [1997] ICJ Rep. 3. The visit, which took place in April 1997, was the first to be made by the ICJ. See P. Tomka and S. S. Wordsworth, 'The first site visit of the International Court of Justice in fulfilment of its judicial function' (1998) 92 *AJIL*, 133.

[3] *Military and Paramilitary Activities in and against Nicaragua*, Merits, Judgment [1986] ICJ Rep. 14.

[4] See K. Highet, 'Evidence, the Court and the Nicaragua case' (1987) 81 *AJIL*, 1. These problems were anticipated in the same author's 'Litigation implications of the US withdrawal from the Nicaragua case' (1985) 79 *AJIL*, 992.

[5] *Armed Activities on the Territory of the Congo (Democratic Republic of the Congo v. Uganda)* [2005] ICJ Rep. 168. And see P. N. Okowa, Note (2006) 55 *ICLQ*, 742.

armed aggression against it, committed numerous violations of human rights law and international humanitarian law and illegally exploited its natural resources. As these allegations related to activities during a lengthy civil war involving at least seven other states, as well as numerous rebel groups, establishing the facts and deciding Uganda's responsibility proved a very demanding task.

In the *Genocide Convention* case,[6] similarly, the question was whether Serbia had committed genocide in Bosnia and Herzegovina during the conflict in the Balkans which followed the violent break-up of Yugoslavia. As in the previous case, this inquiry called for the Court to examine a mass of evidence relating to both the atrocities themselves and official policies on the matter. However, since some of these issues had already been investigated by the International Criminal Tribunal for the Former Yugoslavia, the Court was able to make use of some of the Tribunal's findings of fact, describing them as 'highly persuasive'.

In the case *Certain Activities Carried Out by Nicaragua in the Border Area (Costa Rica v. Nicaragua)* decided in 2018,[7] the Court similarly dealt with complex issues arising from the contention of Costa Rica that Nicaragua had occupied parts of Costa Rican territory in connection with the construction of a canal ('*caño*') linking the San Juan River with Harbor Head Lagoon, and carried out dredging works on the San Juan River. The Court had to examine detailed documentary evidence, including aerial and satellite imagery of the area.[8] While Nicaragua had argued that only an 'inspection on the ground' could provide certainty because of the thick vegetation, the Court considered that such would not be useful in light of the fact that the Court was asked to assess the situation before 2010. The Court also dismissed the evidentiary power of the aerial and satellite imagery because of its 'general lack of clarity', and declined to give evidential weight to affidavits, since these had been provided by Nicaraguan state officials and had been drafted after the initiation of proceedings.[9]

Because international litigation is complex and the Court is now very busy, various measures to speed up the handling of cases have been introduced in recent years. These include several changes to the Court's

---

[6] *Application of the Convention on the Prevention and Punishment of the Crime of Genocide (Bosnia and Herzegovina v. Serbia and Montenegro)*, Merits, Judgment [2007] ICJ Rep. 43; and see S. Sivakumaran, Note (2007) 56 *ICLQ*, 695.

[7] *Certain Activities Carried Out by Nicaragua in the Border Area (Costa Rica v. Nicaragua) and Construction of a Road in Costa Rica along the San Juan River (Nicaragua v. Costa Rica)*, Judgment, [2015] ICJ Rep. 665.

[8] *Certain Activities Carried Out by Nicaragua in the Border Area (Costa Rica v. Nicaragua) and Construction of a Road in Costa Rica along the San Juan River (Nicaragua v. Costa Rica)*, Judgment, [2015] ICJ Rep. 665, paras 79–82.

[9] On the evidentiary value of affidavits, see also: *Application of the Convention on the Prevention and Punishment of the Crime of Genocide (Croatia v. Serbia)*, Judgment [2015] ICJ Rep. 78, para. 196.

Rules, and some important Practice Directions,[10] as well as a series of other measures designed to simplify its procedures.[11] Steps with a particular bearing on the presentation of evidence include a requirement that documents annexed to a party's written pleadings should be strictly selected; a restriction on the production of new documents after the closure of the written proceedings; and encouragement to the parties to focus their oral statements on the issues which divide them. Other measures are intended to limit the number of rounds of written pleadings. In adopting these measures, the Court is seeking to promote efficiency without unduly constraining a party's ability to make its case, a policy requiring a balancing act of some delicacy.

9.1.2 Scientific Evidence and Experts

Another situation that may present difficulties is where the Court has to deal with a case involving technical and scientific evidence.[12] This is because the distinction between disputes about legal and factual questions, which are the Court's province, and the resolution of scientific controversies, which is not, may not be clear-cut. In the *Pulp Mills on the River Uruguay* case,[13] for example, several judges were rightly critical of the handling of the parties' scientific evidence. However, in the more recent *Whaling in the Antarctic* case,[14] the Court took a fresh approach and, adopting what has been described as 'a strict and rapid schedule',[15] produced a more satisfactory decision. Scientific and technical issues are increasingly important since international tribunals are often presented with various kinds of disputes concerned with the environment. As we shall see in Chapter 11, the World Trade Organization frequently has to

---

[10] See Practice Directions IX, IX*bis*, IX*ter*, and XI*quater*, as amended and promulgated in 2006. The Practice Directions are available at www.icj-cij.org/en/practice-directions.

[11] See R. Higgins, 'Respecting sovereign states and running a tight courtroom' (2001) 50 *ICLQ*, 121 and the Notes by S. Rosenne in (2002) 2 *Global Community YBILJ*, 207 and J. G. Merrills in (2003) 3 *Global Community YBILJ*, 277.

[12] See generally M. M. Mbengue, 'Scientific fact-finding at the International Court of Justice: an appraisal in the aftermath of the Whaling Case' (2016) 29 *Leiden Journal of International Law*, 529–50 and J. d'Aspremont and M. Mbengue, 'Strategies of engagement with scientific fact-finding in international adjudication' (2014) 5 *Journal of International Dispute Settlement* 240–72.

[13] *Pulp Mills on the River Uruguay (Argentina v. Uruguay)*, Judgment [2010] ICJ Rep. 14 and see C. R. Payne, Note (2011) 105 *AJIL*, 94.

[14] *Whaling in the Antarctic (Australia v. Japan: New Zealand Intervening)*, Judgment [2014] ICJ Rep. 225 and see S. E. Rolland, Note (2014) 108 *AJIL*, 496.

[15] C. R. Payne, 'Australia v. Japan: ICJ halts Antarctic whaling' (2014) 18 *ASIL Insights*, Issue 9. See also M.M. Mbengue, 'Scientific fact-finding at the International Court of Justice: an appraisal in the aftermath of the Whaling Case' (2016) 29 *Leiden Journal of International Law* 529–50.

deal with cases of this type. Finding the proper way to handle the evidence in such cases is therefore now a significant challenge.

The Statute and Rules contain a number of provisions designed to enable the Court to supplement the parties' evidence with its own investigations. It is entitled to request the parties to call witnesses or experts and may call for the production of any other evidence on points of fact in regard to which the parties are not in agreement. Article 30(2) of the Statute permits the Court to appoint assessors to sit with it during the proceedings and is intended to ensure that the decision takes account of the latest scientific knowledge and contains no technical errors. Under Article 50 of the Statute, the Court is empowered to commission an inquiry or expert opinion.[16] Although this power has rarely been used, its value was demonstrated in the *Corfu Channel* case[17] and in the reparations phase of the *Armed Activities on the Territory of the Congo* case.

In the *Corfu Channel* case, after hearing the conflicting evidence of the parties' witnesses and expert witnesses, the Court appointed a committee of experts, composed of senior officers of the Dutch, Norwegian and Swedish navies, which submitted two reports concerning the mining of the channel. After the second report, which resulted from a visit to the scene, the Court was satisfied that Albania's responsibility had been established. This raised the question of compensation and further technical issues. The Court therefore appointed another committee of experts, consisting of two senior officers of the Dutch navy. Their conclusion, that the British claim represented a fair and accurate estimate of the damage sustained, was accepted by the Court and formed the basis of its final judgment.

In the *Armed Activities on the Territory of the Congo* case, the Court appointed four experts to determine the reparation to be made by Uganda and the Congo. While the case had already been decided on the merits in 2005, the parties were unable to settle the question of the amount of reparation through bilateral negotiations. After having been seized by the Congo in 2015 to settle the question of reparation, the Court decided pursuant to Article 50 of the Statute to request an expert opinion for several heads of damage including loss of human life, loss of natural resources and property damage.[18] The Court recalled in its 2020 Order that 'it will be for the Court to determine what weight, if any, to be given to the assessments contained in the expert report'.[19] Despite opposition from

---

[16] See generally L. Boisson de Chazournes, M.M. Mbengue, R. Das and G. Gros, 'One size does not fit all – uses of experts before international courts and tribunals: an insight into the practice' (2018) 3 *Journal of International Dispute Settlement* 477–505.

[17] See [1949] ICJ Rep. 142, 152 and 258.

[18] *Armed Activities on the Territory of the Congo (Democratic Republic of the Congo v. Uganda)*, Order of 8 September 2020 and Order of 12 October 2020.

[19] *Armed Activities on the Territory of the Congo (Democratic Republic of the Congo v. Uganda)*, Order of 12 October 2020, p. 3.

Uganda to three of the experts proposed by the Court, the Court confirmed the appointment of the experts it had proposed to the parties. The committee of experts consists of a Professor of Public Health, an Environmental Governance Advisor, an accountant, and a Professor of the Peace Research Institute, Oslo.

9.2 Identifying the Law

The sources of law which the Court is to utilise are set out in Article 38(1) of the Statute, and it is clear that the way in which these are applied is likely to exercise a major influence on states' attitudes towards judicial settlement. In the work of the Court, as in that of municipal courts, the essential problem is to reconcile continuity with innovation. Internationally, however, the problem is complicated by three factors: the lack of a single legal culture; the relatively undeveloped state of international law; and the tensions of a period of radical changes in international society.

The cultural dimension is well illustrated by the *Western Sahara* case.[20] There, Spain argued that whether the territory was *terra nullius* at the time of colonisation must be determined by the criteria of classical international law, while Algeria and Mauritania argued that the Court should acknowledge the existence of an Arab–Islamic civilisation, outside the traditional legal framework, of which the Western Sahara formed an integral part. In its advisory opinion, the Court preferred Spain's argument on this point and rejected the more radical view. However, when the Court turned to the issue of 'legal ties' with the territory, it examined the special characteristics of the region in great detail and made the Arab–Islamic elements in the case the focal point of its opinion. From a bookish standpoint, it is easy to criticise this attempt to blend a traditional approach with the concepts of non-Western legal cultures. Yet it is inevitable that broadening the Court's membership should bring with it a widening of the basis of its decisions. Moreover, it is right that it should do so. For, if judicial decisions are to be an acceptable means of resolving disputes, the Court must recognise the diversity of its audience and frame its judgments in language which the bulk of the members of the international community can support and understand.

A President of the Court has observed that its decisions 'must continue to provide that core of predictability that distinguishes law from politics', while doing so 'in a way that is responsive to the legitimate needs and aspirations of the international community'.[21] This tension can be seen in

---

[20] Western Sahara, Advisory Opinion [1975] ICJ Rep. 12. For discussion of this aspect of the case, see M. Shaw, 'The Western Sahara case' (1978) 40 *BYBIL*, 118.

[21] Speech by HE Judge Rosalyn Higgins at the sixtieth anniversary of the inaugural sitting of the Court, ICJ Press Release 2006/15 (12 April 2006).

the *Arrest Warrant* case,[22] where the Court decided that a foreign minister enjoys complete immunity from the jurisdiction of courts in other states, even with regard to allegations of war crimes and crimes against humanity. In the absence of a clear body of state practice on this issue, the Court based its conclusion on functional criteria and, while careful to distinguish immunity from impunity, rejected arguments based on international public policy. In this case, then, the Court proceeded cautiously. In contrast, in the *LaGrand* case,[23] a few months earlier, it had accepted that Article 36(1) of the 1963 Vienna Convention on Consular Relations confers rights on individuals, as well as on states, thereby endorsing the then progressive view that in modern international law a convention does not have to be a human rights treaty in order to confer such rights.

Adjudicating in an era of social and legal change requires both a technique for resolving disputes when state practice provides no clear guidance, and, after things begin to settle down, a way of deciding when new trends in practice, as evidenced in non-binding declarations, codes, guidelines and other 'soft' materials, cross the threshold of normativity and merit recognition as law. In the *Gabcikovo-Nagymaros* case,[24] for example, the Court held that a treaty concluded by Hungary and Czechoslovakia in 1977 had to be interpreted and applied in light of subsequent developments in international law relating to the protection of the environment. That in itself was a ruling of some significance in the present context, but tantalisingly left open the question of which of the various instruments cited in argument qualified as 'law' for this purpose.

A situation in which practice was in a state of flux and provided no clear guidance had to be addressed by the Court in the *Fisheries Jurisdiction* case of 1974.[25] The questions on which the United Kingdom sought a decision were whether Iceland's claim to a fifty-mile exclusive fishery was contrary to international law; whether the claim was opposable to the United Kingdom; and whether the conservation of fish stocks in the disputed area was a matter for unilateral regulation by Iceland. In the face of a wide diversity in state practice, however, the Court declined to address the question of customary international law and based its decision on the

---

[22] *Arrest Warrant of 11 April 2000 (Democratic Republic of the Congo v. Belgium)*, Judgment [2002] ICJ Rep. 3. For comment, see C. Wickremasinghe, Note (2003) 52 *ICLQ*, 775.
[23] *LaGrand Case (Germany v. United States)*, Judgment [2001] ICJ Rep. 466. For comment, see M. Menneke and C. J. Tams, Note (2002) 51 *ICLQ*, 449.
[24] *Gabcikovo-Nagymaros Project (Hungary/Slovakia)*, Judgment [1997] ICJ Rep. 7. For comment, see P. N. Okowa, Note (1998) 47 *ICLQ*, 688.
[25] *Fisheries Jurisdiction (United Kingdom v. Iceland)*, Merits, Judgment [1974] ICJ Rep. 3. For a critical comment, see R. R. Churchill, 'The Fisheries Jurisdiction cases: the contribution of the International Court of Justice to the debate on coastal states' fisheries rights' (1975) 24 *ICLQ*, 82.

non-opposability of Iceland's regulations to the United Kingdom in view of the latter's historic rights.

Although the Court's approach was criticised, in the circumstances of the case it had much to recommend it. The Court was here being called upon to act at a sensitive time and avoided a 'legislative' decision by deciding the case on the narrowest possible ground. Indeed, the Court went out of its way to emphasise that, as a judicial tribunal, political and other movements which have yet to achieve the status of international law cannot provide a basis for its decisions. This, however, is rather deceptive. The Court was unable to recognise the emerging concept of the exclusive economic zone, but took into account Iceland's 'preferential rights', a concept for which the evidence of state practice was certainly less than compelling. The explanation is not hard to find. The Court was ensuring that the orientation of its decision corresponded to the trends at the Third United Nations Conference on the Law of the Sea (UNCLOS III), which was then in session. While denying its ability to revise the law and refusing to abandon established principles altogether, it nonetheless achieved a substantial measure of legal innovation.

The tension between continuity of the law and the development of international law also is visible in the 2019 opinion of the Court in *Legal Consequences of the Separation of the Chagos Archipelago from Mauritius in 1965*.[26] The ICJ was faced with the question of the application of international law to historical events, as the request for an advisory opinion asked the Court to consider whether the process of decolonisation of Mauritius had been completed in 1968 in light of the separation and the continued administration by the United Kingdom of the Chagos Archipelago. The Court first needed to identify the relevant time period in order to ascertain the applicable law, finding it to be between the separation of Chagos from Mauritius in 1965 and its independence in 1968. The Court recalled that

> while its determination of the applicable law must focus on the period from 1965 to 1968, this will not prevent it, particularly when customary rules are at issue, from considering the evolution of the law on self-determination since the adoption of the Charter of the United Nations and of resolution 1514 (XV) of 14 December 1960 entitled 'Declaration on the Granting of Independence to Colonial Countries and Peoples'. Indeed, State practice and opinio juris, i.e. the acceptance of that practice as law (Article 38 of the Statute of the Court), are consolidated and confirmed gradually over time.[27]

---

[26] *Legal Consequences of the Separation of the Chagos Archipelago from Mauritius in 1965*, Advisory Opinion, [2019] ICJ Rep. 95.

[27] *Ibid.*, para. 142.

Furthermore, the Court found that it may rely on legal instruments which postdate the period between 1965 and 1968, where those instruments confirm or interpret the application of the existing rules or principles.[28] The Court finally concluded that the unlawful detachment of the Chagos Archipelago from Mauritius, and its subsequent 'incorporation into a new colony' implied that the process of decolonisation of Mauritius was not lawfully completed when Mauritius acceded to independence in 1968. The United Kingdom was therefore found to be under an obligation to bring to an end its administration of the Chagos Archipelago as rapidly as possible.

9.3 Extension of the Court's Function

The cases discussed so far indicate that the Court's obligation to apply the law has not in practice prevented it from broadening the basis of its decisions to take account of cultural diversity, from refining and elaborating the law and from taking account of changing circumstances. Enough has been said, however, to indicate that the demands of continuity impose certain limits which the Court could only ignore at the cost of ceasing to be a court of law. If, therefore, the parties regard the law as unsatisfactory or inadequate, then a decision must be sought on some other basis.

When considering how the judicial function may be extended, a point to appreciate at the outset is that the Court must always respect both the limits of the jurisdiction conferred by the treaty or other instrument, and the scope of the dispute as defined in the parties' pleadings. In the *Kasikili/Sedudu Island* case,[29] for example, the special agreement asked for a ruling on the boundary between Botswana and Namibia and the status of the disputed island. In its judgment in the case, the Court answered these questions, but then rather surprisingly went on to hold that in the two channels around the island the vessels and nationals of both states were entitled to equal treatment. This was a broad view of the Court's function, but one which could be justified in light of an earlier undertaking by the parties dealing with cooperation, and which could be regarded as relevant to the interpretation of their special agreement. However, one member of the Court would have gone further and required the parties to negotiate a joint regulatory regime for the island and waterway as a means of environmental protection.[30] This, no doubt, was a laudable objective, but so expansive a view of the judicial role is hard to reconcile with what the parties had actually asked the Court to do and with the special agreement providing the basis for its jurisdiction.

---

[28] *Ibid.*, para. 143.
[29] *Kasikili/Sedudu Island (Botswana/Namibia)*, Judgment [1999] ICJ Rep. 1045. For a summary, see M. N. Shaw, Note (2000) 49 *ICLQ*, 964.
[30] See the dissenting opinion of Judge Weeramantry, *ibid.*, paras 114–16.

9.3.1 Agreement of the Parties

Under Article 38(2) of the Statute, the Court may at the request of the parties give a decision *ex aequo et bono*. This has the merit of achieving complete flexibility, but at the price of complete uncertainty as to the criteria for decision. Perhaps for this reason the Court has never been asked to decide a case under this provision. A less drastic alternative is to refer a case to the Court for a decision on an agreed basis. This too is rare, though common enough in arbitration, as already noted. Directives of this kind also sometimes lead to disagreements as to what the parties really intended. Thus, in the *Kasikili/Sedudu Island* case, the special agreement requested a decision on the basis of a treaty concluded in 1890 and 'the rules and principles of international law'. Botswana argued that the Court was not permitted to take into account arguments which Namibia had put forward on prescription and acquiescence as these were not covered in the agreement. The Court, however, disagreed and held that in referring to 'the rules and principles of international law' the agreement authorised it not only to interpret the treaty in light of those rules and principles, but also to apply them independently.

An example of the Court being given a very specific directive may be seen in the special agreement in the 1986 *Frontier Dispute* case. This asked a chamber of the Court to define the frontier between Mali and Burkina Faso and expressed the parties' desire that the line should be 'based in particular on respect for the principle of the intangibility of frontiers inherited from colonization'.[31] Although this reference to the principle of *uti possidetis* appeared in the Preamble to the special agreement, not in the main text, the chamber held that the parties had expressly requested it to resolve their dispute on this basis, and proceeded to do so. As the chamber explained, the principle it was required to apply here was not so much a special rule, as a principle of general relevance to territorial issues in Africa, the countries of Spanish America, and elsewhere. It is therefore probable that, even without the special agreement, the principle of *uti possidetis* would have featured in the decision. By drawing specific attention to it, however, the parties ensured that it received the attention they considered it merited, and effectively became the pivot of the case.

A less oblique directive is to be found in the special agreement in the *Tunisia–Libya Continental Shelf* case. This asked the Court to decide what principles and rules of international law were applicable to the delimitation of the continental shelf in the disputed area, and required it to take its decision 'according to equitable principles, and the relevant circumstances

---

[31] *Frontier Dispute*, Judgment [1986] ICJ Rep. 554 at 557.

which characterize the area, *as well as the new accepted trends in the Third Conference on the Law of the Sea*'.[32]

It is evident that, by this directive, the Court was required to reconcile its role as a traditional court of law with a function devised for it by the parties – that of a forward-looking, quasi-legislative instrument of dispute settlement. In discharging this burden, it achieved a not uncharacteristic compromise. While emphasising its role as a judicial organ, it acknowledged the directive in the *compromis* and was at pains to demonstrate the congruence between its premises and the proceedings at UNCLOS III. To complete the circle, however, it further justified its decision by reference to established principles. Although it would be wrong to assume that the inclusion of 'new accepted trends' in the Court's mandate had no effect on its decision, its concern for the existing law produces almost a mirror-image of the *Fisheries Jurisdiction* case considered earlier. There, current developments played a larger and more constructive part than the Court's emphasis on the *lex lata* might lead one to expect; in the *Tunisia–Libya* case, where the Court was authorised to cast its net more widely, with equal prudence it elected to buttress its decision with the established law.

In both the cases just mentioned, the parties were able to modify the Court's function by indicating the principles it should apply. It may be possible to achieve much the same thing by framing the question in such a way as to limit the range of permissible solutions. Thus, in the *Gulf of Maine* case,[33] the special agreement asked the chamber to decide the course of the 'single maritime boundary' between their respective continental shelves and fisheries zones, and specified the points between which the boundary should run. Commenting on these prescriptions, the chamber observed that neither was contrary to the requirements of international law, and went on to draw the boundary accordingly. Even so, had it been free to choose, the chamber might have held that different boundaries were needed for continental shelf and fisheries purposes, and similarly might well have selected different terminal points. By ruling out such possibilities, the parties directed the chamber's attention to what they considered important, while excluding solutions which would be unacceptable, a result very similar to specifying the applicable law.

Whether the Court has an inherent power to use equity and thereby to extend its function on its own initiative is a question which raises issues of

---

[32] See *Continental Shelf (Tunisia/Libyan Arab Jamahiriya)*, Judgment [1982] ICJ Rep. 18 at 23 (emphasis added). For comments on this and other aspects of the case, see M. B. Feldman, 'The Tunisia–Libya Continental Shelf case: geographic justice or judicial compromise?' (1983) 77 *AJIL*, 219.

[33] *Delimitation of the Maritime Boundary in the Gulf of Maine Area*, Judgment [1984] ICJ Rep. 246.

some complexity.[34] On the one hand, the Court is a legal tribunal, and, without express authorisation, is not entitled to perform a general legislative function, whether under the guise of equity or on some other ground.[35] The view that the Court should ignore the existing law, and boldly decide all its cases 'equitably' – assuming it still had any – therefore has nothing to be said for it. On the other hand, to demand that every decision be justified by reference to a specific pre-established rule is not only quite unrealistic, given the patchwork nature of the modern law, but ignores what all courts do in practice which, as we have already suggested, is certainly to innovate, albeit within rather ill-defined conventions.

9.3.2 Equity *Infra Legem*

One of the recognised methods of introducing flexibility into the law is the use of equity *infra legem*. In the *Frontier Dispute* case, the chamber described this as 'that form of equity which constitutes a method of interpretation of the law in force, and is one of its attributes'.[36] It can be seen therefore that what is involved here is not especially radical. Nevertheless, this form of equity can provide the Court with a useful extra resource, as the judgment in this case demonstrates. For, having found that there were no special circumstances pointing to a different solution, the chamber used equity as its justification for dividing a frontier pool between the parties equally.[37]

A limited recourse to equity in the way just described is unlikely to be controversial. It was pointed out in a previous chapter that courts of arbitration regularly employ equity *infra legem* and the International Court is no less entitled to seek sensible solutions. If, however, the Court goes further and relies on equitable considerations of a more general character, then questions about the role of adjudication are bound to arise. In the *Fisheries Jurisdiction* case, for example, the Court decided that, according to customary international law, the states concerned were under a legal obligation to undertake negotiations in good faith for the 'equitable solution' of their differences concerning their respective fishing rights. This conclusion, which in the Court's view followed from its earlier ruling that Iceland enjoyed preferential, but not exclusive, rights in the area concerned, can be regarded as a constructive attempt to provide a legal answer to a difficult problem. Presumably, however, in the event of the parties failing to negotiate an equitable solution, they would be entitled to return

---

[34] For an excellent discussion of this issue, see M. B. Akehurst, 'Equity and general principles of law' (1976) 25 *ICLQ*, 801.
[35] On the 'lawmaking' role of judicial institutions, see A. von Bogdandy and I. Venzke, 'International courts as lawmakers', in R. Wolfrum, and I. Gätzschmann (eds), *International dispute settlement: room for innovations?*, Heidelberg, 2013, pp. 161–213.
[36] [1986] ICJ Rep. 567–8.   [37] *Ibid.*, 633.

to the Court and ask it to indicate the solution required. Would it be able as a court of law to do so? It is this which raises questions about the role of the adjudication.

Subsequent developments in the law of the sea, specifically the general recognition of the rights of states to an exclusive economic zone, meant that the Court was never asked to indicate an equitable solution in a fisheries dispute. However, in another part of the law of the sea, the application of this form of equity is very much a live issue. In the first case on continental shelf delimitation, the *North Sea Continental Shelf* cases of 1969,[38] the Court held that, under customary international law, states were obliged to negotiate their continental shelf boundaries 'in accordance with equitable principles'. However, in its judgment in the *Tunisia–Libya Continental Shelf* case of 1982, the Court, influenced as we have seen by UNCLOS III, modified the requirement to an obligation to seek an 'equitable result'. This was a controversial step, and, both here and in the subsequent *Gulf of Maine* case, where a chamber of the Court followed the same approach, strong criticism was expressed by one member of the Court.

The thrust of the argument advanced by Judge Gros was that, by emphasising the result, the Court had indulged in 'an equity beyond the law, detached from any established rules, based solely on whatever each group of judges seized of a case declares itself able and free to appreciate in accordance with its political or economic views of the moment'.[39] In light of this criticism, it is interesting to note that in more recent cases on delimitation the Court has put less emphasis on achieving an equitable result and more on its methodology, first establishing a provisional boundary line based on equidistance, then, where appropriate, applying equity as a corrective.[40] While this approach does not remove the element of discretion in decisions on delimitation, it does tend to make the process more predictable and consequently seem less like court-sponsored conciliation. Since conciliation, as Judge Gros pointed out, is something which judges are not normally called upon to do, and may have no qualifications to undertake, this is a welcome evolution.

9.3.3 Recommendations

Another way in which the Court has extended its function is by using the opportunity presented by the proceedings to address recommendations to

---

[38] *North Sea Continental Shelf*, Judgment [1969] ICJ Rep. 3.   [39] [1984] ICJ Rep. 388.
[40] See, for example, *Maritime Delimitation in the Black Sea (Romania v. Ukraine)* [2009] ICJ Rep. 61. And see C. G. Lathrop, Note (2009) 103 *AJIL*, 543. Also *Maritime Dispute (Peru v. Chile)*, Judgment [2014] ICJ Rep. 3. And see A. G. Jain, Note (2015) 109 *AJIL*, 379. For a good account of this approach to delimitation, see Y. Tanaka, 'Reflections on maritime delimitation in the Cameroon/Nigeria case' (2004) 53 *ICLQ*, 369.

the parties, reminding them of their obligations under the general law in addition to any specific consequences of the Court's decision. Thus, in the *Armed Activities on the Territory of the Congo* case, the Court urged 'all those involved in the conflict to support the peace process in the Democratic Republic of the Congo and other peace processes in the Great Lakes area in order to ensure respect for human rights in the region',[41] and has made similar calls in other recent cases.

Recommendations are not binding, and so are quite different from the findings of law or fact in judgments or orders of interim protection. If used judiciously, however, recommendations are a way of stressing the parties' wider responsibilities and putting their dispute in context with a view to encouraging a peaceful settlement. As such, they can be thought of as a modest, but legitimate, extension of the Court's function.

9.4 Legal and Political Disputes

At the beginning of 1985, the United States announced that it would take no further part in the case brought against it by Nicaragua in the Court. This action, which we have noted had important procedural consequences, was stated to be justified by two reasons: first, that the Court had erred in finding that it had jurisdiction to decide the case; and, second, that, quite apart from the issue of jurisdiction, the Court should have held the case to be inadmissible on the ground that it raised a political and therefore a non-justiciable issue. As the official explanation put it, in the view of the United States the decision that the case could be heard on the merits represented 'an overreaching of the Court's limits, a departure from its tradition of judicial restraint and a risky venture into political waters'.[42]

The *Nicaragua* case is not the first to raise the question of whether adjudication has any place in the resolution of political disputes, and is unlikely to be the last. For this is a key aspect of justiciability in both international and domestic law. At the international level, however, it raises issues which concern the very possibility of adjudication. For courts are legal institutions and normally have no authority to decide political questions. Yet states are political entities whose disputes invariably have a political dimension. The Court, with the responsibility of deciding disputes between states, is therefore in a particularly delicate position.

As we discussed in Chapter 1, when deciding whether the political aspect of a dispute has any bearing on its power to adjudicate, the Court has always sought to apply two principles. The first is that, if a question is referred to the Court which cannot be resolved by applying legal criteria,

---

[41] [2005] ICJ Rep. 168, para. 221. For a thoughtful survey, see J. d'Aspremont, 'The recommendations made by the International Court of Justice' (2007) 56 *ICLQ*, 185.
[42] See the State Department's background paper quoted in (1985) 79 *AJIL* 438 at 441.

then, unless its competence has been extended by the parties, it must decline to adjudicate. This follows from the fact that the normal function of a court is to apply the law, and has the effect of preventing the Court from deciding disputes and issues of an exclusively political or non-legal type. As already noted, it was because he considered that the Court had lost sight of this principle that Judge Gros dissented in the *Gulf of Maine* case.

The second principle, which is a corollary of the first and no less fundamental, is that, provided a case raises a question of international law, then to fulfil its function the Court must give a decision, whatever the background or political complications may be. This point was made by the Court in a number of advisory opinions concerned with the interpretation of the United Nations Charter, and has been reiterated in a number of later cases.

In one of Turkey's communications to the Court in the *Aegean Sea Continental Shelf* case, for example, the suggestion was made that the dispute between Greece and Turkey was 'of a highly political nature'. This led the Court to consider whether the case might be said to concern a political rather than a legal dispute. Explaining that 'a dispute involving two States in respect of the delimitation of their continental shelf can hardly fail to have some political element', the Court held that it was clear from the parties' arguments that the dispute between them involved a conflict as to their respective rights. Concluding that 'there are certain sovereign rights being claimed by both Greece and Turkey, one against the other and it is manifest that legal rights lie at the root of the dispute that divides the two States',[43] the Court decided that a legal dispute existed between them in respect of the continental shelf in the Aegean.

Similarly, in the *Diplomatic Staff in Tehran* case, Iran maintained that the Court was precluded from taking cognisance of the case by the fact that the proceedings would be confined to the issue of the hostages' detention. For, Iran stated:

> this question only represents a marginal and secondary aspect of an overall problem, one such that it cannot be studied separately, and which involves, *inter alia*, more than 25 years' continual interference by the United States in the internal affairs of Iran, the shameless exploitation of our country, and numerous crimes perpetrated against the Iranian people, contrary to and in conflict with all international and humanitarian norms.[44]

In its order of December 1979 relating to interim measures of protection, the Court made it clear that the seizure of the United States' diplomatic premises and the detention of internationally protected persons could not be regarded as something 'secondary' or 'marginal' in view of the

---

[43] *Aegean Sea Continental Shelf*, Judgment [1978] ICJ Rep. 3 at 13.

[44] *United States Diplomatic and Consular Staff in Tehran*, Judgment [1980] ICJ Rep. 3 at 19.

importance of the legal principles involved. It further pointed out that no provision of the Statute or Rules prevents the Court from taking cognisance of one aspect of a dispute merely because the dispute in question has other aspects, and concluded by reminding the Iranian government that, if it considered the alleged activities of the United States in Iran to have a close connection with the subject matter of the dispute, it could present its arguments concerning those activities either as a defence or by way of a counter-claim.

When, in 1980, the Court came to consider the question of its jurisdiction to decide the merits, it repeated its earlier comments, and then noted that, since the preliminary proceedings, Iran had taken no steps to submit evidence and arguments in support of its contentions. In these circumstances, the Court decided that it could not accept the Iranian argument. The Court proceeded from the assumption that its duty is to decide legal questions and that to regard political considerations as an obstacle would be to abrogate its function. In the Court's words:

> legal disputes between sovereign States by their very nature are likely to occur in political contexts and often form only one element in a wider and long-standing political dispute between the States concerned. Yet never has the view been put forward before that, because a legal dispute submitted to the Court is only one aspect of a political dispute, the Court should decline to resolve for the parties the legal questions at issue between them ... [I]f the Court were, contrary to its settled jurisprudence, to adopt such a view, it would impose a far-reaching and unwarranted restriction upon the role of the Court in the peaceful solution of international disputes.[45]

In the *Nicaragua* case, the Court took this point further. There, at the jurisdictional stage, the United States maintained that the case was non-justiciable, but, although the argument was put in various ways, the United States did not try to say that the Court should refuse to deal with the case on the broad ground that the whole matter was political. Instead, it took a more specific point and argued, inter alia, that adjudication was incompatible with the Contadora process, which was generally recognised as the appropriate means of dealing with the problems of Central America. The United States pointed out that Nicaragua was asking the Court to examine only certain issues involved in the Contadora process and that a judicial decision would therefore disrupt the balance of the negotiations, which should be allowed to continue as a comprehensive, integrated process, without interference from the Court.

Not surprisingly, the Court rejected this argument, which it regarded as essentially similar to Iran's argument in the earlier case. In both cases, said the Court, the respondent was suggesting that it should refrain from

---

[45] *Ibid.*, 20.

deciding certain legal questions because the case raised larger issues. The Court's job, however, is to decide whatever legal issues a case raises without reference to its wider context. Since the use of force in the *Nicaragua* case raised a legal issue in the same way as the previous case raised an issue of diplomatic law, in both cases the Court was entitled to proceed.[46]

Because all international disputes have a political dimension of some kind, arguments like those which were advanced and rejected in these cases could in theory be raised whenever a dispute is taken to the Court. In most cases, however, the objection that a dispute is too political for the Court to decide is not put forward for the simple reason that, by electing to have their dispute adjudicated, the parties have already agreed that its legal and political aspects should be separated. In other words, what distinguishes the cases in which the Court has to address this aspect of justiciability is not that these kinds of disputes are political whereas others are not, rather that, though all international disputes are political, some can be depoliticised by the parties, whereas in others depoliticisation, that is, separation of the legal from the political aspects of the case, must be done by the Court.

The cases in which the Court's competence to handle politically charged disputes has been questioned have all been referred unilaterally and involved a basic disagreement as to how the dispute should be characterised. For the applicant, the legal aspect was paramount and the intention in taking the case to the Court was to vindicate a claim based on legal rights. For the respondent, on the other hand, the core of the issue was political, and so, though legal issues might be involved, the case was unsuitable for adjudication. Faced with this incomplete depoliticisation, the Court has taken the only position open to a legal tribunal and, having established that it has the right to decide the issue of characterisation, has ruled that, whatever the politics of a dispute may be, the applicant has the right to a decision, provided only that the case presents a legal issue.

The Court, then, is prepared to depoliticise a dispute if the parties are unable to do so. However, though it has been correct to assume this responsibility, the consequences may sometimes be unfortunate. Separating the legal from the political aspects of disputes is bound to mean that there will be difficulties in securing acceptance of certain judicial decisions, and, as we shall see in a moment, this limits the contribution which adjudication can make to the solution of international disputes. 'The whole political dossier of the relations between Iran and the United States over the last 25 years', which Iran saw as the context of the *Diplomatic Staff in Tehran* case, or 'the complex of interrelated political, social, economic and security matters that confront the Central American region', which the

---

[46] A similar point was raised in the *Construction of a Wall* case (2004), but this and other arguments against the Court's giving an advisory opinion were rejected. For the outcome, see Chapter 8; and, for the United States' position on justiciability, see (2004) 98 *AJIL* 361.

United States saw as relevant in the *Nicaragua* case, are obviously not the kinds of matters that are justiciable in legal proceedings. Yet, these were the matters which concerned the respondent states. It follows, then, that, if the isolation of the legal element is to result in a decision which can be implemented, it is important to ensure that the respondent's interests are recognised elsewhere.

Thus, to appreciate the significance of cases in which highly political disputes have been held to be justiciable, it is necessary to keep in mind the many important matters which are not justiciable. If the Court, rightly, holds that it is entitled to decide a case on the ground that it presents legal issues, and at the same time, and no less rightly, takes the view that 'issues which no legal rules can be found to touch are not justiciable, irrespective of any sense of grievance a disputant may feel',[47] then, unless those grievances can be dealt with somewhere, the Court's decision is unlikely to be respected.

9.5 Effect of Judgments

Decisions in contentious cases are legally binding. Does it follow that they are effective in settling disputes?[48]

9.5.1 The Finality of the Court's Decisions

The first point to notice is that litigation can serve different functions. So, when states refer a case to the Court, they may not be seeking a definitive settlement but merely a decision which will narrow the differences between them, or in some other way move the dispute nearer to resolution. In the *Ambatielos* case,[49] for example, the sole question was whether the United Kingdom was under an obligation to refer a commercial dispute with Greece to arbitration. The Court decided that it was, and arbitration was then attempted. Similarly, in the *North Sea Continental Shelf* cases, instead

---

[47] S. Roberts, *Order and Dispute: An Introduction to Legal Anthropology*, Harmondsworth, 1979, p. 21. For further discussion of this issue, see E. Gordon, 'Legal disputes under Article 36(2) of the Statute', in L. F. Damrosch (ed.), *The International Court of Justice at a Crossroads*, New York, 1987, p. 183; and T. Sugihara, 'The judicial function of the International Court of Justice with respect to disputes involving highly political issues', in A. S. Muller, D. Raic and J. M. Thuránszky (eds), *The International Court of Justice*, The Hague, 1997, p. 117. Also S. V. Scott, 'Litigation versus dispute resolution through political processes', in N. Klein (ed.), *Litigating International Disputes*, Cambridge, 2014, p. 24.

[48] See generally L. Boisson de Chazournes and A Angelini, 'After "the court rose": the rise of diplomatic means to implement the pronouncements of the International Court of Justice', (2012) 11 *Law and Practice of International Courts and Tribunals*, 1–46.

[49] *Ambatielos*, Merits, Judgment [1953] ICJ Rep. 10. For similar use of the Court's advisory jurisdiction, see *Applicability of the Obligation to Arbitrate under Section 21 of the United Nations Headquarters Agreement of 26 June 1947*, Advisory Opinion [1988] ICJ Rep. 12.

of asking, as they might have done, for the Court to delimit their continental shelf boundaries in the North Sea, the parties asked only for an indication of the relevant 'principles and rules', leaving the delimitation itself to subsequent negotiation.[50] Step-by-step solutions of this kind are attractive to states which are willing to sacrifice a measure of control over their disputes, and so tend to produce few problems of implementation.

Although it is often clear that the parties are using adjudication as no more than a stage in the settlement of a dispute, there is sometimes room for argument as to their precise intentions. In such a case, which arises when there is a real or imagined ambiguity in the *compromis*, the Court's first task is to resolve the disagreement and establish the scope of its competence. Thus, Article 1 of the special agreement in the *Libya–Malta Continental Shelf* case asked the Court to decide what principles and rules of international law were applicable to their respective areas of continental shelf and also 'how in principle such principles and rules can be applied by the two Parties in this particular case in order that they may without difficulty delimit such areas', with this to be done by an agreement which was provided for in a later article.[51] Malta argued that, to perform its function, the Court would have to draw the boundary on a map, as in the *Tunisia–Libya* case. Libya, on the other hand, maintained that the situation was more like the *North Sea Continental Shelf* cases and that all that was needed was an indication of the relevant principles and rules. After hearing these arguments, the Court decided in the end that it was appropriate to draw a boundary line, though it did not accept Malta's argument in its entirety. Like other cases on the scope of jurisdictional instruments, this decision shows how, even when states have committed themselves to the Court in principle, the extent of their commitment may need to be clarified.

Of course, in many cases, states go to court with the clear aim of securing a definitive settlement. Provided both parties are willing litigants – and this is an important qualification – the resulting decision will usually be all that is required to end the dispute. In the *Minquiers and Ecrehos* case,[52] for example, where France and the United Kingdom went to the

---

[50] For a review of the Court's 'conciliatory' function in this and other cases, see C. F. Murphy, 'The World Court and the peaceful settlement of disputes' (1977) 7 *Ga J Int. and Comp. L*, 551.

[51] See *Continental Shelf (Libyan Arab Jamahiriya/Malta)*, Judgment [1985] ICJ Rep. 13 at 16. In a similar way, Cameroon's application in the *Land and Maritime Boundary* case asked the Court 'to specify definitively' the course of the land boundary which led to some argument between the parties as to the exact nature of its task. See J. G. Merrills, Note (2003) 52 *ICLQ*, 788 at 790.

[52] *Minquiers and Ecrehos*, Judgment [1953] ICJ Rep. 47. For comment, see D. H. N. Johnson, 'The Minquiers and Ecrehos case' (1954) 3 *ICLQ*, 189. 'Arm in arm' is from S. Rosenne, *The World Court*, 3rd ed., Deventer, 1974, p. 142. On the issue of compliance generally, see C. Paulson, 'Compliance with final judgments of the International Court of Justice since 1987' (2004) 98 *AJIL*, 434. See also C. Schulte, *Compliance with Decisions of the International Court of Justice*, Oxford, 2004. Also Y. Shany, *Assessing the Effectiveness of International Courts*, Oxford, 2014.

Court on an issue of territorial sovereignty 'arm in arm', there was never any doubt that the decision (which went against France) would be implemented. There is nothing surprising about this. Litigation is not an intrinsically hostile act, but a convenient way of depoliticising and settling a dispute by submitting it to third-party decision. A state which is willing to litigate will therefore be most unlikely to repudiate a decision, since to do so, apart from its inherent costs, would simply return the dispute to the political arena and so defeat the object of the exercise.

9.5.2 Implementation of Decisions

In certain cases of this kind, there may be difficulties of implementation attributable to technical factors. Boundary awards, for example, often require implementation through a subsequent process of demarcation. After the *Arbitral Award* case,[53] there were further negotiations between the parties concerning demarcation and a mixed commission was established by the Inter-American Peace Committee to settle certain outstanding problems. In the *Frontier Dispute* case, the issue of implementation was actually dealt with in the special agreement. Anticipating that, when the chamber made its award, they would need assistance in establishing the boundary on the ground, the parties agreed to demarcate the frontier within twelve months of the decision, and asked that, in its judgment, the chamber should nominate three experts to assist them in this work. In its decision in 1986, the chamber supported this arrangement in principle, but stated that, before nominating experts, it wished to ascertain the views of the parties 'particularly as regards the practical aspects of the exercise'.[54] Consequently, the three experts, a French lawyer, an Algerian cartographer and a Dutch geodetic consultant, were named by an order of the chamber in 1987.[55]

There are a number of other ways in which the parties can seek to minimise any problems of implementation. Thus, the special agreement in the *Gulf of Maine* case contained elaborate provisions on geographic coordinates, charts and other technical matters probably designed to avoid the problems of implementation encountered in the *Channel* arbitration.[56]

---

[53] *Arbitral Award Made by the King of Spain on 23 December 1906*, Judgment [1960] ICJ Rep. 192. See also the 1994 Agreement between Libya and Chad providing for implementation of the Court's judgment in the *Territorial Dispute* case [1994] ICJ Rep. 6. Text of the Agreement in (1994) 33 ILM 619.

[54] [1986] ICJ Rep. 648.

[55] *Frontier Dispute*, Nomination of Experts, Order of 9 April 1987 [1987] ICJ Rep. 7. The Court recently performed a similar function in the *Burkina Faso/Niger Frontier Dispute* case, see the Court's Order of 22 July 2013 [2013] ICJ Rep. 226.

[56] For the text of the Special Agreement, see (1981) 20 ILM 1378. On the problems in the *Channel* arbitration, see J. G. Merrills, 'The United Kingdom–France continental shelf arbitration' (1980) 10 *Calif. Western Int. LJ.*, 314 at 349–55.

Moreover, as a further safeguard, the agreement provided for the appointment of an expert to assist the chamber in technical matters and specifically in carrying out the parties' wishes as regarded the preparation and depiction of the maritime boundary. The expert who was appointed, a distinguished hydrographer, was supplied with copies of the parties' pleadings, and, besides being present at the oral proceedings, was available to the chamber throughout for consultation.

Another feature of the agreement in this case was a provision which entitled either side to request negotiations concerning the further extension of the parties' maritime boundary, following the chamber's decision. It went on to provide that, if such negotiations were held and no agreement was reached within a specified time, then, unless the dispute was referred to some other form of binding third-party procedure, either state was at liberty to bring it to the chamber. This interesting arrangement was a way of building on the parties' current commitment so as to provide in advance for the resolution of a possible future dispute. In contrast, in the special agreement under which the *Gabcikovo-Nagymaros* case was referred to the Court, the parties agreed that, following the judgment, they would 'enter into negotiations on the modalities for its execution' and that, if they were unable to reach agreement within six months, either party could request the Court for an 'additional judgment' on this issue.[57] This turned out to be a wise precaution, because, when efforts to secure implementation of the judgment proved unsuccessful, Slovakia was able to return to the Court in 1998 to request a further judgment.

In the *Armed Activities on the Territory of the Congo* case, the Court decided in 2005 that both Uganda and the Congo were under an obligation to make reparation to the other state for the injury caused.[58] Both parties attempted to settle the question of reparation through negotiations, but since the attempts proved unsuccessful, the case was brought again before the Court in 2015. The Court had, in its 2005 judgment, indicated that failing agreement between the Parties, the question of reparation due to Uganda and the Congo would be settled by the Court.

Another possibility is to include in the special agreement a provision allowing either party to return to the Court to seek clarification of its decision. In 2002, for example, Benin and Niger concluded a special agreement to take a boundary dispute to a chamber of the Court which included a provision laying down that the parties would begin the work of demarcation within eighteen months of the judgment being handed down, and that, in case of difficulty over implementation, either party could refer the matter back. Article 3 of the agreement in the *Tunisia–Libya*

---

[57] See Article 5 of the 1993 Special Agreement, text in (1993) 32 ILM 1293; and Appendix E.
[58] *Armed Activities on the Territory of the Congo (Democratic Republic of the Congo v. Uganda)* [2005] ICJ Rep. 168.

Continental Shelf case was to the same effect. In the *Avena* case,[59] Mexico sought to use Article 60 of the Court's Statute in a similar way. It will be recalled that this provision deals with interpretation and forms part of the Court's incidental jurisdiction. Mexico's complaint was that the United States had failed to implement parts of the Court's 2004 judgment concerning review of the convictions and sentences of certain Mexicans convicted of murder in the United States. The Court, however, decided that Mexico's request related to matters that had not been decided in the earlier judgment, with the result that it could not be entertained under Article 60.

In the event of a refusal to implement a decision, the successful party in a case has a number of options. The United Nations Charter requires states to comply with the Court's decisions (Article 94(1)) and Article 94(2) allows recourse to the Security Council which 'may make recommendations or decide upon measures to give effect to the judgment'. However, returning a case to the political arena in this way is difficult and a state may prefer to ask the Court to interpret the original judgment, if its meaning is genuinely disputed, or even bring a new case. In 2012, for example, the Court established the boundaries between the continental shelves of Nicaragua and Colombia, but the latter then repudiated the decision. In 2013 Nicaragua therefore initiated further proceedings against Colombia,[60] claiming that its actions represented a violation of Nicaragua's sovereign rights, as well as involving an unlawful threat of the use of force. Clearly, further proceedings may not always be possible, and like interpretation, are subject to the same problem of enforcement as the original judgment. In appropriate circumstances, however, they each provide options which may be more attractive than resort to the Security Council.

Suppose one of the states involved in the dispute is an unwilling party to the litigation. It has already been seen that unwillingness does not prevent the Court from deciding a case provided there is consent. Under Article 53 of the Statute, even the refusal of a party to appear is no obstacle, provided the Court has jurisdiction and is satisfied that the applicant's case is well founded in fact and in law.[61] Moreover, a state may be a most

---

[59] *Request for Interpretation of the Judgment of 31 March 2004 in the Case concerning Avena and Other Mexican Nationals (Mexico v. United States of America)*, Judgment [2009] ICJ Rep. 3; and see (2009) 103 *AJIL* 362.

[60] See *Alleged Violations of Sovereign Rights and Maritime Spaces in the Caribbean Sea*, ICJ Press Release 2013/36 (27 November 2013).

[61] For analysis of the problems posed by Art. 53, see Sir Gerald Fitzmaurice, 'The problem of the "non-appearing" defendant government' (1980) 51 *BYBIL*, 89; I. Sinclair, 'Some procedural aspects of recent international litigation' (1981) 30 *ICLQ*, 338; and J. I. Charney, 'Disputes implicating the institutional credibility of the Court', in L. F. Damrosch (ed.), *The International Court of Justice at a Crossroads*, New York, 1987, p. 288.

unwilling litigant and yet still carry out a decision. In the *Temple* case,[62] for example, Thailand strenuously contested the Court's jurisdiction, but accepted a decision assigning disputed territory to Cambodia. It is clear, however, that disputes in which states are brought to court against their will are those in which a settlement is least likely to be achieved by litigation.

There have unfortunately been several cases in which a decision against an unwilling state failed to settle a dispute. These include the *Fisheries Jurisdiction* cases (1974), the *Diplomatic Staff in Tehran* case (1980) and the *Nicaragua* case (1986). In the first, developments in the law of the sea soon made attempts at enforcement seem inappropriate; in the second case, any attempt to secure enforcement of the judgment through the Security Council could be blocked by a Soviet veto; while, in the *Nicaragua* case, the United States was in the same position. In all three cases, although there were legal issues which the Court could and did decide, these were bound up with wider issues which in the respondent's view made the case non-justiciable. Thus, in each of the cases, when the applicant made a unilateral attempt to depoliticise the dispute by referring it to the Court, the respondent refused to appear and the Court had to invoke Article 53.

The fact that willingness is often no less important than consent in achieving a judicial settlement does not, as is sometimes suggested, make independent recourse to the Court pointless. Apart from the obvious consideration that an unwilling respondent may be persuaded to change its policy, a state which is ready to litigate can use this fact to its advantage in a number of ways. When both sides have clearly accepted the Court's jurisdiction by treaty or in some other way, the initiation of litigation indicates that the applicant takes such arrangements seriously, as well as demonstrating its support for the principle that disputes about legal rights ought to be settled by adjudication. Britain's decision to take its dispute with Iceland to the Court achieved both these objectives. Because litigation is a way of depoliticising a dispute, a state which goes to the Court is also signalling its desire to reduce tension and pursue a peaceful settlement. This can be extremely important if feelings are running high, or both sides are engaged in warlike preparations, as was the case in the *Aegean Sea Continental Shelf* case. Finally – and here both the *Diplomatic Staff in Tehran* case and the *Nicaragua* case are very much in point – a state which takes its case to the Court and wins, gains vindication for its position from

---

[62] *Temple of Preah Vihear*, Merits, Judgment [1962] ICJ Rep. 6. For commentary, see D. H. N. Johnson, 'International Court of Justice, judgments of May 26, 1961 and June 15, 1962' (1962) 11 *ICLQ*, 1183. However, see the subsequent proceedings on interpretation described in Chapter 6 and necessitated by disagreement between the parties as to the meaning of the judgment.

an authoritative and disinterested source, which may be useful in securing the support of neutral opinion and consolidating that of allies.

9.6 Significance of the Court

Since it was established in 1945, the Court has dealt with nearly 180 contentious cases and requests for advisory opinions. It has delivered around 150 judgments and almost 600 orders, including orders on interim measures and procedural orders. Adding those advisory opinions which in substance concerned disputes between states does little to change the picture of a situation in which litigation remains exceptional and the vast majority of disputes are handled by other means. It would therefore be easy to conclude that the Court makes an insignificant contribution to dispute resolution. But that would be to underestimate its importance. The number of cases referred to the Court has risen considerably in recent years, and it is now not unusual for there to be ten or more cases on its list, denoting an unprecedented growth in popularity. Many treaties provide for the reference of disputes to the Court, and the number of states with declarations of some kind under the optional clause is slowly rising. It was pointed out earlier that commitments of this kind tend to discourage disputes, and so this 'background' role of the Court should not be overlooked. Furthermore, several disputes have been settled following reference of the matter to the Court, without requiring a decision.[63] Although cases which are settled out of court do not call for judgments, they are, of course, a further illustration of the contribution which the availability of adjudication makes to dispute resolution.

Notwithstanding the points which have just been made, it is clear that, by comparison with domestic courts, international courts and tribunals occupy a relatively insignificant position. Many explanations have been advanced for this situation, including the reluctance of states to surrender control over their disputes, particularly where important interests are involved, an unwillingness to trust the individuals who make up the Court, and the feeling that international law supplies inadequate answers to current problems.

Analysis of the cases which states are prepared to litigate, and, perhaps more significantly, those which they are not, suggests that there is a measure of truth in all of these explanations and over the years a major

---

[63] See the *Passage through the Great Belt* case, Order of 10 September 1992 [1992] ICJ Rep. 348, (1993) 32 ILM 101; the *Phosphate Lands in Nauru* case, Order of 13 September 1993 [1993] ICJ Rep. 322; the *Maritime Delimitation* case, Order of 8 November 1995 [1995] ICJ 423; and the *Aerial Incident of 3 July 1988*, Order of 22 February 1996 [1996] ICJ Rep. 9, (1996) 90 *AJIL* 278. In 2003, Libya agreed to discontinue the two *Lockerbie* cases against the United States and the United Kingdom: see ICJ Press Release 2003/29 (10 September 2003). See also the *Aerial Herbicide Spraying* case (2013) discussed in Chapter 2.

part of the literature concerning the Court has been devoted to considering how the present position can be improved.[64]

Various suggestions for encouraging use of the Court will be made in the final chapter, but one general point should perhaps be made here. It is that too much is sometimes expected of judicial settlement.[65] Even at the municipal level, litigation is the exception not the rule and most disputes are settled by other means. Therefore, while it is certainly worth considering what can be done to improve the Court, it is important not to become fixated with adjudication and overlook the contribution which can be made by other techniques such as conciliation. As we shall see in Chapter 10, both legal and non-legal methods of settlement are prominent features of the 1982 Law of the Sea Convention.

The fact that not all disputes are suitable for adjudication has been recognised by the Court itself, which on a number of occasions has made the point that judicial tribunals have no general mandate to decide all matters of international controversy, but occupy a specialised place in the machinery of dispute settlement. It is clear, for example, that because the Court can only adjudicate in cases where there is a 'dispute', as was also discussed in Chapter 1, its competence in contentious cases is limited to situations in which the parties' disagreement has achieved a measure of concretisation; or, to put it in a slightly different way, the function of the Court, like that of other judicial bodies, is not to head off disagreements before they become serious, nor to alleviate situations of amorphous tension, but to intervene only when called upon to resolve a particular crisis in the parties' relations.

The way in which adjudication is circumscribed underlines the part which political institutions and non-judicial processes can play at an earlier stage. So, as we shall see in Chapter 12, under Article 34 of the United Nations Charter, the Security Council may investigate 'any dispute or any situation which might lead to international friction or give rise to a dispute', while consultation through bilateral arrangements or regional institutions provides a way of avoiding disputes which need never reach the judicial stage.

Another way in which the role of the Court is limited can be seen by recalling our discussion of the justiciability of political disputes, in this

---

[64] See, for example, the essays in C. Peck and R. S. Lee (eds), *Increasing the Effectiveness of the International Court of Justice*, The Hague, 1997; and earlier in L. Gross (ed.), *The Future of the International Court of Justice*, New York, 1976. See also M. N. Shaw, 'The International Court of Justice: a practical perspective' (1997) 46 *ICLQ*, 831.

[65] See R. A. Falk, 'Realistic horizons for international adjudication' (1970–1) 11 *Va. JIL*, 314; R. B. Bilder, 'Some limitations of adjudication as a dispute settlement technique' (1982–3) 23 *Va. JIL*, 1, and 'International dispute settlement and the role of adjudication', in L. F. Damrosch (ed.), *The International Court of Justice at a Crossroads*, New York, 1987, p. 155. Also, N. Klein (ed.), *Litigating International Disputes*, Cambridge, 2014.

chapter and in Chapter 1. There are actually two limitations demonstrated here. One is that, although the Court can establish its competence in a case like *Nicaragua* at the technical level, its decisions, though not to be entirely discounted, clearly cannot solve disputes which raise much wider issues. The other limitation, which is related to the first, is that many disputes lie outside the Court's formal competence altogether, because they do not raise legal issues. So, as we have seen, unless the Court has been authorised to give a decision *ex aequo et bono*, it will not deal with questions which call for, say, a political or economic assessment, rather than a decision on legal grounds. Thus, in the *Haya de la Torre* case,[66] the Court refused to specify the manner in which its judgment in the *Asylum* case should be executed, on the ground that the way in which an unlawful grant of political asylum should be terminated depends on considerations of practicality or political expediency, which it is not the Court's function to assess.

A related point was raised by one of the preliminary issues in the *Western Sahara* case. In its request for an advisory opinion, the General Assembly asked the Court two questions: was the Western Sahara at the time of Spanish colonisation a territory belonging to no one (*terra nullius*)? If not, what were the legal ties between the territory and the neighbouring territories of Morocco and Mauritania? Spain argued that, since its title to the Western Sahara was not in issue, questions concerning the status of the territory at the time of colonisation, almost 100 years before, were only of historical interest and on grounds of propriety should not be answered. In the view of the Court, however, the object of the request was not to disinter a dead issue, but to obtain an opinion which might be of assistance to the General Assembly in dealing with the decolonisation of the territory. As such, the issues raised were sufficiently relevant to overcome any objection on grounds of propriety. Here, and in the earlier *Northern Cameroons* case,[67] the Court was in effect deciding when legal history is no longer a matter for litigation. The crucial difference was that, in the *Western Sahara* case, decolonisation had just begun, so legal considerations had a contemporary relevance, whereas in the *Northern Cameroons* case, since the essential decision had already been taken, raking over the ashes could serve no useful purpose.

Events occurring while a case is before the Court may raise analogous issues and further emphasise the distinctive characteristics of adjudication. The parties are at liberty to discontinue proceedings at any time and will normally do so when they have come to some arrangement outside the

---

[66] *Haya de la Torre*, Judgment [1951] ICJ Rep. 71. For commentary, see A. E. Evans, 'The Colombian–Peruvian Asylum case: termination of the judicial phase' (1951) 45 *AJIL*, 755.
[67] *Northern Cameroons*, Judgment [1963] ICJ Rep. 15. For analysis, see D. H. N. Johnson, 'The case concerning the Northern Cameroons' (1964) 13 *ICLQ*, 1143.

Court and further proceedings would serve no useful purpose. However, if a case is discontinued, this is regarded as the parties' prerogative and the Court will respect their decision without asking why they have done so. Unlike the position in certain other tribunals, therefore, there is no question of the Court retaining a case against the wishes of the parties.[68] Sometimes, moreover, the Court itself decides that the object of bringing a case has been achieved and that further proceedings are unnecessary. As we saw in Chapter 1, this was the situation in the *Nuclear Tests* cases,[69] where attaching exaggerated significance to French actions outside the Court enabled it to rule that the case had become moot and to dispose of a particularly awkward dispute without having to address the merits.

The *Nuclear Tests* cases had a sequel which provides further evidence of how the Court regards its function. The original proceedings were dismissed when France gave what the Court viewed as an undertaking that no further atmospheric nuclear tests would be carried out in the Pacific. The Court also stated that, if 'the basis' of its judgment were to be affected by future events, it would be open to the applicants 'to request an examination of the situation in accordance with the provisions of the Statute'.[70] In 1995, France announced that it intended to carry out a series of underground nuclear tests in the Pacific, which prompted New Zealand, one of the original applicants, to refer the situation back to the Court in reliance on the passage quoted.[71]

In the 1995 proceedings (*Nuclear Tests II* case), there were essentially two questions: whether it was open to the Court (in effect) to reopen the 1974 proceedings; and, if so, whether the necessary conditions were fulfilled for it to do so. The Court's answers were 'yes' to the first question, but 'no' to the second. The negative answer was based on its ruling that underground nuclear testing could not affect the basis of a judgment concerned only with atmospheric tests. Thus, here, the Court rejected the arguments of those who favoured expanding its role.[72] On the other hand, in answering the first question positively, the Court showed that, if France

---

[68] For discussion of the position of the European Court of Human Rights on this issue, see J. G. Merrills, *The Development of International Law by the European Court of Human Rights*, 2nd ed., Manchester, 1993, pp. 60–3.

[69] *Nuclear Tests*, Judgments [1974] ICJ Rep. 253 and 457. For criticism of these decisions, see P. Lellouche, 'The Nuclear Tests cases: judicial silence v. atomic blasts' (1975) 16 *Harv. Int. LJ.*, 614. In the *Arrest Warrant* case (2002), Belgium argued that events subsequent to the filing of the application had deprived the case of its object, but the Court rejected the argument: see para. 32 of the Judgment.

[70] *Nuclear Tests (New Zealand v. France)*, Judgment [1974] ICJ Rep. 457 at 477 (para. 63).

[71] See *Request for an Examination of the Situation in accordance with Paragraph 63 of the Court's Judgment of 20 December 1974 in the Nuclear Tests (New Zealand v. France) Case*, Order of 22 September 1995 [1995] ICJ Rep. 288. For commentaries, see M. C. R. Craven, Note (1996) 45 ICLQ, 725; and P. H. F. Bekker, Note (1996) 90 *AJIL*, 280.

[72] See the dissenting opinions of Judges Weeramantry, Koroma and Sir Geoffrey Palmer.

had resumed atmospheric tests, New Zealand could have challenged its action without having to bring fresh proceedings. As there is nothing in the Statute which expressly permits a case to be resurrected in this way, this was a bold piece of judicial legislation and an unusual enhancement of the Court's powers.

That the scope of the judicial function is limited and that states are reluctant to refer disputes to the Court are findings which could have been anticipated from our earlier discussion of arbitration. What, then, in conclusion, are the advantages of having an international court?

The first, and the most clear-cut, is that the existence of a standing court relieves states of the need to set up a new tribunal whenever a justiciable dispute arises. Besides saving the time and effort involved in creating such a tribunal (and the cost of financing its operation), the ability to refer a case to a tribunal with an established composition and procedure avoids the need to negotiate about the membership of the tribunal and related matters, and thereby avoids the problems which can arise with arbitration. Of course, the other side of the coin is that the flexibility of arbitration makes it the more attractive option when there are special requirements, a consideration which, as we have seen, has led the Court in recent cases to consider how it can adapt itself to the parties' wishes.

Second, to the extent that the avoidance and settlement of disputes are assisted by the development of international law, permanent courts, with their ability to develop a consistent jurisprudence,[73] may be expected to contribute more to legal progress than occasional arbitrations. Whether they can do so in fact depends, as already noted, on a number of factors, not least on the provision of suitable opportunities and the judges' perception of their role, but the possibility that through litigation 'the law can find some concrete measure of clarification and development'[74] is undeniably improved.

A final advantage is that a permanent tribunal provides a constant reminder to states of the availability of litigation as a means of peaceful settlement. True, there are now other standing tribunals of various kinds, including the International Tribunal for the Law of the Sea, discussed in the next chapter, and the Appellate Body of the World Trade Organization,

---

[73] See on this E. De Brabandere, 'The use of precedent and external case law by the International Court of Justice and the International Tribunal for the Law of the Sea' (2016) 15 *The Law and Practice of International Courts and Tribunals*, 24–55.

[74] [1970] ICJ Rep. 65 (Judge Fitzmaurice). For discussion of this aspect of the Court's work, see M. Lachs, 'Some reflections on the contribution of the International Court of Justice to the development of international law' (1983) 10 *Syr. J Int. L and Com.*, 239; and R. Y. Jennings, 'The judiciary, international and national, and the development of international law' (1996) 45 *ICLQ*. See also P. Kooijmans, 'The ICJ in the 21st century: judicial restraint, judicial activism, or proactive judicial policy' (2007) 56 *ICLQ*, 741. And Tams and Sloan (eds), *The Development of International Law* (n. 1).

examined in Chapter 11. Accordingly, the emblematic significance of the International Court has been reduced. On the other hand, since the newer courts and tribunals are all rather specialised, the International Court is still the only court with general competence in the sense that disputes relating to any aspect of international law may be brought before it. Thus, the fact of the Court's existence, together with a simple procedure for establishing its jurisdiction, continue to give a prominence to adjudication in the international field it would not otherwise enjoy.

9.7 Further Reading

9.7.1 General References on the International Court of Justice

d'Aspremont, J., and M. Mbengue, 'Strategies of engagement with scientific fact-finding in international adjudication' (2014) 5 *Journal of International Dispute Settlement*, 240–72.

Becker, M. A., and C. Rose, 'Investigating the value of site visits in inter-state arbitration and adjudication' (2017) 8 *Journal of International Dispute Settlement*, 219–49.

von Bogdandy, A., and I. Venzke, 'International courts as lawmakers', in R. Wolfrum, and I. Gätzschmann (eds) *International dispute settlement: room for innovations?*, Heidelberg, 2013, pp. 161–213.

Boisson de Chazournes, L., and A. Angelini, 'After "The Court Rose": the rise of diplomatic means to implement the pronouncements of the International Court of Justice' (2012) *The Law and Practice of International Courts and Tribunals*, 1–46.

Cancado Trindade, A., 'A century of international justice and prospects for the future', in M. Andenas and E. Bjorge (eds), *A Farewell to Fragmentation: Reassertion and Convergence in International Law*, Cambridge, 2015, pp. 56–86.

De Brabandere, E., 'The use of precedent and external case law by the International Court of Justice and the International Tribunal for the Law of the Sea' (2016) 15 *The law and practice of international courts and tribunals*, 24–55.

Devaney, J. G., *Fact-finding before the International Court of Justice*, Cambridge, 2016.

Eisemann, P.-M., and P. Pazartzis (eds), *La jurisprudence de la Cour internationale de Justice*, Paris, 2008.

Llamzon, A. P., 'Jurisdiction and compliance in recent decisions of the International Court of Justice' (2007) 18 *European Journal of International Law* 815–52.

Mbengue, M. M., 'Scientific Fact-finding at the International Court of Justice: An Appraisal in the Aftermath of the Whaling Case' (2016) 29 *Leiden Journal of International Law*, 529–50.

Odermatt, J., 'Patterns of avoidance: political questions before international courts' (2018) 14 *International Journal of Law in Context*, 221.

Pelet, A., 'Shaping the Future in International Law: The Role of the World Court in Law-Making', in *Looking to the Future – Essays on International Law in Honor of W. Michael Reisman*, Leiden/Boston, 2010, pp. 1065–83.

Schulte, C., *Compliance with Decisions of the International Court of Justice*, Oxford, 2004.

Tams, C. J., and J. Sloan (eds) *The Development of International Law by the International Court of Justice*, Oxford, 2013.

Tomka, P., and S. Wordsworth, 'The first site visit of the International Court of Justice in fulfilment of its judicial function' (1998) 92 *American Journal of International Law*, 133–40.

Venzke, I., 'Public interests in the International Court of Justice – A comparison between nuclear arms race (2016) and South West Africa (1966)' (2017) 111 *AJIL Unbound*, 68–74.

Wojcikiewicz Almeida, P., and J.-M. Sorel (eds), *Latin America and the International Court of Justice: Contributions to International Law*, London, 2017.

9.7.2 Treaties, Official Documents and Collections of Documents

Patel, B., *The World Court Reference Guide. Judgments, Advisory Opinions and Orders of the Permanent Court of International Justice and the International Court of Justice (1922–2000)*, The Hague, 2002.

Patel, B., *The World Court Reference Guide and Case-Law Digest. Judgments, Advisory Opinions and Orders of the Permanent Court of International Justice and the International Court of Justice (2001–2010) and Case-Law Digest (1992–2010)*, The Hague, 2014.

10

The Law of the Sea Convention

The methods of settlement considered so far can be used in all types of disputes and are available to all states. Alongside these general methods are to be found specialised procedures created by particular groups of states for the resolution of disputes in a specific subject area. We have already seen the specific nature of investor-state arbitration in Chapter 7. The machinery available for the settlement of disputes in other special fields will be considered in subsequent chapters. Chapter 11 examines dispute settlement in international trade law, while this chapter provides an outline and review of the arrangements for dispute settlement to be found in the 1982 United Nations Convention on the Law of the Sea (hereafter 'the Convention' or 'UNCLOS').

The 1982 Law of the Sea Convention came into force in November 1994, twelve months after the date of deposit of the sixtieth instrument of ratification or accession in accordance with Article 308. A little earlier, in July 1994, the UN General Assembly had adopted Resolution 48/263 with an annexed Agreement relating to the Implementation of Part XI of the 1982 Law of the Sea Convention,[1] the aim of which was to modify the provisions on the international seabed in order to make them acceptable to the industrialised states. The Agreement, which had been under negotiation for several years, does not affect the existing arrangements for dispute settlement, but, as a revision of the Convention, it must naturally be applied by the International Tribunal for the Law of the Sea (ITLOS) and other (arbitral) tribunals when exercising their jurisdiction. With the Agreement in place, the Convention looked set to achieve general acceptance, and so attention turned to the question of implementation.

The 1982 Convention contains 307 articles and eleven annexes and was eight years in negotiation.[2] With an instrument of such length and complexity, dealing with matters in which virtually all states have an interest of

---

[1] Text in (1994) 33 ILM 1309. For analysis of the Agreement and discussion of its significance, see B. H. Oxman, 'The 1994 Agreement and the Convention' (1994) 88 *AJIL*, 687; and D. H. Anderson, 'Further efforts to ensure universal participation in the United Nations Convention on the Law of the Sea' (1994) 43 *ICLQ*, 886.

[2] The evolution of the Convention can be conveniently traced through a series of articles published by J. R. Stevenson and B. H. Oxman in the *American Journal of International Law* between 1974 and 1982. For an excellent survey of the impact of the Conference, see R. R. Churchill and A. V. Lowe, *The Law of the Sea*, 3rd ed., Manchester, 1999.

some kind, certain issues naturally proved more difficult than others. Not surprisingly, dispute settlement was one of the most contentious issues and the provisions which now comprise Part XV of the Convention went through several versions before the text was finally agreed.

10.1 The Convention and its Dispute Settlement System

The Third United Nations Conference on the Law of the Sea (UNCLOS III) held its first substantive session at Caracas in 1974 and decided that the issue of dispute settlement should be dealt with by each Main Committee to the extent that the matter was relevant to its work. It soon became clear, however, that the three Main Committees were likely to be preoccupied with other issues and would be able to give little time to this question. An informal group was therefore established to consider the issue of dispute settlement, and the working paper which it produced supplied a focus for the Conference's early discussions. At the third session in 1975, the group was reconstituted as the Settlement of Disputes Group, and at the end of that session the Informal Single Negotiating Text, prepared by the President of the Conference, included a set of draft provisions on the subject.

After discussion at the fourth session, the President's draft was revised, and was considered again at the fifth session in 1976. Further revisions were incorporated in the Revised Single Negotiating Text in 1977 and the Informal Composite Negotiating Text in 1978. The identification of certain particularly difficult questions led to further discussions at the eighth session in 1979 and more modifications at the ninth session in the following year. Even as late as the tenth session in 1981, changes in the arrangements for dispute settlement were still being introduced, and the articles in question assumed their final form only when the Convention as a whole was approved and opened for signature in 1982.[3] The Convention came into force in November 1994.

At the outset, it is important to note that the UNCLOS does not allow the states party to the Convention to make any reservations, unless expressly permitted by certain specific articles of this Convention (Article 309). No such possibility exists in Part XV, which means that states party to the UNCLOS cannot 'opt out' of its dispute settlement provisions. However, as we will see, there are several ways in which the parties to a dispute can nonetheless avoid the compulsory methods of settlement provided for under Section 2. But the principle remains that UNCLOS

---

[3] For analysis of the provisions of the Convention relating to dispute settlement and discussion of their evolution, see S. Rosenne and L. B. Sohn (eds.), *United Nations Convention on the Law of the Sea 1982: A Commentary*, vol. V, Dordrecht, 1988; and A. O. Adede, *The System for Settlement of Disputes under the United Nations Convention on the Law of the Sea*, Dordrecht, 1987. Also N. Klein, *Dispute Settlement in the UN Convention on the Law of the Sea*, Cambridge, 2005.

provides a general system of dispute settlement to which the parties to the UNCLOS cannot make any reservations.

10.1.1 General Provisions and Voluntary Methods of Settlement

The Convention's dispute settlement provisions are situated in Part XV of the Convention and is divided into three sections. Section 1 contains general provisions on the peaceful settlement of disputes including voluntary dispute settlement methods. Section 2 contains compulsory methods of settlement, which in principle come into play only when a dispute has not been settled by recourse to Section 1. Section 3 finally contains exceptions and limitations to the compulsory methods of settlement. These sections are complemented by several annexes: Annex V (procedure for conciliation), Annex VI (Statute of the ITLOS), Annex VII (procedure for arbitration), and Annex VIII (procedure for special arbitration).

Section 1 of Part XV of the Convention proceeds from the basic principle that the states which are parties will settle any dispute between them concerning its interpretation or application by peaceful means in accordance with Article 2(3) of the United Nations Charter (Article 279). This has a double effect. It extends the obligation contained in the Charter to non-members of the United Nations if they become parties to the Convention; and, for all states, it confirms that disputes relating to the Convention must be settled by peaceful means. The Convention goes on to provide that nothing in Part XV of the Convention impairs the right of states to settle such a dispute by any peaceful means of their own choice (Article 280), and as a consequence gives the parties to a dispute the right to freely determine how their dispute will be settled. This may include resort to diplomatic means or legal methods of settlement, including the submission of the dispute to the ITLOS or the ICJ. This emphasis on the parties' autonomy is of course consistent with general practice and was not controversial. However, the principle of free choice of means is elaborated in later articles which underline its implications. These implications are notably, as we will see in Section 1.2 of this chapter, that resort to the compulsory methods of settlement under Section 2 of Part XV is excluded if a settlement has been reached by recourse to the voluntary methods of settlement under section 1 (Article 286).

Aside from article 280 which gives the parties the choice to freely determine how their dispute will be settled, when a dispute arises, the parties are under an obligation to 'proceed expeditiously to an exchange of views' as to the means of settlement to be adopted (Article 283(1)). This important provision, on which there is some significant case law,[4] is clearly

---

[4] See, for example, *Barbados/Trinidad and Tobago*, Award on Jurisdiction and Merits, (2006) 45 ILM 800. For an outline of earlier jurisprudence on Art. 283, see Klein, *Dispute Settlement in the UN Convention* (n. 3) pp. 62–4.

designed to emphasise negotiation or consultation and provide the obligation to use peaceful means with a procedural buttress. The precise meaning of the obligation to proceed to an 'exchange of views' has been discussed in several recent cases. Several tribunals have considered that in general the provision aims at an 'exchange of views' concerning the way in which the dispute will be settled rather than an obligation to negotiate the merits of the dispute. The Arbitral Tribunal in *Chagos Marine Protected Area Arbitration (Mauritius* v. *United Kingdom)*,[5] explained that the provision

> requires the Parties to exchange views regarding the means for resolving their dispute; it does not require the Parties to in fact engage in negotiations or other forms of peaceful dispute resolution. As a matter of textual construction, the Tribunal considers that Article 283 cannot be understood as an obligation to negotiate the substance of the dispute.[6]

This position has been endorsed by other arbitral tribunals such as in the *South China Sea Arbitration (the Philippines* v. *China)* arbitration,[7] and the *Arctic Sunrise (Netherlands* v. *Russia)* arbitration.[8]

The ITLOS also has on several occasions been confronted with the question of whether the requirement for an 'exchange of views' has been exhausted. In the *'ARA Libertad' (Argentina* v. *Ghana)* case, the Tribunal confirmed its position in the *Mox Plant* case that 'a State Party is not obliged to continue with an exchange of views when it concludes that the possibilities of reaching agreement have been exhausted'.[9] In the *M/T 'San Padre Pio' Case (Switzerland* v. *Nigeria)*, the Tribunal similarly held that, since Switzerland received no response from the Nigerian authorities to its various communications, 'Switzerland could reasonably conclude that the possibility of reaching agreement was exhausted'.[10] In these cases, however, the ITLOS has not explicitly confirmed that the 'exchange of views' requirements concerns only the way in which the dispute will be settled and not the merits of the dispute.

In any event, the obligation to exchange views also arises when a settlement has been reached and 'the circumstances require consultation regarding the manner of implementing the settlement' (Article 283(2)) and also when a procedure has been used unsuccessfully. In this last situation,

---

[5] *Chagos Marine Protected Area Arbitration (Mauritius* v. *United Kingdom)*, PCA Case Nr. 2011-03, Award, 18 March 2015.
[6] *Ibid.*, para. 378.
[7] *The South China Sea Arbitration (The Republic of Philippines* v. *The People's Republic of China)*, PCA Case No. 2013-19, Award on Jurisdiction and Admissibility, 29 October 2015, paras 332 ff.
[8] *Arctic Sunrise (Kingdom of the Netherlands* v. *Russian Federation)*, PCA Case No. 2014-02, Merits, Award of 14 August 2015, para. 151.
[9] "ARA Libertad" *(Argentina* v. *Ghana)*, Provisional Measures, Order of 15 December 2012, ITLOS Reports 2012, p. 332, para. 71. See also *MOX Plant (Ireland* v. *United Kingdom)*, Provisional Measures, Order of 3 December 2001, ITLOS Reports 2001, p. 95, at p. 107, para. 60.
[10] *The M/T "San Padre Pio" Case (Switzerland* v. *Nigeria)*, Provisional Measures, Order of 6 July 2019, para. 73.

as has been pointed out, the effect is to ensure that a move from one means of settlement to another is never automatic, which inevitably reduces the impact of the Convention's own arrangements.[11]

10.1.2 'Avoiding' Compulsory Settlement: Articles 281 and 282 UNCLOS

No less significant is the provision laying down that, when the parties have selected a particular means of peaceful settlement, the procedures laid down later in the Convention apply only if such means prove unsuccessful and the agreement between the parties does not exclude any further procedure (Article 281). Moreover, any agreement of a general, regional, bilateral or other nature providing for the submission of a dispute to a procedure involving a binding decision supplants the procedure laid down later in the Convention, unless the parties otherwise agree (Article 282). Both articles have been discussed in several cases, and their precise meaning and implications have been the subject of discussion and debate.[12]

In general terms, both articles have a similar aim, that is to enable the parties by agreement in advance to avoid the settlement machinery provided in the Convention.[13] However, both articles cover different situations. Article 281 ('Procedure where no settlement has been reached by the parties') is worded as follows:

> 1. If the States Parties which are parties to a dispute concerning the interpretation or application of this Convention have agreed to seek settlement of the dispute by a peaceful means of their own choice, the procedures provided for in this Part apply only where no settlement has been reached by recourse to such means and the agreement between the parties does not exclude any further procedure.
> 2. If the parties have also agreed on a time-limit, paragraph 1 applies only upon the expiration of that time-limit.

Article 281 generally 'refers to agreements between the parties that may derogate from the principle of compulsory and binding third-party settlement set forth in Article 286'.[14] Article 281 applies notably to non-binding settlement procedures.[15] As another author explained, the context for which the provision is designed is

---

[11] See A. O. Adede, 'The basic structure of the disputes settlement part of the Law of the Sea Convention' (1982) 11 *Ocean Devel. and Int. L.*, 125 at 129.
[12] See amongst others B. H. Oxman, 'Complementary Agreements and Compulsory Jurisdiction', (2001) 95 *American Journal of International Law*, 277 and N. Bankes, 'Precluding the applicability of Section 2 of Part XV of the Law of the Sea Convention' (2017) 48 *Ocean Development & International Law*, 268.
[13] It should be noted, however, that disputes concerning the seabed are subject to the special provisions of Part XI, Section 5, described below. Interpretation of Article 281 was crucial in the *Southern Bluefin Tuna* arbitration (2000), described in the text accompanying note 31 below.
[14] B. H. Oxman, 'Complementary Agreements and Compulsory Jurisdiction' (n. 12), 281.
[15] N. Bankes, 'Precluding the Applicability of Section 2 of Part XV of the Law of the Sea Convention' (n. 12), 259.

one in which the parties to an UN Convention on the Law of the Sea dispute are seeking a negotiated settlement and agree to resort, for example, to conciliation. If this does not result in settlement, then the parties would remain free to resort to the UN Convention on the Law of the Sea procedures unless they had specifically agreed otherwise.[16]

As explained by the Arbitral Tribunal in *Barbados* v. *Trinidad and Tobago*:

> Article 281 is intended primarily to cover the situation where the Parties have come to an ad hoc agreement as to the means to be adopted to settle the particular dispute which has arisen.[17]

Article 281 applies only under the following conditions. The parties to a dispute concerning the interpretation or application of this Convention (1) 'have agreed to seek settlement of the dispute by a peaceful means of their own choice'; (2) 'no settlement has been reached by recourse to such means'; and (3) 'the agreement between the parties does not exclude any further procedure'.

Article 282 ('Obligations under general, regional or bilateral agreements') in turn is worded as follows:

> If the States Parties which are parties to a dispute concerning the interpretation or application of this Convention have agreed, through a general, regional or bilateral agreement or otherwise, that such dispute shall, at the request of any party to the dispute, be submitted to a procedure that entails a binding decision, that procedure shall apply in lieu of the procedures provided for in this Part, unless the parties to the dispute otherwise agree.

Article 282 has been described as dealing with 'choice of forum: the means of compulsory and binding third-party settlement set forth in the Convention do not supplant a forum for such settlement otherwise chosen by both parties.'[18]

In order for the procedure mentioned in Article 282 to apply in lieu of the 'compulsory methods' under Section 2 of Part XV of the Convention, the following is required: (1) an agreement through a general, regional or bilateral agreement or otherwise, (2) an agreement that a dispute shall, at the request of any party to the dispute, be submitted to a procedure that entails a binding decision, and (3) the absence of an agreement of the parties to the contrary. The mention of 'otherwise', after general, regional or bilateral agreement as instruments by which states can agree to a procedure entailing a binding decision, has been interpreted as implying, for example, 'an agreement to the jurisdiction of [the International Court

---

[16] A. Boyle, 'The Southern Bluefin Tuna Arbitration' (2001) 50 *ICLQ*, 447 449.
[17] *Barbados* v. *Trinidad and Tobago*, PCA Case 2004-02, Award of the Arbitral Tribunal, 11 April 2006, para. 200.
[18] B. H. Oxman, 'Complementary Agreements and Compulsory Jurisdiction' (n. 1) 280.

of Justice] that is expressed in optional clause declarations.'[19] The situation which may occur that the agreement to dispute settlement through a procedure that entails a binding decision itself contains a reservation either for disputes which either are related to the issues covered by the UNCLOS, or for disputes which the parties have agreed to settle via other means. Both instances were discussed by the ICJ in *Maritime Delimitation in the Indian Ocean (Somalia v. Kenya)*. In relation to the first situation, the Court held that:

> if a reservation to an optional clause declaration excluded disputes concerning a particular subject (for example, a reservation excluding disputes relating to maritime delimitation), there would be no agreement to the Court's jurisdiction falling within Article 282, so the procedures provided for in Section 2 of Part XV would apply to those disputes, subject to the limitations and exceptions that result from the application of Section 3.[20]

In relation to the second situation, the Court held that an optional clause declaration which excludes from the jurisdiction of the Court disputes as to which the parties have agreed on another method of settlement, as Kenya had made:

> falls within the scope of [Article 282] and applies 'in lieu' of procedures provided for in Section 2 of Part XV, even when such declarations contain a reservation to the same effect as that of Kenya. The contrary interpretation would mean that, by ratifying a treaty which gives priority to agreed procedures resulting from optional clause declarations (pursuant to Article 282 of UNCLOS), States would have achieved precisely the opposite outcome, giving priority instead to the procedures contained in Section 2 of Part XV. Consequently, under Article 282, the optional clause declarations of the Parties constitute an agreement, reached 'otherwise', to settle in this Court disputes concerning interpretation or application of UNCLOS, and the procedure before this Court shall thus apply 'in lieu' of procedures provided for in Section 2 of Part XV.[21]

The difference between both articles is not always clear in practice, however. The Tribunal in the *South China Sea* arbitration for example, analysed the application of both provisions to virtually the same 'agreements': The Convention on Biological Diversity (CBD), the 2020 China–ASEAN Declaration on the Conduct of Parties in the South China Sea, and the 1976 Treaty of Amity and Cooperation in Southeast Asia. This would imply that both provisions could in theory apply to similar situations.

---

[19] *Maritime Delimitation in the Indian Ocean (Somalia v. Kenya)*, Preliminary Objections, Judgment, ICJ Reports 2017, p. 3, para. 126.
[20] *Maritime Delimitation in the Indian Ocean (Somalia v. Kenya)*, Preliminary Objections, Judgment, ICJ Reports 2017, p. 3, para. 128.
[21] *Maritime Delimitation in the Indian Ocean (Somalia v. Kenya)*, Preliminary Objections, Judgment, ICJ Reports 2017, p. 3, para. 130.

Under both Article 281 and 282, the dispute moreover must be 'a dispute concerning the interpretation or application of this Convention'. As several cases have shown, many disputes in relation to the law of the sea can fall under both the Law of the Sea Convention, and another treaty. Examples are the *OSPAR Convention*,[22] the Convention for the Conservation of Southern Bluefin Tuna (CCSBT),[23] the Convention on Biological Diversity (CBD)[24] or bilateral treaties.[25] The question then is whether such disputes can be 'separated'.

The arbitral tribunal in the *Southern Bluefin Tuna* case argued that a dispute existed under both the Convention for the Conservation of Southern Bluefin Tuna (CCSBT) and the Law of the Sea Convention; it considered that it would be 'artificial' to treat both disputes as distinct disputes.[26] As a consequence, it considered that the parties had agreed under Article 281 to settle the dispute through the dispute settlement mechanism of the CCSBT rather than those under the Law of the Sea Convention. However, most decisions rendered after the *Southern Bluefin Tuna* case, did accept that disputes falling both under the Law of the Sea Convention and another 'agreement', could be separated. For example, in the *South China Sea* arbitration, the Tribunal acknowledged an 'overlap' between the obligations contained in both the Law of the Sea Convention and the Convention on Biological Diversity (CBD).[27] The Tribunal however argued that 'the two treaties establish parallel environmental regimes that overlap in a discrete area', and concluded, endorsing the position of the Philippines, that '[a] dispute under UNCLOS does not become a dispute under the CBD merely because there is some overlap between the two. Parallel regimes remain parallel regimes'.[28]

Section 1 in general shows that the Convention's first principle is peaceful settlement with free choice of means. But what happens if the parties cannot agree upon a means of settlement, or if they choose a means which proves unsuccessful? At this stage, after the exchange of views

---

[22] *MOX Plant (Ireland. United Kingdom)*, Provisional Measures, Order of 3 December 2001, ITLOS Reports 2001, p. 95.

[23] *Southern Bluefin Tuna Case (Australia and New Zealand v. Japan)*, Award on Jurisdiction and Admissibility (2000), text in (2009) 39 ILM 1359.

[24] *The South China Sea Arbitration (The Republic of Philippines v. The People's Republic of China)*, PCA Case No. 2013-19, Award on Jurisdiction and Admissibility, 29 October 2015.

[25] E.g. *The South China Sea Arbitration (The Republic of Philippines v. The People's Republic of China)*, PCA Case No. 2013-19, Award on Jurisdiction and Admissibility, 29 October 2015; *Dispute Concerning Coastal State Rights in the Black Sea, Sea of Azov, and Kerch Strait (Ukraine v. the Russian Federation)* PCA Case No. 2017-06, Award on Preliminary Objections, 21 February 2020.

[26] *Southern Bluefin Tuna Case (Australia and New Zealand v. Japan)*, Award on Jurisdiction and Admissibility (2000), text in (2009) 39 ILM 1359, para. 54.

[27] *The South China Sea Arbitration (The Republic of Philippines v. The People's Republic of China)*, PCA Case No. 2013-19, Award on Jurisdiction and Admissibility, 29 October 2015, para. 284.

[28] *Ibid.*, para. 285.

required by Article 283 has taken place, and provided that Articles 281 and 282 do not apply, Section 2 of Part XV, entitled 'Compulsory Procedures Entailing Binding Decisions', comes into play.

10.2 Principle of Compulsory Settlement

Whether or not the Convention should incorporate articles providing for the compulsory settlement of disputes was a question which provoked considerable disagreement. The corresponding provisions of the 1958 Conventions on the Law of the Sea were merely an optional protocol to the Conventions, and one view was that the same approach should be adopted in the new Convention. However, many found this unacceptable on the ground that the interpretation and application of an instrument containing so many innovations was bound to generate disputes which could only be resolved by the use of a third-party procedure which was both obligatory, in the sense that it had to be used, and binding in its result. As noted earlier, the knowledge that recourse to such procedures is ultimately possible also discourages unreasonableness and so acts as a means of dispute avoidance, and this too was no doubt a salient consideration. It was therefore eventually decided that compulsory procedures of some kind should be incorporated.

10.2.1 Choice of Methods of Binding Settlement

Article 286 provides that, where no settlement has been reached by recourse to Section 1, at the request of a party to a dispute concerning the interpretation or application of this Convention, the dispute may be submitted at the request of any party to the court or tribunal having jurisdiction under Section 2. The compulsory methods of settlement under Section 2 thus come into play only when a dispute has been settled by application of the rules and methods provided for in Section 1.

The first problem in establishing a procedure for securing binding decisions in an instrument such as the Convention is to find a method which all the parties to the instrument can accept. The International Court was not universally supported, yet was preferred by some states to alternatives such as permanent tribunals with restricted jurisdiction, or ad hoc arbitration. At the Conference, it became clear that there was so much disagreement that it was unlikely that a single method could be nominated.[29] Whereas several states wished disputes to be referred to the International Court and pointed to the contribution which its decisions had already made to the development of the law of the sea, others

---

[29] See Rosenne and Sohn, *Commentary* (n. 3) pp. 41–5.

considered that disputes relating to the 'new' law of the sea could be more appropriately handled by a new tribunal. A third group regarded any kind of standing court as too rigid and emphasised the flexibility of arbitration, while a fourth group considered that the technical issues raised by many law of the sea disputes called for a functional approach and the creation of specialised bodies. Faced with this wide divergence of views, the negotiators of the Convention took the only practicable course and resolved the problem by again invoking the principle of freedom of choice, this time in the form of a choice of methods of binding settlement, which has been termed a 'cafeteria approach'.[30] Article 287 gives the parties to the UNCLOS a choice in different methods of binding settlement. The Convention provides for states to make a written declaration accepting that disputes may be referred to one or more of the following tribunals: the 'International Tribunal for the Law of the Sea'; the International Court; or an arbitral tribunal, or a special arbitral tribunal, with both forms of arbitral tribunal to be constituted in accordance with the Convention. Where both parties to a dispute have accepted the same procedure, that procedure is to be used, unless the parties otherwise agree. Where, however, they have accepted different procedures (or one party has not accepted any procedure), then the dispute may be referred to arbitration.[31] These arrangements, which are set out in Article 287 of the Convention, represent a neat solution to the problem of choice of forum and, subject to a point considered below, can be said to establish a useful and flexible system of compulsory jurisdiction.

The articles which comprise the remainder of Section 2 of Part XV of the Convention deal with a number of matters relevant to the functioning of the system of obligatory settlement. The unique role of another body, the 'Seabed Disputes Chamber', is recognised in Article 287(2). The crucial question of jurisdiction *ratione materiae* is dealt with in Article 288, which provides for the reference of disputes concerning the interpretation or application of the Convention and any international agreement 'related to the purposes' of the Convention. Article 289 provides for the appointment of scientific or technical experts. Another provision reminiscent of the Court's Statute, Article 290, authorises the prescribing of provisional measures of protection (though only at the request of a party to the dispute), while Article 292, which was difficult to negotiate, but has proved very important in practice, deals with the problem of securing the prompt

---

[30] A. Boyle, 'Dispute settlement and the Law of the Sea Convention,' (1997) 46 *International and Comparative Law Quarterly*, 37, 40.

[31] Attempts to use the International Court of Justice or the International Tribunal for the Law of the Sea for this purpose were abandoned in 1977; see A. O. Adede, 'Prolegomena to the dispute settlement part of the Law of the Sea Convention' (1977–8) 10 *NYUJ Int. L and Politics*, 253 at 340.

release of vessels and crews detained by national authorities. These procedures will be discussed later in this chapter.

An unusual provision permits a court or tribunal exercising compulsory jurisdiction to determine whether a claim 'constitutes an abuse of legal process or whether *prima facie* it is well founded' (Article 294). If the claim is determined to be an abuse of legal process, or prima facie unfounded, the court or tribunal in question is to take no further action in the case. This provision was inserted at quite a late stage to meet the concern of certain coastal states that they might be hampered in exercising their rights within the exclusive economic zone by a proliferation of groundless applications. It resembles Article 35(3) of the European Convention on Human Rights[32] in that it provides a way of disposing of frivolous applications and should also have a tendency to discourage them. The Arbitral Tribunal in the *South China Sea* arbitration has considered that it is entitled to determine *proprio motu* whether a claim constitutes an abuse of legal process.[33]

Another provision with a counterpart in the European Convention is Article 295, which confirms that exhaustion of local remedies is a condition of admissibility for certain claims.[34] However, this only applies when such exhaustion is 'required by international law'. The effect is therefore to preserve the requirement for those disputes where the existence of local remedies would normally be relevant, without imposing it in disputes involving the direct interests of states, or other situations, in which it has not traditionally been necessary.

10.2.2 The Applicable Law and the Jurisdiction of Tribunals under Section 2

The question of choice of law is dealt with by a directive to courts and tribunals having jurisdiction under Article 293(1), which provides

> A court or tribunal having jurisdiction under this section shall apply this Convention and other rules of international law not incompatible with this Convention.

This provision thus implies that tribunals established under the Convention will primarily apply the Convention itself. In the earlier

---

[32] Article 35(3) provides: 'The Court shall declare inadmissible any individual application submitted under Article 34 which it considers incompatible with the provisions of the Convention or the protocols thereto, manifestly ill-founded, or an abuse of the right of application'. In the original Convention, the corresponding provision was Art. 27(2). For discussion of Art. 294, see T. Treves, 'Preliminary proceedings in the settlement of disputes under the United Nations Law of the Sea Convention: some observations', in N. Ando, E. McWhinney and R. Wolfrum (eds), *Liber Amicorum Judge Shigeru Oda*, The Hague, 2002, p. 749.
[33] *The South China Sea Arbitration (The Republic of Philippines v. The People's Republic of China)*, PCA Case No. 2013-19, Award on Jurisdiction and Admissibility, 29 October 2015, para. 128.
[34] See Art. 35(1), formerly Art. 26, of the European Convention.

discussion of arbitration and judicial settlement, we saw that the basis of an international tribunal's decision is a matter to which states, for obvious reasons, attach very great importance. Bearing in mind the widely held view that the reluctance of 'new' states to use the International Court in the immediate post-colonial period stemmed from a distrust of traditional international law, it is not difficult to see why the 'new' law of the sea, reflecting as it does the influence of those states in many of its elements, should have been given such priority in the Convention.

However, there is also room for the application of 'other rules of international law'. As was noted by the Arbitral Tribunal in *Arctic Sunrise*

> In order properly to interpret and apply particular provisions of the Convention, it may be necessary for a tribunal to resort to foundational or secondary rules of general international law such as the rules of State responsibility.
>
> In the case of some broadly worded or general provisions, it may also be necessary to rely on primary rules of international law other than the Convention in order to interpret and apply particular provisions of the Convention. Both arbitral tribunals and ITLOS have interpreted the Convention as allowing for the application of relevant rules of international law. Article 293 of the Convention makes this possible. For instance, in M/V 'SAIGA' No. 2, ITLOS took account of general international law rules on the use of force in considering the use of force for the arrest of a vessel.[35]

As we noted in the introductory chapter, the question of jurisdiction is different from that of the 'applicable law'.[36] The 'applicable law' defines the law to be applied by the court or tribunal to the merits of the case, and is regulated by Article 293, which we have just discussed. Jurisdiction, however, is regulated by Article 288 of the Convention. As explained by the Arbitral Tribunal in the *Mox Plant* case, 'there is a cardinal distinction between the scope of its jurisdiction under article 288, paragraph 1, of the Convention, on the one hand, and the law to be applied by the Tribunal under article 293 of the Convention, on the other hand'.[37] There is, however, a close interaction between jurisdiction and applicable law, as was noted in the introductory chapter.[38]

---

[35] *Arctic Sunrise (Kingdom of the Netherlands v. Russian Federation)*, PCA Case No. 2014-02, Merits, Award of 14 August 2015, paras 190–1.

[36] On the distinction and its consequences, see M. Wood, 'The International Tribunal for the Law of the Sea and general international law', (2007) 22 *Int'l J. Marine & Coastal L.*, 351.

[37] *The MOX Plant Case (Ireland v. United Kingdom)*, PCA Case No. 2002-01, Order No. 3, Suspension of Proceedings on Jurisdiction and Merits, and Request for Further Provisional Measures, 24 June 2003, para. 19. See also *Arctic Sunrise (Kingdom of the Netherlands v. Russian Federation)*, PCA Case No. 2014-02, Merits, Award of 14 August 2015, para. 188.

[38] See in general: K. Parlett, 'Beyond the four corners of the convention: expanding the scope of jurisdiction of Law of the Sea Tribunals' (2017) 48 *Ocean Development & International Law*, 284 and J. Harrison, 'Defining disputes and characterizing claims: subject-matter jurisdiction in Law of the Sea Convention litigation' (2017) 48 *Ocean Development & International Law*, 269.

Although a Tribunal's competence can be extended by agreement of the parties to a dispute so as to encompass jurisdiction over disputes concerning the interpretation or application of an international agreement related to the UNCLOS,[39] the Tribunal in principle has no jurisdiction over disputes arising under general international law.[40] The Arbitral Tribunal in *Arctic Sunrise* explained that the applicable law clause in Article 293 in principle does not extend the jurisdiction of a tribunal:

> Article 293(1) does not extend the jurisdiction of a tribunal. Rather, it ensures that, in exercising its jurisdiction under the Convention, a tribunal can give full effect to the provisions of the Convention. For this purpose, some provisions of the Convention directly incorporate other rules of international law.
>
> Article 293 is not [...] a means to obtain a determination that some treaty other than the Convention has been violated, unless that treaty is otherwise a source of jurisdiction, or unless the treaty otherwise directly applies pursuant to the Convention.[41]

It should be reminded that, as discussed in Chapter 6, several jurisdictional questions have arisen in the work of arbitral tribunals established under Annex VII of the UNCLOS on precisely the question of whether certain claims could be considered to fall under the issues referred to by the parties to the dispute. We refer the reader to Chapter 6, where these cases were discussed in detail, but it is important to re-emphasise the main points here. An issue that has arisen in several recent international arbitrations concerns the question of whether an arbitral tribunal is authorized to settle questions of territorial sovereignty of the states parties to the dispute as 'ancillary' questions.

It was explained in Chapter 6 that questions relating to the application and interpretation of the UNCLOS often imply questions in respect of a dispute over land sovereignty, and hence trigger the question of whether the tribunal has jurisdiction to decide that aspect of the case. In the *Dispute Concerning Coastal State Rights in the Black Sea, Sea of Azov, and Kerch Strait (Ukraine v. the Russian Federation)* arbitration,[42] which concerned the question of coastal state rights of both states in the Black Sea, Sea of Azov, and Kerch Strait, the Tribunal established that a sovereignty dispute existed, and concluded that the dispute regarding sovereignty over Crimea 'is not a minor issue ancillary to the dispute concerning the interpretation

---

[39] Articles 21(2) and 22 ITLOS Statute; Article 288(2) UNCLOS.
[40] Wood, 'The International Tribunal for the Law of the Sea and General International Law' (n. 36) 351, 357.
[41] *Arctic Sunrise (Kingdom of the Netherlands v. Russian Federation)*, PCA Case No. 2014-02, Merits, Award of 14 August 2015, paras 181 and 1921.
[42] *Dispute Concerning Coastal State Rights in the Black Sea, Sea of Azov, and Kerch Strait (Ukraine v. the Russian Federation)* PCA Case No. 2017-06, Award on Preliminary Objections, 21 February 2020.

or application of the Convention'.[43] The Tribunal as a consequence concluded that it had no jurisdiction over Ukraine's claims, to the extent that a ruling of the tribunal would necessarily require it to decide, directly or implicitly, on the sovereignty of either party over Crimea.

In the *Chagos* arbitration, the Arbitral Tribunal confirmed that 'where a dispute concerns the interpretation or application of the Convention, the jurisdiction of a court or tribunal pursuant to Article 288(1) [UNCLOS] extends to making such findings of fact or ancillary determinations of law as are necessary to resolve the dispute presented to it'.[44] The Tribunal declined jurisdiction over certain parts of Mauritius' claim, including the question of whether the United Kingdom was entitled to declare a 'Marine Protected Area' zone in the *Chagos Archipelago*, since this would have implied for the Tribunal to decide whether the United Kingdom was the 'coastal state' and hence had territorial sovereignty.

In 2021, an ITLOS Special Chamber has again discussed the matter in the case *Dispute concerning delimitation of the maritime boundary between Mauritius and Maldives in the Indian Ocean (Mauritius/Maldives)*. In its decision on preliminary objections,[45] the Special Chamber was confronted to the question of whether it had jurisdiction over the question of who holds sovereign rights over the Chagos Archipelago. The Maldives had argued that there is a sovereignty dispute between Mauritius and the United Kingdom, which would not only require the United Kingdom to be a participant in the case, but also result in the ITLOS declining jurisdiction. The difference between the case before the ITLOS Special Chamber, and the case before the *Chagos* Arbitral Tribunal, lies in the fact that in 2019 the International Court of Justice rendered an advisory opinion on the question of the separation of the Chagos Archipelago from Mauritius in 1965,[46] in which it held that, following the separation of the Chagos Archipelago, the process of decolonisation of Mauritius was not lawfully completed when that country acceded to independence in 1968 and that the United Kingdom was under an obligation to bring to an end its administration of the Chagos Archipelago as rapidly as possible.

The ITLOS Special Chamber considered that it was 'competent to assess the Parties' dispute as to the consequences of the advisory opinion to the

---

[43] *Dispute Concerning Coastal State Rights in the Black Sea, Sea of Azov, and Kerch Strait (Ukraine v. the Russian Federation)* PCA Case No. 2017-06, Award on Preliminary Objections, 21 February 2020, para. 195.
[44] *Chagos Marine Protected Area Arbitration (Mauritius v. United Kingdom)*, PCA Case Nr. 2011-03, Reasoned Decision on Challenge, 30 November 2011, para. 220.
[45] *Dispute concerning delimitation of the maritime boundary between Mauritius and Maldives in the Indian Ocean (Mauritius/Maldives)*, Preliminary Objections, Judgment of 28 January 2021.
[46] *Legal Consequences of the Separation of the Chagos Archipelago from Mauritius in 1965*, Advisory Opinion, ICJ Reports 2019, p. 95.

extent necessary to determine its jurisdiction',[47] presenting the issue as one relating to the effect of the advisory opinion of the ICJ, rather than a dispute over sovereignty as such. The Special Chamber argued that it was competent to consider the Parties' disagreement on the consequences of the *Chagos* advisory opinion falls outside its jurisdiction since, under article 288(4) of the Convention, the Special Chamber has the competence to decide its own jurisdiction.[48] It then concluded, based on the advisory opinion of the ICJ, that

> Mauritius can be regarded as the coastal State in respect of the Chagos Archipelago for the purpose of the delimitation of a maritime boundary even before the process of the decolonization of Mauritius is completed. In the Special Chamber's view, to treat Mauritius as such State is consistent with the determinations made in the *Chagos* arbitral award, and, in particular, the determinations made in the *Chagos* advisory opinion which were acted upon by UNGA resolution 73/295.[49]

Finally, it is noteworthy that the parties may agree to request a decision *ex aequo et bono* (Article 293(2)), but, unless they do so, the clear intention is that the Convention will prevail over other sources of obligation.

10.2.3 Exceptions and Limitations to the Principle of Compulsory Settlement

The third and final Section of Part XV of the Convention is headed 'Limitations and Exceptions to the Applicability of Section 2' and concerns disputes which are not, or need not be, subject to the procedures just described, and in certain cases may be referred to another compulsory procedure instead. Thus, if the principle of Section 2 is that disputes which the parties have failed to settle by means of their own choice are, as a general rule, to be submitted to some form of binding method of settlement, Section 3 proceeds on the assumption that certain disputes ought not to be subject to obligatory settlement at all, while others call for a procedure not involving adjudication.

Section 3 contains two important exceptions to the principle of compulsory settlement: Article 297 ('Limitations on applicability of section 2') which concerns the exercise by coastal states of sovereign rights or jurisdiction (freedoms of navigation, fisheries, marine scientific research ...),[50]

---

[47] *Dispute concerning delimitation of the maritime boundary between Mauritius and Maldives in the Indian Ocean (Mauritius/Maldives)*, Preliminary Objections, Judgment of 28 January 2021, para. 190.
[48] Ibid., para. 191.   [49] Ibid., para. 250.
[50] For a comprehensive overview of the application of the Article, see S. Allen, 'Article 297 of the United Nations Convention on the Law of the Sea and the scope of mandatory jurisdiction' (2017) 48 *Ocean Development & International Law*, 313.

and Article 298 ('Optional exceptions to applicability of section 2') which concerns the possibility for states to exclude from compulsory settlement certain categories of disputes such as sea boundary delimitation and military activities. The details of Section 3, which went through many forms during the negotiations, are complex and closely bound up with the substantive provisions of the Convention. Their significance, however, can be grasped without an exhaustive analysis of each provision.

Article 297 reflects the view of coastal states that certain decisions relating to the exercise of sovereign rights or jurisdiction, especially those concerning the exercise of discretion, should not be subject to challenge in any form of adjudication. In respect of the exercise by a coastal state of its sovereign rights or jurisdiction, Article 297(1) provides that the compulsory procedures of Section 2 apply to certain cases.[51] As explained by the arbitral tribunal in *Southern Bluefin Tuna*:

> Article 297 of UNCLOS [...] provides significant limitations on the applicability of compulsory procedures insofar as coastal States are concerned. Paragraph 1 of Article 297 limits the application of such procedures to disputes concerning the exercise by a coastal State of its sovereign rights or jurisdiction in certain identified cases only, i.e.: (a) cases involving rights of navigation, overflight, laying of submarine cables and pipelines or other internationally lawful uses of the sea associated therewith; and (b) cases involving the protection and preservation of the marine environment.[52]

Despite the title of Article 297, i.e. 'Limitations on applicability of section 2', the first paragraph of the provision thus confirms rather than excludes the application of the compulsory methods of settlement under Section 2.[53] Article 297 thus lays down that disputes involving coastal states' rights with respect to marine research and fisheries shall be submitted to the procedures under Section 2 in certain cases, and to conciliation in others (Article 297 (2) and (3)).[54] As summarised by the arbitral tribunal in *Southern Bluefin Tuna*:

---

[51] In *Chagos Marine Protected Area Arbitration (Mauritius v. United Kingdom)*, however, the tribunal considered that Article 297(1) is not to be read as confirming the application of Section 2 (compulsory methods) *only* in these three cases. It confirmed that Article 297(1) 'does not restrict a tribunal from considering disputes concerning the exercise of sovereign rights and jurisdiction in other cases'. See *Chagos Marine Protected Area Arbitration (Mauritius v. United Kingdom)*, PCA Case No. 2011-03, Award, 18 March 2015, paras 308 and 317.

[52] *Southern Bluefin Tuna Case (Australia and New Zealand v. Japan)*, Award on Jurisdiction and Admissibility (2000), text in (2009) 39 ILM 1359, para. 61.

[53] *Chagos Marine Protected Area Arbitration (Mauritius v. United Kingdom)*, PCA Case No. 2011-03, Award, 18 March 2015, para. 307.

[54] For comments on this approach, see S. Rosenne, 'Settlement of fisheries disputes in the exclusive economic zone' (1979) 73 *AJIL*, 89; and J. P. A. Bernhardt, 'Compulsory dispute settlement in the law of the sea negotiations: a reassessment' (1978–9) 19 *Va. JIL*, 69.

Paragraph 2 of Article 297, while providing for the application of section 2 compulsory procedures to disputes concerning marine scientific research, exempts coastal States from the obligation of submitting to such procedures in cases involving exercise by a coastal State of its rights or discretionary authority in its exclusive economic zone (EEZ) or its continental shelf, and cases of termination or suspension by the coastal State of a research project in accordance with article 253. Disputes between the researching State and the coastal State concerning a specific research project are subject to conciliation under annex V of UNCLOS. Under paragraph 3 of Article 297, section 2 procedures are applicable to disputes concerning fisheries but, and this is an important 'but', the coastal State is not obliged to submit to such procedures where the dispute relates to its sovereign rights or their exercise with respect to the living resources in its EEZ, including determination of allowable catch, harvesting capacity, allocation of surpluses to other States, and application of its own conservation and management laws and regulations.[55]

An important point here is that, while the use of conciliation in the cases specified is obligatory, the Convention is careful to state that the coastal state's exercise of its discretion cannot be questioned (Article 297 (2)(b) and (3)(c)), and the Conciliation Commission's report is in any event not binding on the parties.

In an early version of the dispute settlement provisions, the exclusion of the procedures of Section 2 depended in all cases on a declaration to that effect by the state concerned.[56] In disputes covered by Article 297, the system of opting out was subsequently replaced by the comprehensive exclusion just described. It survives, however, in Article 298.

Article 298 ('Optional exceptions to applicability of section 2')[57] deals with three types of disputes which states may exclude from any or all of the procedures of Section 2 by written declaration. These are disputes involving sea boundary delimitations or historic bays or titles (Article 298(1)(a));[58] disputes concerning military activities or law enforcement activities in regard to the exercise of sovereign rights or jurisdiction excluded from the jurisdiction of a court or tribunal under Article 297,

---

[55] *Southern Bluefin Tuna Case (Australia and New Zealand* v. *Japan)*, Award on Jurisdiction and Admissibility (2000), text in (2009) 39 ILM 1359, para. 61.

[56] See A. O. Adede, 'Settlement of disputes arising under the Law of the Sea Convention' (1975) 69 *AJIL*, 798 at 813–14. For the transition to the final version, see the same author's Note in (1977) 71 *AJIL*, 305; and Rosenne and Sohn, *Commentary* (n. 3) pp. 87–106.

[57] For a comprehensive overview of the application of the Article, see K. Zou and Q. Ye, 'Interpretation and Application of Article 298 of the Law of the Sea Convention in recent Annex VII arbitrations: an appraisal' (2017) 48 *Ocean Development & International Law*, 331.

[58] For a comprehensive discussion of the controversy over delimitation, see A. O. Adede, 'Toward the formulation of the rule of delimitation of sea boundaries between states with opposite or adjacent coasts' (1978–9) 19 *Va. JIL*, 209; P. C. Irwin, 'Settlement of maritime boundary disputes: an analysis of the law of the sea negotiations' (1980) 8 *Ocean Development & International Law*, 105; Rosenne and Sohn, *Commentary* (n. 3) pp. 116–35; and P. Weil, *The Law of Maritime Delimitation: Reflections*, Cambridge, 1989.

paragraph 2 or 3 (Article 298(1)(b));[59] and disputes in respect of which the United Nations Security Council is exercising its functions under the Charter (Article 298(1)(c)).[60]

In the case of sea boundary delimitations and other disputes in the first category, the Convention provides that a dispute which arises after the Convention has entered into force may be subject to compulsory conciliation and then, if this does not result in an agreement, to the procedures laid down in Section 2 (Article 298(1)(a)). However, this elaborate arrangement has no application to such a dispute if it also involves sovereignty or other rights over land territory, and there is no corresponding provision concerning disputes in the second and third categories. It should also be noted that declarations can be made or withdrawn at any time and are expressly stated to be reciprocal in their effect (Article 298(3)). In other words, a state which makes a declaration excluding disputes of a particular type from the procedures of Section 2 secures an immunity to the extent permitted by this provision, but also loses the right to bring a claim arising out of such a dispute against other states. While this is in accordance with the usual principle governing limitations on international jurisdiction, it indicates that, if states were to make extensive use of the opportunities offered by Article 298,[61] the resulting erosion of the principle of compulsory settlement would be very significant. The exclusions in Article 298 have been discussed in several cases.

In *The South China Sea Arbitration*, China refused to participate, but the Tribunal discussed in detail the application of the exceptions under Article 298 since China had indeed declared to not accept the application of the compulsory methods under Section 2 for the three categories of disputes provided for in Article 298(1)(a)–(c). In relation to first exception under Article 298(1)(a) ('disputes concerning the interpretation or application of articles 15, 74 and 83 relating to sea boundary delimitations, or those involving historic bays or titles'), the Tribunal distinguished disputes concerning sea boundary delimitations, from disputes concerning an entitlement to maritime zones. It noted:

> a dispute concerning the existence of an entitlement to maritime zones is distinct from a dispute concerning the delimitation of those zones in an area where the entitlements of parties overlap. While fixing the extent of parties' entitlements and the area in which they overlap will commonly be one of the first matters to be addressed in the delimitation of a maritime boundary, it is

---

[59] For analysis of this exception, see M. W. Janis, 'Dispute settlement in the Law of the Sea Convention: the military activities exception' (1977) 4 *Ocean Development & International Law*, 51.

[60] Unless, of course, the Security Council calls upon the parties to employ the means of dispute settlement provided in the Convention.

[61] For details, see the website of the UN's Division for Oceans and the Law of the Sea, available atwww.un.org/Depts/los/settlement_of_disputes/choice_procedure.htm.

nevertheless a distinct issue. A maritime boundary may be delimited only between States with opposite or adjacent coasts and overlapping entitlements. In contrast, a dispute over claimed entitlements may exist even without overlap, where—for instance—a State claims maritime zones in an area understood by other States to form part of the high seas or the Area for the purposes of the Convention.[62]

The Tribunal in *Dispute Concerning Coastal State Rights in the Black Sea, Sea of Azov, and Kerch Strait* also considered that

> one of the key questions is whether there are entitlements and whether there is an area of overlapping maritime entitlements. If such area exists, the question of delimitation inevitably arises and the delimitation exception may be triggered.[63]

In relation to disputes involving historic bays or titles, also an exception under Article 298(1)(a), the Tribunal in the *South China Sea* arbitration distinguished historic *title* from historic *rights*:

> the reference to 'historic titles' in Article 298(1)(a)(i) of the Convention is accordingly a reference to claims of sovereignty over maritime areas derived from historical circumstances. [...] Other 'historic rights', in contrast, are nowhere mentioned in the Convention, and the Tribunal sees nothing to suggest that Article 298(1)(a)(i) was intended to also exclude jurisdiction over abroad and unspecified category of possible claims to historic rights falling short of sovereignty.[64]

In relation to the exception for military activities under Article 298(1)(b), the Tribunal in the *South China Sea* arbitration clarified that the exception applies only to *disputes concerning military activities*, and not to military activities as such.[65] In other words, it is not so much the employment of the military in relation to the dispute which triggers the exception, but the existence of a dispute concerning military activities.[66] The Tribunal in the *Black Sea* arbitration endorsed this position and held that the exception is not triggered 'simply because the conduct of the Russian Federation

---

[62] *The South China Sea Arbitration (The Republic of Philippines* v. *The People's Republic of China)*, PCA Case No. 2013-19, Award on Jurisdiction and Admissibility, 29 October 2015, para. 156.
[63] *Dispute Concerning Coastal State Rights in the Black Sea, Sea of Azov, and Kerch Strait (Ukraine* v. *the Russian Federation)* PCA Case No. 2017-06, Award on Preliminary Objections, 21 February 2020, para. 381.
[64] *The South China Sea Arbitration (The Republic of Philippines* v. *The People's Republic of China)*, PCA Case No. 2013-19, Award, 12 July 2016, para. 226. See also para. 402.
[65] *The South China Sea Arbitration (The Republic of Philippines* v. *The People's Republic of China)*, PCA Case No. 2013-19, Award, 12 July 2016, para. 1158.
[66] The Tribunal in the end accepted that most constriction activities were civilian in nature rather than military, but did consider that in one particular situation, a stand-off between ships from China's Navy and from China's Coast Guard and the Philippines' armed forces around Thomas Shoal, fell within the exception under Article 298(1)(b). See *The South China Sea Arbitration (The Republic of Philippines* v. *The People's Republic of China)*, PCA Case No. 2013-19, Award, 12 July 2016, paras 938, 1028 and 1161.

complained of by Ukraine has its origins in, or occurred against the background of, a broader alleged armed conflict'.[67]

The Tribunal in *Arctic Sunrise* was confronted with a declaration of the Russian Federation which excluded 'disputes concerning law-enforcement activities in regard to the exercise of sovereign rights or jurisdiction'. The declaration, however, did not explicitly mention that the exclusion applies only to law enforcement activities 'in regard to the exercise of sovereign rights or jurisdiction excluded from the jurisdiction of a court or tribunal under article 297, paragraph 2 or 3', as is mentioned in Article 298(1)(b). The Tribunal considered that a broad general exclusion for 'law enforcement activities' is not permitted under the Convention, and that only those law enforcement activities in regard to the exercise of sovereign rights or jurisdiction which are also excluded from the jurisdiction of a court or tribunal under paragraph 2 or 3 of Article 297 can validly be excluded.[68] The intricate provisions of Section 3 are an attempt to balance the desire to be a judge in one's own cause against the principle of binding third-party settlement. The exclusion of certain types of disputes from the procedures of Section 2 in Article 297 and the opportunity to exclude others provided by Article 298 reflect both traditional sensitivities – territorial sovereignty and military activities, for example – and the special concerns of developing states, whose voting power at the Conference, as the so-called 'Group of 77',[69] secured the exclusions relating to fishing and research. It is arguable, of course, that for certain disputes (over the exercise of discretion, for example) conciliation is a more appropriate means of settling disputes than adjudication. Be that as it may, it is clear that, without the limitations and exceptions provided for in Section 3, the adoption of machinery for the binding settlement of disputes as an integral part of the Convention would not have been generally accepted.

Although the effect of Section 3 is to cut down the scope for compulsory settlement of disputes under the Convention, two further points about these provisions should be noted which, in a non-technical sense, qualify these limitations. The first is that whether a state can rely on Articles 297 or 298 in a particular case is not a matter to be decided by the state unilaterally, but, as the Convention makes plain, is an issue for the court or tribunal whose jurisdiction is in question. This is another example of the

---

[67] *Dispute Concerning Coastal State Rights in the Black Sea, Sea of Azov, and Kerch Strait (Ukraine v. the Russian Federation)* PCA Case No. 2017-06, Award on Preliminary Objections, 21 February 2020, para. 331.
[68] *Arctic Sunrise (Kingdom of the Netherlands v. Russian Federation)*, PCA Case No. 2014-02, Award on Jurisdiction, 26 November 2014, para. 69.
[69] On the influence of the Group of 77, see A. G. Friedman and C. A. Williams, 'The Group of 77 at the United Nations: an emergent force in the law of the sea' (1978–9) 16 *San Diego L. Rev.*, 555; and G. A. Pierce, 'Dispute settlement mechanisms in the Draft Convention on the Law of the Sea' (1980–1) 10 *Denver J. Int. L. and Pol.*, 331.

Convention incorporating a recognised principle of international law, and does not, of course, prevent the various limitations and exceptions from being utilised in an appropriate case. What it does do, however, is to discourage the abuse of these provisions which would certainly follow if they were subject to self-serving interpretation. The other point is that, while the intention behind Section 3 is to prevent certain disputes from falling under the Convention's compulsory procedures automatically, the Section's final provision, Article 299, permits the parties to use these procedures, even for a dispute in an excluded category, so long as they agree to do so. In other words, where Articles 297 and 298 apply, their effect is to prevent the unilateral reference of a dispute to the Convention's procedures, without prejudice to the parties' right to employ such procedures by agreement. This is therefore a further example of the Convention's fundamental principle of freedom of choice. As Sohn and Rosenne put it:

> The last article of Part XV thus concludes in the spirit of section 1, emphasizing that even in matters where dispute settlement is restricted, there is still the possibility, by agreement of the parties, to find a dispute settlement procedure which would enable the parties to resolve their dispute amicably and peacefully.[70]

10.3 Conciliation

Conciliation is the only method of third-party settlement specifically mentioned in Section 1 of Part XV, dealing with the settlement of disputes by any means chosen by the parties.[71] Moreover, as has been seen, conciliation is obligatory for certain types of disputes excluded from adjudication in Section 3. Conciliation can therefore be said to occupy a prominent place in the Convention and could, at least in theory, be used twice in relation to certain disputes, first as the procedure chosen by the parties and then, if the initial attempt was unsuccessful, as the compulsory arrangement under Section 3. The procedure to be followed in voluntary or mandatory conciliation is set out in Annex V to the Convention. In general, the provisions which make up Annex V follow those of other recent multilateral treaties, though they are more elaborate in certain respects and also differ in certain details.

10.3.1 Procedure under Annex V of the Convention

Like its predecessors, the Convention provides for the submission of disputes to ad hoc commissions rather than to permanent bodies. Unless

---
[70] Rosenne and Sohn, *Commentary* (n. 3) p. 146.
[71] See Art. 284. References in early drafts to arbitration and judicial settlement were subsequently deleted; see Adede, 'Prolegomena' (n. 31) 282.

the parties agree to a different arrangement, a commission is established by each party appointing two members, who then appoint an additional member as chairman. Thus, a commission will normally contain five members. In the event of a failure to agree, the chairman may be appointed by the Secretary-General of the United Nations, who can also act should a party fail to appoint its own members. To facilitate the appointment of commissions, each party to the Convention is entitled to nominate four conciliators to a list to be compiled by the Secretary-General.[72] In setting up a commission, preference is to be given to candidates on the list, though only the Secretary-General is bound by it, and a state cannot select more than one of its own nationals. The qualification for nomination to the list is 'the highest reputation for fairness, competence and integrity' (Article 2). A conspicuous, but not unprecedented,[73] omission is the absence of any reference to legal qualifications.

In accordance with the usual practice, a commission normally determines its own procedure and takes decisions relating to its report, its recommendations and other matters by majority vote. With the consent of the parties to the dispute, it may invite any party to the Convention to submit its views orally or in writing and, if the parties agree, can presumably extend this facility to other states.[74] In the course of its proceedings, a commission may also draw attention to any measures which might facilitate an amicable settlement.

The functions of a commission are to 'hear the parties, examine their claims and objections and make proposals to the parties with a view to reaching an amicable settlement' (Article 6). This formula, which is taken from the 1969 Vienna Convention on the Law of Treaties,[75] was originally put forward to emphasise the point that, although conciliation is not arbitration, legal, as well as factual, issues may be examined. The directive that, if the dispute has not been settled, the commission's report shall record 'its conclusions on all questions of fact or law relevant to the matter in dispute' is also reminiscent of the Vienna Convention and was similarly intended to underline the judicial element in the commission's work by requiring it to present its conclusions. The earlier Convention, however, envisaged conciliation by 'qualified jurists'. Whether the conciliators appointed under the Convention will in practice be competent to draw conclusions on questions of law remains to be seen.

[72] Originally, the Registrar of the Law of the Sea Tribunal. See Adede, *ibid.*, 350.
[73] See Art. 85 of the Vienna Convention on the Representation of States in their Relations with International Organizations of a Universal Character, 1975. Text in (1975) 69 *AJIL* 730.
[74] See Rosenne and Sohn, *Commentary* (n. 3) p. 319.
[75] Vienna Convention on the Law of Treaties, 1969, Annex, Art. 5. Text in (1969) 63 *AJIL* 875. On the negotiation of the dispute settlement provisions of this convention, see R. D. Kearney and R. E. Dalton, 'The treaty on treaties' (1970) 64 *AJIL*, 495 at 554.

The provisions just discussed incline towards what was termed in Chapter 6 'quasi-arbitration'. However, there is no lack of emphasis on conciliation as a distinctive process. In addition to the point already noted, that in certain cases a state's discretion cannot be challenged, the commission's conclusions are only to be presented when the parties, despite the commission's assistance, have failed to reach an agreement. Thus, an important part of its task is the attempt to secure a settlement of the dispute while the proceedings are in progress. Moreover, any conclusions in its report must be accompanied by 'such recommendations as the commission may deem appropriate for an amicable settlement' (Article 7). And the commission's report, including its conclusions and recommendations, is, of course, not binding on the parties.

The fact that in some situations the Convention envisages conciliation as a compulsory procedure is reflected both in the arrangements for filling vacancies on a commission and in provisions indicating that a state is obliged to submit to such proceedings (Article 11) and cannot prevent them by non-cooperation (Article 12). As might be expected, any disagreement as to whether a commission has competence is to be decided by the commission (Article 13).

10.3.2 The 'Timor Sea Conciliation'

Although it cannot be excluded that other conciliations have taken place but remained confidential, so far only one known case has been referred to conciliation under the Convention's arrangements: the 'Timor Sea Conciliation' (Timor-Leste v. Australia) which was also discussed in Chapter 5. The conciliation between Australia and the Democratic Republic of Timor-Leste ('Timor-Leste') in the establishment of their maritime boundaries in the Timor Sea was submitted to the compulsory conciliation procedure under Section 2 of Annex V of the UNCLOS in 2016 and proved successful. Previous negotiations on the dispute had not resolved the dispute but the conciliation successfully resulted in the settlement of the dispute.

On 11 April 2016, the maritime boundary dispute between Timor-Leste and Australia was submitted to the compulsory conciliation procedure under the Convention on the Law of the Sea. Between July 2016 and February 2018, the Commission met regularly with the parties.

The Commission first needed to resolve Australia's objection to the competence of the Commission. In its Decision on Australia's Objections to Competence of 19 September 2016,[76] following hearings on the question, the Commission confirmed its jurisdiction. It decided, inter alia that a

---

[76] "Timor Sea Conciliation", 'Decision on Australia's Objections to Competence' PCA Case No 2016-10 (19 September 2016).

2003 exchange of letters between Prime Ministers Alkatiri and Howard did not constitute an agreement under Article 281 of the Convention which would have had the effect of precluding recourse to conciliation, as was discussed in Section 1 above. The Commission also discarded the argument that the 2006 Treaty on Certain Maritime Arrangements in the Timor Sea (CMATS) would constitute an agreement 'to seek settlement of the dispute by a peaceful means of [the Parties'] own choice', as required under Article 281.[77]

Article 298 was invoked as the basis of the compulsory conciliation since Australia had made a declaration excluding the compulsory methods under Section 2 for disputes relating to sea boundary delimitations. Australia, however, objected to the competence of the Commission, arguing that the requirements under Article 298 had not been met. Notably, it argued that the dispute arose prior to the entry into force of the Convention, and that an agreement within a reasonable period of time could be reached in negotiations between the parties. The Commission decided that the dispute had arisen prior to the entry into force of the Convention as between the parties in 2013, but not prior to the entry into force of the Convention in general in 1994, and argued that the entry into force of the Convention in general was determinant. Finally, the Commission argued that negotiations had taken place and were unsuccessful.

On 30 August 2017, an agreement on measures was reached on the basis of a proposal made by the Commission. In October 2017, the Commission assisted the parties in reaching an agreement on the text of a draft treaty to formalise the agreement of 30 August. This has led to the conclusion and signing of the 'Treaty Between Australia and the Democratic Republic of Timor-Leste Establishing Their Maritime Boundaries in the Timor Sea' (the Maritime Boundary Treaty) on 6 March 2018. The successful conciliation of this dispute is an important example of the significance of the role played by conciliation in general and under the Law of the Sea Convention.[78]

10.4 Arbitration under Annex VII

According to the Convention, law of the sea disputes may be referred to arbitration in three different ways. Under Section 1 of Part XV, the parties may by agreement select any peaceful means and so can decide to set up an arbitral tribunal along traditional lines. Under Section 2, both parties may make declarations nominating arbitration as a preferred means of

---

[77] Ibid., para. 62.
[78] See for a discussion D. Tamada, 'The Timor Sea Conciliation: the unique mechanism of dispute settlement', (2020) 31 *European Journal of International Law*, 321.

settlement, in which case arbitration will be governed by the provisions of the Convention. Alternatively, if there is no common declaration under Section 2, arbitration under the Convention will be deemed to have been accepted as the relevant obligatory procedure. Since only about one-quarter of the parties to the Convention have made declarations nominating a means of settlement,[79] this fall-back arrangement is very significant. It is arbitration under the Convention, the arrangements for which are set out in Annex VII to the Convention, with which we are here concerned.

The arrangements for constituting a tribunal resemble the provisions described earlier concerning conciliation, and much of what was discussed in Chapter 6 also is applicable to Annex VII arbitration. However, Annex VII does contain certain specific procedural questions relating, amongst others, to the constitution of the arbitral tribunal.

A list of arbitrators is to be drawn up by the Secretary-General, and each party to the Convention may make four nominations. The persons nominated are to be 'experienced in maritime affairs and enjoying the highest reputation for fairness, competence and integrity' (Article 2(1)). While these qualifications are clearly most desirable, the omission of any reference to the legal competence of prospective arbitrators is again disquieting.[80] Unless a dispute involves more than two parties, or the parties otherwise agree, a tribunal is to consist of five members, one nominated by each party and three, including the president, appointed by agreement. The 'neutral' element, it will be noticed, is larger here than in conciliation commissions and will normally consist of non-nationals. In constituting a tribunal, preference is to be given to arbitrators on the Secretary-General's list.

It was explained in Chapter 6 that the failure of a state to appoint its members of an arbitral tribunal, or disagreement between the parties as to the neutral element, are matters that must be expressly provided for, to guard against difficulties in getting an arbitration under way. The Convention deals with the problem by providing that unfilled places on the tribunal, and disagreement over the president, shall be resolved either by a person or third state chosen by the parties, or by the President of the International Tribunal for the Law of the Sea. All such appointments are to be made from the Secretary-General's list and in consultation with the parties. In an obvious attempt to provide assurance on the crucial issue of neutrality, the Convention lays down that members of the tribunal appointed in this way must also be of different nationalities and may not

---

[79] See n. 16 above.
[80] According to Adede, 'it was observed in this connection that the problems of interpretation of the Convention did not require experts on the law of the sea *per se* and that the tribunal could be tailored to suit a particular dispute by including experts on various matters'. Adede, 'Prolegomena' (n. 31) 354.

be 'in the service of, ordinarily resident in the territory of, or nationals of, any of the parties to the dispute' (Article 3(3)).

The provisions dealing with procedure and related matters contain a number of points of interest. The tribunal is normally to decide its own procedure, 'assuring to each party a full opportunity to be heard and to present its case' (Article 5), and takes decisions by majority vote. Frustration of the proceedings by members of the tribunal is discouraged by an unusual provision stating that 'the absence or abstention of less than half the members shall not constitute a bar to the tribunal reaching a decision' (Article 8). In accordance with the usual practice, the tribunal's expenses are normally borne by the parties. The parties to the dispute are also obliged to facilitate the work of the tribunal by providing it with documents, facilities and information, access to witnesses and experts, and the means to visit the localities to which the case relates. However, the Convention's directive here is qualified by a provision that such assistance shall be 'in accordance with their law and using all means at their disposal' (Article 6), a formula which permits a state to plead lack of resources and, more seriously, to set up its own law to restrict its obligations.

Failure to appear or to defend a case is dealt with in terms similar to those of Article 53 of the Statute of the International Court. While such default cannot prevent a decision, before making an award the tribunal must satisfy itself that it has jurisdiction and that the claim is well-founded in fact and in law. The award, which is binding on the parties, must be reasoned and limited to the subject matter of the dispute and may include separate and dissenting opinions. As is generally the case with arbitration, the award is final and without appeal unless the parties otherwise agree.[81] However, it is surprising to find that, according to Article 12, disagreements relating to the interpretation or manner of implementation of an award may apparently be submitted by either party to the original tribunal at any time, or to another court or tribunal by agreement. Like several other parts of the Convention, the provisions of Annex VII apply *mutatis mutandis* to disputes involving international organisations.

The value of these arrangements, along with some of their limitations, may be seen from the use which has been made of arbitration since the Convention came into force.

In the *Bay of Bengal Maritime Boundary* case,[82] an Annex VII Tribunal delimited the maritime boundary between the territorial sea, the exclusive

---

[81] This does not, of course, exclude the possibility of annulment of an award in appropriate circumstances, in which connection the requirement of Art. 10 that the award 'shall be confined to the subject-matter of the dispute' could be particularly important. See Rosenne and Sohn, *Commentary* (n. 3) p. 435.

[82] *Bay of Bengal Maritime Boundary (Bangladesh v. India)*, Annex VII Arbitral Tribunal, 7 July 2014 and see D. H. Anderson, Note (2015) 109 *AJIL*, 146.

economic zone and the continental shelf within and beyond 200 nautical miles of Bangladesh and India, and at the same time determined the starting point of the maritime boundary in an area where the coast of the two states is highly unstable. Maritime boundaries were also an issue in the *Barbados/Trinidad and Tobago* case[83] and the *Guyana/Suriname* case,[84] in the second of which there was also an issue concerning the threat of force. In the *Land Reclamation* case[85] between Malaysia and Singapore, on the other hand, which concerned reclamation projects in the Straits of Johore, the dispute was settled through negotiations while the arbitration was in progress, and so the tribunal made an award on agreed terms.

Sometimes a case is begun before an arbitral tribunal, but then discontinued. In the *MOX Plant* case,[86] for example, between Ireland and the United Kingdom, and which concerned alleged threats to the marine environment, an Annex VII tribunal exercised its power to prescribe provisional measures of protection under Article 290(1) of the Convention, but also decided to suspend proceedings, pending clarification of certain jurisdictional issues by the European Court of Justice. Following the Court's ruling, Ireland decided to discontinue the case.

Other cases have begun before an Annex VII tribunal and have then been transferred to ITLOS. This happened in the *Bangladesh/Myanmar* case, described below, and in the *MV Saiga No. 2* case, decided in 1999. Similarly, in the *Swordfish* case, between Chile and the European Community, Chile began proceedings before an Annex VII tribunal, but then, after discussions between the parties, the case was transferred to a Special Chamber of ITLOS.[87] A similar situation occurred in *Dispute concerning delimitation of the maritime boundary between Mauritius and Maldives in the Indian Ocean (Mauritius/Maldives)*, where the parties agreed through a special agreement to transfer their dispute concerning the delimitation of the maritime boundary between them in the Indian Ocean to a Special Chamber of the ITLOS after the initiate of Annex VII Arbitral Proceedings.[88]

---

[83] *Barbados/Trinidad and Tobago*, Award on Jurisdiction and Merits, (2006) 45 ILM 800. For comment, see B. Kwiatkowska, Note (2007) 101 *AJIL*, 149.

[84] *Guyana/Suriname*, Award (2007), (2008) 47 ILM 166. For comment, see S. Fietta (2008) 102 *AJIL*, 119.

[85] *Case concerning Land Reclamation by Singapore in and around the Straits of Johor*, Award on Agreed Terms (2005), available at www.pca-cpa.org. See also J. G. Merrills, 'New horizons for international adjudication' (2006) 6 *Global Community YBILJ*, 47 at 48–57.

[86] See the *MOX Plant Case (Ireland v. United Kingdom)*, Order No. 3, Suspension of Proceedings on Jurisdiction and Merits and Request for Further Provisional Measures (June 2003), text in (2003) 42 ILM 1187. In Order No. 4 in November the suspension was extended, and in Order No. 6 in June 2008 the proceedings were terminated. For a review of the proceedings in this case and the related *OSPAR (Article 9)* arbitration, see R. R. Churchill and J. Scott, 'The MOX Plant litigation: the first half-life' (2004) 53 *ICLQ*, 643.

[87] See notes 53, 54 and 60 above.

[88] *Dispute concerning delimitation of the maritime boundary between Mauritius and Maldives in the Indian Ocean (Mauritius/Maldives)*, Preliminary Objections, Judgment of 28 January 2021.

In most cases the jurisdiction of an Annex VII tribunal has been challenged, and often the jurisdictional challenges relate to the application of Article 281 and 282, as was discussed in Section 10.1.2 of this chapter. In the *Southern Bluefin Tuna* case,[89] for example, where Australia and New Zealand claimed that Japan had failed to comply with certain conservation obligations, the arbitration tribunal, in a controversial decision, adopted a strained interpretation of Article 281 of the Convention and dismissed the case on jurisdictional grounds. In contrast, in the *South China Sea* arbitration,[90] in which the Philippines disputed a number of China's maritime claims, the tribunal took a more expansive approach and held that it was competent to adjudicate on some matters, but that others were outside its jurisdiction, as discussed above.[91] Jurisdictional challenges on these and other grounds also occurred in other recent arbitrations.[92]

In different ways, therefore, the record to date shows that arbitration is available under the Convention for disputes on a variety of matters, although its functioning in practice must be seen in relation to other means of peaceful settlement.

10.5 Special Arbitration under Annex VIII

The maritime activities of states, like many aspects of the contemporary international scene, are so complex that disputes often involve technical issues which arbitrators with no specialist qualifications may find difficult to handle. A partial attempt to meet this problem was made in the third of the 1958 Conventions on the Law of the Sea, which provided for the appointment of experts to decide disputes relating to fishing and conservation. When such a dispute arose, the procedure laid down by that Convention envisaged a special commission of five members established by agreement between the parties. The members were to be drawn 'from amongst well-qualified persons being nationals of states not involved in the dispute and specializing in legal, administrative or scientific questions relating to fisheries, depending upon the nature of the dispute to be settled' (Article 9(2)). The decisions of special commissions were to be made in

---

[89] *Southern Bluefin Tuna Case (Australia and New Zealand* v. *Japan)*, Award on Jurisdiction and Admissibility (2000), text in (2009) 39 ILM 1359; and see A. E. Boyle, Note (2001) 50 *ICLQ*, 447.

[90] *Arbitration between the Republic of the Philippines and the Peoples' Republic of China* (2015).

[91] This was, incidentally, one of a number of cases referred to Annex VII arbitration in which, owing to disagreement between the parties, the President of ITLOS was called upon to appoint arbitrators under the emergency arrangements described earlier.

[92] See e.g. *Arctic Sunrise (Kingdom of the Netherlands* v. *Russian Federation)*, PCA Case No. 2014-02, Award on Jurisdiction, 26 November 2014; *Dispute Concerning Coastal State Rights in the Black Sea, Sea of Azov, and Kerch Strait (Ukraine* v. *the Russian Federation)* PCA Case No. 2017-06, Award on Preliminary Objections, 21 February 2020; *The 'Enrica Lexie' Incident (Italy* v. *India)*, PCA Case No. 2015-28, Award, 21 May 2020.

accordance with scientific and technical criteria set out in the Convention and were binding on the states concerned. This functional approach to dispute settlement is taken considerably further in Annex VIII to the Convention concerning special arbitration.

Special arbitration is one of the binding methods of settlement which a party to the Convention can accept in advance by a declaration under Section 2 of Part XV of the Convention. It may therefore be initiated unilaterally whenever a dispute of the appropriate type arises and both parties have deposited a declaration in appropriate terms. The disputes for which special arbitration may be employed are those concerning the interpretation or application of the articles of the Convention relating to: fisheries; protection and preservation of the marine environment; marine scientific research; and navigation, including pollution from vessels and by dumping. Since a state is free to accept special arbitration for all or any of these categories, it is essential for jurisdictional purposes that both parties' declarations cover the type of dispute in question.

To assist states in setting up a tribunal, lists of experts in each of the four fields are to be maintained by, respectively, the Food and Agriculture Organization, the UN Environment Programme, the Inter-Governmental Oceanographic Commission and the International Maritime Organization. Each state party may nominate to each list two experts 'whose competence in the legal, scientific or technical aspects' of the field is established and 'who enjoy the highest reputation for fairness and integrity' (Article 3). The inclusion here of a reference to legal competence and the corresponding omission in the provisions on conciliation and arbitration perhaps suggest that law is regarded more as another type of useful expertise, than, as might be thought, a primary qualification for interpreting and applying a major international convention.

The arrangements for constituting a tribunal essentially follow the pattern of conciliation, rather than arbitration, in that each party selects two members, preferably from the appropriate list, and the president is chosen by agreement. Similarly, vacant places must be filled from the appropriate list by the Secretary-General, not the President of the International Tribunal for the Law of the Sea. However, as might be expected, the provisions concerning the disqualification of certain candidates follow those on arbitration, and, in exercising his powers of appointment, the Secretary-General must consult with both the parties and the relevant international organisation.

The job of a special arbitral tribunal, as the name implies, will normally be adjudication. However, the last provision of Annex VIII (Article 5) provides that, in certain circumstances, its functions can be broadened to include fact finding and conciliation. By agreement, the parties may set up a special arbitral tribunal to carry out an inquiry into the facts of any dispute of a type amenable to special arbitration. An interesting point here is that, unless otherwise agreed, such a tribunal's findings of fact are conclusive as between the parties. Here, then, in contrast to the cases considered in Chapter 3, we have the phenomenon of 'binding inquiry'. Moreover, if the parties so request, such a tribunal may formulate non-binding recommendations to provide the basis for a review by the parties of the questions giving rise to the dispute. Thus, in a suitable case and with the parties' agreement, the machinery of special arbitration can be employed as an additional form of conciliation. The term 'special arbitration' hardly seems appropriate to describe either inquiry or inquiry with conciliation. However, as we saw when considering the *Red Crusader* and other cases discussed earlier,[93] considerable expertise may be necessary to unravel the circumstances of an incident at sea. These facilities can therefore be regarded as a useful adjunct to the Convention, but so far no cases have been brought under Annex VIII of the Convention.

10.6 The International Tribunal for the Law of the Sea (ITLOS)

Among the several new institutions created by the Law of the Sea Convention is a court, the International Tribunal for the Law of the Sea (ITLOS).[94] The idea that disputes of a particular type are best handled by tribunals set up for the purpose is nothing new – the machinery of the European Convention on Human Rights is a well-established example – and the Convention's arrangements for special arbitration clearly reflect the same impulse. However, since the law of the sea can scarcely be said to be so specialised as to be beyond the competence of existing tribunals, the creation of ITLOS may be thought to indicate a certain lack of confidence in the International Court. In light of this, it is interesting to compare the Tribunal's Statute, which contains forty articles and forms Annex VI to the Convention, with that of the International Court.

10.6.1 The Structure and Composition of the ITLOS

ITLOS, whose seat is in Hamburg, has twenty-one members, elected for a nine-year term. At meetings of the states parties in 1994 and 1995, arrangements were made to hold the first election of the members of ITLOS, an Acting Registrar for the Tribunal was appointed, and English and French were designated as its official languages.[95] It was also decided that the remuneration of the members of the Tribunal should consist of three

---

[93] See Chapter 3.
[94] For a detailed description of the structure and working methods of the Tribunal, see G. Eiriksson, *The International Tribunal for the Law of the Sea*, The Hague, 2000.
[95] See S. Rosenne, 'Establishing the International Tribunal for the Law of the Sea' (1995) 89 *AJIL*, 806.

elements: an annual allowance, a special allowance for each day that a member is engaged in the work of the Tribunal, and a subsistence allowance for each day of attendance. This arrangement, which contrasts with the annual salary paid to members of the International Court, reflects the fact that all the judges, apart from the President, currently work on a part-time basis. Although ITLOS and its offshoot, the Seabed Disputes Chamber (SBDC), are standing tribunals, demand for their services has been hard to predict. Consequently, to begin in a limited way, with capacity to expand if demand makes this necessary, is a prudent and economical approach.

The first election of members of the Tribunal took place in 1996. Article 2(1) of the Statute requires of the members 'recognised competence in the field of the law of the sea' and, not surprisingly, several of those elected had taken part in UNCLOS III or the negotiation of the 1994 Agreement, as legal advisers, government representatives or academic experts. To enable a system of triennial elections to operate, lots were drawn after the election to determine which seven members would serve for three or six years and which for the full nine-year term.

Those elected included five each from the African and Asian groups, four each from the Latin American and Caribbean group, and the Western European and others group, and three from the Eastern European states. This provides a representative Tribunal in accordance with Article 2(2) of the Statute, and is a composition which has been maintained in subsequent elections. The vital matter of distribution of seats is dealt with by requiring that 'the representation of the principal legal systems of the world and equitable geographical distribution shall be assured' (Article 2(2)). To clarify this point, it is provided that no two members of the Tribunal may be nationals of the same state and that 'there shall be no fewer than three members from each geographical group as established by the General Assembly of the United Nations' (Article 3(2)). At the time of the Third UN Conference on the Law of the Sea, there were five such geographical groups, but, as no number is mentioned in Article 3, the Convention is flexible in this respect. Election is by a two-thirds majority of the parties to the Convention and from a list of candidates which they have nominated. This is of course a quite different arrangement from that governing elections to the International Court, and means that the Permanent Members of the Security Council have no guarantee of a seat on the Tribunal.[96]

The provisions dealing with disqualification of a member in a particular case contain the usual reference to previous participation as agent, counsel, etc., and are modelled on Article 17 of the Statute of the International

---

[96] On this and other aspects of the Tribunal, see Adede, 'Prolegomena' (n. 31) 361–73. At the first election for the Tribunal in 1996, those elected included candidates from China, Russia and the United Kingdom, but not from France or the United States.

Court. The treatment of incompatible activities of members of the Tribunal, however, expands the earlier Statute's prohibition on political and administrative functions to include active association or financial interest 'in any of the operations of any enterprise concerned with the exploration for or exploitation of the resources of the sea or the sea-bed or other commercial use of the sea or the sea-bed' (Article 7). As with the International Court, a member of the Tribunal is not disqualified by being a national of one of the parties to a dispute, and an ad hoc member may be appointed by a party or parties currently unrepresented.[97]

In light of the International Court's successful effort to encourage the use of chambers, it is interesting to see that the Tribunal's Statute provides for these in terms very similar to those of the earlier instrument. Chambers of three or more members may be formed for dealing with particular categories of cases. A five-member chamber of summary procedure is to be formed for the 'speedy despatch of business' (Article 15(3)). And a chamber may be formed to deal with a particular dispute if the parties so request. In the last case, the Statute makes it clear that the composition of the chamber is to be determined by the Tribunal 'with the approval of the parties' (Article 15(2)), a provision which appears to meet the point which initially caused difficulty in the *Gulf of Maine* case.[98] The Statute also provides for a special Seabed Disputes Chamber, which is further discussed below.

At their various meetings before the election, the states parties had wisely decided to refrain from trying to regulate the Tribunal's internal processes. This was therefore the first task for its newly elected members, and so at meetings in 1996 and 1997 they arranged to set up the SBDC, together with a Chamber for Fisheries Disputes and one for Marine Environment Disputes, and at the same time dealt with various other administrative and organisational matters. The latter included adopting the Tribunal's Rules, and also guidelines on the preparation and presentation of cases before the Tribunal and a resolution concerning its internal practice. In 2007, a further Chamber was created for Maritime Delimitation Disputes. While the Tribunal's treatment of these matters predictably drew on the experience of the International Court, several departures and adaptations reflect differences between the two bodies' jurisdictions, as well as an effort to make the Tribunal's proceedings efficient, cost-effective and 'user-friendly'.[99]

---

[97] See Article 17. On the problem of determining the applicability of this provision if entities other than states parties claim the right to appoint ad hoc judges, see Rosenne and Sohn, *Commentary* (n. 3) p. 368.
[98] See Chapter 6.
[99] See D. Anderson, 'The International Tribunal for the Law of the Sea', in M. D. Evans (ed.), *Remedies in International Law: The Institutional Dilemma*, Oxford, 1998, 71; and T. Treves, 'Introductory Note' (2001) 1 *Global Community YBILJ*, 269.

10.6.2 Jurisdiction of the ITLOS

The competence of ITLOS raises a number of points of interest. As already noted in Sections 10.1.1 and 10.2.1 above, a dispute may be referred to the Tribunal when both parties have made a declaration accepting its jurisdiction. It also has jurisdiction when any agreement so provides, or when all the parties to any treaty concerning the law of the sea already in force agree that disputes may be so referred.

In terms of jurisdiction *ratione personae,* and unlike the International Court of Justice, the Tribunal is open to entities other than states, including international organisations in certain circumstances (Article 20(2)), and under the same provision may be used by states which are not parties to the Convention. The Statute further provides in Article 37, which is situated in the section concerning the Seabed Disputes Chamber (see below section 10.7), that the Seabed Disputes Chamber shall be open to the states parties, the Seabed Authority and the other entities referred to in Part XI, Section 5: the Enterprise, state enterprises and natural or juridical persons.

Its choice of law, as we have seen, is governed largely by the Convention. Procedural arrangements are straightforward and in general resemble those of the Statute of the International Court. Each party to a case normally bears its own costs, while the running expenses of the Tribunal are borne by the parties to the Convention and the International Seabed Authority on terms to be agreed.[100]

Article 31 allows a state which considers that it has an interest of a legal nature in the outcome of a case to request permission to intervene, and Article 32 gives parties to the Convention, or to other international agreements being considered, the right to intervene in proceedings before the Tribunal. These are both modelled on the Statute of the International Court. The Court, as we have seen, has been reluctant to allow intervention on the few occasions when it has been attempted; it remains to be seen whether the Tribunal's policy will be equally restrictive.

The provision governing default (Article 28) is likewise very similar to the Statute and the Convention's own articles on arbitration. Decisions, for which a quorum is eleven elected members, are by majority vote and may include separate opinions. Like decisions of the International Court, the Tribunal's decisions are final, but may be interpreted by the Tribunal at the request of any party. Similarly, they are binding only as between the parties and in respect of the particular dispute.

If judgments in contentious cases are not very numerous so far, the same cannot be said of the special procedure under Article 292, by which the Tribunal can be asked to order the prompt release of a detained vessel which has been invoked so frequently that use of this provision may be said

---

[100] On the thinking behind this arrangement, see Rosenne and Sohn, *Commentary* (n. 3) p. 372.

to have become something of a regular occurrence. The same can be said in respect of provisional measures, notably under Article 290(5), which gives ITLOS competence for requests for provisional measures of protection pending arbitration proceedings.

10.6.3 Provisional Measures

ITLOS, like other courts and tribunals forming part of the Convention system, also has the power to prescribe provisional measures at the request of a party to a dispute (Article 25 ITLOS Statute and Article 290 UNCLOS). Such orders, like judgments under Article 292, not only help to resolve the specific dispute, but also serve to resolve significant procedural questions and to clarify the meaning of key provisions of the Convention.

An interesting feature is that provisional measures may be ordered by the Tribunal if it considers it appropriate under the circumstances 'to preserve the respective rights of the parties to the dispute', but also 'to prevent serious harm to the marine environment, pending the final decision' (Article 290(1) UNCLOS). In general, the requirements that must be satisfied for the ITLOS to order provisions measures are similar to those applicable at the International Court of Justice, as discussed in Chapter 8: *prima facie* jurisdiction, plausibility of the rights invoked, a link between the measures requested and the rights invoked, and a risk of irreparable prejudice.[101] While there are certain differences in the application of these requirements,[102] they largely follow the ICJ practice and hence we refer the reader to the discussion in Chapter 8.

Aside from the ITLOS's right to order provisional measures, the Tribunal can order provisional measures under Article 290(5) in response to requests for provisional measures of protection, pending arbitration proceedings, termed a residual jurisdiction.

Article 290(5) provides that

> Pending the constitution of an arbitral tribunal to which a dispute is being submitted under this section, any court or tribunal agreed upon by the parties or, failing such agreement within two weeks from the date of the request for provisional measures, the International Tribunal for the Law of the Sea or, with respect to activities in the Area, the Seabed Disputes Chamber, may prescribe, modify or revoke provisional measures in accordance with this article if it considers that prima facie the tribunal which is to be constituted would have

---

[101] See e.g. *Dispute Concerning Delimitation of the Maritime Boundary between Ghana and Côte d'Ivoire in the Atlantic Ocean (Ghana/Côte d'Ivoire)*, Provisional Measures, Order of 25 April 2015, *ITLOS Reports 2015*, p. 146, paras 33 ff.
[102] See Yoshifumi Tanaka, *The Peaceful Settlement of International Disputes*, Cambridge, 2018, pp. 255–9.

jurisdiction and that the urgency of the situation so requires. Once constituted, the tribunal to which the dispute has been submitted may modify, revoke or affirm those provisional measures, acting in conformity with paragraphs 1 to 4.

While the general requirements for the ITLOS to order provisional measures in contentious proceedings before the Tribunal itself apply similarly to requests for provisional measures pending the constitution of an arbitral tribunal, there are certain specific features that need to be mentioned. First, when requested to order provisional measures pending the constitution of an arbitral tribunal under Annex VII, the competence of the ITLOS is different. Article 290(5) requires that the parties first seek to agree to 'any court or tribunal' to submit a request for provisional measures; it is only failing such agreement within two weeks from the date of the request for provisional measures, that the ITLOS (or the Seabed Disputes Chamber in case of activities in the area) may exercise its jurisdiction to order provisional measures.

Second, it is important to point out that the ITLOS' competence to order such measures is provided for by Article 290(5). However, when establishing the existence of prima facie jurisdiction, the ITLOS is required to establish whether the *arbitral tribunal* to be constituted has prima facie jurisdiction. In other words, the ITLOS' competence to order provisions measures is based on its own jurisdiction under Article 290(5), and the prima facie jurisdiction of the arbitral tribunal to which the dispute has been submitted.

10.6.4 Prompt Release of Vessels

Article 292 provides that the Tribunal can be asked to order the prompt release of a detained vessel. This provision has been invoked frequently and the use of this provision may be said to have become something of a regular occurrence since the inauguration of the ITLOS.[103]

According to Article 292, in the event of the detention by a state party of a vessel flying flag of another state party in alleged violation of the Convention, a state may request 'any court or tribunal agreed upon by the parties' to decide on the release from detention of the vessel or its crew. Alleged violations of the Convention in this respect are limited to the failure of the detaining state to comply 'with the provisions of this Convention for the prompt release of the vessel or its crew upon the posting of a reasonable bond or other financial security', as required notably by Article 73 of the Convention.

---

[103] For an assessment, see Seline Trevisanut, 'Twenty years of prompt release of vessels: admissibility, jurisdiction, and recent trends' (2017) 48 *Ocean Development & International Law*, 300.

Absent an agreement on the court or tribunal within 10 days from the time of detention, the case may be brought either before a court or tribunal accepted by the detaining state under article 287 (the general choice of compulsory dispute settlement method in Section 2), or to the ITLOS, unless the parties otherwise agree. This specific form of competence of the ITLOS calls for several observations.

First of all, the procedure relates only to the release of the vessel or its crew and is not concerned with the merits of the detention, which will typically be decided before a domestic court. It is an 'autonomous procedure'.[104]

Second, as noted in Article 292(2), 'the application for release may be made only by or on behalf of the flag State of the vessel'.

Third, despite the possibility for such disputes to be submitted, failing an agreement on the court or tribunal to decide the release within ten days, to 'a court or tribunal accepted by the detaining State under article 287', such a scenario will in practice unlikely occur since proceedings before an arbitral tribunal or the ICJ will cause a serious delay in the proceedings.[105] In practice, therefore, such cases will most often end up at the ITLOS. So far, the ITLOS has decided approximately ten prompt release of vessels cases, out of a total of slightly less than thirty cases.

10.6.5 Advisory Opinions

In contrast with the SBDC which, as we will see in the next section, is authorised to give advisory opinions under Article 191 of the Convention, no provision of either the Convention or the ITLOS Statute permits the Tribunal to issue advisory opinions. However, this omission has been rectified in Article 138 of the ITLOS Rules which confers this competence where an international agreement related to the purposes of the Convention specifically provides for such a request.[106]

Article 138 of the Rules of Procedure[107] provide that 'the Tribunal may give an advisory opinion on a legal question if an international agreement related to the purposes of the Convention specifically provides for the submission to the Tribunal of a request for such an opinion'. This competence which is asserted only in the Rules of Procedure, has been met with some criticism, especially in light of the fact that it had not been envisaged in the Convention itself and in fact such a competence had been met with

---

[104] *Ibid.*, 301.   [105] Tanaka, *The Peaceful Settlement of International Disputes* (n. 102) p. 262.

[106] For a critical assessment of this competence, see T. Ruys and A. Soete, '"Creeping" advisory jurisdiction of international courts and tribunals? The case of the International Tribunal for the Law of the Sea', (2016) 29 *Leiden Journal of International Law*, 155.

[107] Rules of the Tribunal (ITLOS/8), as adopted on 28 October 1997 and amended on 15 March 2001, 21 September 2001, 17 March 2009, 25 September 2018 and 25 September 2020, available at www.itlos.org/en/main/basic-texts-and-other-documents/.

reluctance during the negotiation of the UNCLOS.[108] It has however been described as a 'consensual solution' between those who considered that absent an explicit provision in the Convention itself such a competence could not be included, and those who considered that requests for advisory proceedings are possible based on Article 288(2) of the Convention which, as we have seen, mentions that 'a court or tribunal referred to in article 287 shall also have jurisdiction over any dispute concerning the interpretation or application of an international agreement related to the purposes of this Convention, which is submitted to it in accordance with the agreement'.[109]

The procedure is similar to the one set in relation to the advisory proceedings before the Seabed Disputes Chamber (Article 138(3) ITLOS Rules of Procedure).

While the requirements for the ITLOS to exercise this competence, have been termed to contain 'a high threshold which makes it rather unlikely that States may use this option',[110] in light of the need for an international treaty to be concluded to that effect, in 2013, the Tribunal received a request from the Sub-Regional Fisheries Commission (SRFC), a West African organisation, for an advisory opinion on a number of questions concerning unlawful fishing in the Exclusive Economic Zone (EEZ). In 2015, the Tribunal handed down its opinion[111] which clarified the position under the Convention on a number of matters, including the obligations and liability of flag states in relation to illegal, unreported and unregulated fishing. This was the Tribunal's first advisory opinion and, like the cases mentioned above, provides helpful legal guidance.

10.7 Seabed Disputes Chamber

Disputes concerning the complex arrangements envisaged in the Convention for the exploration and exploitation of the deep seabed are dealt with in a series of provisions separate from those relating to other types of dispute. Indeed, it was originally suggested that, because seabed disputes raise a variety of special problems, they should be handled by a distinct tribunal with no connection to the ITLOS. However, it was eventually decided that, though such disputes required a functional approach, the best arrangement would be to create a Seabed Disputes Chamber (SBDC) of ITLOS with its own constitution and jurisdiction.[112]

---

[108] For a discussion, see R. Wolfrum, 'Advisory Opinions: are they a suitable alternative for the settlement of international disputes?', in R. Wolfrum and I. Gätzschmann (eds), *International Dispute Settlement: Room for Innovations?* Heidelberg, 2013, p. 35, at 55.
[109] *Ibid.*, p. 35, at 54.   [110] *Ibid.*
[111] *Request for Advisory Opinion submitted by the Sub-Regional Fisheries Commission*, Advisory Opinion, 2 April 2015, [2015] ITLOS Reports.
[112] On the integration of the system for settling seabed disputes into the general system of the Convention, see the Note by A. O. Adede in (1978) 72 *AJIL*, 84.

As a result of this change of policy, the provisions governing the SBDC are to be found in two places in the Convention, Part XI, Section 5, dealing with the administration of the International Seabed Area, and Annex VI, setting up ITLOS.

10.7.1 Composition and Functioning of the Seabed Disputes Chamber

The SBDC consists of eleven members chosen for a three-year term by the twenty-one elected members of the ITLOS from among their number. In electing the Chamber, they are required to ensure that the principal legal systems of the world are represented and that equitable geographical distribution is achieved. Since the Tribunal may have as few as three members from a particular geographical group, the element of choice in the election will sometimes be quite limited.[113] At one time, it was proposed that elections should be in the hands of a political body, the Assembly of the International Sebed Authority. However, it was eventually accepted that, since the members of the Tribunal are elected by the parties to the Convention, their involvement in the election of the members of the SBDC was unnecessary. The Assembly was therefore restricted to making recommendations of a general nature relating to representation and the distribution of seats, which are provided for in Article 35(2) of Annex VI.

A quorum in the SBDC is seven, but for certain purposes a smaller ad hoc chamber of three may be formed (Article 36). The composition of this 'chamber of a chamber' is to be determined by the SBDC with the approval of the parties. If they cannot agree, it is to be set up in the same way as an arbitral tribunal, with each party appointing one member and the third appointed by agreement or, if necessary, by the President of the SBDC. The possibility of creating ad hoc chambers may appear to be an unnecessary complication in an already elaborate set of provisions, but is explained by the need to compromise between states which wished disputes relating to Part XI of the Convention to be dealt with by the regular SBDC, and those which would have preferred arbitration. Allowing chambers to be created gave the latter a measure of control over the composition of the Tribunal, which was what they wanted, while preserving the principle that the law relating to this new and important area would be developed by a single set of judges.[114]

10.7.2 Competence of the Seabed Disputes Chamber

The competence of the SBDC is bound up with the complex arrangements for the administration of the International Seabed Area, details of which

---

[113] See Rosenne and Sohn, *Commentary* (n. 3) p. 406.   [114] *Ibid.*, 409.

must be sought elsewhere.[115] It is relevant to note, however, that the SBDC's jurisdiction, which is set out in Article 187,[116] covers disputes between states; between a state and the International Seabed Authority; between the International Seabed Authority and a prospective contractor; and between the parties to a contract, including state enterprises and natural or juridical persons. Thus, although the privileges traditionally accorded to states are by no means ignored,[117] the Convention seeks to ensure that machinery for the settlement of disputes is available to all prospective participants in the International Seabed Area.

The law to be applied by the SBDC corresponds to the nature of its jurisdiction. In addition to the provisions of Article 293, which, as noted earlier, all tribunals are to apply, the SBDC is to apply 'the rules, regulations and procedures of the Authority' adopted in accordance with the Convention, together with 'the terms of contracts concerning activities in the Area in matters relating to those contracts' (Annex VI, Article 38). While it can perhaps be argued that the scope of Article 293 is wide enough to make such particularisation unnecessary, the aim here was presumably 'to specify, with a view to greater clarity by means of emphasis, those parts of the law of the Convention itself which would be likely always to be relevant in proceedings before the Seabed Disputes Chamber, but which would be less likely to be of significance in proceedings before the full Tribunal'.[118]

The SBDC has a jurisdiction which is automatically accepted by all parties to the Convention. In respect of certain disputes there are nevertheless alternative procedures available. Thus, the principle of freedom of choice, already encountered in the general provisions of the Convention, emerges again in the treatment of seabed disputes. As an alternative to the SBDC, a dispute between states concerning the seabed articles of the Convention may be referred to an ordinary chamber of the ITLOS by agreement. As a further alternative, it may, at the request of any party to the dispute, be referred to the type of ad hoc chamber of the SBDC already described (Article 188(1)(b)). Similarly, unless the parties otherwise agree, disputes concerning the application or interpretation of a contract can be referred at the request of either party to binding commercial arbitration in accordance with the UNCITRAL Arbitration Rules. The Arbitral Tribunal, however, has no authority to interpret the Convention and any such issue must be referred to the SBDC for a ruling (Article 188(2)(a)), a procedure

---

[115] See note 50 above; and Churchill and Lowe, *Law of the Sea* (n. 2) ch. 12. Also Y. Tanaka, *The International Law of the Sea*, Cambridge, 2012, pp. 170–85.

[116] In addition to the jurisdiction conferred by Art. 187, the SBDC is competent to prescribe provisional measures under Art. 290.

[117] In proceedings involving natural or juridical persons, Art. 190 gives a right of appearance and participation to sponsoring states.

[118] A. R. Carnegie, 'The Law of the Sea Tribunal' (1979) 28 *ICLQ*, 669 at 680.

similar to a request for an advisory opinion.[119] This unusual arrangement, which may give rise to difficulties in practice, is clearly an attempt to combine the established advantages of commercial arbitration with the need for a uniform interpretation of the Convention.

The exclusion of certain issues on the ground of non-justiciability provides another parallel between the general provisions of the Convention and those relating to the SBDC. Article 189 prohibits the latter from questioning the exercise by the International Seabed Authority of its discretionary powers under the Convention. Moreover, unless the SBDC is asked for an advisory opinion on the point, it may not 'pronounce itself on the question of whether any rules, regulations and procedures of the Authority are in conformity with this Convention, nor declare invalid any such rules, regulations and procedures'. Essentially, therefore, its jurisdiction is confined to questions concerning the application of the Convention and its associated legislation. Like the provisions on the discretion of coastal states considered earlier, these prohibitions are an uncompromising assertion of the controversial proposition that certain disputes concerning the exercise of legal powers are unsuitable for adjudication. Within its allotted sphere, decisions of the SBDC are binding and the Convention provides that in the territories of the states parties, such decisions shall be enforceable 'in the same manner as judgments or orders of the highest court of the State Party in whose territory the enforcement is sought' (Annex VI, Article 39).

10.7.3 Advisory Opinions

Under Article 191 of the Convention, the SBDC has the power to give advisory opinions at the request of the Assembly or the Council of the International Seabed Authority (ISA) 'on legal questions arising within the scope of their activities'.

In 2011 the Chamber exercised this power for the first time when it handed down its advisory opinion in the *Activities in the Area* case.[120] The ISA Council had been asked by Nauru to request an opinion clarifying the possible future obligations of a state mining in international waters. The Council then reformulated Nauru's request into three questions which provided the basis for the Chamber's advisory opinion. The most significant feature of the case is the Chamber's discussion of the obligations of sponsoring states to exercise due diligence, including their obligation to provide environmental impact statements, which makes an important

---

[119] Wolfrum, 'Advisory Opinions' (n. 108) p. 35, at 55.
[120] *Responsibilities and Obligations of States with respect to Activities in the Area*, Advisory Opinion, 1 February 2011, [2011] ITLOS Reports 10 and see D. Freestone, Note (2011) 105 AJIL, 755.

contribution to environmental law. This was not only the first request to the SBDC for an advisory opinion, but also the first case of any kind to be referred to the Chamber.

10.8 Significance of the Convention and its Dispute Settlement Provisions

When the ITLOS was founded, doubts were expressed in some quarters that the new tribunal might not have enough business to justify its existence. However, these fears have not been realised.

In an essay in 1975, a leading commentator suggested that the establishment of an effective system for the settlement of disputes arising out of the 1982 Convention should be regarded as 'one of the pillars of the new world order in the ocean space itself'.[121] The arrangements which were eventually negotiated are, as has been seen, both complex and less than ideal in certain respects. Regarded, however, as an exercise in the art of the possible, they represent a remarkable achievement, the influence of which on both the handling of disputes and the law of the sea itself has already been profound.

10.8.1 The Increasing Use of UNCLOS Dispute Settlement and the ITLOS

In the first years after its inauguration, the ITLOS decided several important cases. In the *MV Saiga No. 2* case,[122] the Tribunal decided that Guinea must pay compensation for arresting and detaining a tanker registered in St Vincent and the Grenadines because the disputed actions could not be justified under the Convention. In the *Bangladesh/Myanmar* case[123] it established a single maritime boundary between the two states in the Bay of Bengal, delimiting each state's territorial sea, as well as its exclusive economic zone (EEZ) and continental shelf. This, the Tribunal's first maritime boundary decision, proved influential when an Annex VII arbitration tribunal subsequently delimited the corresponding Bangladesh/India maritime boundary. And in the *M/V Virginia G* case[124] between Panama and Guinea-Bissau, the Tribunal decided that the refuelling of vessels fishing in the EEZ is subject to regulation by the coastal state and that confiscation of the tanker and its cargo is a permissible penalty for violation of the coastal state's fishing regulations. However, because

---

[121] Adede, 'Settlement of disputes' (n. 13) 798.
[122] *MV Saiga (No. 2) Case (Saint Vincent and the Grenadines v. Guinea)*, Judgment [1999] ITLOS Reports 10, also (1999) 38 ILM 1323; and see L. de La Fayette, Note (2000) 49 *ICLQ*, 467.
[123] *Delimitation of the Maritime Boundary in the Bay of Bengal (Bangladesh/Myanmar)*, Judgment, [2012] ITLOS Reports 4, and see D. H. Anderson, Note (2012) 106 *AJIL*, 817.
[124] *MV Virginia G (Panama/Guinea-Bissau)*, Judgment [2014] ITLOS Reports 4, also (2014) 53 ILM 1164, and see B. H. Oxman and V. P. Cogliati-Banz, Note (2014) 108 *AJIL*, 769.

confiscation was not necessary in the circumstances of this case, Panama was awarded damages. In recent years, the Tribunal's docket has also increased, and several arbitrations under Annex VII have also been initiated or decided, as we have seen.

Various other features of the Tribunal's record shed further light on its significance and its potential. In the *Swordfish* case, as mentioned earlier, Chile originally referred its dispute with the European Community to Annex VII arbitration, but then, after discussions between the parties, the case was transferred to ITLOS, a special chamber being set up under Article 17(2) of the Tribunal's Statute at the end of 2000 for this purpose.[125] Although proceedings were subsequently suspended, the case is notable as the first contentious case between a state and an organisation to be referred to an international court, as well as a demonstration of the flexibility of the Convention's procedures. It is also a reminder of the value of obligatory jurisdiction in encouraging accommodation, a point also apparent from the *Chaisiri Reefer 2* case,[126] another prompt-release application under Article 292, which was entered on the Tribunal's list in 2001, but was then discontinued following an agreement between the parties.

A perceptive observer has noted that '[t]he experience of most international courts is to start slowly and steadily build up their docket'.[127] This may well be the route that the ITLOS will follow. A member of the Tribunal described its judicial policy as 'to administer justice diligently, thoroughly and fairly, in accordance with the applicable law, without any unnecessary expense or delay'.[128] The Tribunal's work to date has shown its commitment to these objectives – its speed in dealing with cases under Article 292 and the constructive use of its discretion in responding to requests for provisional measures of protection being particularly commendable. As its intention to develop 'user-friendly' procedures is also evident from current practice, the record of ITLOS to date is far from negligible and contains encouraging signs for the future.

Although the 1982 Law of the Sea Convention has been ratified by more than 160 states, and there has been increasing practice under Part XV, there is much that has not yet been tested. Consequently, how well it will achieve its purpose still remains to be seen. But, if the record so far can

---

[125] See the Tribunal's Order of 20 December 2000. On this and the subsequent suspension of the proceedings, see A. Serdy, 'See you in port' (2002) 3 *Melbourne JIL*, 79.

[126] On this case, brought by Panama against Yemen, see T. L. McDorman, Note (2001) 12 *YBIEL*, 592.

[127] See the speech of the President of the ICJ, Rosalyn Higgins, on the occasion of the tenth anniversary of ITLOS in 2006, quoted in T. Treves, 'The International Tribunal for the Law of the Sea in 2006' (2007) 7 *Global Community YBILJ*, 231 at 232.

[128] See Anderson, 'The International Tribunal' (n. 99) p. 79. See also P. Chandrasekhara Rao, 'The International Tribunal for the Law of the Sea: an evaluation', in N. Ando, E. McWhinney and R. Wolfrum (eds), *Liber Amicorum Judge Shigeru Oda*, The Hague, 2002, p. 667.

provide some pointers to the future, the treatment of dispute settlement in the Convention is in itself highly significant, for it shows the issues which arise in attempting to create a regulatory framework for a major area of state activity, and the means available for handling such issues in the contemporary world.

10.8.2 Dispute Settlement under the UNCLOS as a 'Comprehensive System'?

The first, and in many ways the most important, question is whether the provision of machinery for the settlement of disputes is to be an integral part of the treaty. One of the most encouraging features of the Convention is that this question is answered positively, as states cannot make reservations to the dispute settlement provisions under Part XV. It must be remembered, of course, that the arrangements set out in the Convention come into play only when the parties have not made other arrangements and in that sense are essentially ancillary. Even so, the recognition that the Convention must contain provisions dealing with dispute settlement was a key step forward, contrasting sharply with previous conventions on the subject. With this basic issue resolved, the characteristics of the machinery to be provided are a matter of who, what, when and how.

The Convention, as we have seen, deals with the issue of 'who' by utilising all the traditional means of dispute settlement including negotiation, the International Court and commercial arbitration. It then adds (in effect) two new courts – ITLOS and its associated SBDC – and a variety of ad hoc bodies in the form of conciliation commissions and general and special tribunals of arbitration. To some extent, this proliferation of tribunals is accounted for by the variety and complexity of the Convention's provisions. There is, however, reason to believe that a feeling by the Group of 77 that new tribunals would more accurately reflect their views was also influential. When ITLOS started to work, some questioned whether a new court, dedicated to law of the sea disputes, was really necessary, especially as the International Court, which has dealt with many such cases, is currently enjoying something of a resurgence.[129] This raises wider issues about the proliferation of international tribunals generally, which will be considered in Chapter 14. All that needs to be said here is that ITLOS was conceived to meet a demand which was real enough at the time and

---

[129] See S. Oda, 'Dispute settlement prospects in the law of the sea' (1995) 44 *ICLQ*, 863; and earlier E. Lauterpacht, *Aspects of the Administration of International Justice*, Cambridge, 1991, pp. 19–22. For the contrary view, see J. I. Charney, 'The implications of expanding international dispute settlement systems: the 1982 Convention on the Law of the Sea' (1996) 90 *AJIL*, 69; and A. E. Boyle, 'Dispute settlement and the Law of the Sea Convention: problems of fragmentation and jurisdiction' (1997) 46 *ICLQ*, 37.

through its developing jurisprudence has an opportunity to answer its detractors.

The question 'what' is answered by the creation of an elaborate series of overlapping and exclusive jurisdictions, reflecting a desire to see technical disputes handled functionally, certain issues excluded from third-party review altogether and other issues dealt with by conciliation rather than adjudication. On the last two points, the influence of the Group of 77 is again apparent. As one would expect, several parties to the Convention, including a number of industrialised states, have taken advantage of the opportunity to opt out of the compulsory procedure which is offered by Article 298. However, whereas most have excepted all three categories of disputes specified therein, others have made exceptions which are more limited. A point of some importance with regard to both Article 298 and the scheme of the Convention generally is that, where a dispute involves several issues, the Convention's 'salami-slicing' approach means that not all aspects of the dispute may be subject to compulsory and binding settlement.[130] So, for example, if a dispute involves both high seas freedoms and a coastal state's rights in its exclusive economic zone, resolving the whole dispute through ITLOS or arbitration will require both parties' agreement.[131]

The possibilities for states to either avoid the binding settlement procedures in Section 2, by either deciding on a different method of settlement under Section 1 or by relying on the exceptions in Section 3, however, result in the reality that the UNCLOS Dispute Settlement System is not as comprehensive as it might seem. As explained by the Arbitral Tribunal in the *Southern Bluefin Tuna* case,

> It thus appears to the Tribunal that UNCLOS falls significantly short of establishing a truly comprehensive regime of compulsory jurisdiction entailing binding decisions.[132]

It is probably also because the Convention contains possibilities for states to either avoid the binding settlement procedures in Section 2, by either deciding on a different method of settlement under Section 1 or by relying on the exceptions in Section 3 that on several occasions states have refused to participate in arbitral proceedings under Annex VII, being convinced that the tribunal lacked jurisdiction in the case. A notable example is the *South China Sea* arbitration. From the outset, China rejected the Philippines' initiation of arbitration and decided to not participate in

---

[130] See Boyle *ibid.*, 41–7.
[131] For discussion of just such a dispute, see P. G. G. Davies, 'The EC/Canadian fisheries dispute in the North Atlantic' (1995) 44 *ICLQ*, 927.
[132] *Southern Bluefin Tuna Case (Australia and New Zealand v. Japan)*, Award on Jurisdiction and Admissibility (2000), text in (2009) 39 ILM 1359, para. 62.

the proceedings.[133] Article 9 of Annex VII of UNCLOS anticipates the possibility of one of the parties to a dispute not participating in proceedings and confirms that non-participation does not stop those proceedings from going ahead. Under Article 9, the participating party must request that proceedings continue, which was expressly done by the Philippines. Similarly, in the *Arctic Sunrise* case, in which Russia refused to participate, the Tribunal also extensively discussed its jurisdiction and the merits of the claim, emphasising that Article 9 of Annex VII to the Convention requires that '[b]efore making its award, the arbitral tribunal must satisfy itself not only that it has jurisdiction over the dispute but also that the claim is well-founded in fact and in law'.[134]

In answering the question 'when', the Convention places great emphasis on the parties' choice of means at all stages and, in respect of certain disputes, enables entities other than states to set the machinery in motion. It seems clear that, in relation to the provisions on obligatory settlement in particular, this element of choice was crucial to the acceptability of the Convention. The consequences of adopting what has been termed the 'cafeteria' approach to compulsory settlement[135] will only become fully apparent as practice under the Convention develops. However, it may be indicative that, in making their choices under Article 287, several states have nominated ITLOS, while a few have chosen the International Court of Justice, and some, as they are entitled to do, have opted for different forums for different purposes. Many states, on the other hand, have expressed no preference as yet, which suggests that arbitration, as the residual procedure, will continue to be prominent. In spite of the limitations already noted, the Convention's arrangements for obtaining binding decisions are actually quite extensive. Given the notorious difficulty of securing agreement on such procedures, this is a considerable achievement.

The last issue, 'how', raises the question of choice of law and the object of proceedings. The former, as we have indicated, is dealt with by according a dominant role to the Convention. The importance of this guarantee that the 'new' law of the sea will be the framework for decisions has already been explained. It should not be forgotten, however, that in conciliation proceedings the object is not to apply rules but to promote an amicable settlement. As conciliation occupies an important place in both the optional and obligatory machinery of the Convention, the inference to

---

[133] This is discussed in detail in the decisions on jurisdiction and on the merits. See *The South China Sea Arbitration (The Republic of Philippines v. The People's Republic of China)*, PCA Case No. 2013-19, Award on Jurisdiction and Admissibility, 29 October 2015; Award, 12 July 2016.

[134] *Arctic Sunrise (Kingdom of the Netherlands v. Russian Federation)*, PCA Case No. 2014-02, Merits, Award of 14 August 2015, paras. 4 ff and Award of 26 November 2014, para. 9.

[135] See Boyle, 'Dispute settlement and the Law of the Sea Convention' (n. 129) 40–1.

be drawn from the resolution of the *Jan Mayen* conciliation[136] – that in the law of the sea there are many problems 'which are better solved other than on a basis of strict law, or, indeed, cannot by their nature be solved on such a basis'[137] – appears to have been fully recognised. The same can be said of the 'Timor Sea' Conciliation, as we have seen.

10.8.3 UNCLOS Dispute Settlement and Related Agreements

As already noted, Article 288 envisages the use of the machinery of Part XV to deal with disputes involving other international agreements related to the 1982 Convention. The value of this provision and the wider potential of the Convention's arrangements for dispute settlement may be seen in a subsequent treaty intended to fill one of the gaps in the 1982 Convention, namely, the Straddling Stocks Agreement of 1995.[138] The Agreement provides in Article 30(1) that the provisions of Part XV of the 1982 Convention shall apply to all disputes concerning its interpretation or application, whether or not the states concerned are parties to the 1982 Convention. This in itself is significant, but Articles 30(2) and 30(5) of the Agreement add two new features to Part XV, widening its reach even further. The former extends its provisions to disputes concerning regional and other fisheries agreements, while the latter requires a court or tribunal having jurisdiction to apply not only the relevant provisions of the 1982 Convention and the 1995 Agreement, but also those of any regional or other fisheries agreement 'as well as generally accepted standards for the conservation and management of living marine resources'. By utilising Part XV and extending its scope, the Agreement is thus intended to encourage states which have assumed obligations with regard to straddling and migratory fish stocks to carry them out, whatever their legal origin.

For Article 30(2) of the Straddling Stocks Agreement to apply it is, of course, essential for the parties to a dispute to have ratified the Agreement, as well as the relevant regional treaty. It is therefore significant that a number of treaties establishing regional fisheries management organisations contain provisions similar to Article 30(1) of the Agreement, extending the dispute settlement machinery of the 1982 Convention to

---

[136] See Chapter 4.
[137] *Settlement of Disputes* (Australian Paper), 21 March 1975, quoted by Adede, 'Settlement of disputes' (n. 3) 80.
[138] Text in (1995) 34 ILM 1542. For analysis, see D. A. Balton, 'Strengthening the law of the sea: the new Agreement on Straddling Fish Stocks and Highly Migratory Fish Stocks' (1996) 27 *Ocean Development & International Law*, 125; see also D. H. Anderson, 'The Straddling Stocks Agreement of 1995' (1996) 45 *ICLQ*, 463. F. Orrego Vicuña, *The Changing International Law of High Seas Fisheries*, Cambridge, 1999, ch. 10; and A. Boyle, 'Problems of compulsory jurisdiction and the settlement of disputes relating to straddling fish stocks' in O. S. Stokke (ed.), *Governing High Seas Fisheries*, Oxford, 2001, p. 91.

disputes arising from the regional treaty, whether or not the states concerned are also parties to the 1995 Agreement. For example, the 2006 Southern Indian Ocean Fisheries Agreement contains a provision of this kind.[139] In this way, then, the obligations of the 1982 Convention may be extended beyond parties to the 1982 Convention itself and the 1995 Agreement to all those accepting the particular regional treaty.

However, to avoid misunderstanding, it must also be pointed out that several fishery conventions contain dispute settlement arrangements weaker than those of the 1982 Convention which will apply when the state or states concerned are not parties to the 1995 Agreement. Likewise, the numerous conventions concerned with marine pollution generally contain their own arrangements for dealing with disputes.[140] These, as noted earlier, will displace the machinery of the 1982 Convention by virtue of Articles 281 and 282 of the 1982 Convention, and there is also nothing to prevent states utilising the International Court, or traditional arbitration, to resolve their law of the sea disputes, if they so choose. The significance of the 1982 Convention is thus not that it aims to provide exclusive machinery for dealing with law of the sea disputes, but rather that it establishes a residual framework for treating such disputes seriously.

10.9 Further Reading

10.9.1 General References on Dispute Settlement under the UNCLOS

Allen, S., 'Article 297 of the United Nations Convention on the Law of the Sea and the Scope of Mandatory Jurisdiction' (2017) 48 *Ocean Development & International Law*, 3–4.

Bankes, N., 'Precluding the applicability of Section 2 of Part XV of the Law of the Sea Convention' (2017) 48 *Ocean Development & International Law*, 3–4, 239.

del Castillo, L. (ed.), *Law of the sea, from Grotius to the International Tribunal for the Law of the Sea: Liber Amicorum Judge Hugo Caminos*, Leiden/Boston, 2015.

Chinese Society of International Law, 'The South China Sea arbitration awards: a critical study' (2018) 18 *Chinese Journal of International Law*, 207.

Churchill, R., 'The general dispute settlement system of the UN Convention on the Law of the Sea: overview, context, and use' (2017) 48 *Ocean Development and International Law*, 216.

Espósito, C., J. Kraska, H. N. Scheiber and M.-S. Kwon, (eds), *Ocean Law and Policy: 20 Years under UNCLOS*, Leiden/Boston, 2017.

Forteau, M., and J. M. Thouvenin (eds), *Traité de droit international de la mer*, Paris, 2017.

---

[139] See R. Churchill, 'Trends in dispute settlement in the law of the sea: towards the increasing availability of compulsory means', in D. French, M. Saul and N. D. White (eds), *International Law and Dispute Settlement: New Problems and Techniques*, Oxford, 2010, p. 143 at p. 158.

[140] See Churchill, 'Trends in dispute settlement' (n. 139) pp. 163–6.

García-Revillo, M., *The Contentious and Advisory Jurisdiction of the International Tribunal for the Law of the Sea*, Leiden/Boston, 2016.

Gautier, P., 'Access to international courts and tribunals in Law of the Sea Disputes', in G. Eiriksson, J.C. Sainz-Borgoand and H. Guđmundsdóttir (eds), *Liber amicorum: in honour of a modern Renaissance man: His Excellency Guđmundur Eiríksson*, Delhi, 2017, pp. 165–93.

Harrison, J., 'Defining disputes and characterizing claims: subject-matter jurisdiction in Law of the Sea Convention litigation' (2017) 48 *Ocean Development & International Law*, 3–4, 269.

Kolodkin, A. L., V. N. Gutsuliak and I. V. Bobrova, *The World Ocean: International Legal Regime*, The Hague, 2010.

Linkevičius, J., 'International Tribunal for the Law of the Sea: the limits of compulsory jurisdiction' (2012) 11 *Baltic Yearbook of International Law*, 153–72.

Nordquist, M. H., N. R. Grandy, S. N. Nandan, and S. Rosenne (eds), *United Nations Convention on the Law of the Sea, 1982: A Commentary*, Dordrecht/Leiden/Boston, 1985–2011 (7 volumes).

Oda, S., *Fifty Years of the Law of the Sea: With a Special Section on the International Court of Justice*, Dordrecht, 1993.

Oral, N., 'Implementing Part XII of the 1982 UN Law of the Sea Convention and the Role of International Courts', in N. Boschiero, T. Scovazzi, C. Pitea and C. Ragni (eds), *International Courts and the Development of International Law: Essays in Honour of Tullio Treves*, The Hague, 2013, pp. 403–23.

Parlett, K., 'Beyond the four corners of the convention: expanding the scope of jurisdiction of Law of the Sea Tribunals' (2017) 48 *Ocean Development & International Law*, 3–4, 284–299.

Perez, B., 'The Permanent Court of Arbitration and its contribution to dispute settlement under the Law of the Sea' (2017) 42 *L' Observateur des Nations Unies*, 107–16.

Pinto, M., 'Asia and Dispute Settlement: the Law of the Sea', in R. Wolfrum, M. Seršić and T. M. Šošić (eds), *Contemporary developments in international law: essays in honour of Budislav Vukas*, Leiden/Boston, 2016, pp. 755–69.

Sands, P., 'Of Courts and Competition: Dispute Settlement under Part XV of UNCLOS', in R. Wolfrum (et al.) (eds), *Contemporary developments in international law: essays in honour of Budislav Vukas*, Leiden/Boston, 2016, pp. 789–98.

Trevisanut, S., 'Twenty Years of Prompt Release of Vessels: Admissibility, Jurisdiction, and Recent Trends' (2017) 48 *Ocean Development & International Law*, 300–12.

Vitzthum, W., and G. Hafner, *Handbuch des Seerechts*, München, 2006.

Zou, Keyuan, and Qiang Ye, 'Interpretation and application of Article 298 of the Law of the Sea Convention in recent Annex VII arbitrations: an appraisal' (2017) 48 *Ocean Development & International Law*, 331–44.

10.9.2 Treaties, Official Documents and Collections of Documents

Patel, B. N., *Law of the Sea: International Tribunal for the Law of the Sea, Jurisprudence: Case Commentary, Case-Law, Digest and Reference Guide (1994–2014)*, Lucknow, 2015.

Lowe, V., and S. Talmon (eds), *The Legal Order of the Oceans: Basic Documents on the Law of the Sea*, Oxford, 2009.

Rao, P. C., and P. Gautier, *International Tribunal for the Law of the Sea: Law, Practice and Procedure*, Cheltenham, 2018.

Sohn, L. B., J. E. Noyes, E. Franckx and K. Gustafson (eds), *Cases and Materials on the Law of the Sea*, Leiden, 2014.

11

International Trade Disputes

The development of special arrangements to deal with disputes involving international trade began in the middle of the last century and has now produced one of the most effective, as well as one of the most important, systems of international dispute settlement. Thus, in contrast to law of the sea disputes, which we have seen are subject to a system which came into force in 1994, trade disputes can be dealt with through arrangements which have been progressively refined, based on regional as well as general agreements. Since limitations of space preclude examining this complex network in detail, this chapter focuses on the central element and outlines the dispute settlement system of the World Trade Organization (WTO).

11.1 From GATT (1947) to the World Trade Organization

As the Second World War drew to a close, governments were forced to consider the shape of the post-war world. First among their considerations was the issue of international peace and security, which led to the creation of the United Nations. However, not far behind came financial and economic issues, including international trade, which also had institutional implications. The 1930s had been an anarchic period in every sense, and to avoid repeating the experience the leaders of the post-war era resolved to establish arrangements which would reflect the realities of economic interdependence. The institutions created in this period, which include the International Monetary Fund, the World Bank and the General Agreement on Tariffs and Trade (GATT), have provided the framework for international economic relations ever since, supplemented, of course, by numerous subsequent instruments and organisations, including regional arrangements, set up for particular purposes.[1]

The 1947 GATT was originally intended as a provisional agreement for the liberalisation of tariffs, pending the establishment of permanent arrangements through a new body to be known as the International Trade Organization (ITO). However, the ITO was never formed owing

---

[1] See J. H. Jackson, 'Reflections on problems of international economic relations', in M. K. Young and Y. Iwasawa (eds), *Trilateral Perspectives on International Legal Issues*, Irvington on Hudson, NY, 1996, p. 263. See also D. L. M. Kennedy and J. D. Southwick (eds), *The Political Economy of International Trade Law*, Cambridge, 2002.

to domestic opposition within the United States. As a result, the GATT became a permanent system of great complexity, evolving into an institution with organs and decision-making powers. The failure of the ITO left a gap which the evolution of the GATT went some way to fill, but numerous problems remained. In areas not covered by GATT law, such as international movements of services, persons and capital, protectionist practices re-emerged, and, even in areas which were covered, governments often failed to observe their obligations.[2] An attempt to address some of these problems was made at the Tokyo Round of trade negotiations between 1973 and 1979, but it was not until the subsequent Uruguay Round, which began in 1986, that they were tackled comprehensively.

After much hard bargaining, the Uruguay Round concluded in 1994 with the signing of the Final Act, which contains the Agreement Establishing the World Trade Organization ('Marrakesh Agreement').[3] The aim of the Agreement, which entered into force on 1 January 1995, is ambitious, being nothing less than the creation of an integrated legal system for world trade, intended to reconstruct the foundations of the international economic order. To this end, the Agreement creates an entirely new international institution, the World Trade Organization, to provide structural coherence, and in comprehensive substantive provisions brings together into a single legal framework all previous GATT agreements and new Uruguay Round agreements, covering matters such as trade in services which previously lacked regulation.[4] The vital issue of dispute settlement is addressed in a new Understanding on Rules and Procedures Governing the Settlement of Disputes (commonly referred to as 'Dispute Settlement Understanding' or 'DSU')[5] annexed to the main Agreement.

11.2 The WTO Dispute Settlement Understanding

If rules to promote fair trading are to be effective, they need to be accompanied by provisions for settling disputes, for only thus can self-serving interpretation be exposed and unilateralism discouraged. There is an obvious parallel here with the law of the sea where, as noted earlier, similar thinking led many governments to see the provisions of Part XV as

---

[2] See E.-U. Petersmann, *The GATT/WTO Dispute Settlement System*, Dordrecht, 1997, p. 90, and, earlier, the same author's 'The dispute settlement system of the World Trade Organization and the evolution of the GATT dispute settlement system since 1948' (1994) 31 *Common Market L Rev.*, 1157 at 1160.
[3] Text in (1994) 33 ILM 1125.
[4] Petersmann, *The GATT/WTO System* (n. 2) pp. 44–54. For the important issue of transitional arrangements, see P. M. Moore, 'The decisions bridging the GATT 1947 and the WTO Agreement' (1996) 90 *AJIL*, 317.
[5] WTO Understanding on Rules and Procedures Governing the Settlement of Disputes, 15 April 1994 (1994) 33 ILM 1226.

a vital component of the 1982 Law of the Sea Convention. In the trade context, such considerations had prompted the development within the GATT of a relatively sophisticated procedure for dealing with disputes even before the 1994 Agreement.[6] While the new Dispute Settlement Understanding develops the procedure in various ways, it is firmly rooted in established practice under the GATT. To understand its content and to see what it adds, it is therefore necessary to say a few words about the earlier system.

11.2.1 Dispute Settlement under the GATT

The original GATT Treaty of 1947 dealt only briefly with dispute settlement, although it did provide in Articles 22 and 23 for consultation, followed, if necessary, by the submission of issues to the GATT Contracting Parties. In the early years, disputes were often referred to working parties, consisting of the representatives of states and always including the parties to the dispute.[7] The working party's function was to examine the question and produce a report setting out the various views. This method of dealing with disputes was essentially a kind of mediation, since the aim of the process was to encourage the protagonists to resolve their differences by bringing the influence of outside states to bear. Before long, however, a more rule-oriented system was evolved and the practice developed of referring disputes to 'panels', composed of individuals rather than governmental representatives, whose findings and recommendations were passed to the GATT Council, representing the Contracting Parties.

Panels proved increasingly popular and eventually supplanted the working party procedure. As reports began to focus on the issue of treaty violations, the procedure became increasingly legalistic and acquired some of the characteristics of arbitration. It is important to appreciate, however, that, as the primary aim was still to achieve an agreement between the parties to the dispute, elements of conciliation were present throughout the process. Moreover, as the report of a panel required adoption by all the Contracting Parties, by consensus by the GATT Council, it did not in itself create binding obligations. It was therefore largely 'a power-based system of dispute settlement through diplomatic negotiations'.[8]

---

[6] See Petersmann, *The GATT/WTO System* (n. 2) pp. 66–92; I. Van Bael, 'The GATT dispute settlement procedure' (1988) 22 *J. World Trade*, 67; and E. Canal-Forgues and R. Ostrihansky, 'New developments in the GATT dispute settlement procedures' (1990) 24 *J. World Trade*, 67.

[7] See Y. Iwasawa, 'Settlement of disputes concerning the WTO Agreement: Various means other than panel procedures', in M. K. Young and Y. Iwasawa (eds), *Trilateral Perspectives on International Legal Issues*, Irvington on Hudson, NY, 1996, p. 377 at pp. 386–9.

[8] P. Van den Bossche and W. Zdouc, *Law and Policy of the World Trade Organization*, 4th ed., Cambridge, 2017, 296.

As well as panels and working groups, it was possible for Contracting Parties to make use of the good offices of the Director-General of GATT, to set up inquiries and to refer disputes to arbitration. Between 1947 and 1995, more than 150 disputes were referred to the Contracting Parties and most were settled through its procedures.[9] However, despite this generally successful record, a number of weaknesses in the system had become apparent and were the subject of attention during the Uruguay Round. An obvious weakness of the panel procedure was that, since both setting up a panel and the adoption of its report required consensus in the GATT Council, it was possible for a state whose actions were challenged to block effective action, for example in relation to the formation of Panels and the adoption of Panel reports in the GATT Council.[10] A second weakness was that arrangements for securing the implementation of decisions were weak or unclear. And a third was that, since the various GATT and Tokyo Round agreements contained different substantive rules and different arrangements for dispute settlement, both 'norm shopping' (seeking the most favourable rule) and 'forum shopping' (seeking the most favourable procedure) were possible.[11]

The Dispute Settlement Understanding, as we shall see, incorporates many features of the existing GATT procedures. However, to deal with the deficiencies identified above, a number of major innovations are also introduced.[12] To deal with norm and forum shopping, the DSU establishes a unified dispute settlement system for the whole GATT/WTO system, including the issues of services and intellectual property. To deal with implementation, new and clearer procedures are laid down. And, to deal with the problem of political interference, the role formerly carried out by the GATT Council is assigned to a new organ called the Dispute Settlement Body (DSB). Although still made up of states, the DSB can refuse to establish a panel, or decline to approve a report, only if there is a consensus (a negative or reverse consensus); these actions therefore become virtually automatic. Since this change effectively removes the political check on panel procedures, an appellate procedure is included as a further innovation. The general effect of the DSU is thus to consolidate existing procedures and at the same time bring them up to date.

---

[9] Ibid., 377.
[10] Mitsuo Matsushita, Thomas Schoenbaum, Petros C. Mavroidis, Michael Hahn, *The World Trade Organization: Law, Practice, and Policy*, 3rd ed., Oxford, 2015, p. 85.
[11] See Petersmann, *The GATT/WTO System* (n. 2) p. 90.
[12] For a concise overview, see A. F. Lowenfeld, 'Remedies along with rights: institutional reform in the new GATT' (1994) 88 *AJIL*, 477; and P. T. B. Kohona, 'Dispute resolution under the World Trade Organization' (1994) 28(2) *J World Trade* 23. For a more detailed treatment, see D. Palmeter and P. C. Mavroidis, *Dispute Settlement in the World Trade Organization: Practice and Procedure*, 2nd ed., Cambridge, 2004.

11.2.2 The WTO DSU: Main Principles and Jurisdiction

Dispute settlement under the WTO is compulsory and exclusive. It is compulsory because the WTO member states are automatically bound by the provisions of the DSU, which is an annex (Annex 2) to the Agreement Establishing the World Trade Organization. There is, in other words, no possibility to make reservations to or otherwise opt out of the dispute settlement system contained in the DSU.[13] Additional consent to settle a specific dispute moreover is not needed.

A second important feature is the exclusive nature of the dispute settlement system. The WTO member states have no other option than to settle their disputes arising under the WTO Agreement by the means and procedures laid out in the DSU. This is confirmed by several provisions of the DSU. Article 1(1) DSU confirms that 'the rules and procedures of this Understanding shall apply to disputes brought pursuant to the consultation and dispute settlement provisions of the agreements listed in Appendix 1 to this Understanding'. Furthermore, Article 23(1) states that

> when Members seek the redress of a violation of obligations or other nullification or impairment of benefits under the covered agreements or an impediment to the attainment of any objective of the covered agreements, they shall have recourse to, and abide by, the rules and procedures of this Understanding.

As far as jurisdiction *ratione personae* is concerned, only WTO member states have access to the dispute settlement system. The latter is thus purely an inter-state method of settlement, to the exclusion of individuals, corporations and international organisations.

In terms of jurisdiction *ratione materiae*, as noted in Article 1(1) DSU, the dispute settlement applies to disputes arising under 'covered agreements', which are the agreements listed in Appendix 1 to the DSU. These include amongst others the WTO Treaty itself, the GATT 1994, the General Agreement on Trade in Services (GATS), the Agreement on Trade-Related Aspects of Intellectual Property Rights (TRIPS), and the Agreement on Government Procurement (a plurilateral agreement to which not all WTO members are parties).

The DSU contains interesting features in terms of jurisdiction *ratione materiae*. As mentioned in the introductory chapter, the question of whether a 'dispute' exists between parties is essential to establish and delimit the issues upon which a court or tribunal is empowered to

---

[13] Article XVI(5) WTO Agreement: 'No reservations may be made in respect of any provision of this Agreement. Reservations in respect of any of the provisions of the Multilateral Trade Agreements may only be made to the extent provided for in those Agreements. Reservations in respect of a provision of a Plurilateral Trade Agreement shall be governed by the provisions of that Agreement.'

pronounce itself resulting in a final and binding decision. However, the WTO DSU does not limit settlement to 'disputes', but extends also to 'situations' and 'non-violation complaints' in case a benefit under a WTO Agreement is being nullified or impaired.[14]

The broad scope of application of *ratione materiae* is mentioned, for example, in Article 3(3) DSU, which more generally refers to the overall objective of dispute settlement:

> The prompt settlement of situations in which a Member considers that any benefits accruing to it directly or indirectly under the covered agreements are being impaired by measures taken by another Member is essential to the effective functioning of the WTO and the maintenance of a proper balance between the rights and obligations of Members.

It should be kept in mind however that the 'covered agreements' may contain provisions relating to dispute settlement, which also apply. According to Article 1(2) DSU

> The rules and procedures of this Understanding shall apply subject to such special or additional rules and procedures on dispute settlement contained in the covered agreements as are identified in Appendix 2 to this Understanding.

This means that the provisions relating to dispute settlement in the covered agreements play an important role alongside the DSU and the WTO Agreement. For example, Article XXIII(1) GATT entitled 'Nullification or Impairment' extends dispute settlement to the situation where a contracting party considers that 'any benefit accruing to it directly or indirectly under this Agreement is being nullified or impaired or that the attainment of any objective of the Agreement is being impeded' as a result of:

(a) the failure of another contracting party to carry out its obligations under this Agreement, or
(b) the application by another contracting party of any measure, whether or not it conflicts with the provisions of this Agreement, or
(c) the existence of any other situation,

It is beyond the scope of this chapter to discuss in detail the measures capable of falling under the jurisdiction *ratione materiae* of the WTO DSU,[15] but Article XXIII(1) GATT clearly illustrates that not only a 'failure to carry out obligations' ('violation complaints'), but also the application of a measure which is not 'in conflict with a provision' ('non-violation complaints'), or 'any other situation' ('situation complaints') may result

---

[14] See Art. 3(3) WTO DSU and Article XXIII GATT.
[15] See on this: Van den Bossche and Zdouc, *Law and Policy of the World Trade Organization* (n. 8) pp. 168–79.

in triggering the dispute settlement mechanism.[16] Situation and non-violation complaints are rare.[17]

Before looking at the main methods of settlement and their functioning, the pivotal role of the Dispute Settlement Body (DSB) needs to be mentioned. The DSB in fact is the WTO General Council (which is composed of representatives of all WTO member states) but convenes as the DSB when discharging its functions in relation to dispute settlement. Its importance in relation to dispute settlement cannot be overstated, since, as was mentioned, it has the authority to

> establish panels, adopt panel and Appellate Body reports, maintain surveillance of implementation of rulings and recommendations, and authorize suspension of concessions and other obligations under the covered agreements.[18]

It is important to emphasise here again that when the DSB establishes panels, and adopts the panel and Appellate Body reports, it does so by 'reverse consensus'.[19]

The main features of the DSU may now therefore be considered in a little more detail.

11.3 Consultations

The aim of the GATT procedures has always been to resolve disputes, whenever possible, through agreement between the parties, rather than by seeking to identify treaty violations. Accordingly, consultation, which it will be recalled is also a good way of avoiding disputes, has always been prominent in those procedures. Articles XXII(1) and XXIII(1) of the GATT provide for bilateral consultations in general terms, and the DSU, based substantially on provisions agreed in 1989,[20] spells out the implications in some detail.

Article 4(3) contains an obligation to enter into consultations in good faith on request, and Article 4(5) reflects a preference for this method by giving consultations priority over other procedures:

> In the course of consultations in accordance with the provisions of a covered agreement, before resorting to further action under this Understanding, Members should attempt to obtain satisfactory adjustment of the matter.

Consultations are not only a matter of preference. The DSU conditions the rights of the parties to a dispute to request the Dispute Settlement Body to

---

[16] For a discussion, see Legal Affairs Division and the Rules Division of the WTO Secretariat, and the Appellate Body Secretariat, *A Handbook on the WTO Dispute Settlement System*, 2nd ed., Cambridge, 2017, 47 ff.
[17] Van den Bossche and Zdouc, *Law and Policy of the World Trade Organization* (n. 8), 181.
[18] Article 2(1) DSU.   [19] See Articles 6(1) and 17(14) DSU.
[20] See Canal-Forgues and Ostrihansky, 'New developments' (n. 6) 68–70.

establish a panel to settle the dispute to a prior exhaustion of a mandatory consultation for sixty days.[21] A request to establish a panel may be made before if both parties agree, or if the other member either 'does not respond within 10 days after the date of receipt of the request, or does not enter into consultations within a period of no more than 30 days, or a period otherwise mutually agreed, after the date of receipt of the request' (Article 4(3)).

An obligation to consult, like an obligation to negotiate, can be used by an unscrupulous government to postpone resort to other procedures, perhaps indefinitely, unless the precise scope of the obligation is carefully defined. To remove the possibility of abuse, and also to imbue the parties with a sense of urgency, the DSU contains strict time limits. The state to which a request for consultations is submitted has just ten days to respond and must enter into consultations within thirty days of the request (Article 4(3)). Consultations must also be concluded within sixty days of the request (Article 4(7)). Even stricter deadlines apply in urgent cases (Article 4(8)) and failure to meet any of the deadlines immediately entitles the complaining party to request the establishment of a panel.

When consultations take place they are confidential and without prejudice to the rights of the states concerned (Article 4(6)). However, it is important to appreciate that the reference to confidentiality here relates to the content of the discussions, not to the fact that they are taking place or to their outcome. Articles 4(4) and 3(6) make it clear that the occurrence and outcome must both be notified to the DSB and relevant bodies. Such notification was not required before 1989, and so this was an innovation. Incorporating this requirement into the DSU has the effect of placing bilateral consultations under the control of the WTO, so helping to integrate the dispute settlement system.

International trade disputes, like some of the disputes considered in earlier chapters, are not exclusively bilateral but often involve the interests of third parties. Because this is frequently the situation in trade relations, the DSU contains a number of provisions concerned with disputes of a multilateral character. As regards consultation, the relevant provision is Article 4(11), which allows a third state which considers that it has 'a substantial trade interest' in any consultations under Article XXII GATT 1994, Article XXII GATS, or the corresponding provisions in other covered agreements, to indicate a desire to join them. It may then do so, provided the member to which the request was made agrees that the claim of substantial interest is well-founded. A study in 1994 found more than twenty instances in which third-party joinder had been permitted under an earlier version of this provision,[22] and the facility has been extensively used

---

[21] Article 4(7) WTO DSU. [22] See Iwasawa, 'Settlement of disputes' (n. 7) p. 381.

since, indicating its practical value. If a request for joinder is refused, the applicant can, of course, seek separate bilateral consultations under Article 4 (3).

The significance of consultation as a means of dealing with international trade disputes can be seen from the record, which shows that around one-fifth of the disputes brought to settlement under the DSU have been settled by consultation.[23] The high success rate is no doubt partly because a round of consultation may sometimes be all that is needed to reach an agreement. It is worth pointing out, however, that consultation can be a continuing process, since governments often maintain a dialogue while the panel procedure or other moves are in progress. Thus, the initial obligation to try consultation by no means exhausts its possibilities, for, as the situation and the parties' perceptions change, a solution may emerge at a later stage, even if the first contacts are unsuccessful.[24]

11.4 Good Offices, Conciliation and Mediation

A system which has consistently emphasised the settlement of disputes through agreement might be expected to recognise the role of good offices and mediation, which are both informal ways of bringing the parties together, and also of conciliation, which, as noted in Chapter 5, is a more structured process. In various forms, good offices, conciliation and mediation have all featured in the GATT system and demonstrated their usefulness. As mentioned earlier, these 'diplomatic' methods cannot always be sharply distinguished from each other in practice and this has certainly been so in the present context. While the DSU contains more detail on these methods than previous instruments,[25] it groups them together in a single article, which visibly highlights their interconnection.

Good offices, conciliation and mediation are voluntary procedures and require the parties' agreement (Article 5(1)). This immediately distinguishes them from consultation which, it will be recalled, is mandatory. They may, however, be requested by a state at any time and at any point in a dispute. They can also be terminated at any time and, once terminated, entitle the complaining party to request the establishment of a panel,

---

[23] Van den Bossche and W. Zdouc, *Law and Policy of the World Trade Organization* (n. 8) p. 165. On the use of consultations, see M. L. Busch and E. Reinhardt, 'Testing international trade law: empirical studies of GATT/WTO dispute settlement' in D. L. Kennedy and J. D. Southwick (eds), *The Political Economy of International Trade Law*, Cambridge, 2002, p. 457 at pp. 467–70.

[24] Moreover, panels have been known to suggest further consultations as a means of avoiding difficult decisions: see Iwasawa, 'Settlement of disputes' (n. 7) pp. 380–1. It has been suggested, however, that a greater emphasis on consultations would be beneficial: see T. J. Schoenbaum, 'WTO dispute settlement: praise and suggestions for reform' (1998) 47 *ICLQ* 647 at 648–52.

[25] On the treatment of good offices, conciliation and mediation in the 1989 'Improvements', see Canal-Forgues and Ostrihansky, 'New developments' (n. 6) 70–1.

provided the sixty-day consultation period has elapsed (Article 5(3) and (4)). Under some of the Tokyo Round agreements, certain disputes had to be referred to a conciliation commission of member states before a state could request a panel. But this requirement, which tended to polarise positions, has now been abandoned.[26] As with consultations, proceedings involving good offices, conciliation and mediation are confidential and without prejudice to the parties' rights, and a further similarity is that, as might be expected, if the parties agree, these procedures can continue while panel proceedings are in progress (Article 5(5)).

Who performs good offices, conciliation and mediation? In theory, if states employ those processes, they can refer a trade dispute to any competent individual, group or organ. In practice, however, the choice is more limited. Unlike the 1982 Law of the Sea Convention and many other treaties, the DSU contains no arrangements for establishing conciliation commissions and similar bodies, apart from the provisions on panels which we shall come to shortly. Indeed, the only possibility which is specifically mentioned in this section is the reference of a dispute to the Director-General of the WTO, who under Article 5(6) is authorised to offer good offices, conciliation or mediation, acting in an *ex officio* capacity.

References to the good offices of the Director-General of the GATT are to be found in earlier instruments, but initially the facility does not appear to have been much used. There are, however, under the GATT, a number of cases which illustrate both the characteristics of this form of intervention and its value. In the *Copper* case[27] in 1987, the European Community (EC) and Japan jointly requested the good offices of the Director-General in their dispute over copper ores and concentrates. The Director-General appointed a distinguished expert to act on his behalf, and the latter, after hearing the parties' representations, produced an 'advisory opinion' at their request. This concluded that Japan had not violated any of its GATT obligations, but recommended that the parties should negotiate with a view to reducing Japanese tariffs. Here, and in the *Wet Salted Cod* case[28] between the EC and Canada the following year, the Director-General's intervention helped the parties to resolve their dispute.

In the above cases, the Director-General's involvement, though termed 'good offices', was really a kind of conciliation since the parties were offered a specific set of conclusions and recommendations as a basis for further action. But more significant than the question of classification is the point that cases of this type show the value of procedures which enable third parties to go beyond the question of whether the rules have been broken and to suggest a solution in situations where the action complained of may be lawful, but there is nevertheless a dispute needing resolution. As

---

[26] See Iwasawa, 'Settlement of disputes' (n. 7) p. 386.
[27] For an outline of this case, see ibid., 385.   [28] Ibid.

we saw in Chapter 5, one of the strengths of conciliation is that by encouraging flexibility it is a way forward in just such cases, an advantage which it will be recalled is also recognised in the Law of the Sea Convention. However, good offices, conciliation and mediation under the WTO DSU have so far not often been used.

There is a qualification, relating to the position of least developed countries, which should be mentioned. Article 24(2) of the DSU provides that, in a dispute involving a least developed country member which has not been resolved through consultations, the Director-General or the Chairman of the Dispute Settlement Body shall offer their good offices, conciliation or mediation on the request of the member concerned before a request for a panel is made. Of course, the exercise of these functions requires the consent of both parties; however, by identifying a role for such intervention in a specific group of cases, the DSU plainly encourages the use of good offices, conciliation and mediation before recourse to panel procedures, so further advertising their value.

11.5 Panel Proceedings

Important though consultations and the various other means of encouraging agreement are, in order to be fully effective a dispute settlement system must include arrangements for resolving differences by obtaining an authoritative decision from an independent body. For such a procedure may not only settle disputes which prove impervious to negotiation; it also encourages the parties to negotiate more seriously, and, as we saw when considering the work of the International Court, can provide an incentive to continue the search for a negotiated solution, when litigation has begun. In the GATT/WTO system, the mechanism for obtaining independent decisions is through panel proceedings, a practice which was first codified in 1979 at the end of the Tokyo Round.[29] The DSU now incorporates various changes which were agreed in 1989,[30] together with several further refinements.

11.5.1 The Mandate of Panels

The purpose of panels is to assist the Dispute Settlement Body in discharging its responsibilities under the DSU. Article 7(1) DSU determines the terms of reference of panels as follows, 'unless the parties to the dispute agree otherwise within 20 days from the establishment of the panel':

---

[29] See Van Bael, 'The GATT dispute settlement procedure' (n. 6) 68.
[30] See Canal-Forgues and Ostrihansky, 'New developments' (n. 6) 71–8.

To examine, in the light of the relevant provisions in (name of the covered agreement(s) cited by the parties to the dispute), the matter referred to the DSB by (name of party) in document ... and to make such findings as will assist the DSB in making the recommendations or in giving the rulings provided for in that/those agreement(s).

The 'standard' terms of reference[31] therefore define the subject matter or *ratione materiae* jurisdiction of the panels in relation to the reference made to the DSB by the parties in order to establish a panel. A panel can 'examine only those measures identified in the panel request and only with respect to the provisions of the covered agreements specifically stated in that request'.[32] These two elements – measure(s) identified and legal basis of the complaint – are therefore primordial. This stresses the import function of panel requests since the content of the panel request will indeed delimit the jurisdiction of the panel.

When a case is referred to a panel, it is required to make an objective assessment of the facts and the law and to 'make such other findings as will assist the DSB in making the recommendations or in giving the rulings provided for in the covered agreements' (Article 11). A panel is also required to 'consult regularly with the parties to the dispute and give them adequate opportunity to develop a mutually satisfactory solution' (ibid.). It is therefore evident that panel proceedings have a special character, including, on the one hand, many of the typical features of arbitration, and, on the other, an underlying emphasis on conciliation. The establishment of a panel requires a decision from the DSB, but, as already mentioned, a request can now be refused only if there is consensus, that is a negative or reverse consensus. This means that there is effectively a 'right to a panel' and the procedure can no longer be frustrated by a state with objections to the procedure. Likewise, there is a provision to ensure that, when a panel is requested, the necessary decision is made promptly (Article 6(1)). When a panel is established, its terms of reference are normally in standard form, along the lines just indicated (Article 7(1)), but it is open to the parties to vary them by agreement.[33]

11.5.2 Composition of Panels

In any procedure involving compulsory decisions, the composition of the authoritative organ is clearly a crucial matter. It is therefore no surprise to

---

[31] The current standard terms are slightly modified compared to the one incorporated in the DSU just cited. See Legal Affairs Division and the Rules Division of the WTO Secretariat, and the Appellate Body Secretariat, *A Handbook on the WTO Dispute Settlement System* (2nd ed.), Cambridge, 2017, 64. Special terms of agreement, however, are very exceptional. See ibid.
[32] Ibid., 65.
[33] The provision for standard terms of reference, which was first introduced in 1989, is also intended to eliminate delays: see Kohona, 'Dispute resolution' (n. 12) 36.

find elaborate attention to this issue in the WTO system. Panels are normally composed of three members, but may be composed of five, if the parties agree (Article 8(5)).

The qualifications of panel members, which include relevant governmental or non-governmental experience,[34] are laid down in Article 8(1), and it is the task of the Secretariat to maintain a list of suitably qualified persons, indicating their particular areas of expertise (Article 8(4)). The selection of panels must be made 'with a view to ensuring the independence of the members, a sufficiently diverse background and a wide spectrum of experience' (Article 8(2)). In disputes between a developed and a developing country member, the panel shall, if the latter requests, include at least one panellist from a developing country member (Article 8(10)). However, nationals of the parties to a dispute are ineligible to serve, unless the parties otherwise agree, and the same restriction applies to the nationals of intervening third parties (Article 8(3)). Panellists are nominated by the Secretariat and may only be objected to for 'compelling reasons' (Article 8(6)). In the event of disagreement over the composition of a panel, the necessary appointments are made by the Director-General in consultation with the Chairman of the DSB and the parties (Article 8(7)).

Although the panel system is essentially an elaboration of the GATT arrangements, the selection of panels has run into a number of problems in practice.[35] Because the WTO procedures have proved very popular, there has been a great demand for panels, which has led to a shortage of well-qualified panellists. The situation has been exacerbated by the increasing burden placed on panellists, as cases have become more complex and taken longer, and are also liable to generate related proceedings. All this has led to the WTO Secretariat playing a significant role in the supporting the panellists with drafting reports. At the same time, parties to disputes have become more fastidious and now regularly object to nominees, with the result that the Director-General is frequently called upon to make the necessary appointments. A solution to these problems might be to replace the present system of ad hoc panellists with a permanent body from which panels could be formed when needed. Such a 'court of international trade'[36] would have

---

[34] On the increasing emphasis on the value of non-governmental experience, which is symptomatic of the increasingly legalistic approach to dispute settlement in GATT practice, see Kohona, 'Dispute resolution' (n. 12) 36; and Canal-Forgues and Ostrihansky, 'New developments' (n. 6) 74.

[35] See W. J. Davey, 'A permanent body for WTO dispute settlement: desirable or practical?', in D. L. M. Kennedy and J. D. Southwick (eds), *The Political Economy of International Trade Law*, Cambridge, 2002, p. 496.

[36] See A. Porges, 'Comment: step by step to an international trade court', in D. L. M. Kennedy and J. D. Southwick (eds), *The Political Economy of International Trade Law*, Cambridge, 2002, p. 528.

many advantages and seems a logical development of the current architecture.

In practice, panels are most often composed of government officials specialised in international trade, diplomats, and occasionally also academics and practitioners.[37] Although government officials are permitted to serve as panellists, the DSU emphasises that panellists serve in their individual capacities and not as representatives of states or organisations. The element of independence, which we have seen in previous chapters is vital to the work of international judicial bodies, is not only made explicit in the DSU but is also addressed in Rules of Conduct for those acting on behalf of the WTO which were adopted in 1996.[38] The Rules, which apply to panellists, to members of the Appellate Body, to arbitrators and to experts, are contained in detailed provisions designed to ensure independence and impartiality, and which also stress the obligation to maintain confidentiality. To further its objectives, the Rules require panellists and others to disclose information which could affect or give rise to doubts as to their independence or impartiality, including information relating to financial interests, professional interests, family interests and previous statements of opinion. Procedures are also provided for dealing with allegations of non-disclosure relating to panellists and others.

The point was made earlier that the kinds of disputes with which the WTO is concerned often involve more than two parties. In the DSU provisions relating to panels, the multilateral nature of many trade disputes is taken into account in two ways. First, where more than one member requests the establishment of a panel in relation to the same matter, a single panel is to be used where possible to examine the complaints, taking into account the rights of all the members concerned (Article 9(1)). Second, any member having a substantial interest in a matter before a panel must be given an opportunity to be heard by the panel and to make written submissions (Article 10(2)). Although not termed 'intervention' in the DSU, this facility resembles those to be found in the corresponding provisions of the Statutes of the International Court of Justice (Articles 62 and 63) and the International Tribunal for the Law of the Sea (Articles 31 and 32), although it will be noted that the conditions under which intervention is authorised are defined differently.[39]

---

[37] Van den Bossche and Zdouc, *Law and Policy of the World Trade Organization* (n. 8), p. 218.

[38] WTO, Rules of Conduct for the Understanding on Rules and Procedures Concerning the Settlement of Disputes, adopted 3 December 1996. Text in (1997) 36 ILM 477.

[39] The WTO provisions are used very frequently: see Y. Iwasawa, 'Third parties before international tribunals: the ICJ and the WTO', in N. Ando, E. McWhinney and R. Wolfrum (eds), *Liber Amicorum Judge Shigeru Oda*, The Hague, 2002, p. 871.

11.5.3 Procedure

In a detailed section on procedures, which is further elaborated in an appendix, the DSU provides for strict time limits to be observed in panel proceedings and establishes arrangements to govern the parties' submissions resembling those of an arbitration. Thus, in normal circumstances, a final report should be delivered within six months, or within three months in cases of urgency (Article 12(8)). These standard time frames however are in practice exceeded, and panel proceedings have lasted around 13 to 16 months.[40] In any event, it is important to point out that the panel may suspend its work at any time at the request of a complaining party for a period not exceeding twelve months (Article 12(12)). The panel's authority lapses if the suspension exceeds twelve months. The parties' initial submissions are normally made consecutively, to permit a response, but simultaneous submissions can be authorised (Article 12(6)). Subsequent written submissions are always simultaneous and, in keeping with the normal practice, the documents submitted and the deliberations of the panel are confidential.

Since trade disputes often involve highly technical questions, the DSU lays down that a panel has the right to seek information and specialist advice from any source[41] and provides specifically for it to request an advisory opinion from an expert review group (Article 13(2)). The formation and activities of such groups are regulated in an appendix to the DSU but are not used often in practice.[42]

However, experts often are consulted individually, that is outside the context of the expert review group. This may be explicitly provided for, as for example in Article 11(2) of the Agreement on the Application of Sanitary and Phytosanitary Measures (SPS Agreement) which provides:

> In a dispute under this Agreement involving scientific or technical issues, a panel should seek advice from experts chosen by the panel in consultation with the parties to the dispute [...]

The report of a panel is produced in three stages. First, after receiving the parties' written submissions and hearing the oral argument, the panel submits the descriptive sections of its draft report (i.e. the section setting out the facts and the parties' arguments) to the parties for comment. Then

---

[40] Legal Affairs Division and the Rules Division of the WTO Secretariat, and the Appellate Body Secretariat, *A Handbook on the WTO Dispute Settlement System* (2nd Ed), Cambridge, 77; Van den Bossche and Zdouc, *Law and Policy of the World Trade Organization* (n. 8) p. 249.

[41] On the controversy over the scope of this power, which has been in issue in a number of recent cases, see E. Baroncini, 'The WTO Appellate Body and amicus curiae briefs' (2002) 2 *Global Community YBILJ*, 181; and J. Darling and D. Hardin, 'Amicus curiae participation in WTO dispute settlement: reflections on the past decade', in R. Yerxa and B. Wilson (eds), *Key Issues in WTO Dispute Settlement*, Cambridge, 2005, p. 221.

[42] See further J. Pauwelyn, 'The use of experts in WTO dispute settlement' (2002) 51 *ICLQ*, 325.

the panel issues an interim report, including both the descriptive sections and the panel's findings and conclusions. The parties have an opportunity to comment on this and then the panel produces its final report (Article 15 (2)). Where the matter has been settled, the report is limited to a brief description of the case and to recording that a solution has been reached (Article 12(7)). Otherwise, the report must be reasoned and, if the dispute involves a developing country member, it must explicitly indicate the form in which account has been taken of relevant provisions on differential and more favourable treatment for the developing country (Article 12(11)).

When a final report has been produced, it is issued to all members of the WTO and then considered by the DSB. Members may object to the report, giving written reasons, and, when the DSB considers the report, the parties to the dispute have the right to participate fully in its consideration. Thus, a party whose arguments have been rejected by a panel can reiterate its position. However, within sixty days of a panel report being issued to the members, the DSB must adopt the report, unless there is a consensus not to do so, or a party has notified its intention to appeal. Thus, a state which objects to a panel report can no longer prevent its adoption by refusing to accept it, but, if it wishes to pursue the matter, it must invoke the procedure for appellate review.

Although panel reports can be, and frequently are, appealed, it would be a serious mistake to underestimate their importance. Not only are appeals, as we shall see, confined to matters of law, which makes panels the final arbiters of all questions of fact, but. as we will see in the next section, the distinction between facts and law is not always clear. It is always possible for a dispute to be settled on agreed terms during the course of panel proceedings. This happened, for example, in the *Japan – Laver* case,[43] which was settled after the descriptive part of the panel's report had been issued, but before circulation of the interim report. Finally, a number of important cases have been dealt with on the basis of panel reports alone without recourse to the appeal procedure. In *EC – Biotech*,[44] for example, which raised complex scientific and technical issues, a panel decided that certain restrictions on the import and marketing of genetically modified plants and products were inconsistent with the Agreement on the Application of Sanitary and Phytosanitary Measures (SPS Agreement). Likewise, in *China – Intellectual Property*,[45] a panel upheld one of three

---

[43] *Japan – Import Quotas on Dried Laver and Seasoned Laver*, Panel Report, WT/DS 323 (2006). See also J. Gomula, 'Introductory note' (2007) 7 *Global Community YBILJ*, 241.

[44] *European Communities – Measures Affecting the Approval and Marketing of Biotech Products*, Panel Report, WT/DS 291/R, WT/DS 292/R and WT/DS 293/R (2006). See S. Lester, Note (2007) 101 *AJIL*, 453; and M. A. Young, 'The WTO's use of relevant rules of international law: an analysis of the Biotech case' (2007) 56 *ICLQ*, 907.

[45] *China – Measures Affecting the Protection and Enforcement of Intellectual Property Rights*, Panel Report, WT/DS 362/R (2009). See D. Gervais, Note, (2009) 103 *AJIL*, 549.

complaints against certain features of Chinese intellectual property law and practice, on the basis of the Agreement on Trade-Related Aspects of Intellectual Property Rights (TRIPS Agreement). Both clearly raised fundamental issues, but for reasons that can only be conjectured, neither case was appealed.

11.6 Appellate Review

Under the GATT dispute settlement procedure, panel reports were submitted to the GATT Council, on which all the contracting parties were represented, and approved only if there was a consensus. In contrast, under the WTO system, as we have seen, reports are adopted by the DSB unless there is a consensus not to do so. This makes adoption almost automatic and means that the parties to a dispute are no longer in a position to prevent adoption. With the significance of panel reports having increased so dramatically, and procedures for their implementation (as described below), it is not surprising that a mechanism for appellate review was considered essential. The organ created to perform this function is called the Appellate Body (AB).

11.6.1 Composition and Mandate of the Appellate Body

The Appellate Body is a standing organ consisting of seven individuals, of whom three, selected in rotation, serve for each case. The persons concerned are appointed by the DSB for a four-year term and may be reappointed, but only once. They must be 'persons of recognised authority, with demonstrated expertise in law, international trade and the subject matter of the covered agreements generally' (Article 17(3)). They must also be independent and broadly representative of membership in the WTO. Although serving on the Appellate Body is not a full-time occupation, members must be 'available at all times and on short notice' (ibid.) and must stay abreast of relevant WTO activities. As one would expect, they may not adjudicate in any case where there would be a conflict of interest.

The Appellate Body's task is to hear appeals from panel cases. Only parties to the dispute may make such an appeal, but it will be recalled that, during panel proceedings, third parties can present submissions if they have notified the DSB of a substantial interest in the matter, and a similar right extends to appellate proceedings. Third parties, however, cannot appeal panel reports, but can, under certain conditions, participate in the appeals procedure.

Appeals are limited to 'issues of law covered in the panel report and legal interpretation developed by the panel' (Article 17(6)). Since panel reports often contain extensive findings of fact, this is an important restriction on the Appellate Body's functions. The distinction between what constitutes an 'issue of law' and what constitutes findings of fact, however, is not always easy to make.[46] The AB in *EC-Hormones* explained that 'the determination of whether or not a certain event did occur in time and space is typically a question of fact', as is the 'determination of the credibility and weight properly to be ascribed to (that is, the appreciation of) a given piece of evidence'.[47] Legal questions, or questions of legal characterisation, on the other hand, are for example 'the consistency or inconsistency of a given fact or set of facts with the requirements of a given treaty provision is'.[48] However, the AB also argued that

> Whether or not a panel has made an objective assessment of the facts before it, as required by Article 11 of the DSU, is also a legal question which, if properly raised on appeal, would fall within the scope of appellate review.[49]

The AB's reports may 'uphold, modify or reverse the legal findings and conclusions of the panel' (Article 17(13)).[50]

In practice, however, the AB has also completed the legal analysis of panel reports. This can happen when, for example, a panel report on issue X is reversed, which in turn would warrant a decision on issue Y which had not been discussed by the panel.

The proceedings are subject to strict time limits, the normal duration of proceedings being no more than sixty days from the notification of the intention to appeal and the maximum duration no more than ninety days (Article 17(5)). As with panel proceedings, here also the proceedings have extended beyond the standard time frame. As of 2011, the AB has in general not been able to submit its reports within ninety days.[51]

11.6.2 Procedure

The proceedings of the Appellate Body, like those of panels, are confidential (Article 17.10 DSU), and, similarly, opinions expressed in its report are anonymous. However, over the past years, the proceedings have, as panel proceedings, been increasingly open,[52] ranging from an increased access of

---

[46] For a discussion, see Van den Bossche and Zdouc, *Law and Policy of the World Trade Organization* (n. 8) pp. 238–43.
[47] *China – Measures Affecting the Protection and Enforcement of Intellectual Property Rights*, Panel Report, WT/DS 362/R (2009). *European Communities – EC Measures Concerning Meat and Meat Products (Hormones)*, Appellate Body Report, WT/DS26/AB/R; WT/DS48/AB/R (16 January 1998), para. 132.   [48] Ibid.   [49] Ibid.
[50] Van den Bossche and Zdouc, *Law and Policy of the World Trade Organization* (n. 8), 244.
[51] Van den Bossche and Zdouc, *Law and Policy of the World Trade Organization* (n. 8), 249.
[52] See P. Delimatsis, 'Institutional Transparency in the WTO', in A. Bianchi and A. Peters (eds), *Transparency in International Law*, Cambridge, 2013, pp. 112–41 and J. Waincymer, 'Transparency of dispute settlement within the World Trade Organization' (2000) 24 *Melbourne University Law Review*, 797.

non-disputing parties to submit *amicus curiae* briefs[53] to public hearings.[54]

Each appellate report is submitted to the DSB and unconditionally accepted by the parties to the dispute unless the DSB decides by consensus not to adopt it within thirty days of its being issued to the members (Article 17(14)). This emphasis on speedy decision-making is further reinforced in Article 20, laying down the overall time frame for DSB decisions. This provides that, unless otherwise agreed by the parties to the dispute, the period from the establishment of a panel to the consideration of the report shall not normally exceed nine months where there is no appeal, or twelve months where the report is appealed.

Article 17(9) of the DSU requires the Appellate Body to draw up its working procedures in consultation with the Chairman of the DSB and the Director-General. Accordingly, in February 1996, before its first case was heard, the Appellate Body issued a wide-ranging set of Rules covering all aspects of its procedures.[55] Three aspects of the Rules demonstrate the Body's conception of its function and are of particular interest. First, in setting time limits and dealing with other procedural issues, the Rules reflect the need for due process in what are plainly judicial proceedings. Second, there is an emphasis in the Rules on the independence and impartiality of the members of the Appellate Body which confirms this conception. Third, in establishing how decisions will be taken and by whom, the Rules implement the principle of rotation, but skilfully combine it with the principle of collegiality. Thus, while a three-member division is selected for each case randomly, all members of the Appellate Body receive the documents on every case and have the opportunity to comment before the final decision (Rules 4.2 and 4.3). In this way, while the decision in a case remains the responsibility of the division assigned to it, and can be given by a majority vote if there is no consensus (Rule 3.2), consistency and coherence in decision-making, desirable in any rule-based system, are also strongly encouraged.

11.6.3 The Importance of the Appellate Body

An illustration of the kinds of issues which come before the Appellate Body is provided by the *EC – Seal Products* case,[56] decided in 2014. The dispute

---

[53] See Eric De Brabandere, 'NGOs and the "public interest": the legality and rationale of amicus curiae interventions in international economic and investment disputes' (2011) 12 *Chicago Journal of International Law*, 85.
[54] A. Alvarez-Jiménez, 'Public hearings at the WTO Appellate Body: the next step' (2010) 59 *International and Comparative Law Quarterly*, 1079.
[55] World Trade Organization Appellate Body, Working Procedures for Appellate Review, 15 February 1996, (1996) 35 ILM 495.
[56] *European Community – Measures Prohibiting the Importation and Marketing of Seal Products*, WT/DS 401/AB/R (2014). See G. Shaffer and D. Pabian, Note (2015) 109 *AJIL*, 154.

arose out the action of the European Union in prohibiting the importation and sale of seal products. The reason given for the ban was animal welfare, although there was an exception for seal products from traditional hunts conducted by indigenous communities (termed the 'IC exception'), and also for seals hunted for the purposes of marine resources management. Today, few countries hunt seals and trade in seal products, but among those that do are Canada, Norway and Greenland, of which only the last was allowed to enter the EU market under the IC exception. Canada and Norway therefore challenged the EU measures, arguing that they contravened both the WTO Agreement on the 1994 Technical Barriers to Trade (TBT Agreement) and the GATT.

In their submissions Canada and Norway complained that there were violations of the TBT Agreement because the disputed measures were discriminatory, contrary to Article 2(1) and more trade-restrictive than necessary, contrary to Article 2(2). As regards GATT, their complaint was that the measures violated Article 1, which is the most favoured nation provision, and Article 3(4), the national treatment clause. The EU, on the other hand, entered a defence to the claims under GATT, relying on Article 20(a) which permits measures 'necessary to protect public morals' and Article 20(b) which allows measures 'necessary to protect . . . animal . . . life or health'. The reason these defences were relevant was that since seals live on ice-floes and in other difficult terrain, hunting them requires clubbing, shooting or harpooning, although Canada and Norway had both adopted regulations intended to ensure that killing was humane. The panel held that the TBT Agreement applied and that the EU measures violated Article 2(1) because they were discriminatory. However, when the case reached the Appellate Body it disagreed and on technical grounds decided that the TBT Agreement did not apply. This part of the complaint was therefore dismissed. As regards the claims under GATT, the Appellate Body agreed with the panel that Articles 1 and 3 applied, with the result that the case turned on the scope of the defences under Article 20. Here the Appellate Body reviewed the scope of the 'public morals' exception in the light of the facts and decided that it was applicable in the present circumstances. However, the EU lost the case because the Appellate Body ruled that it had failed to show that the disputed measures did not lead to arbitrary or unjustifiable discrimination, as the chapeau of Article 20 requires.

The Appellate Body's report was adopted by the DSB within a month and shortly afterwards Canada and the EU signed a joint statement concerning access to the EU market under the IC exception.

This case, typical of many dealt with by the Appellate Body, is a clear demonstration of the value of a juridical procedure. For it is evident that the proceedings here were successful, not only in the sense that they resolved the dispute, but also because they clarified important legal issues relating to the scope for environmental measures under current trading agreements. Indeed, although there is no doctrine of *stare decisis* in the WTO, a feature of the dispute settlement system is the way in which reports of the Appellate Body, along with adopted panel reports, are treated as part of the GATT *acquis* and as such provide an ever-expanding body of legal precedent.[57]

Recent cases which have had the effect of elucidating members' obligations generally include *United States – Tuna*,[58] another case interpreting the TBT Agreement, and which raised the issue of the relation between WTO law and general international law; *China – Raw Materials*,[59] which concerned the scope of a state's power to restrict trade in its natural resources; and *Canada – Renewable Energy/Feed-in Tariff*,[60] where the panel and Appellate Body had to consider the compatibility of measures to address climate change with the WTO Rules prohibiting subsidies. In this last case, the first to deal with the issue of climate change, the Appellate Body held that by encouraging renewable energy producers to feed into the national grid on favourable terms, Canada had violated certain WTO obligations. In wider perspective, however, the decision reviewed the whole question of subsidy and incentive arrangements in government-supported renewable energy products.

With regard to the significance of practice, it is notable too that, while the Appellate Body has as its primary function clarification of states' obligations under the covered agreements, a key ancillary role is resolving procedural issues relating to the scope and operation of the DSU itself.[61] Thus, cases have called for rulings on issues such as standing, burden of proof, jurisdiction of panels and admissibility of evidence, as well as substantive matters. In the *EC – Bananas* case,[62] for example, the Appellate Body held that a member can bring a complaint without having to demonstrate a 'legal interest' in the matter; while, in the *United States –*

---

[57] See D. Palmeter and P. C. Mavroidis, 'The WTO legal system: sources of law' (1998) 92 *AJIL*, 398; and J. Cameron and K. R. Gray, 'Principles of international law in the WTO Dispute Settlement Body' (2001) 50 *ICLQ*, 248. Also P. C. Mavroidis, 'No outsourcing of law? WTO law as practiced by WTO courts' (2008) 102 *AJIL*, 241.

[58] *United States – Measures Concerning the Importation, Marketing and Sale of Tuna and Tuna Products*, WT/DS 381/AB/R (2012). See G. Shaffer, Note, (2013) 107 *AJIL*, 192.

[59] *China – Measures Related to the Exportation of Various Raw Materials*, WT/DS 392/AB/R (2012). See S. E. Rolland, 'China – Raw Materials: WTO rules on Chinese natural resources export dispute' (2012) 16 *ASIL Insights*, Issue 21.

[60] *Canada – Certain Measures Affecting the Renewable Energy Generation Sector* and *Canada – Measures Relating to the Feed-in Tariff Programme*, WT/DS 412/AB/R and WT/DS 426/AB/R (2013). See S. Shadikhodjaev, Note (2013) 107 *AJIL*, 864.

[61] See Cameron and Gray, 'Principles of international law in the WTO Dispute Settlement Body' (n. 57) 272–92. See also D. P. Steger, 'The Appellate Body and its contribution to WTO dispute settlement', in D. L. M. Kennedy and J. D. Southwick (eds), *The Political Economy of International Trade Law*, Cambridge, 2002, p. 482 at pp. 487–92.

[62] *European Communities – Bananas*, Appellate Body Report, WT/DS 27/AB/R (1997).

Shrimp case,[63] it ruled that panels have the discretion to accept unsolicited *amicus curiae* briefs submitted by non-governmental organisations.

As we shall see shortly, the WTO system places considerable emphasis on procedures to ensure the effective implementation of its rulings. It is therefore not surprising that a good deal of the time of the Appellate Body is taken up with cases concerned in one way or another with issues of implementation. In *United States – Continued Suspension*,[64] for example, it had to consider whether the European Communities (EC) had complied with the ruling in the *EC – Hormones* case[65] and thus whether the continued imposition of sanctions on the EC by the United States could be justified. In *United States – Upland Cotton (Article 21.5)*,[66] on the other hand, the question was whether the United States had itself done enough to comply with an earlier ruling. *Mexico – Taxes*[67] was yet another compliance case, although there Mexico sought to justify the imposition of taxes on certain soft drinks and beverages on the ground that the United States had refused to resolve a related dispute under a regional trade agreement. However, Mexico's attempt to use the WTO Agreement to justify counter-measures for breach of a separate international obligation was unsuccessful.

Since there is always a great deal at stake in trade disputes, and the right of appeal under the DSU is automatic, one could anticipate that cases would be referred from panels to the Appellate Body as a matter of routine and that the latter would accordingly be very busy. The 2020 Report from the Appellate Body shows that over the years, the percentage of panel reports that have been appealed ranges from 27 per cent to 100 per cent, with an overall average of 66 per cent.[68]

The fact that more than half the cases referred to panels are appealed, indicates the value that states attach to this facility.

Although not all panel reports are appealed, the large number of cases being referred to the WTO has created a formidable workload for the Appellate Body, an effect compounded by the range and complexity of the cases, which, as has been seen, now sometimes involve claims under the

---

[63] *United States – Shrimp*, Appellate Body Report, WT/DS 58/AB/R (1998), also in (1999) 38 ILM 121. See A. H. Qureshi, 'Extraterritorial shrimps, NGOs and the WTO Appellate Body' (1999) 48 *ICLQ*, 199, and n. 27 above.

[64] *United States – Continued Suspension of Obligations in the EC – Hormones Dispute*, Appellate Body Report, WT/DS 320/AB/R (2008). See Sungjoon Choo, Note (2009) 103 *AJIL*, 299.

[65] *European Communities – Measures Concerning Meat and Meat Products (Hormones)*, Appellate Body Report, WT/DS 26/AB/R (1998). See D. A. Wirth, Note (1998) 92 *AJIL*, 755.

[66] *United States – Subsidies on Upland Cotton Recourse to Article 21.5 of the DSU by Brazil*, Appellate Body Report, WT/DS 267/AB/RW (2008). See K. H. Cross, Note (2009) 103 *AJIL*, 110.

[67] *Mexico – Taxes on Soft Drinks and Other Beverages*, Appellate Body Report, WT/DS 308/AB/R (2006). See J. Gomula, 'Introductory note' (2007) 7 *Global Community YBILJ*, 241 at 243.

[68] See WTO, Appellate Body Annual Report for 2019–2020, WT/AB/30 (31 July 2020), p. 176, available at www.wto.org/english/tratop_e/dispu_e/ab_an_rep_e.htm.

new Uruguay Round agreements, as well as more traditional claims under the GATT. Proposals to expand the Appellate Body were considered, but not taken up, when the DSB reviewed the DSU in 1998 and 1999, and other proposals for modifying its workings have been made subsequently.[69] Since the speedy resolution of disputes is one of the main aims of the DSU, changes may well need to be made. In a relatively short time, however, the Appellate Body has established a record of solid competence and contributed significantly to the success of the whole system. However, in 2019, the AB became dysfunctional following the refusal by the United States to agree to the appointment of new AB members.

11.6.4 The Dysfunction of the Appellate Body in 2019

On 10 December 2019, the AB became dysfunctional as two of its three remaining members' four-year terms came to an end. There were therefore no sufficient AB members to form a division to deal with appeals.

The crisis arose from the blocking by the United States of the appointment of new members to the AB from 2016 onwards. The reasons behind the blocking of appointments by the US are explained in a February 2020 Report on the Appellate Body of the World Trade Organization issued by the US.[70] The document details the position of the US regarding its claim that the AB 'has not functioned according to the rules agreed by the United States and other WTO Members'.[71] In particular the US claims that the Appellate Body has added obligations and diminished rights by failing to comply with WTO rules, notably by interpreting WTO agreements beyond the original intention of the parties. The US also challenged certain procedural practices, such as the fact that the AB has since 2011 not been able to issue its report within the agreed ninety days period,[72] and the fact that the AB has engaged in reviewing factual findings by panels and panel findings concerning the meaning of domestic law, which the US considers to be 'a clear issue of fact in WTO dispute settlement'.[73]

In March 2020, the EU and twenty-two WTO members established a 'multi-party interim appeal arbitration arrangement' (MPIA) for trade disputes as a reaction to the dysfunction of the AB.[74] Participating

---

[69] See Steger, 'The Appellate Body' (n. 61) pp. 485–6.
[70] Office of the United States Trade Representative, 'Report on the Appellate Body of the World Trade Organization' (February 2020), available at https://ustr.gov/sites/default/files/Report_on_the_Appellate_Body_of_the_World_Trade_Organization.pdf.
[71] Ibid., p. 1 (introduction).   [72] Ibid., p. 28.   [73] Ibid., p. 37.
[74] 'Multi-Party Interim Appeal Arbitration Arrangement Pursuant to Article 25 of the DSU' (27 March 2020), available at https://trade.ec.europa.eu/doclib/docs/2020/march/tradoc_158685.pdf. See also WTO, 'Statement on a Mechanism for Developing, Documenting and Sharing Practices and Procedures in the Conduct of WTO Disputes – Multi-Party Interim Appeal Arbitration Arrangement Pursuant to Article 25 of the DSU' JOB/DSB/1/Add.12, 30 April 2020.

members include Australia, Brazil, Canada, China, Chile, Colombia, Costa Rica, the European Union, Guatemala, Hong Kong, Mexico, New Zealand, Norway, Singapore, Switzerland and Uruguay. The main features of the interim appeal are contained in Articles 1 and 2 of the MPIA:

1. The participating Members indicate their intention to resort to arbitration under Article 25 of the DSU as an interim appeal arbitration procedure (hereafter the 'appeal arbitration procedure'), as long as the Appellate Body is not able to hear appeals of panel reports in disputes among them due to an insufficient number of Appellate Body members.
2. In such circumstances, the participating Members will not pursue appeals under Articles 16.4 and 17 of the DSU.

The MPIA is based on Article 25 DSU which covers arbitration (see below Section 11.8 of this chapter), and procedurally, the interim appeal arbitration arrangement is based on the procedure for appellate review contained in Article 17 of the DSU.

Under Article 4 MPIA, the participating members envisage that under the appeal arbitration procedure, appeals will be heard by three appeal arbitrators selected from a pool of ten standing appeal arbitrators composed by the participating members in accordance with Annex 2 of the Agreement.

At the time of writing, the dysfunction of the AB was not solved, nor has the MPIA been used.

11.7 Implementation of Rulings and Recommendations

Article 19(1) of the DSU concerns the results of the panel process and provides that, where a panel or the Appellate Body concludes that a measure is inconsistent with a covered agreement, it must recommend that the member concerned bring the measure into conformity with the agreement. In addition, the panel or Appellate Body may suggest ways in which the member could implement the recommendations. With adoption of the report of the panel or Appellate Body by the DSB now subject only to the negative consensus procedure, the question of implementation of recommendations and rulings received close attention during the negotiation of the DSU, and two quite detailed provisions finally emerged: Article 21, concerned with surveillance by the DSB, and Article 22, concerned with compensation and the suspension of concessions.

11.7.1 Surveillance of Implementation of Recommendations and Rulings

Article 21 is based on the principle that prompt compliance with recommendations or rulings of the DSB is essential for effective dispute resolution, and therefore specifies a strict time frame. Within thirty days of the adoption of a panel or Appellate Body report, the member concerned must inform the DSB of its intentions with regard to implementation. If immediate compliance is impracticable, the member has a reasonable period in which to comply, but this must not normally exceed fifteen months from the date of adoption of the report. In the event of a dispute over the period of time allowed, the matter is to be determined by binding arbitration (Article 21(3)(c)). If, on the other hand, there is a dispute over whether the necessary measures have been taken, it is to be resolved through the normal procedures of the DSU, using the original panel wherever possible (Article 21(5)) (termed a 'compliance panel'). The DSB is required to keep the whole issue of implementation under surveillance and, when doing so, specifically to take into account the interests of developing states.

The principle of surveillance was first adopted in 1989, along with the concept of a reasonable time for compliance, and so neither is new. However, no means of determining what a reasonable time might be was laid down, and so in this respect the DSU represents a significant step forward. It must be appreciated, however, that implementation of dispute settlement rulings is not automatic, and, as a leading commentator has pointed out, in practice 'will continue to be influenced by the relative economic and political weight of the parties to the dispute'.[75] This lends particular significance to Article 22, concerned with the remedies available when recommendations and rulings are not implemented within a reasonable time.

11.7.2 Compensation and the Suspension of Concessions

The relevant remedies are compensation (i.e. trade concessions by the losing party) and suspension of concessions, the difference between them being that compensation requires an agreement between the states concerned and involves recompense, whereas suspension of concessions is essentially a penalty at the disposal of the state which brought the complaint, if compensation cannot be agreed.[76] Article 22(1) codifies existing GATT practice by laying down that both compensation and suspension of concessions are temporary measures and that full implementation,

---

[75] Petersmann, *The GATT/WTO System* (n. 2) p. 192. For the record on implementation under GATT and the WTO, see Busch and Reinhardt, 'Testing international trade law' (n. 23) pp. 470–4.

[76] Whether the penalty's function is to induce compliance, or simply to restore the balance of trade benefits, is a question on which there are differing views. See, for example, A. Kotera, 'On the legal character of retaliation in the World Trade Organization system', in N. Ando, E. McWhinney and R. Wolfrum (eds), *Liber Amicorum Judge Shigeru Oda*, The Hague, 2002, p. 911; and D. Palmeter and S. A. Alexandrov, '"Inducing compliance" in WTO dispute settlement', in D. L. M. Kennedy and J. D. Southwick (eds), *The Political Economy of International Trade Law*, Cambridge, 2002, p. 646.

avoiding the need for either, is preferred. Although compensation is voluntary, a state which has failed to comply with a recommendation or ruling within a reasonable time must enter into negotiations with the complaining state, if requested 'with a view to developing mutually acceptable compensation' (Article 22(2)). If no satisfactory compensation has been agreed within twenty days of the expiry of the reasonable period of time, the complaining state may request the DSB to authorise the suspension of concessions or other obligations under the covered agreement in relation to the state in default.

Counter-measures, which is what suspension of concessions or other obligations are, can be an effective means of encouraging compliance with rulings and recommendations, but also have the potential to disrupt international trade very seriously, which plainly runs counter to the aims of the DSU. To keep retaliation within bounds and control its effects, the DSU first specifies the nature of the counter-measures permitted, then places such measures within a tight regulatory framework.[77] Thus, on the first point, Article 22(3) requires that, wherever possible, an injured member shall limit its retaliation to the same sector, and Article 22(4) that the level of suspension of concessions shall be equivalent to the level of transgression.

Procedurally, members agree that retaliation must be authorised by the DSB (Article 23(2)(c)). It is true that authorisation of retaliation is subject to the negative consensus procedure and will therefore usually be automatic. However, to prevent abuse, a state which objects to the level of suspension proposed, or claims that inappropriate measures have been imposed, is entitled to have these matters determined by binding arbitration (Article 22(6) and (7)). Article 22(6) DSU provides that

> Such arbitration shall be carried out by the original panel, if members are available, or by an arbitrator appointed by the Director-General and shall be completed within 60 days after the date of expiry of the reasonable period of time. Concessions or other obligations shall not be suspended during the course of the arbitration.

In practice, it is often a panel – original where available – which decides the dispute, and hence the reference to 'arbitrator' is somewhat misleading.

As one would expect, any suspension of concessions applies only until the failure which made it necessary has been removed, or a mutually satisfactory solution has been agreed upon. The situation will in any case

---

[77] See Kohona, 'Dispute resolution' (n. 12) 42–3. For discussion of the operation of the counter-measures regime and possible alternatives, see J. Pauwelyn, 'Enforcement and countermeasures in the WTO' (2000) 94 *AJIL*, 335; and S. Charnovitz, 'Rethinking WTO trade sanctions' (2001) 95 *AJIL*, 792. See also S. Charnovitz, 'Should the teeth be pulled? An analysis of WTO sanctions', in D. L. M. Kennedy and J. D. Southwick (eds), *The Political Economy of International Trade Law*, Cambridge, 2002, p. 602.

continue to be monitored by the DSB, since the surveillance obligation in Article 21(6) extends to cases where compensation has been provided or concessions have been suspended.

Experience with these arrangements in practice has revealed the not unexpected fact that, while the DSU is generally good at generating adopted reports, securing their implementation, particularly in sensitive or controversial cases, may be subject to considerable delay. One reason, as a shrewd observer has pointed out, is that the system provides cost-free opportunities for foot-dragging by the losing party.[78] In the *EC – Hormones* case, for example, the report of the Appellate Body was adopted in February 1998, but the EC asked for arbitration to determine a reasonable time for compliance in accordance with Article 21(3)(c). In May 1998, this was set at fifteen months from the date of adoption of the report (February 1998), giving a deadline of May 1999. At that deadline, however, the EC had still not complied with the report and so the United States requested authorisation to suspend concessions. This in turn produced a further request for arbitration from the EU under Article 22(6). It was therefore only when that arbitration had taken place, in July 1999, that the retaliatory tariffs, authorised by the WTO and intended to encourage compliance with a ruling some eighteen months earlier, finally came into effect.

A similar lesson may be learned from *United States – Gambling*.[79] In 2005 the Appellate Body decided this case, which concerned US restrictions against online gambling, in favour of the complainant, Antigua. As noted above, an unsuccessful party has a reasonable time to comply with a ruling, but here the parties could not agree on what this should be, and so an arbitrator was called upon and ruled that the time for compliance expired in April 2006. However, no steps to comply were taken by the United States and so Antigua requested consultations over the issue. When these were unsuccessful, Antigua requested a compliance panel, which in 2007 ruled in favour of Antigua. The next event was an announcement from the United States that it was withdrawing its original commitment, to allow the cross-border provision of gambling and betting services. Although this was permissible, withdrawal required the compensation of any affected WTO members. Accordingly, six states, in addition to Antigua, filed compensation claims. The United States reached agreement with the six but not with Antigua for whom the remote gaming industry was of major economic importance. In 2007 Antigua was authorised to

---

[78] See G. N. Horlick, 'Problems with the compliance structure of the WTO dispute resolution process', in D. L. M. Kennedy and J. D. Southwick (eds), *The Political Economy of International Trade Law*, Cambridge, 2002, p. 636.

[79] *United States – Measures Affecting the Cross-Border Supply of Gambling and Betting Services*, WT/DS 285/AB/R (2015). See J. P. Trachtman, Note (2015) 99 *AJIL*, 861.

retaliate against the United States to the value of US$21 million, which was deemed to be the amount it had lost. Over the next five years further negotiations took place, but were again unsuccessful. Finally, in 2013 Antigua was granted authorisation to suspend certain concessions and obligations it had towards the United States in respect of intellectual property rights. Like *EC – Hormones*, this is an example of the obstacles which an unsuccessful party can put in the way of implementation and, more particularly, the problems which small states may have in securing respect for rulings in their favour.

The elaborate provisions of Articles 21 and 22 are further evidence of the shift towards a legalistic approach to dispute settlement in the WTO system. After 'legalising' panel procedures and creating the Appellate Body, it was a logical step to tighten the arrangements for implementation and address the issue of noncompliance. The option of avoiding retaliation by agreeing to compensation is in keeping with the general emphasis in the DSU on encouraging the parties' agreement, while the regulation of counter-measures, and in particular the undertaking that such measures will not be taken outside the WTO system, is a significant advance. There is, as we have seen, also recognition that disputes over the application of these provisions are inevitable. It is in keeping with the general approach in the DSU that the procedure laid down for dealing with such disputes should include mandatory arbitration, resulting in a binding decision.

11.8 Arbitration under Article 25 DSU

Arbitration has always been available as a means of dispute settlement which parties to the GATT could select, but until recently was rarely used in practice. This is no doubt because the need for a rule-based method of dealing with disputes was largely satisfied by the development of panel procedures, which, especially in their latest form, have much in common with arbitration. However, the two processes are still distinct, and the latter is the subject of a separate article in the DSU, which recognises that expeditious arbitration within the WTO 'can facilitate the solution of certain disputes' (Article 25(1)). This point is borne out by a number of disputes under the GATT in which arbitration has been used successfully and its designation in the DSU as the mandatory procedure in the cases noted earlier.

In 1990, Canada and the EC agreed to use arbitration in a dispute over Article 28 of the GATT, known as the *Article XXVIII Rights* case. The dispute, which concerned negotiation rights with regard to wheat, was referred to a single arbitrator, who concluded that, in a bilateral agreement of 1962, Canada had retained certain rights under Article 28, but relinquished others. Nearly thirty years earlier, in 1962, a dispute between the EC and the United States over the value of poultry exports was referred for an 'advisory opinion' to a panel appointed by the GATT Council.[80] Despite appearances, this too was an arbitration, since the award, which involved issues of law as well as fact, was presented directly to the parties and treated by them as binding. These awards settled the disputes concerned, and, though exceptional, show that, in trade disputes, as elsewhere, arbitration can be useful.

To date, arbitration under Article 25 has been used only on one occasion by WTO member states, and moreover occurred at the implementation stage.[81] However, as discussed in Section 6.4, in March 2020, the EU and twenty-two WTO members established the MPIA in which they agree to resort to arbitration under Article 25 of the DSU as an interim appeal arbitration procedure. The MPIA ensures that its participants can continue to benefit from a two-step dispute settlement system and is explicitly based on Article 25 of the DSU. The MPIA is not intended to supplant the AB, but to function as a temporary solution. So far, no disputes have been heard under the MPIA.

Arbitration under Article 25 DSU requires mutual agreement, and, since the DSU has no provisions at all on relevant procedures, it is for the parties to arrange the details, including the names of the arbitrators, and the procedure to be followed. This makes WTO involvement more limited than in the panel process, a difference which is emphasised by the fact that arbitration awards are binding on the parties immediately and do not need adoption by the Dispute Settlement Body. By the same token, of course, arbitral awards are binding *only* on the parties and cannot create obligations for third parties. Consequently, whereas the DSU contains provisions to protect the interests of third parties in panel proceedings which have already been mentioned, it makes it clear that, when arbitration takes place, the normal rule applies and third states can only become a party to the proceedings with the agreement of the litigating states (Article 25(3)).

Although the DSU reflects the party autonomy that has traditionally been the hallmark of international arbitration, its provisions are designed to ensure that the arbitration of trade disputes does not become an exclusively bilateral affair, but is integrated into the WTO system. Thus, states proposing to employ arbitration must notify other members of their agreement before the process begins to give them an opportunity to apply to become a party (Article 25(2)). When the award is made, it must be notified to the DSB and to the council or committee of any relevant agreement, where any member may raise a point relating to it (Article 25(3)).

---

[80] See Iwasawa, 'Settlement of disputes' (n. 7) pp. 390–1; and H. Walker, 'Dispute settlement: the chicken war' (1964) 58 *AJIL*, 671.
[81] Award of the Arbitrators, US – Section 110(5) Copyright Act (Article 25); see Legal Affairs Division and the Rules Division of the WTO Secretariat, and the Appellate Body Secretariat, *A Handbook on the WTO Dispute Settlement System* (2nd ed), Cambridge, 2017, 175.

This is likely to be particularly important if other states disagree with the arbitrators' conclusions, and provides an opportunity for the DSB as a whole to indicate any reservations.

Whether others agree or not, the award is always binding on the parties and Article 25(4) underlines this by providing that at the implementation stage, involving Articles 21 and 22, the role of the DSB with regard to arbitral awards and panel reports which have been adopted is identical.

11.9 Regional Trade Systems

As we shall see in Chapter 11, there are today many regional organisations of various kinds. Many of these are concerned with issues of international trade and nearly all include arrangements for dealing with disputes, some with elements similar to the WTO system, while others are quite different. It is not possible to mention, let alone describe, the assortment of regional trade systems here.[82] Regional trade agreements, in the form of Customs Unions and free trade areas, are allowed under the WTO, for instance under Article XXIV GATT. There are numerous so-called preferential trade agreements (PTAs) in place and their number is steadily growing. The prime example of a customs union is the European Union (EU).

11.9.1 The European Union

The centrepiece of the EU's arrangements for dispute settlement is the European Court of Justice (ECJ). The Court, which sits in Luxembourg, has one judge from each member state, together with eleven Advocates General. The Court is divided into three bodies: the Court of Justice which deals with requests for preliminary rulings from national courts, together with certain actions for annulment and appeals; the General Court which deals with actions for annulment brought by individuals, companies and EU governments. This means that in practice the General Court is mainly concerned with competition law, state aid, trade, agriculture and trademarks. And, third, the Civil Service Tribunal which deals with disputes between the EU and its staff. The broad functions of the ECJ are to ensure that EU law is applied uniformly across the member states and to provide a remedy for those who consider that an EU institution has infringed their rights. Thus national courts are entitled to ask the Court to clarify a point of EU law, action can be taken against national governments who fail to comply with EU law, and EU legal acts can be annulled and where necessary compensation awarded.

---

[82] For a more detailed treatment see J. Collier and V. Lowe, *The Settlement of Disputes in International Law*, Oxford 1999, pp. 104–16; also P. Sands and P. Klein (eds), *Bowett's Law of International Institutions*, 5th ed., London, 2001.

When a case comes before the Court of Justice it is assigned to a judge and an advocate-general. At the first stage the parties supply the Court with written statements, which may be supplemented by observations from third parties. The documentation is then discussed at a general meeting which decides how many judges will hear the case (depending on its importance) and also whether there will be an oral stage and whether an opinion from the advocate-general is needed. If there is an oral stage, the parties present their arguments and subsequently receive the Opinion of the advocate-general. The Court then gives its verdict. The General Court's procedure is similar, except that most cases are heard by three judges and an advocate-general is not involved. The EU is the world's most integrated regional organisation, with a range of activity which now goes well beyond international trade. As we shall see shortly, its institutional arrangements have provided a model for other regional organisations, although, owing to different political circumstances, their evolution is at an earlier stage.

11.9.2 The 2020 United States–Mexico–Canada Agreement

The 2020 United States–Mexico–Canada Agreement (USMCA) (its predecessor was the 1992 North American Free Trade Agreement (NAFTA)), is another example of a regional exception in the form of a preferential trade agreement. It is a treaty to which Canada, Mexico and the United States are parties. Its objectives include eliminating barriers to trade in goods and services, promoting fair competition and investment, and protecting intellectual property rights in the member states. In addition to a large number of provisions dealing with substantive obligations, it contains a chapter on dispute settlement, Chapter 31.

11.9.3 The Economic Community of West African States (ECOWAS)

The Economic Community of West African States (ECOWAS), founded in 1975, is another example of this kind and currently has fifteen members, all in West Africa. Its aims include cooperation and harmonisation of national policies in economic fields, including agriculture, industry, natural resources and tourism and the creation of a customs union and an economic and monetary union, following the example of the European Union. However, ECOWAS does not have powers to change law in the member states, but, as will be seen in Chapter 13, does engage in peacekeeping in the region. The official languages of ECOWAS are English, French and Portuguese and the implementation of its policies is in the hands of two institutions: the ECOWAS Commission and the ECOWAS Bank for Investment and Development. The settlement of disputes is the responsibility of the ECOWAS Community Court of Justice, an institution which has undergone considerable changes in the twenty-five years it has been in existence.

The Court was created in 1991, but did not begin operation until 1996. The jurisdiction of the Court is set out in Articles 9 and 76 of the 1993 Revised Treaty of the Community. It may decide contentious cases between member states or between states and ECOWAS institutions with regard to the interpretation or application of the Revised Treaty which are not settled amicably by direct agreement. Unlike the ECJ, all disputes arising under the Treaty are inter-state disputes and individuals and legal persons do not have standing. However, under Article 10 the Court may provide the ECOWAS Council with advisory opinions on legal questions. In 2005 in a far-reaching step, the Court was given the authority to deal with human rights complaints and has made extensive use of these powers.[83] Indeed, since the aim of regional economic integration is still far from realisation, there is reason to regard the human rights jurisprudence of the ECOWAS Court as its major achievement.

11.9.4 The Common Market for Eastern and Southern Africa (COMESA)

The Common Market for Eastern and Southern Africa (COMESA) is a free trade area with twenty member states, extending from Libya to Swaziland. Formed in 1994, its official languages are English, French and Portuguese and it has various decision-making organs. Dispute settlement is the responsibility of the COMESA Court of Justice whose decisions have precedence over those of national courts. The Court is open to states and also natural and legal persons who may bring actions against the COMESA Council to determine the legality of its actions. They are also able to sue a state where the lawfulness of its actions under the Treaty is in question. As in the EU, national courts may refer questions of application or interpretation of the Treaty to the Court. The Court also has jurisdiction over claims brought by COMESA employees and third parties against COMESA or its institutions. In addition, it may act as an arbitration tribunal on any matter arising from a contract to which COMESA, or any of its institutions is a party. Lastly the Court can deal with any dispute between the member states if they agree to have recourse to it. In 2005 the Court was divided into two divisions, the Court of First Instance and the Appellate Division. Although this change was implemented successfully, the Court is underfunded, with the result that it currently has a significant backlog of cases.

---

[83] See K. J. Alter, L. R. Helfer and J. R. McAllister, 'A new international human rights court for Africa: the ECOWAS Community Court of Justice' (2013) 107 *AJIL*, 737.

11.9.5 The 'Mercado Común del Sur' (MERCOSUR)

Finally, Mercado Común del Sur, or MERCOSUR, is a sub-regional block in Latin America. It has five full members: Argentina, Brazil, Paraguay, Uruguay and Venezuela, a number of associate countries and two observers, New Zealand and Mexico. It has the aim of promoting the free movement of goods, people and currency and has Spanish, Portuguese and Guarani as its official languages. Since it was founded in 1991, it has undergone many developments and now fully merits its alternative title of the Southern Common Market. Originally disputes were to be settled by direct negotiations, but as a result of subsequent agreements complaints of breaches of the Treaty made by states or individuals may be submitted to the national sections of the Inter-State Mercosur Trade Commission and after that to the Trade Commission itself which proceeds by consensus. If no solution is reached, the matter is referred to the intergovernmental Common Market Group, or ultimately to an ad hoc arbitration panel. There are also arrangements for mixed arbitrations to deal with investment disputes.

11.10 The WTO System in Context

The Agreement Establishing the World Trade Organization came into force in January 1995, together with the Dispute Settlement Understanding which is in Annex 2 to the WTO Agreement. Judged by the extent to which the DSU is actually used, it has been outstandingly successful, until the Appellate Body became dysfunctional in 2019. To date more than 600 requests for consultations have been made. Thus, the WTO system is plainly one that the members of the WTO are prepared to use. There are, of course, other criteria to consider as well. An effective dispute settlement must do more than generate rulings – it must produce good, in the sense of prompt and adequately reasoned, decisions and also be an effective procedure for resolving disputes. The point has been made above that reports of the panels and the Appellate Body are generally of good quality, and, while compliance is an issue that often needs attention, given what is at stake in trade disputes, the record is in this respect a vast improvement on less structured arrangements. There is also the point that, as explained in earlier chapters, the existence of an arrangement for compulsory dispute settlement has in itself a significant, though immeasurable, effect in discouraging extreme claims and promoting moderation. If practice, which is more fully examined in the specialist literature on the WTO, is one aspect of the DSU calling for consideration, it is also useful to make a more general assessment and place these developments in context, a task which is, of course, greatly assisted by the fact that, in many respects, the DSU constitutes a distillation of four decades of experience and has already been the subject of a good deal of analysis. When reviewing the corresponding provisions of the 1982 Law of the Sea Convention in the previous chapter, it was noted that, once the key decision has been taken to make arrangements for dispute settlement an integral part of a treaty, the characteristics of the particular system are a matter of who, what, when and how. Though styled an 'understanding', the DSU is an integral part of the WTO Agreement, and according to Article 2(2) is legally binding.[84] It will therefore be convenient to put the DSU in context by adopting the same analytical framework.

The DSU, as already noted, deals with the issue of 'who' by utilising the familiar processes of consultation, good offices/conciliation/mediation (which are not distinguished) and arbitration, together with the panel process, a distinctive but established GATT procedure, and a process of appellate review through the Appellate Body. Behind all this stands another organ, the Dispute Settlement Body, with the political responsibility for integrating the dispute settlement system and ensuring its effectiveness. Panel proceedings, which have always been *sui generis*, are brought closer to arbitration by the emphasis in the DSU and the 1996 Rules of Conduct on the independence and impartiality of panellists and by the negative consensus procedure for the adoption of their reports. The latter in turn prompted the creation of the Appellate Body, whose conception of its juridical functions can be seen in the 1996 Working Procedures.

The question 'what' is answered in the provisions dealing with the coverage and application of the DSU which provide that it embraces all the covered agreements. This, as we have seen, reflects the objective of the WTO to bring together old and new agreements in a single instrument, with, as a corollary, a unified system of dispute settlement. Thus, in principle, the procedures laid down in the DSU are available in respect of all the relevant agreements and the jurisdiction of panels and the Appellate Body is not normally restricted as to subject matter. It should be noted, however, that certain covered agreements contain special or additional rules and procedures, and, as these prevail in case of conflict, some disputes are subject to different arrangements.[85] Moreover, wide though the WTO system is, it is limited to the covered agreements. Accordingly, disputes involving only bilateral treaties, or regional agreements lie outside the DSU and must be dealt with elsewhere.

In answering the question 'when', the DSU contains a number of features of interest. In the first place, the choice of means, which is such an important feature of Part XV of the Law of the Sea Convention, is almost wholly absent. Although states are encouraged to settle their

---

[84] See Kohona, 'Dispute resolution' (n. 12) 45.
[85] See Art. 1(2) of the DSU; and Petersmann, *The GATT/WTO System* (n. 2) pp. 223–32, examining the problems to which this provision could give rise to.

disputes by agreement, if they fail to do so, the complaining party can request a panel. After the panel has reported, recourse to the Appellate Body is again a matter of right, and, when the 'litigation' stage is complete, the DSB takes over. It is true that there is no obligation to request a panel and that arbitration is mentioned as a possible alternative. This is nevertheless conceptually a 'one-track' system.

In the same connection, it is relevant to note that, by subscribing to the WTO Agreement, states not only forgo the right to impose unilateral sanctions, but also undertake to resolve pertinent disputes through the DSU exclusively. So, for example, if a dispute arises which could be resolved either through the DSU or through the procedures of an agreement such as the USMCA, the former should be employed.[86] A final point concerns the relation between the DSU and domestic litigation. The WTO Agreement includes numerous provisions designed to strengthen judicial and other procedures at the national level, because here, as elsewhere, effective domestic arrangements tend to minimise international disputes. On the other hand, under the WTO Agreement, as under the GATT, exhaustion of domestic remedies is not a condition for activating the DSU system. Thus, even if domestic litigation is in progress, because trade disputes involve treaty rights, a state is entitled to begin the DSU procedure immediately, without waiting for the outcome.[87] Moreover, it is worth noting that WTO law does not necessarily enjoy direct effect in national jurisdictions.

The last issue, 'how', concerns the criteria for decision-making and the object of the proceedings. These are particularly significant aspects of the DSU system in view of the changes which emerged during the Uruguay Round in the way many of the participants approach trade disputes and want to see them handled. The primary goal of the DSU, as of the former arrangements, is to secure a mutually acceptable solution. However, whereas under the old system this 'political' approach predominated, under its successor, if accommodation proves impossible, juridical machinery of a somewhat inexorable character comes into play. This switch from what has been termed a 'power-oriented' approach to a 'rule-oriented' approach[88] is exemplified in the change from positive to negative consensus for decision-making in the DSB, in the increasing assimilation of panel proceedings to arbitration, in the creation of the Appellate Body, and in the

---

[86] See Iwasawa, 'Settlement of disputes' (n. 7) p. 400. For an outline of the NAFTA arrangements, which influenced the drafting of the DSU, see J. L. Siqueiros, 'NAFTA institutional arrangements and dispute settlement procedures' (1992/3) 23 *Calif. Western Int. L.J.*, 383.

[87] For discussion of the merits of this approach, see Petersmann, *The GATT/WTO System* (n. 2) pp. 233–40.

[88] See M. M. T. A. Brus, *Third Party Dispute Settlement in an Interdependent World*, Dordrecht, 1995, p. 31; and J. H. Jackson, 'Perspectives on the jurisprudence of international trade: costs and benefits of legal procedures in the United States' (1984) 82 *Mich. L Rev.*, 1570 at 1571–2.

stricter arrangements for supervising decisions. It is therefore no surprise to find the purpose of the DSU defined in Article 3(2) as 'to preserve the rights and obligations of Members under the covered agreements, and to clarify the existing provisions of those agreements in accordance with customary rules of interpretation of public international law'.[89]

The DSU, has therefore already provided its value and, while a developing system, can never be thought of as a finished product, its impact to date has been very positive. When considering the future, however, two general points concerning the relevance of a rule-oriented approach to disputes in this field should be borne in mind. The first is that trade disputes are complex, often involve changing economic and political interests and are capable of arousing strong national passions. If this makes peaceful methods of resolving such disputes indispensable, it also means that methods which provide opportunities for accommodation and addressing new situations are at least as important as those which emphasise existing rules.[90] As already noted, this has not been lost sight of in the DSU. The other general point is that, in international trade law, as elsewhere, an insistence on established rules can only be effective if the rules in question are not only interpreted competently, but also regarded as appropriate, and as such command general acceptance. In the WTO system, interpretation is the responsibility of panels and the Appellate Body, but the rules they apply are made by states, which thus bear a legislative, as well as an executive, responsibility for the future of the Dispute Settlement Understanding.[91]

11.11 Further Reading

11.11.1 General References on WTO Dispute Settlement

Ascencio, H., *Droit international économique*, Paris, 2018.

Hoekman, B. M., and P. C. Mavroidis, *The World Trade Organization: Law, Economics and Politics*, 2nd ed., 2015, Abingdon.

Legal Affairs Division and the Rules Division of the WTO Secretariat, and the Appellate Body Secretariat, *A Handbook on the WTO Dispute Settlement System*, 2nd ed., Cambridge, 2017.

---

[89] See further J. Pauwelyn, 'The role of public international law in the WTO: how far can we go?' (2001) 95 *AJIL*, 535; and the references in n. 34 above. See also J. Pauwelyn, *Conflict of Norms in Public International Law*, Cambridge, 2003.

[90] In this connection it is significant that Art. 3(7) of the DSU provides that: 'Before bringing a case, a Member shall exercise its judgment as to whether action under these procedures would be fruitful'; see, on this point, Kohona, 'Dispute resolution' (n. 12) 29.

[91] See N. Saiki, 'WTO procedures for the settlement of disputes – their formation: a practitioner's view', in M. K. Young and Y. Iwasawa (eds), *Trilateral Perspectives on International Legal Issues*, Irvington on Hudson, NY, 1996, p. 403 at p. 417. See also L. Bartels, 'The separation of powers in the WTO: how to avoid judicial activism' (2004) 53 *ICLQ*, 861; and J. H. Jackson, *Sovereignty, the WTO and Changing Fundamentals of International Law*, Cambridge, 2006.

Matsushita, M., T. Schoenbaum, P. C. Mavroidis, M. Hahn, *The World Trade Organization: Law, Practice, and Policy*, 3rd ed., Oxford, Ch. 4, 'Dispute Settlement'.

Subedi, S. P., 'The WTO Dispute Settlement Mechanism as a New Technique for Settling Disputes in International Law', in D. French, M. Saul and N.D. White (eds), *International Law and Dispute Settlement: New Problems and Techniques*, London, 2010, pp. 173–90.

Van den Bossche, P., and W. Zdouc, *Law and Policy of the World Trade Organization*, 4th ed., Cambridge, 2017, Ch. 3.

11.11.2 Treaties, Official Documents and Collections of Documents

Choukroune, L., and J. Nedumpara, *International Economic Law: Text, Cases and Materials*. Cambridge, 2021.

World Trade Organization, *The WTO Dispute Settlement Procedures. A Collection of the Relevant Legal Texts*, 3rd ed., Cambridge, 2012.

World Trade Organization, *WTO Dispute Settlement: One-Page Case Summaries 1995–2018*, Geneva, 2019, available at www.wto.org/english/res_e/booksp_e/dispu_settl_1995_2018_e.pdf.

12

The United Nations

The reference of disputes to international political institutions has a history as long as that of arbitration. For present purposes, however, it is unnecessary to go further back than 1919, when, with the creation of the League of Nations as a reaction to the First World War, the first attempt was made to establish a universal organisation with broad responsibilities in this area. Following the failure of the League, or more accurately its member states, to take effective action to forestall a second bloodbath, a fresh effort to bring disputes within the field of operations of a world organisation was made with the creation of the United Nations Organisation in 1945.[1]

The purposes of the United Nations, as set out in Article 1 of the Charter, are to maintain international peace and security; to develop friendly relations among nations; to achieve international cooperation in solving problems of an economic, social, cultural or humanitarian character and in promoting human rights; and to be a centre for harmonising the actions of states in attaining these ends. Of these interrelated purposes, the maintenance of international peace and security occupies the primary place. Here, according to the Charter, the Organisation has two distinct responsibilities: to bring about the cessation of armed conflict whenever it occurs, and to assist the parties to international disputes to settle their differences by peaceful means. The scope of the Organisation's powers in this second area, the ways in which they are exercised in practice and the effectiveness of the United Nations' contribution are the subject of this chapter.

While United Nations peacekeeping and the powers of the Security Council under Chapter VII of the UN Charter play an important role in the maintenance of international peace and security, these activities are not always questions of dispute settlement. Moreover, United Nations

---

[1] There is an enormous literature dealing with all aspects of the United Nations. In addition to the works cited below, the following studies contain particularly useful reviews of the activities of the Organization in the field of dispute settlement: K. V. Raman (ed.), *Dispute Settlement through the United Nations*, New York, 1977; UNITAR, *The United Nations and the Maintenance of International Peace and Security*, Dordrecht, 1987; A. Roberts and B. Kingsbury (eds), *United Nations, Divided World*, 2nd ed., Oxford, 1993; N. D. White, *Keeping the Peace*, Manchester, 1993; and C. Peck, *The United Nations as a Dispute Settlement System*, The Hague, 1996. See also J. A. Mingst and M. P. Karns, *The United Nations in the Post Cold-War Era*, 2nd ed., Boulder, CO, 2000; and N. D. White, *The United Nations System*, Boulder, CO, 2002.

peacekeeping has been the subject of many detailed studies.[2] The same is true for Chapter VII of the Charter which enables the Security Council to adopt economic sanctions and military measures where there is a 'threat to the peace, breach of the peace or act of aggression', thereby equipping it with enforcement powers in disputes or situations that are particularly serious.[3]

Since this book is concerned with peaceful methods of dispute settlement, a detailed analysis of both UN peacekeeping and the coercive potential of Chapter VII, and the concept of collective security generally, would be out of place. I refer the reader to the referenced detailed studies which cover both areas in detail.

12.1 Machinery of the Organisation

There are three organs of the United Nations with principal roles to play in the peaceful settlement of disputes: the Security Council, the General Assembly and the Secretariat.

12.1.1 The Security Council

The Security Council's powers derive from Chapter VI of the Charter, which is wholly concerned with the pacific settlement of disputes. Apart from Article 38, which entitles the Council to make recommendations with a view to the settlement of any dispute if all the parties so request, its competence is limited to disputes 'the continuance of which is likely to endanger the maintenance of international peace and security' (Article 33 (1)). It is therefore clear that, although Article 2(3) imposes a general obligation on member states to settle disputes by peaceful means (as was discussed also in the first chapter), only the more serious disputes, or those which have become serious, are regarded as the Council's concern.

The specialised role of the Security Council receives further emphasis in Article 33(1), which provides that the parties to such a dispute shall 'first of all' seek a solution by negotiation or some other peaceful means of their own choice, and Article 52(2), which provides that members of regional

---

[2] Useful studies include A. James, *Peacekeeping in International Politics*, London, 1990; A. Parsons, *From Cold War to Hot Peace*, London, 1995; and D. Warner ed., *New Dimensions of Peacekeeping*, Dordrecht, 1995. An invaluable collection of primary material is the four-volume series by R. Higgins, *United Nations Peace-Keeping Documents and Commentary*, Oxford, 1969–81. On the latest activities, see N. D. White, *The United Nations System* (n. 1), 161–97; and C. Gray, *International Law and the Use of Force*, 4th ed., Oxford, 2018, chs 7 and 8.

[3] For good overviews, see N. D. White, *The Law of International Organizations*, Manchester, 1996, ch. 7; and A. Hurrell, 'Collective security and international order revisited' (1992) 11 *Int. Rel.*, 37. See also N. D. White, The *United Nations System* (n. 1) ch. 6; and C. Gray, *Use of Force* (n. 2) chs. 7 and 8 and A. Orakhelashvili, *Collective Security*, Oxford, 2011.

arrangements or agencies 'shall make every effort to achieve pacific settlement of local disputes' through such arrangements or agencies before referring them to the Security Council. However, it is worth noting that, despite these priorities, the Council has the right to recommend appropriate procedures or methods of adjustment under Article 36(1) at any time. Furthermore, the effect of Articles 11(3), 35(1) and 99 is to enable the Council to consider a matter at the request of the General Assembly, a member state or the Secretary-General, whether or not the states involved consent to it doing so.[4]

Of course, it is for the Council to decide by vote whether to place a particular matter on its agenda, but the important point is that its authority to consider a dispute, unlike that of a conciliation commission or court of arbitration, does not depend on the consent of the states concerned. Moreover, in deciding whether it should take a matter up, the Council is free to adopt a broader conception of an international 'dispute' than might be acceptable in a judicial forum, as was discussed in the first chapter. When this is combined with the authority under Article 34 to act in 'any *situation* which might lead to international friction',[5] as well as in disputes, it can be seen that the Council's jurisdiction can be extended to virtually all matters of international significance.

Finally, if the provisions of Chapter VII are read alongside those of Chapter VI, it is evident that a dispute or situation which leads to an actual 'threat to the peace, breach of the peace or act of aggression' activates the provisions of the Charter concerned with political and military action under that Chapter. As a result, the Council's authority in the field of dispute settlement, unlike that of, say, the International Court, is complemented, at least on paper, by powers of enforcement in the very circumstances in which they are most likely to be needed.

12.1.2 The General Assembly

The powers of the General Assembly are less elaborate and can be dealt with more briefly. Under Articles 10 to 14 of the Charter, the Assembly is given broad powers of discussion and recommendation. Its powers of discussion cover any questions or matters within the scope of the Charter. This plainly includes the settlement of all disputes except those which are 'essentially within the domestic jurisdiction of any state' as

---

[4] For a more detailed account of these provisions, see D. W. Bowett, 'The United Nations and Peaceful Settlement', in C. M. H. Waldock (ed.), *International Disputes: The Legal Aspects*, London, 1972, pp. 179–80. Bowett points out that, under Art. 35(1) of the Charter, any member of the United Nations has a right of recourse to the Security Council, and, under Art. 37(1), the parties to a dispute have a duty to refer it to the Council should they fail to settle it by negotiation, etc.

[5] Emphasis added.

provided by Article 2(7). However, this limitation, which applies to all United Nations organs, including the Security Council, is less significant than it may appear. In practice it has not prevented the General Assembly from discussing human rights, civil conflict and other highly sensitive 'domestic' issues.

The Assembly's powers of recommendation likewise cover the settlement of disputes and under Article 14 extend to the recommendation of 'measures for the peaceful adjustment of any situation, regardless of origin, which it deems likely to impair the general welfare or friendly relations among nations'. It is evident here that the Assembly's powers of recommendation are not confined to issues of peace and security and so are somewhat broader than those of the Security Council. It must be noted, however, that Article 14 is subject to Article 12(1), which provides that:

> While the Security Council is exercising in respect of any dispute or situation the functions assigned to it in the present Charter, the General Assembly shall not make any recommendation with regard to that dispute or situation unless the Security Council so requests.

This limitation also applies to the Assembly's broad powers of recommendation under Article 10, its competence in the field of international peace and security under Article 11(2) and its proceedings in respect of matters brought to its attention by a non-member state under Article 35(2). Thus, although the role which the Charter assigns to the General Assembly in relation to disputes is by no means negligible, as regards issues of peace and security the intention was to preserve the primacy of the Security Council.

The powers of the Secretariat are contained in Articles 98 and 99 and will be considered later (see Section 12.3).

12.2 Security Council and General Assembly in Action

Both the Security Council and the General Assembly have made extensive use of their powers to make recommendations to states concerning the settlement of disputes.

12.2.1 Recommendations Concerning the Settlement of Disputes

Under Article 33(2) of the Charter the Council may call upon the parties to settle a dispute by the peaceful means specified in Article 33(1), and under Article 36(1) it can recommend the specific means to be employed. Thus in 1976 the Council called upon Greece and Turkey 'to resume direct negotiations over their differences' with regard to the Aegean Sea dispute and appealed to them 'to do everything within their power to ensure that this results in mutually acceptable solutions'.[6] The General Assembly exercises similar powers, and, like the Security Council when it acts under Articles 37(2) and 38, can go so far as to recommend possible terms of settlement. In 1948, for example, in a recommendation addressed to the incipient Arab–Israeli struggle, the General Assembly set out an elaborate plan for the future of Palestine. The recommendation, incidentally, like so many others on this intractable issue, did nothing to resolve the dispute, a reminder of the self-evident, but basic, point that recommendations, which are not binding on the members of the United Nations, are also highly variable in their effects.

In recent years, however, the recommendations issued by the Security Council in relation to the peaceful settlement of disputes occur mostly in connection with intra-state conflicts. These recommendations most often relate to issues that exceed the traditional understanding of dispute settlement, and include, notably:

> (a) to cease hostilities and implement ceasefires; (b) to implement inclusive national reconciliation processes; (c) to fully implement existing peace agreements; (d) to engage in dialogue to ensure the peaceful transfer of power and the resolution of political and institutional crises; and (e) to engage in dialogue to resolve long-standing disputes.[7]

12.2.2 Fact-Finding

Another activity in which the Security Council and the General Assembly have been extensively engaged is fact-finding, and on numerous occasions both bodies have exercised their powers to set up subsidiary organs for this purpose.

Article 34 of the Charter provides explicitly for the Security Council to 'investigate' disputes:

> The Security Council may investigate any dispute, or any situation which might lead to international friction or give rise to a dispute, in order to determine whether the continuance of the dispute or situation is likely to endanger the maintenance of international peace and security.

In the *Corfu Channel* dispute, the Security Council established a fact-finding sub-committee to investigate evidence relating to the incident which had already been laid before the Council. Usually, however, the

---

[6] Security Council Resolution 395 (1976) referred to by the International Court in the *Aegean Sea Continental Shelf*, Interim Protection, Order of 11 September 1976 [1976] ICJ Rep. 3 at 12.

[7] United Nations, Repertoire of the Practice of the Security Council – Supplement 2016–2017, UN Doc. Nr. ST/PSCA/1/Add.20, p. 332.

purpose of establishing such a body has been to conduct an on-the-spot investigation. Among examples of such bodies are the Commission of Investigation set up by the Security Council to investigate incidents on the Greek frontier in 1947, a purely fact-finding operation, and the Special Committee on the Balkans set up by the General Assembly later in the same year, which combined fact-finding activities in the area with elements of mediation and conciliation. More recently, the Security Council appointed an International Independent Investigation Commission to assist the Lebanese authorities with the investigation of the terrorist bombing that killed former Prime Minister Rafiq Hariri in 2005.[8]

In practice, most 'missions' established by the Security Council often do not directly relate to the settlement of disputes in the narrow sense, but more broadly aim to 'to support peace processes and to assess the situation on the ground and the status of implementation of its resolutions' and are not 'explicitly charged with investigative tasks'.[9]

In recent years, the Security Council has often entrusted the Secretary-General with 'investigative' functions, including the creation of commissions of enquiry. Recent examples include a request to the Secretary-General to establish an international commission of enquiry to

> investigate reports of violations of international humanitarian law, international human rights law and abuses of human rights in [the Central African Republic] by all parties since 1 January 2013, to compile information, to help identify the perpetrators of such violations and abuses, point to their possible criminal responsibility and to help ensure that those responsible are held accountable, and calls on all parties to cooperate fully with such a commission.[10]

Another example is the request by the Security Council in Resolution 2379 (2017), to the Secretary-General to 'establish an investigative team, headed by a Special Adviser, to support domestic efforts in Iraq to hold ISIL (Da'esh) accountable by collecting, preserving and storing evidence in Iraq of acts that might amount to war crimes, crimes against humanity and genocide by the terrorist group'.[11]

---

[8] Security Council Resolution 1595 (2005). The Commission's report led to the Council's setting up a special tribunal, composed of Lebanese and international judges, to try those accused of the crime. See N. D. White and M. Saul, 'Legal means of dispute settlement in the field of collective security: the quasi-judicial powers of the Security Council', in D. French, M. Saul and N. D. White (eds), *International Law and Dispute Settlement: New Problems and Techniques*, Oxford, 2010, at p. 191 and p. 202.

[9] United Nations, Repertoire of the Practice of the Security Council – Supplement 2016–2017, UN Doc. Nr. ST/PSCA/1/Add.20, 314–15.

[10] Security Council Resolution 2127 (2013), UN Doc. S/RES/2127 (2013) (5 December 2013), para. 24.

[11] See for a discussion United Nations, Repertoire of the Practice of the Security Council – Supplement 2016–2017, UN Doc. Nr. ST/PSCA/1/Add.20, p. 318.

12.2.3 Mediation, Good offices and Conciliation

Assisting the parties to a dispute with negotiation, for which mediation and conciliation, together with good offices, provide possible means, is the third and perhaps the most important step open to the Organisation.[12] The existence of the United Nations itself facilitates diplomacy by bringing together ambassadors in a setting in which unobtrusive contacts are easily arranged and outside states can make an effort to encourage settlement behind the scenes, without the publicity and complications of formal intervention.

When quiet diplomacy is not enough, more open methods may be attempted. One such method, much favoured in the early years of the United Nations, is to establish a special committee to assist negotiations. In 1947, the Security Council set up a Committee of Good Offices, consisting of the representatives of Belgium, Australia and the United States, to promote the resumption of negotiations over the independence of Indonesia and to supervise the implementation of a cease-fire between Dutch and Indonesian forces. This was later reconstituted as the United Nations Commission for Indonesia, and supervised the transition to independence. Likewise, in 1950, the General Assembly set up (among other bodies) a Good Offices Committee, consisting of the President of the Assembly and the representatives of Sweden and Mexico, to explore the possibility of a settlement of the Korean War.

Although such committees can be useful, and in the first case mentioned certainly helped to produce the desired result, their tendency to reflect the political divisions of the parent organ and the slowness and indecision characteristic of committees everywhere have handicapped their operations and encouraged the search for alternatives.[13] From the earliest days of the United Nations, the exercise of good offices was sometimes entrusted to individuals rather than to the representatives of member states, and, while this in no sense guarantees success, its advantages have led to its being utilised on an increasing scale. Thus, in 1948, the General Assembly appointed Count Bernadotte United Nations Mediator for Palestine, with the task of arranging for the operation of essential common services, securing the protection of the holy places and promoting 'a peaceful adjustment of the future situation' in Palestine.[14] Similarly, in the dispute

---

[12] An excellent study of this form of assistance may be found in the editor's contribution to Raman, *Dispute Settlement* (n. 1) pp. 367–517. For recent activities of this kind by the UN in Abkhazia, Croatia and El Salvador, see M. C. Greenberg, J. H. Barton and M. E. McGuinness, *Words over War*, Lanham, MD, 2000, at pp. 15, 76 and 161.

[13] See M. W. Zacher, 'The Secretary-General and the United Nations' function of peaceful settlement' (1966) 20 *Int. Org.*, 724.

[14] For an account of this mission and Bernadotte's previous work, see R. Hewins, *Count Folke Bernadotte: His Life and Work*, London, 1949. It will be recalled that Bernadotte's assassination

between India and Pakistan over Kashmir, the Security Council appointed a Canadian, General McNaughton, to act as 'informal mediator' on the question of demilitarisation of the area in 1949; an Australian, Sir Owen Dixon, as 'United Nations Representative' with a similar brief in 1950; an American, Dr Frank Graham, as his successor in 1951; and a Swede, Dr Gunnar Jarring, with essentially the same task in 1957.[15]

The reference of disputes to individual mediators received its most important boost with the election of Dag Hammarskjöld as Secretary-General in 1953. In 1954, he was instructed by the General Assembly to seek the release of eleven American airmen held by the Chinese since their aircraft had been shot down during the Korean War some twenty months before. Instructed to use 'the means most appropriate in his judgment', Hammarskjöld secured an invitation to Peking and, after discussion and some delay, the airmen were eventually returned. Not surprisingly, the success of this personal diplomacy led to further requests to act in this capacity and, as we shall see, to a more active role for the Secretariat generally.

12.2.4 Referral of Disputes to Regional Organisations and the International Court of Justice

Leaving aside the option of taking coercive measures under Chapter VII, which is the prerogative of the Security Council and discussed below, a final possibility open to the Security Council and the General Assembly is to refer a dispute to a regional organisation[16] or another body for settlement. Under Article 11(2) of the Charter, the General Assembly must refer questions relating to the maintenance of international peace and security on which action is necessary to the Security Council 'either before or after discussion'. Other questions may be referred at any time. Although there is no corresponding duty on the Council to refer disputes to the Assembly, a power to make such references may be presumed.

Besides referring disputes to each other, the Council and Assembly can refer disputes to other organs of the United Nations. This has occasionally been done by the Council and more rarely by the Assembly. Article 36(3) of the Charter lays down that, in making recommendations for settlement, the Security Council should take into consideration that legal disputes should 'as a general rule' be referred to the International Court. However, neither the Council nor the Assembly can really be said to have

---

precipitated the International Court's advisory opinion in the *Reparation for Injuries* case [1949] ICJ Rep. 174.

[15] For further details, see E. Luard, *A History of the United Nations*, vol. I, London, 1982, ch. 14.

[16] The relation between regional organisations and the United Nations is discussed in the next chapter.

encouraged use of the Court. In 1947, the Council recommended that the parties to the *Corfu Channel* dispute refer the case to the Court, but, to date, this is the only contentious case where this has occurred.

12.2.5 Advisory Opinions

Requests for advisory opinions have also been sparse. As we have seen in Chapter 7, there can be no question of using advisory proceedings to nullify the consensual basis of the Court's contentious jurisdiction. But the fact that the reference of the *Peace Treaties* case[17] by the Assembly in 1949 was the only occasion on which the legal aspects of a dispute were referred to the Court in the first twenty-five years of the United Nations indicates a clear preference for the use of political means of settlement. This is still the case, although the reference of the *Namibia* case[18] by the Council in 1970, the *Western Sahara* case[19] by the Assembly in 1974, and the *Chagos* case[20] by the General Assembly in 2017 suggest a willingness to make use of the Court for disputes over decolonisation.

Other kinds of issues too have been referred on occasion, as was discussed in Chapters 6 and 7. Thus, the *Nuclear Weapons* case[21] was decided in 1996, the *Construction of a Wall* case[22] in 2004, and the *Kosovo* case[23] in 2010, in each instance at the request of the General Assembly. These opinions would never have been asked for by the Security Council (which has only once requested an advisory opinion from the Court, in the *Namibia* case), where involving the International Court was opposed by Permanent Members. This clearly demonstrates the Assembly's independence. At the same time, however, the impact of an advisory opinion is always likely to be affected by the procedure leading to the request and the connection between the requested opinion and an ongoing dispute, and so this too is a factor to be borne in mind.

12.2.6 Peacekeeping Operations and Action under Chapter VII

United Nations peacekeeping has been the subject of many detailed studies.[24] Consequently, all that is needed here is an outline of the types of

---

[17] [1950] ICJ Rep. 65 and 221. For discussion of this advisory opinion, see Chapters 6 and 7.
[18] [1971] ICJ Rep. 16.   [19] [1975] ICJ Rep. 12.
[20] [2019] ICJ Rep. 95. For discussion of this advisory opinion, see Chapters 6 and 7.
[21] [1996] ICJ Rep. 66.   [22] [2004] ICJ Rep. 136.   [23] [2010] ICJ Rep. 403.
[24] Useful studies include James, *Peacekeeping in International Politics* (n. 2); Parsons, *From Cold War to Hot Peace* (n. 2); and Warner, *New Dimensions of Peacekeeping* (n. 2). An invaluable collection of primary material is the four-volume series by Higgins entitled *United Nations Peace-Keeping Documents and Commentary* (n. 2). On the latest activities, see White, *The United Nations System* (n. 1) pp. 161–97; and C. Gray, *International Law and the Use of Force*, 2nd ed., Oxford, 2004, chs. 7 and 9.

activity undertaken by the Organisation and their contribution to the work of dispute settlement. A preliminary point to note is that the classification of the various peacekeeping groups established by the United Nations is difficult. Some were, from the beginning, intended to fulfil more than one function, while others, whose operations have spanned a decade or more, have in several instances performed different functions at different times. Moreover, the functions themselves, as we shall see, tend to merge and overlap. At the cost of some simplification, then, the following forms of operation can be distinguished.

Observation involves the sending of a team of United Nations personnel to a disturbed area in the hope that their presence and the knowledge that they are reporting what they see may have the effect of preventing, or at least discouraging, the crossing of international boundaries or other unauthorised activities. Observation is often combined with other peace-keeping functions, but on occasion has provided either the sole or the main objective of a United Nations presence. For example, the UN Observer Group in the Lebanon (UNOGIL), set up by the Security Council in 1958 to monitor alleged Syrian infiltration, was exclusively concerned with observation, whereas the UN Special Committee on the Balkans (UNSCOB), established by the General Assembly in 1947, acted as an observer group on the Greek border, and, as noted earlier, performed a number of other functions.

To improve relations in a sensitive border area, something more than observation may be needed. Attempts to have UNOGIL assume an extended role in the Lebanon were unsuccessful, but the assumption of a positive role can be seen in the practice of United Nations observer groups elsewhere in the Middle East and in Kashmir. The UN Truce Supervision Organization (UNTSO) developed from the arrangements devised by the Mediator for Palestine, whose work has already been mentioned. The group, which was steadily enlarged, had as its task the observation of the Arab–Israeli borders, together with the settlement of incidents and the negotiation of a cease-fire, should an outbreak of fighting occur. In less difficult circumstances, the UN Military Observer Group in India and Pakistan (UNMOGIP) has performed the same function in Kashmir from 1949 to the present day.

In situations in which fighting has broken out, it will often be easier to negotiate a cease-fire if arrangements for the disengagement of forces can be supervised by a third party. Here, then, is another function which peacekeeping forces can perform. In 1963, for example, the Security Council authorised the creation of a UN Observer Group in the Yemen (UNYOM) with the task of supervising the withdrawal of Egyptian and Saudi Arabian troops which had intervened in the civil war there, and, two years later, following the three-week war between India and Pakistan over Kashmir, set up the UN India–Pakistan Observation Mission (UNIPOM) to supervise a cease-fire and troop withdrawals from the disputed area. In 1988, the UN Good Offices Mission in Afghanistan and Pakistan was set up to perform a similar function in Afghanistan.[25]

Following a disengagement, it may be necessary to ensure that the rival forces remain separated. Although the groups already described can help achieve this to some extent, the task involved extends beyond observation and supervision, which can often be performed by relatively small groups, and calls for the deployment of more substantial forces. The creation of a force comparable to national military forces is beyond the capacity of the United Nations, and in any case the consent of the parties in dispute (which is essential) would hardly be given to the deployment of such a force on national territory. Fortunately, no such arrangements are necessary. What is required here is not a force capable of large-scale fighting but a group large enough to occupy a sensitive frontier area and to act as a buffer between the parties. An example of the usefulness of such a group is the UN Emergency Force in the Middle East (UNEF I), a force whose initial task was to supervise the withdrawal of French and British forces from Egypt in 1956 patrolled the Egypt–Israel border until 1967.

Although it is no part of the United Nations' function to intervene in domestic affairs, there are situations in which a breakdown of order in a state may become a matter of international concern on account of the risk of foreign intervention. Similarly, there are circumstances in which the implementation of the terms of an international settlement could be threatened by internal disorder. In situations of this type, United Nations forces may be employed with another objective, that of restoring or maintaining order. The foremost example of an operation with this purpose is the UN Operation in the Congo (ONUC).[26] There, following a mutiny of local troops, Belgian forces had intervened and the dispatch of United Nations forces, though highly controversial at the time, played a valuable role in preventing a further deterioration of the situation.

From time to time, suggestions have been made that this or that disputed territory should be handed over to the United Nations to become the object of international administration. Although permanent administration will generally be out of the question,[27] a transitional arrangement as

---

[25] See White, *Keeping the Peace* (n. 1) p. 223; and (1988) 27 ILM 577.
[26] See Higgins, *United Nations Peace-Keeping* (n. 2) vol. III; and G. Abi-Saab, *The United Nations Operation in the Congo 1960–1964*, Oxford, 1978.
[27] Although the Saar was administered by the League of Nations for fifteen years following the First World War, the failure of the United Nations to implement similar schemes in respect of Trieste and Jerusalem indicates the difficulty of obtaining and maintaining the degree of support necessary to carry such schemes through. See on this: Eric De Brabandere, *Post-conflict Administrations in International Law. International Territorial Administration, Transitional Authority and Foreign Occupation in Theory and Practice*, Leiden/ Boston, 2009.

part of the process of changing sovereignty over a disputed area may be a more promising possibility.

Operations like UNTAG, UNMIK and UNTAET reflect what has been termed the 'integrated and pacific' approach to peacekeeping,[28] in which the parties to a conflict are persuaded to accept a UN presence not just to stabilise the situation as in Kashmir, Cyprus and elsewhere, but to support proposals for a settlement which UN forces then help to implement.

In contrast, the Congo operation and a number of recent operations which have not yet been mentioned represent a line of development which has been termed the 'quasi-enforcement' approach to peacekeeping.[29] Here, there are elements of peacekeeping in the traditional sense, but the activities of the UN involve a use of force beyond that required in self-defence and, while not amounting to enforcement action under Chapter VII, are difficult to reconcile with the normal peacekeeping requirements of neutrality, cooperation and consent. In 2013, for example, the Security Council established an 'Intervention Brigade', as part of the peacekeeping mission in the Democratic Republic of the Congo (MONUSCO) which had been in operation since 2010 and with responsibilities including carrying out 'targeted offensive operations'. In the same year it established a mission in Mali (MINUSMA) with authorisation to carry out parts of its mandate, using 'all necessary means'. And in 2014 the Council established a mission in the Central African Republic (MINUSCA) with similar powers.[30]

Although the constitutional problems surrounding the creation and operation of UN forces are not a subject which is possible to enter into here,[31] it should be noted that peacekeeping operations are quite distinct from the kind of collective security operation envisaged in Chapter VII of the Charter and discussed below. Rather, they represent improvised responses to particular situations with no very clear constitutional basis, and it is here that practical and theoretical difficulties have arisen.

As already noted, Chapter VII of the Charter enables the Security Council to adopt economic sanctions and military measures where there is a 'threat to the peace, breach of the peace or act of aggression', thereby equipping it with enforcement powers in disputes or situations that are

---

[28] See N. D. White, 'UN peacekeeping: development or destruction' (1994) 12 *Int. Rel.*, 129 at 137–49, and *The Law of International Organizations*, Manchester, 1996, p. 184.

[29] See White, 'UN peacekeeping' (n. 28 above) 149–58; and M. Bertrand, 'The confusion between peacemaking and peacekeeping' in D. Warner (ed.), *New Dimensions of Peacekeeping*, Dordrecht, 1995, p. 163. See also White, *The United Nations System* (n. 1) pp. 161–5; and Gray, *Use of Force* (n. 24) pp. 217–27.

[30] On the three missions mentioned, see J. K. Cogan, 'Stabilization and the expanding scope of the Security Council's work' (2015) 109 *AJIL*, 324 at 330.

[31] See A. Cassese (ed.), *United Nations Peacekeeping: Legal Essays*, Alphen aan den Rijn, 1978; and White, *Keeping the Peace* (n. 1) ch. 8.

particularly serious. Since this book is concerned with peaceful methods of dispute settlement, analysis of the coercive potential of Chapter VII, and the concept of collective security generally, would be out of place.[32] However, something needs to be said about this part of the Charter, partly in order to appreciate the role of Chapter VI, and partly because, since the ending of the Cold War, the provisions of Chapter VII have acquired a practical importance with far-reaching implications.

To bring Chapter VII into play, Article 39 lays down that it is for the Security Council to determine that the necessary conditions are present. The first question therefore is what qualifies as a 'threat to the peace, breach of the peace or act of aggression'.[33] The term 'threat to the peace' has been interpreted very flexibly and extended beyond the obvious case of one state threatening another, to cover situations within a state, such as civil wars, which have international repercussions. In 1961, for example, the Security Council characterised the civil war in the Congo in this way and subsequently made similar determinations in relation to the conflicts in Yugoslavia (1991) and Liberia (1992). The 'third generation' peacekeeping operations in Kosovo and East Timor (1999) were also authorised under Chapter VII on this basis. In contrast, the terms 'breach of peace' and 'act of aggression' have so far mostly been confined to situations in which force has been used between states, as in, for example, the Argentine invasion of the Falkland Islands in 1982 and the Iraqi invasion of Kuwait in 1990.

A survey of how the Security Council has used Article 39 shows very clearly that whether it is prepared to activate Chapter VII depends on political rather than legal considerations. Thus, although there have been numerous international wars and other cases of force being used between states in the United Nations era, only a handful have been characterised by the Security Council as involving a breach of the peace. Conversely, in the activist period following the end of the Cold War, the concept of a threat to the peace has been extended beyond civil conflicts to cover support for terrorism in the case of Libya (1992) and the denial of democracy in the case of Haiti (1993). More recently, the Security Council has characterised as threats to the peace, the security situation in the Central African Republic (2013), the Ebola outbreak in Africa (2014), and the humanitarian situation in Syria (2014). But, while the Charter invests the Security Council with sanctioning powers and purports to define the conditions for their use, there is nothing automatic about this process. Because any

---

[32] For good overviews, see N. D. White, *The Law of International Organizations*, Manchester 1996, ch. 7; and A. Hurrell, 'Collective security and international order revisited' (1992) 11 *Int. Rel.* 37. See also White, *The United Nations System* (n. 1) ch. 6; and Gray, *Use of Force* (n. 24) chs. 7 and 8 and A. Orakhelashvili, *Collective Security*, Oxford, 2011.

[33] See White, *The Law of International Organizations* (n. 32) pp. 172–4. Also, J. K. Cogan, 'Stabilization and the expanding scope of the Security Council's work' (2015) 109 *AJIL* 324.

determination under Article 39 requires a political decision, the potential of Chapter VII may be neglected in some situations and exploited in others according to the particular circumstances.

Once a determination under Article 39 has been made, it is open to the Security Council to make recommendations, or to decide what measures shall be taken in accordance with Articles 41 and 42 to maintain or restore international peace and security. Article 41 permits the employment of measures 'not involving the use of armed force' and is primarily concerned with economic sanctions. Although the intention behind this provision was to enable mandatory sanctions to be imposed on a delinquent state, in practice lack of agreement has often compelled the Security Council to call only for voluntary (i.e. non-obligatory) measures. These, as might be expected, are usually ineffective and demonstrate that, even when a situation is being considered under Chapter VII, political factors govern the ultimate decision.

The Security Council's power to impose military sanctions rests on Article 42 of the Charter, which authorises it to 'take such action by air, sea or land forces as may be necessary to maintain or restore international peace and security'. Article 43 goes on to provide for member states to conclude agreements with the UN under which their forces will be available for use when needed. This arrangement would, in effect, have provided the UN with a standing army. In the event, however, such agreements were never concluded on account of East–West tensions. As a result, instead of initiating military action with its own forces, the Security Council has been limited to recommending military action by member states and has been forced to rely on their voluntary provision of forces.

12.3 Role of the Secretary-General

The work of the Secretary-General in the field of dispute settlement falls into two distinct parts. On the one hand, there are the functions delegated by the Security Council, as discussed in the previous section, and General Assembly under Article 98; on the other hand, there are the various actions undertaken at the request of interested parties, or on the Secretary-General's own initiative by virtue of his powers under Article 99.

12.3.1 Actions undertaken by the Secretary-General

The authority to investigate the possibilities of settlement given to the Secretary-General by the General Assembly in 1954 in the dispute over the detained American airmen set a precedent which has been followed in many subsequent cases.[34] In its resolution on the crisis caused by the

---

[34] See T. M. Franck, *Fairness in International Law and Institutions*, Oxford, 1995, ch. 6.

detention of the United States diplomatic and consular staff in Tehran, for example, the Security Council called on Iran to release the personnel of the embassy immediately and requested the Secretary-General to lend his good offices for the immediate implementation of the resolution. In pursuance of his mandate to take all appropriate measures to this end, Secretary-General Waldheim first visited Tehran, and then set up a commission to investigate the dispute. The Commission was unable to resolve the crisis, but at least maintained contact, demonstrating that, when called upon for his good offices, the Secretary-General enjoys a wide measure of discretion and may, if he thinks it necessary, establish subordinate bodies.

In January 1980, shortly after the Soviet invasion of Afghanistan, the General Assembly passed a resolution asking the Secretary-General to use his good offices with regard to the situation. This was the first of a number of resolutions on this question, which ultimately led the Secretary-General to appoint one of his subordinates, Diego Cordovez, to serve as his personal representative in negotiations between Pakistan, the Soviet Union and Afghanistan on the procedure for removing Soviet troops from the territory. Negotiations were conducted by shuttling between Kabul and Islamabad and between separate rooms allocated to the parties in the Geneva headquarters of the United Nations. Progress towards a settlement was slow and complicated by the absence from the negotiations of the Afghan resistance leaders. Eventually, however, a settlement was agreed and the withdrawal of the last Soviet troops took place in 1989.

In cases where armed conflict has broken out, the Secretary-General's mandate has generally included a request that he use his good offices in an attempt to secure a cease-fire. For example, when India and Pakistan went to war over Kashmir in 1965, the Security Council requested the Secretary-General to 'exert every possible effort' to achieve an end to the fighting. Similarly, after the outbreak of hostilities over the Falkland Islands, the Security Council in its Resolution of May 1982 requested the Secretary-General to enter into contact immediately with Argentina and the United Kingdom 'with a view to negotiating mutually acceptable terms for a ceasefire'.[35] Subsequently, following Security Council Resolution 598 of July 1987, the Secretary-General visited Iran and Iraq to assist with the negotiation of the cease-fire in the Iran–Iraq War which took effect in August 1988.

In a situation of armed conflict, it may also be possible for the Secretary-General to take certain steps with a view to restraining parties and limiting the scope of the fighting. Thus, in the war with Iraq, Iran asked the Security Council to investigate the use of chemical weapons by the Iraqi forces. As

---

[35] Security Council Resolution 505 (1982). For the full text, see (1982) 21 ILM 680. For an evaluation of the Security Council's role in the Falklands crisis, see J. F. Murphy, *The United Nations and the Control of International Violence*, Manchester, 1982, pp. 67–71.

we have seen in Chapter 4, this led the Secretary-General to appoint a group to inquire into this issue. The resulting studies confirmed that chemical weapons had been used and were the basis for the Security Council's condemnation of the use of such weapons in March 1986. During the same conflict, a public appeal by the Secretary-General succeeded in obtaining from the belligerents an undertaking not to attack each other's civilian population.[36] This was intended as part of an incremental solution to the conflict and as such was not immediately successful. It did, however, have the effect of restraining the parties' conduct of hostilities for a period and preventing further deterioration.

A third function often assigned to the Secretary-General has in practice been one of the most important, namely, the organisation and administration of United Nations peacekeeping operations of various kinds. Thus, the negotiations envisaged in the resolution on the Falklands were to include 'if necessary, arrangements for the dispatch of United Nations observers to monitor compliance with the terms of the cease-fire'. In this instance, the group in question was never formed, but peacekeeping operations and the supervision of a United Nations 'presence' have been a prominent feature of the mandates of successive Secretaries-General over the years.

Article 99 of the UN Charter allows the Secretary-General to 'bring to the attention of the Security Council any matter which in his opinion may threaten the maintenance of international peace and security.' Official or explicit invocations of or references to Article 99 are uncommon,[37] despite the fact that several Security Council member states 'encouraged the Secretary-General to fully exercise his power under Article 99 and to strengthen the effectiveness of his good offices' in 2018.[38]

With the exception of peacekeeping operations, which always require a mandate, the Secretary-General's exercise of his powers under Article 99 has involved him in activities similar to those already described. As noted by the Security Council, 'the work of the Council regarding conflict prevention and the peaceful settlement of disputes has, however, required the involvement of the Secretary-General in all relevant aspects of that

---

[36] See D. Cordovez, 'Strengthening United Nations diplomacy for peace: the role of the Secretary-General', in UNITAR, *The United Nations and the Maintenance of International Peace and Security*, Dordrecht, 1987, p. 161 at p. 172.

[37] Since 2016, the Secretary-General has not used his powers under Article 99. See United Nations, Repertoire of the Practice of the Security Council – Supplement 2016–2017, UN Doc. No. ST/PSCA/1/Add.20, p. 313; United Nations, Repertoire of the Practice of the Security Council – Supplement 2018, UN Doc. No. ST/PSCA/1/Add.21, p. 291, United Nations, Repertoire of the Practice of the Security Council – 22nd Supplement 2019, available at https://www.un.org/securitycouncil/content/repertoire/structure, p. 10.

[38] United Nations, Repertoire of the Practice of the Security Council – Supplement 2018, UN Doc. No. ST/PSCA/1/Add.21, p. 313.

agenda.'[39] This involvement mostly relates to 'the good offices work of the Secretary-General, as well as that of his special representatives and envoys, in support of efforts to end violent conflict, of peace and reconciliation processes, and the resolution of outstanding disputes'.[40]

Thus, in 1958, in an attempt to alleviate the border tension between Thailand and Cambodia, Secretary-General Hammarskjöld discussed the issue with the parties, consulted members of the Security Council, and at the parties' invitation sent Ambassador Johan Beck-Friis of Sweden to the area as his Special Representative. As a result of the latter's efforts, the parties eventually resumed diplomatic relations. Similarly, in the Cuban missile crisis of 1962, Secretary-General U Thant devoted his efforts first to the formulation of various proposals to reduce the immediate tension and gain time, and then to discussions with the Government of Cuba over possible arrangements for a United Nations presence.[41]

In these disputes, the Secretary-General's primary objective was to discourage precipitate action which might make a difficult situation worse; in other words, by filling a dangerous political vacuum to create a breathing space and the opportunity for a settlement later. In other cases his actions have been more obviously directed towards procedural or substantive solutions. In the dispute between the United Kingdom and Iran over the status of Bahrain, for example, U Thant spent many months discussing the issue with the parties. Then, following a formal request that he should act as mediator and ascertain the wishes of the inhabitants of the area, he appointed a personal representative to conduct an inquiry. The latter's report, which favoured independence for Bahrain, was subsequently accepted by the Security Council and formed the basis of the final settlement.[42]

The *Bahrain* dispute not only drew attention to the possibility of combining mediation with fact-finding, but also showed the usefulness of the Secretary-General's position in a dispute in which non-recognition could have caused difficulties, because Bahrain was not recognised by Iran. At about the same time, U Thant was making strenuous efforts to promote peace in Vietnam, where non-recognition was again a problem. The Secretary-General's ability to bypass such difficulties through the use

---

[39] United Nations, Repertoire of the Practice of the Security Council – 22nd Supplement 2019, available at www.un.org/securitycouncil/content/repertoire/structure, p. 43.
[40] *Ibid.* [41] U Thant, *View from the UN*, London, 1978, ch. 8.
[42] See H. Al-Baharna, 'The fact-finding mission of the United Nations Secretary-General and the settlement of the Bahrain–Iran dispute' (1973) 22 *ICLQ*, 541. In 1996, a proposal by Secretary-General Boutros-Ghali to send a fact-finding mission to investigate frontier incidents between Cameroon and Nigeria was supported by both the Security Council and the International Court. See *Land and Maritime Boundary between Cameroon and Nigeria*, Provisional Measures, Order of 15 March 1996 [1996] ICJ Rep. 13. See also the Report on the *Flotilla Incident*, organised by the Secretary-General in 2010, and described in Chapter 4.

of quiet diplomacy is an important feature of his role. However, as U Thant's refusal to become involved in the Nigerian civil war and the rejection by the United Kingdom of his offer to intercede in Northern Ireland demonstrate, the exclusion of matters of domestic jurisdiction from the United Nations is a major limitation on its powers.

The good offices role of the Secretary-General can on occasion also exploit the possibilities of utilising legal procedures for the settlement of international disputes. The Secretary-General was evidently instrumental in persuading Libya and Malta to take their dispute over continental shelf delimitation to the International Court in 1985,[43] and, in the following year, the Secretary-General himself acted as arbitrator in the *Rainbow Warrior* case[44] between France and New Zealand. In the latter instance, as we have seen in Chapter 6, the parties had succeeded in resolving some of their differences by negotiation, but outstanding issues included the future of the French agents imprisoned in New Zealand, and the question of compensation. In his award, the Secretary-General resolved these and certain other matters to the parties' satisfaction, and the incident was declared closed. Although the procedure in this case differed in some respects from that of a conventional arbitration, it had many of the same advantages. The decision was accepted in advance, so minimising the problem of implementation, while the source of the decision, a third party of unimpeachable independence, had the effect of legitimising a result which would have been difficult, if not impossible, to arrive at in direct negotiations.

Over recent years, as was also noted in relation to the recommendations made by the Security Council, the work of the Secretary-General has been important mostly in connection with intra-state disputes or situations. The Secretary-General's good offices and mediation role is therefore often related to

> the cessation of hostilities and the implementation of permanent ceasefires, the implementation of inclusive reconciliation processes, the full implementation of peace agreements, the peaceful transfer of power and the resolution of political and institutional crises, the resolution of protracted conflicts and the addressing of cross-border challenges.[45]

12.3.2 The Independence of the Secretary-General

In exercising the initiatives described, the Secretary-General's activity has usually been closely related to that of the other organs of the United

---

[43] Cordovez, 'Role of the Secretary-General' (n. 36) p. 171.
[44] See *Ruling pertaining to the Differences between France and New Zealand arising from the Rainbow Warrior Affair* (1986). Text in 74 ILR 241 and Appendix G.
[45] United Nations, Repertoire of the Practice of the Security Council – Supplement 2016–2017, UN Doc. Nr. ST/PSCA/1/Add.20, pp. 337–8.

Nations, as was also discussed in Section 12.2. In the Cuban missile crisis, the dispute was before the Security Council throughout the period of the Secretary-General's involvement, and in both the Falklands and Kashmir disputes a period of active diplomacy by the Secretary-General preceded his Security Council mandate. Even in cases such as the Thailand–Cambodia dispute, where the matter is never formally considered by the Council, its members will expect to be kept informed. If, however, it would be wrong to see the efforts of the Secretary-General in isolation, it is clear that his ability to take the initiative will often have the advantage of enabling a potentially significant influence to be brought to bear on a dispute at a very early stage.

Although the Secretary-General must be prepared to coordinate his activity with that of the Security Council and General Assembly, the strength of his position clearly lies in his independence. The preservation of his independence must therefore be a primary goal, since without it little could be achieved. Its value is evident in many ways. It was, for example, the Secretary-General's independence which made his good offices acceptable to both sides in the diplomatic hostages crisis and the negotiations on Afghanistan. It was similarly his independent position which enabled him to address his appeal to the parties in the Cuban missile crisis and the Iran–Iraq war, and which enabled him to arbitrate in the *Rainbow Warrior* case. On several occasions during the Afghanistan negotiations, the Secretary-General privately told the parties that he might discontinue his efforts on account of a lack of progress. This produced strenuous pleas for him to continue, and shows how the Secretary-General can sometimes exploit his position to move the parties forward.

To preserve the Secretary-General's independence, it is important not only that he acts without fear or favour, but also that he stays within his constitutional competence.[46] Action which brought him into conflict with the other organs would lead inevitably to accusations that he was taking sides and ultimately render his position untenable. In this respect, the issue of independence is concerned with more than the question of how he does his job, but poses the basic question of what precisely the job consists of. Faced with a situation in which the political organs are unable to act effectively, it is tempting to believe that the Secretary-General should always step into the breach. That, however, would be a mistake. The objections to such a policy are not only constitutional, they are also practical. For, as former Secretary-General Pérez de Cuéllar has written, 'the temptation to aggrandizement can discredit the institution of Secretary-General, and thus the organization as a whole, because it can

---

[46] See N. Elaraby, 'The office of the Secretary-General and the maintenance of international peace and security', in UNITAR, *The United Nations and the Maintenance of International Peace and Security*, Dordrecht, 1987, p. 177 at pp. 181–7.

lead the Secretary-General into courses of action which are not realistically sustainable'.[47]

This does not mean that it is necessary to take the opposite position and regard the Secretary-General as merely the chief administrative officer of the Organisation with no peace-making function. On the contrary, 'situations can, and do, arise when the Secretary-General has to exercise his powers to the full, as the bearer of a sacred trust, and as the guardian of the principles of the Charter',[48] and, in practice, as we have seen, this is a view which successive holders of the office have taken, though with differences of emphasis. But it is worth bearing in mind that, while the Secretary-General's scope for initiative is extensive, the decision to invoke Article 99 is a matter for his discretion. Efforts to make intervention a duty, rather than a power, were resisted on the ground that the Secretary-General was the best judge of whether action was appropriate. The wisdom of this decision is now apparent. Since the timing of initiatives is often crucial in the settlement of disputes, and much of the Secretary-General's work is in any case 'quiet diplomacy', treating the Secretary-General's authority under Article 99 as another facet of his independence was much better than trying to impose it as a duty.

A final point concerns the responsibility of the members of the Security Council and, to a lesser extent, the members of the General Assembly. The possibility noted earlier of a Secretary-General seeking to usurp the role of the other organs cannot be said to be a real risk at the present time. Unfortunately, the same cannot be said of the converse situation, that is, one in which the members of the Security Council fail to discharge their obligations in the field of peace and security, and matters are left to the Secretary-General. A moment's reflection will demonstrate that this situation, which is likely to arise whenever the major states find themselves at loggerheads, cannot provide a sustainable basis for international peace-making. To demand that the other organs deal with every problem, always adopt the measures most likely to be effective and invariably provide the Secretary-General with precise instructions is, no doubt, quite unrealistic. What is vital, however, is the point which has already been made, that the functions of the Secretary-General should be treated as complementary to those of the other organs. This means that neither the Security Council nor the General Assembly can abrogate their political responsibility for peace and security and expect the Secretary-General to bear the burden. This moreover, was pointed out by the Secretary-General in his 1982 Annual Report:

---

[47] See J. Pérez de Cuéllar, 'The role of the UN Secretary-General', in A. Roberts and B. Kingsbury (eds), *United Nations, Divided World*, 2nd ed., Oxford, 1993, p. 124 at p. 126.
[48] *Ibid.*

[t]here is a tendency in the United Nations for governments to act as though the passage of a resolution absolved them from further responsibility for the subject in question.[49]

The ability of the Secretary-General to take action to promote the settlement of disputes on his own initiative or under Article 98 does not, of course, bring with it any guarantee that such intervention will be successful. For example, following the invasion and occupation of Kuwait in 1990, Secretary-General Pérez de Cuéllar twice sought to engage Iraq in discussions designed to bring about its withdrawal. However, neither the contacts at the beginning of the crisis in August 1990, nor those on the eve of the conflict between Iraq and the US-led coalition in January 1991, were fruitful, owing to Iraq's intransigence on both occasions.[50] As ways of settling disputes, good offices, mediation, conciliation and fact-finding are subject to very much the same constraints whether they are carried out by the Secretary-General and his representatives or by an outside party. But, if the gap between the disputants must sometimes prove unbridgeable, it is not always so. Bearing in mind that the possibilities of a solution can only be identified if they are first explored, a Secretary-General willing and able to undertake that task must be regarded as a major asset to the United Nations system.[51]

12.4 Political Organs and the International Court

Action by the Secretary-General, the involvement of the Security Council or the adoption of measures by the General Assembly all represent ways of attempting to deal with international disputes at the political level. In addition to these procedures, which are essentially discretionary, it is of course possible for states to seek to employ arbitration or judicial settlement to obtain a decision based on international law. Since the distinctive features of legal means of settlement have been considered earlier, they need not be described again here. One point, however, does need to be examined because it is directly concerned with the subject matter of this chapter. It is the relation between the International Court, the 'principal

---

[49] UN Doc. A/37/1, at 3.
[50] See L. Freedman and E. Karsh, *The Gulf Conflict 1990–1991*, London, 1993, pp. 160–1, 268–70 and 274.
[51] For further information on the work of the Secretary-General, see Zacher, 'The Secretary-General' (n. 13); L. Gordenker, *The UN Secretary-General and the Maintenance of Peace*, New York, 1967; V. Pechota, 'The quiet approach', in K. V. Raman (ed.), *Dispute Settlement through the United Nations*, New York, 1977, p. 577; and K. Skjelsbaek and G. Fermann, 'The UN Secretary-General and the mediation of international disputes', in J. Bercovitch (ed.), *Resolving International Conflict: The Theory and Practice of Mediation*, London, 1996, p. 75. Also S. Chesterman (ed.), *Secretary or General? The UN Secretary-General in World Politics*, Cambridge, 2007.

judicial organ of the United Nations',[52] and the political organs. This question has two aspects. The first, examined here, is whether, as a matter of principle, the Court's competence is affected if a political organ is also dealing with a dispute. The second, considered later, is whether, when a case is properly before the Court, it may exercise judicial control by holding the action of one of the political organs to be unconstitutional.

12.4.1 The Competence of the International Court of Justice in Relation to Simultaneous Security Council Action

How far recourse to the Court is compatible with simultaneous use of the political organs was a question which was raised by a number of the arguments put forward by the United States in the *Nicaragua* case.[53] For, in addition to various objections to the jurisdiction of the Court, which have been discussed in Chapter 8, the United States maintained that the case should be declared inadmissible on the ground that a ruling on the merits would transgress the boundaries of the judicial function and involve the Court in issues which are the prerogative of the Security Council. The argument was put in two ways. First, it was said that Nicaragua's claim required the Court to decide whether the United States had used unlawful force and that questions of this kind fall within the exclusive jurisdiction of the political organs. Second, and as a development of the first point, the United States maintained that, by bringing the case to the Court, Nicaragua was in effect seeking to appeal from an adverse ruling on its complaints by the Council. Since the Charter makes no provision for such an appeal, the Court, according to the United States, lacked 'subject-matter jurisdiction'[54] over the claim.

The Court rejected both arguments. On the first point, it explained that, while Article 24 of the Charter confers on the Council 'primary responsibility for the maintenance of international peace and security', this is different from exclusive responsibility. As the Court and the Security Council have quite separate functions, neither the fact that a matter is under consideration by the Security Council nor the fact that a case concerns the use of force is legally any bar to judicial proceedings. As to the proceedings being an appeal from the Security Council, the Court rejected this argument on the facts. The Court pointed out that it was 'not asked to say that the Security Council is wrong in its decision, nor that there is anything inconsistent with law in the way in which the members of

---

[52] Article 1 of the Statute of the Court provides: 'The International Court of Justice established by the Charter of the United Nations as the principal judicial organ of the United Nations shall be constituted and shall function in accordance with the provisions of the present Statute'.
[53] *Military and Paramilitary Activities in and against Nicaragua*, Jurisdiction and Admissibility, Judgment [1984] ICJ Rep. 392.
[54] *Ibid.*, para. 91.

the Council employed their right to vote'. On the contrary, the Court said that it was 'asked to pass judgment on certain legal aspects of a situation which has also been considered by the Security Council, a procedure which is entirely consonant with its position as the principal judicial organ of the United Nations'.[55] This objection too was therefore rejected.

The Court's decision on these points was unanimous, and its ruling is clearly correct. Not only is the decision to treat the case as admissible in line with its previous jurisprudence, but it is only necessary to reflect on what was at stake here to appreciate that acceptance of either of the United States' arguments would produce grotesque results. If the Court had accepted that claims relating to the use of force are outside its competence, it would have disqualified itself from dealing with a wide range of important international disputes and relegated the rules of international law which govern these matters to a second-class status. If, on the other hand, it had accepted the jurisdictional point and agreed that, when a matter has been vetoed in the Security Council, litigation amounts to an appeal from 'the decision which the Security Council did not take',[56] it would have extended the veto of the Permanent Members from the political to the legal arena. While the Charter invests the Security Council, and consequently the Permanent Members, with major responsibilities in the area of peace and security, it also recognises a role for legal procedures which the Court, as the institution's legal organ, has a duty to protect.

In drawing its conclusions in the *Nicaragua* case, the Court placed a good deal of reliance on its decision in the *Diplomatic Hostages in Tehran* case[57] in 1980. In that case, the question which the Court had to consider was not specifically concerned with the articles of the Charter relating to the use of force, but with the more general issue of the relation between the Court and the political organs. In addition, because the Secretary-General had established a Special Commission to look into the dispute, the Court took the opportunity to examine how far this type of initiative, which, as we have seen, is not uncommon, is compatible with the pursuit of judicial remedies. Both the general question and the specific matter of the Commission touched on issues which had been considered before, but which, like the questions of justiciability raised in the *Nicaragua* case, go to the root of the United Nations system.

The question of the Court's role *vis-à-vis* the political organs arose in this case because shortly before the United States made its application to the Court, the occupation of the embassy and the detention of the staff as hostages were referred to the Security Council by both the United States and the Secretary-General. Although the matter was actively being considered by the Council, and the Secretary-General had already been given a

---

[55] *Ibid.*, para. 98. [56] *Ibid.*, para. 91, referring to the United States' argument on this point.
[57] *United States Diplomatic and Consular Staff in Tehran*, Judgment [1980] ICJ Rep. 3.

mandate to use his good offices in the matter, the Court decided, in December 1979, that it was competent to entertain a request from the United States for provisional measures of protection and went on to make such an order. Commenting on this in its judgment of May 1980, the Court made the following observation about its action and the scope of its authority:

> [I]t does not seem to have occurred to any member of the Council that there was or could be anything irregular in the simultaneous exercise of their respective functions by the Court and the Security Council. Nor is there in this any cause for surprise. Whereas Article 12 of the Charter expressly forbids the General Assembly to make any recommendation with regard to a dispute or situation while the Security Council is exercising its functions in respect of that dispute situation, no such restriction is placed on the functioning of the Court by any provision of either the Charter or the Statute of the Court. The reasons are clear. It is for the Court, the principal judicial organ of the United Nations, to resolve any legal questions that may be in issue between parties to a dispute; and the resolution of such legal questions by the Court may be an important, and sometimes decisive, factor in promoting the peaceful settlement of the dispute.[58]

Having made the point that the involvement of the Security Council was not in itself an obstacle to the exercise of its jurisdiction, the Court proceeded to examine in some detail the Special Commission which the Secretary-General had established with the authority of the Council and which had already begun its work. With reference to the circumstances in which the Commission was set up, the Court made the important point that its creation was evidently not intended to postpone consideration of the dispute by the Court. It would have been open to the parties to agree to use the Commission for this purpose, but the Court said that it could 'find no trace of any understanding on the part of either the United States or Iran that the establishment of the Commission might involve a postponement of all proceedings before the Court until the conclusion of the work of the Commission and of the Security Council's consideration of the matter'.[59]

As regards the actual function of the Commission, the Court found that it had not been set up to decide disputed matters of fact or law, but rather to carry out mediation, conciliation or negotiation in an attempt to ease the tension between Iran and the United States. Its establishment could not therefore 'be considered in itself as in any way incompatible with the continuance of parallel proceedings before the Court'.[60] Here the Court was really saying two things. It was confirming a view that it had previously expressed that mediation, conciliation and negotiation are normally compatible with judicial settlement. Then, by implication, it was recognising

---

[58] *Ibid.*, para. 40.   [59] *Ibid.*, para. 42.   [60] *Ibid.*

that a body which was empowered to decide 'matters of fact or law in dispute between Iran and the United States' would displace the Court by virtue of the recognised principle of litispendence.[61] However, as there was no question of litispendence here, it held that neither the Secretary-General's mandate, nor the setting up of his Commission, could be regarded as an obstacle to the exercise of jurisdiction.

In the *Genocide Convention* case[62] in 1993, the Court again had to consider the relation between its power to order provisional measures under Article 41 of its Statute and the actions of the Security Council. The situation in the former Yugoslavia was taken to the United Nations in 1991 before the initiation of proceedings by Bosnia against the Federal Republic of Yugoslavia and was under review by the Security Council throughout the Court's consideration of the case. Moreover, the Security Council had taken decisions on the basis of Article 25 of the Charter, and, when imposing an arms embargo and taking various other measures, had indicated that it was acting under Chapter VII. As a result, when Bosnia made its first request for interim protection, Yugoslavia argued that, so long as the Council was acting under these provisions, 'it would be premature and inappropriate for the Court to indicate provisional measures, and certainly provisional measures of the type which have been requested'.[63]

The Court, however, rejected the argument and ordered certain provisional measures, recalling that, at the jurisdiction and admissibility stage of the *Nicaragua* case, it had made the point that, in the absence of any provision in the Charter giving the Security Council priority over the Court, both organs can 'perform their separate but complementary functions with respect to the same events'.[64] This was therefore a rejection of the view that the involvement of the Security Council, even in disputes falling under Chapter VII, is per se an obstacle to the consideration of a case under Article 41. The Court's view of its relationship to the Security Council was further demonstrated six months later when Bosnia made a further request for interim protection, following further Security Council resolutions.[65] Deciding that what was needed was not additional measures but the immediate and effective implementation of those already ordered, it reaffirmed the measures in its previous order, showing again that Security Council action in itself is no bar to measures under Article 41.

---

[61] For an exhaustive examination of this issue, see D. Ciobanu, 'Litispendence between the International Court of Justice and the political organs of the United Nations', in L. Gross (ed.), *The Future of the International Court of Justice*, New York, 1976, p. 209.

[62] *Application of the Convention on the Prevention and Punishment of the Crime of Genocide*, Provisional Measures, Order of 8 April 1993 [1993] ICJ Rep. 3.

[63] *Ibid.*, para. 33.   [64] *Ibid.* The words quoted are to be found in [1984] ICJ Rep. 435, para. 95.

[65] See the Court's Order of 13 September 1993, [1993] ICJ Rep. 325.

In the *Construction of a Wall* case, the Court's relation to the political organs had to be considered in the context of its advisory jurisdiction and, more specifically, in a situation where the General Assembly and the Security Council were in disagreement. The issue of Israel's wall in the Occupied Palestinian Territory was taken up by the General Assembly when the Security Council was unable to adopt a resolution on the matter owing to the exercise of a United States veto. Addressing the question of its jurisdiction to give an advisory opinion, the Court held that the General Assembly's request was within the latter's competence and did not violate Article 12(1) of the Charter. Since the Court went on to find that the question presented was a 'legal question' for the purposes of Article 65(1) of its Statute and Article 96(1) of the Charter, it also concluded that it had jurisdiction to respond to the request.

To reach this conclusion, the Court had to consider the position of the General Assembly vis-à-vis the Security Council in some detail and by implication rejected any notion that a 'decision which the Security Council did not take' can restrict its competence to give advisory opinions at the request of the General Assembly. It is notable, too, that, when the Court went on to consider and reject various arguments to the effect that it should exercise its discretion and not give an advisory opinion, it pointed out that the value of its opinion to the General Assembly was a matter for the Assembly, and not the Court, to determine. This confirms that the role of advisory opinions is to provide the requesting organs with the information they seek, helping them in performing their functions, but without encroaching on their responsibilities.

These cases provide a clear and consistent picture of the relation between the jurisdiction of the International Court and the political organs of the United Nations, and indicate that in general the reference of a dispute to the Security Council is no bar to consideration of the same matter by the Court. Moreover, the *Diplomatic Hostages in Tehran* case shows that there is no inherent conflict between litigation and action by the Secretary-General. It may be recalled from Chapter 2 that, when called upon to consider the relation between negotiation and litigation in the *Aegean Sea* case, the Court rejected the view that the two were incompatible, and we shall see shortly that it has taken the same view of regional political procedures. As the Court itself has often said, legal and political means of settling disputes are complementary.

12.4.2 Are Decisions of Political Organs Open to Legal Challenge?

Whether decisions of the Security Council or the other political organs can be challenged before the International Court is a complex and sensitive question. For, although states have no right to bring proceedings against the UN or to challenge decisions directly, the issue of *ultra vires* is one which can arise in both advisory and contentious cases. In the *Lockerbie* cases, for example, a crucial issue was whether the Security Council had acted lawfully in adopting Resolutions under Chapter VII of the Charter and whether the Court was competent to examine this question. The disputed Resolutions were intended to compel Libya to surrender two terrorist suspects and the issue of legality was raised first in 1992, when Libya requested interim protection under Article 41 of the Statute, and then again in 1998, when the Court had to consider questions of admissibility and jurisdiction.

The background to these proceedings was rather unusual. When Libya refused to surrender two of its nationals who were suspected terrorists, the United States and the United Kingdom took the issue to the Security Council, which, in January 1992, adopted Resolution 731 urging Libya to cooperate. Libya then instituted proceedings in the International Court against the United States and the United Kingdom, seeking a declaration that it had complied with its obligations under the 1971 Montreal Convention and at the same time requesting interim protection. However, three days after the close of the hearings on the request, the Security Council adopted Resolution 748. This resolution, unlike Resolution 731, expressly invoked Chapter VII of the Charter, and, stating that Libya's failure to renounce terrorism constituted a threat to international peace and security, laid down that Libya must comply with the earlier Resolution. Resolution 748 also imposed economic sanctions which were to apply until the Security Council decided that Libya had complied with this directive. The Court decided that it had no option but to reject Libya's request for interim protection.[66] Under Article 25 of the Charter, member states are obliged to carry out decisions of the Security Council, and the Court considered that prima facie this obligation extended to the decision contained in Resolution 748. Moreover, according to Article 103 of the Charter, this obligation prevailed over those in any other international agreement, including the Montreal Convention. The Court therefore concluded that 'the rights claimed by Libya under the Montreal Convention cannot now be regarded as appropriate for protection by the indication of provisional measures'.[67]

The Court's decision was unanimous on this point and appears unavoidable. Once the Security Council had taken action under Chapter VII, compliance with Libya's requests would have needed a ruling that Resolution 748 was unconstitutional. Whatever the Court's powers to deal

---

[66] *Questions of Interpretation and Application of the 1971 Montreal Convention Arising from the Aerial Incident at Lockerbie*, Provisional Measures, Orders of 14 April 1992 [1992] ICJ Rep. 3 and 114. See F. Beveridge, 'The Lockerbie affair' (1992) 41 *ICLQ*, 907.

[67] [1992] ICJ Rep. 15, para. 40.

with such questions, it is difficult to see how they could be properly addressed in incidental proceedings. The situation in the *Lockerbie* cases was therefore one in which there was a direct challenge to Security Council action and was thus quite different from that in earlier cases under Article 41. A year later, however, a parallel case occurred when, in its second request in the *Genocide Convention* case, Bosnia requested certain interim measures which would have been inconsistent with the arms embargo on the former Yugoslavia imposed by Security Council Resolution 713. On that occasion, the Court was able to avoid dealing with the point by ruling that this aspect of the request lay outside its jurisdiction as defined by the 1948 Genocide Convention.[68] Had it been necessary to address the issue directly, however, there can be little doubt that it would have dismissed Bosnia's request by relying on Article 103 of the Charter, exactly as it did in the *Lockerbie* cases.

In 1998, when the Court had to consider various issues of admissibility and jurisdiction in the *Lockerbie* cases, it found that it had jurisdiction, but by putting its decision on the narrowest grounds avoided having to examine the legality of the Security Council's actions.[69] This left open the possibility that the Court's powers of review would be considered when it finally decided the merits. In the event, however, the matter was never tested because an agreement was reached providing for the trial of the two suspects before a Scottish criminal court sitting in the Netherlands. After one of the accused was convicted and imprisoned, Libya agreed to pay compensation for the atrocity, and in 2003 the cases in the International Court were discontinued.

The Court's refusal to question the Security Council's action in the truncated *Lockerbie* proceedings does not, of course, mean that there are no situations in which it can do so. Indeed, once it is recognised that the Security Council, like other international bodies, is bound by international law, questions as to the role of the Court arise quite naturally. Accordingly, it is not surprising that, in both 1992 and 1998, a number of judges in the *Lockerbie* cases considered this matter in their individual opinions. Nor is this the first time it has been judicially discussed.[70] However, the issue here is complex, and to avoid confusion it is essential to separate three distinct questions: whether the Court possesses a power of judicial review; if so, what aspects of the decisions of the political organs are reviewable; and,

---

[68] See [1993] ICJ Rep. 344–5, para. 41.
[69] [1998] ICJ Rep. 9 and 115. See P. H. F. Bekker, Note (1998) 92 *AJIL*, 503; and F. Beveridge, Note (1999) 48 *ICLQ*, 658.
[70] See, for example, the *Namibia* case [1971] ICJ Rep. 16, and the *Expenses* case [1962] ICJ Rep. 151, in which various aspects of this issue were considered by the Court and by individual judges.

finally, with regard to such decisions, what standard of review should be applied.[71]

As regards the first question, there is nothing in the United Nations Charter or the Statute of the Court which expressly confers a power to review the actions of the political organs. Equally, however, there is nothing which expressly prohibits such review. The answer therefore depends on whether this power is implied by the provisions of the Statute concerned with the Court's substantive jurisdiction. It will be recalled from Chapter 7 that the Court's contentious jurisdiction extends to any question of international law, while its advisory jurisdiction covers any legal question. If, as suggested above, it is accepted that the political organs are subject to international law, then questions about the validity of their decisions are clearly legal questions and accordingly subject to review, provided that the other requirements of the Statute are satisfied.

What aspects of the decisions of the political organs are reviewable, assuming that there is room in principle for judicial review, is a question on which little has yet been decided and different views have been expressed. In the *Lockerbie* and *Genocide Convention* cases, as we have seen, the issue was raised in relation to the exercise of the Security Council's powers under Chapter VII of the Charter, and, although other contexts can be imagined, this situation is particularly critical. The key, it is submitted, is to distinguish determinations calling for political appreciation from those involving legal standards. Accordingly, it has been persuasively argued that a decision by the Council under Article 39 that a situation constitutes a threat to the peace, breach of the peace or act of aggression is not reviewable and that the same is true of a decision as to whether a certain measure is likely or necessary to restore or maintain the peace.[72] On the other hand, while the Court cannot question these essentially political assessments, it can decide that the measure is not open to the Council because it transgresses basic principles of international law, or is otherwise beyond its powers.

The standard of review, like the standard applicable in other courts engaged in review,[73] involves deciding how far the Court should defer to the political organ when assessing its actions. Here, there is some guidance from the case law which suggests, as might be expected, that there is a prima facie presumption in favour of validity.[74] This has the effect of

---

[71] For a more detailed review of these questions, see D. Akande, 'The International Court of Justice and the Security Council: is there room for judicial control of decisions of the political organs of the United Nations?' (1997) 46 *ICLQ*, 309.

[72] *Ibid.*, 336–41.

[73] For example, the application of the 'margin of appreciation' doctrine by the European Court of Human Rights, examined in J. G. Merrills, *The Development of International Law by the European Court of Human Rights*, 2nd ed., Manchester, 1993, ch. 7.

[74] See Akande, 'The International Court of Justice and the Security Council' (n. 71) 341.

putting the burden on the state which wishes to challenge the action in question, enables the Security Council to perform its functions without judicial sniping and avoids the risk of constant conflict. It does not prevent the Court from exercising its review function, nor in an appropriate case from finding a decision *ultra vires*. It should, however, mean that such cases will be exceptional.

It should be obvious from what has been said that the issue of judicial review poses difficult questions, and that at this stage any answers must necessarily be tentative.[75] Whereas it is clear that the Court is entitled to proceed with a case which is also being considered by the political organs and, as indicated earlier, it has made this point many times, its power to question decisions made by such organs raises constitutional issues going to the very heart of the international system which are still controversial. When dealing with the earlier point, it will be recalled that the Court observed that legal and political procedures are complementary. The approach to judicial review sketched in above, though not yet supported by a comparable weight of judicial authority, proceeds from the same assumption.

12.5 Effectiveness of the United Nations

To assess the effectiveness of the United Nations as a dispute-handling institution calls for an investigation of two quite separate questions: the extent to which the Organisation is regularly involved in international disputes, and the degree to which, in cases in which the United Nations is involved, its participation is successful in the sense of achieving or encouraging a settlement.[76]

Because the Secretary-General's power to bring a matter to the attention of the Security Council has been rarely used, most disputes which come to the United Nations are brought by the parties or by outside states. The reference may be by both parties; more commonly, however, one party will seek United Nations involvement and the other will resist it. Reference by an outside state may be on behalf of a party, where for example a dispute

---

[75] For other views on this matter, see, for example, W. M. Reisman, 'The constitutional crisis in the United Nations' (1993) 87 *AJIL*, 83; J. E. Alvarez, 'Judging the Security Council' (1996) 90 *AJIL*, 1; and K. Skubiszewski, 'The International Court of Justice and the Security Council' in V. Lowe and M. Fitzmaurice (eds.), *Fifty Years of the International Court of Justice*, Cambridge, 1996, p. 606.

[76] For wide-ranging surveys showing the historical evolution, see F. S. Northedge and M. D. Donelan, *International Disputes: The Political Aspects*, London, 1971; J. G. Ruggie, 'Contingencies, constraints and collective security: perspectives on UN involvement in international disputes' (1974) 28 *Int. Org.*, 493; E. B. Haas, 'The collective management of international conflict, 1945–1984', in UNITAR, *The United Nations and the Maintenance of International Peace and Security*, Dordrecht, 1987, p. 1; and Parsons, *From Cold War to Hot Peace* (n. 2).

involves a non-member. Alternatively, raising the matter may simply reflect concern from outside states over a dispute which the parties themselves have no desire to see referred to the Organisation. It follows that many disputes are never considered by the United Nations because no incentive to raise them is present, while, of those which are considered, the extent, and ultimately the effectiveness, of institutional action is likely to depend very much on the nature of the dispute and the circumstances in which the reference to the United Nations is made.

Confrontations involving the Permanent Members of the Security Council are the clearest example of disputes in which the United Nations is likely to play at best a marginal role. Mediation in such cases, whether by the Secretary-General or third states, is extremely difficult; measures proposed by the General Assembly cannot be effectively implemented, while all but limited action by the Security Council can be prevented by use of the veto. As a result, disputes of this kind either do not come before the United Nations at all, as with the dispute over Berlin between 1958 and 1961, or, if they do, as in the Cuban missile crisis of 1962, the Organisation provides a sounding board for each side's claims, and an opportunity for third parties, including the Secretary-General, to exert what influence they can, but beyond this little by way of substantive contribution to any settlement.

Closely related to confrontations, and no less impervious to intervention, are disputes in which major states consider that their interests are directly involved and unlikely to be furthered by United Nations action. This is the case, for example, with claims to act in a hegemonial capacity in a region of special strategic interest. Although the United Kingdom and France over Suez in 1956, and South Africa over Namibia, were unable to block United Nations measures, in the Cold War era the United States and the Soviet Union were politically in a much stronger position. Thus, while the Soviet interventions in Hungary in 1956 and in Czechoslovakia in 1968 were all raised in the United Nations, there was really no possibility of the Organisation's becoming deeply involved in these issues. Relations between the United States and the countries of Latin America are not directly comparable, but here too efforts to bring disputes involving the dominant regional power before the United Nations have usually been strongly and effectively opposed.

Although hegemonial claims are the clearest case of disputes from which the United Nations has been excluded, they are by no means the only example. Indeed, the fact that for more than forty years the United States and the Soviet Union engaged in a worldwide struggle for power and influence led to a situation in which almost any dispute could be regarded as a matter of critical interest to be dealt with outside the world organisation. Thus, until fairly recently, the scope for United Nations action in the field of dispute settlement tended in practice to be restricted to situations in which either there was no such objection to the Organisation's involvement, or, more rarely, the two states saw the Organisation's involvement as positively advantageous.

What kinds of disputes does the United Nations deal with? Generalisation is difficult and the kinds of dispute with which the United Nations has been concerned have varied with the changing balance of political forces within the Organisation. However, it is clear that, for many years, the cases of most active involvement tended to be those in which the central question was decolonisation or some related issue. So, taking peacekeeping operations as an example, Cyprus, the Congo, West Irian, Kashmir, the Yemen and Namibia all come under this heading, while the long involvement with Israel, which, it will be recalled, was created after the termination of the British mandate over Palestine, is essentially similar in origin.

Among cases which do not fall into the above category are the Soviet disengagement from Afghanistan, the crisis in Central America and the Iran–Iraq war. In all three there was a significant degree of United Nations involvement, including in the first two situations the deployment of peacekeeping forces. These demonstrate that even during the Cold War the Organisation could act in other types of situations, but the special features of these cases, and in particular the position of the superpowers, should be noted. In the case of Afghanistan, where the Soviet invasion caused a major international crisis, the General Assembly passed its first resolution in 1980, but it was not until the Soviet Union was prepared to contemplate withdrawal that exploration of the possibilities of a settlement became feasible. In these cases, therefore, the involvement of the United Nations depended on a reassessment of interests by the hegemonic actor. The Iran–Iraq war was rather different because neither superpower was directly involved. There, however, there was no incentive for Security Council action until the conflict threatened to expand and engulf other states in the region. Since this would have drawn in the United States and possibly the Soviet Union, by 1987 both realised that they had an interest in trying to stop the war.

The ending of the Cold War had the effect of widening the field of UN involvement by removing the paralysing influence of East–West rivalry, and also because with the end of Soviet hegemony in Eastern Europe and the break-up of the Soviet Union itself came a host of new problems requiring attention. The first of these effects was quickly apparent when the invasion of Kuwait in 1990 prompted an immediate response from the Security Council which would have been unthinkable a short time earlier, and both the continuing UN involvement with Iraq and the willingness to intervene in places such as Angola and Cambodia have a similar explanation. New problems are exemplified by the situation in the former Yugoslavia where civil conflict arising out of ethnic rivalry led to UN involvement in Bosnia, foreshadowing crises in parts of the former Soviet Union such as Georgia, which have also been taken up.[77]

Thus, the field of dispute settlement with which the United Nations has been concerned has been defined by the major political forces of the post-1945 period. One, the tension between the United States and the Soviet Union, excluded a major group of disputes from the Organisation, while permitting or requiring its involvement in others; another, the process of decolonisation, changed the political complexion of the United Nations and provided its major area of concern; while a third, the ending of the Cold War, opened up new possibilities for cooperation, but at the same time has given rise to new matters of concern. If we add to these political factors a major institutional development, in the form of regional organisations to be considered in the next chapter, and a traditional constraint in the shape of domestic jurisdiction, the pattern of United Nations involvement in dispute settlement begins to fall into place.

To answer our second question, we must consider the successes, partial successes and failures of the Organisation.

Tension between East and West effectively wrecked the United Nations as a collective security system. Thus, during the Cold War, in all but exceptional circumstances the sanctioning provisions of Chapter VII of the Charter proved to be a dead letter. At the same time, the disregard of Security Council Resolutions in the diplomatic hostages crisis, the Iran–Iraq war, the Falklands dispute and other crises, showed that the force of collective opinion is hardly an adequate substitute. On some issues, moreover, dissension within the United Nations created a situation in which steps towards the settlement of a dispute had to be taken outside the Organisation. The Camp David Agreements, for example, were concluded by Israel, Egypt and the United States without any reference to the Security Council. Moreover, in 1982, in a development of considerable significance, these Agreements led to the creation of a 3,500-strong peacekeeping force, the Multinational Force and Observers (MFO), again outside the United Nations.[78]

The reactivation of Chapter VII, although only one aspect of the UN's activity in relation to disputes, means that, for the first time, the use of economic and military coercion has become a real option. Both were used effectively when Iraq invaded Kuwait, although the limitations of these methods are also evident, and in view of their complex ramifications it would be wrong to see either as anything but a last resort. Also significant in terms of the United Nations' effectiveness in this context has been the

---

[77] See M. Webber, 'Coping with anarchy: ethnic conflict and international organisations in the former Soviet Union' (1996) 13 *Int. Rel.*, 1.

[78] For the protocol between Egypt and Israel establishing the MFO, see (1981) 20 ILM 1190. For discussion, see R. W. Nelson, 'Peacekeeping aspects of the Egyptian–Israeli Peace Treaty and consequences for United Nations peacekeeping' (1980) 10 *Denver J Int. L and Pol.*, 113.

recent tendency to combine its efforts with those of regional organisations. Thus, in Haiti, economic sanctions were imposed by the Security Council following earlier action by the Organisation of American States; in Bosnia, NATO was used to supply military support while diplomatic efforts were conducted jointly with the EC; and, in Central America, both United Nations Observer Group in Central America (ONUCA) and United Nations Observer Mission in El Salvador (ONUSAL) originated in regional initiatives.[79] As we shall see in the next chapter, the coordination of regional and United Nations action is a subject on which much remains to be done, but has already contributed something to the Organisation's effectiveness.

If the reactivation of Chapter VII continues to provide opportunities for constructive action the other side of the picture is that, when members of the Security Council are divided on an issue, action through the Organisation will not be possible. In such circumstances, one of two things will happen. Either nothing at all will be done, or individual members will act unilaterally, perhaps, as we have seen, citing previous expressions of Security Council concern as a disingenuous justification. Thus, NATO intervened in Kosovo in 1999 when it became clear that measures against Yugoslavia under Chapter VII would be limited to censure, and the military actions against Iraq taken by the United States and the United Kingdom, which culminated in the invasion of 2003, reflected an impatience with the supervision of Iraq's disarmament by the Security Council, together with a desire to achieve regime change.

Where does this leave the balance sheet? It was noted at the beginning of this chapter that the responsibilities of the United Nations in the field of peace and security were to terminate armed conflict and to assist the parties to international disputes to settle their differences by peaceful means. While no observer of international affairs since 1945 could conclude that the United Nations has been successful in terminating conflict whenever it has occurred, it would be difficult to deny that, through peacekeeping operations and in other ways, it has sometimes made a significant contribution to that end. As far as aiding the settlement of disputes is concerned, all three major organs have had successes and, when reckoning the score, it is important to understand that the quiet diplomacy of the Secretary-General, by its very nature, will often leave no mark on the diplomatic record. But, if success has sometimes been achieved, it is only necessary to recall the cases mentioned earlier and the perennial issues – the Arab–Israeli dispute, Kashmir, Cyprus and the Lebanon – to see disputes on which the Organisation has apparently had little impact.

---

[79] For these and other cases of inter-organisational co-operation, see A. K. Henrikson, 'The growth of regional organisations and the role of the United Nations', in L. Fawcett and A. Hurrell, *Regionalism in World Politics*, Oxford, 1995, p. 122 at pp. 142–59. See also Gray, *Use of Force* (n. 24) ch. 9.

In *An Agenda for Peace*,[80] his 1992 report to the Security Council, Secretary-General Boutros-Ghali examined the potential of the United Nations in the fields of preventive diplomacy, peacekeeping, peace-making and post-conflict peace-building. It is clear from the record that efforts so far have been mainly directed to the first two activities, which are also where most has been achieved. Thus, the fact that the United Nations has often been more successful in arranging truces and supervising periods of relative calm than in dealing with underlying problems has often been noted, and peacekeeping operations, until quite recently, have certainly been less concerned with dispute settlement than with the prevention of violence. Such 'prophylactic' operations are valuable, of course, and may provide a vital foundation for a final settlement. On the other hand, this is by no means guaranteed, and though much better than nothing, operations which are interminable or repetitious may become in effect a substitute for a settlement, a perpetual treatment of symptoms rather than causes.

To see why all this is so is to begin to understand the nature and limitations of the United Nations system. The Organisation is a reflection of the social and political relations of states. Largely as a result of the efforts of the Secretariat, the whole is now a little greater than the sum of the parts and the institution has acquired a degree of authority in dispute situations. However, effective action by the United Nations is possible only insofar as states are prepared to relinquish attempts to control disputes by the use of their own power. When things become sufficiently serious, a United Nations presence or other initiative may be acceptable, but, unless what is wanted is simply a face-saving arrangement, settling the basic issue is likely to be much more difficult. In cases like those which have been mentioned, prophylactic measures may be all that is politically possible, yet the fact that a festering dispute remains on the agenda will be accounted another failure of the Organisation.

In a trenchant observation, U Thant explained the true position:

> Great problems usually come to the United Nations because governments have been unable to think of anything else to do about them. The United Nations is a last-ditch, last-resort affair, and it is not surprising that the Organization should often be blamed for failing to solve problems that have already been found to be insoluble by governments. More often than not, the United Nations is criticised for failing to resolve a crisis or to enforce an action. It is not generally realised that the failure of the United Nations is the failure of the international community, and the failure to enforce an action is due to the refusal of the party or parties concerned to comply with the Organization's decisions.[81]

---

[80] SC Doc. S/24111, 17 June 1992. Text in (1992) 31 ILM 953. See also *Supplement to Agenda for Peace*, S/1995/1.

[81] U Thant, *View from the UN* (n. 41) p. 32.

The United Nations, then, is in no sense a world government, but a diplomatic forum in which persuasion, argument, negotiation and a search for consensus are the means available for handling international disputes. Like any human institution, its organisation and procedures are imperfect and could be improved.[82] At root, however, its activities – successes as well as failures – are less a matter of institutional arrangements than a reflection of the statesmanship, or otherwise, of those responsible for the direction of affairs.

12.6 Further Reading

12.6.1 General References on the United Nations

Blokker, Niels M., *Saving Succeeding Generations from the Scourge of War*, Leiden, 2020.

Ratner, Steven R., 'Image and reality in the UN's peaceful settlement of disputes' (1995) 6 *European Journal of International Law*, 426–44.

Schermers, H. G., and N. Blokker, *International Institutional Law* 6th ed., Leiden, 2018, Chs 1 ('Introduction'), 3 ('Rules for international organs'), 9 ('Interpretation and settlement of disputes').

Simma, Bruno, Daniel-Erasmus Khan, Georg Nolte, Andreas Paulus and Nikolai Wessendorf, *The Charter of the United Nations*, 3rd ed., Oxford, 2012.

Viñuales, J.E., *The UN Friendly Relations Declaration at 50: An Assessment of the Fundamental Principles of International Law*, Cambridge, 2020.

12.6.2 Treaties, Official Documents and Collections of Documents

Legal Consequences of the Construction of a Wall in the Occupied Palestinian Territory, Advisory Opinion, 9 July 2004, ICJ Reports 2004, especially paras. 87 and 138–42.

Report of the Special Committee on Principles of International Law Concerning Friendly Relations and Co-operation Among States, 1964, UN Doc A/5746, 82.

UN General Assembly, *Declaration on Principles of International Law concerning Friendly Relations and Cooperation among States in accordance with the Charter of the United Nations*, 24 October 1970, A/RES/2625(XXV).

UN General Assembly, *Definition of Aggression*, 14 December 1974, A/RES/3314.

UN General Assembly, *Manila Declaration on the Peaceful Settlement of Disputes*, 15 November 1982, UNGA Res 37/10.

UN General Assembly, *Solemn Appeal to States in Conflict to Cease Armed Action forthwith and to Settle Disputes between Them through Negotiations*, UN Doc A/RES/40/9.

---

[82] For some suggestions as to how this might be done, see Chapter 13.

13

Regional Organisations

The growth and development of the United Nations as the major universal organisation has been accompanied by a no less dramatic increase in the number and range of organisations with membership drawn from the states of a particular region. Such regional organisations frequently become involved in the resolution of disputes.[1] Sometimes this is because dispute settlement has been defined as a goal of the organisation. Article 4(e) of the Constitutive Act of the African Union, for example, lays down as one of its aims the peaceful resolution of conflicts between member states, and similar provisions can be found in the constitutions of other organisations. But even organisations whose primary concern is with matters of no present relevance may find themselves involved in some form of settlement activity. For bringing states together in an institutional setting provides the parties to a dispute with an opportunity to settle their differences and regional neighbours with the chance to add their encouragement, assistance and pressure as an incentive.

13.1 Range of Regional Organisations

The role played by a particular regional organisation depends very much on the characteristics of the organisation concerned: where it is located, how it is structured and what resources it commands. For this reason, though detailed treatment must be sought elsewhere,[2] a glance at some of the leading regional organisations may be useful. Europe, which contains an exceptional number and variety of organisations, is an instructive place to begin.

---

[1] On the role of regional organisations, see L. Fawcett and A. Hurrell (eds), *Regionalism in World Politics*, Oxford, 1995; F. S. Northedge and M. D. Donelan, *International Disputes: The Political Aspects*, London, 1971, ch. 11; E. Luard, *The International Regulation of Frontier Disputes*, London, 1970, ch. 4; L. B. Sohn, 'The role of international institutions as conflict-adjusting agencies' (1960–1) 28 *U Chi. L Rev.*, 205. See also C. Peck, *Sustainable Peace*, Lanham, MD, 1998; and C. Gray, *International Law and the Use of Force*, 2nd ed., Oxford, 2004, ch. 9. On particular organisations, see the works cited below.

[2] For general surveys, see the references in 'Further Reading' at the end of this chapter.

13.1.1 Regional Organisations in Europe

The Council of Europe was founded in 1949 for the discussion of matters of common interest, to promote conventions on such matters and with the specific aim of promoting and protecting human rights. The Council is in no sense a supranational organisation, but has achieved a great deal by way of consultation and cooperation. In the field of dispute settlement, the Council's major achievement has been the European Convention on Human Rights, an agreement by European states to respect the rights defined in the Convention and to submit disputes concerning its application and interpretation to international supervisory machinery.

The European Union (EU) represents a radically different approach. In 1952, the European Coal and Steel Community was created as an instrument of economic integration and later expanded with the addition of the European Economic Community and the European Atomic Energy Community in 1957. Subsequent developments, notably the Single European Act (1986) and the Treaty of Maastricht (1992), furthered the process of integration, introducing political objectives and the concept of the European Union (EU) and consolidating institutional arrangements which already included majority voting and executive powers. Further evolution took place through the Treaty of Amsterdam (1997) and the Lisbon Treaty which came into force in 2009. Under the current arrangements, the settlement of disputes is the responsibility of the Court of Justice of the European Union (CJEU) and its General Court, with an extensive jurisdiction covering member states, community organs and natural and legal persons.

Turning from economic to military integration, the North Atlantic Treaty Organization (NATO), founded in 1949 as a regional security organisation, includes in its membership the United States, Canada and Iceland, as well as many European states. Although primarily an alliance against external aggression, NATO is also concerned with promoting cooperation in the non-military field and the settlement of disputes between its members. In 1956, NATO's supreme organ, the North Atlantic Council, made this commitment quite explicit when it resolved that, with certain exceptions, disputes which cannot be settled by direct negotiation should be submitted to a good offices procedure within NATO before resort to any other organisation.[3] The same resolution recognised that the Secretary-General and each member have both a right and a duty to draw the Council's attention to matters capable of threatening the

---

[3] See C. M. H. Waldock (ed.), *International Disputes: The Legal Aspects*, London, 1972, p. 256. Also F. L. Kirgis, 'NATO consultations as a component of national decision-making' (1979) 73 *AJIL*, 372.

solidarity or effectiveness of the alliance. Moreover, the Secretary-General was authorised to offer his good offices to the parties to a dispute at any time, and with their consent to facilitate procedures of inquiry, mediation, conciliation or arbitration.

The Eastern European equivalent of NATO was the Warsaw Treaty Organisation, a military alliance founded by the Soviet Union and covering most of Eastern Europe. The corresponding economic organisation was the Council for Mutual Economic Aid, established in 1949 as an instrument of economic co-operation but, like the Warsaw Pact, with apparently no formal machinery for the settlement of disputes. Between 1949 and 1989, Europe was sharply divided between East and West, with the rival military and economic organisations in static and seemingly permanent confrontation. However, when the Soviet Union at last withdrew support from its clients in Eastern Europe, the way was clear for non-communist governments to emerge. With the ending of the Cold War, the basis for the Warsaw Pact and its economic counterpart disappeared and both arrangements collapsed, along with the Soviet Union itself, and were replaced in 1991 by a new regional body, the Commonwealth of Independent States (CIS),[4] led by the Russian Federation.

These momentous changes had important effects on Europe's other institutions. In 1994, the Conference on Security and Co-operation in Europe (CSCE), a series of meetings which since 1975 had dealt with East–West affairs, was renamed the Organization for Security and Co-operation in Europe (OSCE) in recognition of its transformation from a loose arrangement of conferences to a fully-fledged organisation with permanent arrangements concerning human rights, security, dispute settlement and other matters.[5] With a membership of more than fifty states, including the United States and Canada, the OSCE is now the largest European organisation.

The three organisations mentioned earlier have also been profoundly affected. Thus, membership of the Council of Europe has been extended to many of the former communist states, including Russia itself. And, in 1997, decisions were taken to expand both the EC and NATO by inviting a number of Eastern European states to join, which took place soon afterwards.[6] These organisations have therefore all recently increased their membership significantly and may well expand further in the future.

---

[4] For the texts of the 1993 Commonwealth of Independent States Charter and the CIS Treaty on Creation of Economic Union, see (1995) 34 ILM 1279 and 1298.

[5] See M. Sapiro, 'Changing the CSCE into the OSCE: legal aspects of a political transformation' (1995) 89 *AJIL*, 631.

[6] For the significance of these developments, see J. Woodliffe, 'The evolution of a new NATO for a new Europe' (1998) 47 *ICLQ*, 174.

13.1.2 The Organisation of American States

On the other side of the Atlantic, the main regional organisation is the Organization of American States (OAS). Founded in 1948 in order to place earlier arrangements for inter-American cooperation on a firmer and broader constitutional basis, the OAS and its predecessors have been concerned with a wide range of matters of common interest, including, on numerous occasions, the settlement of disputes between member states.

The legal framework for the OAS is provided by three treaties, which however are not in force for all OAS member states. The Inter American Treaty of Reciprocal Assistance (Rio Treaty, 1947) creates a defensive alliance comparable in some ways to NATO, in which the parties undertake to exercise their collective right of self-defence under Article 51 of the United Nations Charter and to use the institutional machinery of the OAS for consultation. That machinery is largely contained in the Charter of Bogotá (1948), which lays down the principles of the Organization and defines its institutional arrangements. Significant changes to the Charter, including provisions to consolidate democracy, were introduced in the 1992 Protocol of Washington,[7] which came into force in 1997. The third treaty, the American Treaty on Pacific Settlement (Pact of Bogotá, 1948), which was also discussed in the first chapter, is exclusively concerned with the settlement of disputes and contains elaborate arrangements for mediation, inquiry, conciliation and judicial settlement. The treaty, which was not ratified by all OAS member states, has provided the basis on which a significant number of cases have been taken to the International Court, but in other respects has had only limited use. Consequently, OAS activity in the field of dispute settlement has usually been channelled through the various organs created by the Charter.[8]

There are five organs of the OAS of interest for present purposes. The supreme organ is the Inter-American Conference, or General Assembly. It 'decides the general action and policy of the Organization and determines the structure and function of its Organs, and has the authority to consider any matter relating to friendly relations among the American States'.[9] Its brief therefore includes the settlement of disputes, but the fact that the Conference's regular meetings are scheduled to take place at five-yearly intervals greatly restricts its significance in practice.

The Meeting of Consultation of Ministers of Foreign Affairs is much more important. It acts as the organ of consultation on matters of peace

---

[7] Text in (1994) 33 ILM 1005 and see E. Lagos and T. D. Rudy, 'The Third Summit of the Americas and the thirty-first session of the OAS General Assembly' (2002) 96 *AJIL*, 173.

[8] For a useful account of the contrast between the theory and practice of the OAS system, see R. Scheman and J. W. Ford, 'The Organization of American States as mediator', in S. Touval and I. W. Zartman (eds), *International Mediation in Theory and Practice*, Boulder, CO, 1985, p. 197.

[9] Charter of Bogotá, 1948, Art. 33.

and security under the Rio Treaty. It can also meet at any time to consider urgent matters of common interest to the American states and in practice therefore tends to act as the supreme organ of the institution. Requests to convene a Meeting of Consultation may be made by any member and are addressed to the Permanent Council. The Council, as the standing political organ of the OAS, is permanently in session in Washington. Subordinate to the Council is the Inter-American Committee on Peaceful Settlement, consisting of five member states, elected by the Council. Created in 1970 to replace the earlier Inter-American Peace Committee,[10] the new Committee has the function of assisting in the resolution of disputes through inquiry, mediation and recommendations on appropriate means of settlement.

The other body that needs to be mentioned is the Secretariat. Under Article 116 of the OAS Charter, the Secretary-General participated 'with voice but without vote in all meetings of the Organization'. This offered a more limited scope for initiative than Article 99 of the United Nations Charter, but in 1985 was amended to allow the Secretary-General, like his UN counterpart, to bring to the attention of the Assembly or Council 'any matter which in his opinion might threaten the peace and security of the hemisphere or the development of the Member States'.[11] This indicates an intention on the part of the member states to see the Secretary-General playing a more active role in the settlement of disputes, an impression which was confirmed soon afterwards when he was entrusted with a mandate relating to the situation in Central America and, together with the UN Secretary-General, gave assistance to the Contadora Group.[12]

13.1.3 The African Union

No regional organisation in Africa or Asia is as structurally complex as the OAS, but two, the African Union (AU), formerly the Organization of African Unity (OAU), and the Arab League, have dispute settlement as a major objective. The OAU was founded in 1963 with the aim of encouraging and coordinating the activities of African states on matters of common interest, including the peaceful settlement of disputes and defence against external aggression.[13] Despite the similarity between these objectives and those of the OAS, the OAU was a much looser type of regional organisation with an emphasis on moral rather than legal

---

[10] See C. Sepulveda, 'The reform of the Charter of American States' (1972) 137 *Hague Recueil des Cours*, 83; and J. C. Drier, 'New wine and old bottles: the changing inter-American system' (1968) 22 *Int. Org.*, 477.

[11] Protocol of Cartagena de Indias, 1985, Art. 116.

[12] See H. Caminos and R. Lavalle, 'New departures in the exercise of inherent powers by the UN and OAS Secretaries-General: the Central American situation' (1989) 83 *AJIL*, 395.

[13] See T. O. Elias, 'The Charter of the Organization of African Unity' (1965) 59 *AJIL*, 243.

obligations and on respect for the members' sovereignty. This difference was clearly evident in the main organs of the OAU which were four in number.

The supreme organ both in theory and in fact was the Assembly of Heads of State and Government, which met annually or sometimes in extraordinary session. It could discuss and pass resolutions on any matter, but only as recommendations, and there was no power to enforce decisions, or expel members for noncompliance. The Council of Ministers, which normally met twice a year, was made up of the foreign ministers of member states and had the task of implementing the Assembly's decisions, while a third organ, the General Secretariat, was run by an 'administrative secretary-general' whose functions, as the name implies, were intended to be more limited than those performed by the Secretary-General in the United Nations and other international organisations.

The specific issue of dispute settlement was originally intended to be the responsibility of a fourth major organ, the Commission of Mediation, Conciliation and Arbitration.[14] The Protocol setting up the Commission in 1964 contained elaborate provisions for the creation of boards of mediation, conciliation or arbitration from a panel elected by the Assembly. However, the Commission, whose jurisdiction rested on the consent of the parties to a dispute, never became operational.[15] As a result, the institutions of the OAU, including the administrative secretary-general, were more actively involved in dispute settlement than might have been anticipated. Recognising the ineffectiveness of the Commission, the Assembly established a 'Mechanism for Conflict Prevention, Management and Resolution' in 1993.[16] This was intended to put conflict management and dispute avoidance on a formal basis, using both the influence of the member states and contributions from the Secretary-General, and seems to have been quite useful.

In 2001, the Constitutive Act of the African Union came into force, setting up a new regional organisation which is expected to have, among other organs, its own Parliament, Court of Justice and Central Bank.[17] This

---

[14] See T. O. Elias, 'The Commission of Mediation, Conciliation and Arbitration of the Organization of African Unity' (1964) 40 *BYBIL*, 336; and H. A. Amankwah, 'International law, dispute settlement and regional organisations in an African setting' (1981) 21 *Ind. J. Int. L.*, 352.

[15] See T. Maluwa, 'The peaceful settlement of disputes among African states, 1963–1983: some conceptual issues and practical trends' (1989) 38 *ICLQ*, 299; and W. J. Foltz, 'The Organization of African Unity and the resolution of Africa's conflicts', in F. M. Deng and I. W. Zartman (eds), *Conflict Resolution in Africa*, Washington, 1991, p. 347. See also G. J. Naldi, *The Organization of African Unity*, 2nd ed., London, 1999, pp. 24–9.

[16] See Naldi, ibid., 32–3; and Peck, *Sustainable Peace* (n. 1) pp. 162–7.

[17] See K. D. Magliveras and G. J. Naldi, 'The African Union: a new dawn for Africa?' (2002) 51 *ICLQ*, 415; and C. A. A. Packer and D. Rukare, 'The new African Union and its Constitutive Act' (2002) 96 *AJIL*, 365. Although the Act establishing the Union outlines its structure, details of its organs were left for later protocols.

major development, which was foreshadowed in the 1991 Treaty Establishing the African Economic Community, represents, at least potentially, a huge stride in institutional arrangements in Africa. In a further development, the AU Assembly adopted a Protocol in 2008 with the aim of establishing a new African Court of Justice and Human Rights.[18] In terms of the implications for dispute settlement in the region, the most significant features of the Union are that it has been created to replace the OAU, and that the Constitutive Act, unlike the OAU Charter, both recognises the need for and encourages a collective response to internal conflict in certain circumstances. However, the Act also reaffirms the principles of domestic sovereignty and non-intervention. Accordingly, much will depend on how the powers of the AU are interpreted in practice, a matter in the hands of its supreme decision-making organ, the Assembly of Heads of State and Government, as in the OAU.

13.1.4 The Arab League and the Organisation of the Islamic Conference

A number of members of the AU are also members of the Arab League.[19] This was founded in 1945 to coordinate the members' activities in economic and financial affairs, commercial relations and a variety of political and social matters. An even looser arrangement than the OAU, the League has as its supreme organ a Council, which takes decisions unanimously, each member having one vote. Although members have agreed to renounce force in the settlement of their disputes and to accept decisions of the Council as binding, they are under no obligation to take a dispute to the Council. In the absence of other machinery, the settlement of disputes is therefore entirely a matter for the parties, prompted by whatever informal assistance may be offered by the Secretariat of the League and the other members.[20]

An attempt to provide a more formal procedure for the resolution of disputes has been put forward by another institution with a membership drawn from more than one region, the Organization of the Islamic Conference (OIC).[21] The Charter of the Conference, which was agreed in

---

[18] See G. J. Naldi, 'Aspects of the African Court of Justice and Human Rights', in D. French, M. Saul and N. D. White (eds), *International Law and Dispute Settlement: New Problems and Techniques*, Oxford, 2010, p. 321.

[19] For discussion of the activities of the League, see B. Boutros-Ghali, 'The Arab League (1945–1970)' (1969) 25 *Rev. Egypt. Droit Int.*, 67; and S. J. Al Kadhem, 'The role of the League of Arab States in settling inter-Arab disputes' (1976) 32 *Rev. Egypt. Droit Int.*, 1. See also P. Sands and P. Klein, *Bowett's Law of International Institutions*, 5th ed., London, 2001, pp. 237–40.

[20] However, in 1996, the League resolved to set up a 'Mechanism for the Prevention, Management and Resolution of Conflicts among Arab States' and also to create an Arab Court of Justice. For the text of this resolution, see (1996) 35 ILM 1289.

[21] For a comprehensive account of the structure and activities of the OIC, see H. Moinuddin, *The Charter of the Islamic Conference*, Oxford, 1987, Part II.

1972, provides for co-operation among Muslim states in accordance with the principle of Islamic solidarity and several agreements relating to economic cooperation have been concluded. At the Third Summit Conference of the OIC in 1981, it was decided to establish an International Islamic Court of Justice, and, at the Fifth Conference in 1987, a Statute for the Court was adopted as an amendment to the Charter.[22] It is evidently intended that the new court will provide a forum for the resolution of inter-Islamic disputes under Islamic law, and so provide Islamic states with an alternative to the International Court. However, the Court is not yet functioning.[23]

In this brief survey, it has been impossible to mention, let alone examine, every regional organisation whose work may have a bearing on dispute settlement. Moreover, it is worth pointing out that, within regions, there are often to be found sub-regional organisations, whose contributions can also be important. Though space precludes discussion of these, of the numerous river commissions and of other organisations with specialised functions, as other regional organisations such as the Association of Southeast Asian Nations (ASEAN), CARICOM and the dozens of regional economic integration organisations, enough has been said to demonstrate the variety of purposes for which states set up regional organisations and their very different institutional structures.

So much for theory. What have regional organisations been able to contribute to the resolution of disputes?

13.2 Role of Regional Organisations in Disputes

One of the most useful functions of a regional organisation is to provide its members with a forum for consultation and negotiation in actual or potential dispute situations. The opportunities for informal contact which the meetings of an organisation provide can be particularly valuable where a dispute has caused normal diplomatic relations to be suspended.

13.2.1 Consultation, Negotiation, and Good Offices

In both the dispute over the status of Cyprus, involving Britain, Greece and Turkey, and the various 'Cod Wars' between Britain and Iceland, the fact that all the states concerned were members of NATO ensured that lines of communication remained open, despite a degree of bitterness and hostility which on several occasions led to the use of force.

---

[22] Resolution 13/5 – P [IS] (1987); see F. E. Vogel, 'Review' (1989) 83 *AJIL*, 228.
[23] For a discussion of the Court, see M. Lombardini, 'The International Islamic Court of Justice: towards an international Islamic legal system?' (2001) 14 *Leiden Journal of International Law*, 665.

In 1961, Anglo-Icelandic contact through NATO helped to secure a negotiated settlement of the dispute over Iceland's twelve-mile fishing zone. Fifteen years later, when the issue was a 200-mile zone, NATO again played a constructive role. As in the previous disputes, Iceland's attempts to enforce its new limits had met with a forceful response from the Royal Navy and relations between Britain and Iceland were at a low ebb. However, through the good offices of the Norwegian foreign minister and the Secretary-General of NATO, the two sides were brought together during a meeting of the foreign ministers of the NATO countries in Oslo and shortly afterwards negotiated an agreement to end the dispute.[24]

An example of the provision of good offices over an extended period is provided by the OAU's handling of the border dispute between Algeria and Morocco in 1963.[25] The OAU established an ad hoc commission which held a number of meetings with the parties, and, with the aid of the commission's good offices, agreements were negotiated concerning the withdrawal of troops, the return of prisoners and the restoration of diplomatic relations.

No doubt one can exaggerate the part regional organisations played in securing a settlement in these and similar cases. In the Cod Wars, Britain, which made most of the concessions, badly needed a settlement, and resolution of the Algeria–Morocco dispute in 1970 was finally achieved by an agreement in which the OAU commission played no part. But, if the settlement of these disputes ultimately depended on the parties' willingness to agree, it is clear that their respective regional organisations provided them with an opportunity which would not otherwise have been available, and with encouragement and assistance in surmounting critical obstacles to negotiation.

13.2.2 Mediation

It is a short step from good offices to mediation, and regional organisations, through their officials and member states, are often well placed to act in this capacity. In 1957, for example, the OAS intervened as mediator in the dispute between Honduras and Nicaragua over the arbitral award of the King of Spain.[26] Following complaints of aggression from both states, the Council of the OAS met in special session and appealed to the parties to refrain from provocative acts. It then appointed a committee, consisting of representatives of five member states, with the task of considering the

---

[24] See H. Jónsson, *Friends in Conflict*, London, 1982, pp. 179–81.
[25] See P. B. Wild, 'The organization of African unity and the Algerian–Moroccan border conflict' (1966) 20 *Int. Org.*, 18.
[26] See C. G. Fenwick, 'The Honduras–Nicaragua boundary dispute' (1957) 51 *AJIL*, 761. For further examples, see S. Touval and I. W. Zartman, *International Mediation in Theory and Practice*, Boulder, CO, 1985, p. 197.

dispute. The committee visited the two capitals and soon secured agreements providing for a cease-fire and mutual troop withdrawals. When the committee returned to Washington, its report was adopted by the Council, which then appointed the same members to an ad hoc committee with the task of devising an acceptable procedure for settling the dispute. Here, the committee's attempts at mediation proved unsuccessful, but, as a result of a further effort by the Council, the parties were eventually persuaded to resolve the dispute by referring it to adjudication.[27]

Mediation has proved to be one of the most useful functions performed by the CSCE/OSCE. In 1993, for example, a CSCE mission was deployed in Moldova to assist negotiations on the status of the disputed Dneister region and on the withdrawal of Russian troops based in the area. In the following year, Moldova accepted a CSCE plan recommending autonomy for the Dneister and the withdrawal of Russian troops was agreed in principle. It is better, of course, if, instead of being called upon to resolve disputes, an organisation can act at an earlier stage with a view to avoiding them. As well as mediating, the OSCE therefore assigns long-duration missions to likely trouble spots as a form of preventive diplomacy. In 1994, for example, it had nine such missions in operation, all in the former Soviet Union or ex-Yugoslavia.[28]

The OAU was also often involved in mediation, sometimes in conjunction with other organisations. In 1998, for example, following an outbreak of fighting between Ethiopia and Eritrea, the OAU assisted the parties to negotiate a peace agreement which came into force in 2000. As part of the settlement, the two states agreed to establish both a boundary commission to delimit their disputed frontier, and a claims commission to resolve issues arising out of the war. The regional mediation effort here was greatly assisted by support from the United Nations which contributed a peace-keeping force (UNMEE), as well as the services of the Cartographic Section of the UN Secretariat to help with mapping.[29]

---

[27] See *Arbitral Award Made by the King of Spain on 23 December 1906*, Judgment [1960] ICJ Rep. 192. For discussion of the Court's decision, see Chapter 5. Mediation by the OAU played a part in persuading Libya and Chad to refer another long-standing dispute to the ICJ leading eventually to the judgment in the *Territorial Dispute* case [1994] ICJ Rep. 6. See S. G. Amoo and W. Zartman, 'Mediation by regional organisations: the Organization for African Unity (OAU) in Chad', in J. Bercovitch and J. Z. Rubin (eds), *Mediation in International Relations*, London, 1992, p. 131.

[28] See M. Webber, 'Coping with anarchy: ethnic conflict and international organisations in the former Soviet Union' (1996) 13 *Int. Rel.*, 1.

[29] See B. Simma and D.-E. Khan, 'Peaceful settlement of boundary disputes under the auspices of the Organization of African Unity and the United Nations: the case of the frontier dispute between Eritrea and Ethiopia', in N. Ando, E. McWhinney and R. Wolfrum (eds), *Liber Amicorum Judge Shigeru Oda*, The Hague, 2002, p. 1179. Also J. G. Merrills, 'Reflections on dispute settlement in the light of recent arbitrations involving Eritrea', in A. Constantinides and Zaikos (eds), *The Diversity of International Law*, Leiden, 2009, p. 109.

Instead of providing mediation through its own officials or organs, a regional organisation may encourage settlement of a dispute by lending its authority to, and thereby legitimising, mediation from another source. In 1972, for example, a dispute occurred between Tanzania and Uganda when the latter was invaded by supporters of the recently deposed president, who had taken refuge in Tanzania.[30] Uganda responded by bombing Tanzanian border villages, and fighting involving both states' forces broke out. With the assistance of the administrative secretary-general of the OAU, the President of Somalia intervened as mediator and succeeded in persuading both sides to agree to a truce, negotiations and troop withdrawals, and to undertake to respect each other's sovereignty. An observer mission under a Somali general supervised the execution of these arrangements and, following the OAU summit meeting in 1973, relations between the two states were temporarily restored.

13.2.3 Inquiry and Conciliation

Inquiry and conciliation are relatively formal processes which regional organisations with the necessary resources and institutions can also use to good effect. The Chaco Commission, set up by the Conference of American States in 1929 to investigate a border dispute between Bolivia and Paraguay, was described in Chapter 5. It will be recalled that the Commission combined the functions of inquiry and conciliation, and by emphasising the latter succeeded in obtaining the parties' agreement to a settlement. In 2008, the European Union established an Independent International Fact-Finding Mission on the Conflict in Georgia, following an outbreak of hostilities there earlier in the year. The Mission investigated the conflict and, after consulting widely, issued its report[31] in the following year. Although termed a 'fact-finding' mission, its brief was a good deal wider and, as a consequence, the report not only went into the facts in some detail, but also dealt with a number of issues of international law, humanitarian law and human rights.

Conciliation also occupies a prominent place in the various arrangements set up by the OSCE. It will be recalled from Chapter 5 that the Valletta Procedure, agreed in 1991, is essentially a process of mandatory conciliation, with elements of mediation and inquiry, and in 1992 was complemented by the creation of formal arrangements for voluntary and

---

[30] See B. D. Meyers, 'Intraregional conflict management by the Organization of African Unity' (1974) 28 *Int. Org.*, 345 at 359–60. For subsequent developments, see M. Shaw, 'Dispute settlement in Africa' (1983) 37 *Yearbook of WA*, 149 at 156–7. For further examples, see M. Wolfers, 'The Organization of African Unity as mediator', in S. Touval and I. W. Zartman (eds), *International Mediation in Theory and Practice*, Boulder, CO, 1985, p. 175.

[31] See C. Henderson and J. A. Green, 'The Jus ad Bellum and entities short of statehood in the Report on the conflict in Georgia' (2010) 59 *ICLQ*, 129.

directed conciliation. In addition, by subscribing to the 1992 Stockholm Convention, OSCE states can assume a legal commitment to employ conciliation or arbitration. While the Convention is binding only on the states which are parties to it, the other procedures represent a political commitment on the part of all the OSCE states. In so far as its procedures can be effectively employed in dispute situations, they have a reach and legitimacy unique among European organisations.[32]

The role of OSCE in diffusing tension in the recent conflict between Ukraine and Russia is a recent example of the regional organisation's role in disputes. In a Permanent Council decision of March 2014, the OSCE deployed a special monitoring mission to Ukraine, to 'contribute … to reducing tensions and fostering peace' (Article 2). The mission is tasked with a monitoring role, but it also has tasks relating to fact-finding: 'gathering information', and 'establishing and reporting facts in response to specific incidents and reports of incidents, including those concerning alleged violations of fundamental OSCE principles and commitments'.

The value of an organisation's ability to deploy resources also is well illustrated by two disputes between Costa Rica and Nicaragua which came before the OAS soon after its creation.[33] In the first, in 1948, the OAS set up an 'Information and Study Committee' to examine Costa Rican allegations that Nicaragua had supported an invasion of its territory. In light of its committee's investigation, the OAS decided that both sides were partly to blame, set up a commission to supervise the border and persuaded the parties to sign a Pact of Amity, pledging respect for each other's sovereignty. The second dispute, in 1955, followed a similar pattern. Again, Costa Rica complained of aggression and a committee was established to investigate the complaint. A more comprehensive system of border supervision, involving aerial surveillance and the creation of a demilitarised zone, was set up, and, in January 1956, a new agreement (which proved more durable than its predecessor) was signed by the two states.

Even more elaborate were the various initiatives in the same region which together made up the Contadora Process.[34] In 1983, alarmed by the dangerous tension in Central America, the foreign ministers of Colombia, Mexico, Panama and Venezuela met on Contadora Island, Panama, to consider the contribution which their countries could make to the resolution of the problems of the region. This was followed by a series of visits to Nicaragua, Honduras, Costa Rica, El Salvador and

---

[32] See Webber, 'Coping with anarchy' (n. 28) 8.
[33] On these disputes and the Haiti–Dominican Republic dispute, see P. Lyon, 'Regional organisations and frontier disputes' in E. Luard, *The International Regulation of Frontier Disputes*, London, 1970, p. 109 at pp. 126–7.
[34] A detailed account of the Contadora Process and its aftermath can be found in pars. 70–5 and 81–8 of the judgment of the International Court in the *Border and Transborder Armed Actions Case* [1988] ICJ Rep. 69. The Court's decision in this case is discussed below.

Guatemala which set in motion an elaborate multilateral negotiation. From 1985, the process was joined by the foreign ministers of Argentina, Brazil, Peru and Uruguay, who became known as the 'Support Group', and, in 1986, this phase of the process culminated in the Act of Contadora, a proposed regional agreement, which was unfortunately rejected by several of the protagonists. In 1987, however, the presidents of the five Central American states made a new agreement, known as the Esquipulas II Accord. This provided for free elections, the termination of hostilities and an end to assistance for irregular forces. The Contadora Group and the Support Group were enlisted to provide security, verification and control, and, as mentioned earlier, the OAS Secretary-General and the UN Secretary-General were also involved.

In 2000, the OAS undertook a similar constructive role in a long-standing dispute between Guatemala and Belize over their common boundary. Here, the OAS sponsored a 'Facilitation Process', in essence a type of conciliation which involved each side nominating a Facilitator, who would then be assisted by the Secretary-General of the OAS in proposing confidence-building measures, examining the substance of the dispute and recommending a solution. Subsequently, the two Facilitators were joined by a third, nominated by Honduras, to assist with discussions relating to maritime areas in the Gulf of Honduras. Initially, efforts were devoted to developing confidence-building measures in order to relieve tension in the border area, and a series of such measures was agreed, including the creation of a mixed commission to promote cooperation. With additional assistance from the OAS, the parties have discussed further ways of improving relations.[35] The dispute eventually was referred to settlement by the International Court of Justice in 2019, following the holding of referenda in both states (in 2018 and 2019), as had been provided in the 2008 special agreement in which the parties agreed to submit the dispute to the ICJ. This case is pending before the Court at the time of writing.

13.2.4 Collective Action by Regional Organisations

From the cases considered so far, it is evident that much of the work of regional organisations in the field of dispute settlement is simply an application of familiar techniques in an institutional setting. In other words, it is often more accurate to speak of settlement *through* rather than *by* regional organisations. This is not the whole picture, however. Regional organisations can also make a contribution which is uniquely their own. Through collective action the members of a body like the AU or OAS may

---

[35] See J. G. Merrills, 'The Belize–Guatemala territorial dispute and the Legal Opinion of January 2002' (2002) 2 *Global Community YBILJ*, 77 at 81 and 93–4.

be able to achieve something which would be difficult or impossible for any state acting alone.

In 1964, the OAU agreed by an overwhelming majority to respect the boundaries of each member state as they existed on the achieving of national independence.[36] The endorsement of this principle was clearly intended to stabilise the status quo and thus to avoid disputes about African boundaries. It has had that effect by demonstrating to potential troublemakers that challenges to the status quo would be costly, and, when this was not enough, by imposing some constraints on their actions.[37] The resolution has therefore been quite successful in practice and shows that collective legitimisation, already noted as relevant to mediation, can operate at an earlier stage, and prevent, or at least discourage, disputes from arising.

For some types of disputes or situations, a collective declaration of non-intervention, for which a regional organisation supplies a convenient forum, can be a way of avoiding escalation. Individual declarations of non-intervention, in, for example, a civil war or a revolution, may be politically disadvantageous, or dismissed as misleading propaganda. Issued collectively, however, and buttressed by reciprocity, such declarations are both easier to make and harder to break and by reducing the danger of outside involvement can make a real contribution to peaceful settlement.

Collective action can also take a positive form. In 1960, the Meeting of Foreign Ministers of the OAS heard a complaint brought by Venezuela against the Dominican Republic in which acts of intervention were alleged to have culminated in an attempt on the life of Venezuela's Chief of State.[38] An OAS committee had earlier found the charges to be true, and, in light of this, it was decided, for the first time in the Organization's history, to apply sanctions under Articles 6 and 8 of the Rio Treaty. The Organ of Consultation decided to break diplomatic relations with the Dominican Republic and to suspend the sale of arms, a measure which was later extended to petrol and trucks.

Regional organisations have also taken part in peacekeeping operations of various kinds. In 1996, the CIS Council adopted a far-reaching policy statement related to the prevention and settlement of conflicts in the member states, indicating their intention to further develop peacekeeping and related activities. Particularly interesting features of this statement are

---

[36] See S. Touval, 'The Organization of African Unity and African borders' (1967) 21 *Int. Org.*, 102; and A. O. Cukwurah, 'The Organization of African Unity and African territorial and boundary problems 1963–1973' (1973) 13 *Ind. J Int. L*, 176.

[37] See I. W. Zartman, 'Conflict reduction: prevention, management and resolution', in F. M. Deng and I. W. Zartman (eds), *Conflict Resolution in Africa*, Washington, 1991, p. 299 at p. 317.

[38] See R. St J. Macdonald, 'The Organization of American States in action' (1963–4) 15 *U Toronto LJ*, 359 at 367–72.

the emphasis on the possible role of the CIS in conflict prevention and the elaborate arrangements for cooperation with other international organisations, especially the UN and the OSCE. In a further decision at the same time, the Council adopted a statute on collective peacekeeping forces,[39] covering their legal basis, composition, functions, training and other matters, in considerable detail, confirming that more operations of this type are envisaged.

In recent years, a number of peacekeeping operations have been carried out in Africa under the auspices of regional or sub-regional organisations.[40] In 2004, the African Union, in one of its first initiatives, agreed to send peacekeeping troops to Darfur in western Sudan to back up AU observers who were already in the country. These subsequently formed part of a hybrid operation with the United Nations.

An earlier example of regional enterprise is provided by the actions of the Arab League over Kuwait.[41] When Kuwait achieved full independence in 1961, Iraq immediately laid claim to the territory. The Sheikh of Kuwait protested to the Arab League and asked for British troops to protect the territory. The troops were sent, but attempts to raise the matter in the Security Council were unsuccessful. The Arab League dispatched its Secretary-General on a mediation mission which also proved abortive, but subsequently decided first to admit Kuwait as a member, thereby acknowledging its claim to independence, and then to substitute Arab for British forces. An Arab defence force was created which replaced the British forces. Although Iraq boycotted the League and continued to press its claim, it was unable to improve its position and, in 1963, following a change of government, diplomatic relations with Kuwait were established.[42]

A final point worth mentioning is that reaction from regional organisations may sometimes provide an incentive for action by the United Nations. This was the case, for example, with Libya in 2011 where the brutal behaviour of the Qaddafi regime led the Arab League to suspend Libya's membership and to condemnation by the African Union, the Gulf Cooperation Council and the Organization of the Islamic Conference, culminating in the action by the Security Council under Chapter VII of

---

[39] Text in (1996) 35 ILM 792; the text of the CIS 'Concept', can also be found at ibid., 786.
[40] For analysis of the operations by ECOWAS, CEMAC and CEN-SAD mentioned in this paragraph, see Gray, *Use of Force* (n. 1) pp. 302–22.
[41] See M. D. Donelan and M. J. Grieve, *International Disputes: Case Histories 1945–1970*, London, 1973, pp. 220–2.
[42] When Iraq invaded and occupied Kuwait in August 1990, the Arab League immediately condemned the action and called for withdrawal. At the same time, arrangements were made for the dispatch of Arab troops to Saudi Arabia as part of the multinational force confronting Iraq. See L. Freedman and E. Karsh, *The Gulf Conflict 1990–1991*, London, 1993, p. 99.

the Charter, described in the previous chapter. However, while regional concern can prompt a UN response, its results cannot be guaranteed.

13.2.5 Regional Courts

Another way in which regional organisations can contribute to the settlement of disputes is through the activity of regional courts, where these exist. This is not the place to examine the work of the CJEU, the European and Inter-American Courts of Human Rights, the African Court of Human and Peoples' Rights (AFCHPR) and similar bodies, but it is worth noting that the jurisdiction of these courts often includes both inter-state cases and cases brought by individuals and their decisions may make a significant contribution to international law. In the *African Commission* v. *Libya* case,[43] for example, the AFCHPR ordered provisional measures against Libya in a case arising out of serious human rights abuses. Similarly, in *Hadijatou Mani Kouraou* v. *Niger*,[44] the ECOWAS Community Court of Justice delivered an important ruling on slavery. As well as human rights, we saw in Chapter 11 that there are also a number of new courts dealing with economic matters, such as the East African Court of Justice, the ECOWAS Court of Justice, and the Caribbean Court of Justice. All these courts vary in their significance and effectiveness, but, individually and collectively, regional and sub-regional courts unquestionably constitute a notable development.

The link between regional organisations and international courts in general will be discussed in Section 13.4 below.

13.3 Limitations of Regional Organisations

That regional institutions have a useful part to play in the settlement of international disputes is clear from the examples of constructive involvement already mentioned. But it is important not to overstate the case, for neither the possibility nor the desirability of regional action can be taken for granted.

In all the disputes considered so far, the parties were states within a single region. Although this is to be expected, it underlines the point that both the authority of regional institutions and their capabilities are restricted geographically. Some types of disputes are almost always intra-regional – boundary disputes are an example – but to the solution of the multitude of inter-regional disputes that occur, including some territorial

---

[43] *African Commission on Human and Peoples' Rights* v. *Great Socialist Libyan Arab Jamahiriya*, Order for Provisional Measures (2011, App. No. 004/2011). And see E. Polymenopoulou in (2012) 61 *ICLQ*, 767.

[44] Judgment, Case No. ECW/CCJ/APP/08/07 (2008). See also K. J. Alter, L. R. Helfer and J. R. McAllister, 'A new international human rights court for West Africa: the ECOWAS Community Court of Justice' (2013) 107 *AJIL*, 739.

disputes, regional organisations generally have little to contribute. Indeed, by providing the antagonists with the diplomatic and material support necessary to continue the struggle, regional organisations may actually make accommodation more difficult. In the *Falklands* dispute, for example, Britain and Argentina saw their membership of the then EEC and OAS as a way of mobilising support for military action and sought to exploit their respective regional alliances for that end. Although each organisation also tried to exercise a restraining influence on its member, they clearly lacked the capacity to act as peace-makers, with the result that the prospects of a non-military solution, as noted earlier, rested on the efforts of the United States and the United Nations.

External limitations on the influence of regional organisations are matched by an internal limitation of comparable importance: the inability to deal effectively with disputes *within* member states. Regional organisations are created to further cooperation *between* states, and only in special cases, such as the European human rights system or the European Union, are they given jurisdiction over internal affairs. Within the EU, Article 344 of the Treaty on the Functioning of the European Union provides for an exclusive competence of the Court of Justice of the EU to settle disputes between its Members States concerning the interpretation or application of the Treaties. The difficulty in dealing with disputes within states can be illustrated by the fate of the SADC Tribunal. The Tribunal became dysfunctional following a series of decisions by the Tribunal against Zimbabwe, such as *Mike Campbell (Pvt) Ltd et al.* v. *Republic of Zimbabwe*.[45] The case had been brought by a Zimbabwean national against the Zimbabwean government, and the Tribunal had found that the SADC Treaty had been violated by Zimbabwe. The 2010 SADC Summit then ordered 'a review of the role, functions and terms of reference of the SADC Tribunal',[46] resulting in a de facto suspension of the Tribunal.[47] Following the 2012 SADC Summit, it was decided 'that a new Protocol on the Tribunal should be negotiated and that its mandate should be confined to interpretation of the SADC Treaty and Protocols relating to disputes between Member States'.[48] Later that year, the Tribunal was suspended; the 18 August 2014 'Protocol on the Tribunal in the Southern African Development Community', which sought to reconstitute the Tribunal with limited interstate jurisdiction, has not yet entered into force.

---

[45] *Mike Campbell (Pty) Limited & Others* v. *The Republic of Zimbabwe*, SADC (T) 11/2008; *William Michael Campbell & Another* v. *The Republic of Zimbabwe*, SADC (T) 03/2009.

[46] SADC, Communiqué of the 30th Jubilee Summit of SADC Heads of State and Government (Windhoek, 17 August 2010), para. 32.

[47] See generally: Laurie Nathan, 'The Disbanding of the SADC Tribunal: A Cautionary Tale' (2013) 35 *Human Rights Quarterly*, 870.

[48] SADC, Final Communiqué of the 32nd Summit of SADC Heads of State and Government (Maputo, 18 August 2012), para. 24.

In practice, the usual inability to deal effectively with disputes *within* member states does not altogether rule out regional intervention over matters of internal government if regional neighbours become sufficiently alarmed, and the OSCE and CIS, as we have seen, already have considerable experience in such situations. It will also be recalled that the Constitutive Act of the African Union indicates that traditional views on this issue are now being modified. Often, however, revolutions, civil wars and other disruptive events within states will so divide the membership as to make regional initiatives politically impossible. With such obstacles to overcome, regional organisations seem likely to continue to show a marked disinclination to become involved in domestic affairs.

The next point concerns the significance of regional solidarity as a factor in dispute settlement. It is sometimes assumed that, except for situations involving domestic jurisdiction, the regional environment is peculiarly suited to the settlement of local disputes. That is to say, the members of a regional organisation have common interests and loyalties which provide them with an incentive to encourage the settlement of conflicts and increase the chances that, when such efforts are made, they will be successful. However, this assumption is open to question. Expressions of regional loyalty and hemispheric solidarity have certainly been prominent in the inter-American system and are now to be found in all regional institutions. The significance of such sentiments for dispute settlement is difficult to assess, but the evidence suggests that they can sometimes prompt constructive interventions that would not otherwise occur, particularly when there is an established tradition of involvement, as in the OAS, or where the policy of a regional organisation is directly determined by heads of state, as in the African Union and its predecessor, the OAU.

From the point of view of the parties to a dispute, regional loyalties are perhaps mainly significant as a way of legitimising both the search for a peaceful settlement and the terms of the settlement itself. As explained earlier, the involvement of third parties as mediators, or in some other capacity, can make it easier for states to agree to arrangements which might be difficult to concede in direct negotiations. This tendency is no doubt encouraged when accommodation can also be presented as motivated by considerations of regional solidarity.

Too much should not be expected of regional loyalties, however. Regions, after all, are large areas, made up of a variety of states. As a result, certain states may not be members of their local organisation, and others, which are members, may have more in common with states outside the region than with those within it.[49] Both are factors which can limit the

---

[49] See C. Moneta, 'The Latin American Economic System as a mechanism to control conflicts', in M. A. Morris and V. Millán (eds), *Controlling Latin American Conflicts*, Boulder, CO, 1983, p. 99 at p. 104.

possibility of concerted regional action very significantly. Thus, the fact that South Africa did not become a member of the OAU until 1994, though easily explained, greatly limited the scope of that organisation's influence, while in the *Falklands* dispute the English-speaking members of the OAS provided Britain with a useful source of support and helped to offset Argentina's influence in the Organization.

Even when special factors are not present, regional solidarity cannot be assumed, especially if substantial interests are at stake. All regional organisations are less united than their ceremonial rhetoric or constitutions might suggest, and disputes between the members can place institutions under great internal strain. In the Cod Wars, Iceland obtained a good deal of political leverage by threatening to leave NATO, hardly an inspiring example of regional loyalty; while a major reason for the relative ineffectiveness of the Arab League has been the deep division of opinion in the membership on major issues of policy. Sometimes, indeed, dissension may undermine the whole idea of regional solidarity and pose a threat to the very existence of the organisation. In 1982, for example, the split between the moderate and the radical members of the OAU was so serious that it proved impossible to hold the meeting of the Organization's Council, despite two attempts to do so.[50]

The fact that regional loyalties may on occasion be more apparent than real lends added significance to the existence of the sub-regional groups mentioned earlier. Here, relations will normally be closer than in the larger institution and intervention with a view to dispute settlement correspondingly easier. In 1964, for example, the Union Africaine et Malagache (UAM), comprising the French-speaking states of Africa, played a constructive role in the settlement of a territorial dispute between Dahomey (Benin) and Niger;[51] and, more recently, as we have seen, the Contadora Group was actively involved in efforts to avoid war in Central America. A particularly striking example of action by a sub-regional organisation is provided by the intervention of ECOWAS in the civil war in Liberia. In 1990, the Liberian government accepted a peace proposal put forward by ECOWAS as a result of which a 4,000-strong peacekeeping force, ECOMOG, arrived in the country and soon became involved in the fighting. In 1992, the Security Council took up the issue, and, when a peace agreement was concluded in 1993, created an observer mission to work alongside ECOMOG. As already noted, the first phase of ECOWAS involvement concluded in 1997, but was then followed by further operations in 2003.

---

[50] In August 1982, the issue was the admission of the Saharan Arab Democratic Republic, which caused Morocco to leave the organisation; in November, the issue was the representation of Chad. After considerable uncertainty, a meeting was finally held in June 1983.

[51] See Cukwurah, 'Territorial and boundary problems' (n. 36) 191–3.

A final point concerns resources. Regional organisations, it is worth remembering, are largely dependent on the willingness of member states to provide whatever may be necessary for a given operation. Thus, the provision of border surveillance in the *Costa Rica/Nicaragua* dispute, and peacekeeping forces in Kuwait in 1961, depended on the members' readiness to make the appropriate resources available. Of course, all organisations have some resources of their own, but even something as simple as mediation may present difficulties for certain organisations as the combination of a small budget and limited personnel may restrict the activities which can be undertaken. In 1982, for example, a peacekeeping force which the OAU sent to Chad had to be withdrawn, having failed to achieve any improvement in the situation. Although logistic and financial difficulties were not the only reason for its failure, they do seem to have been a contributory factor.[52] Similarly, the fact that the Commission of Mediation, Conciliation and Arbitration never became operational was due in part to a lack of political support, and in part to the budgetary problems which were always a weakness of the Organization.[53]

The resource requirements of regional action, then, like the political factors with which they are linked, are an important element in the settlement of disputes. As a result, if interest in a dispute is lacking, or if the price of intervention is too high, or if a matter is highly controversial, attempts to secure a peaceful settlement from within a region are conceivably no more likely than attempts from outside.

13.4 Regional Organisations and Adjudication

Adjudication and regional organisations are linked in many different ways. A procedure for the reference of disputes to a tribunal may be laid down in a regional agreement and a regional court created for this purpose. The European Court of Human Rights and the Court of Justice of the European Union are regional tribunals of this kind, and the Inter-American Court of Human Rights and the projected International Islamic Court of Justice are further examples. Alternatively, a regional treaty may provide for the reference of disputes to the International Court of Justice, or to arbitration. Thus, Article 31 of the Pact of Bogotá provides:

> In conformity with Article 36, paragraph 2, of the Statute of the International Court of Justice, the High Contracting Parties declare that they recognize, in

---

[52] See G. J. Naldi, 'Peace-keeping attempts by the Organization of African Unity' (1985) 34 *ICLQ*, 593 at 595.
[53] See Maluwa, 'Conceptual issues and practical trends' (n. 15) 313. When the OAU celebrated its twenty-fifth anniversary in 1988, it had an annual budget of US$23 million. Of this sum, only US$5 million had been paid, and thirty-three states were behind in their contributions. Other arrears amounted to US$26 million; see *Independent*, 25 May 1988, p. 12.

relation to any other American State, the jurisdiction of the Court as compulsory *ipso facto*, without the necessity of any special agreement so long as the present Treaty is in force, in all disputes of a juridical nature that arise among them concerning:

- The interpretation of a treaty;
- Any question of international law;
- The existence of any fact which, if established, would constitute the breach of an international obligation;
- The nature or extent of the reparation to be made for the breach of an international obligation.

In addition to arrangements establishing legal obligations, regional organisations can also provide effective support for adjudication at the political level.

13.4.1 Support for Adjudication

When a dispute arises between states within a region, the pressure of other regional states can be a way of persuading the parties to settle it by adjudication. Similarly, when judgment has been given, the members of a regional organisation may have a part to play in encouraging the parties to implement the decision, or helping them to do so. We have seen that, in the *Arbitral Award* case, the OAS performed both functions: first, persuading Honduras and Nicaragua to refer the dispute to the International Court; then, when the case was decided, assisting the parties with implementation of the judgment.[54] More generally, the OAS has over the past years played an important role in supporting the submission of territorial disputes to the International Court of Justice. It has to this effect established 'The Fund for Peace: Peaceful Settlement of Territorial Disputes' ('Peace Fund')[55] to 'provide member states of the Organization that so request with financial resources to assist with defraying the costs of proceedings previously agreed to by the parties for the peaceful resolution of territorial disputes among member states.' The Fund has been used to assist amongst others the settlement of the border dispute between El Salvador and Honduras, and more recently the territorial dispute between Belize and Guatemala which was submitted to the ICJ in 2019. The kind of mutually supportive relationship which existed, amongst others, in the

---

[54] For the OAS contribution before the reference to the Court, see the text accompanying n. 25 above; for the post-adjudication phase, see the text accompanying n. 39 in Chapter 7, and J. G. Merrills, 'The International Court of Justice and the adjudication of territorial and boundary disputes' (2000) 13 *Leiden JIL*, 873 at 899, and C. Schulte, *Compliance with Decisions of the International Court of Justice*, Oxford, 2004, pp. 126–32.

[55] OAS General Assembly Resolution 'Fund for Peace: Peaceful Settlement of Territorial Disputes' AG/RES. 1756 (XXX-O/00) (6 June 2000).

Arbitral Award case cannot, of course, be guaranteed. In some situations the search for a political solution may be under way in a regional organisation, while at the same time, and quite independently, an attempt is being made to have the dispute adjudicated. This raises the question of whether the two processes are compatible and, if priorities have to be determined, how this is to be done. As the issue here is the respective areas of competence of political and judicial organs, this is a matter with a vital bearing on the role of regional organisations.

13.4.2 The Interplay between the Political Role of Regional Organisations and Judicial Settlement

In the *Nicaragua* case,[56] the United States sought to persuade the International Court that its competence was affected by the Contadora negotiations in which Nicaragua, the applicant in the case, was involved. Specifically, the United States argued that Nicaragua was obliged to exhaust the possibilities of a political settlement through the Contadora Process, before submitting the legal aspects of its dispute with the United States to judicial settlement. The Court, however, rejected the argument. Relying on cases which have been mentioned earlier,[57] it held that, even if negotiations were currently in progress, this would be no bar to the Court's exercising its functions under the United Nations Charter. It therefore concluded that, in the present situation, there was no 'requirement of prior exhaustion of regional negotiating processes as a precondition to seising the Court'.[58] In other words, there was no incompatibility between participation in the Contadora Process, a regional procedure of a political nature, and simultaneous recourse to the International Court.

At an earlier stage of the case, the Court had considered another aspect of this issue. When Nicaragua asked the Court to indicate interim measures of protection, the United States resisted the claim, putting forward, amongst other arguments, the point that interim measures might prejudice the Contadora Process. The submission, which lacked plausibility, was summarily rejected.[59] In a different situation, however, an argument of this type might merit attention. At the corresponding stage of the *Aegean Sea* case, where the ruling was that interim measures were unnecessary, the Court appears to have been influenced by the fact that the Security Council was actively seised of the matter.[60] Thus, there seems no reason why, in an

---

[56] *Military and Paramilitary Activities in and against Nicaragua*, Jurisdiction and Admissibility, Judgment [1984] ICJ Rep. 392.
[57] See Chapter 1.   [58] [1984] ICJ Rep. 440.
[59] *Military and Paramilitary Activities in and against Nicaragua*, Provisional Measures, Order of 10 May 1984 [1984] ICJ Rep. 169.
[60] See *Aegean Sea Continental Shelf*, Interim Protection, Order of 11 September 1976 [1976] ICJ Rep. 3.

appropriate case, the fact that a dispute is being dealt with by a regional body should not also carry weight.

In the *Border and Transborder Armed Actions* case[61] in 1988, the relation between regional and judicial procedures was given further consideration. The case was referred to the International Court by Nicaragua, which alleged that Honduras was allowing armed bands to operate from its territory. The basis of jurisdiction relied on by Nicaragua was Article 31 of the Pact of Bogotá, which has already been quoted. Both states were parties to the Pact, but, before the Court could address the merits of the case, it had to deal with a number of preliminary objections raised by Honduras, some of which, like the United States' objections in the *Nicaragua* case, concerned the relation between adjudication and other means of settlement.

As regards the issue of jurisdiction, the Court decided that, despite the similarity between Article 31 of the Pact and Article 36(2) of the Court's Statute, the Pact establishes an independent basis of jurisdiction. This was important because it meant that it was unnecessary for the Court to decide whether Honduras had validly modified its declaration under Article 36(2) in 1986, and in addition meant that any reservations in the latter were irrelevant to the obligations of Honduras under the Pact. The Court also decided that the jurisdiction which Article 31 invested in the Court was quite separate from the arrangements for conciliation and arbitration provided for in Article 32 and could therefore be invoked by Nicaragua before the latter had been attempted.

As regards the admissibility of the claim, the issues before the Court concerned various aspects of the Contadora Process. Article 2 of the Pact provides for use of its procedures for disputes which 'in the opinion of the parties cannot be settled by direct negotiations through the usual diplomatic channels'. Honduras submitted that the present dispute failed to satisfy this requirement and cited the Contadora Process as evidence that negotiations were in progress. The Court, however, rejected the argument. After examining the origin and character of the Contadora Process, the Court concluded that, at the relevant time, it was 'primarily a mediation, in which third States, on their own initiative, endeavoured to bring together the viewpoints of the States concerned by making specific proposals to them'.[62] As such, the process was markedly different from 'direct negotiations through the usual diplomatic channels' and consequently fell outside Article 2.

---

[61] *Border and Transborder Armed Actions*, Jurisdiction and Admissibility, Judgment [1988] ICJ Rep. 69. This case was subsequently withdrawn; see the Court's order of 27 May 1992 [1992] ICJ Rep. 222.
[62] [1988] ICJ Rep. 99.

Honduras next argued that the claim was barred by Article 4 of the Pact, which provides that, when any 'pacific procedure' has been initiated, no other procedure may be commenced until that procedure has been concluded. Honduras maintained that the Contadora Process was a 'pacific procedure' and had not yet been concluded. The Court, however, again disagreed. Without deciding whether the original Contadora Process of mediation could be regarded as a 'pacific procedure', the Court held that the Process had ended in June 1986 when the states concerned put forward the unsuccessful Act of Contadora. What followed, 'the Contadora – Esquipulas II process', was, in the Court's view, 'an independent mechanism of multilateral negotiation'[63] and as such must be treated as a new procedure.

Since the original Contadora Process had therefore been concluded, Article 4 did not have the effect of barring Nicaragua's claim.

A final argument was that, whatever the status of the Contadora Process under the Pact, Nicaragua was barred by the principle of good faith from referring the case to the Court while the Process continued. This submission, which was not unlike the argument put forward by the United States in the *Nicaragua* case, was also rejected. As on the previous point, the Court considered that it was significant that the original Contadora Process had terminated, and pointed out that in any case there had never been any suggestion that the use of the Contadora Process was intended to be exclusive.

The *Border and Transborder Armed Actions* case has been discussed here in some detail because it is a good illustration of the issues which can arise when adjudication and regional procedures are employed simultaneously. Of course, the precise questions which the Court had to answer stemmed from the language of the treaty under which the dispute had been referred. However, the analysis which was required of the nature and effect of the Contadora Process at its various stages shows the sort of review which is called for when a treaty provides several procedures for the settlement of disputes and, as will usually be the case, is also intended to regulate the relation between them. Moreover, the decision confirms the point which was crucial in the *Nicaragua* case, that, where different procedures are being used simultaneously, diplomatic methods have priority over legal methods only insofar as this is provided for.

In the *Land and Maritime Boundary* case[64] between Cameroon and Nigeria, the Court again had to consider the role of regional procedures, on

---

[63] Ibid., 105. Although 'the Contadora–Esquipulas II Process' could also be argued to be a 'pacific procedure', Nicaragua had filed its application before this second regional procedure began. It was therefore irrelevant for the purposes of Art. 4.

[64] *Land and Maritime Boundary between Cameroon and Nigeria*, Preliminary Objections, Judgment [1998] ICJ Rep. 275.

this occasion in a dispute over territory. One of the many issues in that case was the location of the frontier in the vicinity of Lake Chad where, according to Nigeria, a body called the Lake Chad Basin Commission had 'exclusive power in relation to issues of security and public order'.[65] Nigeria argued that this rendered Cameroon's reference of the boundary issue to the International Court inadmissible, but the Court disagreed. Ruling that the Commission was neither a judicial body intended to displace the Court, nor a regional organisation acknowledged under Chapter VIII of the UN Charter, it reiterated the point made in earlier cases, that in any event the mere existence of procedures for regional negotiation cannot prevent the Court from carrying out its functions.

It is clear that, if the parties to a dispute have agreed that a regional procedure, or some other means of settlement, shall be used exclusively, or in priority to adjudication, then they will be held to their agreement.

There are countless examples of governments agreeing either that judicial settlement must take second place to other procedures, or that some other means of settlement must be used instead. Governments are at liberty to make such arrangements, and they will be given effect. The point which the International Court was making in the cases above was not that judicial settlement has a privileged status, but simply that the overriding objective is a peaceful settlement, and so, in principle, unless they have made special arrangements, the parties to a legal dispute are free to employ any of the means set out in Article 33 of the Charter, including regional procedures, without prejudice to their juridical position.

13.5 Regional Organisations and the United Nations

The place of regionalism within a universal political organisation was an issue which taxed the founders of the League of Nations after the First World War.[66] After some debate, the matter was eventually dealt with by Article 21 of the League of Nations Covenant, which provided that: 'Nothing in this Covenant shall be deemed to affect the validity of international engagements, such as treaties of arbitration or regional understandings like the Monroe Doctrine, for securing the maintenance of international peace.' A quarter of a century later, a more elaborate treatment of regional arrangements formed Chapter VIII of the United Nations Charter (Articles 52–54), while 'resort to regional agencies or arrangements' is one of the methods available for settling disputes whose

---

[65] Ibid., para. 66.
[66] See R. A. Akindele, 'From the Covenant to the Charter: constitutional relations between universal and regional organisations in the promotion of peace and security' (1973) 8 *Israel L Rev.*, 91.

continuation is likely to endanger the maintenance of international peace and security, under Article 33.

During the period of the Cold War, the relationship between regional organisations and the United Nations gave rise to controversy on a number of occasions. Disagreement, a reflection of political rivalry in the form of inter-organisational competition, centred on two issues: the limits of the authority of regional organisations in matters concerning international peace and security, and whether regional means of settlement must be exhausted before a dispute can be considered by the Security Council.[67] With the ending of the Cold War the debate about Chapter VIII has taken a more constructive turn and attention has been given to how regional organisations and the UN can work together.[68] The framework for such cooperation is, however, still based on the Charter. Accordingly, before we examine the latest developments, something should be said about the constitutional position.

The crucial limitation on the authority of regional organisations is contained in Article 53(1) of the Charter, which provides that 'no enforcement action shall be taken under regional arrangements or by regional agencies without the authorisation of the Security Council'. The question of what constitutes 'enforcement action' has been exhaustively considered elsewhere[69] and need not be investigated here. Two cases in which the question was raised will, however, indicate its importance.

In the *Dominican* case, mentioned earlier, the Soviet Union argued in the Security Council that the diplomatic and economic sanctions imposed on the Dominican Republic by the OAS constituted 'enforcement action', requiring the authorisation of the Council under Article 53(1). During the Cuban missile crisis of 1962, on the other hand, the United States proceeded on the assumption that no Security Council authorisation was required for the interdiction of Cuba by the US Navy and various other coercive measures approved by the OAS.

Neither interpretation of Article 53(1) is really very convincing. The Soviet view has the curious consequence that states are denied the right to do collectively what they would clearly be entitled to do individually, and deprives regional organisations of an opportunity to make a real contribution to dispute settlement by bringing political pressure to bear on a

---

[67] See R. St J. Macdonald, 'The developing relationship between superior and subordinate political bodies at the international level' (1964) 2 *Can. Yearbook Int. L.*, 21.

[68] See, for example, B. Rivlin, 'Regional arrangements and the UN system for collective security and conflict resolution: a new road ahead?' (1992) 11 *Int. Rel.*, 95; and A. K. Henrikson, 'The growth of regional organisations and the role of the United Nations', in L. Fawcett and A. Hurrell (eds), *Regionalism in World Politics*, Oxford, 1995, p. 122.

[69] See M. Akehurst, 'Enforcement action by regional agencies with special reference to the Organization of American States' (1967) 42 *BYBIL*, 175, with references to previous literature. See also Gray, *Use of Force* (n. 1) ch. 9.

recalcitrant member. The United States view, on the other hand, allows a state to be the target of military coercion, perhaps directed by a dominant regional member, a situation in which the rest of the world has an overwhelming interest in preserving the requirement of Security Council authorisation.

Reconciling effective regional action with the interests of the international community is a major element in the other issue to be considered: the priority to be given to regional means of settlement. On several occasions a state has sought to bring a dispute to the Security Council before a regional organisation has had an opportunity of dealing with the matter. In the border dispute between Morocco and Algeria, for example, Morocco's initial instinct was to take the matter to the Security Council rather than the OAU, perhaps because it believed that the former might have more sympathy with its demand for frontier revision. In this type of situation, which is likely to occur whenever a state perceives an advantage in having its case considered in a wider forum, there is clearly a potential conflict of jurisdiction between the regional and universal organisation. In the *Guatemala* case in 1954, the United States sought to argue that a case which was being handled by the OAS was beyond the competence of the Security Council, an assertion which was strongly challenged by the Soviet Union. Following the invasion of Czechoslovakia by Warsaw Pact forces in 1968, however, it was the Soviet Union that denied the Council's competence and the United States that called for United Nations action.[70] The self-serving character of these arguments is clear, and Security Council practice, though not always consistent, provides little support for these extreme versions of the regionalist approach.

The intention of those who drafted the Charter was to create a presumption in favour of the use of regional institutions and the view that regional procedures should be tried first has, as one would expect, been vigorously endorsed by the major regional organisations. It is, however, widely recognised that regional organisations cannot remove the Security Council's ultimate responsibility for the maintenance of international peace and security. States cannot therefore be deprived of the right to take a dispute or situation to the Security Council, if they consider it necessary to do so. Of course, it does not follow that the Council will necessarily wish to deal with the matter, nor that, if it decides to do so, it will be able to do anything effective, but the right to have the matter put before the Council is something which regional organisations, however insistent, can never take away.

In his 1992 report to the Security Council, entitled *An Agenda for Peace*, UN Secretary-General Boutros-Ghali observed that the Cold War 'impaired the proper use of Chapter VIII' and that in that era 'regional

---

[70] See R. A. Akindele, 'The Warsaw Pact, the United Nations and the Soviet Union' (1971) 11 *Ind. J Int. L.*, 553.

arrangements worked on occasion against resolving disputes in the manner foreseen in the Charter'.[71] There was, as we have seen, ample justification for that assessment, but, with the Cold War over, it has been possible to see the relation between the United Nations and regional organisations in a new light and to explore the possibilities for cooperation between them. In his report, the Secretary-General described what he saw as the contribution of regional organisations in this context, emphasising that a variety of bodies, including 'regional organisations for mutual security and defence' and 'groups created to deal with a specific political, economic or social issue', may all have a role to play.[72]

The thrust of the Secretary-General's argument, with which it is easy to agree, is that regional bodies plainly possess a potential which can be utilised in serving the functions identified in *An Agenda for Peace*. These, it will be recalled, are preventive diplomacy, peacekeeping, peace-making and post-conflict peace-building. As might be expected, the point is made that regional organisations must act in a manner consistent with the Charter and that the Security Council has primary responsibility for maintaining international peace and security. However, so long as these constitutional limitations are respected, regional action is valuable because 'as a matter of decentralisation, delegation and co-operation with United Nations efforts could not only lighten the burden of the Council but also contribute to a deeper sense of participation, consensus and democratisation in international affairs'.[73]

As the former Secretary-General has indicated, cooperation between regional organisations and the UN is particularly useful in situations which call for peacekeeping forces or related action, and a number of cases which have already been mentioned show how institutions can perform complementary functions when the political atmosphere is favourable. We have seen how in the complex situation in Central America the main diplomatic work was carried out through the Contadora Process, but when security arrangements were needed a UN force (ONUCA) was established by the Security Council. In the Liberian crisis, local peacekeeping forces were supplied by ECOWAS and subsequently supported both politically and on the ground by the UN. In Georgia, on the other hand, a UN observer mission was already in place when CIS forces arrived, and coordination was then overseen by the Security Council.

Similarly, the initial response to the coup in Haiti came from the OAS, but only became effective when backed up by the UN, while, in the complex and protracted crisis in Bosnia, the EC intervened with diplomatic and economic measures, but, when the Security Council became involved and military action was needed, NATO was utilised as the organisation

---

[71] SC Doc. S/24111, 17 June 1992. Text in (1992) 31 ILM 953.   [72] Ibid., para. 61.
[73] Ibid., para. 64.

with the necessary capabilities. Cooperation between the UN and regional organisations has therefore been extensive in recent years, with many Security Council Resolutions authorising or approving regional action of various kinds and a number of joint peacekeeping operations in different parts of the world. The record thus suggests that the potential of regional organisations in what *An Agenda for Peace* called 'this new era of opportunity'[74] is now being realised.

Assessing the role of regional organisations in relation to the United Nations comes down in the end to appreciating both the limitations and the advantages of delegation. As regards limitations, securing agreement within a regional organisation on peacekeeping or other measures may be no easier than within the United Nations, not least when it calls for resources which members of the organisation may be unable or unwilling to provide. Regional action, particularly when it involves the use of force, may well raise the issue of impartiality, and, when it is authorised by the Security Council, still needs to be properly controlled, which can present its own difficulties.[75] Finally, there is, of course, no guarantee that, when regional solutions are attempted, they will be successful. It is clear therefore that, on account of their various limitations, regional organisations are in no sense a panacea. On the other hand, although co-operation between the UN and regional organisations can be very valuable, when a body like the African Union or the OAS is seised of a dispute, Security Council involvement will only be needed if regional measures are inadequate. Regional organisations, as has been seen, can often make a constructive contribution to dispute settlement without outside help. Encouraging regional organisations to use their own resources enables the United Nations to reserve its efforts for inter-regional disputes and the more intractable intra-regional conflicts, and thereby achieves a useful division of labour. Insisting that the Security Council should always be involved, on the other hand, would tend to discourage regional organisations from taking responsibility, while perhaps introducing complications in the form of outside states' involvement, which treatment at the regional level may be able to avoid.

13.6 Further Reading

13.6.1 General References on Dispute Settlement and Regional Organisations

Cogen, M., *An Introduction to European Intergovernmental Organizations*, London, Routledge, 2015.

---

[74] B. Boutros-Ghali, *An Agenda for Peace*, SC Doc. S/24111, 17 June 1992, para. 63. Text in (1992) 31 ILM 953.

[75] See Gray, *Use of Force* (n. 1) pp. 326–7.

Cremona, M., A. Thies and R. A. Wessel, *The European Union and International Dispute Settlement*, Oregon, 2017.

Dorosh, L., and O. Ivasechjo, 'The OSCE institutional and operational possibilities in the modern conflict resolution: by example of the activity of the OSCE special monitoring mission to Ukraine' (2020) 30 *Security and Human Rights*, 1.

Hoffmeister, F., 'The European Union and the peaceful settlement of international disputes' (2012) 11 *Chinese Journal of International Law*, 77.

Kachuyevski, A., 'The possibilities and limitations of preventative action: the OSCE High Commissioner on National Minorities in Ukraine' (2012) 17 *International Negotiation*, 389.

Remler, P., 'Ukraine, protracted violence and the OSCE' (2015) 26 *Security and Human Rights*, 88.

13.6.2 Treaties, Official Documents and Collections of Documents

Craig, P., and G. de Búrca, *EU Law: Text, Cases, and Materials*, Oxford, 2020. Ch. 2 ('EU Membership: tensions and challenges'); Ch. 11 ('EU international relations law').

14

Trends and Prospects

Having reviewed the various ways of attempting to resolve international disputes individually, we are now in a position to consider what this survey as a whole demonstrates about the possibilities open to a state when confronted with a dispute, the factors which influence decisions on whether to use a particular procedure and the prospects for improving this situation in the future. To deal with these issues it will be necessary to consider separately some of the legal and political factors which form the context in which decisions relating to the conduct of disputes are taken, and then to suggest some ways of modifying or developing current methods of settlement with a view to making them more effective and easier to use. First, however, it may be useful to recall in brief outline what our study has revealed about the present situation.

14.1 International Dispute Settlement Today

The idea that international disputes should be settled by peaceful means rather than by the use of force has a long history. From the survey in the preceding pages, however, it is clear that the attempt to devise techniques and institutions with this objective is a more recent phenomenon, much of what exists today having been created in a period of little more than 100 years. What has all the interest which states have shown in this subject succeeded in producing?

In one respect, at least, remarkably little. It was explained at the beginning of this book that the basic means of resolving disputes peacefully is still negotiation. Noteworthy developments here, however, are the increasing use of consultation and related techniques as a means of avoiding disputes and new forms of diplomacy associated with the growth of international organisations. All disputes are likely to involve negotiation at some stage, but as a method of settlement it is evidently subject to serious limitations. To some extent these can be overcome by good offices and mediation, yet these in turn are circumscribed in various ways and, like negotiation, wholly dependent on the readiness of the parties to agree. With the introduction of inquiry and conciliation we find third-party assistance institutionalised, in the shape of permanent or ad hoc commissions, and objectified, in the sense that the necessary findings or recommendations are arrived at independently and passed to the parties for assimilation. Inquiry, as we have seen, has principally been employed when the disputed issue is one of fact. Conciliation, on the other hand, has often been used as a form of quasi-arbitration in cases concerned with present or future legal rights. The usefulness and flexibility of both procedures are shown by the variety of cases in which they have been used successfully. Thus, although both have features which make them unsuitable for certain types of dispute, each has a potential which ought to be, and in the case of conciliation is, coming to be more widely recognised.

From the perspective of the parties to a dispute, inquiry and conciliation offer the benefit of a third-party opinion with no commitment to accept the result. Although the non-binding character of these procedures is plainly an advantage to a party whose ultimate object is a negotiated settlement, a state which is prepared to relinquish such control can reap the additional advantages of judicial settlement or arbitration. It has been explained that these legal means offer the possibility of a binding decision for individual disputes or whole classes of disputes. Given the type of dispute which a judicial tribunal is capable of handling, the prerequisites here are a court which the parties are prepared to trust – thus the constitution and composition of the tribunal are of major importance – and agreement on terms of reference, an issue involving both the nature of the dispute and the adequacy of international law. To these should be added a willingness to carry out the decision. For on this the effectiveness of all binding methods of settlement actually depends.

The factors which determine the approach of states to the different methods of dispute settlement emerge with particular clarity in the provisions of the 1982 Law of the Sea Convention. Recognising that suitable arrangements must be an integral part of the Convention, states have here succeeded in combining the principle of free choice of means with exploitation of the full range of existing techniques and many novelties. The machinery of the Convention thus provides the framework for a flexible and useful system, the value of which is now being demonstrated. Though open to criticism in certain respects, the provisions of the Convention are also an indication of a positive attitude towards dispute settlement and the kind of results that a major effort can achieve.

The dispute settlement system of the World Trade Organization, though no less progressive, represents a quite different approach. Like the Law of the Sea Convention, the 1994 Dispute Settlement Understanding utilises established methods for dealing with disputes in its particular field, and also develops them. Thus, consultations and panel proceedings, which have been employed in trade disputes for several decades, are not only formalised in the DSU, but also supplemented by a system of appellate review and implementation. However, a key difference is that, whereas the Law of the Sea Convention, with its emphasis on choice of means, creates, as it were, a lateral system of competing methods, the DSU employs what is plainly intended as a vertical system with the various methods available successively, and in accordance with a strict timetable, until a solution is achieved. The difference may be accounted for by the capacity of unresolved trade disputes to inflict a great deal of damage quickly, which makes resolution a matter of urgency, and also perhaps by the fact that, while trade disputes are often complex, they tend to be less diverse than maritime disputes, making a uniform procedure for dealing with them easier to agree. Be that as it may, the extensive use now being made of the DSU reflects states' confidence in the system. At the same time, the recent dysfunction of the Appellate Body is a reminder that the success of the 1994 Dispute Settlement Understanding remains subject to the need for states to maintain that confidence.

Our final reflections concerned the United Nations and regional organisations. The former, it was noted, is not a world government, or an international policeman, but essentially a body through which pressure and influence can be brought to bear on states whose disputes come before the Organisation. The ending of the Cold War, though enabling the Security Council to make significant use of its powers under Chapter VII, has not changed this basic situation. Consequently, although the Secretary-General exercises a role of considerable importance and peacekeeping operations can reduce international tensions, it is more accurate to speak of settlement through, rather than by, the United Nations. Of course, many disputes never reach the United Nations, while of those that do many remain unsettled. Regional organisations, however, can sometimes help by providing a forum for negotiation, or involving regional neighbours in the capacity of mediators or conciliators. There is also now the real possibility of combining regional action with action by the United Nations. Again, though, action in the form of legitimisation or sanctions is less important in practice than the use of regional machinery by the parties themselves. Organizations, then, like the other institutions we have considered, represent not so much a transformation of the international scene, as a new arena in which the sovereign state can exercise its traditional power to pursue (or not to pursue) a settlement of its disputes.

14.2 A Political Perspective

What has been said so far is enough to demonstrate that, although a great many different ways of handling disputes have been developed, there is often a considerable gap between what is possible in theory and what states are prepared to do in practice. Moreover, as we have frequently had occasion to note, even when a particular method of settlement is available and utilised, there is no guarantee that it will be effective in a given case. Before we consider what can be done to improve this state of affairs, it is worth considering just why international disputes are so difficult to deal with, beginning with some features of their political context.

From the political perspective, international disputes can be thought of as having three dimensions: the social, the material and the temporal. The social dimension is concerned with where a dispute occurs, and establishes who the protagonists are. The material dimension relates to what the dispute is about and identifies its subject matter. And the temporal dimension concerns when the dispute occurs, how long it lasts and when it is resolved. All three dimensions are present in every dispute and can exercise a crucial influence on the effectiveness of peaceful means of settlement.

14.2.1 The Social Element

The social element is important because the traditions, interests and attitudes of states are very different, as also is the power which each can bring to bear in a particular situation. In Western Europe, for example, there is now a high degree of political and economic integration, a readiness to lay aside historical animosity, and a high level of economic prosperity. In these circumstances, it is not surprising that governments generally make every effort to avoid disputes and that, when disputes do occur, they are normally settled quite quickly, often through the use of regional procedures. In contrast, the situation in Africa and Latin America is much more volatile. There are fewer procedures for avoiding disputes within the region, and there is less political and economic integration, or at least fragmented into different regional integration schemes. To be sure, these factors do not preclude the use of peaceful means of settlement, and many such cases have already been noted. They do, however, mean that approaches to international conduct which can be taken for granted in Europe cannot be regarded as universal and that whether a dispute is settled peacefully or by force – and indeed whether a disagreement becomes a dispute in the first place – may well depend on its location.

The greater the interaction between states, the more opportunity there is for disagreement. Consequently, the majority of international disputes involve states which are neighbours, and so the nature of the regional environment is extremely significant. However, some disputes cross regional boundaries and here too the social factor is important. When states have a great deal in common, then, even if they happen to be separated geographically, the chances that they will be able to resolve their disputes peacefully are good. For example, it is difficult to imagine any dispute between the United States and the United Kingdom which would be comparable to the diplomatic hostages dispute between the United States and Iran. In the Anglo-American situation, both sides have an incentive to maintain good relations and to resolve any disputes peacefully;

in the latter case, as we have seen, cultural, as well as historical and political, factors not only brought about the crisis, but also made resolution of it exceedingly difficult. It is noteworthy that several new cases between the United States and Iran are currently pending before the Court. In the same way, it is instructive to contrast the long-standing dispute between the United Kingdom and Spain over Gibraltar with the not dissimilar issues raised by the dispute with Argentina over the Falkland Islands. In the first case, though the dispute has not been resolved and must be regarded as an irritant in Anglo-Spanish relations, neither side is interested in provoking a crisis. In the case of the Falklands, on the other hand, while the British tended to assume that the situation was broadly similar, Argentina was in fact prepared to regard force as an available option, and, when negotiation proved unsuccessful, had no compunction in mounting an invasion.

Finally, in relation to the social dimension, recent years have demonstrated that despite the different political power each party can bring to a particular situation, states have not shied away from initiating proceedings before the International Court of Justice, with an attraction of judicial settlement offering a more level playing field than diplomatic methods of settlement. The choice of the Marshall Islands to file an application to institute proceedings against the United Kingdom amongst other states in 2014 to the ICJ is an example of this.

14.2.2 The Material Dimension

The significance of the material dimension stems from the fact that, other things being equal, the difficulty of resolving a dispute depends on what is at stake. Thus, a dispute over a technical obligation under a treaty will usually be easier to dispose of than a disagreement over a major issue of policy. Similarly, a dispute concerning an isolated point is normally more straightforward than one which is bound up with larger aspects of the parties' relations. Thus, the diplomatic hostages crisis was exceptionally difficult because the particular dispute became a symbol for Iran of the repudiation of all things American in the period immediately after the Islamic Revolution. In the Falklands dispute, on the other hand, the issue itself was not bound up with larger questions, but raised issues of national sovereignty and self-determination on which all states, including the protagonists, are extremely sensitive.

The material element also has a bearing on which methods of peaceful settlement may be appropriate. As we saw when considering inquiry, for this procedure to be relevant it is essential for there to be a disputed issue of fact. Conciliation, on the other hand, addresses the issue of what should be done, rather than what happened, and so is more appropriate for accommodating differences of policy. Likewise, arbitration and judicial settlement are clearly most suitable for disputes involving legal questions. It is, of course, necessary to add that these are not inflexible prescriptions. Just as disputes themselves often combine issues of fact, law and policy in varying proportions, so it may be necessary for a particular method of settlement to perform more than one function. The differences are nevertheless important. Thus, conciliators should not be criticised for failing to apply the law, and, by the same token, judges should not normally be thought of as conciliators. The fact that states can, if they wish, modify the position and introduce elements of arbitration into conciliation, or conciliation into judicial settlement, does not alter this, but rather serves to emphasise the distinctions between these processes which exist under normal circumstances.

A further point is that the material element in a dispute is not a fixed quantity but depends on the parties' perceptions. The easiest disputes to resolve are those in which the states concerned agree about how the dispute is to be classified; the hardest are those where this is a matter of disagreement. Thus, the *Diplomatic Staff in Tehran* case[1] was not resolved by the International Court because only the United States was prepared to treat it as a legal dispute. Similarly, the *Korean Air Lines Flight 007 Incident*[2] was not amenable to inquiry because, despite appearances, the dispute was not about how a civilian aircraft came to be so far off course, but about the Soviet policy of shooting it down. It follows that, in the preliminary stages of a dispute, one of the main functions of negotiation is to establish an agreed classification of the dispute in order to decide the best way of handling it.

14.2.3 The Temporal Dimension

The final dimension which needs to be considered is time. Whether a disagreement becomes a dispute, which, if any, method of peaceful settlement is tried and whether, to the extent that such methods are used, they are successful, may all depend on when a dispute occurs. The political significance of a dispute within a state is also related to its timing and is conditioned by the style and traditions of its political leadership. Some British governments might not have gone to war over the Falklands, just as most Argentine governments would not have taken the risk of invasion. Similarly, some British governments would have avoided a crisis altogether by either negotiating a settlement of the dispute at an earlier stage, or ensuring that the islands were properly defended, just as many leaders in General Galtieri's position would have accepted the terms which were on

---

[1] *United States Diplomatic and Consular Staff in Tehran*, Judgment [1980] ICJ Rep. 3.
[2] See Chapter 5.

offer during the various attempts at mediation. That these alternatives can all be conceived without straining the imagination confirms that the war of 1982 was the result of a particular combination of unfavourable historical circumstances and thus underlines the significance of timing in determining the course of an international dispute.

If the timing of the Falklands crisis was unfortunate, time can sometimes have a beneficial effect by effectively removing the causes of a dispute. In 1973, for example, the United Kingdom challenged Iceland's extension of its exclusive fishing zone to fifty miles and took the dispute as far as the International Court. This was in line with a traditional policy of seeking to protect freedom of the seas which successive British governments had followed for many years. In 1975, however, when Iceland extended its claim to 200 miles, although there was an initial protest, the matter was not pursued. This was because an increasing number of states were now making such claims and, rather than maintain a futile rearguard action, the United Kingdom, together with the other members of the EEC, elected to make its own 200-mile claim.[3] Here, then, developments in state practice had legitimated actions which would formerly have been unacceptable. Time had eliminated a possible source of dispute. The old saying, 'when rain falls, water disputes turn to bubbles', makes the same point.

Sometimes, the time element is not concerned with an individual dispute but with a whole class of disputes. A particularly clear illustration of this may be seen today in Eastern Europe and Russia. At the end of the Second World War, Eastern Europe fell under the domination of the Soviet Union, with the result that normal political relations between the states of the region, including the promotion and defence of national interests, were effectively suspended. In 1989, however, as Soviet power retreated, these states were able to reassert their national sovereignty and rejoin the international political system. Similarly, with the break-up of the Soviet Union itself in 1991, an entirely new group of states with separate national interests came into being. These dramatic developments do not mean that, with so many new possibilities for public assertiveness, Eastern Europe and the Commonwealth of Independent States are bound to be torn apart by chauvinism and aggrandisement. But disputes, as we have seen, are a regular part of international politics. Consequently, in addition to many long-standing grievances which were masked by Soviet hegemony, these states must now deal with the differences with their neighbours and with other states which are a normal incident of independence.

---

[3] For an account of events following the 1974 judgment of the International Court, see C. Schulte, *Compliance with Decisions of the International Court of Justice*, Oxford, 2004, pp. 151–5.

14.3 A Legal Perspective

The relevance of law and legal institutions to the settlement of international disputes is a subject which has generated abundant and varied literature. To some, the answer to all the world's problems is to be found in legal codes and international tribunals. To others, observing the disregard for legality which is a feature of most international crises, law at best has a marginal role in world affairs, and at worst is a pious illusion. Although it is unnecessary to pursue this controversy here, legal methods bulk large in any discussion of peaceful means of settlement, and three chapters have already been devoted to outlining the main features of arbitration and judicial settlement. It may therefore be appropriate to identify a number of general considerations with a bearing on our theme. These will also be useful later, when we consider how the present legal means of settlement might be improved.

14.3.1 The Connection between Law and Adjudication

The first point to make is that the role of law and the role of adjudication are two issues, not one. While it is difficult to imagine adjudication without law, law without adjudication is actually the normal situation in international affairs. Even within states, this position is more common than is generally appreciated once the practical obstacles to litigation are taken into account. In international affairs, where even 'compulsory' jurisdiction is voluntary, law frequently stands alone, totally unsupported by institutional arrangements.

Is there any value in legal rules without procedures for adjudication? The answer is yes: first, because in practice where legal rules exist they are normally followed; and, second, because, although international disputes are generally resolved without adjudication, law will frequently play a significant part in defining the points in issue, and in providing a framework for negotiation, conciliation or the presentation of a state's case in a political forum. Law can, of course, also supply an acceptable vehicle for a settlement in the form of a treaty. To draw attention to the fact that international law is significant in practice is not to suggest that law is the key to international relations, nor that states live under the rule of law in the same sense as citizens within a state. Neither is it to imply that adjudication is irrelevant, or not worth improving. The point is simply that to appreciate the place of legal methods of settlement one must first be clear about the role of law.

14.3.2 The Nature and Characteristics of Adjudication

Turning now to adjudication, the most fruitful approach is perhaps to consider the special features of legal methods of settlement and to see how these govern their usefulness. This is a matter which can be analysed in different ways,[4] but for our purposes the following characteristics are particularly relevant.

Probably the most striking feature of adjudication is that it is dispositive. Because the decisions of courts and tribunals are treated as binding, litigation is a good way of disposing of a troublesome issue when the resolution of a dispute is considered to be more important than the result. Conversely, when the result is all-important, adjudication is unlikely to be used because it is simply too risky. These attitudes are reinforced by the fact that adjudication is not merely dispositive, but tends to produce a winner-takes-all type of solution. This can obviously render an unfavourable outcome a catastrophe and so encourages states to choose other procedures for disputes which they cannot afford to lose.

Because adjudication is dispositive, the attitude of states towards compulsory jurisdiction is conspicuously ambivalent. On the one hand, there is a good deal of support for the principle of the optional clause and similar arrangements, since the idea of establishing a binding system to resolve international disputes is an attractive one. On the other hand, as soon as such arrangements are established, states become aware of the risks involved in a commitment to litigate disputes which cannot be foreseen and begin to have second thoughts. The result, as we have seen, is a reluctance to subscribe to the more general arrangements for compulsory jurisdiction and a preference for agreements concerned either with particular types of cases or individual disputes.

A second characteristic of adjudication is that the binding decision is given by judges who are impartial. Looking to individuals who are neutral for assistance in settling disputes is by no means unique to adjudication and is also to be found in other third-party methods such as conciliation. In relation to adjudication, however, impartiality is not only by tradition a definitive feature, but also assumes a crucial importance owing to the consequences of the decision. While bias on the part of conciliators is no doubt regrettable, on the part of a court empowered to make a binding decision it is far more serious. However, an impartial process also offers great advantages. Referring a dispute to a court which is demonstrably impartial can be very useful when a government is anxious to settle a dispute, but is under pressure not to make concessions. As the decision is not the government's responsibility, then, provided it has been arrived at fairly, a strong case can be made for accepting it even if it is unfavourable.

---

[4] For excellent surveys of this issue, see R. B. Bilder, 'International dispute settlement and the role of adjudication', in L. F. Damrosch (ed.), *The International Court of Justice at a Crossroads*, New York, 1987, p. 155; and R. Y. Jennings, 'The proper work and purposes of the International Court of Justice', in A. S. Muller, D. Raic and J. M. Thuránszky (eds), *The International Court of Justice*, The Hague, 1997, p. 33.

Since international law is more controversial than domestic law, the international judge is more like a US Supreme Court justice, deciding a point of constitutional interpretation, than a domestic judge with a routine case. It follows that it may be better to ensure that a court as a whole represents a range of views rather than to expect each individual to be able to synthesise all approaches. Alternatively, states can seek to ensure that their cases are heard by judges whose general legal philosophy they accept. It will be recalled that both ways of dealing with the issue of impartiality are employed internationally: the first by the provision requiring the representation of 'the main forms of civilization' and 'the principal legal systems of the world' on the International Court for example, and the second by the control which states exercise over the composition of arbitral tribunals and the possibilities offered by chambers of the International Court and the Law of the Sea Tribunal.[5]

A further aspect of adjudication, bound up with the issue of impartiality and hinted at above, is that the resolution of disputes by legal means employs a special sort of justification. For the reference of a dispute to arbitration or to an international court or tribunal demonstrates more than a desire for an impartial decision. It also shows that the parties want a decision which can be justified in a particular way, in terms of rules or principles rather than expediency or the judges' whim. This requirement is the basis of many of the rules relating to the nullity of awards, including the rule that a judgment should be reasoned and that an arbitrator must follow instructions as regards the applicable law. Because it is founded on principles, adjudication supplies a way of settling disputes which is rational, orderly and authoritative. No doubt the rationality of the judicial process can be exaggerated, and no one who has ever been involved in litigation is likely to think of it as a bloodless procedure. It is nevertheless true that, as methods of dealing with serious and sensitive issues go, adjudication is as rational a process as fallible mortals can make it.

The orderly quality of adjudication has been well described as follows:

> The well-established structure of the adjudicative process provides a framework for the orderly presentation and development of the opposing arguments concerning the dispute. Where complex and difficult factual and technical questions are involved – as may be the case, for example, in land or maritime boundary disputes – the adjudicative process may facilitate a more orderly and thorough examination of the issues than might otherwise be the case. Adjudication also typically requires at least some contact and co-operation between the parties. At the least, this may lead to a more thorough examination of the issues by each party and a fairer disposition of the controversy. Conceivably, it may lead to a

---

[5] See further T. M. Franck, *Fairness in International Law and Institutions*, Oxford, 1995, ch. 10.

better understanding by the parties themselves of the respective merits of each other's positions concerning the issue in dispute, and to their own negotiation of a settlement.[6]

Adjudication is authoritative because the decision is reasoned and the jurisdiction of the tribunal has been accepted by the parties. It is therefore vital to ensure that these conditions are maintained. In the last analysis, authority depends on substantive, not formal, considerations, and so a decision which is not convincingly reasoned or is handed down in circumstances where there is reason to doubt whether jurisdiction has been accepted will lack authority in the eyes of the parties, whatever the status or reputation of the tribunal. In the same way, one of the advantages of adjudication is that the decision legitimates the successful party's claim in the view of the international community more generally and not only the opposing party. However, this will only be achieved if the court pays scrupulous attention to the demands of its role. For it is not the fact of obtaining judgment which vindicates a claim, so much as the reasoning by which the decision is supported.

14.3.3 The Impact of Decisions

Judgments based on principles cannot avoid having an impact as precedents, and this feature of the judicial process has both advantages and disadvantages. The advantage is that it enables the settlement of individual disputes to make a contribution to the development of international law. This is especially significant on issues such as human rights, where abstract principles require concrete application, and the law relating to evidence, jurisdiction and procedure, where the formulation of principles by tribunals is of direct assistance to adjudication. The disadvantage is that states are sometimes anxious for a dispute to be resolved in a way which will not prejudice their position in other disputes. In such a situation, they are likely to regard adjudication as much less attractive than methods such as negotiation or conciliation, where the precedential effect of the outcome can be minimised.

A further aspect of adjudication, related to its precedential significance, is that this method of resolving disputes tends to be conservative. This is because law itself is conservative, resting as it does on principles to be found in past practice and, in a broader way, because the purpose of adjudication is to decide disputes by reference to certain criteria which qualify as legal, while excluding others which, however much a part of the dispute, do not. The conservative element in law makes adjudication attractive in any situation where there is broad agreement about the

---

[6] Bilder, 'International dispute settlement' (n. 4) p. 165.

relevant law and resolution of the dispute is a matter of establishing who has the better case. It is totally unsuitable for disputes in which there is a fundamental disagreement about what the law is, or should be. The parties to a dispute can, of course, counteract the conservatism of the law by providing their own directive to the tribunal, and adjudication, as we have noted, is flexible enough to respond to such initiatives. Moreover, law itself is far from inflexible and is always being adapted to new situations. Adjudication, however, is not a free-ranging legislative operation and so is unlikely to be effective in settling disputes where the adequacy of the law is the central issue.

The same conclusion can be drawn where the parties classify a dispute in completely different ways. The question here is not whether a legal tribunal is competent, which will depend on technical considerations of admissibility and jurisdiction, but rather whether a legal decision can contribute anything to the solution of a dispute. In the *Diplomatic Staff in Tehran* case, as was mentioned earlier, the United States emphasised the legal aspects of the dispute, whereas Iran saw it as part of a wider political issue. In the *Nicaragua* case,[7] it was the United States which defined the dispute politically and Nicaragua which sought a legal judgment. In both cases, the International Court, having held that it had jurisdiction, proceeded to examine the case within the legal framework relied on by the applicant. As a legal tribunal it was right to do so. However, although the judgments in these cases were not without effect, no one expected them to resolve the underlying disputes and they did not do so. Adjudication by its nature is well suited to dealing with the legal aspect of disputes; for disputes which raise other issues, however, different methods are needed, as was discussed in the first chapter.

14.3.4 Adjudication and Multilateral Disputes

The last feature of adjudication which merits attention was thrown into prominence in one of the cases which have just been mentioned. It will be recalled that one of the arguments of the United States in the *Nicaragua* case related to the absence from the proceedings of certain third parties whose presence was said to be indispensable. Similarly, it will be recalled that various cases have posed the question of when a third state can intervene in the Court, and, as noted in Chapter 8, in 1990 this question was raised in relation to proceedings before a chamber.[8] What these cases

---

[7] *Military and Paramilitary Activities in and against Nicaragua*, Jurisdiction and Admissibility, Judgment [1984] ICJ Rep. 392. For discussion, see Chapters 6 and 7.

[8] See *Land, Island and Maritime Frontier Dispute (El Salvador/Honduras)*, Application to Intervene, Order of 28 February 1990 and Judgment [1990] ICJ Rep. 3 and 92.

have in common is that, in different ways, they all present problems which concern the position of third parties in international litigation.

It is clear from the history of arbitration and judicial settlement that because international adjudication is consensual it works best for bilateral disputes and not so well for multilateral disputes. When a case involves the interests of a third state, there are two difficulties. The first, exemplified by the *Monetary Gold* case,[9] is the problem of the third state whose rights are in issue but which does not wish to litigate; the second, raised by the cases on intervention, is the third state which does wish to litigate, but whose presence is objected to by the main parties. In both situations, the root of the problem is that a bilateral procedure is being employed for what are effectively multilateral disputes and that reconciling the interests of the parties with those of the third state is a virtually impossible task.

In the first situation, too much protection for the third state will prevent the states which are present from obtaining a decision. This no doubt accounts for the International Court's rejection of the American argument in the *Nicaragua* case. In the second situation, admitting the would-be intervenor may cause the original parties to withdraw the case, preferring to settle the matter outside the courtroom, rather than defend a flank against a third party. This probably explains the Court's restrictive stand on intervention. The treatment of both issues is open to criticism, but it is as well to recognise that no answer to this problem is wholly satisfactory because the real difficulty is with the attitudes of states. If all the states concerned are prepared to resolve a dispute by adjudication, the procedures exist for enabling them to do so. If, on the other hand, some of them are not, no amount of tinkering with rules can transcend the practical limitations of adjudication.

14.4 Improving the Capacity of Political Methods and International Organisations

The Charter of the United Nations, as critics of the Organization never fail to point out, was intended to put the conduct of international relations on a new footing. It is therefore part of a tradition which includes the League Covenant and the various schemes for a new world order put forward by thinkers before 1945 and subsequently. Clearly, the UN has not worked; or, to be more accurate, it does not work in the way that a reading of the Charter suggests that it should. It is nevertheless by far the most important international political organisation and, as we have seen, is often in a

---

[9] *Monetary Gold Removed from Rome in 1943*, Judgment [1954] ICJ Rep. 19. For discussion of this case and its subsequent interpretation, see Chapter 6. For a review of the general issue, see L. F. Damrosch, 'Multilateral disputes', in L. F. Damrosch (ed.), *The International Court of Justice at a Crossroads*, New York, 1987, p. 376.

position to contribute to the resolution of disputes. It is therefore an appropriate focus when thinking about improvements in political means of settlement.

14.4.1 The United Nations Security Council

The first suggestions for change relate to the Security Council. It will be recalled that under the Charter, the Security Council has the primary responsibility for maintaining international peace and security and dealing with disputes, and for these purposes is equipped with extensive powers under Chapters VI and VII. In the Cold War era between 1946 and 1989, little use could be made of Chapter VII, and, although some initiatives were possible under Chapter VI, there too the scope for initiatives was severely constrained. In recent years, with greater co-operation among the Permanent Members, the situation has changed and the Security Council has been much more active. While there is still a tendency to neglect disputes until they become critical, and although preventive measures are rarely considered, cases which reach the Security Council now often receive a positive response. However, as the Security Council has become more active, especially in employing Chapter VII, questions have been raised about its authority which have yet to be satisfactorily answered.

An organ which acts on behalf of the international community, which can authorise the use of force, set up peacekeeping forces and take other far-reaching measures must, if its actions are to be regarded as legitimate, be adequately representative. When the United Nations was founded, it had about fifty members, and nine were represented on the Security Council. Since the membership is now nearly 200 and the Security Council is a mere fifteen, the problem here is plain. The composition of the Security Council has been extensively discussed, but the outcome remains to be seen.[10]

Changing the composition of the Security Council or redefining its powers would each be significant institutional developments, and are therefore difficult. There are, however, steps which could be taken now to enhance the Council's authority because the way it takes its decisions and the decisions themselves also have a bearing on the issue of legitimacy. As regards the decisions which are taken, while the merits of this or that Resolution can be debated, the general point is that, if the Security Council

---

[10] See further A. Parsons, 'The United Nations in the post-Cold War era' (1992) 11 *Int. Rel.*, 189; P. Wilenski, 'The structure of the UN in the post-Cold War period' in A. Roberts and B. Kingsbury (eds), *United Nations, Divided World*, 2nd ed., Oxford, 1993, p. 437; and L. Willson, 'Changing the Charter: the United Nations prepares for the twenty-first century' (1996) 90 *AJIL*, 115. See also K. A. Mingst and M. P. Karns, *The United Nations in the Post-Cold War Era*, 2nd ed., Boulder, CO, 2000, pp. 202–5; and Y. Z. Blum, 'Proposals for UN Security Council reform' (2005) 99 *AJIL* 632.

is to be respected, it must be seen to act fairly.[11] As regards the way decisions are taken, the need is for the Council to operate with greater transparency and to consult more widely with the membership.[12] This is more than a matter of presentation, for, as Secretary-General Boutros-Ghali observed in 1992, 'agreement among the Permanent Members must have the deeper support of the other members of the Council, and the membership more widely, if the Council's decisions are to be effective and endure'.[13] Recognising this point, the Security Council has already introduced a number of changes in its working methods and procedure,[14] but further attention to these matters is needed.

14.4.2 The United Nations Secretary-General

Another possible area for change is the Secretariat. Although reform of the Security Council is important, whatever changes are made there, the good offices work of the Secretary-General is likely to remain the United Nations' most practical contribution in many dispute situations. Secessionist conflicts, for example, or civil wars within states, have increased in recent years, but for various reasons the Security Council has often been slow to act. If, therefore, there is to be UN involvement at an early stage, the Secretary-General may have to provide the response. There are, however, a number of ways in which the potential of the office could be improved.[15] Some of the proposed changes are concerned with the resources which are available to do the job; others are related to the job itself.

Improving the Secretary-General's resources is partly a matter of ensuring that, when an opportunity occurs to promote the settlement of a dispute, lack of available funds is not a significant constraint. Resources, however, are not just a matter of money. If action is to be effective, there is a need for information and individuals who can process it and decide what should be done. Here, also, improvements can be suggested. A previous Secretary-General has drawn attention to the fact that the position of the UN is much inferior to that of its member states and indeed most

---

[11] See Franck, *Fairness in International Law* (n. 5) ch. 7.
[12] See F. L. Kirgis, 'The Security Council's first fifty years' (1995) 89 *AJIL*, 506 at 518–19; and C. Peck, *The United Nations as a Dispute Settlement System*, The Hague, 1996, p. 219.
[13] B. Boutros-Ghali, *An Agenda for Peace*, SC Doc. S/24111, 17 June 1992, para. 78. Text in (1992) 31 ILM 953.
[14] See M. C. Wood, 'Security Council working methods and procedure: recent developments' (1996) 45 *ICLQ*, 150. Also J. K. Cogan, 'Stabilization and the expanding scope of the Security Council's work' (2015) 109 *AJIL*, 324.
[15] See also Wilenski, 'The structure of the UN' (n. 10) pp. 449–56; and S. Chesterman (ed.), *Secretary or General? The UN Secretary-General in World Politics*, Cambridge, 2007, Part IV.

transnational corporations.[16] In an attempt to improve the information flow and facilitate preventive diplomacy, various changes have been made in the internal organisation of the Secretariat. However, problems have been encountered in relation to two matters.[17] One is the need to integrate the work of those who gather and analyse information with the activities of those in the Secretariat who decide what action, if any, should be taken in response. The other is the difficulty of maintaining staffing and providing essential resources in the face of frequent cost-cutting and downsizing. While the responsiveness problem is essentially organisational and bureaucratic, the resource issue is ultimately the responsibility of the member states, specifically the major contributors, who, if they wish the UN to have the capacity to provide early warning, must be prepared to pay for it.

Finally, it was pointed out in Chapter 12 that the Secretariat does not work in isolation, but as an integral part of the whole United Nations system. This is relevant to the issue of reform when the contribution of the Secretary-General to the prevention and settlement of disputes is seen in relation to the work of the Security Council. The latter, as we have noted, tends to find itself dealing with disputes late in the day and should be prepared to intervene earlier. It has to be said, however, that the Secretariat, which has generally been reluctant to exercise its power to bring issues to the Council under Article 99, cannot escape all responsibility for this state of affairs. The fact that the Secretary-General has been very active in performing a good offices function is, no doubt, some compensation for this deficiency, but the Secretariat could make an even greater contribution to the effectiveness of the Charter system by ensuring that the members of the Security Council are aware of potential disputes at an early stage and, where necessary, by placing the matter on its agenda.

In relation to the question of peacekeeping mandates, we saw in Chapter 12 that peacekeeping operations can take many forms and that confusion over the nature of a mission, or the related phenomenon of 'mission creep' (i.e. the expansion of a mission's mandate through force of circumstances after it has begun) are highly undesirable. The Brahimi Report, reflecting experience with peacekeeping in Somalia, Rwanda and the former Yugoslavia over the previous decade, emphasised the need for clear, credible and achievable mandates, and its recommendations to that effect have been accepted by the Security Council.[18] For such a policy to be

---

[16] J. Pérez de Cuéllar, 'The role of the UN Secretary-General', in A. Roberts and B. Kingsbury (eds), *United Nations, Divided World*, 2nd ed., Oxford, 1993, p. 124 at p. 136.

[17] See C. Peck, *Sustainable Peace*, Lanham, MD, 1998, pp. 71–5. For earlier efforts, see B. G. Ramcharan, *The International Law and Practice of Early-Warning and Preventive Diplomacy: The Emerging Global Watch*, Dordrecht, 1991, chs. 2 and 4; and Peck, *The United Nations* (n. 12) ch. 7.

[18] In Resolution 1327 (2000). See Security Council Resolution 1327 (2000), text in (2001) 40 ILM 503 and C. Gray, *International Law and the Use of Force*, 2nd ed., Oxford, 2004, p. 243.

effective, however, it will be necessary either to develop a broader resource base for peacekeeping operations, or for the Security Council to limit its ambitions. Either way, ensuring that UN peacekeeping always has a clear, credible and achievable mandate is another way in which it can be improved.

14.4.3 Regional Organisations

Although the focus here has been on the United Nations system, this is not intended to suggest that the traditional diplomatic means for handling disputes cannot be improved, nor that the record of regional organisations is completely satisfactory. In relation to the latter, however, it is unnecessary to add to the general comments of the previous chapter, and proposals concerning specific organisations may be found elsewhere. As regards other political procedures, perhaps the point which emerges most clearly is the need to encourage consultation both as an informal practice and, where appropriate, in an institutional setting. This could be done by, for example, making its advantages more widely known and ensuring that states with little experience of its benefits are provided with examples of good practice and help in setting up their own arrangements. While the record demonstrates that states are reluctant to restrict their prerogatives, there are many situations where consultation, when once established, is an excellent way of promoting and protecting interests. This being so, it is reasonable to suppose that a wider dissemination of information, accompanied by practical assistance, might increase its use significantly.

14.5 Improving the Capacity of Legal Methods

Reform of the legal methods for handling disputes has been a subject of concern to those with an interest in international affairs from the earliest days of arbitration. The creation of the Permanent Court in 1919 and its successor, the present International Court, far from propitiating the advocates of change, made adjudication the focus of even greater attention. As a result, everything done by international judges and arbitrators is now studied, analysed and criticised in minute detail and the would-be reformer is presented with an almost embarrassing wealth of suggestions.

This is, of course, excellent because it indicates that the ideals which animated the pioneers of adjudication are still alive, and, pragmatically, because informed criticism is indispensable if institutions are to retain their relevance and improve. On the other hand, though the reform of legal institutions is no less important than that of political institutions, here, as with the proposals we have just been considering, suggestions which ignore the constraints within which legal and political arrangements operate are not at all helpful. Into this category, for example, fall proposals for making adherence to the optional clause compulsory, or prohibiting reservations to states' acceptances, because these treat problems which are a reflection of the political context of adjudication as though they were merely technical. What is needed is not prescriptions for an ideal world, but practical proposals. The following, though not exhaustive, are thought to fulfil this requirement.

14.5.1 The Costs of Adjudication

The first improvement is already being implemented. It is to make litigation more attractive to states by reducing its cost.[19] In 1989, the UN Secretary-General announced that he was setting up a Trust Fund to assist states in settling their disputes through the International Court.[20] Stating that he saw himself as having a special responsibility to promote judicial settlement, the Secretary-General indicated that the object of the Fund is to assist states which are prevented from using the Court by either lack of legal expertise or lack of money. Initially two categories of cases would be considered eligible for assistance: first, cases where there is a joint agreement to submit a dispute to the Court and consequently no question of disputed jurisdiction; second, cases where the parties are ready to implement a judgment which has already been given, but one or both are unable to do so on account of a lack of funds or expertise.

Administration of the Fund is the responsibility of a panel of experts whose task is to examine each application and make recommendations regarding the sums to be awarded and the expenses to be covered. The latter may include 'counsel fees, the costs of translation and interpretation, [and] expenses for producing cartographic materials', as well as costs relating to the execution of a judgment such as the demarcation of boundaries. The panel to consider each application consists of three persons 'of the highest judicial and moral standing', who work in strict confidentiality and must 'be guided solely by the financial needs of the requesting State and the availability of the funds'. The Fund is not part of the regular UN budget but is financed by voluntary contributors who can include individuals, national and international organisations and corporations, as well as states. More than fifty states initially made significant contributions to the Fund, and others indicated that they would be prepared to offer support in response

---

[19] See generally: B. McGarry, 'Achieving greater access to justice through cost-efficiency: a comparative assessment across state-to-state dispute settlement institutions', in E. De Brabandere (ed.), *International Procedure in Interstate Litigation and Arbitration: A Comparative Perspective*, Cambridge, 2021.

[20] Text in (1989) 28 ILM 1584. For a contemporary reaction, see T. Bien-Aime, 'A pathway to the Hague and beyond: the United Nations Trust Fund proposal' (1991) 22 *NYUJ Int. L. and Politics*, 671.

to particular applications.[21] The sums involved are not large, but it has been possible to provide assistance in several cases, an early beneficiary being Chad, which was given help in the *Territorial Dispute* case.[22]

Following the above example, a number of other courts and tribunals have made arrangements to provide prospective litigants with financial assistance.[23] The Permanent Court of Arbitration has set up a Financial Assistance Fund for this purpose, and the Secretariat of the World Trade Organization has been authorised to provide technical and legal assistance to developing member states for cases being dealt with through the procedures described in Chapter 9. One of the latest organs to benefit from an arrangement of this kind is the International Tribunal for the Law of the Sea, for which the UN General Assembly established a Trust Fund by resolution in 2000. The Fund is administered by the Secretary-General and is similar in many respects to that already available for the International Court. There are, however, also some significant differences; for example, there is no need for a special agreement between the litigants.[24] The creation of these new sources of assistance is an imaginative way of encouraging adjudication and as such is to be welcomed. What is required now is for those who approve of these measures in principle to continue supporting them financially.

14.5.2 Preserving the Integrity of the Judicial and Arbitral Process

The second issue concerns a matter which until recently had received relatively little attention, namely the question of fraud in international litigation and the wider issue of preserving the integrity of the judicial process.[25] In the *Maritime Delimitation and Territorial Questions* case,[26] a significant quantity of documentary evidence which Qatar had put forward to support its case was challenged as fraudulent by Bahrain. Following exchanges between the parties, Qatar announced that it would no longer

---

[21] See P. H. F. Bekker, 'International legal aid in practice: the ICJ Trust Fund' (1993) 87 *AJIL*, 659. See also A. Eyffinger, *The International Court of Justice 1946–1996*, The Hague, 1996, pp. 365–6.

[22] *Territorial Dispute (Libyan Arab Jamahiriya/Chad)*, Judgment [1994] ICJ Rep. 6. During the oral proceedings, the Agent of Chad revealed that help had been received: see Bekker, 'International legal aid' (n. 21) 666, n. 45.

[23] See D. Anderson, 'Trust funds in international litigation', in N. Ando, E. McWhinney and R. Wolfrum (eds), *Liber Amicorum Judge Shigeru Oda*, The Hague, 2002, p. 793.

[24] Similarly, although the main aim of the new Fund is to provide assistance for proceedings on the merits, where jurisdiction is not an issue, 'in exceptional circumstances' assistance can be provided for any phase of the proceedings. For further discussion, see Anderson, 'Trust funds in international litigation' (n. 23) pp. 801–3.

[25] See W. M. Reisman and C. P. Skinner, *Fraudulent Evidence before Public International Tribunals*, Cambridge, 2014.

[26] *Maritime Delimitation and Territorial Questions between Qatar and Bahrain*, Judgment [2001] ICJ Rep. 40. For discussion of the contested documents, see M. Mendelson, 'The curious case of Qatar v. Bahrain in the International Court of Justice' (2001) 72 *BYBIL*, 183 at 197–201.

rely on the documents, with the result that the International Court was never called upon to examine the documents' authenticity. Nevertheless, it is evident that this was an unscrupulous attempt to deceive the Court which was only averted by Bahrain's diligence. Unfortunately, this is by no means the only attempt to mislead courts and tribunals in recent years and analogous problems have been encountered when enterprises have sought to invoke investment protection arrangements after themselves engaging in bribery and other unwholesome practices.[27]

A lesson which might be drawn from the *Qatar/Bahrain* case is that since Qatar was allowed to replead its case without penalty when the fraud was discovered, putting forward false evidence is something of a win/win situation for the errant state. This seems completely wrong, but dealing with it is not a simple matter. International courts and tribunals are not well equipped to investigate allegations of fraud, the range of potentially reprehensible conduct is wide and varies in gravity, while proving fraud in a given case may be very difficult. Moreover, since accusing another government of fraud is a serious matter, the accuser must be sure of its case. In addition, there is what one commentator has termed 'the temptation to find excuses in *la raison d'État*',[28] that is, to excuse the use of illicit means on the grounds that the perpetrators are pursuing a public, not a private objective. In relation to fraud by foreign investors, the issue is further complicated by the fact that bribery and corruption of public officials by the investor also inevitably implicates the respondent.

As regards wider threats to the integrity of the judicial process, concerns that come to mind include frivolous challenges to the qualifications of judges and arbitrators, noted earlier in Chapter 7, and repudiation of judicial decisions and orders, despite jurisdiction having been previously accepted. The second problem is hardly new, but threatens to undermine the new systems of compulsory jurisdiction laid down in the Law of the Sea Convention and elsewhere. In 2013, for example, Russia rejected the provisional measures of protection ordered by ITLOS in the *Arctic Sunrise* case.[29] Article 9 of Annex VII UNCLOS anticipates the possibility of one of the parties not participating in the proceedings and confirms that non-participation does not preclude the conduct of proceedings. However, in 2015 China refused to recognise the decision on jurisdiction given by an Annex VII tribunal in the *South China Sea* arbitration.[30] We also saw that in that case, the Tribunal did take measures to ensure procedural fairness

---

[27] See A. P. Llamzon, *Corruption in International Investment Arbitration*, Oxford, 2014.
[28] J. Paulsson, 'Review' (2015) 62 *Neth. Int. L. Rev.*, 513 at 515.
[29] '*Arctic Sunrise*' *(Kingdom of the Netherlands v. Russian Federation)*, Provisional Measures, Order of 22 November 2013 [2013] ITLOS Reports 230. In its Award in 2015, the Annex VII Arbitral Tribunal held that Russia's failure to comply with the Order has breached its obligations towards the Netherlands.
[30] *Arbitration between the Republic of the Philippines and the Peoples' Republic of China* (2015).

between the parties by referring to arguments which China had raised outside the proceedings. Not to be overlooked too is Australia's brazen attempt to interfere with Timor-Leste's communications with its legal adviser which prompted the *Questions relating to the Seizure and Detention of Certain Documents* case[31] of 2014.

Of course, the above episodes do not constitute a single problem and by the same token may require different solutions. Nevertheless, each in its own way suggests that if adjudication is to play its proper role, threats to its integrity of all kinds need to be taken seriously. Solutions to these types of problems, like many challenges in international law and relations, are essentially in the hands of governments, for whom the game of litigation performs a valuable function. Unless, however, they are prepared to approach it honestly and in good faith, they may wake up one day and find they no longer have a game to play.

14.5.3 The Quality of Decisions and Awards

The next issue is more traditional. It is the contribution which can be made to the Court's efficacy by the quality of its judgments. Good judgments help to develop and maintain confidence in the Court by giving users of adjudication the kinds of results they are entitled to expect. Poor judgments have the opposite effect. What constitutes a good judgment? The fact that a decision is criticised, or even that a state refuses to carry it out, are not in themselves reasons for regarding a judgment as defective. In a case of any complexity, it will usually be possible to justify more than one conclusion and so the critic can almost always find something to object to. Equally, there will always be bad losers, and consequently the rejection of a decision by a state may be no more than a sign that the Court has done what it is supposed to do and has applied the law without fear or favour. The criticisms which matter are those which question whether the Court is adequately discharging its function and here, it is suggested, there may be scope for improvement.

The essential purpose of adjudication is to resolve disputes by reference to law, or, where this is authorised, on some other basis. This requires a reasoned decision which addresses the arguments put forward by the parties and explains the Court's conclusion. It follows that judgments which are inconsistent, inadequately reasoned, based on points not raised in argument, or which evade crucial issues, are defective. The point is not that better judgments will increase the readiness of states to use adjudication, which seems unlikely, nor even that better judgments will mean that cases will have different results, though no doubt this will sometimes

---

[31] See Chapter 6.

happen. The point is rather that, as a technique for dealing with international disputes, adjudication has properties which are uniquely valuable, but to survive requires practitioners both willing and able to preserve its integrity.

14.5.4 The Multiplication of International Courts and Tribunals

This leads to a related point concerning the multiplication of international tribunals and its consequences.[32] Far more judicial bodies exist today than was once the case, and the number is constantly increasing. Thus, as already noted, recent decades have seen the creation of the International Criminal Tribunals for the Former Yugoslavia (1993) and for Rwanda (1994), the World Trade Organization's Appellate Body (1995) and the International Tribunal for the Law of the Sea (1996). This proliferation poses two challenges, one procedural and one substantive. The procedural challenge is to establish priorities, given that in some situations more than one tribunal may have jurisdiction and that views may differ as to how a dispute should be handled. The substantive challenge is to ensure that, when different tribunals are dealing with similar legal issues, their decisions are consistent.

It is not possible to deal fully with this complex matter here, but thinking about it will be easier if several distinct issues of legal policy are separated. The first of these is the factors to be taken into account when proposals are being considered to set up a new tribunal. It would be absurd to establish bodies to duplicate the work of existing tribunals, but it would be equally absurd to believe that our present range of tribunals can supply all that will ever be needed. It is only necessary to consider the four tribunals mentioned in the previous paragraph to appreciate that new bodies will always be required when there are demands which for one reason or another cannot be met by existing arrangements. A proliferation of tribunals in itself is therefore neither good nor bad. Everything depends on their justification.

A second issue of policy concerns the jurisdiction of the new courts and tribunals, more specifically how they interpret and apply their powers when these are challenged. The Law of the Sea Convention, the WTO Agreement and similar treaties, as we have seen, create elaborate systems of essentially compulsory jurisdiction over most disputes relating to their subject matter. When a dispute involving the treaty arises, it is therefore

---

[32] See E. Lauterpacht, *Aspects of the Administration of International Justice*, Cambridge, 1991, ch. 2; and G. Guillaume, 'The future of international judicial institutions' (1995) 44 *ICLQ*, 848. See also the essays by H. Caminos and others in N. Ando, E. McWhinney and R. Wolfrum (eds), *Liber Amicorum Judge Shigeru Oda*, The Hague, 2002, pp. 569–667; and Y. Shany, *The Competing Jurisdictions of International Courts and Tribunals*, Oxford, 2003.

necessary to decide whether it is one falling within the system, if the point is contentious, as happened, for example, in the *Southern Bluefin Tuna* case,[33] where an Annex VII arbitral tribunal decided that it did not have jurisdiction over the case brought by Australia and New Zealand against Japan. How questions of this kind are resolved is plainly crucial if attempts to extend compulsory jurisdiction and make it effective in practice are to succeed. Accordingly, while the limits of states' commitments must be respected, it is also important for new courts and tribunals to avoid jurisdictional decisions that are too restrictive.[34]

A third issue of policy concerns the problem of priorities which may arise when more than one court or tribunal has jurisdiction over a dispute. This situation is unavoidable as networks of compulsory jurisdiction multiply, and there can be no objection in principle to separate aspects of a dispute being addressed by different tribunals.[35] However, matters become more complicated when different tribunals are asked to deal with similar questions, leading to the possibility of conflicting decisions.[36] Although in one sense a procedural problem, this has substantive aspects since it may involve conflicting treaty obligations, for example where trade and environmental treaties relate to the same activities, as well as procedural concepts such as *res judicata* and litispendence. As there is no hierarchy of international courts, these questions are currently resolved in an ad hoc manner by the tribunals concerned,[37] and, as there seems no prospect of establishing such a hierarchy, this will probably continue for the foreseeable future. It would, however, be useful if thought could be given to codifying the relevant rules and principles of international law in

---

[33] *Southern Bluefin Tuna Case (Australia and New Zealand v. Japan)*, Award on Jurisdiction and Admissibility (2000), text in (2000) 39 ILM 1359; and see A. E. Boyle, Note (2001) 50 *ICLQ*, 447.

[34] It is instructive to compare the restrictive approach adopted by the tribunal in the *Southern Bluefin Tuna* case with the broader view favoured by its counterpart in the *MOX Plant* case (2003). For discussion of this point, see R. R. Churchill and J. Scott, 'The MOX Plant litigation: the first half-life' (2004) 53 *ICLQ*, 643 at 652–7.

[35] In the *MOX Plant* dispute, for example, the question of access to information was dealt with by means of an arbitration in 2003 under the OSPAR Convention. On those proceedings, see Churchill and Scott, 'The MOX Plant litigation' (n. 34) 645–7.

[36] For example, in the *Swordfish* case, mentioned in Chapter 8, the EC submitted elements of the dispute to WTO procedures, but Chile initially invoked Annex VII arbitration under the Law of the Sea Convention. See A. Serdy, 'See you in port' (2002) 3 *Melbourne JIL*, 79; and Churchill and Scott, 'The MOX Plant litigation' (n. 34) 654.

[37] See, for example, the tribunal's suspension of proceedings in the *MOX Plant* case in 2003, pending clarification of certain jurisdictional issues by the European Court of Justice. On this aspect of the case, see Churchill and Scott, 'The MOX Plant litigation' (n. 34) 647–52. On the general issue see M. A. Young, *Regime Interaction in International Law*, Cambridge, 2012; D. Pulkowski, *The Law and Politics of International Regime Conflict*, Oxford, 2014; L. E. Salles, *Forum Shopping in International Adjudication: The Role of Preliminary Objections*, Cambridge, 2014; and Y. Shany, *Questions of Jurisdiction and Admissibility before International Courts*, Cambridge, 2016.

this area and perhaps developing them by reference to the treatment of similar questions in national law.

14.5.5 The Relationship between Adjudication and the Other Processes

This leads to a more general policy issue which concerns the relationship between adjudication and the other processes of international relations. If we think of adjudication as simply a way of resolving a dispute for the benefit of the parties, we miss the crucial link between the decision of a court or tribunal and the context in which it occurs. As a leading scholar has explained, the fact that a dispute can be resolved by adjudication does not mean that the decision of a court or tribunal is the best way of doing so.[38] Indeed, referring certain types of disputes to adjudication, although something the parties are entitled to do, may mask, or even impede the resolution of wider issues. Where this is so, the key point is not that the parties should be discouraged from litigating, which may be quite impractical, but rather that the underlying problem should be addressed elsewhere, and that the adjudicator's decision should be sensitive to this.

A good illustration of this limitation of adjudication may be seen in the situation when the law is changing. To confirm the old law in such a case may be technically correct, but is likely to slow the emergence of new law, as well as making the judges seem out of touch. As we saw in Chapter 9, when faced with this dilemma in the *Fisheries Jurisdiction* case, the International Court's ingenious solution was to decide the case on a narrow point, and to omit discussion of fishing rights under customary law. The same limitation of litigation can be seen in cases which raise the question of the relation between different international tribunals, mentioned above. Further examples are the type of case that arises from a political impasse such as the *Diplomatic Staff in Tehran* case,[39] where a judicial decision is unlikely to solve the problem, or where, on account of its effect, the correct legal decision may have completely impractical consequences.[40] In all of these situations the blunt instrument of litigation may need tempering by the adoption of suitable measures in other forums.

14.5.6 The Role of Adjudication in International Society

Thus a final suggestion is directed not to judges and arbitrators but to the states which they exist to serve. Because adjudication is primarily a matter

---

[38] See V. Lowe, 'The function of litigation in international society' (2012) 61 *ICLQ*, 209. Also N. Klein (ed.), *Litigating International Disputes*, Cambridge, 2014.
[39] See Chapter 7.
[40] See, for example, the *Marckx* case, ECHR, Series A, No. 31, para. 58 (decision on inheritance rights held not to be retrospective).

of applying rules to facts, the future of courts and tribunals is intimately linked with that of the law itself. As a leading commentator puts it: 'Settling disputes is not just about "settling disputes". It is also about how issues are addressed, regulated and engaged with. It is about *how* law is generated, about *what* law is generated and about the manner in which it is engaged with and responded to.'[41] To be sure, it is wrong to think of adjudication as a mechanical process, to deny the significance of judicial creativity[42] or to ignore the functions which various non-legal criteria can perform. Nor is it true that the creation of new rules of international law is in itself a guarantee that they will be used to settle international disputes. All that having been said, however, adjudication needs a basis in law and the responsibility for developing new law lies not with judges but with states.

To the extent that states discharge their responsibility by taking the difficult political decisions which are needed to formulate new legal principles, they strengthen the process of adjudication by providing courts and tribunals with a legitimate basis for their decisions. On the other hand, if they avoid their responsibility, the task of the international judge becomes immeasurably more difficult and perhaps even impossible. This is not because adjudicators lack the skill to produce solutions to international problems, but because it is unreasonable to expect them to do so alone. If adjudication is to work, there must first be a substantial measure of agreement on the rules of decision. For it is this agreement which, if a judgment is also competent technically, makes a ruling legitimate. Thus, a commitment to the progressive development of international law offers both a way of bringing the conduct of international politics within a legal framework and real support for the process of adjudication.

14.6 Conclusion

The peaceful settlement of international disputes is the most critical issue of our time. Although human rights, the environment, climate change,[43] and economic and financial issues, among other matters, present challenges which must be addressed if our planet is to have a future, the problems which these subjects pose are always going to generate an abundance of international disputes. However, the use of force in certain disputes could result in the destruction of civilisation. Even without such nuclear nightmares, it is clear that the destructiveness of modern warfare is

---

[41] M. D. Evans, 'Foreword', in D. French, M. Saul and N. D. White (eds), *International Law and Dispute Settlement: New Problems and Techniques*, Oxford, 2010, p. viii (emphasis in original).

[42] See generally A. von Bogdandy and I. Venzke, 'In whose name? An investigation of international courts' public authority and its democratic justification' (2012) 23 *European Journal of International Law*, 7–41.

[43] See M. Wewerinke-Singh, *State Responsibility, Climate Change and Human Rights under International Law*, Oxford, 2019.

such as to inflict suffering on an unprecedented scale. And, leaving aside for a moment the terrible risks associated with force, for states, as for individuals, a persistent failure to resolve disputes leads only to wasted effort and antagonism.

In this book, we have tried to show how the intelligence and resourcefulness that have produced contemporary weapons have also developed methods of dispute settlement that can make the use of force unnecessary. To suppose that a time will come when all international disputes are resolved by peaceful means is perhaps unrealistic. Yet the present situation can and must be improved. The tools are already to hand. Now, more than ever, it is the responsibility of leaders, advisers and citizens to see that they are used.

14.7 Further Reading

Alvarez, J., 'The new dispute settlers: (half) truths and consequences', (2003) 38 *Texas International Law Journal*, 405–44.

De Brabandere, E., 'Non-State Actors and the Individualization and Proliferation of International Dispute Settlement', in Bob Reinalda (ed.), *The Ashgate Research Companion to Non-State Actors*, Farnham, 2011, pp. 347–59.

Giorgetti, C., 'Horizontal and vertical relationships of international courts and tribunals – how do we address their competing jurisdiction?' (2015) 30 *ICSID Review*, 98.

Jayakumar, S., R. L. Beckman and T. Koh, *The South China Sea Arbitration: The Legal Dimension*, Massachusetts, 2018.

Keohane, R. O., A. Moravcsik and A.-M. Slaughter, 'Legalized dispute resolution: interstate and transnational' (2000) 54 *International Organization*, 457.

Oellers-Frahm, K., 'Multiplication of international courts and tribunals and conflicting jurisdiction – problems and possible solutions' (2001) 67 *Max Planck UNYB*, 67–104.

Proulx, V. J., 'The world court's jurisdictional formalism and its lost market share: the Marshall Islands decisions and the quest for a suitable dispute settlement forum for multilateral disputes' (2017) 30 *Leiden Journal of International Law*, 925.

Sands, P., 'Reflections on international judicialization' (2017) 27 *European Journal of International Law*, 885.

Wittke, C., 'The politics of international law in the post-Soviet space: do Georgia, Ukraine and Russia 'speak' international law in international politics differently?' (2020) 72 *Europe-Asia Studies*, 180.

Appendices

A Agreement between Argentina and the United Kingdom establishing an Interim Reciprocal Information and Consultation System, 1990

Both parties agree to establish an Interim Reciprocal Information and Consultation System for movements of units of their Armed Forces in areas of the South West Atlantic. The aims of this system are to increase confidence between Argentina and the United Kingdom and to contribute to achieving a more normal situation in the region without unnecessary delay. The system consists of the following provisions:

I. Direct Communication Link

A. A direct communication link will be established between the respective military authorities – under the supervision of both Foreign Ministries – in order to:
   – reduce the possibility of incidents and limit their consequences if they should occur;
   – increase common knowledge of activities in the South West Atlantic.
B. The respective military authorities will be:
   British Authority: Commander British Forces Falkland Islands (Malvinas).
   Argentine Naval Authority: Commandante del Area Naval Austral (Ushuaia).
   Argentine Air Authority: Jefe de la Novena Brigada Aérea (Comodoro Rivadavia).
C. It is agreed to establish a direct radio link between the respective authorities which will include voice and/or telex transmissions. The link will be manned on a 24 hour basis and will be tested at least once a week. Technical information relating to equipment, frequencies and modalities of use will be exchanged through diplomatic channels.
D. It is agreed to establish a communications plan for radio links between units and stations of the parties. Technical information will be exchanged through diplomatic channels.

II. Definition of Units

A. Ship:

Any ship belonging to the naval forces of the parties bearing the external marks distinguishing warships of its nationality, under the command of an officer duly commissioned by the governments and whose name appears in the naval list, and manned by a crew who are under regular naval discipline, and British Fleet Auxiliaries.

B. Aircraft:

Any aircraft belonging to the Armed Forces of the parties, manned by a military crew who are under regular Armed Forces discipline.

C. Combatant Units:

Any ship or aircraft equipped with weapons systems or means of offensive power or offensive projection capabilities (naval examples: aircraft carriers, cruisers, destroyers, frigates, corvettes, submarines, fast patrol boats, amphibious ships or ships carrying troops: aircraft examples: strike aircraft, fighters, bombers, missile or troop-carrying aircraft).

III. Reciprocal Information about Military Movements

1. Reciprocal written information will be provided through diplomatic channels, not less than 25 days in advance, about:
   I.1.A. Movements of naval forces involving four or more ships;
   I.1.B. Movements of aerial forces involving four or more aircraft;
   I.1.C. Exercises involving more than 1,000 men or more than 20 sorties by aircraft;
   I.1.D. Amphibious or airborne exercises involving more than 500 men or more than 20 sorties by aircraft.

   The areas of application of this measure are:

   For British Forces: the area south of parallel 40°S, west of meridian 20°W and north of 60°S.
   For Argentine Forces: within rhumb lines joining the following geographical coordinates in the specified order: 46S 63W, 50S 63W, 50S 64W, 53S 64W, 53S 63W, 60S 63W, 60S 20W, 46S 20W, 46S 63W.
   Each party will accept the presence of an observer ship from the other party in the vicinity of naval forces involving four or more ships engaged in manoeuvres within the relevant area of application.

2. Reciprocal notification of identity, intended track and purpose will be given, not less than 48 hours in advance, of a ship or an aircraft that intends to approach closer to coasts than 50 miles by sea or 70 miles by

air. When specific movements of the kind described in this paragraph are intended to be carried out by combatant units and might cause political difficulty to the Argentine Government or to the British Government, the notifying party will be informed immediately and mutual agreement will be necessary to proceed.

IV. Verification

Verification of compliance with the reciprocal information arrangements in provision III above will be by national means, by observer ships (as provided for in III.1), and by consultations through the direct communication link. If disagreement should persist, the parties shall have recourse to the diplomatic channel.

V. Reciprocal Visits

Reciprocal visits to military bases and naval units may be agreed through the diplomatic channel on a case by case basis.

VI. Applicability of International Practice

In situations not specifically covered above, it is understood that normal international practice will be applied on a reciprocal basis.

VII. Duration

This system, including the reciprocal information measures, shall be reviewed at regular diplomatic–technical meetings. The first of these meetings shall take place within one year after the entry into force of the system and shall be convened at a date to be agreed through the diplomatic channel.

[*Source*: Falkland Islands Department, Foreign and Commonwealth Office, February 1990]

B Report of the Commission of Inquiry into the Red Crusader Incident, 1962 (extract)

1. Facts Leading up to the Arrest of the Red Crusader and Circumstances of the Arrest

... [T]he Commission finds:

(1) that no proof of fishing inside the blue line has been established, in spite of the fact that the trawl was in the water inside the blue line from about 21.00 hours until 21.14 hours on May 29, 1961;

(2) that the *Red Crusader* was with her gear not stowed inside the blue line from about 21.00 hours until 21.14 hours on May 29, 1961;
(3) that the first signal to stop was given by *Niels Ebbesen* at 21.39 hours and that this signal and the later stop-signals were all given outside the blue line.

2. Events between the Arrest of the Red Crusader and the Meeting with the British Naval Vessels

... [T]he Commission finds:

(1) The *Red Crusader* was arrested. This conclusion is established by Captain Sølling's declarations as well as by the evidence given by Skipper Wood. Even if the Skipper formally denied his guilt, his answers clearly implied that he considered at the time that he had been duly arrested for illegal fishing. Notes made in the Skipper's red pocket-book and the *Red Crusader*'s log-book also leave no doubt on that point.
(2) Skipper Wood, after having obeyed for a certain time the order given him by Captain Sølling, changed his mind during the trip to Thorshavn and put into effect a plan, concerted with his crew, whereby he attempted to escape and to evade the jurisdiction of an authority which he had at first, rightly, accepted.
(3) During this attempt to escape, the Skipper of the *Red Crusader* took steps to seclude Lieutenant Bech and Corporal Kropp during a certain period and had the intention to take them to Aberdeen.
(4) In opening fire at 03.22 hours up to 03.53 hours, the Commanding Officer of the *Niels Ebbesen* exceeded legitimate use of armed force on two counts: (a) firing without warning of solid gun-shot: (b) creating danger to human life on board the *Red Crusader* without proved necessity, by the effective firing at the *Red Crusader* after 03.40 hours. The escape of the *Red Crusader* in flagrant violation of the order received and obeyed, the seclusion on board the trawler of an officer and rating of the crew of *Neils Ebbesen*, and Skipper Wood's refusal to stop may explain some resentment on the part of Captain Sølling. Those circumstances, however, cannot justify such violent action.

The Commission is of the opinion that other means should have been attempted, which, if duly persisted in, might have finally persuaded Skipper Wood to stop and revert to the normal procedure which he himself had previously followed.
(5) The cost of the repair of the damage caused by firing at and hitting of the *Red Crusader* submitted by the British Government has been considered reasonable by the Danish Agent.

3. Events after the Meeting with the British Naval Vessels

... [T]he Commission finds:

> that Commander Griffiths and the other officers of the British Royal Navy made every effort to avoid any recourse to violence between *Niels Ebbesen* and *Red Crusader*. Such an attitude and conduct were impeccable.

[*Source*: 35 ILR 486–500]

C Conciliation Commission on the Continental Shelf Area between Iceland and Jan Mayen, May 1981

Summary of Recommendations

1. For the purposes of these recommendations the Commission proposes a specified area defined by the following coordinates: 70̱35° N. Lat. 68° N. Lat. 10̱30°W. Long. 6̱30°W. Long.
2. Taking the demarcation line between the 200 mile economic zone and the Norwegian fisheries zone as a dividing line, the specified area has two parts: the part north of the demarcation line comprises some 32.750 km². The area south of this line comprises some 12.725 km².
3. The Commission proposes a joint cooperation arrangement for the area so defined.
4. In the pre-drilling stage, which includes a systematic geological mapping of the specified area mainly by seismic surveys, the Commission recommends that such surveys should be undertaken jointly by the Norwegian Petroleum Directorate and the equivalent government organisation of Iceland. These seismic surveys should be carried out by the Norwegian Petroleum Directorate according to plans elaborated by the two governments jointly. The costs of such surveys should be borne by Norway unless otherwise agreed by the parties. Icelandic and Norwegian experts should have the opportunity to participate in the seismic surveys on an equal footing. The results and evaluations of the surveys should be equally available to both parties.

    If any profits accrue from the sale of the seismic surveys to interested companies or organisations, such profits should be shared by the two countries on a basis to be negotiated.
5. If the surveys justify further exploration, drilling and possible exploitation activities, the Commission proposes that concession contracts with joint-venture arrangements between the two parties and oil companies be negotiated.
6. In the part of the specified area north of the Icelandic 200 mile economic zone Iceland should have the opportunity to acquire a 25 per cent interest in any joint venture arrangement. In negotiations with oil companies an

effort should be made to assure that the costs of both Norwegian and Icelandic state participation are 'carried' by the oil companies up to the moment when a commercial find has been declared.

Should the oil companies refuse to 'carry' the state participation wholly or in part, the Conciliation Commission refers to its proposals made for such event in the foregoing Section VI [*not reproduced here*].

Norwegian legislation, oil policy and control, safety and environmental regulations and administration would apply to the activities in this part of the specified area.

7. In the part of the specified area south of the northern demarcation line of the Icelandic 200 mile economic zone, Norway should have an option to acquire a 25 per cent interest in any joint-venture arrangement. It should not be expected that Iceland will accommodate Norway with a carried-interest arrangement in the same manner and to the same extent proposed for the Norwegian part of the specified area. However, Norway should be allowed to participate in the negotiations with the oil companies.

Icelandic legislation, oil policy control, safety and environmental regulations and administration would apply to the activities in this part of the specified area.

8. In the development phase in any part of the specified area it is understood that each of the two States parties would carry a share of the development costs proportional to its share of State participation.

9. The Commission at the end of Section VI has made certain recommendations for dealing with deposits on both sides of the 200-mile demarcation line or overlapping some part of the specified area boundary and refers to its proposals in this respect and considers them included among the present recommendations.

[*Source*: 62 ILR 134]

D Arbitration Agreement between the United Kingdom and France, July 1975

The Government of the United Kingdom of Great Britain and Northern Ireland and the Government of the French Republic ... have agreed as follows:

Article 1

1. The Court of Arbitration (hereinafter called the Court) shall be composed of:
   Sir Humphrey Waldock, nominated by the United Kingdom Government.

Messrs Paul Reuter, nominated by the French Government.
Herbert Briggs.
Erik Castren.
Endre Ustor.
The President of the Court shall be: Mr Erik Castren.

2. Should the President or any other Member of the Court be or become unable to act, the vacancy shall be filled by a new Member appointed by the Government which nominated the Member to be replaced in the case of the two Members nominated by the United Kingdom and French Governments, or by agreement between the two Governments in the case of the President or the remaining two Members.

Article 2

1. The Court is requested to decide, in accordance with the rules of international law applicable in the matter as between the Parties, the following question:

   What is the course of the boundary (or boundaries) between the portions of the continental shelf appertaining to the United Kingdom and the Channel Islands and to the French Republic, respectively, westward of 30 minutes west of the Greenwich Meridian as far as the 1,000 metre isobath?

2. The choice of the 1,000 metre isobath is without prejudice to the position of either Government concerning the outer limit of the continental shelf.

Article 3

1. The Court shall, subject to the provisions of this Agreement, determine its own procedure and all questions affecting the conduct of the arbitration.
2. In the absence of unanimity, the decisions of the Court on all questions, whether of substance or procedure, shall be given by a majority vote of its Members, including all questions relating to the competence of the Court, the interpretation of this Agreement, and the decision on the question specified in Article 2 hereof.

Article 4

1. The Parties shall, within 14 days of the signature of the present Agreement, each appoint an Agent for the purpose of the arbitration, and shall communicate the name and address of their respective Agents to each other and to the Court.

2. Each Agent so appointed shall be entitled to nominate an Assistant Agent to act for him as occasion may require. The name and address of an Assistant Agent so appointed shall be similarly communicated.

Article 5

The Court shall, after consultation with the two Agents, appoint a Registrar and establish its seat at a place fixed in agreement with the Parties. Until the seat has been determined the Court may meet at a place provisionally chosen by the President.

Article 6

1. The proceedings shall be written and oral.
2. Without prejudice to any question as to burden of proof, the Parties agree that the written proceedings should consist of:
   (a) a Memorial to be submitted by each Party not later than six months after signature of the present Agreement:
   (b) a Counter-Memorial to be submitted by each Party within a time limit of six months after the exchange of Memorials:
   (c) any further pleading found by the Court to be necessary. The Court shall have power to extend the time-limits so fixed at the request of either Party.
3. The Registrar shall notify to the Parties an address for the filing of their written pleadings and other documents.
4. The oral hearing shall follow the written proceedings, and shall be held in private at such place and time as the Court, after consultation with the two Agents, may determine.
5. The Parties may be represented at the oral hearing by their Agents and by such Counsel and advisers as they may appoint.

Article 7

1. The pleadings, written and oral, shall be either in the English or in the French language; the decisions of the Court shall be in both languages.
2. The Court shall, as may be necessary, arrange for translations and interpretations and shall be entitled to engage secretarial and clerical staff, and to make arrangements in respect of accommodation and the purchase or hire of equipment.

Article 8

1. The remuneration of Members of the Court shall be borne equally by the two Governments.

2. The general expenses of the arbitration shall be borne equally by the two Governments, but each Government shall bear its own expenses incurred in or for the preparation and presentation of its case.

Article 9

1. When the proceedings before the Court have been completed, it shall transmit to the two Governments its decision on the question specified in Article 2 of the present Agreement. The decision shall include the drawing of the course of the boundary (or boundaries) on a chart. To this end, the Court shall be entitled to appoint a technical expert or experts to assist it in preparing the chart.
2. The decision shall be fully reasoned.
3. If the decision of the Court does not represent in whole or in part the unanimous opinion of the Members of the Court, any Member shall be entitled to deliver a separate opinion.
4. Any question of the subsequent publication of the proceedings shall be decided by agreement between the two Governments.

Article 10

1. The two Governments agree to accept as final and binding upon them the decision of the Court on the question specified in Article 2 of the present Agreement.
2. Either Party may, within three months of the rendering of the decision, refer to the Court any dispute between the Parties as to the meaning and scope of the decision.

Article 11

1. A Party wishing to carry out, at any time before the Court has rendered its decision on the question specified in Article 2, any activity in a portion of what it considers to be its continental shelf within the area submitted to arbitration shall, subject to the remaining provisions of this Article, obtain the prior consent of the other Party.
2. If such a request for consent is made by one Party the other Party may not withhold its consent for more than one month nor if it consents within this period, subject its consent to conditions, except on the ground that the proposed activity relates to an area which it intends to claim or might claim as part of its own continental shelf at any stage in the course of the arbitration.
3. The Party withholding consent or subjecting its consent to conditions shall, when notifying the Party making the request, briefly state the grounds upon which it justifies its position.

4. The Party making the request may, if dissatisfied with the justification provided, refer the issue to the Court for a ruling.
5. Without prejudice to paragraph 4, either Party may refer any dispute as to the interpretation or application of this Article to the Court for a ruling.
6. The Court shall give, as soon as possible, a ruling on any issue referred to it pursuant to paragraph 4 or 5, and may order such provisional measures as it considers desirable to protect the interests of either Party.

Article 12

The present Agreement shall enter into force on the date of signature.
[*Source*: 54 ILR 13]

E Special Agreement for Submission to the International Court of Justice of the Differences between the Republic of Hungary and the Slovak Republic Concerning the Gabcikovo–Nagymaros Project (1993)

The Republic of Hungary and the Slovak Republic:

Considering that differences have arisen between the Czech and Slovak Federal Republic and the Republic of Hungary regarding the implementation and the termination of the Treaty on the Construction and Operation of the Gabcikovo–Nagymaros Barrage system signed in Budapest on 16 September 1977 and related instruments (hereinafter referred to as 'the Treaty'), and on the construction and operation of the 'provisional solution'; Bearing in mind that the Slovak Republic is one of the two successor States of the Czech and Slovak Federal Republic and the sole successor State in respect of rights and obligations relating to the Gabcikovo–Nagymaros Project;

Recognising that the Parties concerned have been unable to settle these differences by negotiations;

Having in mind that both the Czechoslovak and Hungarian delegations expressed their commitment to submit the differences connected with the Gabcikovo-Nagymaros Project in all its aspects to binding international arbitration or to the International Court of Justice;

Desiring that these differences should be settled by the International Court of Justice;

Recalling their commitment to apply, pending the Judgment of the International Court of Justice, such a temporary water management régime of the Danube as shall be agreed between the Parties;

Desiring further to define the issues to be submitted to the International Court of Justice,

Have agreed as follows:

Article 1

The Parties submit the questions contained in Article 2 to the International Court of Justice pursuant to Article 40, paragraph 1, of the Statute of the Court.

Article 2

(C.B.1) The Court is requested to decide on the basis of the Treaty and rules and principles of general international law, as well as such other treaties as the Court may find applicable,

(C.B.1.a) whether the Republic of Hungary was entitled to suspend and subsequently abandon, in 1989, the works on the Nagymaros Project and on the part of the Gabcikovo Project for which the Treaty attributed responsibility to the Republic of Hungary;

(C.B.1.b) whether the Czech and Slovak Federal Republic was entitled to proceed, in November 1991, to the 'provisional solution' and to put into operation from October 1992 this system, described in the Report of the Working Group of Independent Experts of the Commission of the European Communities, the Republic of Hungary and the Czech and Slovak Federal Republic dated 23 November 1992 (damming up of the Danube at river kilometre 1851.7 on Czechoslovak territory and resulting consequences on water and navigation course);

(C.B.1.c) what are the legal effects of the notification, on 19 May 1992, of the termination of the Treaty by the Republic of Hungary.

(C.B.2) The Court is also requested to determine the legal consequences, including the rights and obligations for the Parties, arising from its Judgment on the questions in paragraph 1 of this Article.

Article 3

(1) All questions of procedure and evidence shall be regulated in accordance with the provisions of the Statute and the Rules of the Court.
(2) However, the Parties request the Court to order that the written proceedings should consist of:
  (a) a Memorial presented by each of the Parties not later than ten months after the date of notification of this Special Agreement to the Registrar of the International Court of Justice;
  (b) a Counter-Memorial presented by each of the Parties not later than seven months after the date on which each has received the certified copy of the Memorial of the other Party;

(c) a Reply presented by each of the Parties within such time-limits as the Court may order;
(d) the Court may request additional written pleadings by the Parties if it so determines.
(3) The above-mentioned parts of the written proceedings and their annexes presented to the Registrar will not be transmitted to the other Party until the Registrar has received the corresponding part of the proceedings from the said Party.

Article 4

(1) The Parties agree that, pending the final Judgment of the Court, they will establish and implement a temporary water management régime for the Danube.
(2) They further agree that, in the period before such a régime is established or implemented, if either Party believes its rights are endangered by the conduct of the other, it may request immediate consultation and reference, if necessary, to experts, including the Commission of the European Communities, with a view to protecting those rights; and that protection shall not be sought through a request to the Court under Article 41 of the Statute.
(3) This commitment is accepted by both Parties as fundamental to the conclusion and continuing validity of the Special Agreement.

Article 5

(1) The Parties shall accept the Judgment of the Court as final and binding upon them and shall execute it in its entirety and in good faith.
(2) Immediately after the transmission of the Judgment the Parties shall enter into negotiations on the modalities for its execution.
(3) If they are unable to reach agreement within six months, either Party may request the Court to render an additional Judgment to determine the modalities for executing its Judgment.

Article 6

(1) The present Special Agreement shall be subject to ratification.
(2) The instruments of ratification shall be exchanged as soon as possible in Brussels.
(3) The present Special Agreement shall enter into force on the date of exchange of instruments of ratification. Thereafter it will be notified jointly to the Registrar of the Court.

[*Source*: (1993) 32 ILM 1293]

F Optional Clause Declarations

Japan (6 October 2015)

I have the honor, by direction of the Minister for Foreign Affairs, to declare on behalf of the Government of Japan that, in conformity with paragraph 2 of Article 36 of the Statute of the International Court of Justice, Japan recognizes as compulsory *ipso facto* and without special agreement, in relation to any other State accepting the same obligation and on condition of reciprocity, the jurisdiction of the International Court of Justice, over all disputes arising on and after 15 September 1958 with regard to situations or facts subsequent to the same date and being not settled by other means of peaceful settlement.

This declaration does not apply to:

(1) any dispute which the parties thereto have agreed or shall agree to refer for final and binding decision to arbitration or judicial settlement;
(2) any dispute in respect of which any other party to the dispute has accepted the compulsory jurisdiction of the International Court of Justice only in relation to or for the purpose of the dispute; or where the acceptance of the Court's compulsory jurisdiction on behalf of any other party to the dispute was deposited or notified less than twelve months prior to the filing of the application bringing the dispute before the Court;
(3) any dispute arising out of, concerning, or relating to research on, or conservation, management or exploitation of, living resources of the sea.

The Government of Japan reserves the right at any time, by means of a written notification addressed to the Secretary-General of the United Nations, and with effect as from the moment of such notification, either to amend or terminate the present declaration.

Marshall Islands (24 April 2013)

I have the honor to declare on behalf of the Government of the Republic of the Marshall Islands that:

(1) The Government of the Republic of the Marshall Islands accepts as compulsory *ipso facto* and without special convention, on condition of reciprocity, the jurisdiction of the International Court of Justice, in conformity with paragraph 2 of Article 36 of the Statute of the Court, until such time as notice may be given to terminate the acceptance, over all disputes arising after 17 September 1991, with regard to situations or facts subsequent to the same date, other than:

i) any dispute which the Republic of Marshall Islands has agreed with the other Party or Parties thereto to settle by some other method of peaceful settlement;

ii) any dispute in respect of which any other Party to the dispute has accepted the compulsory jurisdiction of the International Court of Justice only in relation to or for the purpose of the dispute.

(2) The Government of the Republic of the Marshall Islands also reserves the right at any time, by means of notification addressed to the Secretary-General of the United Nations, and with effect as from the moment of such notification, to add to, amend or withdraw either of the foregoing reservations or any that may hereafter be added.

Romania (23 June 2015)

Romania declares that it recognises as compulsory *ipso facto* and without special agreement, in relation to any other State accepting the same obligation, meaning on the condition of reciprocity, the jurisdiction of the International Court of Justice, in accordance with Article 36(2) of the Statute of the Court, in relation to all legal disputes related to facts or situations arising after this declaration is made, other than:

(a) any dispute in regard to which the parties thereto have agreed or shall agree to have recourse to some other method of peaceful settlement for its final and binding decision;

(b) any dispute with any State which has accepted the compulsory jurisdiction of the International Court of Justice under Article 36(2) of the Statute less than twelve months prior to filing an application bringing the dispute before the Court or where such acceptance has been made only for the purpose of a particular dispute;

(c) any dispute regarding to the protection of the environment;

(d) any dispute relating to, or connected with, hostilities, war, armed conflict, individual or collective self-defence or the discharge of any functions pursuant to any decision or recommendation of the United Nations, the deployment of armed forces abroad, as well as decisions relating thereto;

(e) any dispute relating to, or connected with, the use for military purposes of the territory of Romania, including the airspace and territorial sea, or maritime zones subject to its sovereign rights and jurisdiction;

(f) any dispute relating to matters which by international law fall exclusively within the domestic jurisdiction of Romania.

This Declaration shall remain in force until such time as notice may be given to the Secretary-General of the United Nations withdrawing or modifying this declaration, and with effect from the moment of such notification.

United Kingdom of Great Britain and Northern Ireland (22 February 2017)

1. The Government of the United Kingdom of Great Britain and Northern Ireland accept as compulsory *ipso facto* and without special convention, on condition of reciprocity, the jurisdiction of the International Court of Justice, in conformity with paragraph 2 of Article 36 of the Statute of the Court, until such time as notice may be given to terminate the acceptance, over all disputes arising after 1 January 1987, with regard to situations or facts subsequent to the same date, other than:
    (i) any dispute which the United Kingdom has agreed with the other Party or Parties thereto to settle by some other method of peaceful settlement;
    (ii) any dispute with the government of any other country which is or has been a Member of the Commonwealth;
    (iii) any dispute in respect of which any other Party to the dispute has accepted the compulsory jurisdiction of the International Court of Justice only in relation to or for the purpose of the dispute; or where the acceptance of the Court's compulsory jurisdiction on behalf of any other Party to the dispute was deposited or ratified less than twelve months prior to the filing of the application bringing the dispute before the Court;
    (iv) any dispute which is substantially the same as a dispute previously submitted to the Court by the same or another Party;
    (v) any claim or dispute in respect of which the claim or dispute in question has not been notified to the United Kingdom by the State or States concerned in writing, including of an Intention to submit the claim or dispute to the Court failing an amicable settlement, at least six months in advance of the submission of the claim or dispute to the Court;
    (vi) any claim or dispute that arises from or is connected with or related to nuclear disarmament and/or nuclear weapons, unless all of the other nuclear-weapon States Party to the Treaty on the Non-Proliferation of Nuclear Weapons have also consented to the jurisdiction of the Court and are party to the proceedings in question.
2. The Government of the United Kingdom also reserves the right at any time, by means of a notification addressed to the Secretary-General of the United Nations, and with effect as from the moment of such notification, either to add to, amend or withdraw any of the foregoing reservations, or any that may hereafter be added.

[*Source*: ICJ website]

G Ruling Pertaining to the Differences between France and New Zealand Arising from the Rainbow Warrior Affair (extract)

Introduction

1. On 10 July 1985 a civilian vessel, the 'Rainbow Warrior', not flying the New Zealand flag, was sunk at its moorings in Auckland Harbor, New Zealand, as a result of extensive damage caused by two high explosive devices. One person, a Netherlands citizen, Mr Fernando Pereira, was killed as a result of this action; he drowned when the ship sank.
2. On 12 July, two agents of the French Directorate General of External Security (DGSE) were interviewed by the New Zealand Police and subsequently arrested and prosecuted. On 4 November they pleaded guilty in the District Court in Auckland, New Zealand, to charges of manslaughter and wilful damage to a ship by means of an explosive. They were sentenced to ten years' imprisonment each; they are presently serving their sentences in New Zealand prisons.
3. A communiqué issued on 22 September 1985 by the Prime Minister of France confirmed that the 'Rainbow Warrior' had been sunk by agents of the DGSE upon instructions. On the same day, the Minister of External Affairs of France pointed out to the Prime Minister of New Zealand that France was ready to undertake reparations for the consequences of that action. He also declared he was ready, as the Prime Minister of New Zealand had already suggested, to meet with the Deputy Prime Minister of New Zealand on 23 and 25 September in New York. Such a meeting did take place for the purpose of discussing the possible ways to find a solution to the problems arising from the Rainbow Warrior affair.
4. A number of subsequent meetings took place between officials of the two countries in the months that followed, but it did not prove possible to reach a settlement.
5. In June 1986 I was formally approached by the Governments of France and New Zealand, who referred to me all the problems between them arising from the Rainbow Warrior affair for a ruling which both sides agreed to abide by. I then informed both Governments that I was prepared to undertake such a task. On 19 June, in Paris and in Wellington, both Governments made public announcements to that effect, and in New York on the same day I publicly confirmed that I was willing to undertake that task and to make my ruling available to the two Governments in the very near future ...

Ruling

The issues that I need to consider are limited in number. I set out below my ruling on them which takes account of all the information available to me. My ruling is as follows:

1. Apology

New Zealand seeks an apology. France is prepared to give one. My ruling is that the Prime Minister of France should convey to the Prime Minister of New Zealand a formal and unqualified apology for the attack, contrary to international law, on the 'Rainbow Warrior' by French service agents which took place on 10 July 1985.

2. Compensation

New Zealand seeks compensation for the wrong done to it and France is ready to pay some compensation. The two sides, however, are some distance apart on quantum. New Zealand has said that the figure should not be less than US Dollars 9 million, France that it should not be more than US Dollars 4 million. My ruling is that the French Government should pay the sum of US Dollars 7 million to the Government of New Zealand as compensation for all the damage it has suffered.

3. The Two French Service Agents

It is on this issue that the two Governments plainly had the greatest difficulty in their attempts to negotiate a solution to the whole issue on a bilateral basis before they took the decision to refer the matter to me.

The French Government seeks the immediate return of the two officers. It underlines that their imprisonment in New Zealand is not justified, taking into account in particular the fact that they acted under military orders and that France is ready to give an apology and to pay compensation to New Zealand for the damage suffered.

The New Zealand position is that the sinking of the 'Rainbow Warrior' involved not only a breach of international law, but also the commission of a serious crime in New Zealand for which the two officers received a lengthy sentence from a New Zealand court. The New Zealand side states that their release to freedom would undermine the integrity of the New Zealand judicial system. In the course of bilateral negotiations with France, New Zealand was ready to explore possibilities for the prisoners serving their sentences outside New Zealand.

But it has been, and remains, essential to the New Zealand position that there should be no release to freedom, that any transfer should be to custody, and that there should be a means of verifying that.

The French response to that is that there is no basis either in international law or in French law on which the two could serve out any portion of their New Zealand sentence in France, and that they could not be subjected to new criminal proceedings after a transfer into French hands.

On this point, if I am to fulfil my mandate adequately, I must find a solution in respect of the two officers which both respects and reconciles these conflicting positions.

My ruling is as follows:

(a) The Government of New Zealand should transfer Major Alain Mafart and Captain Dominique Prieur to the French military authorities. Immediately thereafter, Major Mafart and Captain Prieur should be transferred to a French military facility on an isolated island outside of Europe for a period of three years.

(b) They should be prohibited from leaving the island for any reason, except with the mutual consent of the two Governments. They should be isolated during their assignment on the island from persons other than military or associated personnel and immediate family and friends. They should be prohibited from any contact with the press or other media whether in person or in writing or in any other manner. These conditions should be strictly complied with and appropriate action should be taken under the rules governing military discipline to enforce them.

(c) The French Government should every three months convey to the New Zealand Government and to the Secretary-General of the United Nations, through diplomatic channels, full reports on the situation of Major Mafart and Captain Prieur in terms of the two preceding paragraphs in order to allow the New Zealand Government to be sure that they are being implemented.

(d) If the New Zealand Government so requests, a visit to the French military facility in question may be made, by mutual agreement by the two Governments, by an agreed third party.

(e) I have sought information on French military facilities outside Europe. On the basis of that information, I believe that the transfer of Major Mafart and Captain Prieur to the French military facility on the isolated island of Hao in French Polynesia would best facilitate the enforcement of the conditions which I have laid down in paragraphs (a) to (d) above. My ruling is that that should be their destination immediately after their transfer.

4. Trade Issues

The New Zealand Government has taken the position that trade issues have been imported into the affair as a result of French action, either taken or in prospect. The French Government denies that, but it has indicated that it is willing to give some undertakings relating to trade, as sought by the New Zealand Government. I therefore rule that France should:

(a) Not oppose continuing imports of New Zealand butter into the United Kingdom in 1987 and 1988 at levels proposed by the Commission of the European Communities in so far as these do not exceed those

mentioned in document COM(83)574 of 6 October 1983 that is to say, 77,000 tonnes in 1987 and 75,000 tonnes in 1988; and
(b) Not take measures that might impair the implementation of the agreement between New Zealand and the European Economic Community on Trade in Mutton, Lamb and Goatmeat which entered into force on 20 October 1980 (as complemented by the exchange of letters of 12 July 1984).

5. Arbitration

The New Zealand Government has argued that a mechanism should exist to ensure that any differences that may arise about the implementation of the agreements concluded as a result of my ruling can be referred for binding decision to an arbitral tribunal. The Government of France is not averse to that. My ruling is that an agreement to that effect should be concluded and provide that any dispute concerning the interpretation or application of the other agreements, which it has not been possible to resolve through the diplomatic channel, shall, at the request of either of the two Governments, be submitted to an arbitral tribunal under the following conditions:

(a) Each Government shall designate a member of the tribunal within 30 days of the date of the delivery by either Government to the other of a written request for arbitration of the dispute, and the two Governments shall, within 60 days of that date, appoint a third member of the tribunal who shall be its chairman;
(b) If, within the times prescribed, either Government fails to designate a member of the tribunal or the third member is not agreed, the Secretary-General of the United Nations shall be requested to make the necessary appointment after consultations with the two Governments by choosing the member or members of the tribunal;
(c) A majority of the members of the tribunal shall constitute a quorum and all decisions shall be made by a majority vote;
(d) The decisions of the tribunal, including all rulings concerning its constitution, procedure and jurisdiction, shall be binding on the two Governments.

6.

The two Governments should conclude and bring into force as soon as possible binding agreements incorporating all of the above rulings. These agreements should provide that the undertaking relating to an apology, the payment of compensation and the transfer of Major Mafart and Captain Prieur should be implemented at the latest on 25 July 1986.

7.

On one matter I find no need to make a ruling. New Zealand, in its written statement of position, has expressed concern regarding compensation for the family of the individual whose life was lost in the incident and for Greenpeace. The French statement of position contains an account of the compensation arrangements that have been made; I understand that those assurances constitute the response that New Zealand was seeking.

[*Source*: 74 ILR 256]

Index

Introductory Note

References such as '178–79' indicate (not necessarily continuous) discussion of a topic across a range of pages. Wherever possible in the case of topics with many references, these have either been divided into sub-topics or only the most significant discussions of the topic are listed. Because the entire work is about 'international dispute settlement', the use of this term (and certain others which occur constantly throughout the book) as entry points has been restricted. Information will be found under the corresponding detailed topics.

acquiescence, 202, 240
ad hoc appointment of judges, 226
ad hoc arbitration, 189–90, 269
ad hoc chambers, 225, 298–9
ad hoc commissions, 46, 106, 281, 391, 413
ad hoc judges, 219, 223–4, 226, 229
ad hoc tribunals, 165, 175
ADF (Arab Deterrent Force), success, 397
adjudication
   and concilliation, 60
   and negotiation, 54–61
   and regional organisations, 402–7
   arbitration, similarity to, 194
   characteristics, 420–5
   costs, 430–1
   financial assistance for *see* trust funds for.
   good judgments, importance, 433
   law, role, 420
   legal perspective, 420–5
   negotiation as precondition, 54–8
   prejudicial link with negotiation, 60
   proliferation of adjudicatory bodies, 434
   regional organisations, 402–3
   substantive relation to negotiation, 59–61
   third party interventions, 425
admirals, 85–7
admissibility, 9, 32–6, 55, 199, 204, 216, 218, 371, 373–4
advisory jurisdiction, 204, 218–21, 372, 375
advisory opinions, 218–21, 236, 238, 254, 256, 274–5, 296–7, 300–1, 355, 372
affidavits, 231, 233
Afghanistan, 357, 361, 365, 378

Africa, cultural and political factors, 236
African Court of Human and Peoples' Rights (AFCHPR), 398
African Union, 383, 387–9, 397, 400, 411
   dispute settlement provision, 383
   peace-keeping operations, 397
Agenda for Peace report, 411
aggression, 82, 196, 233, 348–9, 358–9, 375, 391, 394
   external, 384, 387
air pollution, 45, 153
Åland Islands dispute, 98
Albania, 203, 235
   adjudication by ICJ, 235
Algeria, 68–9, 71–2, 74, 76, 79–80, 236, 391, 409
   adjudication by ICJ, 236
   Ben Bella affair, 113
   experts from, use, 250
   mediation, 68–9, 71–2, 76, 79–81
   OAU intervention, 391, 409
amicus curiae briefs, 183, 328, 330
ancillary questions, 149, 273
Angola, 378
Annex VII arbitration, 285, 287, 302
Annex VII tribunals, 168, 286–8, 301, 432
annulment, 21–3, 189–90, 208, 339
   grounds for, 23, 186
   of arbitral awards, 161–5
Antarctic, 43, 51, 204, 215, 234
anticipatory co-operation, 43
Antigua, 336–7
antitrust proceedings, consultation, 39

appeal arbitration procedures, 333, 338
appeals, 21–2, 59, 158–9, 164, 325–8, 331–3, 339, 365, 368–9
  arbitration awards, 159
  DSU, 328–32, 342–5
  ICJ, 216–17
  interim, 332–3, 338
Appellate Body, 22, 258, 323, 336–7, 342–5, 415, 434
  composition and mandate, 326–7
  dysfunction, 332–3
  functions, 326
  importance, 328–32
  procedure, 327–8
  reports, 316, 329, 334
appellate review, 325–33, 343, 414
applicable law, 27, 152–3, 181, 185–7, 238, 241, 271–2, 302, 422
  clauses, 186, 273
appointing authorities, 137–8, 140
appointments, 136–42, 145, 162, 184, 222, 224, 285, 288–9, 332
Arab League, 387, 389, 397, 401
  dispute settlement provision, 389
  division within, 401
Arab states, non-recognition of Israel, 61
Arab-Israeli conflict
  Camp David Agreements, 379
  ICJ advisory jurisdiction, 220
  non-recognition issues, 61
  UN intervention, 351, 353
arbitral awards, 22–3, 35, 161–2, 165, 168–70, 188–9, 208, 338–9, 403–4
  annulment, 161–5
  international, 169–70
  interpretation, revision and rectification, 159–61
arbitral process, 181, 431
arbitral tribunals, 19–21, 29–30, 136–7, 139–43, 148–9, 185–6, 271–4, 284–5, 294–6
  special, 270, 289
  work, 148–9, 273
arbitration, 132–70
  adjudication differing, 132
  agreements, 117, 136, 140, 142, 149, 154, 158
  and negotiation, 55
  Annex VII, 285, 287, 302
  annulment of arbitral awards, 161–5
  appeals, 159

arbitral awards, nullity claims as to, 161–5
arbitration decision, support by regional organisations for implementation, 403
as to compensation payment, 152–8
basis of decisions, 152–8
bilateral agreements, 140
binding, 80, 94, 334–5
by collegiate body, 135
by commission, 133
by foreign head of state or government, 133–4
by specially qualified individual, 134
clauses, 172–4
consent, 162
decision-making criteria, 133–5
definition of issue, 146–8
DSU, 337–9
effect of awards, 158–65
effect of awards in, 158–65
equity, application, 154–6
errors in decisions, correction, 161
essential error as reason for nullifying, 164–5
established after dispute has arisen, 132
established before dispute, 132
failure to give reasons for decision, 163–4
forms, 132–6
fraud as reason for nullifying award, 164
ICSID, 174, 181, 188–90
inquiry differing, 94
inquiry resembling, 90
interpretation, revision and rectification, 159–61
inter-state, 10, 18, 134–6, 143, 149, 169
investment *see* investment arbitration.
investor-state *see* investor-state arbitration.
law applicable to the merits, 152–4
limits to jurisdiction of arbitral tribunals, 148–52
majority vote decision, 135
mixed, 167, 342
municipal law and *ex aequo et bono*, 154–8
nullity claims as to awards, adjudication, 161–5
panels, 112, 191, 342
procedural rules, 144–6
revision of award due to new facts, 160–1
rules, 10, 27, 29, 141, 143–4, 175, 180–1

sovereign, 133–4
special, 102, 263, 288–90
terms of reference, 144–52
treaties of, 91, 137, 156, 407
  negotiation, 91
UNCLOS, 284–8
under municipal law, 153–5
utility, 165–70
arbitrators
  appointing authority, 140
  authority invalid, claims that, 161–2
  independence and impartiality, 141–4, 185
  list, 134, 142, 285
  majority voting, 282
  neutral arbitrators, 137–8, 285
  party-appointed, 137, 139–42
  qualities, 142
  selection and appointment, 136–44
  single, 134–6, 337
  sovereign, 133–4, 163
  terms of reference, 144–52
  third party selection, 137–8
Argentina, 42, 51, 63, 67–8, 70–1, 134, 178–9, 190–1, 208–9, 417
  adjudication by ICJ, 209
  arbitration, 134, 147, 152, 164
  consultation, 41–2
  Contadora process, 395
  mediation, 67–8, 70–1, 76, 82
  negotiations, 51, 63
  severing of diplomatic relations, 61
  treaties of arbitration, negotiation, 91
  UN intervention, 361
armed conflict, 67, 70, 98, 196, 280, 347, 361, 380
armed forces, 2–3, 93–4, 205, 360
arrest, 88–9, 92, 272
ASEAN (Association of Southeast Asian Nations), 267, 390
Asian Development Bank, fact-finding tribunals, 101
Association of Southeast Asian Nations see ASEAN.
asylum, political, 15, 256
atmospheric nuclear tests, 16–17, 257
Australia, 16, 50, 129, 145, 168, 204–5, 283–4, 288, 333
  adjudication by ICJ, 204–5
  good offices, 353
  Law of the Sea Convention arbitration, 288

negotiations, 50
proliferation of adjudicatory bodies, problems arising from, 435
UN intervention, 353
Austro-Hungary inquiry, 86
authority, discretionary, 219, 277
automatic competence, 21, 23
autonomy, party, 177, 263, 338

Bahrain, 53–4, 178, 199, 210, 363, 431–2
  adjudication by ICJ, 199, 431–2
  negotiation, 53
  UN intervention, 363
Balkans, UN Special Committee on (UNSCOB), 352
Barbados, Law of the Sea Convention, 287
Beck-Friis, Ambassador Johan, good offices, 363
Belgium, 92, 105–9, 112–13, 115, 135, 159, 180, 204, 209
  adjudication by ICJ, 204
  arbitration, 135, 159
  conciliation, 107, 109, 112, 115, 129
  conciliation treaty, 105
  good offices, 353
  inquiry, 92
  UN intervention, 353
Belize, 395, 403
  OAS intervention, 395
Ben Bella affair, 113, 115, 129
Benin
  adjudication by ICJ, 226, 251
  UAM intervention, 401
Bernadotte, Count Folke, good offices, 353
Biafra and Nigeria, mediations between, 70
bilateral agreements, 122, 266, 337
  arbitration, 140
  conciliation, 39, 105, 116–17
  consultation, 39, 42
  negotiation, 51–2
  without prejudice clauses, 51–2
bilateral investment treaties see BITs.
bilateral negotiations, 51, 235
binding arbitration, 80, 94, 334–5
binding decisions, 9, 19–21, 24, 57, 96, 132, 266–7, 414, 421
binding settlement, 269–70, 280, 304
BITs (bilateral investment treaties), 30, 79, 172–5, 178, 180, 186–7, 191
Black Sea, 138, 150, 273, 279
Bolivia, 64, 107, 393

border disputes, 129–30, 391, 393, 403, 409
Bosnia
   adjudication by ICJ, 200, 217, 233
   arbitration, 156
   ICJ and the Security Council, 371
   mediation, 70
   UN intervention, 371, 374, 379, 410
Botswana, adjudication by ICJ, 198, 239–40
boundaries, 148, 152, 164, 169, 197, 208, 239, 241, 249–50, 252
   maritime, 50, 129, 147, 153, 251, 274–5, 278–9, 283–4, 286–7, 301
Boutros-Ghali, Boutros, *Agenda for Peace* report, 409
Brahimi Report, 428
Brazil, 91, 113, 128, 333, 342, 395
   Contadora process, 395
   treaties of arbitration, negotiation, 91
British Guiana, arbitration, 164
Bulgaria, 12, 138–9
   adjudication by ICJ, 139
   arbitration, 138
Burkina Faso, 17, 205, 226, 240
Bush, President George H., meeting with Gorbachev, 47

cafeteria approach, 270, 305
Cambodia
   adjudication by ICJ, 216, 253
   UN intervention, 363, 365, 378
Cameroon
   adjudication by ICJ, 256, 406
   negotiation, 48
Camp David Agreements, 379
Canada, 39, 44–5, 60, 201, 225–7, 329–30, 333, 337, 340, 384–5
   adjudication by ICJ, 201, 225–8, 245
   arbitration, 151, 153–4
   consultation by, 39
   DSU, 319, 329–30
   good offices, 60
   good offices of GATT Director, 319
   Joint Commission with US, 45
   negotiation, 60
   regional organisations, membership, 384–5
Caribbean Court of Justice, 398
categories of disputes, 28, 276, 278, 304
ceasefires, 68, 78, 80, 205, 351, 353, 356–7, 361–2, 364, 392
Central African Republic, 352, 358–9

Central America, 106, 232, 246, 378, 380, 387, 394–5, 401, 410
   OAS, 386–7, 394
   sub-regional organisations, role, 401
   UN intervention, 379–80, 410
Chaco Commission, 107–9, 112–15, 129–30, 393
Chaco War (Bolivia/Paraguay), conciliation, 107, 112–15, 130, 393
Chad
   financial assistance for adjudication, 431
   OAU intervention, 402
Chagos Archipelago, 150, 221, 238–9, 274–5, 355
chambers, 214, 217, 224–8, 240–3, 250–1, 292, 298, 300–1, 422, 424
   further development of procedure, 431
   procedures, 224–9
   special, 274–5, 287, 302
   use, 225, 228, 292
Chile, 64, 68, 71, 75, 82, 91, 95–6, 128, 134, 287
   arbitration, 134, 147, 152, 164
   conciliation treaty, 104
   Law of the Sea Convention arbitration, 302
   mediation, 68, 71, 75, 82
   treaties of arbitration, negotiation, 91
China, 139, 222, 264, 267, 278, 304, 325, 330, 333, 432–3
   Belgrade embassy bombing, 98
   DSU, 326, 330
   ICJ judges panel, representation on, 222
   ITLOS membership, 291
   Security Council membership, 222
   UN intervention, 353–4
choice of law, 186, 271, 293, 305
   ICJ, 236
   Iran-United States Claims Tribunal, 136
   Law of the Sea Convention, 271–2, 305
choice of means
   DSU, 343
   Law of the Sea Convention, 304–5, 348, 414
CJEU (Court of Justice of the European Union), 384, 398, 402
classes of cases in arbitration, 132–6
coastal States, 150, 273–7, 300–1, 304
Cod Wars
   duty to negotiate, 63
   NATO involvement, 391, 401

negotiation, 391
  timing, 419
Cold War
  and regional organisations, 408
  negotiation during, 52
  UN intervention during, 377–8
collective action by regional organisation, 395–8
collegiate body, arbitration by, 135
Colombia, 46, 99, 156, 214, 218, 252, 333, 394
  adjudication by ICJ, 214, 252, 256
  arbitration, 156
  Contadora process, 394
  UN, 99
colonisation and decolonisation
  and ICJ, 219, 236, 256
  and UN, 378
  terra nullius, 236, 256
COMESA (Common Market for Eastern and Southern Africa), 341
commercial arbitration and municipal law, 153
commercial transactions, 176–7
commissions
  arbitration by, 133
  negotiation by, 45–6
commissions of conciliation, 38, 102, 104–8, 111–15, 119–20, 124, 128, 319
  role and powers, 113–16
commissions of inquiry, 84–90, 92–4, 96–8, 100, 102, 106, 127
  introduction of international, 84–5
  League of Nations, 98
committees of experts, 164, 235–6
Common Market for Eastern and Southern Africa see COMESA.
Commonwealth of Independent States (CIS)
  establishment, 385
compensation, 90, 96, 100, 109, 118, 146, 157, 167, 174, 333–7
  arbitration as to, 152–8
  conciliation as to, 109
  DSU provisions as to, 126–7
  ICJ ruling as to, 374
  payment as to
    arbitration as to, 146–7
    conciliation as to, 118
    DSU provisions, 333–4
  payment of
    following inquiry, 90, 95–6

following negotiation, 52
  ICJ, 374
  ITLOS ruling as to, 301
  UN Compensation Commission, 100
competence, 22–3, 26–7, 151–2, 198–200, 222, 283–4, 289–91, 295–8, 368
  automatic, 21, 23
  exclusive, 399
  limited, 27
compétence de la compétence, 27, 198
competent authorities, negotiation via, 45
compliance
  panels, 334, 336
  procedures and conciliation, 126–7
compromis, 6, 95–6, 133, 136, 145, 147–9, 152, 159, 162, 241
compromissory clauses, 6–7, 10, 26, 28, 31, 34, 49, 56, 145, 147
compulsory conciliation, 119, 129, 278, 283–4
compulsory jurisdiction, 3, 6, 196–7, 224, 270–1, 304, 420–1, 432, 434–5
compulsory settlement, 2, 6, 195, 199, 262–3, 266, 269, 276, 278, 280, 284, 296, 305
  principle, 269, 275, 278
concessions, 42, 62, 70, 76, 95, 115, 128, 154, 176, 335–7
  suspension, 277, 316, 324, 331, 333–5
conciliation, 104–31, 278, 281–3
  and adjudication, 61
  and compliance procedures, 126–7
  and the OSCE, 123–6
  as to compensation payment, 109, 118
  bilateral agreements, 39, 105, 116–17
  combined with other methods of settlement, 120–2
  compliance procedures in environmental, 126–7
  compulsory, 119, 129, 278, 283–4
  current trends, 413–14
  DSU, 318–19
  emergence, 104–6
  Law of the Sea Convention, 277, 280–3, 289
  limitations, 129–30
  meaning, 66
  mediation distinguished, 66
  Model Rules, 122
  modern treaty law, 116–22
  multilateral treaties, 117–20

conciliation (cont.)
  nature, 112–13
  negotiation, resemblance to, 112
  non-use, reasons for, 128
  OAS, 394
  OSCE, 123–5, 393–4
  practice, 112–16
  procedures, 120–1, 124, 129, 283
  recent developments, 122–7
  significance, 127–31
  single conciliator, referral to, 110–11
  success, 129
  time-limit for acceptance, 115
  treaties, negotiation, 104–6, 116–17
  type of process, 112
  UNCLOS, 281–4
conciliation commissions, 38, 102, 104–8, 112–15, 119–20, 124, 128, 319
  active role, 114
  confidentiality, 115
  functions defined, 105
  League of Nations resolution recommending, 105
  proposals, 114
  reports, 114
  role and powers, 113–16
  work, 106–12
conciliators, 111, 114–16, 124, 282, 415, 418, 421
  single conciliator, referral to, 110–11, 114
concurrence, meaning, 43
Conference of American States, inquiry and conciliation by, 107
confidentiality, 82, 115, 183, 317, 323, 430
conflicts of interest(s), 11, 143, 326
Congo, 198, 232, 235, 244, 251, 358–9, 378
  Democratic Republic (DRC)
    adjudication by ICJ, 232–3, 244
    negotiation, 55
  Republic of
    adjudication by ICJ, 198
consensuality, 102, 148, 195, 211–12, 218, 297, 355, 425
consensus, 312–13, 321, 325–6, 328, 342, 382, 410
  reverse, 313, 316, 321
consent, 5–8, 21–30, 34, 151, 173–5, 182–3, 194–5, 198, 202–4
  and arbitration, 148
  consultation distinguished, 39–40
  expression, 6, 8, 26, 174, 204

  lack of, 220
  of states, 7, 26, 28, 31–2, 149
  to adjudication by ICJ, 194–5, 203
  to mediation, 69–73
conservation, 50, 237, 277, 288, 306
consistency, 214, 258, 327–8
consultation, 39–44
  ad hoc process, 43
  and dispute prevention, 39–41
  and legislative co-ordination, 43–4
  as form of negotiation, 39
  bilateral agreements, 39, 42–3
  compliance with arrangements for, 42
  consent distinguished, 39–40
  difficulty of institutionalising, 43–4
  growth, 44
  multilateral agreements, 44
  notification distinguished, 39
  overview, 39–45
  role in dispute settlement, 41–3
  stages, 41
  value, 39
Contadora Group, 394, 401
Contadora process, 55, 246, 394, 405–6
contentious jurisdiction, 194–204, 218–20, 224, 355, 375
Cooperation Council of Arab States, 54
Cordovez, Diego, good offices, 361
Corfu Channel dispute
  adjudication by ICJ, 235
  committee of experts, use, 235
  UN intervention, 351
corruption, 23, 164, 190, 432
Costa Rica
  adjudication by ICJ, 203, 214
  arbitration, 135
  Contadora process, 394
  OAS intervention, 394
costs, 71, 74, 77, 109, 202, 226–7, 239, 250, 258, 430
  diplomatic, 69
  of adjudication, 430–1
  political, 73, 168
Council of Europe, dispute settlement mechanism, 384
counter-claims, 1, 217–18, 246
Court of First Instance, 341
Court of Justice of the European Union (CJEU), 384, 398, 402
Croatia, mediation, 70
Cuba, arbitration, 178

Cuban missile crisis, UN intervention, 363, 365, 377, 408
cultural factors, 236, 417
Cyprus, NATO involvement, 390
Czechoslovakia
   adjudication by ICJ, 237
   conciliation, 128
   conciliation treaty, 105
   UN intervention, 377, 409

Da'esh *see* ISIL.
deceit, 23, 164
decisions *ex aequo et bono*, 24, 158, 256, 275
decolonisation, 219, 221, 238–9, 256, 274, 355, 378–9
delimitation, 148–9, 151, 155, 197, 240, 243, 245, 274–5, 278–9, 287
   exception, 279
   maritime, 50, 53, 147–8, 155, 199, 214, 223, 232, 267, 431
Democratic Republic of the Congo *see* DRC.
Democratic Republic of Timor-Leste, 129, 283–4
Denmark
   adjudication by ICJ, 212
   conciliation, 107, 112, 115, 118, 129
   inquiry, 90, 92
   Red Crusader incident, 92–4
detention, 205, 245, 295–6, 361, 369, 433
dialogue, 83, 112, 129, 318, 351
diplomacy, 24, 52, 60, 353, 413
   personal, 72, 354
   preventive, 381, 392, 410, 428
   quiet, 353, 364, 366, 380
diplomatic exchanges, clarification of dispute via, 58
diplomatic methods, 5–6, 24–5, 318, 406, 417
diplomatic negotiations, 47, 113, 156, 312
diplomatic relations, 61, 72, 107, 197, 199, 390–1, 396–7
   severing of, 61
direct negotiations, 38, 48, 61, 67, 77, 342, 350, 364, 400, 405
discretion, 33, 219, 276–7, 280, 300, 302, 361, 366, 372
discretionary authority, 219, 277
discrimination, racial, 12, 49, 55–6, 209–10
dispute settlement
   methods, 2, 5–9, 21, 24, 38, 207, 263, 296, 414

system, 22, 262, 310, 313–14, 317, 320, 330, 338, 343, 414
Dispute Settlement Body (DSB), 31, 313, 316, 320–2, 325–9, 332–6, 338–9, 343–4
   awards reviewed by, 338
   establishment, 313
   good offices, 320
   panel procedures, 320–6
   panel proceedings, 320–6
   responsibilities, 313
Dispute Settlement Understanding (DSU), 9, 22, 31, 311–16, 320–6
   appellate review, 326–32
   arbitration under, 337–9
   cases dealt with by, 102, 325–32, 335–7
   choice of means, 343
   compensation provisions, 126–7
   conciliation, 318–19
   current trends, 414–15
   development from original GATT dispute settlement system, 312–13
   experts, rules for the use of, 325
   good offices, 318–19
   historical background, 310–11
   implementation of rulings and recommendations, 333–7
   innovations introduced by, 313
   Law of the Sea Convention Compared, 311–12
   least developed countries, provisions for, 320
   main principles and jurisdiction, 314–16
   mediation, 318–19
   origins, 310–11
   panel reports, 324
disputed areas, 108, 113, 156, 205, 208, 237, 240, 357–8
disputes
   clarification by diplomatic exchanges, 58
   commitment to peaceful resolution, 1
   court's recognition of existence, 58
   definition, 8–14
   inter-regional, 398, 411
   inter-state, 11, 23, 178, 189, 204, 220, 341
   intra-state, 364
   meaning, 1
   political, 13–14, 67, 72, 77, 244, 246, 248, 255

disputes (cont.)
　territorial, 61, 68, 134, 165, 216, 226, 398, 401, 403, 431
　trade see trade disputes.
dissenting opinions, 15, 48, 286
Dixon, Sir Owen, good offices, 354
documentary evidence, 217, 231–4, 431
Dogger Bank Inquiry, 85–7, 97, 102
domestic courts, 32, 174, 183, 187, 189–90, 254, 296
　significance compared to international courts, 254
domestic jurisdiction, 70, 196, 349, 364, 379, 400
domestic law, 152–4, 170, 186, 244, 332, 422
Dominican Republic
　OAS intervention, 396, 408
　regional commission inquiry, 396
doubts, justifiable, 141, 143–4
DRC (Democratic Republic of the Congo), 55, 232, 244, 358
DSB see Dispute Settlement Body.
DSU see Dispute Settlement Understanding.
dual nationality, 179
dysfunction of Appellate Body, 332–3

East African Community case, 110–11, 114–16, 130–1
East Timor (Timor-Leste)
　adjudication by ICJ, 205
Eastern Europe, 222, 291, 378, 385, 419
　collapse of Soviet Union, effect, 385
　regional organisations, membership, 385
　Warsaw Pact, 385
Economic Community of West African States (ECOWAS), 340–1, 398, 401, 410
economic sanctions, 70, 76, 348, 358, 360, 373, 380, 408
ECOWAS see Economic Community of West African States.
ECOWAS Community Court of Justice, 398
Ecuador, arbitration, 42–3, 156
EEZ see exclusive economic zone.
Egypt, 71, 80, 116, 135, 147–8, 210, 220, 357, 379
　adjudication by ICJ, 220
　arbitration, 135, 147
　Camp David Agreements, 379
　conciliation, 116
　mediation, 71, 80

El Salvador, 203, 214, 217, 226, 380, 394, 403
　adjudication by ICJ, 203, 214, 217, 226
　Contadora process, 394
elections, 71, 221–2, 290–2, 298, 354
Elizabeth II, Queen, arbitration by, 134
enforcement, 81, 168, 170, 189–90, 252–3, 300, 349
　of arbitration decisions, 253, 300
　powers, 348–9, 358
environmental agreements
　conciliation provisions, 126–7
equality
　of the parties, 23
　sovereign, 5, 7–8, 24
equitable geographical distribution of ICJ judges, 222–3
equity, 24–5, 155–6
　and ICJ, 239, 242–3
　infra legem, 242–3
Eritrea
　arbitration, 147, 149, 152, 157, 159, 163
　OAU intervention, 392
errors in arbitration decisions, correction, 161
essential error as reason for nullifying arbitration award, 164–5
Ethiopia
　arbitration, 152, 159
　negotiation, 47–8
　OAU intervention, 392
European Convention on Human Rights (ECHR), Law of the Sea Convention compared, 271
European Court of Human Rights (ECtHR)
　functions, 117–18
　judicial settlement by, 132
European Court of Justice (ECJ)
　suspension of arbitral proceedings pending judgement by, 287
European Union/European Community (EC, EEC, EU), 44, 181–2, 329, 333, 339–40, 384, 393, 399
　dispute settlement provision, 384
　DSU, 319, 325, 329–31
　expansion and integration, 384
　good offices of GATT Director-General, use, 313, 319
　intervention by, 410
　jurisdiction over members' internal affairs, 399–400
　Law of the Sea Convention arbitration, 302

mediation, 69
UN, co-operation with, 380
evidence, 53, 60, 88–9, 107–8, 111, 113, 163–5, 227, 231–5
documentary, 217, 231–4, 431
scientific, 231, 234–6
use in ICJ proceedings, 232–5
excess of authority, 23
exclusive economic zone (EEZ), 148, 197, 238, 243, 271, 277, 286, 297, 301, 304
exhaustion of remedies, 54, 80, 271, 344, 404
experts, 53, 158, 164, 231, 234–6, 250–1, 286, 288–9, 319, 323–4
committees of, 164, 235–6
use
DSU, 324
ICJ, 232–5, 250
Law of the Sea Convention, 270

fact-finding, 80, 87, 97, 100, 123, 232, 351, 363, 367, 394
failure to give reasons for arbitration decision, 163–4
fairness, 142, 282, 285, 289
procedural, 432
Falkland Islands crisis
failure of negotiations, 62–3
Gibraltar dispute contrasted, 417
material dimension, 417
mediation, 67–8, 70, 73, 76–7, 79
regional organisations, role, 399, 401
severing of diplomatic relations, 61
UN intervention, 362, 365
finality, 19–21, 217
ICJ judgments, 248–50
Finland
adjudication by ICJ, 212
Åland Islands dispute, 98
inquiry, 98
First World War, submarine incidents, 88–90
fisheries, 275–7, 288–9
Fitzmaurice, Judge Gerald, 33–4, 48
flag states, 296–7
foreign head of state or government arbitration by, 133–4
foreign investors, 78, 120, 172–4, 180, 189, 432
fork-in-the-road clauses, 174
formalisation, 2
forum prorogatorium, application of, 198

France, 40, 46, 86–7, 105–9, 112–15, 129–30, 159–60, 257
adjudication by ICJ, 135, 198, 200, 257
arbitration, 46, 135–6, 138, 146, 148, 152, 158–61, 249–50
Ben Bella affair, 113, 115, 129
conciliation, 108–9, 115, 129
conciliation treaty, 105
experts from, use, 250
ICJ judges panel, representation on, 222
inquiry, 86–8, 92
mediation, 82
Security Council membership, 222
treaties of arbitration, negotiation, 91
France–Switzerland Commission, 109
Franco-Siamese dispute, 108, 112–13, 129
fraud, 23, 164, 431–2
fraud as reason for nullifying arbitration award, 164
free choice of means of settlement, 7–8
friendly settlements, 18, 117–18

GATS (General Agreement on Trade in Services), 314, 317
GATT (General Agreement on Tariffs and Trade), 9, 310, 312–17, 319, 326, 329, 332, 337–9, 344 *see also* World Trade Organization.
consultations, 316–18
dispute settlement, 312–13
dispute settlement, original system, 312–13
good offices of Director General, 313
historical background, 310–11
origins, 310–11
panels, 9, 312
working groups, 313
General Agreement on Trade in Services *see* GATS.
General Assembly *see* United Nations General Assembly.
general international law, 5, 27, 29, 151, 158, 272–3, 330
Georgia, 34, 49, 55, 223, 379, 393, 410
adjudication by ICJ, 223
EU intervention, 393
UN intervention, 379, 410
Germany
adjudication by ICJ, 214
conciliation, 128
conciliation treaty, 105

Germany (cont.)
  First World War submarine incidents, 88–90
  inquiry, 88–90
Gibraltar
  dispute contrasted with Falkland Islands crisis, 417
  UK–Spain negotiations, 62, 65
Gondra Treaty, 106–7
good faith, 19, 41, 63, 121, 124, 160, 242, 316, 406, 433
good judgments, importance, 433–4
good offices, 24–5, 66–7, 74, 318–20, 353, 361–5, 367, 384–5, 390–1, 427–8
  Director-General, WTO, 319
  DSU, 318–19
  GATT, 313
  individuals, 319
  meaning, 66
  NATO, 391
  Norway, 391
  OAU, 391
  UN Secretary-General, 361–3
  UNGA, 353
  UNSC, 353
Gorbachev, President Mikhail, meeting with President Bush, 47
Graham, Dr Frank, good offices, 354
Greece
  adjudication by ICJ, 59, 207, 215, 245, 248
  conciliation, 129
  negotiation, 53, 59
  UN intervention, 350, 390
Greenwood, Christopher, 142, 144
Gros, Judge André, adjudication by, 243
Group of 77 and Law of the Sea Convention, 280, 303–4
Guatemala, 333, 395, 403, 409
  Contadora process, 394
  OAS intervention, 395
Guinea
  arbitration, 136, 160
  Law of the Sea Convention arbitration, 301
Guinea-Bissau, 136, 160, 162–3, 208, 301
  adjudication by ICJ, 162–3
  arbitration, 136
  Law of the Sea Convention arbitration, 301
Gulf War 1991
  mediation, 82

UN Compensation Commission, role of, 100
UN intervention, 367

Hague Conventions, 84, 86–91, 93, 97–8, 102, 134, 144
  1899, 84–5
    arbitration rules, 144–5
  1907, 87–90
    arbitration rules, 144–5
Hague Peace Conferences, 2–3, 85
Haiti
  OAS intervention, 410
  UN intervention, 380, 410
Hammarskjöld, Dag, good offices, 354
Hariri, Rafiq, assassination, 352
hearings, 182–3, 283, 373
  oral, 93
  public, 115, 328
high moral character, 120, 184–5, 222
highest reputation, 142, 282, 285, 289
historic bays, 277–9
historic rights, 238, 279
historic titles, 153, 279
home states, 172, 174, 179, 181
Honduras, 13, 55, 161, 199, 203, 214, 391, 394–5, 403, 405–6
  adjudication by ICJ, 199, 203, 214
  arbitration, 161
  Contadora process, 55, 394
  negotiation, 55
honour, 15, 85, 87, 97
host states, 32, 120, 172–4, 177–80, 184–6, 189, 191
hostilities, 13, 71, 77, 196, 351, 361–2, 364, 390, 393, 395
Huber, Max, arbitration by, 135
human rights, 18, 117–18, 347, 350, 352, 384–5, 389, 398, 402
  adjudication, 423
  AFCHPR, 398
  arbitration as to, 42, 136
  conciliation, 117–18
  Council of Europe, 384
  ECOWAS Community Court of Justice, 341
  EU, 384, 393, 399
  ICJ and, 138, 233, 237, 244
  OAU, 389
  OSCE, 385
  UNGA, 350

United Nations, 347
violations, 99
Hungary, 12, 63, 70, 138–9, 181, 198, 232, 237, 377
   adjudication by ICJ, 139, 198, 232, 237
   arbitration, 138
   mediation, 70
   negotiations, 63
   UN intervention, 377

ICC *see* International Criminal Court.
Iceland
   adjudication by ICJ, 199, 237–8, 242, 253
   conciliation, 111
   negoriation, 391
   negotiations, 50–1, 62–3
   regional organisations, membership, 384
ICJ *see* International Court of Justice.
ICSID *see* International Centre for the Settlement of Investment Disputes.
immovable property, 176
immunities, 150–1, 199, 237, 278
impairment, 314–15
impartiality, 141–4, 185, 187, 191, 323, 328, 343, 411, 421–2
   independence and, 141–4, 185, 187, 323, 328, 343
implementation, 80–2, 159–60, 249–51, 313, 333–4, 336–7, 352–3, 364
inadmissibility, 33, 36
incidental jurisdiction, 203–18, 252
independence, 141, 143–4, 185, 238–9, 322–3, 353, 364–6, 397
   and impartiality, 141–4, 185, 187, 323, 328, 343
India, 73, 76, 136–7, 150, 166, 196–7, 199, 201, 287
   adjudication by ICJ, 199, 201–2
   arbitration, 138, 152, 154–5
Indonesia, 174, 215, 353
   adjudication by ICJ, 215
   negotiations, 353
innovations, 91, 93, 146, 174, 236, 238, 269, 313, 317
inquiry, 84–103
   1899 Hague Convention, 84–5
   1907 Hague Convention, 87–91
   arbitration differing, 94
   arbitration resembling, 90
   commissions, introduction, 84–5
   compensation following, 52, 84–5, 90
   current trends, 413–14
   first use of a lawyer, 90
   flexibility, 97
   infrequent use, 97–8
   meaning, 84
   non-use, reasons for, 97–8
   overview, 84–103
   post-Second World War practice, 92–7
   regional organisations, 393–5
   treaty practice 1911-1940, 91
   value, 97–103
integrity, 142, 219, 282, 285, 289, 431–4
intellectual property rights, 176, 314, 326, 337
intentions, 64, 75, 144, 154, 161, 247, 249, 325, 327, 333–4
   original, 96, 332
Inter-American Commission on Human Rights, 95
Inter-American Development Bank, fact-finding tribunals, 101
Inter-American Peace Committee
   commission established by, 250
interim appeals, 332–3, 338
interim measures, 204–12, 214, 216, 245, 254, 374, 404
International Bank for Reconstruction and Development (IBRD)
   conciliation, 114
   mediation, 76
International Centre for the Settlement of Investment Disputes (ICSID), 28–9, 172–3, 175–7, 179, 182–3, 190
   arbitration, 174, 181, 188–90
International Civil Aviation Organization (ICAO), inquiry, 100–1
International Committee of the Red Cross (ICRC)
   mediation, 67, 72, 77
International Court of Justice (ICJ), 3, 6–13, 15–23, 25–6, 28–9, 142–4, 194, 274–5, 402–3
   absence of clear legal practice, adjudication in cases where, 237–8
   advantages, 258–9
   advisory jurisdiction, 218–21
   and colonisation/ decolonisation, 219, 236, 256
   and equity *infra legem*, 242–3
   and human rights, 233

International Court of Justice (ICJ) (cont.)
  and UN political organs, 367–72
  chambers, 224–9
  compensation, ruling as to, 374
  consent to adjudication by, 194–5, 203
  contentious jurisdiction, 194–8
  counter-claims, 217–18
  counter-claims, power to consider, 217–18
  cultural factors as to choice of law, 236
  decision-making process, 231–8
  disputes over jurisdiction, 198–204
  documentary evidence, 231–4
  effect of judgments, 248–54
  effects of judgments, 248–54
  elections to, 221–4
  enforcement of arbitration decisions, 253
  equity, application, 239, 242–3
  establishing the facts, 231–6
  establishment, 389
  evidence, use, 232–5
  extension of function, 239–44
  finality of decisions, 248–50
  forum prorogatorium, application of, 198
  good judgments, importance, 433–4
  human rights, 138
  identifying the law, 236–9
  implementation of decisions, 250–4
  improving legal capacity, 429–37
  incidental jurisdiction, 204–18
  interim measures of protection, 204–12
  intervention, 212–15
  ITLOS compared, 290–3
  law, sources of, 236–8
  legal and political disputes, 244–8
  membership, 221–4
  optional clause declarations, 195–7, 200–2
  organisation and procedure, 194–229
  political disputes, adjudication in, 244–8
  recommendations, 243
  referral of cases to, 195–8, 270
  res judicata, application, 216, 435
  revision and interpretation of judgments, 215–17
  revision of judgments, 160–1
  scientific evidence and experts, 234–6
  Security Council, 371
  selection of neutral arbitrators by, 137–8
  significance, 254–9
  soft law, use, 237
  special agreement, consent by, 197–8
  third state intervention, power to allow, 212–15
  third states' consent to adjudication, 203
  transferred jurisdiction, 202
  uti possidetis principle, 240
  work, 231–59
  workload, 254
international courts
  meaning, 194
  significance compared to domestic courts, 254
International Criminal Court (ICC), 14, 143, 175, 182
international friction, 255, 349, 351
International Labour Office (ILO), inquiry, 100
International Law Commission (ILC)
  arbitration rules, 144
International Monetary Fund (IMF)
  conciliation, 114
  concurrence, 43
international organisations, 47–8, 77–9, 128, 218–19, 224, 289, 293, 425, 430
  conciliation mechanisms, 122–7
  mediation, 67
  negotiation, 48
international peace and security, maintenance, 4, 347–8, 351, 354, 362, 368, 407–9
International Seabed Authority (ISA), 28, 293, 298–300
international trade disputes, 310, 317–18 see trade disputes
International Trade Organization (ITO), 310
International Tribunal for the Law of the Sea (ITLOS), 10–11, 28–9, 137–9, 142–4, 261, 263–4, 287, 289–91, 301–4
  advisory opinions, 296–7
  cases dealt with by, 302
  compensation, ruling as to, 301
  financial assistance by, 431
  ICJ compared, 290–3
  judicial policy, 290–2, 302
  jurisdiction, 293–4, 304–5
  prompt release of vessels, 295–6
  provisional measures, 294–5
  referral of cases to, 41, 57
  Special Chamber, 274, 287
  structure and composition, 290–2

interpretation, 10–12, 21–2, 29, 120–1,
    149–50, 159, 215–16, 252, 265–9,
    273–4
inter-state disputes, 11, 23, 189, 204, 220,
    341
intra-state disputes, 364
investment arbitration, 144–5, 154, 167, 169,
    172–91
  investment treaties and consent to
    arbitration, 173–5
  jurisdiction of investment tribunals,
    175–80
  law applicable to the merits, 185–8
  procedural law, 180–5
  validity of awards and implementation,
    188–91
investment treaties, 172–3, 175–80, 183,
    186–8, 191 see also BITs
investors, 78–9, 120, 172–6, 178, 181, 187,
    189, 191, 432
investor-state arbitration, 10–11, 18, 23, 30,
    32, 35, 44, 120, 173–4, 180
  clauses, 30, 56, 174
Iran, 71–4, 76–7, 79–80, 151–2, 168, 245–6,
    361–3, 370, 416–17
  adjudication by ICJ, 200, 218, 245–7
  arbitration, *136–7*, 154
  Kurds, mediation involving, 71
  mediation, 71
  severing of diplomatic relations, 61
  UN intervention, 363
Iran hostages crisis
  court's recognition of dispute, 58
  definition as legal or political issue, 424
  material dimension, 418
  mediation, 68, 71, 74, 79–80
  severing of diplomatic relations, 61
  UN intervention, 361, 369
Iran-Iraq conflict
  mediation, 71–2, 76–7
  UN intervention, 361, 378
Iran-United States Claims Tribunal, 136,
    151, 154, 168, 170
  arbitrators selection, 136–7
  choice of law, 154
  jurisdiction by, 151–2
Iraq, 71–2, 76, 81–2, 352, 361, 367, 378–80,
    397
  Arab League intervention, 397
  compensation, payment, 100
  mediation, 71

Ireland, 18, 136, 287
  arbitration, 136, 287
  Law of the Sea Convention arbitration,
    287
irreparable prejudice, 206, 208
  risk, 294
  risk of, 206–7
ISA *see* International Seabed Authority.
ISIL, 352
Islamic Court of Justice
  establishment, 390
Israel
  adjudication by ICJ, *220, 223*
  advisory opinion by ICJ, 220
  arbitration, 135, 147
  Camp David Agreements, 379
  conciliation, 116
  inquiry, 99
  non-recognition issues, 61
  UN intervention, 372
Italy, 87, 110, 114–15, 134, 150, 174, 178,
    213–15, 218
  adjudication by ICJ, 213–14, 227
  arbitration, 178
  conciliation, 110, 115, 129
  inquiry, 87–8
  sovereign arbitration by, 134
  Turco-Italian war of, 1911–12, 87–8
Italy–Switzerland Commission, 110, 114–15
ITLOS *see* International Tribunal for the
    Law of the Sea.

Jan Mayen case, 111–13, 131
Japan
  adjudication by ICJ, 204
  conciliation, 114, 129
  DSU, 319, 325
  good offices of GATT Director-General,
    use, 319
  Law of the Sea Convention arbitration,
    288
  negotiation, 57
  proliferation of adjudicatory bodies,
    problems arising from, 435
Jarring, Dr Gunnar, good offices, 354
judges
  'equitable geographical distribution',
    222–3
  ad hoc appointment, 223–4
  African and Asian representation, 222
  chambers, 224–9

judges (cont.)
  comparison of municipal and international practice, 224
  competence and qualification, 222
  disqualification, 223
  election, 221–4
judicial functions, 9, 16–17, 59, 219, 239, 258, 368
judicial process, 133, 232, 422–3, 431–2
juridical persons *see* legal persons.
jurisdiction, 25–32
  advisory, 204, 218–21, 372, 375
  and consent, 6
  compétence de la compétence, conferral, 198
  compulsory, 3, 6, 196–7, 224, 270–1, 304, 420–1, 432, 434–5
  contentious, 194–204, 218–20, 224, 355, 375
  disputes over ICJ, 198–204
  domestic, 70, 196, 349, 364, 379, 400
  exercise, 16, 23, 34, 56, 150, 203, 371
  for adjudication, 53–8
  incidental, 203–18, 252
  Iran-United States Claims Tribunal, 151–2
  ITLOS, 293–4
  of investment tribunals, 175–80
  prima facie, 206, 294–5
  ratione materiae, 26–30, 35, 176–8, 270, 314–15, 321, 368
  ratione personae, 26–8, 178–9, 293, 314
  ratione temporis, 14, 26, 30, 180
  ratione voluntatis, 5
  residual, 294
  Seabed Disputes Chamber (SBDC), 298–300
jurisdictional conditions, 26, 31–2, 34–6
jurisdictional questions, 148–9, 273
jurisdictional requirements, 6, 26, 32, 36, 175, 178
justiciability, 14–16, 34, 60, 244, 247, 255, 369
justifiable doubts, 141, 143–4

Kashmir
  mediation, 68, 71–3, 76, 78, 80–1
  UN intervention, 76, 80, 361
KE 007 incident (South Korean airliner shot down over Soviet territory), 100–2
Kenya, 110–11, 267

King of Spain (Alfonso XIII), dispute over arbitral award by
  arbitration, 161–2, 165
  negotiation, 162
  OAS intervention, 391–2, 403
Knox treaties of arbitration, negotiation, 91
kompetenz-kompetenz, 27
Korea, South
  inquiry, 100–2
  KE 007 incident, 100–2
Korean War, UN intervention, 353–4
Kosovo, bombing of
  adjudication by ICJ, 206, 355
Kosygin, Alexei, leverage as mediator, 76, 80
Kurds, mediation involving, 71
Kuwait, 82
  Arab League intervention, 397

land sovereignty, 149, 273
language, 24, 145, 216, 236, 406
Latin America
  relations with US, 377
  UN intervention, 377
Latvia, 18
Law of the Sea Convention (UNCLOS), 28–9, 140–4, 149–50, 167–8, 261–307, 319–20, 414
  and ICJ, 269
  applicable law and jurisdiction of tribunals, 271–5
  arbitration, 270, 284–8
  avoiding compulsory settlement, 265–9
  choice of law, 305
  choice of means, 304–5, 348, 414
  choice of methods of binding settlement, 269–71
  compulsory settlement, 269–81
  conciliation, 277, 280–4, 289
  determination of whether claims well founded, 271
  dispute settlement, basic principles, 262–9
  DSU compared, 311–12
  ECHR compared, 271
  exceptions and limitations to compulsory settlement, 275–81
  experts, use, 270
  fact-finding tribunals, 289
  free choice of referral to, 263–9
  general provisions and voluntary methods of settlement, 263–5

Group of 77's views on, 280
jurisdiction under, 270–1
principles of compulsory settlement, 269–81
protective measures under, 270–1
significance, 301–7
special arbitration, 270, 288–90
lawyers, first use in inquiry, 90
LCIA (London Court of International Arbitration), 182
League of Nations, 105–6, 197, 347, 407
and regional organisations, 407
commissions of inquiry, 98
conciliation treaty, 106
conciliation, resolution as to, 105
election of judges to International Court, 222
failure, 347
least developed countries, DSU provisions for, 320
Lebanon, UN intervention, 380
legal basis, 96, 153, 321, 397
legal interests, 16, 203–4, 214, 330
legal means, settlement by, 132
legal methods, 25, 263, 406, 420, 429
legal persons, 178–9, 293, 299, 341, 384
nationality, 179
legal perspective, 420–5
legal questions, 89, 219, 246–7, 296, 300, 327, 341, 370, 372, 375
legal rights, 16, 61, 109, 157–8, 169, 205, 245, 247, 253, 414
legality, 16, 94, 162, 201, 206, 341, 373–4, 420
Letelier and Moffitt, 95–7, 103
lex specialis, 25, 153, 160
Liberia
ECOWAS intervention, 401
negotiation, 47–8
Libya
adjudication by ICJ, 212–13, 215–16, 228, 240–1, 243, 249
arbitration, 154, 163
NATO intervention, 99
negotiation, 55
UN intervention, 99–100, 364, 373–4
Lithuania, conciliation, 107
London Court of International Arbitration (LCIA), 182
Luxembourg, conciliation, 107

Maine incident, 84–5
maintenance of international peace and security, 4, 347–8, 351, 354, 362, 368, 407, 409
majority vote decision for arbitration, 135
Malaysia
adjudication by ICJ, 198, 215, 287
consultation, 41
Law of the Sea Convention arbitration, 41, 57
Maldives, 274, 287
Mali, adjudication by ICJ, 205, 211, 226, 240
Malta
adjudication by ICJ, 213–14, 228, 249
UN intervention, 364
manifest excess of power, 186
marine environment, 218, 276, 287, 289, 292, 294
maritime boundaries, 50, 129, 147, 153, 251, 274–5, 278–9, 283–4, 286–7, 301
maritime delimitation, 50, 53, 147–8, 155, 199, 214, 223, 232, 267, 431
maritime zones, 148, 150, 155, 278–9
material dimension of disputes, 417–18
Mauritania, adjudication by ICJ, 236, 256
Mauritius, 142, 150, 221, 238–9, 264, 274–5, 287
Mavi Marmara incident, 99
McNaughton, General Andrew, good offices, 354
means of international dispute settlement, 24–5
media precautions regarding sensitive negotiations, 52
mediated settlements, 70, 75–9
implementation, 80–3
mediation, 5–6, 66–84, 318–20, 352–3, 386–8, 391–2, 402
advantages, 66
conciliation distinguished, 66
consent to, 69–73
DSU, 318–19
functions, 74–8
ICRC, 67
limits, 79–80
OAS, 391–2
OAU, 392–3
OSCE, 392
overview, 66–83
politics of accepting, 70–2
refusal, 70

mediation (cont.)
　regional organisations, 391–3
　Secretary-General, 363–6
mediators, 66–70, 79–80, 83, 353–4, 356, 363, 391, 393, 400
　agreeing on, 72–3
　persons acting as, 67–9
　unwillingness to act, 69
MERCOSUR, 342
methods
　compulsory, 2, 266, 278, 284
　diplomatic, 5, 24–5, 318, 406, 417
　legal, 25, 263, 406, 420, 429
　of settlement, 5–8, 24, 59, 120, 196, 261, 267, 304, 413
　peaceful, 38, 345, 348, 359, 417–18
Mexico, 176, 195, 252, 331, 333, 340, 342, 353, 394
　adjudication by ICJ, 252
　arbitration, 133
　Contadora process, 394
　DSU, 331
　UN mediation, 353
　United States–Mexican General Claims Commission, 133
middle-rank states, mediation by, 68
military activities, 276–7, 279–80
mixed commissions, 45–6, 80, 133–4, 250, 395
Model Rules on Conciliation, 122–3
Moffitt, Mr Michael, injury to, 95–6
Moffitt, Mrs Ronni, murder, 95–6
Moldova, CSCE intervention, 392
mootness, 14, 16–18, 34, 257
Morocco, 113, 115, 174, 177, 224, 256, 391, 409
　adjudication by ICJ, 224, 256
　conciliation, 113, 115
　OAU intervention, 391, 409
Mosul dispute, 98
Mox Plant case, 57, 168, 264, 272, 287
MPIA (multi-party interim appeal arbitration arrangement), 332–3, 338
multilateral agreements
　arbitration provisions in regional treaties, 402
　on peaceful settlement, 140, 402
Multinational Force and Observers (MFO), 379
Munich agreement, conciliation, 77

municipal law *see also* domestic law.
　arbitration under, 153
　judicial practice compared with international law, 224
mutual agreement, 42, 63, 137, 338

Namibia
　adjudication by ICJ, 198, 223–4, 239–40
　mediation, 76
　UN intervention, 355, 377
nationality, 142, 178–9, 184, 222–3, 285
　dual, 179
　of legal persons, 179
NATO *see* North Atlantic Treaty Organization.
natural persons, 178–9
natural resources, 233, 235, 330, 340
Nauru, adjudication by ICJ, 300
negotiated settlement, 38, 49, 52, 55–6, 58, 62, 88, 133, 221
negotiation, 38–65
　and adjudication, 54–61
　as precondition to adjudication, 54–8
　bilateral agreements, 51–2
　commissions, 45–6
　conciliation resembling, 112
　consultation as form of, 39
　control of details, 52
　court's competence, 59
　current trends, 413
　diplomatic, 47, 113, 156, 312
　direct, 38, 48, 61, 67, 77, 342, 350, 364, 400, 405
　during Cold War, 52
　duty to negotiate, 62
　forms, 45–9
　in multilateral setting, 47–9
　international organizations, 48
　limitations, 61–5
　means of dispute handling, 38
　media restrictions, 52
　non-recognition issues, 61
　normal diplomatic channels, 45
　official communications relating to controversy over, 53
　package deals, 52
　prejdicial link with adjudication, 60
　sensitivity, 52
　special committees of the UN, assistance by, 353
　splitting of dispute, 50

substantive aspects, 49–54
substantive relation to adjudication, 59–61
time-limit for, 56
without prejudice clauses, 51–2
Netherlands, 90, 92, 135, 174, 178–9, 264, 374
　arbitration, 135
　experts from, use, 235
　First World War submarine incident, 90
　inquiry, 90, 92
　MH17 incident, 101
　UN intervention, 353
neutral arbitrators, selection, 136
neutral members, 133, 136–41, 160
neutrality, 29, 72, 153, 285, 358
new facts, revision of arbitration award due to, 160
New Zealand, 16, 99, 135, 146, 157, 159–60, 168, 204, 215, 364
　adjudication by ICJ, 204, 215, 257–8
　arbitration, 146, 159–60
　Law of the Sea Convention arbitration, 288
　proliferation of adjudicatory bodies, problems arising from, 435
Nicaragua, 161–2, 199, 201–3, 214, 218, 232–3, 252–3, 368–9, 403–6, 424–5
　adjudication by ICJ, 199, 201, 203, 211, 214, 218, 232, 244, 246, 252
　arbitration, 161, 165
　Contadora process, 55, 394
　negotiation, 55
　OAS intervention, 394
Nicaragua-United States dispute
　adjudication by ICJ, 201, 203, 211, 232, 244
　Contadora process, role, 404
　third party interventions, 424
　UN intervention, 368
Niels Ebbesen, 92
Niger
　adjudication by ICJ, 226, 251
　ECOWAS Community Court of Justice, 398
　UAM intervention, 401
Nigeria, 216, 264, 406–7
　adjudication by ICJ, 216–17, 406
　mediation, 70
　refusal of mediation, 70
　UN intervention, 364

non-aggravation, 210–11
non-cooperation, 138, 283
non-intervention, declarations of, 396
non-justiciability, Seabed Disputes Chamber (SBDC), 300
non-participation, 305, 432
non-recognition issues as to negotiation, 61
non-retroactivity, 180
non-violation complaints, 9, 315–16
normal diplomatic channels, negotiation via, 45
North American Free Trade Agreement (NAFTA), 187, 340
North Atlantic Treaty Organization (NATO), 67, 69, 73, 99, 380, 384–6, 390–1, 401, 410
　dispute settlement provision, 384
　disputes, involvement in, 390
　expansion, 385
　good offices, 391
　UN, co-operation with, 410
Norway, 111, 200, 329, 333
　adjudication by ICJ, 200
　conciliation, 111
　DSU, 329
　experts from, use, 235
　First World War submarine incidents, 88–9
　good offices, 391
notification, 32, 39–42, 121, 139, 209, 317, 327
　consultation distinguished, 39
nuclear tests, atmospheric, 16–17, 257
nullification, 22, 163, 314–15
nullity, 22–3, 148, 161–3, 165, 169–70, 422

OAS *see* Organisation of American States.
OAU *see* Organization of African Unity.
objections, preliminary, 47, 199, 216, 274, 405
objective assessment, 84, 321, 327
objective determination, 12
objectivity, 12, 73
obligations
　general, 5, 116, 348
　substantive, 6, 42, 56, 180, 340
OEC *see* Organization of Eastern Caribbean States (OEC), 117
OIC (Organization of the Islamic Conference), 389–90, 397
omissions, 79, 180, 282, 285, 289, 296

ONUCA (United Nations Observer Group in Central America), 380, 410
optional clauses, 7, 196–8, 200–3, 206, 254, 421, 430
  declarations, 195–7, 199–202, 267
Organisation of American States (OAS), 67, 386–7, 391, 394–6, 399–401, 403, 408–11
  arbitration decision, support for implementation, 403
  collective action, 396
  conciliation, 394–5
  Contadora process, 394
  dispute settlement provision, 386
  foreign ministers' Meeting of Consultation, 386
  General Assembly, 386
  OAS mediation by, 394–5
  purposes, 386
  resources deployment, 394
  Secretariat, 387
  Soviet Union, 409
Organization for Security and Co-operation in Europe (OSCE), 123–6, 385, 392–4, 397, 400
  and conciliation, 123–6
  conciliation, 393–4
  conciliation provisions, 123–5
  expansion, 385
  mediation by, 392
Organization of African Unity (OAU), 117, 387–9, 391–3, 396, 400–2, 409
  boundaries agreement, 396
  dispute settlement provision, 388–9
  division within, 401
  good offices, 391
  mediation by, 391
  peace-keeping operations, 402
Organization of Eastern Caribbean States (OEC), 117
  conciliation provisions, 117
Organization of the Islamic Conference (OIC), 389–90, 397
  dispute settlement provision, 390
OSCE see Organization for Security and Co-operation in Europe.
overlapping entitlements, 279
ozone layer, conciliation provisions in protocols for protecting, 126–7

package deals linking negotiations, 52
Pakistan, 68, 73, 76–8, 136–8, 154–5, 166, 173–4, 356–7, 361
  adjudication by ICJ, 201–2
  arbitration, 138, 152, 154–5
  mediation, 68
Palestine, 10–12, 200, 351, 353, 356, 378
Palestinians see also Arab-Israeli conflict
  advisory opinion by ICJ, 220
  non-recognition issues, 61
  UN intervention, 98, 372
Panama
  Contadora process, 394
  Law of the Sea Convention arbitration, 301
panel proceedings, 319–27, 338, 343–4, 414
panel reports, 101, 313, 325–7, 330–3, 339
panellists, 322–3, 343
panels, 123, 125, 137, 312–13, 316–35, 344–5, 430
  arbitration, 112, 191, 342
  composition, 321–3
  jurisdiction, 330, 343
  mandate, 320–1
  procedure, 324–6
Papua New Guinea, negotiations, 50
Paraguay, conciliation, 112–13
parallel regimes, 268
party autonomy, 177, 263, 338
PCA see Permanent Court of Arbitration.
PCIJ see Permanent Court of International Justice.
peace agreements, 351, 364, 392, 401
peace treaties, 12, 80, 110, 138–9, 162, 219, 355
peaceful means, agreement to settle disputes by, 413
peaceful methods, 38, 345, 348, 359, 417–18
peaceful settlement of disputes, 2–5, 38, 77–8, 140, 195, 263, 265, 387, 402–3
  importance of issue, 437
peaceful transfer of power, 351, 364
peacekeeping, 340, 348, 358, 381, 396, 410–11, 428–9
  by regional organisations, 396–7
  forces, 356, 378–9, 392, 397, 401–2, 410, 426
  operations, 355, 358–9, 362, 378, 380–1, 396–7, 411, 415, 428–9
  Brahimi report, 428
  by UN Secretary-General, 362
  political capacity, improving, 428

Pérez de Cuéllar, Javier, 365
  good offices, 67, 98
Permanent Court of Arbitration (PCA), 2–3, 15, 134–5, 137, 140–1, 143–5, 166, 173, 222, 431
  continuing role, 134
  financial assistance by, 431
  selection of appointing authority by, 141
Permanent Court of International Justice (PCIJ), 3, 5, 10–12, 96, 102, 106, 194, 201 *see also* International Court of Justice
personal diplomacy, 72, 354
personal jurisdiction *see* jurisdiction, *ratione personae*.
persons of high moral character, 120, 184–5, 222
Peru, 15, 188, 395
  adjudication by ICJ, 256
  Contadora process, 395
Philippines, 139, 215, 264, 268, 288, 304–5
plausibility, 206, 209, 294, 404
Poland
  conciliation treaty, 105
  troops interned in Switzerland, conciliation as to, 109
political asylum, 15, 256
political contexts, 13, 246, 416, 430
political disputes, 13–14, 67, 72, 77, 244, 246, 248, 255
political methods of dispute settlement, improving capacity, 425–9
political perspective on dispute settlement, 417
  material dimension, 417–18
  overview, 415–20
  timing of dispute, 418–20
politics, 108, 236, 247
  domestic, 82
  of accepting mediation, 70–2
Portugal, procedural rules for arbitration, 156
predictability, 20, 236
preferential trade agreements *see* PTAs.
preliminary objections, 47, 199, 216, 274, 405
prima facie jurisdiction, 206, 294–5
procedural fairness, 432
procedural rules, 6, 20, 81, 87, 125, 173, 181, 184–6, 296
  arbitration, 144–6

proliferation of adjudicatory bodies, 434
prompt release of vessels, 270, 295–6
provisional measures, 13, 145, 204, 206, 208–11, 294–5, 302, 371, 373
PTAs (preferential trade agreements), 339–40
public international law, 5, 181, 345

Qatar, 53, 199, 207, 209–11, 431–2
  adjudication by ICJ, 199, 431–2
  negotiation, 53
qualifications of judges and/or arbitrators, 135, 142–3, 184, 222, 243, 282, 285, 322, 432

racial discrimination, 12, 49, 55–6, 209–10
Rainbow Warrior affair, 25, 135, 146, 157–9, 169, 364–5
  arbitration, 159–60
  UN intervention, 135, 157
reasonableness, 60, 70, 185
reasoned awards, 23, 135, 163–4
receivability, 35
recommendations, 41, 91, 111, 119, 243–4, 282–3, 321, 333–5, 349–51, 387–8
reconciliation processes, 351, 363–4
rectification, 21, 159
Red Cross, mediation by, 67, 72, 77
Red Crusader, 92–7, 290
refusal to negotiate, 55–6
regional agencies, 8, 407–8
regional courts, 398, 402
regional organisations, 339–40, 379–80, 383–411, 415
  14.4suggested changes, 429
  and adjudication, 402–7
  and Cold War, 408
  and United Nations, 354, 407–11
  collective action, 395–8
  consultation, negotiation, and good offices, 390–1
  dispute settlement role, 383
  disputes within member states, ability to deal with, 399–400
  geographical limitations, 398
  in Europe, 384–5
  inquiry and conciliation, 393–5
  inquiry by, 102
  jurisdictional conflicts with UN, 408
  League of Nations, 407
  limitations, 398–402

regional organisations (cont.)
  mediation, 391–3
  peacekeeping operations, 396–7
  range of, 383–90
  regional solidarity, influence, 400–2
  resource constraints, 402
  role, 390–8, 404, 411
  sub-regional organisations, importance, 390, 401–2
  survey, 383–90
  trade systems, 339–42
  UN, 397, 407–11, 415
regional solidarity, influence on regional organisations, 400–2
regional trade agreements, 331, 339
regional trade systems, 339–42
remoteness, 7, 96
representatives, 40, 45, 76, 93, 98, 138, 312, 316, 323, 353
reputation, highest, 142, 282, 285, 289
res judicata, application, 216
reservations, 6–7, 126, 195–6, 199–201, 206, 213, 262–3, 267, 303
resources, natural, 233, 235, 330, 340
resubmission of claims, 36
reverse consensus, 313, 316, 321
revision, 21, 159, 161, 215–17, 226, 261–2
rights
  intellectual property, 176, 314, 326, 337
  legal, 16, 61, 109, 157–8, 169, 205, 245, 247, 253, 414
  sovereign, 218, 245, 274–7, 280
Romania
  adjudication by ICJ, 139, 223
  arbitration, 138, 179
  conciliation, 130
  conciliation treaty, 106
royalty payments, 178
rule of law, 20, 58, 420
rules of procedure *see* procedural rules.
Russia, 34, 49, 86, 127, 138, 223, 264, 305, 385, 394
Russian Empire, Dogger Bank incident, 85–7
Russian Federation, 49, 55, 138, 150, 222, 273, 279–80, 385
  adjudication by ICJ, 223
  conciliation, 127
  ICJ judges panel, representation on, 222
  ITLOS membership, 432
  regional organisations, membership, 385
  Security Council membership, 222

Russo-Japanese war, 85–7
Rwanda, negotiation, 55

St Vincent and the Grenadines, Law of the Sea Convention arbitration, 301
Samoré, Cardinal Antonio, mediation by, 68, 72, 75
sanctions, economic, 70, 76, 348, 358, 360, 373, 380, 408
satellite imagery, 233
Sauser-Hall, M. George, arbitration by, 135
SBDC *see* Seabed Disputes Chamber.
SCC *see* Stockholm Chamber of Commerce.
scientific evidence, 234–6
sea boundary delimitations, 276–8, 284 *see also* maritime boundaries
Seabed Disputes Chamber (SBDC), 270, 291–4, 296–301, 303
  ad hoc chambers, 298–9
  advisory opinions, 300
  competence, 298–300
  composition and functioning, 298
  constituting of, 297–8
  enforcement of decisions, 300
  establishment, 303, 306
  jurisdiction, 298–300
  non-justiciability, 300
  role, 270
Security Council *see* United Nations Security Council.
self-defence, 196, 358, 386
self-determination, 238, 417
Senegal, 136, 162, 208–9
  adjudication by ICJ, 204
  arbitration, 136
Serbia
  adjudication by ICJ, 233
  mediation, 70
settlement, notion and functions, 18–23
Seychelles, inquiry, 98
Siam (Thailand), 108
Singapore, 41, 57, 198, 287, 333
  adjudication by ICJ, 198, 287
  consultation, 41
  Law of the Sea Convention arbitration, 57
  negotiation, 57
single legal culture, 224, 236
Slovakia
  adjudication by ICJ, 198, 232
  negotiations, 63
Slovenia, 139–41

small states, mediation by, 337
soft law, ICJ's use, 237
Somalia, 267, 393, 428
   OAU intervention, 393
South Africa
   adjudication by ICJ, 224
   negotiation, 47–8
   OAU membership, 401
South China Sea Arbitration, 139, 264, 267–8, 271, 278–9, 288, 304, 432
Southern Bluefin Tuna, 57, 167, 268, 276, 288, 304, 435
sovereign arbitration, 133–4
sovereign equality, 5, 7–8, 24
sovereign rights, 218, 245, 274–7, 280
sovereignty, 51, 62, 65, 147, 150, 273–5, 278–9, 388, 393–4
   land, 149, 273
   territorial, 40, 147, 149–50, 153, 250, 273–4, 280
Soviet Union
   collapse, 385
   inquiry, 100–2, 418
   KE 007, 100–1
   KE 007 incident, 418
   mediation, 68, 73, 82
   negotiation, 361
   OAS, 409
   refusal of mediation, 70
   regional organisations, membership, 385
   UN intervention during the Cold War, 377–8
Spain, 30, 40, 46, 49, 62, 85, 89, 161–2, 201, 236
   adjudication by ICJ, 201
   arbitration, 46, 138
   inquiry, 85
   Spanish–American war, 84–5
Spanish–American war, 84–5
special agreements, 6, 10, 17, 53, 60, 195, 197–8, 206, 239–41, 249–51
special arbitration, 102, 263, 270, 288–90
special committees of the UN, negotiation assisted by, 352
specially qualified individual, arbitration by, 134
Spender, Judge, opinion by, 48
splitting of dispute, negotiation as to, 50
Sri Lanka, 173
stability, 20, 68–9, 155
state consent, 5–8

state enterprises, 293, 299
statehood, 200
Stockholm Chamber of Commerce (SCC), 175, 182
strict time limits, 317, 324, 327
subject matter, 27–9, 45, 49, 54, 81–2, 91, 203, 209, 321, 326
   jurisdiction, 26–30, 35, 176–8, 270, 314–15, 321, 368
submarine incidents, First World War, 88–90
sub-regional organisations, importance, 390, 401
substantive obligations, 6, 42, 56, 180, 340
Sudan
   arbitration, 164
   AU intervention, 397
Suez Crisis, UN intervention, 377
summit discussions, 46–7
surveillance, 316, 333–4, 336
suspension of concessions, 277, 316, 324, 331, 333–5
Sweden, 90, 98, 104, 128, 138, 179, 353, 363
   Åland Islands dispute, 98
   arbitration, 179
   conciliation treaty, 104
   experts from, use, 235
   inquiry, 90, 98
   selection of neutral arbitrators by, 138
   UN mediation, 353
Switzerland, 105, 109–10, 115–16, 157, 264, 333
   arbitration, 157
   conciliation, 110, 115, 129
   conciliation treaty, 105, 116

Taba dispute, 152
Taft treaties of arbitration, negotiation, 91
Taft, Chief Justice William Howard, arbitration by, 135
Tanzania
   conciliation, 110–11
   OAU intervention, 393
Tavignano Inquiry, 87–9, 92, 97
termination of diplomatic relations, 61
terms of reference, 38, 86, 89, 92, 172, 180, 320–1, 399, 414
   arbitrators, 144–52
terra nullius, 236, 256
territorial disputes, 61, 68, 134, 165, 216, 226, 398, 401, 403, 431

territorial jurisdiction, 26–7
territorial seas, 149, 197, 286, 301
territorial sovereignty, 40, 147, 149–50, 153, 250, 273–4, 280
Thailand
  adjudication by ICJ, 216, 253
  conciliation, 108
  UN intervention, 363, 365
third parties, 24, 66, 151, 183–4, 317, 326, 338, 340–1, 424–5
  disinterested, 84, 133
  interests, 317, 338
third party intervention
  forms, 66
  ICJ power to allow, 120, 425
  whether indespensible, 425
third party selection of arbitrators, 137–8
third states, consent to ICJ adjudication by, 203
third-party settlement, 265–6
Tiger Inquiry, 88–90, 97
time limits, 56, 145, 216, 328
  conciliation, acceptance, 115
  for negotiation, 56
  strict, 317, 324, 327
timing of disputes, 418–20
Timor Sea, 104, 129, 145, 205, 283–4, 306
trade disputes, 310–45, 414–15 *see also* GATT; World Trade Organization.
  appellate review, 326–33
  arbitration, 337–9
  consultations, 316–18
  good offices, conciliation and mediation, 318–20
  implementation of rulings and recommendations, 333–7
  panel proceedings, 320–6
  procedure, 310, 324–6
trademarks, 178, 339
Trail Smelter case, 154
transferred jurisdiction of ICJ, 202
transparency, 182–4, 427
treaties
  investment, 79
  of arbitration, negotiation, 91
  on peaceful settlement, 117
treaty practice, 1911-1940, 91
Trinidad and Tobago, Law of the Sea Convention, 287
troops interned in Switzerland, conciliation as to, 109

trust funds for adjudication
  UN General Assembly's, 431
  UN Secretary-General's, 430
Tubantia Inquiry, 90, 93
Tunisia, adjudication by ICJ, 212–13, 215–16, 240–1, 243
Turco-Italian war of, 1911–12, 87–8
Turkey, 21, 53, 59, 99, 118, 207, 245, 350, 390
  adjudication by ICJ, 59, 207, 245
  conciliation, 118
  inquiry, 98–9
  Mosul dispute, 98
  negotiation, 53, 59
  UN intervention, 350, 390

U Thant, good offices, 363
UAM, intervention by, 401
Uganda, 110–11, 232, 235–6, 251, 393
  adjudication by ICJ, 232
  conciliation, 110–11
  OAU intervention, 393
Ukraine, 101, 138, 150, 223, 273–4, 280, 394
  adjudication by ICJ, 223
  MH17 incident, 101
ultra vires, issue, 372
Umbricht, Dr Victor, work as a conciliator, 110–11, 114
UN Compensation Commission, role, 100
UN Human Rights Council (UNHRC), 98–9
UN Special Committee on (UNSCOB), 352
UNCITRAL Arbitration Rules, 10, 141, 144–5, 172, 175, 180, 182–3, 186, 188, 299
UNCLOS *see* Law of the Sea Convention
Union Africaine et Malagache (UAM), intervention by, 401
United Arab Emirates, 207, 209–11
United Kingdom, 15–16, 62–3, 135–6, 142, 146, 221–2, 237–9, 248–9, 274, 416–17
  adjudication by ICJ, 199, 237–8, 241–2, 248, 253
  arbitration, 55, 135–6, 138, 146–8, 152–3, 155–6, 158–9, 161, 164, 249–50
  British–Venezuelan Commission, 133
  consultation, 41–2
  Dogger Bank incident, 85–7
  inquiry, 92
  judges panel, representation on, 222
  Law of the Sea Convention arbitration, 287

mediation, 67–8, 70
Mosul dispute, 98
negotiations, 51, 57, 62–3, 391
Red Crusader incident, 92–4
Security Council membership, 222
severing of diplomatic relations, 61
sovereign arbitration, 134
treaties of arbitration, negotiation, 91
UN intervention, 361, 363, 390
United Nations (UN), 71–3, 218–20, 347–83, 397–9, 411, 415, 425–7
advisory opinions, 355, *see* old war
and regional organisations, 407–11
assistance with negotiation, provision of, 353–4
Cold War, intervention during, 377–8
colonisation and decolonisation, 378
creation, 347
EC, co-operation with, 380
effectiveness, 376–82
election of judges to International Court, 222
fact-finding, 351–60
human rights, 347
independence of Secretary-General, 364–7
inquiry by specialised agencies, 100–1
machinery of organisation, 348–50
main ogans, 348–50
mediation, good offices and conciliation, 353–5
Model Rules on conciliation, 122
Observer Group in Central America *see* ONUCA.
peacekeeping operations and action under Chapter VII, 355–60
political organs and International Court, 367–76
purposes, 347
recommendations concerning the settlement of disputes, 350
regional organisations, 397, 407–11, 415
role of Secretary-General, 360–7
Secretary-General, suggested changes, 67, 70, 427–9
Security Council and General Assembly in action, 350–60
special committees, 352
United Nations Conference on the Law of the Sea (UNCLOS III), 238
negotiation of dispute settlement provisions, 262–9

United Nations General Assembly (UNGA), 97–8, 122, 220–1, 256, 348–56, 360–1, 365–7, 372
fact-finding by, 97, 351
good offices, 353
recommendations to states, powers to make, 98, 350–1
referral of cases to UNSC, 354
referral to other UN bodies, 354
role, 348–55
United Nations Secretary General
other UN bodies, activities related to, 366
political capacity, improving, 427–8
United Nations Secretary-General
An Agenda for Peace, 381
arbitration by, 135, 138–9, 146, 159–60
arbitraton by, 157
compensation, ruling as to and Contadora process, 387
good offices, 361
independence, 365–6
investigation, power of, 360
mediation, 363–6
mediation by, 67
peace-keeping operations, 362
restraint oof hostilitites, action for, 361
success of intervention, likelihood of, 367
trust funds for adjudication, 430
United Nations Security Council (UNSC), 69, 252–3, 347–56, 358–81, 397, 408–11, 426–9
compensation Commission, 100
ECOWAS peace-keeping operations, support for, 401
fact-finding by, 351
good offices, 353–4
inquiry by, 98
jurisdictional conflicts with regional organisations, 408
membership, 222
political capacity, improving, 426–7
powers, 348–9
recommendations to states, power to make, 349
referral of cases to other UN bodies, 354
referral of cases to UNGA, 354
role, 348–55
suggested changes, 426–7
United States, 67–74, 201–3, 245–6, 330–2, 336–7, 368–70, 377–80

United States (cont.)
  adjudication by ICJ, 199–201, 203, 211, 225–8, 232, 244–7, 368
  and Iran, 61, 68, 72, 74, 416–17
  arbitration, 55, 135–6, *136–7*, 138, 146–7, 153–5, 161
  Camp David Agreements, 379
  Chinese embassy in Belgrade, bombing, 98
  compensation, payment, 98
  conciliation, 107, 128
  conciliation treaty, 106
  consultation, 39
  DSU, 330–1, 336–7
  good offices, 353
  ICJ judges panel, representation on, 222
  inquiry, 85
  Joint Commission with Canada, 45
  mediation, 67, 71
  negotiation, 45, 60
  OAS, 408
  regional organisations, membership, 384–5
  Security Council membership, 222
  severing of diplomatic relations, 61
  Spanish–American war, 84–5
  treaties of arbitration, negotiation, 91
  UN intervention, 353
  UN intervention during Cold War, 377–8
  United States–Mexican General Claims Commission, arbitration by, 133
  United States–Mexico–Canada Agreement (USMCA), 340, 344
urgency, 206–7, 295, 317, 324, 415
Uruguay
  adjudication by ICJ, 209, 234
  Contadora process, 395
Uruguay Round of GATT, establishment of WTO, 311
USMCA (United States–Mexico–Canada Agreement), 340, 344
uti possidetis principle, 240

validity, 22, 100, 119, 164, 169–70, 182, 188, 190–1, 199, 375
Valletta procedure (OSCE conciliation provisions), 123–4, 126

Vatican
  arbitration by, 133
  mediation by, 68, 71–2
Venezuela, 59, 95, 133, 164, 169, 187, 342, 394, 396
  arbitration, 164
  British–Venezuelan Commission, 133
  Contadora process, 394
  inquiry, 95
  MERCOSUR, 342
  OAS, 396
vessels, prompt release, 270, 295–6
Vietnam, UN intervention, 363

Waldheim, Kurt, investigation by, 361
war crimes, 98–9, 237, 352
Warsaw Pact, dispute settlement provision, 385
without prejudice clauses, use, 51
World Bank, 101, 111, 173, 310
World Trade Organization (WTO), 310–11, 314–15, 317, 323, 325–6, 330–2, 342–3
  Dispute Settlement Body *see* Dispute Settlement Body.
  Dispute Settlement Understanding *see* Dispute Settlement Understanding.
  establishment, 311
  financial assistance by, 431
  good offices of Director-General, 319
  in context, 342–5
  Appellate Body *see* Appellate Body.
written submissions, 93, 95, 100, 183–4, 323–4
WTO *see* World Trade Organization.

Yemen
  arbitration, 147, 149, 152, 157, 163
Yugoslavia, 69, 98, 200, 206, 216–17, 233, 359, 371, 380
Yugoslavia, conciliation treaty, 106
Yugoslavia, dissolution, 69
Yugoslavia, dissolution of
  adjudication by ICJ, 200, 206
  cases following, 434
  Chinese embassy bombing, 98
  OSCE missions, 392

Zimbabwe, 399

Made in the USA
Monee, IL
11 July 2025